JACK KENNEDY

The EDUCATION *of a* STATESMAN

W. W. Norton & Company

New York London

JACK KENNEDY

The EDUCATION *of a* STATESMAN

Barbara Leaming

For information about permission to reproduce selections from this book, write to
Permissions, W. W. Norton & Company, Inc., 500 Fifth Avenue, New York, NY 10110

Manufacturing by R.R. Donnelley, Harrisonburg
Book design by Barbara M. Bachman
Production manager: Amanda Morrison

Library of Congress Cataloging-in-Publication Data

Leaming, Barbara.
Jack Kennedy : the education of a statesman / Barbara Leaming.— 1st
ed.
p. cm.
Includes bibliographical references and index.
ISBN-13: 978-0-393-05161-2 (hardcover)
ISBN-10: 0-393-05161-7 (hardcover)
1. Kennedy, John F. (John Fitzgerald), 1917–1963. 2. Presidents—United States—Biography.
3. Presidents—United States—Decision making. 4. United States—Politics and government—
1961–1963. 5. United States—Foreign relations—1961–1963. I. Title.
E841.L345 2006
973.922092—dc22

2005036598

W. W. Norton & Company, Inc., 500 Fifth Avenue, New York, N.Y. 10110
www.wwnorton.com

W. W. Norton & Company Ltd., Castle House, 75/76 Wells Street, London W1T 3QT

1 2 3 4 5 6 7 8 9 0

CONTENTS

JACK KENNEDY

The EDUCATION *of a* STATESMAN

CHAPTER ONE

The Twenty-Five-Year Conversation

L ATE IN THE AFTERNOON ON SATURDAY, JUNE 29, 1963, A HELI-copter's whirling rotors sounded over Chatsworth, the palace of the Devonshire dukes nestled in the Derbyshire countryside. In accord with the American president's wishes, there had been no public announcement of his visit; it was, he said, "of an extremely personal nature," and he hoped it could take place with complete secrecy. To that end, the estate manager had orders to mark the landing ground at the last possible moment; and most of the police called in on special duty had no idea why they were there until the brown United States Army helicopter materialized overhead.

From inside the aircraft, Jack Kennedy had a spectacular view of the vast, golden stone edifice. Sunlight glinted off long rows of gilded window frames, intensifying the effect of sensuous color. As he passed over green parkland, a plume of water shot high into the air from the famous Emperor's Fountain. Finally, the helicopter touched down on the hillside above the house, some hundred yards from the churchyard of the estate's tiny gray-walled village of Edensor. When the door opened, the president, dressed in a single-breasted dark blue suit, gingerly descended some steps.

In the field below waited the 11th Duke of Devonshire. He had rearranged his weekend plans the previous day, when word came of Jack Kennedy's wish for a private visit before he went on to an official meeting with Prime Minister Harold Macmillan, the duke's uncle, and the duke's cousin David Ormsby Gore, who was Kennedy's close personal friend as well as the British ambassador to the United States. Andrew Devonshire escorted his guest across a narrow steel scaffolding bridge, which estate workers had erected overnight between the field and the churchyard. The president and the duke walked together with the easy familiarity of long years of family intimacy. Even now, a quarter century after they had been members of the same London set on the eve of the Second World War, there was something remarkably youthful about these two tall, thin men, a boyish quality unaltered by rank and power or by the tragedies that had linked their lives.

At least thirty uniformed police, under strict orders to stay back lest they intrude on the president's "act of memory and homage," ringed the churchyard where the Cavendish family plot lay. The duke discreetly dropped back as the vicar guided Kennedy to his sister's grave. They stopped in front of a stone marker with the inscription, "In loving memory of Kathleen, 1920–1948, widow of Major the Marquess of Hartington, killed in action, and daughter of the Hon. Joseph P. Kennedy, sometime Ambassador of the United States to Great Britain. Joy she gave—joy she has found."

For a long moment Kennedy stood in silence. From a distance, the Duchess of Devonshire, the former Debo Mitford, who had overseen all the last-minute arrangements to ensure her friend's privacy, watched him place a small, simple bunch of flowers, the stems wrapped in silver foil, on the ground. Then, despite the pain his bad back cost him, Jack lowered himself to his knees and began to pray. Almost exactly fifteen years before, Debo Devonshire had stood in this same churchyard and watched her mother-in-law, then herself the duchess, bury the young American girl her eldest son had loved so intensely. She had seen the look of anguish on the face of old Joe Kennedy, by that time a reviled figure in Britain because of his anti-British pronouncements during the war, as he stood at his daughter's graveside, the only Kennedy present at the funeral. Jack himself had begun the trip from America, but he had only gone as far as New York before turning back without explanation, unable to face the reality of the death of the person who more than any other had always believed in him. Fifteen years later he had come at last, at a time when, after long struggle, he had finally emerged as the man she had always insisted he could be.

When the president's prayers were done, the vicar walked him past the old church to the duke's Bentley. By the time Jack joined the Devonshires in the car, his right arm was clutched tightly against one side, as if the act of kneeling had been almost too much for him. Soon, they crossed a bridge over the river that ran in front of the great house where Kick had once dreamed she would make an exciting political life for herself and her husband when he became the 11th duke. But the war, which had changed everything for the three people in the car, shattered Kick's dreams.

This book tells the story of the lifelong impact on Jack Kennedy of the world his sister introduced him to in London before the war. It tells of the bonds of friendship and family forged in that turbulent time that did so much to shape the man who would become president, and it examines the deep and lasting influence of British history, literature and values on an American leader. It shows how the experience of Britain on the eve of war provisioned him with knowledge and ideas that he would draw on significantly throughout his political career; and it traces Britain's continued impact long after Kathleen's death. Through conversation and reading, Jack Kennedy reinvented himself politically and intellectually in the years that followed the Second World War. In exploring that process, this book shows for the first time Winston Churchill's monumental influence on the thirty-fifth president and lays open the central strategy of the presidency as Kennedy himself saw it.

That Kennedy admired Churchill has long been known. But no historian has yet examined his preoccupation with the ideas in Churchill's speeches and writings, or tracked his attempts to apply them during his years in the White House. As president, Kennedy drew on the full range of Churchillian thought, from insights into how the First World War began to Churchill's program for defeating the Soviets after the Second World War. This book reveals the previously unrecognized influence of David Ormsby Gore, Kennedy's friend from prewar days in London, who helped convey Churchill's defining ideas about the postwar world to the presidential aspirant and counseled him as he made them an integral part of both his campaign and his presidency. Ormsby Gore would speak in later years of Kennedy's "twenty-five-year conversation" with Britain. In the late 1930s, Kennedy had fervently debated with Ormsby Gore and other young aristocrats certain questions—notably, the differences between a politician and a statesman—that would remain unresolved almost until the end of his life. In British books the young Jack Kennedy discovered an image of the man he wanted to be, and he spent much of his life struggling against considerable odds to become that man.

By documenting Kennedy's goals in office and by tracing their sources, this new portrait of the thirty-fifth president differs sharply from previous accounts, which depict him as coming to the White House with far more in the way of attitude than ideas. On inauguration day, Kennedy knew—and stated emphatically—what he hoped to do. The question, in his own terms, was whether he had the "political courage" to try.

WINSTON CHURCHILL SAW the First World War, the Second World War and the postwar struggle with the Soviets as a single, vast narrative, in which the lessons of the first two world wars were crucial to averting a third. An avid student of Churchill's writing, John Fitzgerald Kennedy learned to look at the history of those years in the same way. Kennedy was formed intellectually in the run-up to the Second World War and he claimed his place in history during the postwar era, but his personal story, like Churchill's three-part historical continuum, began with the bloodshed of what was once known as the Great War.

A young father's horror that he might soon himself be sent off to fight lent a turbulent atmosphere to the Kennedy family home in the Boston suburb of Brookline, Massachusetts, where Jack Kennedy was born on May 29, 1917, six weeks after the United States entered the First World War. Following graduation from Harvard University in 1912, Joseph P. Kennedy, the tall, red-haired, freckle-faced son of a Boston-Irish saloonkeeper, had swiftly risen to become Massachusetts's youngest bank president. On the day Jack, as he would be known, was born, his father was named to the board of the Massachusetts Electric Company; still only twenty-seven, he became one of the nation's youngest corporate trustees. Though far from poor, Joe Kennedy was possessed of what his son would later characterize as the poor man's ingrained suspicion that "someone" at the uppermost levels of government meant to betray him by sending him off to be slaughtered. He was vehemently opposed to the United States becoming involved in what he saw as a European war that had nothing to do with American interests. The United States had not been attacked, and it was his conviction that one ought to fight only to protect one's life, family or possessions—not in the name of abstract ideas like democracy. Men who risked their lives for such principles were, as Joe Kennedy saw it, just being used. Thus, intent on career and family, Joe set himself the task of finding a way to escape military service. This lack of patriotism put him at odds with many members of his Harvard class, who, upon the declaration of war, had forsaken their own careers and rushed to sign up. The disdain of Joe's college friends, who accused him of selfishness at a critical moment, contributed to the air of agitation that pervaded the Kennedy household during Jack's first months of life.

Joe Kennedy transferred to a managerial position at the Fore River shipyard, which allowed him to claim participation in the war effort without putting himself anywhere near the line of fire. This new job was so all-consuming that, with the exception of Sundays and of three months in 1919 when he collapsed with physical and mental exhaustion, Joe was at home, by his wife's account, "just long enough to sleep." As a consequence, during his first two years Jack was largely dependent on his mother for attention. Jack craved a kiss, a hug, a caress; but, as he remembered years afterward, these were things Rose Kennedy failed to provide. The fragile, blue-eyed boy with a mop of reddish-brown hair could hardly understand why it should be so, but Rose, unrelentingly rigid and physically distant, was submerged in troubles of her own. She rarely saw her husband; she knew but apparently never openly acknowledged that he cavorted with other women; she missed the big, colorful life she had enjoyed when, prior to her marriage, she had served as political hostess for her father, former Boston mayor John F. Fitzgerald; and she was overwhelmed by the demands of caring for two small sons, Jack and his older brother, Joe Junior, and for a daughter, Rosemary, born in 1918 and later diagnosed as mentally retarded.

Faced with a life that had veered out of control, Rose did the one thing that always worked for her. In an effort to impose order, she tightly reined in her emotions. The entries in her diary confirm that

Rose did perceive little Jack's acute neediness, as well as the anger and resentment that, over time, he began to feel toward her, but she remained sequestered inside the emotional wall she had built round herself. In later years Jack would insist that he could not remember so much as a hug from his mother.

Certainly young Jack knew exactly what physical affection could be like and understood the pleasure it gave him, for in the brief hours when Joe Kennedy passed through his children's lives, he was as warm and demonstrative as Rose was chilly and remote. On Sunday mornings, he might take the little ones into bed to read them a story or just give them a kiss. These joyous interludes offered Jack a generous helping of the physical intimacy for which he was left to hunger during the rest of the week.

The war ended in 1918, and two days after the signing of the Treaty of Versailles in June 1919, Joe left his post at the shipyard. Rather than return to banking, he went to work at Hayden, Stone & Co., a brokerage house in Boston, and would go on to make a fortune as a stock-market operator. As for Rose, her husband's change of employment failed to ease her mounting crisis. At the beginning of 1920 she was eight months pregnant with a fourth child when, in a mist of despair, she packed a suitcase and returned to her father's house. For three weeks, Jack's mother simply vanished from his life. A nanny cared for the three children until their grandfather insisted that, whatever Rose's complaint, she had no choice but to return to her young family, though for her own good she had better make some changes when she did. Rose came home as suddenly and mysteriously as she had disappeared, and hardly was she back when two-year-old Jack fell ill with scarlet fever. She could do nothing to comfort him, for on the very day he was stricken she went into labor in another room of the small house. It was impossible to explain to a two-year-old why his mother, whom he knew to be nearby, could not answer his cries, however much she may have wanted to. Nor could Rose come to him when the baby, a girl named Kathleen, had been safely delivered, as there was reason to worry that she and the baby might also contract the disease.

As Jack lay close to death and unable to grasp why his mother stayed away, his father burst into his life with all the focus and intensity the lonely little boy had missed. For the first time in Jack's experience, the full force of an adult's emotions was concentrated on him for a sustained period of time. It was Joe who held the sick child in his arms and arranged for him to enter a hospital, Joe who perched day after day at his bedside, letting him know that nothing could be more important to the father than his son's survival. Jack remained in the hospital for weeks, not seeing his mother but basking in his father's unreserved love. Joe later confessed to one of the doctors that, never having known any serious illness in his family prior to Jack's, he could never have predicted the power of his own feelings when he realized that the child might die. Joe's intensely emotional reaction to his son's ordeal, combined with Rose's absence, bonded the boy to his father in ways that would long go to the very core of Jack's being.

On his release from the hospital, Jack was sent to Maine to complete his recuperation. By the time he rejoined his family, almost three months had elapsed since he had first fallen ill. He returned to Brookline to find a mother even more distant and self-absorbed than she had been previously. When Rose's father sent her back to Joe and the children, he had advised her that she ought regularly to take some time for herself apart from household responsibilities. At her instigation, Joe moved his family to a larger house with a specially designated room where Rose made it her custom to retreat for hours on end. She sought escape in books and religion, and throve on quiet and solitude. A door emphatically shut against everything and everyone that might impinge on her privacy became Rose's prescription for survival in a life that otherwise brought much unhappiness. To Jack, this was further evidence, if any were needed, of a mother's rejection. He was known to grow enraged when she went off traveling for weeks at a time, leaving him and his siblings in the care of nannies. "Gee, you're a great mother to go away and leave your children all alone," the five-year-old Jack confronted her in 1923. Rose recorded the incident in her diary, but the child's outburst did not prevent her from leaving the next day on a six-week trip to the West Coast with her sister.

Though on this and other occasions Jack voiced resentment against his mother, there was little reason to hope that she would alter her ways. He had, in fact, already given up on her. Joe Kennedy, bursting with volcanic emotion which he never hesitated to express, was all that Jack had—but to the boy's frustration, Jack was far from all that his father had. When Jack was critically ill in 1920, his father made him the center of his universe. The rest of the time, however, no one could doubt his abiding preoccupation with his eldest son. Joe Junior, twenty-two months Jack's senior, had claimed their father's imagination before the second son was born. As such, the older brother posed a formidable obstacle to the thing Jack learned to want most.

On the day of young Joe's birth, Rose's father had lightheartedly assured newsmen that his grandson would grow up to be president. But there was nothing lighthearted about the way Joe Kennedy embraced that prophecy and transformed it into a family mantra. As far as Joe Senior was concerned, his eldest son was the ideal boy—athletic, strong and strikingly handsome. He was the robust, healthy son, while scrawny, "elfin" Jack was often confined to bed with one childhood ailment or another. Jack's brush with death had riveted Joe Kennedy's attention, but at length the boy's identity in the family as the sickly son meant that, in the father's eyes at least, he must remain his brother's inferior.

Joe Kennedy's maxim, "We want winners, we don't want losers around here," suggested that Jack by virtue of poor health stood little chance in the competition for first place in their father's heart. Jack's sensitive, affectionate nature would attract a host of devoted friends from early on, but those were not characteristics prized by Joe Kennedy, who unabashedly favored the bullying, hot-headed, "manly" older boy. Jack, narrow-faced with protruding ears and a dusting of freckles, was frequently the target of his brother's brutality, and Joe Junior was known to laugh at the sight of the smaller, weaker child after he had been hurt. On numerous occasions young Joe pounded Jack's head against a wall, to the horror of their younger siblings. It was almost as if Joe sniffed a threat from Jack. When the brothers fought each other, their father made a point of declining to come between them, though he did insist that should the need arise they join together as Kennedys to battle against outsiders.

Though in health and hardiness Joe Junior was the superior by far, Jack realized that he had significant vulnerabilities. Their father's hopes placed a huge burden on Joe, who, in whatever he said or did, was under constant pressure to live up to the patriarch's glowing image of him. Rose, too, singled out young Joe as the "natural leader" among her offspring. Always on the lookout for ways to impose order on an ever-growing family, she gave him considerable authority over the younger children. Determined to appear mature beyond his years and unquestionably in charge, Joe Junior developed an excruciating sense of his own dignity. Jack, spotting an opening, exploited every opportunity to make Joe seem ridiculous. Then and later, part of Jack's charm was his ability to laugh at himself, and he realized early on that this gave him a distinct edge over his leadenly self-serious, easily provoked older brother. Young Joe, as neat and painstakingly systematic as Jack often seemed the reverse, had inherited their mother's rage for order. At meals he would carefully separate the chocolate frosting from his slice of cake in anticipation of savoring it last. One evening at dinner, as Joe began this ritual, Jack lay in wait. No sooner had his brother set the frosting to one side than Jack's little hand shot across the table, grabbed the frosting off his brother's plate and stuffed it into his own mouth. The spluttering rage that caused Joe Junior to lose his dignity in front of both parents was a far more cherished treat for Jack than the stolen chocolate.

By such stratagems Jack satirized and sabotaged his brother. Still, he also yearned to defeat young Joe on the latter's terms and to prove himself the tough, sturdy sort of boy their father admired. Accordingly, he provoked innumerable fistfights with his older brother, in which Jack, though capable of battling "like fury" when he had to, inevitably got the worst of it. On the athletic field, he repeatedly ignored his physical frailty in an attempt to live up to their father's image of what a Kennedy ought to be. But whatever the battering to which Jack subjected himself, his place in the family pecking order remained unchanged. Winning, the patriarch taught, was all; runners-up were still losers, however valiantly they competed.

Forced to spend much time in bed, whether to recuperate from sickness or simply to conserve his strength, Jack began to read a great deal. His taste ran to the heroes of English and Scottish history. He was drawn to tales of adventure and chivalry, of the strong who protected the weak, and of causes worth dying for. He read and reread the legends of King Arthur and the Round Table. He was entranced by the works of Robert Louis Stevenson and Sir Walter Scott. Like Winston Churchill, who won an award at Harrow for having memorized the most lines of Macaulay's *Lays of Ancient Rome*, he prized the story of Horatio at the gate, laying down his life to defend his city. Jack's reading would expose him to values starkly at odds with those of a father who taught his boys to regard matters such as duty and honor as superfluous. Jack worshipped his dynamic, highly successful father and longed for his approbation, and it would not have occurred to him at that point to question his philosophy. Nonetheless, Jack, who was already physically out of harmony with the Kennedy atmosphere, widened the breach by his reading. He also quietly confirmed his sense of superiority to young Joe. Unlike the older boy, who studied strictly to earn grades that lived up to their parents' expectations, Jack read for pleasure. If a subject failed to interest him, he did not bother.

Jack enjoyed another important advantage over his brother; he could count on his sister Kathleen to cheer him on. Eventually Joe and Rose would have nine children, including, besides the first four, Eunice, born in 1921; Pat, in 1924; Bobby, in 1925; Jean, in 1928; and finally Teddy, in 1932. Of them all, only Kathleen—whose irrepressible nature had earned her the nickname "Kick"—dissented from the prevailing view that Joe was better than his brother. Jack took enormous pleasure in the fact that Kick idolized him, not young Joe. Her good opinion was worth much in the family; as Rose would later say, Kick was her father's "favorite of all the children."

Years afterward, Kick would recall her father's consternation when she insisted that her beloved Jack could do no wrong. It was, she would laugh, "heresy" in the family even to suggest that Jack might be superior to young Joe. But she had consistently said precisely that and managed to get away with it because her father adored and indulged her. Like Jack, Kick possessed the charm that comes from an ability to laugh at oneself, and from the first they had been each other's preferred companion. Kick, Jack would say after her death, had been the one family member to whom he could tell everything, because "I always knew she loved me."

Kick perceived—and valued—who he was, but as far as Jack was concerned his father did not, and he grew increasingly frustrated by Joe's blindness. Finally, in 1929, when Jack was twelve, he saw a chance to tear the veil from his father's eyes. Joe Junior, aged fourteen, had gone off to boarding school that year, while Jack stayed at home. By this time the Kennedys were living in a sprawling brick house set on five thickly wooded acres in Bronxville, New York; Joe Kennedy had already made a fortune in the stock market and prided himself on the fact that the market crash in October had left him "untouched." At Thanksgiving, when young Joe came home for his first visit since starting at Choate, his father was off in Hollywood chasing a second fortune in the film business and a love affair with the actress Gloria Swanson. To Jack's delight, his brother bore physical evidence that his reception at Choate had been quite different from what the family might have expected. The other boys had shown no inclination to regard Joe as a "natural leader"—far from it. Out in the world on his own, Joe had fallen victim to the sort of brutality he himself routinely dispensed at home. Upperclassmen had knocked the idol off his pedestal, and Jack, who had waited years for their father to acknowledge Joe Junior's imperfection, wrote to apprise him of Joe's pathetic fate:

> When Joe came home he was telling me how strong he was and how tough. The first thing he did to show me how tough he was was to get sick so that he could not have any thanksgiving dinner. Manly Youth. He was then going to show me how to Indian wrestle. I then through him over on his neck. Did the sixth formers lick him. Oh Man he was all blisters, they almost paddled the life out of him. He was roughhousing in the hall a sixth former caught him he led him in and all the sixth formers had a swat or two. What I wouldn't have given to be a sixth former. They have some pretty strong fellows if blisters have anything to do with it.

Jack's letter, fueled by rage at his brother's preeminence at home, posed an open challenge to Joe Junior. Its swagger aimed to make the father perceive young Joe as Jack saw him—and to recast himself as his father would have wished him to be.

It irked Jack that when Mr. and Mrs. Kennedy discussed Joe Junior the emphasis tended to be on matters of achievement, but that when the second son was the subject of conversation they inevitably reverted to the question of his delicacy. Determined to break loose from the image of the sickly boy, Jack, when he was enrolled the following year at the Canterbury School in New Milford, Connecticut, immediately went out for the football team. But no amount of will could cover the fact that, underweight and undersized, Jack was far and away the smallest member of the team. The physical disparity between Jack and his teammates was so absurd that he could only laugh at it himself. One player, he wrote home, weighed 145 pounds—"5 lb. heavier than Joe. Awoh!" He went on, "My nose my leg and other parts of my anatomy have been kicked around so much that it is beginning to be funny." He labored to maintain the guise of a normal, robust boy, but whatever hopes he may have had of starting anew at Canterbury were soon dashed when his health again betrayed him. Inexplicably he lost weight and experienced fatigue, blurred vision and dizzy spells. He landed in the infirmary with a case of hives that left him itching madly and frantic for sleep. He was mortified as the headmaster hovered about constantly, insisting he dress warmly, take additional rest periods, drink a tonic, and submit to regular weigh-ins with the goal of increasing his weight to at least 105 pounds. Other students sat at the headmaster's table on occasion; Jack was required to eat all his meals there. The extra attention, he wrote home in near despair, led the other boys to tease him: "I am made out to be an awful baby."

At school, as at home, beloved books offered consolation—and more. With typical self-mockery, Jack conceded that he had been laughable on the football field, but after Christmas he strove to force his father to acknowledge that there was also an area in which he excelled. Jack's English teacher had assigned the class to read Scott's *Ivanhoe*. The experience, a triumph for Jack, prompted the thirteen-year-old to write a poignant plea to his father: "We are reading Ivanhoe in English," Jack exulted, "and though I may not be able to remember material things such as tickets, gloves and so on I can remember things like Ivanhoe and the last time we had an exam I got a ninety eight." It was the letter of a boy hoping to find a way to assert his own worth, to press his father to see him clearly and shift focus from the things that did not matter to the things that did. In this sense, Canterbury had begun to provide something immensely important for Jack. Sadly, there would be no opportunity to learn where it might have led. Jack's Canterbury career ended abruptly when he had to be taken to the hospital for an appendectomy, and his father, then much on the West Coast, decided not to send him back after spring break. Instead, in the fall of 1931, Jack was sent off to Choate to join Joe Junior.

Even before Jack arrived at his new school, the signs were unpromising for a fourteen-year-old who yearned to shake off his identity as a second son. "If Jack is anything like his brother, he can make up his Latin, and go ahead normally with the Third Form," wrote Choate's Frank Wheeler that summer to Hyannis Port, on Cape Cod, where the Kennedys had a beach house. Jack had not even arrived at Choate and already he was being measured in relation to young Joe. Two years previously, Jack had rejoiced at Joe's troubles at Choate, but by the time he caught up with him there Joe had managed somehow to establish the reputation, in the words of Mrs. George St. John, the headmaster's wife, as "one of the big boys of School on whom we are going to depend." No sooner had Jack entered Choate than it became apparent he was doomed to the sort of comparisons that had long exasperated him. Rather than emulate his brother, Jack now chose to disdain anything that earned young Joe praise. At Choate, Jack seemed to all appearances to abandon the fight to displace Joe in their father's eyes. Joe was compulsively neat; Jack became notorious for the disarray of his room and attire. Joe prided himself on efficiency; Jack billed himself as "the boy that doesn't get things done." Joe worked doggedly for grades and rarely relaxed; Jack made a point of seeming hardly to study. Joe was noted for a fierce intensity; Jack, his teachers complained, suffered from an "inability to concentrate effectively."

Having failed to make his father recognize the particular gifts and tastes that distinguished him, Jack finally gave up. If his father, and just about everyone else except Kick, believed him to be inferior to young Joe, he would play along. Kick alone understood that he did not abandon his sense of himself as superior, only the effort to persuade others that it was so. Thenceforth, Jack publicly cast himself as the happy-go-lucky boy, whose apparent absence of ambition and responsibility his father endlessly bemoaned. In private, however, Jack plunged ever more deeply into the serious reading that at length helped produce the man who would be president.

So it was that, on October 31, 1932, a visitor to Peter Bent Brigham Hospital in Boston, where Jack was undergoing tests to determine the cause of a bout of anemia triggered by a knee injury, was astonished to find him absorbed in *The World Crisis*, Churchill's multi-volume history of the First World War. The visitor, Kay Halle, a new friend of his father's who had never met Jack before, happened to walk in on a pivotal episode in the boy's life. As Kick would recall years afterward, when their father spoke of the war to his sons he would inevitably launch into an angry account of the soldiers who had died "for nothing" at the battle of the Somme in 1916. The British, hoping to break through the German lines along a twenty-five-mile front, had methodically bombarded the enemy for seven days. When the British Expeditionary Force finally advanced, it expected minimal resistance. Instead, the Germans, secure in the shelter of deep dugouts, extinguished vast numbers of men in a relentless blast of machine guns. Yet even then, wave upon wave of British troops, aware of the likelihood they would be mown down by enemy fire, continued across no man's land. By nightfall Britain had lost some 58,000 volunteer soldiers, making that day the deadliest its army had ever known. The battle dragged on for five months and resulted in more than 400,000 British casualties. By the time the carnage ended, a generation had been wiped out and no strategic advantage gained. Joe Kennedy, who at the outset of the battle had quarreled with his Harvard friends about their admiration for the troops' spirit of sacrifice, never ceased to believe that the young men who gave their lives for king and country had died for a "delusion."

In *The World Crisis*, his son encountered a dramatically different view that, like the books to which Jack had been drawn as a boy, set duty and honor before self-interest. Though Churchill criticized the planning behind the battle and lamented the outcome, he extolled the high sense of duty that had led the young soldiers—"every man a volunteer, inspired not only by love of country but by a widespread conviction that human freedom was challenged by military and Imperial tyranny"—to give their lives for a cause larger than themselves. The idea of such gallantry appealed immensely to Jack, and *The World Crisis* proved revelatory in other ways as well. Almost certainly Jack's encounter with that work was the start of his lifelong fascination with how wars begin—and how to prevent them. From Churchill, the fifteen-year-old learned about the miscalculations and accidents that had led to the First World War. He read about what can happen when the momentum toward war takes on an energy of its own, and about the danger of allowing oneself to be drawn to the edge of the precipice. He read about the importance of military preparedness and of firm clear words of warning if war is to be avoided.

Thirty years later, these and other lessons from *The World Crisis* would prove central to the Kennedy presidency.

As Jack lay in bed—"so surrounded by books I could barely see him," Kay Halle remembered—America was days from a presidential election that pitted a Democratic challenger, New York's governor Franklin D. Roosevelt, against the Republican incumbent, Herbert Hoover. Joe Kennedy, in the belief that the Great Depression would provoke a national upheaval likely to strip him of his fortune, had emerged as a fervent supporter of Roosevelt and traveled extensively with him. Roosevelt had arrived in Boston earlier in the day in anticipation of a rally that evening which was billed as the climax of his New England tour. While the candidate rested at his hotel, Kennedy and Halle, also a Roosevelt supporter, visited with Jack at the hospital. The picture of Jack amid a heap of books encapsulates the strange discordance of his life in those years. It was as if the pale, bone-thin teenager simultaneously occupied two planes of existence. He was the "problem child"—his father's characterization—who seemed utterly to lack drive and ambition, and he was the avid reader who had already begun to store up ideas and information critical to his future.

Jack, the only member of his class with his own subscription to the *New York Times* (a gift from his father), read the newspaper "every single day from cover to cover," recalled his schoolmate Ralph "Rip" Horton. When a news item particularly interested him, Jack told Rip, "I'll read it, and then I'll force myself to lie down for about a half an hour and go through the total article in my mind, bringing to memory as much as I possibly can and then analyzing the article, and then attacking it and tearing it down." One such item attracted Jack's attention not long after he left the hospital, where doctors had failed to pinpoint the cause of his anemia. In light of his reading at the hospital, it is not difficult to see why Jack would have been mesmerized when, in comments printed in the *New York Times*, Churchill seemed to answer the question posed on the final page of *The World Crisis*: whether the last war had been the end of strife or whether his nation's children would soon "bleed and gasp again in devastated lands." On November 23, 1932, in the House of Commons, the fifty-seven-year-old former First Lord of the Admiralty warned of another fiery confrontation with Germany if steps were not taken immediately. Jack later called those remarks "the opening gun" of Churchill's campaign for British rearmament in the face of German territorial ambitions.

Churchill was responding to an address by Stanley Baldwin, the former prime minister who, as Lord President of the Council, was the real power in Prime Minister Ramsay MacDonald's government. Germany, forbidden by the Treaty of Versailles to rearm, now demanded the right to do precisely that. Baldwin, speaking on behalf of the government, supported Germany's demand on the condition that it pledge along with other nations to renounce the use of force. In comments that, Jack later wrote, "deeply and profoundly impressed the people" and had a "tremendous influence on later British policy," Baldwin called on young people to consider the unprecedented peril of aerial warfare. He predicted that British towns were likely to be bombed "within the first five minutes of war to an extent inconceivable in the last war." He urged his listeners to keep in mind that there was "no power on earth" that could protect them from bombing. In an indelible phrase calculated, as Jack later judged, to create a sense of defenselessness among the civilian population, Baldwin declared, "The bomber will always get through." Churchill, ill with paratyphoid, had been absent from the House at the time of Baldwin's speech, but when he returned on the 23rd he replied to the government's case with the first of his great warnings of the approaching danger—speeches which a young Jack Kennedy would monitor in the *New York Times*, and which years afterward he would cite, as well as emulate, when he ran for president. Churchill deplored Baldwin's sense of fatalism and helplessness and mocked the naïveté of government leaders who failed to perceive Germany's desire for revenge. He warned that, far from merely seeking equal status, a rearmed Germany would soon demand "the return of lost territories and lost colonies." Like *The World Crisis*, Churchill's warnings about the need for Britain to rearm, which began with the November 1932 foreign policy debate, became part of Jack's imaginative landscape.

So did a controversy spurred by Baldwin's appeal to the young to consider that, were there to be another war, "they principally and they alone" would be "responsible for the terrors that have fallen on the earth." Less than three months after Baldwin's assertion that the bomber would always get through, it appeared that British youth had taken his words to heart. In the last war, great numbers of Oxford University students had volunteered. Now, within days of Adolf Hitler becoming German chancellor, the Oxford Union, the renowned debating society where future British prime ministers and members of Parliament honed their skills, voted in favor of the motion, "That this House will in no circumstances fight for its King and Country." The proceedings, on February 9, 1933, mirrored the recent debate in the Commons, with one side playing to the anxieties drummed up by Baldwin and the other echoing Churchill's position that only by a course of rearmament might Britain avert another war. When the pacifist argument prevailed, Churchill growled that the defeatism propounded by Baldwin had done its insidious work by persuading the younger generation that there would be no way to defend themselves in a new war. Speaking at Oxford on February 17, Churchill claimed almost to be able to feel "the curl of contempt" upon the lips of militaristic German youth "when they read this message sent out by Oxford University in the name of young England."

The King and Country resolution, coming as it did so soon after he had read Churchill's powerful account of the young men who had rushed to volunteer in 1914 and who by giving their lives had "fulfilled the high purpose of duty with which they were imbued," made the deepest impression on Jack. Puzzled by the degree to which the heroic Britain of his books seemed to have altered since the last war, Jack followed the Oxford Union affair in the *New York Times* over the course of several days. He concluded that young Britain had grown "decadent"— a judgment later repeated to London friends. In 1933, Churchill remained confident that were war to be declared his nation's young men would perform their duty. The problem with the King and Country resolution, in Churchill's view, was that it might encourage those in other countries to think Britain would not fight, and that that miscalculation might set off another war. Jack's assessment that the British had grown decadent represented precisely the sort of foreign reaction Churchill feared.

Even as he religiously followed the events in Europe and embarked on a many-years' project of reading "every single thing Churchill had ever written," Jack's day-to-day performance at Choate continued to provoke dismay. Most distressing to his father was Jack's apparent imperviousness to rebuke, as though his family's disappointment concerned him not at all. Still there were signs, invisible to Joe, that Jack was not as indifferent as his carefree pose suggested. When Joe Junior graduated in May 1933, he won Choate's award for best all-round athletic and academic achievement. Following the presentation, Jack slipped off with his closest school friend, Kirk LeMoyne "Lem" Billings, himself a second son whose older brother had been a Choate star and prizewinner. When he and Lem were alone, Jack confessed for the first time that he believed he was more intelligent than Joe, though his parents failed to recognize it.

At least the fact that Joe was graduating meant that, for his last two years at Choate, Jack would be free of his brother's suffocating presence. Indeed, the following year Joe would not even be at home during school vacations. He had been accepted to their father's alma mater, but at the suggestion of Harvard law professor Felix Frankfurter, Joe Senior had decided first to send him to Britain. He was to spend a year at the London School of Economics under the guidance of the political scientist Harold Laski, whom Frankfurter recommended as the world's finest educator. Laski presided over packed lecture halls, but it was in the more intimate setting of Sunday afternoon teas at his home that, he liked to say, his most vital work with students occurred. Laski was also a socialist, and Joe Kennedy recognized that in their views he and the professor were "black and white." Kennedy insisted that, while he disagreed with everything Laski had ever written, it would serve young Joe well to know the arguments on the other side. In September 1933, the day before he escorted his eldest son to Europe, Kennedy wrote to the headmaster at Choate, "I feel very pleased and satisfied with the development Joe has shown since he has been under your care, and I am sincerely hopeful of Jack coming out with the same results." Though Jack had improved in the past year, "He still has a tendency to be careless in details and really is not very determined to be a success." Kennedy notified him that, when he and Mrs. Kennedy returned to the United States in November, he would visit Choate to see how Jack was getting along.

Briefly, it seemed as if Jack did intend to alter his profile. Impressed by the caliber of his private reading and by the gusto with which he approached the subject, the history instructor Russell Ayres, whom Joe Kennedy had known at Harvard, pronounced Jack "one of the few great minds" he had ever had in his class. In large part, however, Jack's attitude toward schoolwork did not change. In his brother's absence Jack did blossom, but in ways unlikely to please his father. That fall, Jack gathered round him a mischievous group of friends who offered all the approval he needed. If Mr. and Mrs. Kennedy, along with most of the teachers, continued to believe young Joe was the more outstanding, the claque was no less ardent in its admiration of the second son. Jack was their leader, and as far as they were concerned everything he said or did was cause for applause. As it happened, Kick was also in Connecticut that fall, beginning her first year at a Roman Catholic convent school in nearby Noroton. No sooner had his favorite sister arrived than Jack snuck out with Lem to see her—as if Kick were a great prize that he could hardly wait to show off to his roommate. From that moment Kick, though only thirteen, was incorporated as an honorary member of Jack's group. The boys visited whenever they could and Kick was kept informed by telephone and telegram of the boys' fun. Kick and Lem, in particular, were soon united in a close friendship, based, as they understood from the first, on their shared devotion to Jack. Raised by a devoutly Roman Catholic mother to be innocent and good, Kick sincerely disapproved of bad behavior and never hesitated to let Jack and his friends know it. At the same time, she shared her brother's sense of humor and often seemed to thrill to his recklessness, regarding him as "quite the grandest fellow that ever lived." Though she remained decidedly her mother's daughter, life with father had provided a veneer of sophistication, an ability to mimic certain of the attitudes and racy talk of Joe Kennedy and her older brothers. The mix of innocence and raciness was as amusing as it was incongruous.

If Jack seemed pleased with his new situation, his father emphatically was not. "I can't tell you how unhappy I felt in seeing him and talking with him and feeling that he certainly is not on the right track," Kennedy complained to Jack's headmaster, George St. John, on November 21, 1933, after his visit to Choate. "The observations that I made are not much different than I made before that the work he wants to do he does exceptionally well, but he seems to lack entirely a sense of responsibility, and that to my way of thinking must be developed in him very quickly, or else I am very fearful of the result. The happy-go-lucky manner with a degree of indifference that he shows toward the things he has no interest in does not portend well for his future development." After urging that the school find a way to help Jack cultivate a sense of responsibility, he concluded with the obligatory comparison to young Joe. "Joe you would be proud of. I have left him in London . . . and he is doing a remarkable job. I would very much like to have Jack follow in his footsteps and he can only do that if he senses his own responsibilities."

At Christmas, Jack obtained permission to bring Lem down to the Kennedys' oceanfront house in Palm Beach, Florida. On this visit, Kick consolidated her role in her brother's claque, tagging along as he and Lem, with some others, made the rounds of Palm Beach nightspots. Afterward, Kick appeared to speak for her brother as well when she pronounced it the best vacation ever. Content, even blissful, in the good opinion of Lem and Kick, Jack had insulated himself from his father's criticism and showed no interest in being drawn back into the competition with his brother. But shortly after Jack returned to Choate following the winter break, his life took a turn that instantly pushed aside all of Joe Kennedy's other concerns.

Jack was taken to the infirmary with a case of hives, and at first the episode seemed similar to the one at Canterbury three years previously. This time, however, Jack did not recover quickly. When his temperature soared and blood count plummeted, the school administration had him moved to New Haven Hospital and summoned his father from Palm Beach. Once again Joe Kennedy, drawing on deep reserves of feeling, hovered over a child for whose life he feared—and the bond forged in 1920 became even stronger. For ten days the father who in recent months had expressed such strong displeasure with Jack dwelt on nothing but the boy's survival. Stingy with praise for his second son he may have been, but never with love when Jack most needed it. At Choate, the boys were told that Jack might be near death, and, as George St. John reported, "we pray Jack is better every hour. To see how sorry everybody is when Jack is ill proves the kind of fellow he is."

The doctors were puzzled by Jack's symptoms. One suggested that he was suffering from agranulocytosis, an often fatal blood disease bordering on leukemia, and that his chances of survival were "about five out of one hundred." Specialists from Peter Bent Brigham Hospital in Boston, where Jack had been treated in 1932, and the Mayo Clinic in

Rochester, Minnesota, followed one another through his hospital room until, finally, the danger seemed to pass. The good news was soon tempered by the realization that no one could say with certainty what had been wrong with him. The crisis could recur at any moment, and the next time it might prove fatal. Beginning with this episode in 1934, a terrible indeterminacy weighed heavily on both father and son.

On the assumption that Jack would not soon return to school, Joe Kennedy took him to Palm Beach. But when Jack, who weighed 125 pounds when he left the hospital, managed to put on another fifteen, his father let him go back to Choate after spring break to finish his junior year. That summer, he was sent to the Mayo Clinic for evaluation. Burdened by his identity in the family as the sickly son, Jack could not bear for his claque at Choate to think of him that way. Accordingly, during this and subsequent hospital stays, he spiced his letters with talk of sexually rapacious nurses—"the dirtiest-minded bunch of females I've ever seen"—and other schoolboy fantasies that would head off pity. Jack nearly managed to cast his situation as enviable. "I had an enema given by a beautiful blonde," he reported to Lem on one occasion. "That, my sweet, is the height of cheap thrills." And on another: "The nurses are very tantalizing and I'm really the pet of the hospital. All day they come in and let me tell you nurses are almost as dirty as you, you filthy minded shit." He even claimed that a nurse "wanted to know if I would give her a workout last night." He reported that he had said yes but that the assignation had failed to materialize, the young woman having gone off duty early. As was his nature, Jack distanced himself from his medical ordeal and cloaked his fears in jokes at his own expense. When Lem was the audience, those jokes tended to be dirty.

To Jack's dismay, and even more so to his father's, a month's worth of tests proved inconclusive. "Nobody able to figure out what's wrong with me," Jack reported. "All they talk about is what an interesting case." Jack returned to Hyannis Port no closer to understanding the cause of his medical problems than in 1932, when tests had failed to discover the source of his anemia.

At the time of those earlier tests, Joe Kennedy had expected to be rewarded with a post in the new Roosevelt administration, preferably as secretary of the treasury. Nearly two years had passed without an offer from the White House when finally, that July of 1934, Roosevelt named Kennedy to chair the newly created Securities and Exchange Commission. The appointment of a famous stock-market operator to be Wall Street's cop seemed a travesty to many, but Kennedy quickly made it clear that he intended to disprove his critics. He announced plans to "cut red tape" and to create an atmosphere of cooperation between the SEC and those whose practices it oversaw.

From then on Joe Kennedy spent a great deal of time in Washington, and when he came home to his family—at Bronxville, Hyannis Port or Palm Beach—he invariably had much to say about the world of politics. Though Kennedy would often, through the years, pay lip service to an ideal of public service, it was really only power that interested him—unabashedly so. "I wanted power," he would later reflect on his career. "I thought money would give me power, so I made money, only to discover that it was politics—not money that really gave a man power. So I went into politics."

In the late summer of 1934 both elder sons were in residence at Hyannis Port, Joe Junior having returned from London in anticipation of entering Harvard. At the family table the father lovingly inculcated his sons with his views. The boys were welcome, even encouraged to disagree with anything he said. And though the give-and-take—especially with volatile young Joe, who, to Jack's amusement, seemed during his year abroad to have embraced some left-wing ideas—would often grow fairly contentious, there could be no doubt that the sons held their father in awe. When by turns he lectured, exhorted, questioned, criticized and praised, his sole focus was on his sons, and only a telephone call from President Roosevelt was capable of breaking the spell. Kennedy's comments were so stimulating, Lem Billings recalled, "that you wanted to read and study so that you could take part" in the discussions. Unfortunately for outsiders, Kennedy made no bones about the fact that he was exclusively interested in what his own offspring had to say. He sought to mold and guide them, not other people's children. When Rip Horton sat in on some of these sessions, he was "practically ignored." Once he committed the faux pas of asking a question and was answered "rather curtly, as though [Kennedy] didn't want to be bothered." By contrast, young Joe, Jack or even outspoken Kick—who as a girl was thought to be without the possibility of a political future—could pose no question too trivial but that their father would "go to great lengths" to answer. He insisted that nothing was more important than his children's education.

During Jack's senior year at Choate, Joe Kennedy received word that Jack, along with Lem, Rip and ten other boys, faced expulsion for "corrupting the morals and integrity of the other students in the school." Jack and his group had baptized themselves the Muckers Club, a defiant reference to the headmaster's remark in chapel that "the worst kind of boy" was what he called a mucker and that if he could learn the identities of all the muckers at Choate he would promptly expel them. St. John, apparently perceiving a challenge to his authority when the boys formed their club, announced plans to send all thirteen of them home. According to Rip Horton, Joe Kennedy arrived from Washington "highly irate at young Jack for allowing himself to get into this particular predicament." He negotiated a reprieve for Jack and the others, who would be permitted to finish out their senior year. But though Jack longed to go on to Princeton with Lem and Rip, his father had other plans for him. He wanted Jack to follow his older brother and spend a year with Professor Laski at the London School of Economics.

Jack and his parents, along with Kick, who had been enrolled at a convent school in France, sailed on the French liner *Normandie* on September 25, 1935. As the Kennedys settled in at Claridge's hotel, throughout London the talk of an impending general election vied with anxious discussion of whether Italy's recent invasion of Abyssinia would lead to war. Prior to the attack on July 4, Britain had sent battle cruisers to the Mediterranean as a warning, but Mussolini, reportedly on the basis of the Oxford Union's King and Country resolution, calculated correctly that in this instance Britain would not go so far as to provoke a confrontation. Still, the specter of war changed Joe Kennedy's mind about the wisdom of leaving Jack in London. "Am definitely coming to Princeton," Jack exulted in a letter to Lem on October 9, "as London looks very tense and know Dad will let me so it ought to be very jolly." Soon, however, much as he loathed and resented the idea of emulating young Joe, Jack began to wonder whether he was really in such a hurry to leave after all.

A few months previously, Stanley Baldwin had become prime minister again, when Ramsay MacDonald resigned because of ill health. For three years Jack had been monitoring Churchill's breach with Baldwin on the issue of preparedness, and now matters arranged themselves in an unexpected way. At the Conservative Party conference in Bourne-mouth at the start of October, Churchill emerged as an unlikely supporter of Baldwin, who, in turn, delivered an address pledging rearmament. Churchill, though he had no greater faith in Baldwin than previously, backed the prime minister in the expectation that were the Conservatives to triumph in the general election he would again be named First Lord of the Admiralty. And Baldwin, even as he assured certain audiences that he supported a program of rearmament, was promising others that there would be "no great armaments." "Thus," Churchill later wrote, "the votes both of those who sought to see the nation prepare itself against the dangers of the future and of those who believed that peace could be preserved by praising its virtues were gained." A quarter century later, when Jack Kennedy repeatedly compared Richard Nixon, his opponent in the presidential election, to Stanley Baldwin, he was referring to Baldwin's willingness to say whatever his audience wished to hear.

In 1935, for the first time, Churchill and Jack's father crossed paths. On October 7, Mr. and Mrs. Kennedy were luncheon guests at Chartwell, Churchill's country house. The financier Bernard Baruch, a friend of both men, had proposed the meeting, and in view of Kennedy's reputation as Roosevelt's intimate Churchill had enthusiastically taken up the suggestion. Just before sailing for Britain, Kennedy had stepped down as SEC chairman after a highly successful year, and he was shortly to report back to the president on the European economic picture. At the time of the luncheon, Churchill expected that, by virtue of his support for Baldwin in the general election, he would soon again have his hands on the military machine. Eager to involve Roosevelt in the problems of Europe, Churchill used the meeting with Kennedy to argue that it would be wise for London and Washington to join forces against the German threat. This initial encounter went well enough for Churchill to invite "a distinguished company" to meet Kennedy at the end of the month, but at exactly the wrong moment Jack fell sick. He was hospitalized with a recurrence of the illness that had almost killed him in 1934, and Joe Kennedy sent word that he would be unable to attend the luncheon in his honor.

Within days, Jack improved sufficiently to allay the doctors' fears.

"Dad says I can go home if I want to," he wrote to Lem from the hospital, "but I have decided to stay as figure it would be rather stupid to go home now however, may return at Christmas." Parliament had been called into session one week early to discuss Britain's role in the Abyssinian crisis, and election fever was heating up; Jack was seeing history unroll before his eyes. But whatever Joe Kennedy may have said at first, on consideration he decided to send Jack home "to be near his doctors." On October 19, he wrote Churchill to explain that, "After a week of concern and anxiety, I have sent my boy back to America this morning. I propose following him on Wednesday." The second meeting with Churchill was canceled. By the end of October Jack had joined Lem and Rip at Princeton, where he followed in the press an election that would fascinate him for years to come. On November 7, 1935, the Baldwin government was returned to power, but there would be no Cabinet post for Churchill.

At Princeton Jack remained unwell. When he came home for Thanksgiving it was apparent that, chronically underweight and suffering from bouts of dizziness and fatigue, he was too ill to continue at the university. He soon withdrew, and after much prodding from his father he agreed to return to Peter Bent Brigham Hospital for further evaluation. Jack arrived in Boston in January 1936, but when doctors proposed two months of tests the usually stoic eighteen-year-old rebelled, informing his mother that he had had enough. That he was resistant to yet another battery of tests was hardly surprising, as he had already endured four years of procedures which had often been excruciatingly painful and had left him no closer to an answer—or a cure. Jack preferred to go to Palm Beach, but his father intervened with a passionately argued letter full of love and comprehension of all that Jack was feeling. He urged his son to go through with the tests and learn once and for all what was the matter with him so that he could proceed with his life. Jack reluctantly agreed, but for all of his usual good humor and bravery, certain of his letters betrayed just how perilous he knew his situation to be. "My blood count this morning was 3500," he wrote to Lem. "When I arrived it was 6000. At 1000 you die. They call me '2000 to go Kennedy.'" The fearsome words "agranulocytosis" and "leukemia" were again uttered, but when Jack arrived in Palm Beach at the end of February he and his family were still no closer to an understanding of his condition. For the moment all he could do was to follow doctors' orders to rest in the sun and try to regain strength.

Hardly had Jack arrived in Florida when Churchill's warnings about a rearmed Germany, which Jack had been tracking since 1932, were spectacularly realized. On March 7, 1936, encouraged by Mussolini's success in Abyssinia, Hitler announced the reoccupation of the Rhineland, which the Treaty of Versailles had designated a demilitarized zone, a status reaffirmed by the Treaty of Locarno. As he made the announcement his soldiers crossed over the boundary and swept into the principal German towns of the region. Later that month, Churchill rose in the Commons to deliver a speech whose ideas and words Jack would draw on in later years. Churchill cautioned that whatever Hitler might claim about this being the end of German territorial ambitions, the Rhineland episode was "but a step, a stage, an incident" in the approach of another war. Churchill predicted that far from stopping at the Rhineland, Hitler would next set his sights on Austria. To those who called Churchill a warmonger, he replied that on the contrary he was "looking for a way to stop war." That, he insisted, could not be done by pious sentiments and appeals. He called on Britain to make itself powerful again so that it might "negotiate from strength and not from weakness" and halt the German war machine while time remained. To Churchill's frustration, the Baldwin government persisted in its refusal to rearm adequately—a failure to which Jack would crucially and repeatedly allude during the 1960 presidential campaign.

By mid-April, Joe Kennedy, convinced that Jack was spending too much time at various Palm Beach nightspots when he ought to be resting, obtained doctors' approval to send him to a ranch in Arizona to complete his recuperation. When Jack came home in June he seemed well enough to contemplate a return to college in the fall. The previous year he had been accepted to both Princeton and Harvard; now he agreed to join his brother at the latter. Unhappy to find himself a full year behind Lem and Rip, Jack briefly spoke of trying to complete the usual four-year course of study in three. His father expressed the hope to Harvard's dean of freshmen that such talk might indicate "the beginning of an awakening ambition." But as soon as Jack arrived at Harvard, he made it clear that he planned to concentrate on sports and socializing, and leave the quest for academic laurels to young Joe.

Feeling much better and aware that the life-threatening episodes might recur at any time, Jack set out to enjoy himself as long as his present burst of vigor held out. He played football, swam and golfed. He arranged visits back and forth with the Princeton crowd as well as group trips to New York, where the Stork Club became a favorite haunt. In his parents' absence, he and his friends enjoyed numerous weekends at the Kennedy family home in Hyannis Port. Kick, re-enrolled at Noroton after a year in France, was a frequent participant in these occasions, except when Jack hoped to have sex with a particular girl he had invited along. Then it usually fell to Lem to make sure Kick was not included in the group, often a difficult task as she expected to be part of whatever fun Jack had organized. The Kennedy children had grown up with a father who thought nothing of bringing his mistresses to the family table, where Mrs. Kennedy always went to great lengths to feign obliviousness. Much as Kick adored her father, she was agonized by what she saw as his heartless humiliation of her mother. Though Jack and young Joe accepted their father's behavior as a matter of course and even learned to admire it, in his own actions Jack took care not to put his sister in situations she might find uncomfortable. As he later said, he loved her too much for that.

Jack's good health persisted during freshman year, but the period of grace ended the following summer. His father, who had returned to public service when Roosevelt appointed him chairman of the United States Maritime Commission, had arranged for Jack and Lem to travel in Europe together. The trip, which took the boys to France, Spain, Italy, Germany and Holland, ended badly when in London Jack was again stricken with a fever and hives. Lem had had a long acquaintance with Jack's health problems, but he had never been called on to deal with an episode alone and he found it terrifying. Jack's symptoms vanished as mysteriously as they had appeared, but they served as a warning that his good health of the previous year could not last.

Soon after Jack returned to Harvard as a sophomore, President Roosevelt named Joe Kennedy to replace the ailing Robert Bingham as Ambassador to the Court of St. James's. It was difficult for some observers to imagine the blunt, proudly profane Joe Kennedy in any diplomatic post—and even harder to conceive of a Catholic Irish-American in charge at the London embassy. Nonetheless, he had been an effective leader at the SEC and had brought the same dedication to the Maritime Commission. His financial expertise promised to be a great advantage at a moment when London and Washington were negotiating a reciprocal trade agreement. In London, news of the appointment of an ambassador said to be close to the president was generally well received. The *Daily Telegraph* hailed it as "the greatest compliment Roosevelt could pay to Great Britain." Kennedy himself was thrilled by the status of the position and by the honor thereby conferred on all Irish-Americans. Not least, he saw the ambassadorship as an opportunity to help prevent American involvement in another European war. Nearly two years had passed since the occupation of the Rhineland, and many people in Britain were eager to believe that Hitler was satisfied, that the Baldwin government had been wise to do nothing, and that Churchill's prediction that the Germans would move next against Austria had been alarmist and wrong. Still, should war break out in Europe, Kennedy, who had bitterly opposed US participation in the last war, intended to make it his mission to ensure that his country stayed out of a conflict that, to his mind, had nothing to do with American interests.

Joe and Rose Kennedy planned to make the voyage, along with Kick, Pat, Bobby, Jean and Teddy, in February 1938, but at the last minute Mrs. Kennedy suffered an attack of appendicitis and her husband sailed alone on the US liner *Manhattan*. The others were scheduled to join him later in "installments," with Jack and Joe Junior due to come over together at the end of the school year. Meanwhile Jack, confined to the Harvard infirmary with the flu, was the only one of the children not to see their father off in New York.

On March 11, 1938, ten days after Joe Kennedy arrived in London to take up his post, the situation in Europe altered sharply when Germany invaded Austria. Joe Kennedy was in the visitors' gallery at the House of Commons when Churchill argued that the significance of Hitler's latest move could not be exaggerated. Europe, Churchill declared, was confronted with "a program of aggression, nicely calculated and timed, unfolding stage by stage." As Churchill saw it, the only possible responses were to submit, like Austria, or to take strong measures while time remained to ward off the danger and, if it could not be warded off, to cope with it. He pointed to Czechoslovakia as Hitler's next target and, in a passage that would long intrigue Jack Kennedy, he warned that his country must "declare plainly" where it stood in the matter of Czechoslovakia. Should Hitler move against Czechoslovakia, France, along with Russia, was bound by treaty to come in on the Czech side; Britain in turn was obliged by the Locarno Agreement to defend France against unprovoked aggression by Germany. Churchill maintained that lest Hitler miscalculate in the light of British inaction after the invasions of the Rhineland and Austria, Britain must be quick to offer "a perfectly plain statement" of its intention to come to the support of France and participate in the defense of Czechoslovakia.

On the day of his speech, Churchill privately insisted to Joe Kennedy that sentiment was growing for determined action. "I must say I am not sure he is right," Kennedy wrote to a friend in America, "or at least that the House opinion he describes represents the country in any large measure. Chamberlain's policy of waiting to see what happens would appear to me to be the popular course, so far as an outsider can judge." Rather than risk a new war, Neville Chamberlain, who had become prime minister on Baldwin's retirement in 1937, had resolved to pursue an "all-out" policy of appeasement that would enable Britain to come to terms with Hitler and Mussolini, an approach warmly favored by the new American ambassador. Churchill's predictions—about German territorial ambitions in general and about Austria in particular—had come true thus far, yet Kennedy was correct in his assessment that Chamberlain's perspective still more closely resembled that of a majority of the electorate.

It had only been twenty years since the end of the First World War and memories of the carnage remained fresh. Virtually every family, of every class, had been touched by the slaughter. Much of a generation had been sacrificed, including men who might have been expected to lead their nation in the future. In the cases of some survivors, the ideals that had propelled them to volunteer had spoiled. Many people in Britain were "firmly of the belief that another war could not happen" so soon after the last one. Certainly there was no appetite for another conflict that, with the advent of aerial warfare, threatened to be even more destructive. Baldwin and others had, through the years, made an impression with haunting images of British cities under a hail of German bombs that would make no distinction between soldier and civilian. Further militating against strong action to counter German aggression was the popular belief that Germany had been dealt with unfairly in the Treaty of Versailles, as well as a perception that Russia posed the more formidable threat and that Hitler, the Bolsheviks' avowed enemy, offered Britain a useful bulwark against Communism.

Four days after Churchill urged his country to declare plainly where it stood, Joe Kennedy made a blunt statement of his own at the customary dinner hosted by the Pilgrims' Club to welcome Washington's new man in London. In his first address to a British audience, Kennedy undertook "to tell our British cousins that they must not get into a mess counting on us to bail them out," as had been the case in the last war. Spinning a variation on the theme of self-interest that Jack had often heard addressed at home, he warned the foreign secretary, Lord Halifax, and other dignitaries that in the harsh economic climate of 1938 the average American was primarily concerned with his own financial security and had little interest in international developments, which, regardless of their importance, seemed "vague and far away." American public opinion, Kennedy strongly suggested, would not support participation in another European war. His talk at the Pilgrims' dinner, which one observer called "the most isolationist utterance that has come from any American Ambassador in many years," served as a warning to think twice before taking any steps that might lead to a new confrontation with Germany.

Jack was at New England Baptist Hospital with intestinal flu when, on March 19, the *New York Times* printed his father's speech. For the past six years, he had been studying Churchill's writings and following his campaign to bolster British defenses in the face of the German threat. With the Pilgrims' Club speech, Joe Kennedy assumed a prominent place in the great debate. Four months before Jack was to join his family in London, the father he idolized had positioned himself as the direct and outspoken adversary of Winston Churchill.

CHAPTER TWO

The Aristocratic Cousinhood

O N JULY 4, 1938, AT THE CLOSE OF A FESTIVE TRANSATLANTIC crossing, Jack Kennedy stood at the railing of the *Normandie* as photographers on the dock at Southampton jostled for position. The rawboned, strikingly handsome six-foot-tall young man projected a palpable energy and exhilaration. Yet he had been in and out of the hospital during the spring term at Harvard, and on the occasion of his twenty-first birthday two months previously he had been too exhausted to celebrate. Poor health had made it a struggle just to finish the academic year, and at the close of exams he had returned to New England Baptist Hospital for two additional weeks in the hope that he would be well enough to spend the summer abroad. Joe Kennedy had come back to America that spring to report to President Roosevelt, attend young Joe's graduation, and bring both boys back with him to London. Jack, standing beside the ambassador and Joe Junior, clearly reveled in the excitement. The elder Kennedy had made a strong impression in Britain, where the very qualities that had caused some in the United States to worry about his appointment had swiftly endeared him to his hosts. They enjoyed his colorful conversation, which bristled with slang and profanity; there was also much favorable comment about informal working habits that brought a new and welcome vigor to the embassy. Kennedy often worked in shirtsleeves, barked constantly into telephones like the film industry mogul he had once been, and was known during meetings to swing both feet up on his desk as he talked. In the beginning, at any rate, a good many people in London relished the fact that he was so different from other diplomats—such as his impeccably well-mannered predecessor, Robert Bingham—and from themselves. At the same time, Kennedy had become popular, notably in certain aristocratic circles, because his sense of Churchill as a warmonger and Hitler as a useful ally against the Bolsheviks harmonized with their views. To judge by the crowd of photographers vying for shots of Jack and Joe Junior, some of Britain's fascination with Joe Kennedy had already rubbed off on his sons.

Ordinarily the ambassador loved to pose with his children, but on this occasion there was no time to linger. When they arrived in London, at the American embassy residence in the former J. P. Morgan house at 14, Prince's Gate, opposite Hyde Park, Jack and Joe Junior had only moments to greet their brothers and sisters before changing into evening dress in order to accompany their parents to the Dorchester hotel, where the ambassador was scheduled to speak at the Independence Day dinner and ball sponsored by the American Society of London. At a moment of high suspense as to whether Hitler would move against Czechoslovakia and how Britain would respond to new German aggression, anything Washington's envoy might reveal about the American position was naturally of urgent interest. Rather than press Hitler to stay back, Chamberlain hoped to persuade the Czechs to accede to the Führer's demands on behalf of the German minority in the Sudetenland—demands that included, in addition to autonomy for the Sudeten Germans, the termination of the treaty of mutual assistance with France designed to shield Czechoslovakia against the Germans. Chamberlain's calculated resistance to calls for a firm and clear promise to act should the Germans move against Czechoslovakia left the world in complete uncertainty about British intentions. Kennedy had returned from the United States that day and, as he was known to have conferred with Roosevelt during his visit, his comments were widely and eagerly awaited. That Kennedy's co-speaker was Anthony Eden, who shortly before the new ambassador took up his post had resigned as British foreign secretary in protest against the policy of appeasement, heightened the drama of the evening.

On his exhilarating first night in London in 1938, Jack saw enacted the debate between those like his father who wanted Britain to come to terms with the dictators and those who argued that matters of principle made it impossible to do so. Kennedy emphasized that various people in America had asked him to convey the message that it would be best to settle things quickly, so that Britain could "keep on living comfortably in the family of nations" and avoid a war. His comments offered thinly veiled support for Chamberlain, while suggesting that the British, should they choose to go to war, must not expect any help from Washington. Eden countered that while he did not expect the United States always to be prepared "to pull British chestnuts out of the fire," there had begun to be "quite a few chestnuts" that ought to be of concern to both countries. Just as Kennedy had managed to avoid the name Roosevelt, Eden did not identify Hitler as the common enemy when he called for Anglo-American cooperation based on a shared belief "in constitutional government, in freedom of the individual, in racial and religious tolerance—now almost become rare in this troubled Europe." Later, Kennedy privately offered additional support for Chamberlain's policy. In the course of a report on his trip to the United States, he informed Lord Halifax that while American popular opinion had been sympathetic toward Eden at the time of his resignation, the mood in America had since shifted in the direction of Chamberlain.

Three days after the Independence Day gala, the ambassador took young Joe along with him to Dublin, where he was to receive an honorary degree from the National University of Ireland and be feted by Prime Minister Eamon de Valera at Dublin Castle. Jack was left at Prince's Gate to stand in for his father at Rose Kennedy's side at a dinner party on the evening of Friday, July 8, for some of Kick's new British friends. A large dinner dance was being held that night, after the Eton and Harrow cricket match, and the American-born hostess Viscountess Astor had asked Mrs. Kennedy to preside over one of several small dinners early in the evening for those who would not be dining with the Astors. By the time they arrived at the brightly lit embassy residence, the young people had heard much of Jack, for Kick had spoken constantly of him in recent weeks. More than six decades later, one guest's memory of that evening would be dominated by the sound of Jack and his eighteen-year-old sister laughing uproariously as she tugged him from one group of friends to another. Kick would whisper something to Jack, he would dissolve in laughter, and that would set her off laughing in turn. To a shy, sheltered British debutante, the lanky American in evening clothes who towered above his diminutive sister seemed everything Kick had promised. "He looked very much a boy, all long skinny arms and legs, but very, very attractive!" remembered Lady Lloyd, Jean Ogilvy as she was then. Though Jack's sister had failed to mention it, he moved with "a sort of careless grace" that made him seem exceedingly sure of himself—"not arrogant, but simply confident." Eventually Rose Kennedy, in what another of Kick's British friends would describe as "the ugliest voice I have ever heard, like a duck with laryngitis," warned her daughter that it was time to stop introducing Jack around as she was ready to announce dinner. Mrs. Kennedy had to intervene at least twice, as Kick always seemed to have "one more person" she wanted Jack to talk to before they went in, and began to grow visibly nervous. Nevertheless, Rose, an adroit hostess, fulfilled her duty of ensuring that the young people in her charge reached Lady Astor's dance at ten.

It was said that at Nancy Astor's "one might meet, and did meet, every conceivable kind of person," and it was precisely that mix that made her parties such great fun. At the Astor residence, 4, St. James's Square, Kick and her friends met up with others from their set, an exclusive subgroup within the vaster category of all those participating in the London Season—which extended from May through the Goodwood races at the end of July—when prominent families introduced their daughters to society, as well as to suitable young men. For Jack, the evening demonstrated the remarkable extent to which his sister, after only four months, had acquired membership in a "tight little circle" drawn in part from families that had helped shape the history of England and Scotland. A number of the young people were related to one another many times over, a reflection of the aristocratic tendency to marry within one's own tribe. More often than not, their families were immensely rich and had vast landholdings with castles, mansions and large numbers of tenants who dwelled in the lord's houses, farmed his land, and otherwise worked on his estates. In line with a venerable past, certain of the families continued to wield political power and influence, though by no means as much as in earlier days.

Jack had already encountered a good many of the names of those in Kick's set. In John Buchan's *Montrose* he had learned about the Ogilvys and the Colquhouns; in Churchill's *Marlborough*, about the Devon-shires; and elsewhere, about the Cecils, the Loughboroughs and others. Some of the great houses that figured in their conversation, such as Chatsworth, Hatfield House and Rossdhu, would also have been famil-iar from his books. Thus, a week that had begun with Jack finding him-self propelled to the very center of a debate he had been absorbed in since 1932 ended with the discovery that Kick, in making the particu-lar friends that she did, had gained entrée to a realm of history that had long ago taken hold of his imagination.

Remarkably, Kick had not simply been accepted into that set. Despite a neck too short, shoulders too high and broad, and a figure that, by her own estimate, left much to be desired, Kick had become one of its leading lights. "She had a raving success," said Lady Lloyd of Kick's effect on the members of the aristocratic cousinhood. "We all absolutely adored her." According to Lady Anne Tree, younger daughter of the 10th Duke of Devonshire, Kick "was just a complete star. She was enchanting." By the time Jack joined Kick on the scene, several young aristocrats including Anne's brother Andrew Cavendish, David Ormsby Gore, Hugh Fraser, Tony Loughborough and William Douglas Home had made it known that they were besotted. Kick had won the friend-ship and admiration of girls in their circle as well, including, besides Jean Ogilvy, Debo Mitford, Jane Kenyon-Slaney, Sissie Lloyd Thomas and Fiona Gore. On occasion even some of Kick's new friends wondered quite how she had managed so brilliantly and quickly to launch herself in what was, in the words of Lady Arran—Fiona Gore, as she was then—"a very narrow society" which did not readily admit outsiders.

Largely overlooked, then as in later years, was the fact that, far from brilliant, Kick's introduction to London was, in her own telling, "rather difficult." She had arrived three weeks after her eighteenth birthday with a plan to stay for six months, time enough to be presented at Court in May and have her coming-out party before returning to New York to study at the Parsons School of Design. Though eventually she would come to speak of Britain as her second home, she confessed to Nancy Astor that in the beginning she had been filled with loneliness for her life in America. She had missed the companionship of her brother's claque, and she had been disappointed that, unlike Lem Billings and her other adoring male pals from Jack's group, the first wave of British boys she met had failed to appreciate her jokes and raillery. "Very few of them can take any kidding at all," Kick complained to Lem of the dreary young men whom Debo Mitford, who also came out that Season but whom Kick had yet to meet, liked to call the "CH's", short for chinless horrors. Nor, in the beginning, had Kick been especially fond of any of the British girls. That changed on the occasion of her first country house weekend, beginning Thursday, April 14, 1938, two weeks before the start of the Season, when Nancy Astor arranged for the ambassador's daughter to celebrate Easter with her sons, Jakie and Michael, and some of their young friends. Afterward, without a trace of exaggeration, Kick would describe that weekend as "the best thing that ever happened to me."

When the invitation arrived, Kick had been "scared to death" at the prospect of a weekend with the Astors. Though she had attended dances, teas and dinner parties in London, she had yet to participate in an event that extended over several days; she had never met any of the Astors' other guests; and, to make matters worse, she had been invited without her parents. When she arrived at the portico of Cliveden, a massive Restoration Baroque house with long views of vast shaven lawns, formal gardens, fountains, statuary, tennis courts, woods and the Thames below, she seemed "rather lost." Nancy Astor had put Jean Ogilvy, a year and a half older than Kick, in the next room, in a passage on the first floor where all the best bedrooms were, and instructed her to help the newcomer navigate Cliveden as well as "chum up" with some of the other young people. From the outset, the dark-haired, porcelain-skinned daughter of the Earl of Airlie took the assignment seriously, for she understood how it felt to face one's first Season without so much as a friend in London. As a girl at Cortachy Castle in Scotland, Jean, the eldest of three sisters and three brothers in a family of ancient Scottish lineage, had led an isolated life. Especially when small, she had participated in the occasional visit to and from the Mitfords and other members of the aristocratic cousinhood, but during the rest of the year she saw few people outside her immediate family. By the time she was a teenager and ready to come out in London, she barely knew anyone her own age. Lady Airlie sought to remedy the problem by inviting various relations and other "suitable" young people—an equal number of boys and girls—for a week-long celebration of her daughter's eighteenth birthday. The guests, some of whom Jean had not seen since early childhood, were to dine, play croquet and attend a Highland ball and the Perth race meeting together. Petrified of the boys, Jean insisted she would not be able to think of a thing to say. "You have to!" Lady Airlie replied. "If you start a man on himself it won't be difficult."

As it happened, at Cortachy that September of 1936 Jean forged a special bond of friendship with her eighteen-year-old cousin, William Burlington, the eldest son of the Marquess of Hartington and second in line to the Devonshire dukedom. Their grandmothers were sisters, which, as was said, caused the young people to be somehow "like-minded," though they had not known each other previously. Set to enter Trinity College, Cambridge, in the fall, Billy so loved "a good talk," as he called it, that he would rub the palms of his hands together in luxurious anticipation of one. He would remain Jean's devoted friend for the rest of his short life. During the 1937 Season, when he was nineteen, he invited her to accompany him and his parents to Eton to take his seventeen-year-old brother, Andrew Cavendish, out for a picnic, an occasion that in effect launched the group that Kick, and later her brother Jack, were to become part of the following year. At length, Billy produced their—and Jean's—cousin David Ormsby Gore, Andrew brought in the Astor boys, and David, his Oxford friend Hugh Fraser, putting the nucleus in place.

Andrew, David and Hugh—though not Billy, who made no secret of his dislike for the boisterous atmosphere at Nancy Astor's—were all at Cliveden that weekend. If the American girl had seemed a bit lost at first, whatever Jean Ogilvy said or did upstairs put her at ease. From then on, if she continued to be nervous she gave no sign of it. Long afterward, the 11th Duke of Devonshire—Andrew Cavendish, as he was then—would still be able to picture Kick on the vast staircase at Cliveden, where he first talked to her. "It was her vitality that overwhelmed us," he said, in an effort to characterize the particular spell she cast. "I had never met anyone with such vitality before." And Kick had almost certainly never met anyone quite like Andrew—"the boy who couldn't wait to grow up." On the face of it, he was simply too young to mix with this particular group, certainly too young for eighteen- and nineteen-year-old debutantes who, having entered the matrimonial market, had reason to regard any male not yet at Oxford or Cambridge as "still a child." Boyishly scruffy, he usually went jacketless, with shirt-sleeves rolled up to the elbows, and declined to part his hair properly or to slick it back with a dollop of grease, as young men tended to do to signal they had grown up. Yet, since the 1937 Season when Billy had introduced his younger brother to their Ogilvy cousin, Andrew had striven to establish himself in an older set. Soon after the picnic where they met, Andrew had invited Jean to lunch at Eton. Despite Jean's reminder that he was both "my cousin and a child," Lady Airlie ordered her to refuse, as there would be no chaperone. Undaunted, Andrew devoted himself to making Jean, along with other of Billy's friends, his friends as well. When the older brother invited a group to one of the family houses, Compton Place, near the seaside resort of Eastbourne, the younger made a point of asking all the same people back the follow-ing weekend—without Billy. Most, including the debutantes, accepted despite the fact that they considered themselves "grown up" while their host was, after all, still an Eton boy. "Not you again," precocious little Anne Cavendish said dryly, when cousin Jean returned a week later under Andrew's dubious auspices.

Andrew's stratagem worked. By the time Lady Airlie asked another group of "suitable" young people for a week at Cortachy Castle in cele-bration of Jean's nineteenth birthday, Andrew, despite his age, had earned an invitation. After that, whenever Billy appeared at a country house weekend, it was a safe bet that Andrew would be there as well. "He didn't like being the youngest," Jean Lloyd fondly recalled, "defi-nitely wanted to catch up and be one up on Billy. Have you ever seen a big dog and a small dog? The small dog always wants to outdo the big dog. Well, Andrew was really like that." Billy, unperturbed, accepted responsibility for his brother, who could be fairly wild. At a house party in Scotland at Rossdhu, the family home of their friend Ivar Colquhoun, Billy went so far as to escort Andrew downstairs and lock him out when he suspected him of having had "one too many" to drink. He rejoined the group of young people in the huge drawing room overlooking Loch Lomond, when suddenly Andrew's "little face" materialized in an open window and he vaulted back inside, having climbed up a drainpipe.

Many an Englishman, let alone a newly-arrived eighteen-year-old

American girl, might have found Andrew's conversation hard to follow. He spoke in the rapid-fire, always exciting and often bewildering manner Kick would soon learn to associate with his mother's illustrious Tory family, the Cecils, who "talked all the time about everything under the sun, with animated and fiercely contested verbal contests." They were capable, it has been said, of uttering more words in a minute than most people can in five. Cecil (pronounced to rhyme with "whistle") children were encouraged to express their views and were "expected to be able to defend them" when challenged. Those challenges could be merciless. Adults took care to listen to the child's every remark, but, according to Andrew's uncle David Cecil, they came down "with all the force of their vigorous minds" if they did not like what they heard. The aim of their barbed questions and criticism was to teach the child to argue with facility, and by and large young Cecils regarded the give-and-take as great fun. As a small boy, Andrew would seek out his uncle and proclaim, "David, I have come round to do a little talking." Andrew, then and later, always had much to say, and his sentences tumbled out as if he could not be bothered to finish one thought before he sped on to the next. He was clever, ironic and highly-strung, and exuded a tremendous sense of enjoyment. In the period when Kick first met him, it was said that Andrew, interested in everything, always had a book in his hand, but also that he was never without a copy of the racing form in his back pocket. He spoke entertainingly of books, politics, history, the Newmarket horse races, lawn tennis, gambling, Society and all the best parties and country-house weekends, most of which he had managed to attend.

Another of the marathon talkers Kick met that day was David Ormsby Gore, who would turn twenty the following month. He more than matched Andrew for velocity. Andrew's and David's mothers were sisters, the granddaughters of Queen Victoria's three-time prime minister Lord Salisbury; half in earnest, half in jest, certain of the boys' friends attributed their intellectual panache to their "Cecil brains." Because Billy and Andrew's mother, Mary, known as Moucher (pronounced "Mao-sher"), was so close to David's mother, Beatrice, known as Mima, Billy and Andrew had been brought up to regard David "as a brother." If one closed one's eyes or turned away, the absence of pauses in Andrew and David's frenetic back-and-forth made it hard to know which boy was speaking. Indeed, both often rattled on simultaneously, causing friends to wonder how, or if, they heard each other.

Talking was not the only thing David did at breakneck speed. He also liked to drive fast, and his new set of false teeth testified to a car accident on the way back to Oxford from Newmarket, when he crashed into the rear of a truck and his speedometer froze at ninety-eight miles per hour. The passengers had included Peter Wood, Hugh Fraser, and Jakie Astor, who boasted a dent-like scar on one cheek. "I've lost my memory," Jakie, always ready with a quip, had cried out as he emerged from the wreckage, "has anybody found it?" Nancy Astor liked to say that she had initially believed the episode to be a case of "boys will be boys," but had come to think "boys will be idiots" more fitting.

On Saturday, twenty-year-old Hugh Fraser arrived. The most promising and ambitious fellow in the group, he enjoyed going "nose-to-nose" with the equally large-nosed David Ormsby Gore, arguing about such matters as Czechoslovakia and Hitler—topics, Jean Lloyd remembered, that were then of relatively little interest to her and the other girls. "Hugh and David, and all those, would discuss nothing else. We weren't always listening, but Kick was, you see. That was her great charm and fascination to all these boys—part of it." Kick, a veteran of years of political table talk with her father and brothers, did more than just listen. Curious about everything and unafraid of making a fool of herself, she gamely joined in, and Andrew, David, Hugh and Jakie loved her for it. Soon, whenever the boys gathered round the large tea table in a massive hall furnished with suits of armor, or in the "hideous" room with tobacco-colored paneling to which they also frequently repaired, Kick joined them. She asked questions, made grand statements about the tense situation in Europe and laughed exuberantly at her own mistakes. The delirious, immensely pleasurable talk continued throughout the weekend as the young people rode horses in the woods, boated and played tennis. Years later, Jean Lloyd would laugh that though Nancy Astor assigned her to look after the newcomer, once Kick got started she "didn't need any looking after!"

As soon as Kick returned on Monday to a London largely shut down for the Easter holiday, she was on the phone to Jean. Kick was leaving for Paris the following day to meet her mother and shop for clothes, and by the time she returned Jean would be back in Scotland. For Kick, the past few days had altered everything. "All the loneliness I had for America has disappeared because now England seems so very jolly," she would write to Nancy Astor of her first weekend at Cliveden. Determined not to wait two weeks until Jean was in London again, she asked her to lunch that day. The invitation surprised Jean. In Kick's position, a British girl would not have taken the initiative. Jean thrilled to the American girl's refreshing lack of reserve, but explained that she could not go out because she had her father with her. Lord Airlie then served as the Queen's Lord Chamberlain. Kick shot back that her father was in London as well, so why not make a foursome? So it was that Lord Airlie, whose first name also happened to be Joe, accompanied his daughter to Prince's Gate.

Prior to lunch in the embassy residence dining room, the "two Joes," as Kick and Jean gaily dubbed their fathers, chatted in a sitting room, while the girls played the popular record "Franklin D. Roosevelt Jones" over and over on a wind-up gramophone and talked of Andrew, David, Jakie, Hugh and the other boys. After the meal, Kick took Jean upstairs to see those of her siblings already in residence. Speaking of the Kennedys yet to come, she assured Jean that Jack "already knows almost everything about England" and that she was certain to find him the most charming and amusing young man she had ever met.

The evening of Nancy Astor's party was Kick's first opportunity to show off her brother to "the gang." Jack, who loved to dance, partnered several of Kick's friends, though the debutantes tended to be tongue-tied in his presence and, given his impenetrable Boston twang, were bewildered by his jokes and remarks. By contrast, there was no such barrier between Jack and the voluble, argumentative fellows in Kick's group. Suddenly, Jean Lloyd recalled, Jack's staccato, nasal, high-pitched speech was added to the mix of the young men's voices, as on and off throughout the evening they talked exuberantly of politics, books and "just about everything else under the sun." That first night at Nancy Astor's, Jack fell in easily with young men who had cut their teeth on many of the same books as he, and whose sparring style of conversation delighted him. Adopted by his sister's set, Jack from then on seemed to turn up "at every party." In the weeks that followed, his evenings were filled with dinners and dancing. On many nights in the Season there were at least two dances, in addition to a dinner before-hand. The parties often lasted till the pre-dawn hours and were punctuated by frequent side trips to the 400 Club and other nightspots. But unlike most of the young men in the set, who could never get enough champagne and had a history of car crashes to prove it, Jack, on account of his fragile constitution, rarely drank—not that that ever impeded his capacity for merrymaking.

Jack was also much seen about town in the company of young Joe, with whom he soon shared a regular table near the door at the 400. The debutantes, who had to elude their chaperones if they hoped to visit the 400, christened Joe "the Big One" by contrast with his scrawny brother. Joe looked a good deal older than his age, while Jack was often mistakenly thought to be younger than Kick. When they got to know Jack, the debutantes tended to judge him the nicer and more attractive brother by far. A scene in the semi-darkness at the 400 encapsulated the difference between the young men's temperaments. A third fellow had approached the Kennedy table and made the mistake of attempting to pick up the girl with whom Joe Junior had been flirting. To the alarm and fascination of a group of young people seated nearby, Joe's temper flared while Jack, apparently oblivious to the air of menace at his own table, went on laughing and joking with a strikingly beautiful older woman who seemed enchanted by him.

Though he was often out until dawn, by day there was much that Jack wanted to see and do. Joe Junior already knew London, where he had spent a year as a student. But during his two previous visits Jack had been sick much of the time and had not had the opportunity to explore. Shortly after he arrived this time, his mother took him out for a drive by way of orientation; when they passed the prime minister's residence, he became so excited that he leaned over to Rose's side of the car to see better. He was immensely curious about everything. On a visit to Eton along with his brother and father, who was giving a talk to the Political Society on the theme of "America", Jack impressed Lord Halifax's son Richard Wood, a student there, with numerous well-informed questions about the school. Wood—later Lord Holderness—recalled that there was in turn a great deal of curiosity among the boys, himself included, about the "fabulous" Kennedys, of whom they had heard so much from their parents, older siblings and the press. Rather than appearing shy before a large group of staring students, Jack and Joe Junior smiled broadly and clearly relished the spotlight.

In Britain as in America, Joe constantly spoke of Joe Junior as a future president. As at home, Jack made a point of refusing to compete. The fact that he gravitated to David Ormsby Gore, of all the fellows in Kick's set, is suggestive of how Jack perceived himself at the time and wished to be perceived. The friendship would prove among the most important of Jack's life and have immense historical ramifications when Jack was president and David the British ambassador in Washington. When it began in 1938, it took the form of a bond between exceptionally bright young men who each, for reasons of his own, seemed to lack the ambition and promise of a Hugh Fraser or a Joe Kennedy Junior.

David belonged to what Andrew Cavendish referred to as the second sons' club, whose members had drawn "the short straw in life." Unlike Jack, David had sincerely admired the older brother on whom his family's hopes were pinned. There were six Ormsby Gore children in all, and they had paired off in sets. For as long as anyone could remember Mary, the eldest, had bonded with Gerard; they had been the strong, outgoing siblings everyone noticed, while David, a somewhat withdrawn, sensitive boy who found sanctuary in books and interests such as music and mechanics, languished at the low end of the pecking order. Jack resented Joe Junior, but David idolized Gerard, who seemed to be everything David could never be. Their father, Billy Ormsby Gore, represented the seventh generation from father to son to sit in the House of Commons, and David had thought it fitting that Gerard continue the tradition. In keeping with the unwritten rule of primogeniture, whose purpose was to keep the great estates intact and preserve the political power of the families that owned them, Gerard would, upon succeeding to the Harlech barony, take possession of the extensive family landholdings in Wales and Shropshire. In 1935, the second son who had thought he might pursue a career related to mechanics found himself suddenly "pushed to the fore," as was said in the family, when Gerard died in an automobile accident. Not only had David lost a hero, he had inherited his burdens as well.

When David met the Kennedys three years later, he was still uncertain whether he was up to the political career associated with his new role as the family's "prime runner." Unlike his friends Hugh Fraser and Julian Amery, he was not a member of the Oxford Union and claimed to be unable to think of "anything more ghastly" than the idea of having to make a speech. He excelled at verbal sparring with his cousins and other close friends, yet he lacked confidence as a public speaker. He throve on barbed questions and criticism from members of his set, but he knew himself to be uneasy in other, less nurturing environments. He adored politics, yet, as Richard Holderness, who much admired his intelligence and integrity, would later say, he lacked the ruthlessness necessary for a major career. In 1938, a sense of the inevitability of war permitted, perhaps even encouraged, David to put off any decisions about his future. He simply refused to make plans until the crisis had passed.

David may have inherited his emotional fragility from his father, a quiet, solitary, erudite man who, in a gesture unusual for one of his position, chose to have his study in the nursery wing because he felt happiest in the company of children. An art historian and author of books including *The Florentine Sculptors of the Fifteenth Century* and *A Guide to the Mantegna Cartoons at Hampton Court*, as well as of learned monographs and articles on Africa and other topics, Billy Ormsby Gore would spend hours patiently explaining books and pictures to the youngsters. From his mother, on the other hand, David seems to have derived his liberalism and independent-mindedness. In her youth at Hatfield House, beak-nosed Mima had made it her custom to travel to London by bus, rather than permit a chauffeur to drive her; if her engagement happened to be at the palace, she simply hid her tiara beneath a hat. She had never wanted to marry in the first place, having harbored early on an ambition to be a doctor. Forbidden by her family to pursue a medical career, she experienced further disappointment when her mother, Lady Alice, ruled out one suitor on the grounds that he was Catholic. Ostensibly the Cecils approved of her marriage to Billy Ormsby Gore, but complained among themselves that the eldest daughter of the 4th Marquess of Salisbury really ought to have done better. Never quite accepted by his wife's family, Billy Ormsby Gore appears to have suffered for his connection to them nonetheless, when in the aftermath of his succession to the Harlech barony in 1938 he was forced out of Chamberlain's Cabinet. The announced reason for relieving him of his post as secretary of state for the colonies was that there were then too many peers in the Cabinet; as members of the House of Lords, they could not defend their departments' positions in the Commons. But it was widely believed that the prime minister really wanted him out because of his tie to the family of Lord Cranborne, the Marquess of Salisbury's eldest son and a prominent Tory opponent of the policy of appeasement.

At Oxford in this period David cut a wild figure, even among young men not known for taking academic work seriously. He drank too much, frequented the races at Newmarket, and spent many nights at the George Hotel in Oxford, where he and his friends slapped each other's faces with their steaks and smoked salmon and hurled champagne bottles out the windows—champagne being "very cheap in those days," Julian Amery would subsequently remark. There tended to be an element of innocence in David's revels, as when, on a visit to Cortachy Castle the previous year, he led the boys in dashing from room to room to gather up all the cushions and pile them high on the four-poster beds—his idea of a hilarious stunt. He also liked to listen to jazz records for hours at a time, as, head bowed and eyes closed, he drummed on the back of a chair in ecstatic accompaniment.

Innocence and rowdiness, references to jazz, history, politics, books and other shared interests, as well as a constant flow of jokes and jibes, characterized David's back-and-forth with Jack Kennedy that summer. Then, as later, the setting for many of their discussions would be the golf course, a game both friends enjoyed for, among other pleasures, the opportunity to converse as they walked between shots. The talks blended the Cecil penchant for velocity with Jack's impatience to get to the point of whatever they happened to be discussing. There were no monologues, no long anecdotes or explanations on either side. David lacked skill as a raconteur, which was fine with Jack, who was easily bored. David did have a marvelously dry sense of humor, as well as an unmistakable snickering laugh. Their repartee was swift and sharp; no sooner had one participant uttered a few words than the other shot back a deflating reply, which led in turn to a new counter-statement, and so on. The content would undergo many alterations in the course of twenty-five years, but the distinctive form of their talks had been quickly established.

David, along with the other young men in their group, haunted the visitors' gallery at the House of Commons, where they followed the great debates of the day almost as one would a sporting event. Jack was soon doing the same. On the Monday after Nancy Astor's party, Jack joined some of his new friends when they headed to the Commons to see Churchill weigh in on the Sandys affair. Churchill's son-in-law Duncan Sandys, a member of Parliament and an officer in the Territorial Army, had asked an embarrassing question in the House, based on information acquired in his military capacity, about the inadequacy of London's air defenses. Sandys, threatened with military discipline for a violation of the Official Secrets Act, had invoked a claim of parliamentary privilege and an inquiry had been convened. On July 11 there was to be a debate on the report of the inquiry's Select Committee, and Churchill was set to attend.

No occasion was more keenly anticipated in the House of Commons than an appearance by Churchill. Even his detractors were eager to see him. On the signal that he was about to speak there would be a great stir in the lobbies as members rushed into the chamber. A hunched, hulking figure would rise and, despite a tendency to lisp and stammer, hold the House spellbound with flights of oratory that Neville Chamberlain grudgingly admitted to be "the best show in town." As to whether Churchill's remarks amounted to anything more than superb entertainment, Chamberlain and a good many others expressed doubt. Admirers such as the future prime minister Harold Macmillan went so far as to claim that Churchill, in his great speech on the invasion of Austria, seemed to have been imbued with the spirit of his ancestor and biographical subject the 1st Duke of Marlborough and "spoke as a man outside and above party, only for his country." As a statesman rather than a politician, Churchill, declared his son Randolph, had "the luxury of subordinating party interests to those of the State." That is, he told the truth as he saw it, though he knew that by doing so he might harm himself politically.

For Jack, fascinated since the age of fifteen by Churchill's books and speeches, the July 11 debate, which set Churchill against the prime minister, provided a first opportunity to see and assess the man himself. The young American was ambivalent from the outset. On the one hand, Jack remained powerfully drawn to Churchill; on the other, he had come to see him as his father's opponent, the figure whose views about Hitler Joe Kennedy had made it his mission to contest. Interestingly, Jack shared this ambivalence with a number of his new British friends who, though they worshipped Churchill as an orator and an author and marveled at the frightening accuracy of his predictions, had also heard some of their fathers—men they loved and respected—question Churchill's character and judgment and dismiss him as a warmonger. (An exception in the group was Julian Amery, whose father, Leo Amery, was prominent in the Tory opposition.) Andrew Devonshire, who had heard his own father characterize Churchill as "hysterical," recalled the many ardent debates about the correct course to pursue with Hitler that the newly published *Arms and the Covenant*, a collection of Churchill's speeches since 1932, had provoked.

The speeches in *Arms and the Covenant* comprised the campaign to persuade Britain to rearm in the face of German territorial ambitions, which Jack had been monitoring from the start, after reading *The World Crisis*; he was, therefore, uniquely well equipped to participate in those arguments. Jack's London friends argued about whether Churchill was right that his country ought to have made a stand against Hitler at the time of the Rhineland episode two years previously, as he had urged in "The Violation of the Rhineland" (March 26, 1936), and they argued about whether Britain had indeed wasted years by its failure to rearm. In "The Locust Years" (November 12, 1936), a speech whose rhetoric Jack would reshape to his own purposes when he ran for president, Churchill marshaled facts and statistics to accuse the Baldwin government of an abdication of duty in permitting the country to "drift" while Germany methodically rearmed. In *Arms and the Covenant* Churchill appended Baldwin's reply in the Commons, in which the prime minister asserted that, given the mood of the electorate, had he pressed for rearmament—in the necessity of which he privately believed—he surely would have been defeated in the 1935 election. Baldwin maintained that in subordinating his convictions to political ends he had acted not out of personal ambition but out of concern that the Socialists, whose statements and votes against defense measures were on record, would win and that as a consequence things would be far worse than under his watch. Andrew Devonshire remembered that the Churchill–Baldwin exchange, when it appeared in *Arms and the Covenant*, ignited a particularly fierce debate among the young men about the role of the leader in a democratic society. Was it a leader's duty to take action that, though to his mind right and necessary, might jeopardize his political standing? How much attention ought a leader pay to public opinion? Should he wait for the electorate to catch up, as Baldwin claimed to have done? Or, as Churchill held, should he speak his mind and try to reeducate the public, at whatever potential cost to his own personal and political fortunes? In the course of the next quarter century, Jack and David would often discuss precisely those questions as they related to Jack's political life. Jack would go back and forth between Baldwin and Churchill, between politician and statesman—matters he would not really begin to resolve until the last months of his presidency.

Of all the topics discussed that summer of 1938, none seemed more urgent than Czechoslovakia and whether, in the event that Hitler invaded, the British would live up to their treaty obligations and fight alongside the French. Among people brought up to think of themselves as honorable men, there was much uneasiness at the prospect that their nation might refuse to fulfill a commitment and allow the Czechs to be overrun. There was uneasiness too at the abandonment of a cornerstone of British foreign policy—the principle that no single power should be permitted to gain predominance in Europe. Even many of those who agreed with Chamberlain's decision to provide no firm guarantees in the matter of Czechoslovakia remained painfully at odds with themselves in a way that Jack's father, who failed to share their preoccupation with matters of honor, simply was not. Jack, softening his remarks with self-deprecating jokes that made it hard to take offense at anything he said, routinely sided with his father, saying that Britain must look strictly to its own interests and stay out of a new war.

Despite his seeming embrace of his father's views, Jack had not abandoned the ideals of his reading, which found expression in his veneration of one hero of the Somme in particular, Raymond Asquith. He had read about Asquith in Churchill's *Great Contemporaries* (1917), and he had become fascinated by the legend of the brilliant son of a British prime minister killed in action at the age of twenty-seven, before he had had a chance to fulfill his promise in a political career scarcely begun. Jack, who had already confronted death on more than one occasion, was drawn to the story of the prodigiously gifted young man who had died young. Jack much admired Asquith's attitude that, as a matter of course, one ought to be ready to sacrifice everything for ideals—even one's own life. Having learned long ago to distance himself from his medical troubles, he found inspiration in the sangfroid, the transcendent indifference, with which Asquith, a second lieutenant in the Grenadier Guards, had faced death on the battlefield. Then and in later years, Jack could quote from memory Churchill's tribute to Asquith: "The War which found the measure of so many never got to the bottom of him, and when the Grenadiers strode into the crash and thunder of the Somme, he went to his fate cool, poised, resolute, matter-of-fact, debonair."

In a conversation with Andrew Cavendish's brother Billy, Jack maintained that Asquith's kind no longer existed in Britain. Basing his assessment on the Oxford Union King and Country resolution, Jack declared that the British had become "decadent" since the last war. By comparing the present generation unfavorably to Asquith and the others who had volunteered in 1914, Jack clearly implied that the British, were they the people they had once been, would come to the defense of the Czechs—a very different position from his usual insistence, in line with his father, that the correct policy was to make peace with the dictators. Seen in this light, it was not to their credit that, whatever Hitler might do in Czechoslovakia, the British would, he was sure, refuse to fight.

Honor meant everything to Billy Hartington. (On the death of his grandfather early in the Season, his father had become the 10th Duke of Devonshire and Billy, previously Earl of Burlington, became Marquess of Hartington.) Though only twenty and in some ways supremely innocent, he seemed as sure of who he was and what he wanted to be as Jack was conflicted. Tall, pale and strikingly handsome, Billy spoke slowly and softly, with nothing of the combative verbal style of his brother and his cousin David Ormsby Gore. Having grown up, as his sister Lady Elizabeth Cavendish pointed out, not only among history-makers but among historians such as their great-aunt Mabell Airlie (author of *In Whig Society*, a life of her great-great-grandmother Lady Melbourne) and their uncle David Cecil (then at work on the first volume of a biography of Lord Melbourne, extracts of which he would read aloud to the family), Billy seemed utterly at peace with the role and responsibilities he expected to inherit. His love of privilege was undeniable, but so was his sense of duty; he sincerely regarded the position of a great territorial noble as an opportunity to be useful. Jack predicted that in the matter of Czechoslovakia the British would base their actions on self-interest; Billy insisted that in the end honor would guide them. His country was obliged by treaty to fight, and that, Billy felt certain, was what it would do. Jack's argument that the British, having grown decadent since the last war, would steer clear of a fight struck Billy as so absurd that he could only be amused by it. Through the intermediary of Kick, he would playfully refer back to it in 1942, by which time, as far he was concerned, Britain had disproved any such claim.

As July drew to a close, Jack, along with his mother and most of his siblings, prepared to travel to the south of France, where Joe Kennedy had rented a villa in Cap d'Antibes. With Jack and the others scheduled to leave on the 22nd and the ambassador planning to follow ten days later, Kick asked if she might wait to make the trip with her father. Billy Hartington had talked politics with Jack, but his real interest at Prince's Gate, it turned out, was Kick. Not only did he instantly join her long list of British admirers, he went right to the head of the queue. Immediately after Billy met the American girl who had captivated Andrew, David, Hugh and the others, his mother wrote to ask her to their annual house party at Compton Place, to begin on the eve of the Goodwood races. Following the house party, Billy and Andrew were to accompany their parents to Bolton Abbey, in Yorkshire, to shoot grouse. Kick was eager to accept the duchess's invitation lest she not see Billy again for some time, and obtained permission to linger in London.

In Cap d'Antibes, Jack again fell gravely ill and his mother telegraphed the doctors in Boston for advice. But, as often happened, the crisis passed quickly, and Jack was soon spending most days at Eden Roc, at the Hôtel du Cap, where he and the family swam and had lunch. Swimming offered relief from the back pain for which, on occasion that summer, he wore a brace under his shirt, and he decided early on that there was no place in the world he would rather swim. The film star Marlene Dietrich, who had arrived in the company of her daughter and the actor Jean Gabin, shot some footage of Jack with her home movie camera as, fresh from a swim, he crossed the terrace toward her at Eden Roc. On film, the strikingly photogenic twenty-one-year-old dressed in a white toweling robe over a bathing suit radiates vitality and gives no sign of how sick he had just been.

In anticipation of her visit to the Devonshires, Kick arranged a series of lunches and teas in London with Jean Ogilvy, the purpose of which, it soon became apparent, was to "pump" her about Billy. Jean did not plan to attend Goodwood, yet she did spend the night at Compton Place, as Andrew's guest, just before the others were expected. When Andrew learned of his brother's interest in Kick he was dismayed, he later said, because he "fancied her" himself. Kick and Billy, much photographed at the races, seemed an incongruous couple. Kick was short like her mother, Billy exceptionally tall and large-framed. Kick tended to be informal, Billy so punctilious that he would wear an impeccable gray flannel suit to a summer picnic on the grass, and make no effort to remove his jacket or loosen his tie despite the heat. Kick was full of energy, he so languid that his mother told a story about Billy refusing a cup of coffee because, he drawled, "I can't be bothered to drink it." Kick adored tennis and other sports; he preferred to leave the lovely grass tennis courts at Compton Place to the energetic, fiercely competitive Andrew. Kick had gleefully participated in the raucous games of musical chairs and charades at Cliveden; Billy, everyone accepted, didn't do "that sort of thing," which was why he avoided Lady Astor's house parties. Kick, though raised in an atmosphere of wealth, was always prepared to jump in and do things for herself; Billy, who liked his comforts, expected to be waited on. On his first visit to Cortachy Castle he had been appalled that despite the presence of liveried footmen, Lord Airlie insisted that guests get up and serve themselves breakfast. Billy so loathed disorder that, when for a period he was forced to share a room with the incorrigibly messy Andrew, he had chalked a line down the center of the floor and instructed his brother to remain on his own side.

For all that, Billy was surprisingly able to laugh at his own pomposities, and he reveled in Kick's teasing. He was charming, funny and delightful to talk to. "Conversation," it has been said, "took precedence over all possible activities" at Compton Place. This was the influence of the duchess, who, when first married, had been troubled by the long, languorous silences characteristic of her husband's family. She "loved conversation above all else," remembered her daughter Anne, and once sacked a nanny when the woman announced that she preferred "punctuality to conversation." Under her aegis, discussion extended breakfast into mid-morning, and continued throughout the day. Billy, who was especially fond of political themes, relished the fact that Kick's "passionate love of politics" made her utterly different from the British debutantes he knew. From the first, he and she talked for hours. For her part, Kick found Billy's formidable confidence and serenity, the sense he projected of feeling "all right about things," highly attractive. It seemed that he was burdened by only one abiding doubt: whether young women wished to be with him solely because he was the duke's heir.

After the Devonshires' house party, it was Billy who asked Jean Ogilvy to lunch—to talk about Kick. By then, it was "taken for granted" by friends that he and Kick were falling in love. Ambassador and Mrs. Kennedy, on the other hand, had as yet no idea of quite what had happened at Compton Place. On August 3, Kick accompanied her father to the south of France, and Rose was soon complaining in her diary that she could "almost go mad" listening to the discussion of diets, Kick's to lose weight and Jack's to gain. It appears never to have occurred to Rose that her daughter's sudden aversion to food might have to do with a young man. Jean had invited Kick to Cortachy Castle in September, when Billy Hartington and David Ormsby Gore were due to come for a celebration of Jean's twentieth birthday, before returning to Cambridge and Oxford respectively. In anticipation of seeing Billy again, Kick, like other love-stricken teenagers before and since, labored to make herself thin.

By this time, there was no longer any question of Kick's returning to New York to study at the Parsons School of Design. She was having far too much fun in London and, though she did not say as much to her parents, the romance with Billy would in itself have been enough to make her want to stay on. In June it had been announced that Joe Junior planned to start Harvard Law School in the fall, but now he too decided to remain abroad. The ambassador, in the belief that another year in Europe would offer "a wonderful opportunity . . . to see history made," had arranged for his eldest son to spend September at the American embassy in Paris, a prime vantage point from which to observe the French reaction to whatever Hitler decided to do over Czechoslovakia. Of the three, Jack alone was due to return to America, after he and Kick had made a motor tour of Austria to see the land

Hitler had most recently taken. Jack was fascinated by the drama unfolding in Europe, but, to his frustration, his father ruled that he could not put off his departure as Joe had done, since illness had caused him to miss a full year of school already. It was agreed that, with an eye toward returning to London in the spring, Jack would attempt to obtain a leave of absence to gather information for his senior thesis while working for his father at the embassy.

On August 26, Jack was savoring his last days in Cap d'Antibes when the news broke that Hitler was traveling along the French border to observe German army maneuvers. The next day, Churchill, citing "disquieting signs similar to those which preceded the seizure of Austria," warned that the situation in Europe was steadily moving toward a climax, which could not long be delayed. He argued that Hitler would not have placed large numbers of troops on a war footing without the intention to act in a very limited period of time. Churchill declared that if, as seemed likely, Hitler invaded Czechoslovakia, it would be more than just an attack upon the Czechs, but an outrage against the entire world, leaving every country to ask whose turn would come next. Resolved that Hitler must not be allowed to persist in the belief that the British would stand helplessly by, Churchill cautioned, "Whatever may happen, foreign countries should know—and the Government are right to let them know—that Great Britain and the British Empire must not be deemed incapable of playing their part and doing their duty as they have done on other great occasions which have not yet been forgotten by history."

As an anxious Europe waited for the Nuremberg party rally on September 12, 1938, where it was thought that Hitler would clarify his intentions with regard to Czechoslovakia, Joe Kennedy prepared to return to the embassy. Jack was to sail from Southampton at the beginning of the month, so it was decided that he would accompany his father to London while Kick, young Joe and the rest stayed on in Cap d'Antibes with their mother. On August 28, Jack and his father flew to Paris, where the ambassador talked with other American diplomats, before continuing to London. Father and son arrived at Prince's Gate to reports of further ominous signs from Germany, notably the large-scale requisitioning of food, animals and vehicles. Kennedy conferred with Chamberlain, who said that virtually all of the information he was receiving suggested that Hitler had made up his mind to take Czechoslovakia, whether peacefully or by force of arms. According to Chamberlain, Hitler was indeed convinced that France was not ready to fight and that Britain did not want to. When Kennedy inquired whether Chamberlain had decided to join the French in the defense of Czechoslovakia, the prime minister—who in recent days had declared in the Commons that the British were unwilling to sacrifice their honor for peace—indicated that he was afraid he might be forced into a war, despite his own determination to stay out. That admission was worrying to Kennedy, who was at pains to ensure that, in the event Germany seized Czechoslovakia, Britain looked the other way. After reporting to Washington on his meeting with Chamberlain, the ambassador reviewed a draft of a speech he was to deliver presently in Scotland. At a moment when Churchill was proclaiming that the British, however great their distaste for a new war, would act honorably in accord with their best traditions, Kennedy planned to make the case that whatever Hitler might do in Czechoslovakia, as Britain was not itself at risk there was no reason to go to war. In a phrase cut from Kennedy's final text by the White House, he asserted that he could not see anything in the present crisis "which could be remotely considered worth shedding blood for."

Jack and Billy Hartington had jousted over whether or not the British would act honorably in the event of a German assault on the Czechs. As Jack began his journey home on the German liner *Bremen* on September 3, events in Europe promised to prove one of them wrong.

CHAPTER THREE

Sunset Glow before the Storm

▪ ▪ ▪ ▪

ON SEPTEMBER 8, 1938, FOUR DAYS BEFORE HITLER WAS due to speak at the Nuremberg party rally, Jack Kennedy arrived in New York City. The scene at the dock was comparable to the one that had greeted Joe Kennedy and his sons on their arrival at Southampton in July, but this time, as Jack traveled alone, it fell to him to talk to the press. The reporters were not interested in Jack's own views, of course, but in what he might reveal about his father's estimate of the chances for war. Jack parried their questions, pointing to the fact that his mother and siblings planned to remain in Europe for the year as evidence that his father did not expect war.

Following his encounter with the press, Jack headed for the family house in Hyannis Port. He was feeling unwell again and planned to take to his bed before the start of what promised to be an exceptionally demanding semester. He would be at the Cape when, in four days' time, Hitler's much-anticipated address to his legions was broadcast on the radio. After that, presumably, the world would know what the Germans intended to do about Czechoslovakia.

Chamberlain had concentrated in recent weeks on pressuring the Czechs rather than the Germans to make concessions. In the days before Nuremberg, Joe Kennedy did all he could to scare the Führer. On previous occasions, Kennedy had strongly implied that should the British go to war they must not count on America to bail them out;

now he gave indications that Washington might indeed be ready to help. He made a point of being much seen on his way in and out of the Foreign Office and the prime minister's residence at 10 Downing Street. On the day before Hitler was to speak, Kennedy telephoned Roosevelt to ask that two cruisers be diverted, as a signal that the United States might be gearing up for a fight. Kennedy of course would have been the last person to support any such involvement but, in the interest of keeping Chamberlain out of a confrontation that might lead to war, he had reason to let it be thought in Germany that he had altered his views.

In a further effort "to clear Hitler's mind," Kennedy also supported a proposal that in advance of the Führer's speech the British send a strongly-worded message that they intended to fight in defense of the Czechs. He approved the strategically-timed announcement in the press of British fleet moves, and he even proposed that the Soviets might undertake military measures designed as a warning to Hitler. On the day of Hitler's address, tensions in Czechoslovakia ran so high that citizens listened with gas masks ready lest at the close of the speech German bombers appear in the sky. Yet, in spite of international expectations that the Nuremberg rally speech would amount to an order to march, it provided no such certainty. Hitler heaped abuse on the Czechs, proclaimed the Reich invincible and warned that if the Sudetens did not get "justice" Germany must soon intervene, but he stopped short of a declaration of war.

Despite his rest at the Cape, Jack was still, as he said, "in rotten shape" by the time he started at Harvard. Most weekends he went to Hyannis Port to rest. His leave of absence in the spring was accepted on the condition that he complete extra courses in addition to his regular load. Longing to get back to London, he was determined not to let ill health prove an obstacle. He studied and attended classes regularly, and even forced himself to turn down invitations from pretty girls. His roommate, Torby Macdonald, acknowledged that in this respect Jack had come back from Britain a different man. Previously the sort of student whom professors, in the words of one, "did not cultivate," he abandoned the pose of frivolity and permitted, even encouraged, his teachers to glimpse the seriousness and intelligence which he had long found it useful to conceal.

During this period Jack was one of countless Americans who got up, dressed, ate and worked by their radios. In the atmosphere of chaos and uncertainty after Hitler's address at Nuremberg, Chamberlain had gone to Germany to confer with the Führer, the first in a dramatic series of meetings. Edward R. Murrow reported from London, and Americans heard the voices of all the key players—including Hitler, Chamberlain and the Czech ambassador in London, Jan Masaryk—in a way that gave the tense situation in Europe an unprecedented immediacy. Many people in Britain assumed that Chamberlain had traveled to Berchtesgaden in order personally to make sure that Hitler understood that the British would fight to defend the Czechs, but that was far from what actually took place. Hitler significantly increased his demands. Having previously insisted on autonomy for the Sudeten Germans, he now required outright cession of the Sudetenland to the Reich. Chamberlain, intent on peace at any cost, indicated that while he himself favored acquiescence he would first have to secure his own government's approval. Back in London he met with resistance, even among those who had supported him in the past. Still, he won the approval of his Cabinet, and an Anglo-French plan calling on the Czechs to accept partition was sent on to Prague.

Joe Kennedy and Winston Churchill, each acting on his own behalf rather than in any official capacity, endeavored to influence British opinion. Kennedy had tried to scare Hitler; now he returned to his earlier tactic of scaring the British. With charges flying in London that Chamberlain had sold out the Czechs, Kennedy brought Charles Lindbergh over from France to testify that it would be suicidal to oppose Hitler, whose overwhelming air strength gave him the capacity to destroy Britain. Privately acknowledging that annexation of the Sudetenland by the Reich amounted to "the rape of Czechoslovakia," Kennedy undertook nonetheless to sell appeasement as the only sensible alternative. Churchill, on the contrary, argued for a tough stand. Where Lindbergh would claim that the British were simply too weak to take on the Germans, Churchill insisted in a statement to the press that to capitulate on Czechoslovakia would put Britain in an even weaker and more perilous situation, notably by liberating twenty-five German divisions to threaten the western front. Churchill disparaged as "a fatal delusion" the belief that security might be obtained by tossing a small state to the wolves. The Czechs decried the Anglo-French plan as a base betrayal, but agreed "under extreme duress" to relinquish all areas of Czechoslovakia with more than 50 per cent Sudeten inhabitants. Chamberlain set off again to meet with Hitler at Godesberg, where, to his astonishment, he was greeted with new demands that, if accepted, would amount to the humiliation not just of the Czechs but also of the British and the French.

Hitler insisted on occupying the Sudetenland by October 1, requiring that the Czechs leave behind all military installations and that those residents unprepared to accept German rule forfeit their household possessions and their cattle. Back in London, Chamberlain cited Hitler's promise that the Sudetenland would be his last territorial demand and again recommended acquiescence. The First Lord of the Admiralty, Duff Cooper, countered that to give in to Hitler this time would be to jeopardize "the honor and the soul of England." Cooper declared that, were he a party to persuading or even suggesting to the Czechs that they ought to accept the Godesberg ultimatum, he would never be able to hold up his head again. As for the Czechs themselves, they were no longer prepared to give in to pressure from London. Noting that when his country accepted the Anglo-French plan it had presumed that Britain and France would guarantee its reduced borders, Masaryk refused to back down again, vowing that his country would not become "a nation of slaves." Hitler, in response, set a deadline—2 p.m., Wednesday, September 28—by which time he expected agreement to all his demands at Godesberg.

Anti-aircraft guns were mounted in London, children were evacuated to the countryside, and hospital beds were emptied in anticipation of the first air raids. "People everywhere were talking loudly about war," the novelist Virginia Woolf reported in a letter to her sister, the painter Vanessa Bell. "There were heaps of sandbags in the streets, also men digging trenches, lorries delivering planks, loud-speakers slowly driving and solemnly exhorting the citizens of Westminster 'Go and fit your gas masks.'" Mussolini's use of poison gas against the Abyssinians in 1935 and Hitler's annihilating air attack on Guernica in northern Spain in 1937 led Londoners to expect a level of ruin and carnage that surpassed all imagination. Rumor spread of a coffin shortage and of the need for citizens to donate their old bedsheets.

While Jack followed "the crisis"—as the September events came to be called—on the airwaves, Kick, Billy Hartington, David Ormsby Gore and some of the other members of their set had been doing the same in Scotland, where friends and cousins had gathered at Cortachy Castle to celebrate Jean Ogilvy's twentieth birthday. Kick had undergone a marked physical transformation since anyone in the group had last seen her. Her weeks in Cap d'Antibes had left her deeply tanned, her hair attractively streaked by the sun. Her face and body were much thinner, and she had acquired a habit of drawing attention to her waist by emphatically spanning it with her hands—something she could never have done before. Still, she was hardly about to admit that she had spent the time since Goodwood on a diet. It had been so exceedingly hot in Cap d'Antibes, she said, that she had simply been unable to eat. The explanation failed to convince Jean, who observed that Kick barely ate anything at Cortachy either. She attributed the big change in Kick's appearance to love.

The turreted, cream-colored castle, which had been used as a hunting lodge in the fourteenth century by Robert the Bruce, King of Scotland, and added on to numerous times since, overlooked the rushing, stony South Esk River. According to legend, the ghost of a drummer boy haunted the tower and beat out a summons whenever a member of the Ogilvy family neared death. During the seventeenth century the Ogilvys were supposed to have hurled the drummer boy from the tower window after he failed to warn of an enemy clan's approach. In the romantic setting of Cortachy, where every corner had some legend or bit of history attached to it, the tumultuous happenings of September 1938 seemed in one sense remote. Still, Billy and David wished to talk of almost nothing else; for once, Kick was less than enthusiastic about the young men's choice of topic. "All you can hear or talk about at this point is the future war which is bound to come," she wrote to Lem. "Am so darn sick of it." Billy's high sense of duty was one of the things that had drawn Kick to him; nonetheless, to an eighteen-year-old in love for the first time, the incessant war talk was an unwelcome reminder that her newfound happiness might soon end. As Jean Lloyd remembered, a sense of foreboding made everything that transpired among the young people at Cortachy seem more urgent and intense. It would have been upheaval enough for Billy, who had never been in love before, to have to decide what to do about his feelings for Kick, but now there was the added complication of the approach of war and what that might mean to both their lives. Kick, Billy, David and some of the others left Cortachy on the day of Chamberlain's second meeting with Hitler. The young men returned to London, but Kick stayed on in Scotland, where she was to spend several days at the residence of a business associate of her father's, whose proximity to Perth would allow her to see Jean and a second contingent of Cortachy houseguests at the race meeting on September 28—Black Wednesday, as it came to be called after the Godesberg ultimatum.

"Black Wednesday dawned bright and clear over Paris and London," the historian John Wheeler-Bennett later wrote. "Men and women woke with an eerie feeling that this was 'the last day,' and that by tomorrow night Paris and London might be in flaming ruins. . . . I recall that while shaving that morning the hymnal injunction to 'live this day as if thy last' came into my head and remained with me much of the day." Newspapers reported a state of emergency. The auxiliary air force had been called up and the fleet mobilized. Chamberlain, due to address Parliament at 3 p.m., was rumored to be planning to close his speech with an ultimatum to Hitler. That morning Ambassador Kennedy telephoned his wife, who was also in Scotland, on a golf holiday at the Gleneagles hotel. "Said I should come back tonight," Rose Kennedy recorded in her diary, "as we must make some sort of plans for the children because war imminent. Everyone here depressed and sober." The ambassador had ordered the children's things packed in anticipation of shipping them back to America.

Such was the psychological climate when Kick met up with the Cortachy crowd in Perth. London and Paris might be about to explode in flames, but the race meeting went on regardless. Jean Ogilvy was there, as were Andrew Cavendish, Robert Cecil, Tony Loughborough, and Charlie Lansdowne. They enjoyed themselves hugely, it being Andrew's theory that in view of what was to come the young people were "entitled" to their pleasures. Yet the fact remained that, should Kick's father send her back to America, her romance might be over before it had really had a chance to start. She had come to the race meeting with the expectation of returning to London that evening, but late in the day word of dramatic events at the House of Commons caused Rose to decide they could stay on in Scotland for at least a few days. Chamberlain's address, widely expected to conclude with a statement that would lead to war, had been interrupted by a surprise message from Hitler. When the prime minister disclosed the contents of the note handed to him—Hitler's proposal of a four-power conference the next day in Munich, to include Britain, Germany, Italy and France but, pointedly, not Czechoslovakia, whose fate was to be decided—there was silence in the House before the MPs shouted approval, standing on the benches and waving their order forms. At first the cheers of only one man issued from the visitors' gallery, where spectators were supposed to refrain from displays of emotion. It was the unmistakable rasping voice of Ambassador Kennedy, and soon a good many others joined his. Not everyone present shared in the elation. Churchill remained, in Harold Macmillan's account, "silent and seated—with his head sunk on his shoulders, his whole demeanor depicting something between anger and despair." Harold Nicolson, who also had declined to rise, wrote in his diary afterward, "I find an immense sense of physical relief, in that I shall not be afraid tonight of the German bombs. But my moral anxieties are in no way diminished." In Perth, where Kick and her friends went on to a cocktail party after the races, "nothing else but the war and Munich were spoken of," recalled Jean Lloyd. "We talked of it the whole time."

Chamberlain went to Munich eager to satisfy Hitler, who by the time the four-power meeting was done had gained virtually every significant point he had demanded at Godesberg. As Wheeler-Bennett later wrote, Germany "had inflicted a defeat of the first magnitude on France and Britain without firing a shot." Yet in Britain the response to the last-minute avoidance of war was euphoric, and Chamberlain, accompanied by Lord Dunglass and others, returned on September 30 to a hero's welcome. *The Times* rhapsodized that "no conqueror returning from a victory on the battlefield has come home adorned with nobler laurels," and Chamberlain was hailed as "the Man of our Age" and "the greatest European statesman of this or any other time." At the airport he proudly waved a piece of paper signed by Hitler, a joint pledge on the part of Britain and Germany "never to go to war with one another again." On the way in to London, jubilant people leapt onto the running board of his car and pounded on the windows in appreciation. There were more cheers when at Buckingham Palace the King and Queen, breaking with tradition, appeared with Chamberlain on a balcony to wave to the crowds below. Later, at 10 Downing Street, Chamberlain, speaking from a first-floor window, claimed to have made good on his promise the previous July to win peace without sacrificing British honor. "My good friends," he declared, "this is the second time in our history that there has come back from Germany to Downing Street peace with honor. I believe it is peace for our time." The crowd roared appreciation, leading one observer of the scene to remark, "For all the fun and cheers you might think that they were celebrating a major victory over an enemy instead of merely a betrayal of a minor ally."

In the course of the weekend, people had time to think about exactly what Chamberlain had done at Munich, about the price he had had to pay for peace, and about how long such a peace could last. In an embarrassment to the Chamberlain faction, when the debate on Munich opened in the House of Commons on Monday, October 3, parliamentary rules gave Duff Cooper the right to speak first in order to explain his resignation as First Lord of the Admiralty. Cooper, who spoke for forty-five minutes, said that he had tried to swallow the terms of the Munich agreement but that they had stuck in his throat. He argued that it was not for Czechoslovakia that Britain would have been fighting had it gone to war the previous week. "It was not for Serbia that we fought in 1914. It was not even for Belgium, although it occasionally suited some people to say so. We were fighting then, as we should have been fighting last week, in order that one great Power should not be allowed, in disregard of Treaty obligations, of the laws of nations, and the decrees of morality, to dominate by brute force the Continent of Europe." For that principle, he declared, Britain had fought against Napoleon Bonaparte, and against Louis XIV of France and Phillip II of Spain; for that principle Britain "must ever be prepared to fight." Cooper admitted that by his resignation he had perhaps ruined his political career, but that was of little matter. "I have retained something which is to me of greater value," he concluded. "I can walk about the world with my head erect."

Typically impatient with all talk of principles, Ambassador Kennedy, who heard the speech in person, dismissed it as "a most ordinary defense." Many others saw it as a moral triumph. Harold Macmillan called it "the finest thing I've heard since I've been in the House," and the historian A. J. P. Taylor wrote to Cooper, "May I express my appreciation that in this hour of national humiliation there has still been found one Englishman not faithless to honor and principle and to the tradition of our great name." Wherever one stood on the virtues of Cooper's address, there could be no denying that the opening speaker's argument that Britain had dishonored itself at Munich made a huge impression. Lest anyone persist in the belief that Chamberlain had in fact brought back peace with honor, on the third day of the debate Churchill spelled out the meaning of Britain's failure to come to the aid of the Czechs. Whatever Hitler might have promised, Czechoslovakia would in a matter of years, or even months, "be engulfed in the Nazi regime."

Two months after Jack Kennedy and Billy Hartington had argued about whether the British would fight for the Czechs, Jack had been proven right. During the summer Billy had refused to believe that his nation could fail to act honorably, yet, according to Cooper and Churchill, that was exactly what had occurred. There was a part of Jack that found both Churchill and Cooper, as figures, immensely attractive; in addition to his fascination with Churchill's writings, Jack was also an admirer of Cooper's biography of Talleyrand. Nevertheless, his father's adversarial relation to these and other critics of the Munich agreement seems to have been the determining factor in shaping Jack's response. As Charles Lindbergh would acknowledge in his diary, Ambassador Kennedy had done much to make Munich happen. By bringing Lindbergh to London at a moment when opposition to the policy of appeasement appeared to be hardening, Kennedy had actively helped create the atmosphere of fear that led to Munich. In the aftermath of the sacrifice of the Czechs, Kennedy vigorously defended Chamberlain against accusations that he had shamefully presided over the loss of his country's honor.

For Kennedy, honor had nothing to do with it; the important thing was that Chamberlain had not taken his country to war. Speaking at the British Navy League's Trafalgar Day dinner on October 19, Kennedy urged his audience to accept the need to learn to live with the dictators. "The democratic and dictator countries differ ideologically, to be sure, but that should not preclude the possibility of good relations between them," Kennedy declared. "After all, we have to live together in the same world, whether we like it or not." His remarks set off a firestorm of criticism in America for seeming to confer official US approval on Hitler. In the matter of Munich, American opinion had initially tended to be one of relief that war had been avoided, but disquiet at the fate of the Czechs soon set in. The State Department was quick to distance itself from Kennedy's remarks, stating that the controversial speech had reflected the ambassador's "own personal views," not those of his government. The journalist Walter Lippmann thereupon attacked Kennedy on the grounds that by publicly expressing his own views he had exceeded his ambassadorial mandate. The attacks on his father caused the whole debate over Munich to take on a deeply personal coloration for Jack, who wrote to him in praise of his position: "The Navy Day speech, while it seemed to be unpopular with the Jews etc. was considered to be very good by everyone who wasn't bitterly anti-Facist [sic]. . . ."

At Harvard, the Russian expert Bruce Hopper, one of the university's most charismatic professors, had by this time taken a personal interest in Jack. He counseled him to choose a senior thesis topic that would permit him to benefit from the special access and information he enjoyed as an ambassador's son. In the wake of the attacks on his father, Jack seized on Munich as his theme. But, though he had been quick to support his father on the matter of living with the dictators, his feelings remained complicated and contradictory. Despite an undeniable appetite for his father's views, the young man known to speak rapturously of Raymond Asquith and to recite by heart Churchill's lines on that emblematic hero of the Somme was far from impervious to the claims of honor. Such was his divided spirit that he turned for help to a strong critic of the policy of appeasement. The gesture of seeking out a mentor whose thinking was the very antithesis of his father's was a paradox typical of Jack.

Shortly after Jack had declared his thesis topic, Hopper invited John Wheeler-Bennett to deliver a guest lecture on Munich to his Government 18 class, "New Factors in International Relations: Europe." The thirty-six-year-old English historian, who presided over a weekly seminar at the University of Virginia law school, had been in London during the crisis and returned to the United States shortly thereafter. Though not a traditional academic, he had written important books on the disarmament movement after the 1914 war and had a reputation as an eminent authority on Germany. Attired in an old-fashioned, almost Edwardian manner, he looked less like a scholar than an especially vigorous soldier or sportsman. His features, it was said, "were strangely un-English, almost those of a German princeling." Freed by a private fortune to do as he wished, he had lived in Germany for years and become personally acquainted with major political figures throughout Europe, so a good deal of his knowledge of international affairs was first-hand. He was also a scintillating lecturer, whom Harold Macmillan, who was among his oldest and most intimate friends, would describe years afterward as "one of the best talkers" he had ever met. In short, both the man and the lecture subject were tailor-made to intrigue Jack.

Wheeler-Bennett, speaking with the remnants of a stammer acquired in 1914, when a bomb dropped on his school dormitory, offered a pungent account of life in Britain during the turbulent weeks of the crisis. At the close of his talk, he suddenly produced the gas mask he had carried in London and covered his face with it. After the Harvard boys had given him an ovation, Jack went to the front of the room to introduce himself. Wheeler-Bennett later recalled being struck by the "pleasing, open countenanced, blue-eyed young man" who reminded him that they had met previously at the embassy residence in London in July. At the time, Ambassador Kennedy had pointed out his three eldest sons and said—speaking of them, or so it seemed to Wheeler-Bennett, almost as if they were not present—"I'll tell you about these boys. There's young Joe, he's going to be president of the United States; and there's Jack, he's going to be a university president; and there's Bobby, he's the lawyer." Several months later at Harvard, Jack—silent no more—asked if he might come and talk privately with Wheeler-Bennett, who was staying with Hopper and his wife in Cambridge. He was invited to call the following afternoon. It was a measure of Hopper's regard for Jack that, in the meantime, he asked Wheeler-Bennett to take a personal interest in Jack's thesis on Munich. Wheeler-Bennett withheld his agreement until he had had a chance to talk to Jack and assess his merits.

At their first meeting, Jack and Wheeler-Bennett, who affected a cane and a monocle and wore a carnation in his buttonhole, walked along the banks of the Charles River and talked for two hours. Jack explained that in his thesis he wished to explore Britain's policy of appeasement and how it had culminated in the Munich agreement. As it turned out, Wheeler-Bennett was himself in the early stages of contemplating a book on Munich. Jack's knowledge and manner impressed the older man, and by the time they returned to the Hopper residence Wheeler-Bennett had judged him to be "a highly exceptional young man who surely merited all the help that I could give him." He saw at once that Jack, a staunch proponent of the wisdom of learning to live with the dictators, had been greatly influenced by his father. "Not unnaturally the boy had arrived at a definitely prejudiced point of view," recalled Wheeler-Bennett, who decided to make it his mission "without trying too hard to prejudice him in the opposite direction, at least to expound the other side." Wheeler-Bennett thereby accepted the role of, in Macmillan's fond description, Jack's "tutor," and undertook to educate the son in what he liked to call "the imponderables of the human spirit" that made it possible to defeat Hitler. Periodically, that fall of 1938, he traveled up to Cambridge to walk by the river with Jack and discuss Munich and related topics. In addition to offering a counterbalance to the ambassador's views, he made suggestions for books to read and matters to look into when Jack returned to London in February for a prolonged stay that Wheeler-Bennett hoped would broaden the young man's perspective. Wheeler-Bennett recommended, for instance, that Jack undertake a study of Edmund Burke, whose argument on the impossibility of living with revolutionary France seemed a fitting riposte to those like Chamberlain and Kennedy who thought it not only possible but advisable to come to terms with Hitler. The ambassador, by no means pleased by Wheeler-Bennett's influence, telephoned Jack on a number of occasions to inquire, "What's that limey been telling you?"

Joe Kennedy came home in December to make the case in Washington that Chamberlain's actions at Munich had been inevitable and that Britain, her glory gone, could never have won a war against Hitler. That of course was very different from what Jack had been hearing from his "tutor" during their walks by the river. Opposition to the

Munich agreement had intensified in America, and Joe Kennedy, who had prominently identified himself with the British decision to acquiesce to the dismemberment of Czechoslovakia, was increasingly unpopular. Kennedy, in turn, argued that Americans, overwhelmingly isolationist as he gauged them to be, had no business telling the British what they ought to have done at Munich. The ambassador maintained that since the British would surely have lost, it was not in America's interest for there to have been a war, and Americans should stop suggesting that Britain ought to have fought.

Jack spent Christmas with his father in Palm Beach while the rest of the family vacationed in Switzerland. His health had improved since September, and once his course work was completed he went to the Mayo Clinic for a two-week checkup in anticipation of spending six months in London. Originally he was to have traveled with his father, but the ambassador returned to London early at Chamberlain's request, so on February 25, 1939, Jack sailed alone on the *Queen Mary*. The crossing was a rough one, though, to Jack's relief, it did not leave him feeling sick.

Six months after Chamberlain returned from Munich to a hero's welcome, Jack arrived in London to find every class of society deeply and painfully divided. "Munich divided friends and it divided families," said Andrew Devonshire of that tumultuous time. Friends stopped speaking to one another; marriages were strained to the breaking point; luncheons and dinner parties degenerated into bitter quarrels. On the one hand, Chamberlain and his supporters insisted that the months of peace had amply vindicated the hard decision taken at Munich. On the other hand, Duff Cooper had challenged his countrymen to face the question of what they had done out of fear of war, and in the aftermath of his resignation speech a nation which held honor dear had undergone a grueling process of self-examination. When outspoken critics such as Raymond Asquith's sister Violet Bonham Carter accused the prime minister of having broken with the great and honorable tradition of British foreign policy, which had always refused to truckle to the strong at the expense of the weak, the potency of the charges derived in part from the fact that it was important to Chamberlain's backers to hold to the belief that he had, as he claimed, won peace with honor. Even the most ardent Chamberlainites, no less than the rest of their countrymen, founded their arguments on the conviction that they were persons of principle, who did their duty when called upon.

Among the many whom Munich had plunged into a crisis of identity was Billy Hartington; like Jack, he had seized on Munich as a topic he planned to write about at length as part of his university studies. When Jack had last talked to him the previous summer, Billy had expressed amusement at what he saw as the American's misunderstanding of the British character. Chamberlain's deal with Hitler was hugely troubling to him, not only because he found it impossible to reconcile the betrayal of the Czechs with his conception of Britain as an honorable nation, but also because his father, the under-secretary for the dominions, approved of what the prime minister had done. (The duchess, though she chose not to differ publicly with her husband, privately sympathized with her brother Lord Cranborne and the Tory opposition.) Billy decided to apply cold reason to Munich, to look at it not in emotional but in strictly strategic terms. What, Billy asked, would Talleyrand have done at Munich? How would the master negotiator and notorious political chameleon (from whom Billy's paternal grandmother was descended) have acted if confronted with Hitler's demands? Unguided by considerations of right action, would Talleyrand have thought it tactically useful to sacrifice Czechoslovakia? By stripping away the moral question, Billy hoped somehow to make sense of his father's support for the Munich agreement.

By contrast, Jack seemed untroubled by his own father's position, whatever inroads Wheeler-Bennett believed himself to have made in the young man's thinking. At a moment when Chamberlain was insisting that the Munich agreement had succeeded brilliantly and that everything pointed "in the direction of peace," Jack accepted his father's view: if Chamberlain had indeed averted a war, then that, from the standpoint of British and American interests, was all that really mattered. During these weeks, Jack spent a good deal of time listening to the ambassador while serving as his aide. Dressed in a dashing new cutaway suit which, he said, made him feel "quite important," he accompanied his father to lunches and dinners, met the King, and took tea with the twelve-year-old future queen, Princess Elizabeth, with whom, he jestingly reported to Lem, he had "made a great deal of time." On March 10, 1939, Jack flew with his father to Rome, where

Ambassador Kennedy was to represent the White House at the coronation of Pope Pius XII. That day the British newspapers were full of optimism about the prospects for peace. The press based its assessment on Chamberlain's comment that "the foreign situation is less anxious and gives me less concern for possible unpleasant development than it has for some time." Jack was still in Italy five days later when the euphoria was abruptly shattered.

On March 15, the day the Pope gave little Teddy Kennedy his first communion, word arrived that German troops had entered Prague in flagrant breach of the Munich agreement. The Czech government, robbed of its fortified defenses by the terms of Munich, advised its people not to resist. That night Hitler proclaimed a German protectorate over Czechoslovakia. Clearly, his promise that the Sudetenland would be his last territorial demand had been a sham. Clearly, those critics who insisted that Hitler could not be trusted and that Chamberlain had been wrong to believe him had been correct. In the past Hitler had claimed to seek to return German natives to their homeland, but the march into Prague and the joining of aliens to the Reich could be construed as nothing other than conquest pure and simple.

At first Chamberlain strove to look the other way. "I have," he declared, "so often heard charges of breaches of faith bandied about which did not seem to be founded on sufficient premises that I do not wish to associate myself with any charges of that character." Yet the fall of Prague made it impossible for Chamberlainites to pretend any longer, whether to others or to themselves, that at Munich the prime minister had won either peace with honor or peace for our time. On March 16, the Duke of Devonshire, a minister just below Cabinet rank, made the extraordinary gesture of complaining in public that Chamberlain's policy was "not bearing fruit." The next day, Jack returned from Rome to what Andrew Devonshire would later describe as a country finally united by its sense of shame over what their leader had done in quest of peace. It had taken six months for the process to be completed, but shame over Munich had, in Andrew Devonshire's words, taken "the safety catch off the hunting rifle." Britain was at last ready to face the Germans. Munich had prepared the British for war, not because, as Jack and certain of the Chamberlainites would later claim, it gave the government a year to rearm, but because shame had finally trumped fear.

Years afterward, Anne Tree would say of Billy, Andrew, David and the other young men Jack knew in London in 1939 that the whole experience of Munich had "completely changed their lives." Following Hitler's entry into Prague, they were so ashamed of their country's actions at Munich that they were determined that such a betrayal of the national honor must never be permitted again. Jack could not help but recognize that the spirit of Munich was dead. He acknowledged the feeling, widespread in London, that there would soon be another war, but he failed to grasp that a turning point had been reached. He persisted in the belief that, confronted with German military might, Britain would yet back down. Nothing his British friends said could change his mind. "Everyone thinks war is inevitable before the year is out," Jack wrote to Lem after he had been back in London for six days. "I personally don't, though Dad does."

At the end of March Jack began work as an aide at the US embassy in Paris. He took over the position previously occupied by his elder brother, who in recent months had slipped off to Spain to observe the last days of the civil war. As was the case with everything to do with young Joe, his exploits there had become a major preoccupation of his father's. Warned that it would be risky for an ambassador's son to travel in a war zone, young Joe had traded in his diplomatic passport for a regular one so that the State Department would not be involved should he find himself in trouble. On his return from America in February, Ambassador Kennedy had been greeted with the news that his namesake had gone to Spain in defiance of his wishes; far from irked, he actually seemed delighted by Joe's determination to single himself out. Never one to pass up an opportunity for positive publicity, the ambassador was soon boasting to the press of his son's courage and ingenuity. He explained that Joe had done his undergraduate thesis on the Spanish Non-Intervention Committee and, naturally, wished to have a look around. Joe's trip, he went on, was hardly the first of his adventures in Europe. "During the crisis I started counting noses and Joe was missing," the ambassador declared in his persona as a father of nine. "It turned out he was in Czechoslovakia." And, Kennedy added proudly, Joe had been "prowling around Russia, too." After a letter arrived from young Joe ("Well, I'm on my way—and on my own") the ambassador read it aloud, not once but twice, at a country-house weekend at

Cliveden, where Nancy Astor's guests included Neville Chamberlain, the Duke and Duchess of Devonshire, Charles and Anne Morrow Lindbergh, and Geoffrey Dawson, editor of *The Times*. Other letters followed, and by the time Jack returned to Prince's Gate his father was treating each new report from Spain as nothing less than oracular. Before long, the ambassador was full of plans to have Joe's letters published in magazines and newspapers, and possibly collected between hard covers. He spoke of the "prestige" and "international publicity" they would win for Joe. He approached the *Saturday Evening Post* and other outlets on his son's behalf. Interest was lacking, so he proposed that Joe be commissioned to write a series on Communism, pitching that idea to the *Saturday Evening Post* and the Hearst papers. When that too failed, he transferred his efforts to London, where he attempted to interest Dawson in a piece by Joe on Spain.

Like young Joe, Jack planned to use Paris as a launching pad for his own travels. At the embassy he gravitated to the office of Ambassador William C. Bullitt's private secretary, Carmel Offie, where, strictly for his own edification, he listened to incoming telegrams as they were read aloud and pored over letters and reports. Professor Hopper had suggested that, because of his father's position, Jack had "access to a good deal of material that other people would not have"—and here, certainly, it was. Offie considered some of the documents "none of his business," but as an ambassador's son Jack was free to do nearly as he wished. During his month at the embassy Jack used his status to ask a good many questions and examine every possible piece of official paper—the beginning of a lifelong appetite for vast quantities of raw documentation. Full of smiles and charm, he proceeded with such nonchalance that no one, including his father, seemed to grasp quite how much information he was assimilating, or how swiftly.

Events in Europe took a new turn when, attention having shifted to Poland as Hitler's next target, Chamberlain declared in Parliament on March 31 that the British and the French would come to Poland's defense in the event of an attack. The announcement, a sharp reversal in government policy, served as a reminder of how much had changed in two weeks. But the question remained: In the event that Hitler did move against Poland, could Britain be counted on to live up to its promise? On April 28, Jack joined other staff members at the US embassy in Paris as they listened on the radio to Hitler's two-and-a-half-hour speech to the Reichstag, in which he asserted German claims on the Polish seaport of Danzig, which had been created a "free city" by the Treaty of Versailles. "Just listened to Hitler's speech which they consider bad," Jack wrote to Lem afterward. ". . . However the encouraging thing is that if Hitler was going to go—the time would have been a month ago before Poland and England signed up. That he didn't shows a reluctance on his part so I still think it will be OK. The whole thing is damn interesting and if this letter wasn't going on a German boat and if they weren't opening mail could tell you some interesting stuff."

A week later, Jack flew to London for his parents' dinner party in honor of the King and Queen, who were about to leave on a trip to America. He arrived at Prince's Gate to find Joe Junior already in residence—and in high spirits. Joe had been invited to Cliveden on two separate weekends, to hold forth on his adventures in Spain to an audience of distinguished guests. Nancy Astor had previously been the making of Kick in Britain, and now, as a kindness to the ambassador, she played the same role on young Joe's behalf. During his most recent visit to Cliveden she had strategically put him together with Hugh Fraser, on the principle that both were young men of exceptional political promise, Joe as a future president and Hugh, quite possibly, as prime minister. Before long they were fast friends and were planning a trip together, with Kick in tow, to see the Spanish locales spoken of at Cliveden; they agreed to leave as soon as the Season ended. Joe, who affected an unctuously flirtatious manner with his benefactress, had by the time of Jack's visit emerged as very much the star in certain London circles. But there was a problem with his preeminence, though few people had any inkling. Young Joe's mature appearance and serious demeanor gave an impression of "gravitas," as Hugh Fraser later described it; his writing and ideas were another matter. Rather than admit that his failure to get Joe's Spanish letters published might have anything to do with their quality, Ambassador Kennedy insisted that the reason must be a decrease in public interest in Spain since the capitulation of the Republic in March. He counseled Joe to work up some impressions of other locales, with an eye toward a book-length collection of travel letters. So it was that, after the dinner party, both sons resumed their travels. Joe's purpose was to develop such insights as, "Are we going to continue to accept newspaper reports which always try to state the worst of all the dictatorships because that is the best news?" and "Does it ever occur to people that there are happy people in Italy and Germany?" Jack, unburdened by the pressure to publish, went off because, as he later stated to Lem Billings, "the only way you can really know what is going on is to go to all the countries." The Kennedy brothers promised to be back before June 22, the debut of their sister Eunice, of whom Jakie Astor liked to laugh that she looked "like Jack in a wig."

Jack headed directly for Danzig, which Hitler had described in the Reichstag speech as "perhaps the most painful of all problems for Germany." In the interim, Churchill had publicly suggested that Hitler seemed to think that the people in Britain who had argued that Czechoslovakia was not worth fighting for would now say the same about Danzig. Churchill expressed concern that the Führer, blind to the immense change in British public opinion that had resulted from his breach of the Munich agreement, would be led to miscalculate in the matter of Danzig. During his visit Jack talked to Nazis as well as to others in an effort to get a sense of what Hitler intended and of how the Poles might respond. In Warsaw, he spent a week at the US embassy and talked to more people about the tense situation. Jack's conclusion was that in the event Hitler tried to grab Danzig the Poles would fight, even if it fell to them to fight alone. "The Poles are not the Czechs," he wrote to Lem, "and they will fight." After Poland, he went on to visit Russia, Hungary, Turkey, Palestine, Lebanon, Syria and Greece.

When Jack returned to London in June 1939, he had little choice but to acknowledge that, contrary to anything he had believed to date, Britain was serious about going to war. The government had introduced conscription, requiring males aged twenty and twenty-one to engage in six months of military training. In his Harvard thesis, Jack would cite conscription as evidence that Britain intended to make good on its promise to fight. In a related development, two of the young men in Jack's London circle had finally managed to overturn the Oxford Union's King and Country resolution that, six years before, had persuaded him that the heroic Britain of his books, the Britain of the 1914 war and of Raymond Asquith, had ceased to exist. Hugh Fraser, the new president of the Union, had called on Julian Amery to propose the motion, "In view of this country's commitments and of the gravity of the general situation in Europe, this house welcomes conscription." "After eight years of fatal mistakes in foreign policy," Amery argued, "it has become clear that only a policy of power can save the situation. You will never preserve the peace unless you can persuade the dictators that you would beat them in war." In 1933 Winston Churchill's son Randolph had led a campaign to expunge the King and Country debate from the Union minute book; returning in 1939 to support the new resolution, he delighted the large audience when he chanted, "Onward Conscript Soldiers, marching as to war, you would not be conscripts, had you gone before." The debate, characterized by the *Oxford Mail* as "one of the most outstanding" in the society's history, extended well into the night. When the motion carried, it was a great moment for all who despised the image of "a decadent, degenerate Britain."

Joe Kennedy was still convinced that if he could only persuade the British that Hitler would surely destroy them, they might yet be convinced to look to their own interests and make further concessions to the Reich. It was not, as some in London had begun to say, that he wanted them to be defeated, but, rather, that he sincerely thought they would be. The previous September, he had brought Lindbergh to London to attest to the magnitude of German military might, which had unquestionably had an impact on public opinion. In the belief that the British had deluded themselves into thinking that they could actually win a war against Germany, Kennedy undertook again to show them their error. At a dinner party that June of 1939, Walter Lippmann informed Churchill that Kennedy had been telling friends that in the event of war Britain, faced with inevitable defeat, would surrender to Hitler. Harold Nicolson, who was present at the dinner, recorded that when Churchill heard the word "surrender" he commented, "No, the Ambassador should not have spoken so, Mr. Lippmann; he should not have said that dreadful word. Yet supposing (as I do not for one moment suppose) that Mr. Kennedy were correct in his tragic utterance, then I for one would willingly lay down my life in combat, rather than, in fear of defeat, surrender to the menaces of these most sinister men." Churchill had been long out of harmony with the public; now he spoke for the many who, in the wake of Munich, had decided to base their actions not on whether they could beat Hitler, but on whether it was right to try.

The chasm between Joe Kennedy's sense of the situation and that of his children's friends became clear on an evening when Kick invited Billy, David and some of the other young people to dine at Prince's Gate. Jack was also present, having recently returned to London. In his absence, Billy Hartington had joined the Coldstream Guards, volunteering rather than waiting to be called up. David Ormsby Gore had been eager to do the same, but Lord Harlech, who had already endured the death of his eldest son, was determined to keep David out of the Coldstreams—who would be sent to the most dangerous positions in the front lines—in favor of a less perilous commission. After much disagreement, David reluctantly conceded and joined the Territorial Army.

After dinner, the ambassador invited everyone to his private screening room, where he enjoyed entertaining guests with Hollywood fare. Even the Kennedys' dinner party for the King and Queen the previous month had concluded with a film. This evening, however, it soon became apparent that the ambassador had something other than his guests' pleasure in mind. He had chosen a film about the 1914 war. Images of trench warfare and soldiers "mown down by gunfire" had begun to unroll when the ambassador jumped up in front of the screen and faced the startled audience. Pictures of slaughter, of British soldiers marching defenselessly toward German guns in the trenches, streamed over Joe Kennedy's skin and clothing as he gestured behind him and shouted at Billy and the other fellows, "That's what you'll all be looking like in a month or two!" A number of the young men present had already enlisted, and all expected that they would likely be fighting within months, so the ambassador's outburst provoked considerable embarrassment. He clearly did not comprehend that young men such as Billy and David viewed fighting as a matter of honor and were under no illusions about its cost; win or lose, live or die, it was something they believed they had to do. He failed to detect the sense of shame that had altered the national mood; as far as he was concerned, Munich had been a matter of survival and therefore nothing to be ashamed of. In that failure lay the origin of the ambassador's ignominious fate in a nation that had once delighted in his presence.

Incensed by her father's performance, Kick leaned over to Billy and whispered, "You mustn't pay attention to him. He just doesn't understand the English as I do." Jack, by contrast, sat impassive throughout. He said not a word and gave no sign of where his sympathies lay. Even afterward, when Kick and the others could talk of nothing but what the ambassador had done, Jack, to her frustration, refused to take sides.

Billy, who was completing his last year at Cambridge, had seen a great deal of Kick in the months since they had been together at Cortachy Castle, and their romance had become the talk of London society. Billy had also been giving much thought to his future role as a duke—and to the part Kick might play at his side. Two factors spurred these reflections: one, his work on an undergraduate thesis on the Whig oligarchy, in which his ancestors had played a central role; the other, his parents' move to Chatsworth, the family seat in the Peak District of Derbyshire, where many of the records of previous Devonshire dukes and duchesses were preserved. In the course of researching his thesis Billy had grown absorbed in letters by and about Georgiana, the 5th Duchess of Devonshire, and he used her story as a historical prism through which to view Kick.

In 1775, Georgiana Spencer, the seventeen-year-old eldest daughter of the 1st Earl Spencer, married the 5th Duke of Devonshire. Young and vibrant though not conventionally beautiful, she captivated London society and, inspired by the great Whig politician Charles James Fox whose confidante she became, staked out a formidable position as a political hostess and campaigner. She played a crucial part in the pivotal 1784 Westminster election by taking to the streets to argue Fox's cause, inspiring tales that the duchess had gone so far as to exchange kisses for votes. She was widely credited with having saved Fox's seat in Parliament at a moment when the King wanted him out. According to Richard Holderness, to whom Kick later spoke extensively of her own life, Billy in this period "often talked to her of Georgiana." As their conversations oscillated between the eighteenth and twentieth centuries, Kick began to grasp "the role he had in mind for his future duchess." He offered more than love and admiration, though both certainly were part of the package. Billy hoped to launch a political career and to revive Chatsworth as a center of political and cultural power; he saw Kick, with her immense personal magnetism and passion for politics, as an "ideal partner." As their friends perceived, Kick lent Billy a certain energy he did not himself possess, and he in turn offered her a significant role in life, something her mother had never had. Kick found the prospect enormously appealing.

The 1st Duke had built Chatsworth, its splendor said to rival that of a king's palace, as a reminder in golden stone of the Cavendish role as kingmaker and guarantor of parliamentary power in the Glorious Revolution of 1688. Billy's ancestor had conspired to dethrone the Roman Catholic James II, who aimed to convert England back to Catholicism and limit the power of Parliament in favor of an absolute monarchy on the model of Louis XIV in France. Along with other members of a landed aristocracy that exercised power through seats held in Parliament, the 1st Duke appealed to James's Dutch nephew, William of Orange, a Protestant whose wife, Mary, was James's daughter by his first wife, to seize the throne. William traveled to England, James fled to France, and the revolution was accomplished bloodlessly. Two and a half centuries later, Chatsworth symbolized the 1st Duke's part in initiating an age of constitutional monarchy, as well as Whiggery's historical mission to defend liberty by protecting parliamentary government against the despotism of kings. The house and all it represented—not just great property, but also political and social responsibility—would eventually be Billy's. He had a Whig's love of high living, great houses and beautiful objects, and reveled in the priceless art, rare books, manuscripts and other treasures with which Chatsworth was filled. When the family had moved to Chatsworth the previous December Billy had claimed for himself a corner room in the state apartments designed for the reception of kings; when he awoke in the morning, floor-to-ceiling windows gave long views of much that he expected to possess one day.

In other circumstances, things between Billy and Kick might have progressed at a more leisurely rate. But, as Jean Lloyd recalled, the approach of war caused not just Kick and Billy but others in their set to "grow up more quickly" than they might otherwise have done. With Billy and the other boys preparing to go off to fight, it seemed as if decisions had to be made at once. Still, even as Kick and Billy talked and planned, a huge difficulty presented itself. He was heir to the title of one of the most important Protestant families in Britain. She was a devout Roman Catholic. Their class difference, though immense, was not insurmountable; their religious difference threatened to be so. The problem was far more complicated than the fact that Billy's father was ferociously anti-Catholic. Had Andrew, the second son, been in love with Kick, the trouble would have been limited to family displeasure. Instead, it was the eldest son and heir who had fallen in love with the Kennedy girl, and Devonshire dukes inherited religious as well as secular responsibilities. "My father had the appointment to forty clergy," Billy's sister Anne Tree observed. "He had to interview and say who he would have as clergyman in forty parishes." Billy would undertake that task one day, and his son after him. Though Billy possessed not a trace of his father's fierce anti-Catholicism, he agreed fully on the preposterousness of a Devonshire duke taking a Catholic wife, and of Catholic offspring succeeding to a dukedom founded on the Protestant succession. As Anne Tree recalled, he "felt that he could not appoint clergy if he had a son of a different faith." On the other side, Kick's parents, especially her mother, were as unhappy at the prospect of her marriage to a Protestant as the duke was at the idea of a Catholic daughter-in-law. And even were there to be no opposition from the Kennedys, Kick herself would have refused to consider the possibility of renouncing her own religion in favor of Billy's. For all that, Billy was rarely distressed by dilemmas that would rattle most other people. He tended to be imperturbable and to act as if difficulties simply did not exist. In the absence of his parents, who had left in May for a three-month official visit to South Africa, he and Kick continued to talk of the shared future a number of their friends doubted could ever really be theirs. Hugh Fraser (himself a Catholic), Tony Loughborough, William Douglas Home and other young men in their group continued to dance attendance on Kick, under the assumption that her romance with Billy, however intense, was doomed.

As chance would have it, David Ormsby Gore had also become romantically involved with a Catholic, though his status as heir to a minor barony made the difficulty far less formidable. A year and a half after a Cavendish cousin of Billy's had created a family scandal by eloping with the Catholic Pamela Lloyd Thomas, David emerged as a suitor for Pamela's younger sister Sylvia, known as Sissie. Kick and Sissie had become close the previous Season, their intimacy encouraged by their shared religion. For all the care on the part of Lady Airlie and other parents to fashion a limited and sealed world in which the aristocratic cousinhood would encounter no one who could be judged "unsuitable," there was anxiety that summer among the Cavendish and Cecil families about how many of their young men had become romantically entangled with Catholics. The situation led the duke's uncle Lord Richard Cavendish to bemoan to Lady Alice Salisbury—whose husband had recently had to warn their grandson Robert Cecil, the future Marquess of Salisbury, to end his romance with Hugh Fraser's sister Veronica—"These Catholic girls are a menace!"

David's involvement with Sissie Lloyd Thomas rendered him less available to attend the Season's parties with Jack. So, while Jack continued to see much of David on the golf course and elsewhere, he went to parties and chased girls in the company of Tony Loughborough. Billy Hartington and Kick Kennedy; David Ormsby Gore and Sissie Lloyd Thomas; Andrew Cavendish and Debo Mitford—as war approached, these and other members of the set had entered into serious relationships. In the belief that those of their friends who had rushed into major romances had "gone nuts," Jack and Tony, making the rounds of the parties, targeted blondes and slightly older married women. They dubbed themselves the team of "RossKennedy," Tony being the heir to his grandfather the 5th Earl of Rosslyn, a heavy drinker and gambler who had dissipated the family fortune. Tony's father, Lord Loughborough, had committed suicide in 1929, when Tony was twelve. Since then, Tony had been somewhat rudderless, and when, a decade later, Ambassador Kennedy encountered him he instinctively took a personal interest in the fatherless boy. The ambassador included him in golf foursomes with Jack and Joe Junior, and soon Tony was listening to his remarks as raptly as his own sons did. Tony disagreed with many of the ambassador's opinions—especially on Britain's chances of defeating the Germans—but admired his willingness to speak his mind despite the unpopularity of what he had to say. As British opinion mounted against Kennedy, Tony, who became the 6th Earl of Rosslyn on his grandfather's death that August, cast himself among friends as the ambassador's ardent defender—one of the few he still had.

During the last six weeks of the Season, the team of RossKennedy was observed at dances and dinners, at the 400 Club and at country-house weekends. The MP Henry "Chips" Channon described the 1939 Season in his diary as the "sunset glow before the storm." Convinced that these next few weeks might be their last, the young people strove to enjoy themselves before the men went off to war and German bombs began to fall on London. Even as the orchestras played "Night And Day," "The Lady Is A Tramp," "I've Got You Under My Skin," and "Dancing Cheek To Cheek," the city's great houses were being packed up and emptied of their treasures. Lavish parties were held against backdrops of shipping crates and furniture draped in white sheets, and there were predictions that many great houses would "never again open their hospitable doors." Julian Amery remembered that the round of festivities, made hectic "by a sense of impending danger," seemed "more brilliant than usual." For Jack, as for many participants, the sense that one was witnessing the final moments of a world about to become extinct made the events of those weeks incomparably exciting. At a time when he was first reading David Cecil's newly-published *The Young Melbourne*, Jack delighted in a heady existence that, like the eighteenth-century Whig world painted in Cecil's opening pages, mixed seriousness and frivolity, intellect and earthy exuberance.

Social life on the eve of war allowed Jack to indulge his equally strong tastes for politics and pleasure. He could be supremely serious. "Jack was very intelligent at a dinner table—too intelligent and political for me," remembered Elizabeth Leveson-Gower, who knew him that summer. "He liked to dominate the conversation at a dinner table; he wasn't interested in making small talk. He wanted to discuss serious issues." In other moods, Jack could be boisterous and even silly, as when, at a country-house weekend at Tichborne Park, he and Joe Junior ganged up on Tony Loughborough and pulled his trousers down. On Friday, July 7, RossKennedy attended the ball given by the Duchess of Marlborough at a dramatically floodlit Blenheim Palace. For Jack, the evening provided an opportunity to see Churchill, Eden and other celebrated guests in person. It was also a chance to position himself among the mass of young men gathered around the lovely Duchess of Kent, who ranked RossKennedy among her most ardent admirers. On the following Monday, Chips Channon, having spotted RossKennedy at Blenheim, invited them to his ornately decorated house in Belgrave Square for a luncheon in honor of his young houseguest Princess Cecile of Prussia, the late Kaiser's granddaughter. Following a "hilarious party" in the silver-and-blue rococo dining room (modeled by the French decorator Boudin on the Amelienburg pleasure palace in Munich), Jack and the others rushed off to Parliament to hear the prime minister make a statement on Danzig, on which the whole question of war appeared to hinge. The day, mixing as it did mirth and matters of grave consequence, was the sort that Jack had learned to love— and would strive throughout his life to replicate.

"Never had a better time," Jack wrote to Lem of the 1939 Season, at the close of which he took off to Germany in the company of David Ormsby Gore and Torby Macdonald, his Harvard roommate. Jack's— indeed, all the Kennedys'—readiness to pick up and travel anywhere at any time was one of the qualities about them that thrilled David. When at length David returned to Britain in anticipation of his own and later Billy Hartington's twenty-first birthday celebrations, Jack and Torby joined the Kennedys in the south of France, where the ambassador had rented a villa about five miles outside Cannes. Torby was romantically interested in Kick, who had recently returned from the trip to Spain with young Joe and Hugh Fraser, but she made it clear that she saw him strictly as a friend. Jack and the disappointed Torby went on to Munich and Vienna, before Torby continued alone to Budapest and Jack to Berlin. By this time Jack had no doubt that the British planned to stand by Poland, but he wondered how Hitler assessed the situation. Jack had been fascinated by miscalculation and the momentum of war since he had first read *The World Crisis* at age fifteen; he now believed that the Germans had gone so far with their Danzig propaganda that it was "hard to see them backing down." The central question in determining the likelihood of war was whether, at the decisive moment, Germany would persist in misjudging British resolve. "England seems firm this time," he wrote to Lem from Berlin that August, "but as that is not completely understood here the big danger lies in the Germans counting on another Munich then finding themselves in a war when Chamberlain refuses to give in."

On August 15, Kick's British friends gathered at Chatsworth for Billy Hartington's coming-of-age celebration. The occasion was the last great party before the war, the final emphatic display of a privileged way of life some thought already defunct and few believed likely to survive another war. The party also provided the setting for one last bitter-sweet gathering of the "tight little circle" Kick had joined sixteen months previously. But Kick would not be among the Devonshires' more than 2,500 guests. The previous year, Rose Kennedy had had no idea why her daughter had been so eager to lose weight before she went to Cortachy Castle. No longer in the dark about Billy, Mrs. Kennedy was vehement in her opposition to Kick's romance with a Protestant and had insisted she remain in Cannes.

Over the course of several days of glorious weather, the duke and duchess hosted a series of parties at Chatsworth to celebrate the majority of their son and heir. "The atmosphere had something of the Duchess of Richmond's ball before the Battle of Waterloo," Andrew Devonshire remembered. ". . . We sensed it was the closing of an age." Weeks after the contents of other major houses had been packed away, Chatsworth remained intact—almost defiantly so. Outdoors, Billy, six foot four, hair slicked back, dressed in an impeccably cut dark suit, stood beside his parents shaking hands with a vast line of estate tenants that snaked across the great terraces above the river. Many of the well-wishers were from Chatsworth itself, but there were also contingents from the numerous other family estates. In a spectacle of fealty and affection, the tenants presented the Marquess, to whom it would one day fall to look out for their interests, with precious gifts: silver salvers and goblets, gold cigarette cases and lighters, gold cufflinks, shirt studs, and a copy of a silver tankard presented to the 1st Duke of Devonshire by his tenants. The music of the Coldstream Guards band let no one forget that the heir, like a great many other young men, might soon be at war.

Five days after a select house party of Billy's friends and relatives dispersed, both he and David were called up to their regiments. News had broken that Hitler had signed a non-aggression pact with Stalin which, by detaching the Soviet Union from the western powers, cleared the way for the invasion of Poland. Parliament was recalled and the fleet ordered to its war stations. Britain signed a treaty to formalize the promise given several months previously to come to the aid of the Poles in the event Hitler attacked. Ambassador Kennedy urged all Americans who did not have urgent business in Britain to leave at once. Rose Kennedy, on her husband's instructions, packed up the villa near Cannes. Jack had joined his mother, Kick and the others in the south of France, and accompanied them back to London on August 26. Early on September 1, 1939, Hitler's forces streamed across the Polish frontier, and warplanes launched a massive bombing campaign on military and civilian targets. As Jack had predicted, the Poles fought bravely but vainly, their mounted cavalry no match for Hitler's tanks. In Britain there was anxiety in many quarters that Chamberlain, despite his pledge to defend the Poles, would again be inclined to give way. After it became clear that popular opinion would not abide another Munich-type capitulation, the government delivered an ultimatum to Hitler. At 9 a.m. on Sunday, September 3, Britain gave Germany two hours to reverse course and provide assurances that the march into Poland had been suspended. At a quarter past eleven Chamberlain announced on the radio that no such assurances had been forthcoming. "Consequently," he went on, "this country is now at war with Germany."

Forty-five minutes later, Jack was in the visitors' gallery at the House of Commons when Chamberlain declared, "This is a sad day for all of us, and to none is it sadder than to me." Churchill commented that while it was indeed a sad day, there must also be "a note of thankful-ness" that a new generation of Britons was ready to fight and thereby to prove itself "not unworthy of the days of yore and not unworthy of those great men, the fathers of our land, who laid the foundation of our laws and shaped the greatness of our country." Churchill, who had always refused to tailor his words to what the majority wanted to hear, had long been out of favor. Despite their well-known mutual antago-nism, Chamberlain now offered him his old post as First Lord of the Admiralty, as well as a place in the War Cabinet. Some thought Chamberlain ought to have gone further. Macmillan, for one, won-dered whether "at this moment of failure and disappointment," it would perhaps have been better had Chamberlain passed on the burden of leadership altogether. In a sign of the changing fortunes not only of Churchill but also of Chamberlain and of the US ambassador who had prominently identified himself with the prime minister's now discred-ited policy of appeasement, President Roosevelt initiated a private cor-respondence with Churchill. He wrote to say how glad he was that Churchill was back at the Admiralty and to propose that they continue to communicate directly through diplomatic pouches. Kennedy, who on taking up the ambassadorship had positioned himself as Churchill's adversary, did what he could to undermine him in the president's eyes.

Heretofore, Jack had been merely an observer of great events. When, the following day, Germany torpedoed the British passenger liner *Athenia* off the Hebrides, Ambassador Kennedy cast him in an active role. One hundred and twelve people had been killed, including twenty-eight Americans who had sailed from Liverpool in the hope of getting out before hostilities began. The ambassador sent Jack to Scotland, where the US citizens who had survived the attack had been transported by a British destroyer. The crowd that greeted Jack in a Glasgow hotel lounge demanded US protection when they started home on an American ship the following week. The "schoolboy diplomat"—as the *Telegraph's* correspondent dubbed Jack on the assumption that he was only eighteen— cited Roosevelt's opinion that a convoy was unnecessary, as Germany would not attack an American vessel. This prompted jeers and indignant cries about the idiocy of trusting the Germans. Jack replied, struggling to be heard above the clamor, "You will be safe on a ship flying the American flag under international law; a neutral ship is safe." In the end, all he could do was promise to communicate the survivors' concerns to his father, and this seemed to satisfy them.

Press accounts noted that Jack, with charm and kindliness, had convinced the survivors that the United States government was genuinely interested in their fate. But even as he won them over, he had been coolly assessing the potential political cost should the Roosevelt administration refuse their demand for a convoy. He shared his thoughts with his father, and on September 8 the ambassador informed US Secretary of State Cordell Hull, "Yesterday my son Jack went up to Glasgow to contact the people rescued from the *Athenia*. He came back with the very definite impression that they are in a terrible state of nerves and that to put them on a ship going back to America for seven days without a convoy or some kind of protection would land them back in New York in such a state that the publicity and criticism of the Government would be unbelievable." In the past, young Joe had been the son whose opinions Kennedy liked to quote, as he had two weeks previously when he telegraphed his namesake's comments on Germany to the State Department. Citing the second son was a new development. Savoring his new status, Jack wrote to Harvard to postpone his return so that he might be certain that the survivors of the *Athenia* incident—his special charges—reached home safely.

Jack was not the only young Kennedy reluctant to leave. Kick had been in Europe for eighteen months, and, according to Jean Lloyd, she had come to think of London as the place where her real life and real friends were. At a moment when David Ormsby Gore and Sissie Lloyd Thomas had begun to discuss marriage, Kick was "distraught" at the thought of leaving Billy, who, like David, had received his commission on September 2. She pleaded with her father to allow her to stay, but, partly because he wanted his entire family safe and partly because he and Rose judged it best for Kick to find a husband of her own faith, Ambassador Kennedy refused. She would sail on September 12, along with her mother and several of her siblings.

Before Kick left she invited Billy and some of their friends to a farewell dinner, also attended by Jack, at Prince's Gate. In the course of the evening the ambassador came in and joined Billy and the other uniformed men in a round of toasts. Inevitably conversation turned to the war and the ambassador seemed "rather to relish" stating his opinion that the British were about to be "badly thrashed." It had been one thing to express such sentiments in the past—and there had been a good deal of upset and embarrassment, when he had so graphically warned his daughter's friends of the horrors that waited on the battlefield—but now that war had been declared, such remarks were bound to provoke and offend. Because Americans had died in the sinking of the *Athenia*, there was speculation in London that the incident might help Roosevelt persuade a reluctant Congress to repeal the Neutrality Act, which forbade the delivery of arms to the war zone. Kennedy declared forcefully that there was little or no chance that the Neutrality Act would be repealed or amended.

On the night of the film screening, Jack had refused to take sides. He showed no such hesitation at the farewell dinner. A year before, Jack had insisted that the decadent British would not fight. Now that Billy, attired in the uniform of the Coldstream Guards, was poised to go off to war, Jack accepted that the British would fight—but he continued to miss the point. Like his father, Jack misjudged the impact Munich had had on Billy and his friends, as well as on much of the country. The feeling of shame that had washed over them as they came to terms with their betrayal not just of the Czechs, but of their sense of themselves, had reminded them forcefully of the principles in which they believed. At this point Jack simply did not realize the depth of those beliefs, nor could he fathom the sense of duty that had motivated Billy and the others to volunteer. As he saw the situation, the failure of Munich to stop Hitler had made the British fear that their lives and property were in danger; and to that fear—a perception of their own self-interest, rather than a sense of duty or principle—he attributed their willingness to fight. "Only fear, violent fear," he would write in his thesis, could "change the outlook in a rich, satisfied nation" such as Britain. To his sister's distress, he voiced agreement with his father about the inevitability of defeat. Even if the Neutrality Act were repealed, he argued, Britain lacked the gold to make substantial armaments purchases in the United States. He seemed to think that if only he could make his friends understand that they could not save themselves in a war with the Germans and that they must not count on the United States to come to their aid militarily or economically, Britain might yet be persuaded to sue for peace.

Since the events of March, Jack had heard young men such as Billy and David explain why after Munich there could no longer be a question of acting on anything but principle, and why they would fight even if they thought defeat likely. But the ambassador's voice had drowned out the others, and it seemed as if, for all that Jack had seen and heard to contest his father's perspective, the main impact of his months in England had been to consolidate his father's influence. Though aware that Munich had changed everything for Billy Hartington and the others, Jack left London in September 1939 still not understanding why.

CHAPTER FOUR

The Form Most Pleasing to His Audience

JACK ARRIVED AT HARVARD IN THE FALL OF 1939 TO DISCOVER that a cinema newsreel of his work with the *Athenia* survivors, as well as newspaper coverage of his Glasgow adventure, had considerably enhanced his profile. Everyone had questions for him about the war in Europe. Jack chose to cast his newfound status as a "seer" in a self-deprecatory light even as he reveled in the attention. He had enjoyed his efficacy in dealing with the crowd of angry, frightened survivors, and he had relished having his opinions taken seriously and sent on to Washington by his father. He returned to Harvard intent on continuing to speak out and exercise influence. At a time when his father's views on appeasement were increasingly under assault in the United States, Jack undertook to convince the American public that even now it would be best for Britain to come to terms with Hitler.

Before Jack left London, his father had written to Roosevelt arguing that a prolonged war would bring economic and social collapse to Britain and thereby have a calamitous impact on the United States, and urged him to act as a "savior" by brokering a peace settlement. Cordell Hull swiftly replied that the president had instructed him to reject Kennedy's suggestion, writing, "The people of the United States would not support any move for peace initiated by this Government that would consolidate or make possible a survival of a regime of force and aggression." Kennedy refused to drop the matter. In further communications, he cited reports that if Hitler fell Germany might "very well go communistic and be a menace to Europe," maintaining that it would be best to "curb our sentiments and sentimentality and look to our own vital interests." He sneered at the claim that the British were fighting for ideals and insisted that whatever they might say they had gone to war to protect "their possessions and place in the sun." He reiterated that their war effort was a "hopeless struggle."

In the first important public statement of his career, Jack contributed an unsigned editorial to the October 9, 1939 issue of the *Harvard Crimson*. Jack knew that since March, when the Germans entered Prague, there had been a desire within the Chamberlain camp to forget the words uttered from the window of Number 10 about having brought back "peace for our time." So the title of his editorial, "Peace In Our Time," had a curiously defiant ring. Indeed, Jack wrote as if the events of recent months had not discredited Chamberlain's claim that he had won a lasting and honorable peace. Jack had heard his British friends insist that the dishonor of Munich must never be repeated; in the *Crimson* editorial, he urged the prudence of another deal with Hitler over the conquest of a powerless nation. Billy Hartington and the others were prepared to fight Hitler even in the face of certain defeat; Jack argued that as defeat was certain the British had better look to their own interests and allow Hitler to keep Poland in exchange for peace. Like his father, he dismissed potential critics of his proposal by saying that they based their objections on "sentiments" rather than on cold facts. Like his father, he maintained that the time had come for a third power to step in and end the war in Europe, and that Roosevelt was "in the most logical position to act." And like his father, he believed that, in the end, fear of their fate at the hands of the Germans would make British leaders receptive to the president's timely intervention.

"The restoration of the old Poland is an utter impossibility, come what may," Jack wrote in the wake of the Nazi–Soviet partitioning of Poland and of Hitler's peace offer to the British, which in effect demanded to keep all while conceding nothing. "The war would be ended now not in the light of what should be done but in the light of what can be done." A Roosevelt-brokered deal, he continued, would involve "considerable concessions to Hitlerdom" and a "puppet Poland," but the victory would also be great for the democracies. German aggression having come to an end, Europe would be able to "breathe easy" again, and "there would be peace for our time." Long after Chamberlain had recognized the use of that phrase as a devastating political mistake, Jack repeated it without a trace of irony. At a moment when even Chamberlain and the other appeasers no longer thought it possible to reach a dependable settlement with Hitler, Jack urged precisely that. On October 12, Chamberlain delivered a speech rejecting the German peace plan.

As Jack was to find, there was also much distaste in America for the idea of coming to terms with Hitler. "Everyone here is still ready to fight till the last Englishman," wrote Jack to his father, satirizing the general mood—at once isolationist and eager to see Britain take on the Germans. Jack had worked up a one-hour speech along the lines of the *Crimson* editorial, and though his appearance before a local group was a success, he agreed that it must be his last. Joe Kennedy's friend Judge John Burns, who had often advised young Joe, had warned that in the current climate to go on speaking as Jack had done "might lead to trouble." Burns's intervention was significant. Young Joe was no longer the only Kennedy brother with a claim on the future; Jack, too, had to exercise caution as he also had a future to protect. Jack retreated from the public stage, and shifted his energies to his senior honors thesis. The project began to take shape as a defense of Ambassador Kennedy's position on the Munich agreement.

Like Jack, Kick had come home preoccupied with events in Britain. Her eighteen months there, she wrote shortly before her boat docked in New York, seemed "like a beautiful dream." But whereas Jack had returned to an exciting new project, Kick reverted to a life she had outgrown. She had changed dramatically during her two years in London, but when the young American men she had dated previously began to call again she discovered that they were "just the same." In London she had been at the very center of her group, but hardly had she returned to Bronxville and begun classes at Finch College in New York than she took up her previous position in Jack's orbit alongside Lem, Torby and the rest. By this time the Duke of Devonshire, whose own father had once felt compelled by religious differences to disapprove of a marriage between the Low Church Cavendishes and the High Church Cecils, was openly declaring a Kennedy alliance "not to his liking." He had forbidden the match and he did not intend to budge. Kick's parents had also made it clear that the match was impossible, and she herself failed to see a way around her own strong commitment to her religion. Yet, despite the fact that she began to go out with the young men whom Jack soon dubbed her "boys' club," she persisted in the expectation that she and Billy would eventually be husband and wife. She later confessed that she had always expected to marry him "Someday— somehow." She and Billy continued to correspond, and she savored scraps of information about him from their friends. She had no idea when he would be sent to the front, when the fighting would begin.

Even as she struggled to reestablish herself in America, she remained absorbed in news of British friends. Their country was at war, but she could tell from their letters that life—a life she had come to love—was going on without her. The previous September she had been in Scotland for the Perth race meeting. This year she was negotiating with Lem to take her up to the Cape for weekends with Jack, while Billy and David were both at Cortachy Castle with Jean. Presently, a letter from Nancy Astor brought news of a house party at Cliveden at which, to everyone's surprise, Billy had appeared. Nancy Astor reported that Andrew had been there as well, as had most of Kick's other friends. "They bemoaned your absence," she wrote, in an effort to assuage Kick's fears that her friends might forget her. "They tried to be cheerful and succeeded in part, but it was very difficult." In another letter, Nancy Astor described the response of Dinah Brand, her young niece, to the mere mention of Kick's name. Dinah's "face lighted up and her little ears stood straight on end like a rabbit's."

Kick worried for her friends' safety, though the massive bombing everyone had expected to follow the declaration of war had failed to materialize. London remained quiet, and a jest made the rounds that Hitler was trying to bore the British into peace. Chamberlain called this prolonged pause the "Twilight War." "The whole stage was set for an intensive and early attack by Germany which would have aroused our stubbornness," wrote Harold Nicolson in his diary. "The Government had not foreseen a situation in which boredom and bewilderment would be the main elements. . . . We have all the apparatus of war conditions without war conditions. The result is general disillusion and grumbling, from which soil defeatism may grow." Not everyone was heard to grumble. Despite the tension of waiting for Hitler's next move, London became even more alluring to some of the young people, especially patrician girls whose mothers and other protectors had abruptly decamped. Daughters relished the opportunity to work at jobs by day and—chaperoned dances being a thing of the past—congregate with friends at nightclubs they had previously visited only when their watchdogs were distracted. By November, Jean Ogilvy, longing for a bit of that freedom, had finally persuaded Lady Airlie to allow her to leave Cortachy Castle for London, where she was soon dining regularly with Billy Hartington. It was not long before Kick had news of the wedding of two of her closest friends, when Sissie Lloyd Thomas married David Ormsby Gore at the Roman Catholic church of St. James's, Spanish Place. Billy, attired in military uniform like the bridegroom, served as best man.

Ambassador Kennedy was winning no friends in London with views that ranged from defeatist to, by some perceptions, anti-British and even pro-German. "I trust that Joe Kennedy . . . is wrong," Chips Channon noted in his diary, "for he prophesies the end of everything, and goes about saying that England is committing suicide." The Foreign Office opened a file on the ambassador's comments, and on October 3, 1939, dispatched a secret memo to Lord Lothian, the British ambassador to the United States, to inform him of Kennedy's "defeatist attitude" which might soon require him "to drop a hint in the proper quarter in Washington." The Foreign Office continued to monitor Kennedy when he traveled to the United States in December to report to Roosevelt. He immediately began to speak out publicly against US participation in the war, warning Americans that the struggle against Hitler was not their fight and involvement not in their interest. "As you love America," he implored parishioners at a Boston church where he had once served as an altar boy, "don't let anything that comes out of any country in the world make you believe that you can make a situation one whit better by getting into the war."

Kennedy remained in America for a medical checkup and several weeks of rest before heading back to his post at the end of February 1940. He returned laden with jazz records to be distributed among Kick's friends as well as a fresh stock of candy and chewing gum for

Nancy Astor, whose sweet tooth the Kennedys had undertaken to satisfy during wartime. His public reception in London surprised him by the depth of its hostility. Kennedy had basked in his popularity during the early days of the ambassadorship, and had failed to appreciate how angry his calls for a deal with Hitler had made people now that Britain had united to go to war. On March 8, 1940, Harold Nicolson led the attack in the *Spectator*, writing, "The vast majority of the British people know that there can be no lasting peace until the Prussian legend is shattered, until the frontiers of France, Holland and Belgium are secured against further attack, and until Eastern Europe is reconstituted in such a manner as to be able to defend itself."

The day after the Nicolson piece, Kennedy went to Cliveden, which, unlike many great houses, remained open after war was declared. (There was one exception to Nancy Astor's generosity as a hostess: her candy, especially now that it was in limited supply. When a visitor arrived, she would pull out a box from under a sofa cushion and offer a sweet before swiftly sliding it back into its hiding place.) Prior to the war, a good number of the guests at Lord and Lady Astor's country-house weekends had, like their hosts, been proponents of appeasement, and Kennedy had always felt at home there. Nonetheless, talk of a so-called Cliveden set whose members uniformly hoped for Britain to come to terms with Germany is misleading, as the Astors had also welcomed guests of the opposite persuasion. Nancy Astor, in her capacity as hostess, had vigorously encouraged arguments on both sides of the debate, making of her houses, in the fond recollection of Harold Macmillan—no appeaser himself—"an open forum." Yet her personal opinions were well known, and during much of Kennedy's tenure she and the ambassador had been in agreement. They agreed no more, however. A staunch supporter of the war, she was eager to see America come in and help Britain to defeat Hitler. She considered Kennedy's opposition to US involvement "scandalous," and fought in vain to change her friend's mind. Her son Jakie, alluding to the ambassador's insistence that the Americans ought to steer clear, quipped that it would be just as well if they did, as Britain preferred to win "without America taking credit for it."

Both Jack and Kick had asked to come over to London during the summer holidays, but their father sent word that it was not a good idea.

"They have friends here now," he wrote to Mrs. Kennedy, "but you would be surprised by how much anti-American they have become. . . . So for Kick to see her old friends and get into a discussion about US and the war might undo all the pleasant memories she has." Kick's main reason to visit was to see Billy, but by the time her father's letter arrived Billy was no longer in Britain. His battalion, part of the British Expeditionary Force, had been sent to the Maginot Line, the zone of fortifications at the French–German border. There he was to wait for the German onslaught which some observers—though not all—believed was soon to come.

The Twilight War persisted during the entire time—January–March 1940—that Jack devoted to the composition of "Appeasement at Munich," his senior honors thesis. Ironically, in light of their contrasting perspectives, Jack, like Billy Hartington in his paper on what Talleyrand would have done at Munich, put aside the moral question in an effort to assess Chamberlain's actions from a strictly practical point of view. Claiming that questions of honor and principle had nothing to do with the decisions taken at Munich, Jack undertook to defend his father's controversial position. He began with the observation that in the intense controversy over Munich, the reasons for Chamberlain's deal with Hitler had been buried beneath "a cloud of political emotionalism." Where other commentators had focused on the betrayal of Czechoslovakia, Jack stripped away what he saw as a good deal of unproductive moralizing. With the detachment cultivated in boyhood, he sought to prove that circumstances had compelled Chamberlain to act as he did.

Jack maintained that the Munich agreement was "a 'realist' policy in that it was the inevitable result of factors that permitted no other decision." As Britain had failed to rearm in the 1930s, "Chamberlain could not have fought even if he had wanted to." Unlike those who believed that Britain had been honor-bound to live up to its treaty obligations and come to the aid of the Czechs, Jack insisted that the inadequacy of British defenses left Chamberlain no option but to seek the "year of grace" Munich offered to rearm. Downplaying the claims by Chamberlain and his supporters that he had saved the world from war, Jack argued that the prime minister had consciously bought time for Britain to prepare militarily—this last, as John Wheeler-Bennett has shown, a claim the Chamberlainites did not actually begin to make until the international situation began to deteriorate. "Most of the critics," Jack observed, "have been firing at the wrong target. The Munich Pact itself should not be the object of criticism but rather the underlying factors, such as the state of British opinion and the condition of Britain's armaments, which made 'surrender' inevitable." Rather than focus on what happened at Munich, Jack proposed to tell the story that led up to it. In doing so, his thesis highlighted the issue he had hotly debated with British friends in 1938 apropos the Churchill–Baldwin exchange printed in *Arms and the Covenant*, which would preoccupy him to the end of his days: the role of a leader in a democratic society.

To explain Britain's lack of strength at the time Chamberlain made his deal with Hitler, Jack wrote of the rise of the pacifist movement after the end of the First World War, of the terror of air attacks, of Baldwin's statement that the bomber would always get through, and of the Oxford Union's "startling" resolution not to fight for King and Country. He noted the general complacency in Britain in the face of German rearmament, the pro-German views of certain British aristocrats, and the conviction that Hitler's Germany would serve as "a bulwark against Communism." He referred to the distrust of Churchill that had led the nation to ignore his warnings. He wrote of the 1933 East Fulham by-election, cited by Baldwin in 1936, in which a Labour candidate won an overwhelming victory in a traditionally Conservative district on a platform of peace and disarmament. And he described the pressure on elected leaders—at least, those who wished to be reelected—not to diverge from popular opinion. This last point led Jack to ask whether leaders bore a responsibility to follow their consciences, even at the risk of being voted out of office. As it had been in 1938, Jack's answer was an emphatic no. "A politician," Jack wrote, "will always endeavor to present things in the form most pleasing to his audience."

Jack's case for the inevitability of Munich rested on the defense of Stanley Baldwin. He argued that in the 1935 election Baldwin, who by his own subsequent admission privately recognized the need to rearm, had been right to tailor his statements and policies to those of a largely pacifist electorate. Jack's unabashedly cynical view of politics and politicians gave no quarter to those who put Baldwin "on the pan for having tied up national defense with party politics." "To blame one man, such as Baldwin, for the unpreparedness of British Armaments is illogical and unfair, given the conditions of Democratic government," he wrote. Jack recycled Baldwin's self-justifying argument that the reelection of the Conservatives had been a matter not of personal ambition but of concern for the country, which would have been much worse off had the pacifist-leaning Socialists come to power. In Jack's telling, it was not the leaders but the mass of voters opposed to rearmament who bore responsibility for Britain's lack of preparedness. The unfortunate politicians were merely trying to stay in office.

On the matter of Churchill, Jack proved characteristically ambivalent. He praised the accuracy of Churchill's early warnings about Hitler and closely followed the historical trajectory laid out in Churchill's *Arms and the Covenant*, yet he differed sharply with Churchill's opinion of Baldwin and persisted in defending the deal struck at Munich and the opportunity it afforded to gear up for war. In a gesture typical of a young man torn between irreconcilable sets of values, Jack used *Arms and the Covenant*, along with Wheeler-Bennett's books on disarmament, to make a case for the Munich agreement, which both authors sharply opposed. Jack had in effect enlisted his father's adversaries to testify on his behalf.

Writing with Chamberlain still in office, Jack made the introduction of conscription the end of the particular story he had set out to tell. "The nation was now united on a path to rearmament," he wrote. "As far as singleness of purpose went democratic England could now match its attitude with totalitarian Germany. And the results were immediately apparent." In the *Crimson* editorial Jack had followed his father in suggesting that Britain was likely to be defeated and would do well to come to terms with the enemy. In the thesis he painted a different picture of British prospects, arguing that in the aftermath of Munich Chamberlain had prepared his nation well. By the time war was declared, Jack wrote, "The public was confident of its armaments. It was ready for what might come."

Jack finished writing on March 15, 1940, and went to Florida. While Jack had been laboring on his thesis, young Joe was in his first term at Harvard Law School. Though one of his Spanish letters had finally appeared in the *Atlantic Monthly*, Joe, to his own dismay, had not managed to write the book his father had bid him produce. Presented with a copy of "Appeasement at Munich," Joe told his father that Jack's thesis "seemed to represent a lot of work, but did not prove anything." The ambassador's friend Arthur Krock, of the *New York Times*, took a different view, declaring that it ought to be published and offering to show it to his agent. He even suggested a new, more commercial title, "Why England Slept"—a play on *While England Slept*, the American title of Churchill's *Arms and the Covenant*. On April 4, Krock wrote to London to convey his enthusiasm for Jack's thesis and to ask the ambassador's permission to seek a publisher.

Jack returned to Harvard confident that, should his father give the go-ahead, he could start to revise the manuscript in May, as soon as he finished his exams. He accepted the need for help in cleaning up the prose, but he did not expect to make changes in the substance of his argument. Certainly, Chamberlain's public remarks on the day Krock wrote to the ambassador suggested that matters were quite as Jack had depicted them. Chamberlain announced that Hitler's failure to attack during the past seven months meant he had "missed the bus." Britain, the prime minister stated, was now militarily prepared to "face the future with a calm and steady mind whatever it brings."

In the month that followed, what Churchill called "a cataract of violent surprises" utterly altered the international situation. Even before his father had had a chance to read the text, Germany invaded Denmark and Norway. Britain had failed in an effort to assist the Norwegians, and the debacle meant a huge loss of support for Chamberlain. Great events had proven his leadership inadequate. On May 10, the day Jack finished his exams and turned back to his thesis, Chamberlain fell and Churchill, whose prophecies, in Duff Cooper's words, had come "disastrously true," became prime minister. A defense of Chamberlain written before the end of the Twilight War was no longer publishable. The story had changed direction, and *Why England Slept* would have to catch up with it.

That was not all Jack found he suddenly had to accomplish. When his father commented at last, the changes he called for went to the very grain of Jack's argument. Jack's cynicism owed a nod to his father, who liked to disparage the high-flown motives of others. Yet, whether out of a concern for appearances or because he actually believed it, Joe faulted Jack's uncritical acceptance of the willingness of politicians to do whatever it takes to get elected. Whatever the reason, he was acting to shield Jack from criticism, as Jack in the *Crimson* editorial and the thesis had attempted to defend him. The ambassador reported that he had shown the thesis to a number of people, who thought that Jack had put too much blame on the electorate for Britain's inadequate defenses at the time of Munich and not enough on the nation's leaders. He wrote, "The basis of this criticism is that the National Government was in absolute control from 1931 to 1935, and that it was returned to office in November 1935, with another huge majority. This mandate, it is contended, should have been used to make the country strong. If the country supported such a policy, well and good; if not, then the National leaders should have thrown caution out of the window and attempted to arouse their countrymen to the dangers with which Britain obviously was confronted." The ambassador noted that one reader had been "especially critical" of Jack's treatment of Baldwin. "He contends that if, as you imply, Baldwin did not believe in the policy he was pursuing, it was his sacred duty not only to plump for the policy he did believe in but to go to the country on that issue and not on another. To say that Baldwin went to the country on one issue in order to gain strength to support another does put him in the role of deceiving the public and playing politics with the country's welfare." He continued:

> I believe that the basis of your case—that the blame must be placed on the people as a whole—is sound. Nevertheless, I think that you had better go over the material to make sure that, in pinning it on the electorate, you don't give the appearance of trying to do a complete whitewash of the leaders. I know that in a Democracy a politician is supposed to keep his ear to the ground; he is also supposed to look after the national welfare, and to attempt to educate the people when, in his opinion, they are off base. It may not be good politics but it is something that is vastly more important—good patriotism. I do not see how we can take any other line if we hope to make Democracy work. . . .

When he embarked on the rewrite, Jack took his father's guidance to heart. Anyone reading the manuscript of *Why England Slept* would never have guessed that its author could be the same person who, only weeks before, had written in "Appeasement at Munich," "A politician will always endeavor to present things in the form most pleasing to his audience." Jack abruptly cast aside the cynicism of the earlier version and criticized Baldwin for his "failure to awaken Britain" to dangers of whose existence he had been aware. He who had emphatically excused Baldwin now wrote, "He admits he was 'very worried' about what was happening in Europe. If this was true, it was unquestionably his duty to go to the country on that issue and not on any other. For if Baldwin went to the country on one issue in order 'to gain a mandate' to support another, it puts him in the role of deceiving the public and playing politics with the country's welfare."

Not only did Jack echo the phrasing in his father's letter (which seems itself to have been drafted by an underling); more importantly, he suddenly embraced a position the very opposite of the one that had been his own. Ambassador Kennedy had warned Jack of the negative response his cynicism might provoke, and Jack tailored his views, or at least his presentation of those views, accordingly. As his own subsequent statements to his father indicate, he never really changed his mind. In *Why England Slept* Jack, like the politicians in his thesis, chose to display himself "in the form most pleasing to his audience." It was a measure of Jack's success in suppressing the cynicism his father had objected to that when William Douglas Home, one of Jack's British friends, read the book version in 1945, he queried the author, "The moral —if anything written by a Kennedy can be said to have a moral— would seem to be 'speak the truth.' Am I right?"

In addition to toughening his stance on Baldwin, Jack also had to take into account the tremendous political changes of the past weeks. Conscription could no longer be the end of the story. In the rewrite, he carried on to the replacement of Chamberlain by Churchill, whom the British, he wrote, saw as "the only man who can carry through a successful war policy." Jack concluded, "With this new spirit alive in England my story ends. England was now awake; it had taken a great shock to bring home a realization of the enormity of the task it was facing."

What of his previous argument that with conscription the nation had finally been "united on a path of rearmament"? Recent events compelled Jack to admit that Chamberlain's efforts even after Munich had been flawed. The thesis had offered no hint of the prime minister's ambivalence about the need to rearm. The book told a different story. Chamberlain, Jack observed,

> had so much hope and confidence in his appeasement policy that he could not conceive of a war as being inevitable. The result was that his energies were split. Although, in one sense, his two aims were harmonious, in another sense, they pulled in opposite directions. A boxer cannot work himself into proper psychological and physical condition for a fight that he seriously believes will never come off. It was the same way with England. She so hated the thought of war that she could not believe it was going to happen, and the appeasement policy gave her confidence that this hope had some basis.

In the thesis, Jack had portrayed Chamberlain as having successfully prepared his nation for war. In the book he painted him as vulnerable to criticism for his "failure to bring to the country the realization of the great dangers with which it was faced." That awakening, the book asserted, coincided with Churchill's ascension to power. Still, Jack's need to justify his father's support of Chamberlain required him to recapitulate the defense of Munich much as it had appeared in the thesis, though such a defense jarred with his new conclusion.

Jack took one further step to ensure his manuscript would be publishable. He framed the story of Britain's failure to rearm as a lesson for present-day America and expressed the wish that his country would seize the opportunity to become strong. He wrote, "We must always keep our armaments equal to our commitments. Munich should teach us that; we must realize that any bluff will be called. We cannot tell anyone to keep out of our hemisphere unless our armaments and the people behind these armaments are prepared to back up the command, even to the ultimate point of going to war. There must be no doubt in anyone's mind, the decision must be automatic: if we debate, if we hesitate, if we question, it will be too late."

As Jack worked on, the situation in Europe continued to darken. Kick begged their father for news of Billy, who had been in France waiting for the Germans to move. He had last written from the

Maginot Line, but on May 11, 1940, his regiment had crossed into Belgium, which was then under siege by Hitler. Three days later, German armor had pierced the supposedly impregnable French defensive line at Sedan. The unprecedented velocity and might of the attack swiftly demoralized the French army. The original plan had been for the British Expeditionary Force to fight its way south to the Somme, alongside the French. On May 25, Lord Gort, BEF commander in chief, calculated that with French forces in disarray and King Leopold of Belgium about to surrender, withdrawal to the coast and evacuation by sea offered the best, perhaps the only chance of survival. The strategy was to save as many men as possible so they could fight again, rather than being killed or captured in a battle almost certain to be lost. Churchill—mindful that "wars are not won by retreats, however successful"—vowed that once the soldiers were safely out, Britain would "reconstitute and build up" the expeditionary force. The entirety of its artillery and equipment would no doubt be sacrificed in the evacuation and probably could not be replaced for many months. "But what was that," Churchill later asked, "compared with saving the Army, the nucleus and structure upon which alone Britain could build her armies of the future?" British troops fought their way to the coast, where a motley flotilla, from battleships to small yachts and fishing craft, waited at Dunkirk amid a hailstorm of German bombs. The Mosquito Armada, as it was called, managed to rescue some 335,000 soldiers.

There was jubilation in Britain as great numbers of young men returned and contacted their families, and a crushing defeat took on the guise of a significant victory. Yet to the Devonshires' mounting alarm, as the days passed there was no sign or word of Billy. Finally, the duke learned that his son had been temporarily left behind in Flanders because he could speak French. Repeatedly in the course of two weeks the duke wrote to Billy, and each time his letter was returned. The duke, as was his nature, went ahead with plans to spend the weekend of June 8–9 at Cliveden, where he struggled not to show "by word or deed or slightest sign that anything was wrong"—though Nancy Astor and others knew that Billy had been missing for a fortnight. In spite of the duke's efforts, the "drawn miserable" look on his fine-featured, mustachioed face was unmistakable and the weekend was a sad one for the hostess and her guests. Afterward, hoping there might yet be news, the duke headed north to Churchdale Hall at Ashford-in-the-Water near Chatsworth, where the Devonshires had taken up residence for the duration of the war. Another week passed and still nobody knew where Billy was. The burden was not made lighter by the fact that twenty-year-old Andrew had just been called up and was at home for a final visit before he too left to join the Coldstream Guards.

On June 18, Jean Ogilvy was in the mews cottage behind her parents' house in London when suddenly the door opened and there was Billy. When he was finally ordered to evacuate, he had commandeered a small car and been able to get out of France from St. Nazaire. Despite the fact that he had only just arrived in London, he had managed to put on freshly pressed battle dress, and he seemed at a glance unchanged. But when he sank into a chair and began to talk, Jean realized she had never seen him like this. Billy tended to keep his emotions in check, yet as he told the story of Dunkirk it was evident that he was "very put out." His upset was what made the entire discussion so striking. He emphasized that he had not wanted to leave, that he had expected to stay and fight. "We ran away!" Billy said in shame and disbelief. "We ran and we ran!" The calculations of Churchill and Gort meant nothing to him. Nor did the feeling among many people that the rescue of such a large number of soldiers had bordered on the miraculous. Over and over, he described his flight in the car and his inability to expunge the thought that retreat was dishonorable. Whatever his orders, Billy persisted in the belief that it had been his duty to stay behind and fight to the death. Even when he came to understand the strategic reasons for Dunkirk, he did not feel any better about what he had done. His only comfort was the hope that he might go back one day to finish the fight.

On the day Billy appeared at Jean's door, Churchill went to the Commons to announce the collapse of France and the likelihood that the bombing of Britain was about to begin. He who had long called for greater vigilance now took a stand against those who wished for an inquest in the House of Commons on the conduct of prior governments. In words that would long resonate with Jack Kennedy, Churchill declared, "Of this I am quite sure, that if we open a quarrel between the past and the present, we shall find that we have lost the future."

In June 1940, Harper's, the publishing house where Jack's agent had placed *Why England Slept*, canceled the contract on the grounds that the book was outdated. When Jack learned of the cancellation, two days before he was to graduate from Harvard, he remained cool. After the ceremony he went to New York, where Harcourt turned down the manuscript before Wilfred Funk, Inc. accepted it for publication. In July, six months after Jack first sat down to write his thesis, *Why England Slept* was published in New York. It appeared on national best-seller lists and hit the number one spot in Boston. Curiously, in the chatter generated by the book, aspects of Jack's argument were attributed to utterly opposing forces in his life—his father and his "tutor." There were claims that Jack had done little more than write up certain of Ambassador Kennedy's views, and rumors that John Wheeler-Bennett, thanked on the acknowledgments page "for his very helpful suggestions" and represented in the bibliography by more works than any other authority, had ghost-written the manuscript. But the reviews, including one by Wheeler-Bennett who, as it happened, had read only the book and not the thesis, were favorable. The packet of press clips Jack sent to his father demonstrated that he was now a young man whose opinion was sought after.

The book instantly and dramatically altered Jack's standing in the family. Quite simply, his triumph was supposed to have been young Joe's. But Joe's notes on travel and politics remained a morass. His short pieces, with one exception, had gone unpublished. His proposals had been politely turned down. Not even Ambassador Kennedy's connections had been enough to place Joe's articles in newspapers or magazines. The "prestige" and "international publicity" he was supposed to win with his writings had consistently eluded his grasp. When his literary dreams failed, Joe had pinned his hopes for attention on his role as a delegate to the Democratic convention in Chicago in the summer of 1940. But that was before he had any reason to expect the acclaim Jack would get for his book—which, to make matters worse, he had produced in a matter of months. As if he could not bear to witness Jack's success, Joe went to California instead of coming home after the convention.

Jack, meanwhile, weighed invitations to write articles for *Reader's Digest* and other publications, as well as suggestions from Wheeler-Bennett and others that he embark on another book project immediately. At the time he graduated, he had intended to go on to Yale Law School, but his doctors subsequently ruled against it. "Health is OK," Jack insisted to his father, "but they seem to feel I should take the year off." Instead of Yale, he planned to go out to California to "take it very easy" and audit business courses at Stanford University. He gladly agreed to a proposal from a British publisher to bring out his book in London, the proceeds from which he later donated to Nancy Astor's project to rebuild the bombed city of Plymouth, where her husband was Lord Mayor and which she herself represented in Parliament.

In the end, he decided against further writing assignments—at least for now. His father approved. "I couldn't be more pleased that you got away with such a marvelous start with the book," the ambassador wrote from London, "and I think you are very wise in not attempting to write other articles until this book has had a long run, because, since the critics think this is all right, there is no sense in opening yourself up to attack on some other article you might write which might not go over so well."

The ambassador's vision of attacks and pitfalls where none seemed yet to have suggested themselves reflected his own beleaguered circumstances in Britain, where feeling against him had increased drastically in the months since Harold Nicolson's essay in the *Spectator*. There had been a time when the policy of appeasement still seemed viable to many, and when America's man in London was a government insider, a friend and important supporter of the prime minister. After the declaration of war Kennedy had become a questionable figure, even with Chamberlain still in office; but once Churchill took power, the ambassador's status verged on that of a pariah. From the first, it was evident that Churchill and Kennedy had conflicting goals, one to bring the Americans into the war and the other to keep them out.

Kennedy's earlier predictions of defeat had been offensive enough. Once the German air assault began, there was tremendous ill feeling about his decision to spend nights in a rented house at Windsor. At all hours, German bombs pounded London. Buildings were reduced to ruins, streets engulfed in smoke and flame. Hitler vowed to "rub out" Britain's cities. Yet most citizens strove to face the air attacks with what Wheeler-Bennett characterized as "quiet defiance." Nancy Astor declared that she wished Hitler could see the British response to the bombardment, for he could then harbor no illusion as to which side was winning "this war of nerves." In such an atmosphere, Kennedy's nightly search for safety outside the city struck a good many observers as not only undignified, but cowardly. He earned the epithet "Jittery Joe". At the Foreign Office he was reported to have become "thoroughly frightened," "lost his nerve" and "gone to pieces" as a result of the bombs. People called him "the most frightened man in the realm," and he was the butt of many private jokes.

Mocked by the British, Kennedy seemed at times to be treated little better by his own government. He made no secret of his anguish that he was not being listened to in Washington. He regarded it as an insult when Roosevelt dealt directly with the British ambassador, Lord Lothian, bypassing Kennedy altogether. "Rarely, as a matter of fact, am I ever advised when important conversations are held in Washington with the British Ambassador," Kennedy whined to the president. "While vice versa Lothian is informed by his government in all talks or events of which there is a mutual importance. . . . Frankly and honestly I do not enjoy being a dummy."

To the horror and fascination of his British hosts, Kennedy did not hesitate to make known even to them his grievances against Washington. "The United States Ambassador called to see me today to tell me that he had decided to return home to the United States the week after next and to give up his post as Ambassador here," Halifax reported to Lothian on October 10. "Mr. Kennedy seemed very much out of temper with the United States Government and with the President, his principal complaint being that they had not kept him adequately informed of their policy and doings during the last two or three months. Indeed he said if it had not been for what he learnt in London, he would have known nothing of what was going on. . . . He is plainly a very disappointed and rather embittered man." Kennedy blustered that he had already sent an article to the United States to be published on November 1, in the event he was unable to get home in time for the election, which was "an indictment of President Roosevelt's administration." Kennedy was confident that his article would be "of considerable importance appearing five days before the Presidential election."

Whether because of the bombardment of London, the contempt in which he was held by the British, a sense of his own impotence in office, or a combination of factors, Kennedy was longing to get out of London. Yet, as Rose Kennedy reported to her husband, Roosevelt did not want him to come home before the election "due to your explosive—defeatist point of view" which might unfavorably influence the electorate. Following one of the worst nights of the Blitz, Kennedy sent a cablegram demanding Roosevelt's permission to leave. He also telephoned Under-Secretary of State Sumner Welles to announce his plan to return whether the president agreed or not. He said that he had sent a "full account" of his side of things to the United States, with instructions to release it to the press should he fail to appear in New York "by a certain date." Several hours after Kennedy's threat, the US State Department sent word of Roosevelt's wish that he "come back for consultation during the week commencing October 21." The explanation in London for the ambassador's departure was that his "interests in Wall Street have been attracting him back to that sphere." With Wall Street supporting the president's opponent, Wendell Willkie, it was assumed that Kennedy had "decided to go along," even to carry out his threat to publish an article "to damage Mr. Roosevelt's cause."

A good many observers on both sides of the Atlantic were astonished when, two days after he visited the White House, Kennedy endorsed the very candidate he had been threatening to attack. Later, Roosevelt would be rumored by turns to have warned Kennedy that his betrayal would damage his sons' futures, and to have vowed to support him for president in 1944 if only he would stay on board now. Or perhaps Roosevelt had managed to salve Kennedy's battered ego by assuring him of how much his endorsement mattered. Whatever the reason, Kennedy delivered a long, highly effective radio address on October 29 at 9 p.m., in which he calmly and convincingly urged voters to reelect Roosevelt.

Speaking on 114 stations nationwide, Kennedy reiterated his conviction that America ought to stay out of the war. Listeners who had read *Why England Slept* might have heard an echo of its arguments in sections of the speech. Never had the influence of the father been more legible than when he was citing the son. Kennedy decried Britain's early failure to rearm. He insisted that Chamberlain had negotiated the Munich agreement in order to give his nation time to prepare for war. He pointed out that Britain would not have been able to defend itself in 1938. He characterized the war in Europe as an opportunity for

America to make itself strong. He explained that a democracy is difficult to rally before its people become desperate and frightened.

He made a point of publicly tipping his hat to Jack. "A study of
this was made by my son while he was in England," Kennedy went on.
"His conclusions published in a volume entitled *Why England Slept*
reveal that all the elements of Great Britain were shortsighted in their
failure to appreciate the peril and prepare accordingly. . . . If we now
lack the crusading effort for rearmament, and I hope we do not, it is
certainly not to be laid at the door of the White House. The President
has provided a program and the nation's best specialists, and a
Democratic Congress has provided ample funds." If the country
rearmed fast enough, Kennedy argued, it would be possible to stay out
of the war. He concluded:

> As a servant of the American people I feel that they are entitled to
> my honest conclusions. In my years of service for the Government,
> both at home and abroad, I have sought to have honest judgment
> as my goal. From the other side I sent reports to the President and
> the Secretary of State, which were my best judgment about the
> forces that were moving, the developments that were likely and the
> course best suited to protect America. After all, I have a great stake
> in this country. My wife and I have given nine hostages to fortune.
> Our children and your children are more important than anything
> else in the world. The kind of America that they and their children
> will inherit is of grave concern to us all. In the light of these consid-
> erations, I believe that Franklin D. Roosevelt should be re-elected
> President of the United States.

It should have been a matchless day for Jack. For once, when the
ambassador spoke simply of "my son," he had not meant young Joe.
"Proud to have sponsored you," Jack telegrammed from California.
"Thanks for the plug." Yet by the time he had heard his father's public
words of approbation, he had also discovered that he was to be among
the first called up for the draft. That afternoon, his national lottery
number had been the eighteenth fished out of a bowl. The problem was
not that he wished to avoid serving; it was that he knew he could not
pass a physical. Now that he had finally changed his standing in the

family, the last thing he wanted was to revert to the status of the sickly son, his brother's eternal inferior. "They will never take me into the army—and yet if I don't, it will look quite bad," Jack wrote to Lem of the negative publicity that would accrue should people think influence had been exerted to keep the ambassador's son out of the military. On the very day Jack had been such a credit to his father he had been given reason to fear he was about to become a source of shame.

Jack's predicament gave Joe Junior his opening. Joe had not gotten the attention he had hoped for as a delegate to the Democratic convention in Chicago; he had not written a bestselling book or been inundated with offers to write for major magazines. He was not the son spoken of by their father on national radio. But, nothing if not robust, he was as likely to be accepted into the military as his brother was to be rejected. Accordingly, Joe announced his inclination to quit law school and join the Navy Air Corps. "I think in that Jack is not doing anything, and with your stand on the war, that people will wonder what the devil I am doing back at school with everyone else working for the national defense," Joe wrote from Harvard. ". . . As far as the family is concerned, it seems that Jack is perfectly capable to do everything, if by chance anything happened to me." Joe, as always, had his eye on the future, pointing out that the Navy Air Corps "will do me more good when I get out" than would a stint in the reserves. "The main reason for my wanting to go in," he wrote, "is that there is a chance for some individuality. There are thousands upon thousands of naval reservists, and you are just one of a flock, whereas here if you've got anything, I think there are numerous possibilities, and not only in the flying end." In short, Joe longed to stand out—as Jack had managed to do by publishing his book.

Shortly before the election, Roosevelt appeared beside Kennedy at a rally in Boston. In recognition that many voters—though they viewed Hitler as an abomination and hoped the British would win—did not want American lives sacrificed in another European war, Roosevelt announced, "I have said this before, but I shall say it again and again and again: Your boys are not going to be sent into any foreign wars!" Roosevelt thereby presented himself in the form most pleasing to his audience, and Willkie was quick to accuse him of hypocrisy. Nonetheless, the isolationist tone of the president's speech, coupled with

Kennedy's endorsement which gave credence to his pledge, would later be seen as the key to victory. Kennedy was characterized in the press as "the man who perhaps more than any other single individual helped to re-elect" Roosevelt, and he looked forward to his reward. He met with the president and asked to resign the ambassadorship, which Roosevelt accepted with the request that he postpone his resignation until a successor could be designated. Kennedy left the White House in the belief that the president planned to find "something for me to do in Washington."

He went on to Boston, where in the course of a ninety-minute interview with Louis Lyons of the *Globe* he did immeasurable harm to himself, a spectacle the journalist was happy to depict. In the apparent belief that the conversation was off the record, Kennedy fulminated about world events. The interview was as rabid as the radio address had been measured and persuasive. "I know more about the European situation than anybody else," Kennedy said, setting the tone, "and it's up to me to see that the country gets it." He enraged a good many readers with the assertion that "Democracy is finished in England. It may be here."

"People call me a pessimist," he continued. "I say, 'What is there to be gay about? Democracy is all gone.'" Asked whether he meant in Britain or in the United States as well, he replied, "Well, I don't know. If we get into war it will be in this country too. A bureaucracy would take over right off. Everything we hold dear would be gone." Britain, he said, was fighting not for democracy but for self-preservation. He vowed that America would enter the war over his dead body and promised to spend all he had to keep his country out. He predicted that the inclusion of Labour politicians in a British government of national unity would lead to National Socialism after the war. Even if Hitler triumphed, he said, the United States would continue to trade with Europe.

After the interview was published, Kennedy tried to defuse the controversy by insisting that he had made it clear to Lyons that he was not speaking for publication. His position as ambassador prohibited direct interviews, but he was always happy to provide newsmen with background. Lyons had violated his trust in using the material as he did. He claimed Lyons had misquoted him and that the published interview created "a different impression entirely from the one I would wish to set forth." The explanation failed to satisfy Kennedy's critics, in part because he was known to have expressed similar views in the past. The difference this time was that they had been made public in one concentrated, obnoxious blast.

"A year ago [Kennedy] was generally credited with believing that it was better to try to placate Hitler than to risk fighting him," noted an editorial in the *New York Tribune*. "Today he is reported to have said that democracy is finished in England and may be here. Such an attitude calls for far more explicit explanation, or denial, than Mr. Kennedy has thus far chosen to afford." The editorial stressed that Kennedy had spoken not as a politician but as an ambassador and the man who had perhaps done more than any other to help reelect Roosevelt.

> In Germany his words will therefore be interpreted as meaning
> that the Roosevelt administration may be counted upon not to go
> the limit in helping Great Britain. . . . This is just what the
> Germans have wanted to hear—and to believe. . . . If such senti-
> ments go abroad, with the weight of Mr. Kennedy's official posi-
> tion behind them, and only his present explanation to mitigate
> their tenor, the results cannot but be painful for the cause of
> Britain, which, in this instance, is our own. We believe that the
> American people are entitled to know exactly what Mr. Kennedy's
> real opinions are and the extent to which he represents the policy
> of the Administration whose accredited envoy he still remains.

The next day, Kennedy addressed a luncheon in Los Angeles hosted by Harry Warner, president of Warner Bros., and astonished those present by repeating more or less what he had said in the *Boston Globe* interview. To those remarks he added fresh tidbits for his "almost entirely Jewish audience." He expounded on the rise of anti-Semitism in Britain: anti-Jewish riots in the East End of London, a tendency to blame the war on the Jews, anti-Semitic attitudes in government circles. The actor Douglas Fairbanks Jr. complained to Roosevelt that Kennedy "apparently threw the fear of God into many of our producers and executives by telling them that the Jews were on the spot, and that they should stop making anti-Nazi pictures or using the film medium to promote or show sympathy to the cause of the 'democracies' versus the 'dictators'. . . . He continued to underline the fact that the film business was using its power to influence the public dangerously and that we all, and the Jews in particular, would be in jeopardy if they continued to abuse that power."

One of the Hollywood producers who had attended the luncheon sneered that Kennedy, soon to be out of a job, was simply trying "to scare some of the Jews to get out of the business" in case he himself decided to return. Others took the speech more seriously. According to Fairbanks, "There is no doubt whatsoever that his talk made a very definite impression, and there were many who were susceptible to Joe's undoubted powers of persuasion." The British consulate in Los Angeles noted that Kennedy's speech "caused what was tantamount to a panic" among those who heard it. The speech had been off the record, emphatically so. Yet, given the controversy then surrounding him, he can hardly have believed that his remarks would not turn up in the press. Fairbanks, for his part, suspected that Kennedy knew such statements were capable of attracting "more publicity" than any on the record. He urged Roosevelt to accept Kennedy's resignation immediately and publicly, which would signal that the White House disowned his views. Despite Fairbanks's suspicion that Kennedy had known full well what he was doing when he let fly at the luncheon, in the aftermath the ambassador again claimed that his position had been distorted by the press.

Briefly, Kennedy wavered in his determination to relinquish his post. He confessed to William Randolph Hearst that he was still wondering if he ought to go back to London on the chance that there might yet be a peace settlement with Hitler whose terms he could influence. He claimed to feel sure that "the British people would respond very happily to my return"—an odd sentiment in view of the outrage his recent remarks about democracy being finished in Britain had provoked there. In the end, Kennedy made up his mind to quit. This time Roosevelt gave the go-ahead to make the resignation public. "My plan," Kennedy announced, "is after a short holiday to devote my efforts to what seems to me the greatest cause in the world today, and means, if successful, the preservation of the American form of democracy. That cause is to help the President keep the United States out of war." The syndicated columnists Joseph Alsop and Robert Kintner, by no means the only American newsmen to lambast the departing ambassador, glossed this as Kennedy's intention "to peddle appeasement all across the United States."

Jack had been with his father in California and witnessed his frustration in the face of escalating criticism. Now, he drew up "a rough outline" of points his father might use in an article or articles to "clear the record." Some of it took the form of advice on how to answer his critics, some of actual sentences and paragraphs to be published under the ambassador's own by-line. In only months, Jack had gone from lifting sentences from his father's letter to setting himself up as his ghostwriter.

In a letter to his father on December 6, 1940, Jack recommended that he do everything possible to avoid being labeled an appeaser: "It seems to me that if this label is tied to you it may nullify your immediate effectiveness, even though in the long run you may be proved correct." He counseled him to emphasize that he did not enjoy making gloomy predictions, but believed he would do his country no good if he failed to tell the truth as he saw it. He urged him to remind his audience that he had a history of truth-telling. Looping back to the very point his father had warned him to excise from his thesis, Jack wrote, "You might bring out that it is necessary for politicians to stress the bright side of things—they are in politics and must get the people's vote—you don't care what people think—you are interested only in the long-run point of view and what is best for this country." Whatever he may have written in *Why England Slept*, Jack had never really abandoned his cynical take on politicians; he just did not perceive his father as one of them.

In a highly revealing passage, Jack wrote, in his best approximation of the ambassador's voice:

> I must confess at the outset that my views are not pleasant. I am
> gloomy and I have been gloomy since September 1938. It may be
> unpleasant for America to hear my views but let me note that
> Winston Churchill was considered distinctly unpleasant to have
> around during the years from 1935 to 1939. It was felt he was a
> gloom monger. In the days of the Blitzkrieg the optimist does not
> always do his country the best service. It is only by facing reality
> that we can hope to meet it successfully.

To most eyes, Churchill and Kennedy were antithetical, but Jack saw them in terms of what they shared: a stubborn insistence on stating the truth as they saw it. Churchill and Kennedy held violently opposing views, but Jack esteemed both for what he perceived as the courage that set them apart from the politicians preoccupied, as most in Jack's opinion necessarily were, with the next election. Churchill and Kennedy, he meant for his father to suggest, insisted on telling their countrymen what they needed, but may not have wanted, to hear.

The ambassador decided finally to defend himself in a radio broadcast, rather than in print. His endorsement of Roosevelt had been most effective, and he tried to repeat the magic on his own behalf. But the second radio talk, on January 18, 1941, failed to undo the damage of his by then notorious off-the-record remarks. He would continue to maneuver, as well as to speak out, but in effect his public career had ended. He would be remembered as a self-made man who sought, by promulgating the policy of appeasement, to protect his own considerable financial interests. Jack would persist in seeing his father differently. As the comparison to Churchill suggests, Jack saw a patriot, willing to speak his mind at whatever detriment to his own prospects and popularity.

By this time, Jack had, as expected, failed his draft physical and been turned down by the military. Following a week-long seminar at the Institute of World Affairs in Riverside, California, he traveled east, where doctors advised against his returning to Stanford. If he wished to go to law school at Yale in the fall, he was to avoid all strenuous activity until then. He spent some time in the hospital for his back, before accompanying his mother and Eunice on a trip to South America. Joe Junior, meanwhile, had followed through with his intention to leave Harvard Law School and join the Navy Air Corps. When Jack returned from South America, Joe was already in the Air Cadet program, outside Boston, in anticipation of going on to train as a pilot in Jacksonville, Florida. In this, at least, Joe finally seemed to have bested his brother. Jack, refusing to be written off on account of frailty, pressed their father to use his influence on his behalf. Joe Kennedy asked his former naval attaché in London, now the director of naval intelligence in Washington, for help. On August 5, 1941, Jack passed a Navy physical, despite his troubled medical history. A lifetime of health problems was made to vanish, if only on paper, with a notation in Jack's medical file that he had suffered no more than the "usual childhood illnesses." On September 25, he received his commission as an ensign in the United States Naval Reserve and was soon assigned to the office of naval intelligence in Washington, DC. In Jack's eyes, the post was no match for his brother's status as a pilot in training, but it would have to do for now. Whatever his father might think, Jack had no intention of remaining behind a desk. From the first, his goal was to be reassigned to sea duty.

CHAPTER FIVE

Billy Hartington Wants to Know

IN LATE OCTOBER 1941, TWENTY-FOUR-YEAR-OLD ENSIGN JOHN F. Kennedy reported for his first day of active duty in the Foreign Intelligence Branch of the Division of Naval Intelligence in Washington. He filled his new apartment at Dorchester House, 2680 Sixteenth Street, with furniture from the family house in Bronxville, which had been sold. But it was not merely the familiar furnishings that made Washington seem like home. Kick had recently moved there to begin work as a secretary to the editor of the *Times–Herald* newspaper. She had been at her new job for three weeks when she received a letter announcing Jack's imminent arrival. Inga Arvad, a twenty-eight-year-old Danish woman who wrote a popular column for the paper, watched Kick read a bit of the letter, then leap up and begin "a whirling dance like some delightful dervish." Kick's blue eyes flashed excitement as she announced, "He is coming to Washington. I am going to give a party at the F Street Club. You will just love him. He's positively great." Only then did Kick explain to her puzzled friend that she was talking about her brother. As in London in 1938, Kick built up Jack in advance of his arrival.

"He came—she hadn't exaggerated," Inga remembered years later. "He had the charm that makes birds come out of their trees, he looked like her twin, the same thick mop of hair, the same blue eyes, natural, engaging, ambitious, warm and when he walked into a room you knew he was there, not pushing, not domineering but exuding animal magnetism." Also as in 1938, Jack arrived to discover that Kick had already gathered around her a circle of adoring friends. There were new friends, like Inga and *Times–Herald* writer John White, as well as people like Betty Coxe (later Spalding), Chuck Spalding and Torby Macdonald whom she and Jack had known previously. Most evenings, the brother and sister were in and out of each other's apartments. Together and with the members of their group, they dined, attended parties, went to the movies and, most of all, talked the hours away.

As always Kick was a delightful companion, yet she was in acute emotional distress. Just as the letter announcing Jack's arrival had reached her, she had had word from London that Billy Hartington had decided to marry another woman. Although Kick had long appeared to accept that because of their religious differences she and Billy could never marry, a secret hope remained alive. The message from London, conveyed in person by Nancy Astor's niece Dinah Brand, devastated her. Her upset was made worse several days later when a letter arrived from Billy himself. He continued to love her, he said, but as time passed and hope faded of seeing her again before the war was over, he had finally chosen to accept defeat. His brother Andrew had married Debo Mitford, his cousin and best friend David Ormsby Gore had married Sissie Lloyd Thomas, and now he too planned to marry. Yet even as Billy prepared to announce his engagement to Sally Norton, one of the debutantes who had come out in the 1938 Season, he asked Kick to continue to write him. Feeling as if she were "nearly going mad," Kick had first responded to Billy's letter by trying to get a visa to travel to London, as several of her friends there, including Andrew and Debo, had urged. By the time Jack appeared in Washington, Kick seemed to have accepted that she had lost Billy once and for all. At least her brother was there to console and divert her.

The Jack Kennedy who arrived in Washington that fall of 1941 was very different from the directionless second son whom Kick had excitedly welcomed to London in the late 1930s. In a measure of how much his life had altered since the publication of *Why England Slept*, in Washington he actually began to speak, however playfully, to Kick and their intimate circle of the possibility that he might someday run for president. "Everything was discussed, mainly politics," Inga remembered, "but somehow it always got back to Jack." The discussions had the air almost of a party game which Betty Coxe fondly called "Jack's Future." The tone was unvaryingly light and amusing, and Jack spoke of himself and his hopes with such curious skepticism and detachment that sometimes it was almost as if he was referring to another person.

Kick and Jack sent out copies of *Why England Slept*, personally inscribed by the author, in a campaign to secure invitations to the best parties in Washington. As the war in Europe naturally dominated the talk at Washington dinner tables, the opinions of the best-selling writer and ex-ambassador's son were of great interest. Asked, in the weeks before Pearl Harbor, to state his views on whether the United States ought to come in on the side of the British, Jack cautioned against a "die-hard position on the war." He argued that US policy must be "fluid" and "flexible" if it was to "stay abreast of the changing conditions in the world." Though he had previously been a firm isolationist on the grounds that "the effort necessary by the U.S. to defeat Germany would be so great that that in the end the U.S. would have lost what they were fighting for," he now thought that "if a quick victory could be achieved," he would favor America going in. Most of the time, however, Jack was careful to stick to subjects he had written about in his book. On these he could speak with a degree of assurance and authority that belied his age and that, along with his natural charm and wit, made him a prized dinner guest. To encounter Jack Kennedy in this period was to meet a voluble, beautifully mannered, highly knowledgeable young man with a distinctly British frame of reference. Munich, naturally, was a topic on which he liked to hold forth, as was Stanley Baldwin's decision to pursue a weak policy of rearmament in the interest of staying in office.

Kick, who had believed in Jack from the first, reveled in his reputation in Washington as a rising man. At the end of a social evening she would put on her bathrobe and sit up late with her brother discussing the various people they had met. Inga Arvad was not the only one to say that Jack and Kick resembled twins; John White also saw them that way. Their speech with one another was elliptical and telegraphic; they darted from point to point and rarely finished a sentence. With Kick's blessing, during this period Jack began a love affair with the beautiful, married Inga, whose husband was then out of the country. Inga was a "wonderful talker," and part of their bond was the intensely sympathetic interest she took in his political ambitions, as well as her acute understanding of both his virtues and his limitations. When Inga was not talking to Jack about Jack, she pursued her new favorite subject with Kick. After he had been in town for a month, Inga devoted an installment of her newspaper column to him. Three years before, the young Jack Kennedy had seemed utterly to lack ambition, but now Inga aptly dubbed him "a boy with a future." She informed readers that at twenty-four he was already the author of a "much-praised book" and that "elder men like to hear his views which are sound and astonishingly objective for so young a man."

A little over a week after the column ran, the Japanese bombed Pearl Harbor. The following day, President Roosevelt asked Congress to declare war on Japan; and on December 11, 1941, Germany, Japan's ally, declared war on the United States. Jack, along with his colleagues at the Division of Naval Intelligence, was put on a wartime schedule. Nights and weekends were no longer his own, and the time previously spent at dinner parties now had to be devoted to work. But, as chance would have it, he was not to remain in Washington much longer. A photograph had turned up in the *Times–Herald* morgue showing Inga Arvad in Hitler's private box at the 1936 Olympics, and rumors began to circulate at the newspaper that she might be a German spy. On December 12, Kick told Inga about the speculation. Enraged to hear herself called a spy when in fact she had simply been covering the Olympics for a Danish newspaper, she went to the FBI to report the rumors and to make a firm denial. Inga hoped to clear herself; instead, she merely prompted the FBI to begin to monitor every aspect of her life. Jack soon found himself drawn into the net.

On December 14, the FBI reported that a hatless man, who had tousled hair and wore a gray overcoat with raglan sleeves and gray tweed trousers, regularly arrived to spend the night at Inga Arvad's apartment at 1600 Sixteenth Street. At this stage of the investigation, Inga's mystery man was "known only as Jack." By January 1942, the FBI knew exactly who he was and where he worked, having listened in on her phone calls and bugged her apartment. If Inga was a spy, it would hardly do for her to be having an affair with someone who worked in naval intelligence, and both Jack's father and his bosses were soon angling to get him transferred out of Washington. On January 12, the syndicated columnist Walter Winchell printed a blind item about Jack's affair with Inga. The next day, Jack had word that he was being transferred to a desk job in the Navy Yard in Charleston, South Carolina. Unhappy as he was to be ordered out of Washington, Jack had no intention of ending his relationship with Inga. He had previously encountered a good number of people who had met Hitler, as it had once been quite common for British aristocrats to make pilgrimages to meet the Führer. He scoffed at the notion that the photograph meant that Inga was currently or had ever been in the Nazis' employ.

"They certainly transfer without much notice," Kick grumbled to her mother at the news that Jack would be leaving Washington. But she had good news as well, for her brother's transfer coincided with a jubilant message from Nancy Astor that Billy's engagement was off. While he was engaged, his sadness at having lost Kick had been evident to the members of his family. "My mother was concerned," remembered Billy's sister Anne. "She was very, very close to Billy and knew his passion for Kick." As he had done when he still had hopes of being with Kick, whenever he was on leave and visited his family at Churchdale Hall he would closet himself with Georgiana's letters, which he read and reread as jazz records blasted in the background. It quickly became apparent to all that he could not get Kick out of his thoughts. His friends were glad for him when he broke off the engagement, but no one was happier than Kick. "I long to come over," she wrote at once to Lady Astor, "but it looks quite impossible." Kick had a standing invitation to stay at Cliveden; the hard part was to arrange a way to get there. Assisted by Betty Coxe, she would spend the next several months trying to bring it off. In the meantime, she and Betty, who had enrolled in a foreign-service course in Washington, commandeered Jack's former apartment. Only days after they moved in, Lem Billings reported to Jack in Charleston that his sister had adorned the living-room table with photographs of what Lem described as "countless dukes and lords of the United Kingdom"—that is, the young men who had danced attendance on her in Britain. The display, Lem noted with amusement, included no picture of John White, whom she had been dating in Washington. A flurry of letters arrived from William Douglas Home, Tony Rosslyn and other British admirers, and Kick would sit cross-legged on Jack's big bed and read them aloud to Betty, with whom she evaluated the literary merits of each.

Kick signaled that Billy was back in her life when she wrote to Jack, two months after Pearl Harbor, "Billy Hartington wants to know if you still think the British are decadent. Do you?" Billy's question referred back to their disagreement in the summer of 1938, over whether Britain would defend Czechoslovakia in the event Hitler invaded. Jack had predicted that the British would base their actions on self-interest, Billy that honor would guide them. Not long afterward, Munich had seemed to prove Jack correct, but Billy rejoiced that when shame finally trumped fear, his country had again chosen to base its actions on principle. In the aftermath of the fall of France, Britain had stood alone, bravely and gracefully withstanding the German onslaught. The British had won the battle for mastery of the air over their island, and had compelled Hitler to abandon his plan to invade. They had taken pride in its being a "British war" and had shown the world they could hold their own. It seemed to Billy that they had amply disproved the charge of decadence, and now he playfully challenged Jack to disagree.

As it happened, Billy's challenge was ill-timed. Two days after Kick typed her letter to Jack on *Times–Herald* stationery, there occurred, in Churchill's characterization, "the greatest disaster to British arms which our history records." On February 15, 1942, Singapore, which was regarded as crucial to the British position in the Far East, fell. Capping a series of military misfortunes, the loss of Singapore along with some 85,000 British and Commonwealth troops taken prisoner by the Japanese left Churchill visibly depressed. To Raymond Asquith's sister Violet Bonham Carter, Churchill confided his anxiety that the British were not the soldiers their fathers had been. "In 1915," Churchill said, "our men fought on even when they had only one shell left and were under a fierce barrage. Now they cannot resist dive-bombers. We have so many men in Singapore, so many men—they should have done better." That was Churchill's private opinion, vouchsafed to a close friend. In public he attempted to allay fears with a broadcast from Chequers— the prime minister's official country residence—the night Singapore fell. Churchill called on the British to show, as they had in the past, that they could meet great reverses with dignity and strength. Having long striven to bring the United States into the war, he emphasized that, despite grave setbacks, Britain was no longer fighting alone and that they were now "in the midst of great company." Jack disliked the speech intensely. Five days after the broadcast he spoke of it to Inga Arvad in the course of a rendezvous at the Francis Marion Hotel in Charleston, where her use of the alias "Barbara Smith" did not fool the FBI, who bugged her room. The agent assigned to eavesdrop on Inga's pillow talk was treated to—in the agent's characterization—"quite a discussion with regard to the international situation, particular attention being paid to Churchill's speech of last Sunday." Jack "stated that in his opinion the British Empire was through," insisted that Churchill knew it, and blamed him "for getting this country into the war." Bitter about his father's plight, he said the error had been to stop speaking out, and claimed that Ambassador Kennedy had pulled back because he believed that to do otherwise "might hurt his sons in politics."

Jack touched on similar themes in a letter to Kick on March 10. By way of comment on the fall of Singapore, Churchill's controversial broadcast and the matter of British decline in general, he answered Billy's question in the bantering tone in which it had been posed. Alloying his remarks, as he liked to do, with a dash of irony that made it hard to know at any given point what he truly thought, Jack cast his reply in the form of brotherly advice on the proposal by Nancy Astor and other British friends that Kick rush over and marry at once. Billy had lain down his challenge in the afterglow of Britain's first years at war, but by the time Jack responded Singapore seemed—at least to him—to have changed everything. Far from being the answer Kick or Billy would have hoped for, Jack's letter drew a connection between the issue of decadence and whether his sister ought to take Billy for a husband.

> After reading the papers, I would advise strongly against any voyages to England to marry an Englishman. For I have come to the reluctant conclusion that it has come time to write the obituary of the British Empire. Like all good things, it had to come to an end sometime, it was good while it lasted. You may not agree with this, but I imagine that the day before Rome fell, not many people would have believed that it could ever fall. And yet, Rome was ready for its fall years before it finally fell, though people, looking

only at it through the rosy tinted glasses of its previous history couldn't and wouldn't see it. . . .

It's the same with England. Singapore was only a symptom, the cause goes back long before Chamberlain or Churchill. It goes back, I think, far beyond any special event. It goes back to a state of mind, really, which is a phase of its organic growth. When a nation finally reaches the point that its primary aim is to preserve the status quo, it's approaching old age. When it reaches the point where it is willing to sacrifice part of that status quo to keep the rest, it's gone beyond being old, it's dying—and that is the state of mind England reached some time ago. From a purely psychological viewpoint, the advantage that a country which is on the make, with not much to lose and plenty to win will have over a country like England is obvious. In a war like today's, tradition and a way of life and a great past history are merely excess baggage that impedes movement, and makes the way easy for the enemy. . . .

You might dispute the above, which is mostly theoretical. Well, look at it from a practical point of view . . . any time the Prime Minister of a country will admit to his own people that another country is going to save them—it's on a toboggan . . . any resemblance after this war to the English way of life or its technique of governing to what we know today will be purely coincidental. . . .

Now, those aren't very happy thoughts, are they? But it's good practice for my typewriter, and they're probably not right. I wouldn't bet that they weren't though.

Beyond the banter, there were serious matters in play. Jack had read David Cecil on the inertia that had afflicted the great Whig landowners despite their reputation as upholders of progress, and in his letter he used that understanding to cast a different light on Billy. Where Kick saw liberalism and a desire to be useful, Jack detected a fondness for the status quo, a wish to save that which the war promised to snatch away. A man could scarcely have been more devoted to tradition and a sense of the past than Billy. Jack, though long and powerfully drawn to precisely those elements in British life, disparaged them here as "excess baggage." The Britain of Billy Hartington, he suggested, must soon die.

In important ways, Billy and Jack were still arguing past one another. At the time of the farewell dinner at the American embassy residence in September 1939, Jack had failed to grasp that for Billy and many others the pressing question was not whether Britain could beat Hitler, but whether it was right to try. Now again, while Billy pointed with pride to the year in which the British had stood alone as evidence that they were still the people they had been of old, Jack concentrated on the fall of Singapore and Churchill's assurance that America would save Britain as sure signs that Britain was finished.

The self-deflating finale, the assertion that all he had just said might well be wrong, was quintessential Jack. The realism he prided himself on was a legacy from his father; the irony was Jack's alone. This was far from the first time that Jack, after he had expressed an opinion likely to upset or offend, had dissipated tensions with a jest and a smile. Yet his reference to the letter as "practice for my typewriter" did reflect something new. As Jack languished at a Charleston desk job, and as Kick, still angling to return to Britain, began to contribute film and theater criticism to the *Times–Herald*, he and she conspired to master the craft of writing. She sent on "the drippings from my pen" for Jack's evaluation and, casting herself in the role of "average reader," critiqued his letters to her and to others. Everything the brother and sister wrote to each other in this period was capable of assuming the air of a literary exercise.

Style often seemed to count for more than sincerity, as when Kick claimed that her own best work was a review of a play she had not seen. When Jack drafted a long, supposedly heartfelt letter to Nancy Astor ("Of course . . . isolationism is by no means dead. It was supposed to have died a rather violent death December 7, but it didn't. It's merely recuperating for the second and major round, and it is aided in its convalescence by the disastrous news from the Far East"), he sent it first to Kick. In addition to offering her own opinions, she solicited the comments of Frank Waldrop, the paper's editor, and John White. Nancy Astor, for her part, was delighted by Jack's letter and wrote in reply, "You young people will have a wonderful chance to make a better world. You, Jack, particularly."

Even Jack's intimate letters to Inga became part of his apprenticeship as a writer, when, as he clearly expected her to do, she shared them with his sister. Kick grew defensive when Inga laughed, however affectionately, at juvenile mistakes in his letters. On the phone to Inga, Jack himself ascribed mistakes to poor typing. In the siblings' private correspondence, however, Kick did not flinch from pointing out his misspellings—"neice," "resemblence," "agression," etc.—and other blunders, and he welcomed her corrections. On such matters at least, they tended to be clear-eyed and candid with one other. Though Jack had published a well-received book, his writing was not all he wished it to be. Misspelled words were the least of it; far more important were Kick's remarks on the "life" or lack thereof in his prose. That he experienced such a strong personal response to certain books and authors, that he reacted to particular passages with an almost sensuous delight and was often moved to quote them aloud, made his own limitations at the typewriter the more frustrating.

It was Inga who hit on Jack's most serious flaw if he hoped to achieve greatness: the relentlessly ironical pose that, however charming, cloaked a lack of firmly-held beliefs. In this context, Jack's admission at the end of his March 10 letter to Kick that everything he had just said might not be right was more than just an endearing bit of whimsy. It reflected his habit of distancing himself from his own arguments, which, two years previously, had made it relatively simple for him to adopt a diametrically opposite position when he revised "Appeasement at Munich" for publication. When Clare Boothe Luce, a friend of Joe Kennedy's, declared that Jack had "everything to make a success," Inga warmly agreed, but the lover's private words to Jack showed that she understood him better. Inga praised his ambition, acknowledging that it would put him on the path to the White House. But she suggested that if he wished to attain not just the office and the power, but true greatness, he would also need something more. "If you can find something you really believe in," Inga wrote, "then my dear you caught the biggest fish in the ocean. You can pull it aboard, but don't rush it, there is still time."

Jack seemed attached to nothing, but his great admiration for Raymond Asquith indicated that he hungered for convictions. In this period Jack was fond of reciting from memory some lines from John Buchan's portrait of Asquith in the memoir *Pilgrim's Way*, which echoed Churchill's tribute in *Great Contemporaries*: "Our roll of honor is long, but it holds no nobler figure. He will stand to those of us who are left as an incarnation of the spirit of the land he loved. . . . He loved his youth and his youth has become eternal. Debonair and brilliant and brave, he is now part of that immortal England which knows not age or weariness or defeat." From early on Betty Coxe and Chuck Spalding, like David Ormsby Gore before them, perceived that Jack sought to model himself on Asquith. Drawn to Asquith's air of cool detachment, his disdain for anything that smacked of false sentiment or the appearance of trying too hard, his unruffled courage and gallant behavior under fire, and above all his willingness to sacrifice everything for the principles in which he so staunchly believed, Jack set out to emulate those traits of character in his own conduct. But first, Inga proposed, he was going to have to discover what, if anything, he believed in. And that might take him some time to accomplish.

Meanwhile, Jack learned that on account of his relationship with Inga, the FBI now had him under surveillance as well—hardly an ideal situation for a young man who aspired to political office. In flagrant violation of rules which forbade him to travel more than fifty miles from Charleston, Jack went to Washington to break off the affair. But no sooner had he spent the evening telling Kick that he planned to see Inga no more than he was back on the phone from Charleston begging his lover to see him again. Though the relationship had helped make up Inga's mind to divorce her husband, she concluded that she had no future with Jack, and that given his indecisiveness she would have to be the one to put an end to their liaison. At a time when Jack, bored with his desk job, had been hoping desperately to be reassigned to sea duty, his grave back problems recurred. For two and a half months, he was in and out of various hospitals, and doctors told him that there might be no alternative to surgery. Inga used his hospitalization and her own six-week residency in Reno, Nevada, to force a kind of finality to the affair. On her return from Reno, she shocked and disappointed Jack with the news that she intended to leave Washington and marry an old friend who lived in New York. On July 22, 1942, Jack received orders to report to Chicago to begin a sixty-day officer training course at Northwestern University. Two days later, en route to Cape Cod, where he planned to rest before going on to Chicago, he stopped in Washington to see Inga one last time. The night she saw him, she lamented to a friend, "He looks like a limping monkey from behind. He can't walk at all. That's ridiculous sending him off to sea duty."

Despite his excruciating back pain, Jack applied to train as a PT boat commander. "The requirements are very strict physically—you have to be young, healthy, and unmarried," he reported to Lem Billings, "and as I am young and unmarried—I'm trying to get in." Promoted to Lieutenant, j.g. in October 1942, Jack wisecracked that were he to die in action it would be "good for Joe's political career." Meanwhile his back pain worsened and he considered surgery, but when he learned that it would almost certainly put him out of commission for six months he decided to risk the PT boat training course in his present state. His father did not see how he could last so much as a week. Jack surprised everyone by completing the two-month program on December 2 and was disappointed afterward by his assignment to stay on as an instructor. At length he militated for, and was finally given, sea duty in the Pacific theater.

Notwithstanding his ambivalence about the war, privately expressed to Inga Arvad, Jack was eager to see action. After a final visit with his parents in Palm Beach, he headed for California and the trip to the South Pacific. "I am finally on my way—and will be leaving in a day or so," he wrote to Lem from San Francisco. "I am rather glad to be on my way—although I understand that this South Pacific is not a place where you lie on a white beach with a cool breeze while those native girls who aren't out hunting for your daily supply of bananas are busy popping grapes into your mouth." He arrived in the Solomon Islands, an archipelago east of New Guinea, on March 28, 1943, and soon assumed command of PT 109.

Kick, too, refused to give up on her goal—to return to London and see Billy before he returned to battle. There was still time, as the launching of an amphibious attack against northern Europe had had to be put off until America, which had been caught militarily unprepared, was ready to go. Kick initially thought she could manage to get over to London as a reporter for the *Times–Herald*, but when that plan failed Betty Coxe proposed that they travel to Europe together as members of the Red Cross. Kick, who had taken over Inga's column, quit her job at the paper and entered the Red Cross training program with Betty. There was no assurance that she would be sent to London, of all possible destinations, but she calculated that when the time came her father might be able to help.

While Kick was undergoing her Red Cross training in Washington, she spoke of her hopes to Richard Wood, later Lord Holderness. Halifax's twenty-two-year-old son had served in the Western Desert with the King's Royal Rifle Corps, fighting with the 8th Army from El Alamein to Tripoli. The victory at El Alamein marked a turning point in the war. As Churchill would later declare, "It may almost be said, before Alamein we never had a victory. After Alamein we never had a defeat." After British and American troops landed in North Africa at Algiers, Oran and Casablanca, Churchill had ordered church bells rung all over Britain for the first time during the war. Yet amid the rejoicing there was also great sorrow for lives destroyed. The fighting in the Western Desert would prove particularly costly to Halifax's family. Richard's older brother Peter—one of the boys in the 1937 car crash involving David Ormsby Gore, Hugh Fraser, and Jakie Astor—had been killed at El Alamein. Later, in a desert raid, an unexploded bomb crushed Richard's legs, which had to be amputated under primitive conditions. At first, it seemed as if he too might die. Roosevelt offered to have Halifax—then Britain's ambassador to Washington—flown to Cairo, but he declined on the grounds that the other boys in the hospital with Richard could not have visits, specially arranged by the US president, from their fathers. When a friend read Richard's letter to his parents about all he had endured, she remarked, "The heroism and cheerfulness of it was fantastic. As if he had had a small scratch—full of jokes. Oh! The gallantry of these young men."

When Richard was well enough, he came to Washington to recuperate. From the moment he arrived, he made it clear that, despite the loss of his legs, he was determined to live as normal a life as possible. In addition to doing all he could to encourage other soldiers in similar circumstances, he planned to remain active and enjoy himself to the fullest. At the embassy, Richard's father permitted him to have groups of young people in to dine, and it was then that he met and was "immensely taken" with Kick. She, in turn, marveled that she had never before encountered such spirit as his. They went to parties and restaurants together. She accompanied him to his first baseball game, which they enjoyed contrasting with a cricket match. They compared politics in America and Britain, and enumerated the differences between presidents and prime ministers. She chronicled her adventures in Britain, and he told of his time in the desert. She taught him about Roman Catholicism, and he spoke to her of his Anglican faith. She revealed her feelings for Billy and the dream he had instilled in her of a political partnership, a useful life together.

As to whether that dream was likely to materialize, Jack remained skeptical. "In regard to Kick becoming a Duchess—" he wrote to Lem on May 6, 1943, "I doubt it—but it would be rather nice as I believe it would give me some title or other." The skepticism was not without foundation. After four years, there were no guarantees that when Kick and Billy finally met again they would feel about one another as they had before the war. Kick had been only nineteen when last she saw Billy, who had been twenty-one at the time of her departure. A tremendous amount had happened in both their lives since then. Billy had seen action in France and Belgium and endured, for him, the morally wrenching experience of Dunkirk. He had decided to marry Sally Norton and subsequently broken off the engagement. Kick, as well, was far from the person she had been in 1939. She had lived on her own and flourished in a demanding job. On the one hand, much had altered. Yet, on the other, religion posed no less of a problem than it had when the duke declared the Kennedy alliance not to his liking. In the interim, Kick's determination to be reunited with Billy had been unwavering, but despite the urgings of Nancy Astor, who thought she ought to be prepared to give up Catholicism, she was no less constant in the matter of her religious faith.

On June 23, 1943, Kick set sail for Britain on the *Queen Mary*. Five days later she and the other Red Cross girls disembarked in Glasgow and proceeded by troop train to London. She had been separated from Betty Coxe, who had been sent to North Africa. Kick as yet had no idea about a definite assignment of her own but wrote to her family that she hoped and prayed it would be London. She wanted her arrival to be a surprise to Billy and her other friends. Rather than call Billy first, she decided to let him learn from others that, after numerous false starts, she really was back at last. And how better could she guarantee that he heard quickly than to place her first phone call to David Ormsby Gore? As soon as Kick telephoned, Sissie, now the mother of two, contacted her husband, who was in training near Hatfield, and told him to find a way to come into town immediately. She said only that a marvelous surprise awaited. Billy was in Scotland with his battalion when he received word from David that Kick had returned. He asked for leave and traveled to London as soon as he could. In the meantime, Kick visited Fiona Gore and her husband Arthur, a cousin of both Billy and David, in their gardener's cottage at Pimlico House, outside London. And she saw Tony Rosslyn, Jane Kenyon-Slaney and other friends. "When she came back," remembered Billy's sister Anne, "all of London rejoiced." At least, the members of the cousinhood did—which for them amounted to the same thing.

Kick wrote to her family that she had never been happier. She called Britain her "second home" and felt justified in her "devotion to the British over a period of years" when her father and brothers had taken a different view. Still, those in London who interpreted Kick's reappearance to mean that she had decided to give in with regard to religion, and that an announcement of her engagement might be imminent, were mistaken. On July 10, Kick and Billy were seen out together in London for the first time in four years. When Billy asked her to visit his family at Compton Place, the invitation suggested that he did not intend to submit to interference from his father. He would not sneak about because the duke had prohibited the match. As Kick soon discovered, it was not Billy's father's convictions she needed to worry about; it was his own.

Her romance with Billy had begun at Compton Place as the 1938 Season drew to a close. Five years later, Kick returned to find her feelings unchanged. "Billy is just the same," she reported to Jack, "a bit older, a bit more ducal but we get on as well as ever. It is queer as he is so unlike anyone I have ever known at home or anyplace really." As in the past, he and she liked nothing better than to talk for hours, but this time she was not made happy by all he said. He left no doubt how he felt about her, but he also made it clear that, as matters stood, the religious difficulties were insurmountable. Given the role and responsibilities he expected to inherit, Billy could not accept the prospect of his children being brought up as Roman Catholics. In short, he would not give in either. "It's all rather difficult," she wrote to Jack after the day-and-a-half visit, "as he is very, very fond of me and as long as I am about he'll never marry. However much he loved me I can easily understand his position. It's really too bad because I'm sure I would be a most efficient Duchess of Devonshire in the post-war world and as I'd have a castle in Ireland, one in Scotland, one in Yorkshire and one in Sussex, I could keep my old nautical brothers in their old age."

When Kick visited Cliveden on a day off from her new post at the Hans Crescent Club for soldiers in London, Billy put in a rare appearance. To general astonishment, as every bed in the house was taken he contentedly slept on the floor. For a fellow known to insist on his comforts, that was certainly a change. Clearly, he wanted to be wherever Kick was, discomfort and indignity be damned. Billy tended to be formal and even a bit stiff, and Kick laughed that she wished the duke could have seen him at Cliveden. When she stayed with Fiona and Arthur Gore in their cottage at Pimlico House, Billy would turn up with a sleeping bag. Kick slept in a bathtub upstairs because she insisted it felt "more like a bed," and he would spend the night on the floor of a narrow dining room barely sufficient for a small table and chairs. These were minor adjustments on Billy's part, to be sure. But they were not ones he would ordinarily have been inclined to make, and to people who knew him well they were telling. On visits to the Yorkshire home of his cousin Jean, now the wife of the 2nd Lord Lloyd and the mother of a baby daughter, Kick and Billy "liked to sit up all night and talk and talk and talk." Jean and her husband, who served in the Welsh Guards, would come down in the morning to find their visitors still engaged in animated conversation about politics, history, the war—everything, apparently, except the one subject Billy pointedly refused to broach. By his own account, Billy, knowing all that Kick's faith meant to her, refrained from asking whether they "couldn't find a way out" of the difficulties that made marriage impossible. As far as he was concerned, given his circumstances the only way out would be for her to compromise on religion, and that he was not yet ready to ask her to do. For the time being, though Kick had managed to get back to Billy, matters between them remained at a stalemate.

CHAPTER SIX

Straw in the Wind

▪ ▪ ▪ ▪

THREE MONTHS AFTER ASSUMING COMMAND OF PT 109, Jack Kennedy was living in what he described to his family as rugged conditions. He slept on his boat, dined on beans, Spam and other food that did his delicate stomach no good, and patrolled the dark and dangerous waters nearly every night. As Jack saw it, he had been lucky so far, though he reported one close call when a Japanese plane strafed the deck, leaving the boat full of holes and a few of the men wounded. Typically, he kept his own emotions in check by treating his time in the South Pacific as a sort of curious intellectual experience. "All in all its an education," he wrote, "and there is an undeniable interest & attraction in it." He assured his family that he was convinced nothing was going to happen to him. "Feeling that way—makes me anxious to see as much of it as possible—and then get out of here and get back home."

Hardly had he written in that spirit when a Japanese destroyer rammed PT 109, cutting it in half. The incident left two of Jack's crew dead and Jack and the surviving men stranded in dark waters, far from land. As some of the men clung to the wreckage, Jack swam to a patch of flaming gasoline and helped his engineer, Patrick MacMahon, who was severely burned on the hands, arms and face, to safety. Following that, he swam out again and rescued two more crewmen. By then, other PT boats had spotted the flames and given up Kennedy and his men for dead. After they had clung to the wreckage for hours, Jack judged it about to sink and ordered his crew to make for a tiny island some four miles away. For five hours he towed MacMahon, swimming with the ties of the burned man's lifejacket between his teeth. After they reached land, Jack swam out again into the darkness, against a thrashing tide, in a failed attempt to signal another PT boat. Despite his efforts, five days would elapse before he and his men were rescued. Had he been a healthy man, his actions would have made for a tale of astonishing heroism. Jack suffered from an unstable back and other physical limitations that ought to have kept him out of the Navy altogether; he had spent years in and out of hospitals, often near death. In the past he had proven immensely courageous in dealing with his own poor health, but now, by risking his life repeatedly for his men, he had demonstrated courage of another order entirely. Jack had already won the affection and respect of his men; now he had their lifelong love and loyalty.

Following the loss of the boat, Jack and his crew were presumed dead. Their squadron held a funeral mass for them, and Jack's father was notified that he was missing in action. But Joe Kennedy refused to accept the news, and for five days he suffered alone and in silence, telling no one of the Navy report. Finally, on August 7, 1943, Jack and his crew were rescued. Only then did Joe Kennedy tell Rose and the other children that Jack had been missing. On August 13, Jack himself wrote a brief note to say that he was alive. He reported that he was back at his base and "O.K.," but the reality was more complicated. His fragile back had been damaged when he was thrown backwards as the destroyer rammed his boat. When doctors examined him after the rescue, he described shooting pains from the hip and down the left leg in addition to the familiar lower back pain. Some fifty hours in the water and almost a week without food or drinking water had taken an additional toll; he was covered with cuts and abrasions, particularly on the feet, and he exhibited symptoms of fatigue.

The newspaper stories of Jack's heroism were a source of joy and pride to all but one of the Kennedys. Joe Junior had just arrived in San Diego, California, on a cross-country flying trip for the Navy when he heard that Jack was missing in action. For reasons of his own, Joe did not contact his parents then. Nor did he contact his parents later that day when he saw the headline "Kennedy Son is Hero in Pacific as

Destroyer Splits his PT Boat." He waited nine days before he finally wrote home, a lapse that caused his father to complain of Joe's apparent lack of interest in how Jack was.

Sadly for Joe, the younger brother who had written the timely, important book he himself was supposed to have produced had bested him yet again. The physical arena was the one place where Jack should never have been able to compete, but, astonishingly, he had surpassed his brother there as well. Joe's anguish showed during a visit to Hyannis Port a few weeks later, on the occasion of his father's fifty-fifth birthday, when he was about to leave for a new assignment in England. At the birthday party, Judge John Burns, long a counselor to young Joe, toasted, "Ambassador Joe Kennedy, father of our hero, our own hero, Lieutenant John F. Kennedy of the United States Navy." Family friend Joe Timilty watched Joe Junior, red-faced and smiling tensely, raise his glass in celebration of his father and brother, the latter still in the Pacific theater. That night, Timilty, assigned to share young Joe's room, listened as he wept in the next bed. Clenching and unclenching his fists, Joe muttered, "By God, I'll show them!" The headlines, the toasts, and the praise of a father who had long unabashedly favored his first-born: all, apparently, had become too much. When Joe Junior left London four years previously, he had been the indisputable Kennedy family star. By the time he returned, in September 1943, he was in Jack's shadow in ways he could never have imagined.

Billy Hartington was also deeply bothered by his younger brother's military career, but for reasons of a very different sort. Jean Lloyd's little house in Yorkshire lacked a telephone, so Billy, stationed nearby, had no way of letting her know beforehand that he wished to drop in for a talk. When she opened the door one day in November 1943, she realized that he was "very, very upset." Only once before had she seen him like that, on his sudden return from Dunkirk three years before. This time, the source of Billy's highly uncharacteristic distress was the news that Andrew, who had a baby daughter and another child on the way, was being sent to fight in Italy. Billy's instinct, on learning the news, was to protect Andrew and his young family. That Andrew was to be posted abroad while Billy, unmarried, remained behind struck the latter as unjust. "He's got a wife and a child," Billy protested. "It ought to be me!" But the decision was not Billy's to make. Andrew went to Italy with his battalion, and at the duke and duchess's insistence Debo and their first grandchild moved to Churchdale Hall.

Christmas arrived, and still Billy held back from asking Kick if there were not some way to make marriage possible. To his sister Anne it was evident that "he adored her and she adored him." The time fast approached when he too would have to go off and fight, but it was not until after the holiday that Billy finally brought up the subject he had been avoiding. Billy well understood that, as he perceived his own duty, the only way that their marriage would be possible was if Kick—not he—were willing to give in on the matter of the religious upbringing of their children. He also understood what it meant to ask her to make such a sacrifice, but after Christmas, with the invasion of France looming, he could no longer bear the thought that he might lose her again. Thus it was that shortly after Christmas 1943, some six months after Kick's return to England and five years after they had first met, Billy finally brought himself to suggest that perhaps she could find a way to accept the Anglican faith, or that possibly her father could arrange for a dispensation that would permit her to raise their children as Protestants. He also made it clear that if she felt unable to do as he asked, he would honor his duty as the future Duke of Devonshire and forever give up hope of marrying the woman he loved.

Billy's proposal confronted Kick with the most difficult choice of her life. It had taken her a great deal of time to see that he believed himself unable to compromise and that if there was to be a marriage it was she who would have to make the great concession. She had come finally to comprehend what duty meant to Billy, and that he would do what he believed he must even at the cost of his own happiness. But understanding did not lessen the difficulty of what he was asking of her. Kick found herself faced with a terrible decision: Would she, after all this time and struggle, be the one to end all hope of marriage to Billy?

Once Billy had made his proposal, he and his mother launched a campaign to get Kick to agree. In the days and weeks that followed, all manner of enticements were set before her. She was given jewels, invited to parties, introduced to fascinating people. Kick had acquired her conversational skills at the Kennedy table, but at the Devonshires' she began to develop breadth in encounters with writers, artists and other cultural figures. At Elizabeth Cavendish's dinner dance on

January 8, 1944, Kick was placed next to the duchess's brother, David Cecil. Kick had already earned a reputation in her young set as a brilliant conversationalist, but Cecil's nimble-witted, exceptionally wide-ranging talk left her with a sense, as she reported afterward to her parents, that she had much to learn. Kick also chatted with Evelyn Waugh, three weeks before he began work on *Brideshead Revisited*, his elegy for a doomed world of privilege. By and large, Billy's sisters had been educated through conversations such as those Kick had that night. From the time the girls were quite young, the duke had insisted they dine with their parents and attend dinner parties where they talked to some of the best minds in Britain. Kick started the next phase of her own education in the same manner. Always eager to learn, she relished the experience.

Still, none of this seemed to sway her to make the concession necessary if she and Billy were to be married. Ironically, it was a decision of Billy's violently anti-Catholic father, the one family member who, however much he liked Kick personally, remained less than enthusiastic about the match, that finally led to her decision to give in. Billy's marriage proposal coincided with the duke's still secret plan to place him in Parliament as member for West Derbyshire, which was traditionally a Cavendish seat. The experience of the rough-and-tumble, historically momentous political campaign would provide Kick with a taste of a life that, in the end, proved irresistible.

That December, the duke learned that his brother-in-law Henry Hunloke, who had taken his seat in the House of Commons when the duke moved to the Lords in 1938, was going to resign his seat. The duke made Billy his candidate, unmindful that times were changing and that his tenants might no longer be willing to let him decide on their behalf who their representative was to be. Within his family circle, Billy's father insisted that the election would be a "walkover." The Cavendishes tended to be well-liked by those who lived and worked on their estates, for, as even the duke's severest critic would have had to admit, his life had embodied the Whiggish dictum that great property brought with it great social and political responsibility. Billy, as his coming-of-age celebration had suggested, was personally popular in the constituency, and it was expected that his status as a captain in the Coldstream Guards would be a significant advantage in wartime. Still, the duke, in predicting a walkover, seemed to have forgotten recent history. Though his man Hunloke had triumphed in the previous by-election, the Labour candidate, Charles White, had done surprisingly, even alarmingly well. Since 1885, when the boundaries of the constituency of West Derbyshire were established, only twice had it gone out of family hands. In both instances, 1918 and 1922, it had been the duke himself who had lost to White's father.

The duke also failed to take into account that the wartime truce, by which the three major political parties had agreed not to oppose each other in by-elections, was, as Harold Macmillan cautioned him, "wearing rather thin." Macmillan, who was the duke's brother-in-law, foresaw a hard-fought campaign in West Derbyshire. He warned of the potential for trouble from Alderman White, as well as from Sir Richard Acland, the MP for Barnstaple and head of the Common Wealth Party. If there was to be a significant contest, the duke calculated that Billy would benefit from support for Churchill, since a vote for the Tory candidate would be a vote of confidence in the war against Hitler.

"It was a mistake," Andrew Devonshire said of his father's attempt to keep the seat in the family. "He shouldn't have done it. He should have let it go." The duke quietly arranged for Billy to obtain leave from the army. While Billy went along with his father's wishes that he run, he made it clear that he would only interrupt his military service for the duration of the campaign. He believed his place to be "in the fight"— that is, at war—whether the election was lost or won. Though, as his mother recognized, Billy "hated soldiering," since his return after the Dunkirk evacuation in 1940 he had awaited the day when he would go back to fulfill his duty, as he saw it, and finish the fight.

The only sign that the duke might not have been as serenely confident about Billy's chances in the election as he claimed was his decision to keep the news of Hunloke's resignation secret until Billy was formally chosen as the Conservative candidate and a writ for the by-election moved. His strategy of rushing the election so as to give the opposition a limited chance to mobilize would attract severe criticism later, as well as provide ammunition to those who accused him of treating the seat of West Derbyshire as a family heirloom.

With the election set for February 17, 1944, Kick was invited to join Billy's family for the final days of the campaign. Before that, she went to stay with Richard Wood for a few days at his sister's house in York. The two had become devoted friends during Richard's convalescence in Washington. He had fallen not a little in love with her, but aware as he was of her feelings for Billy, he had taken care that their relationship remained a friendship. When she arrived on February 12, she was delighted to find that Richard not only had gotten wooden legs, but that he was able to drive a car. His resolution and courage made her certain that he was going to reclaim his life. Meanwhile, it was evident to Richard that she was preoccupied with what life with Billy would be like were she to agree to marry. On this visit, much time was taken up by her questioning him about the relations between landlord and tenants on the Halifaxes' estate at Garrowby. "All this interested Kick very much indeed," he would later recall, "in that she was going to be in a position one day of great authority and responsibility for masses of people who lived at Chatsworth." While Richard explained that the situation at Garrowby was by no means comparable to an estate on the scale of Chatsworth, he did his best to answer her questions. He perceived that Kick, having often discussed this sort of thing with Billy, was deeply attracted to the idea that the landowner looked out for those who, in turn, yielded to his political leadership, and to the sense of stability and harmonious cooperation it suggested.

Even as she and Richard spoke, the very traditions she had lately grown so fond of were under assault in West Derbyshire. The by-election was being fought not on the matter of Churchill's conduct of the war, which had gone well since El Alamein, but on what electors hoped a postwar Britain would be like. It had become a referendum on whether the people wanted any longer to defer to aristocratic political leadership or to accept the conception of the social order it implied. A question hovered over the proceedings: The aristocrat might think it his duty to govern, but was it also his right? Instead of the walkover the duke had anticipated, the campaign had quickly turned vicious, as the young Marquess of Hartington, through no doing of his own, emerged as the symbol of everything in British life that a good many in the constituency hoped had been left behind in the prewar world.

The fireworks had begun in the House of Commons on January 26 when another of the duke's brothers-in-law, James Stuart, the chief whip, moved for a new writ for the election of a member for West

Derbyshire to fill the vacancy caused by Hunloke's resignation. Sir Richard Acland, in line with Macmillan's forecast of the previous month, objected. He rose to ask sardonically when the Government Whips' Office intended to learn "political manners," pointing out that this was the first day on which the public knew of the resignation. It was customary to make such announcements at least two or three weeks before a writ was moved, and Acland argued that the practice had been departed from to the embarrassment of the people of the constituency. "These 48,000 people," he went on, "are being treated as if they are the goods and chattel of the Hartington family. You can move your writ. You can have it today, but you are not going to get that seat."

Matters quickly worsened when word got out that a Tory candidate had already been chosen, and that he was the duke's heir. In the days that followed, sneers were heard in reaction to reports that the duke had assured local Conservatives that they need not feel "absolutely bound" to select Billy as their candidate. On another occasion, the duke's side publicly insisted that the constituency was "not tied to the Cavendish family   nothing of the sort." To that, one wit replied in print, "This must mean that, of all the millions of available adults, Lord Hartington was considered on grounds of personal merit, political brilliance, oratorical splendor and general what-have-you, to be the most suitable representative of the people of West Derbyshire in this momentous parliamentary session."

Time and again, cynicism about the duke and his tactics translated into resentment against Billy. "That lad'll get a shock, he won't find it as easy as he thinks to slip into his uncle's seat," said one old fellow, as he clipped a hedge, to one of the army of reporters who rushed up from London to cover the by-election. Less than five years after Billy's coming-of-age party at Chatsworth, the tenants and employees who had stood in line for hours to wish him well were apparently queuing up now to vote for his opponent. The *Sunday Pictorial* painted a picture of growing dissension on the estate: "Even the family retainers are deserting—very secretly of course—the ducal cause. Not only because of the 'jiggery-pokery' they suspect. . . . They don't think much of the brains and ability of the Marquis." According to press reports, the deserters favored the Independent candidate Alderman White, who had the support of the Common Wealth Party. The cobbler's son launched his campaign against the duke's son in the village of his birth in a shilling-a-week cottage.

Electors had a chance to see the candidates together for the first time on an auctioneer's rostrum at Bakewell market, where the speakers' remarks competed with the mooing of cows and the haggling of housewives over second-hand stockings. At a glance, one might have thought twenty-six-year-old Billy and his sixty-three-year-old rival had come from different planets. One had boyish good looks, with a smile journalists characterized as a "bobby dazzler" that "would mean his fortune in Elstree or Hollywood if death duties ever made his removal from Chatsworth a necessity"; the other was stout and rather grim. One was elegant in dress and manner, the other homespun. One was a novice, even halting speaker, who, in the course of five agonizing minutes, frequently consulted notes; the other, seasoned and fluent, spoke extemporaneously for twenty-five. One seemed uninformed on issues of particular interest to the constituency; the other was highly knowledgeable. During the campaign Billy often faltered when questioned on specifics. At times, an expression came upon his face that reminded one commentator of "the gaze of a wounded greyhound." The *Daily Express*'s man, no friend to the Tories, tried to interview Billy at the local Conservative Club but soon gave up, because, he later wrote, "It was too like pulling the wings off a fly."

Notably, though, Billy did not falter when his opponent tried to capitalize on passionate resentment throughout Britain over the recent release from prison of Sir Oswald Mosley, leader of the British Fascists, and his wife, the former Diana Mitford—Debo's sister. The couple had been arrested in 1940 during fears of a German invasion and the installation of a quisling government possibly headed by Mosley. At that time, Churchill, uneasy about the challenge to basic tenets of British liberty that the Mosleys' imprisonment represented, had viewed them as "persons who cannot be proved to have committed any offense known to the law, but who because of the public danger and the conditions of war have to be held in custody." With the danger of invasion having receded, Mosley, in poor health, and his wife, who it had been suspected might act as his agent, had been let out on November 20, 1943. Churchill maintained that their release had been motivated by the belief that no one, however reprehensible his views, ought to be sent to prison in the absence of charges or a fair trial. "Nothing," Churchill declared, "is more abhorrent than to imprison a person or keep him in prison because he is unpopular. This really is the test of civilization." In the prime minister's opinion, it was among the very principles Britain and the United States were fighting for.

Such arguments notwithstanding, the decision triggered a national uproar, and many people suspected the couple had received preferential treatment because they were aristocrats. In the face of demonstrations against their release, Harold Nicolson, who agreed with the decision to free the Mosleys, concluded that the controversy had "widened the class breach." Anything Nicolson might say in defense of the government's action, he reflected, would be dismissed by critics as "'propaganda' and untrue. I feel that it is most dangerous that the working classes should have lost all confidence in their leaders. They will believe anything 'against the Government' and nothing which its defenders can assert." Three months later, when Charles White, shrugging his shoulders "in mute comment," pointed out that Billy Hartington's brother was married to Mosley's sister-in-law, he was playing to the anti-aristocratic sentiment that fueled his campaign, as well as seeking to associate Billy and his family with Mosley's Fascist views. Billy retorted crisply and effectively, "My brother is fighting in Italy. He and his wife are violently anti-Fascist. So am I."

While Billy's opponent had tried to link him to Britain's enemies, his supporters sought to anoint him the "patriotic" candidate. The Duke of Norfolk argued that nothing would give the enemy greater encouragement than to detect disunity and unrest in Britain, saying, "You in West Derbyshire must show the rest of your own country as well as the world that we are united." Col. Manningham Buller, the Conservative MP for Daventry, struck a similar note when he warned that an Independent victory would send a message to Britain's enemies that "if they held out a bit longer opinion would change to such an extent that they would be able to secure a compromise peace."

Churchill himself weighed in with a public letter that proved calamitously tone-deaf to the times: "My Dear Hartington, I see that they are attacking you because your family has been identified for about 300 years with the Parliamentary representation of West Derbyshire. It ought, on the contrary, to be a matter of pride to the constituency to have such long traditions of constancy and fidelity through so many changing scenes and circumstances. Moreover, it is a historical fact that your family and the people of West Derby have acted together on every great occasion in this long period of history on the side of the people's rights and progress." A good many electors found the prime minister's comments unctuous and offensive, a reminder of the very paternalism they despised. As such, his letter, along with Billy's much-touted status as "the Government representative and Mr. Churchill's personal choice," emerged as drawbacks rather than advantages. Billy's failed candidacy, as Debo Devonshire remembered, proved to be the "straw in the wind" that foretold Churchill's own political fate immediately after the war. Churchill could not protect Billy from class resentment, for he too would soon be its victim.

The political fledgling, meanwhile, stood in for Churchill—indeed, for all aristocrats—as day after day he endured the hoots and jeers of the crowd. As a mother would, Moucher Devonshire privately excused the humiliating gaps in Billy's knowledge by citing the existence of Common Wealth Party members in London who worked "all day to find and make out questions on obscure Parliamentary issues with no other purpose than to catch him out." The 1944 by-election, she later told Jack Kennedy, was "the worst & dirtiest fight I ever came across in all the 9 or 10 elections I have fought." To the pride of the duchess, who electioneered vigorously, Billy "would stand up to any amount of heckling of the worst kind." His adversaries "hardly ever hit above the belt," but somehow Billy "never got cross." In the last days of the campaign, he actually seemed to begin to enjoy himself—and to improve.

When Kick arrived in Derbyshire on February 15, two days before the poll, she was pitched into a scene of great excitement. It was clear that this was no ordinary election and that her first campaign was to be one of high drama. She marveled that rather than crumble before hecklers, Billy remained self-possessed; confronted with much booing, hissing and stamping of feet, he simply spoke louder. It had been decided that the participation of Ambassador Kennedy's daughter would do Billy's candidacy no good and that it would be best if she remained out of sight. One afternoon, she was permitted to canvass with Billy's sister Elizabeth in a gig adorned with election posters and pulled by a chestnut pony. For the most part, however, Kick had to be content to look on silently as, in the last hours of the campaign, Billy delivered six speeches and the duchess five. She wrote home that Billy's mother had been absolutely wonderful on the platform. His family would stay up late discussing the election, and Kick would sit and listen and think how lucky she was to be there.

On polling day, the duchess, by her own account, was glad the campaign was over and could not help but laugh when Billy said wistfully as they left the polling place, "It's a pity we are not just starting, isn't it?" The next day, she, Billy, Elizabeth and Kick, along with Charles White and his people, were locked in together at the Matlock Town Hall as the ballot boxes were opened and the votes counted. The laborious process took three hours, during which, Kick observed, Billy had to walk around looking pleased though he knew he faced almost certain defeat. White's victory can have been a surprise to no one, though the size of his majority—more than 4,500 votes—attracted considerable notice. Billy, the young man who had represented the old order while the old man had stood for the new, made a short speech afterward from the balcony. "It has been a hard fight," he told the crowd of about one thousand, "and that is the way it goes. I am going out now to fight for you at the front. After all, unless we win the war, there can be no home front. Better luck next time." The duke, bewildered by the people's rejection after all that he and his ancestors had done for them, lamented in private, "I don't know what the people want." "I do," his heir replied. "They just don't want the Cavendishes."

It was more than simply Billy's family the electors had spurned. The magnitude of White's victory could not be explained solely by the political history of West Derbyshire, or by the candidates' qualifications. For good reason, news of the outcome "caused a pall of the blackest gloom to fall on the P.M.," Churchill's secretary, John Colville, noted in his diary. Chips Channon called the by-election results "disastrous" and "a shattering blow to the Government," and wrote of seeing Churchill glare at White on the "ignominious" occasion of his presentation in the House of Commons. Sir Richard Acland, exultant, viewed the numbers as "proof that Britain will not be content to return to the old 1939 world when we have defeated the enemy." The Duchess of Westminster commented in a lighter vein, but she too pointed to big changes when, alluding to the Westminster election of 1784 in which Georgiana, Duchess of Devonshire, campaigned, she said of Billy's defeat, "Duchesses' kisses are not what they used to be."

The by-election clearly did mark the end of something. For Kick and Billy, it was also a beginning. Billy's mother noted that despite everything he had "loved the fight." He accepted that they lived in changing times but was, as Captain Charles Waterhouse, a Derbyshire neighbor, later wrote, "no less determined to play his part in directing the current, and not merely to be swept away by it." Far from disheartened by the harsh tone of the campaign, Billy had been invigorated. Not by chance his parting words had been, "Better luck next time." He planned to return after the war and launch his political career anew. When he did, he intended to have Kick at his side.

For Kick, the electioneering had proven a revelation. She wrote home that she had never experienced such an interesting week: "That's really the way I like to spend my time." By the time the votes had been counted, it was clear that she had tasted a life she wanted and would do whatever it took to get it, however painful the sacrifice. Billy had failed to secure a seat in Parliament, but in the course of the campaign he had won Kick's hand.

Following the by-election, Kick heard from her mother that the ambassador had had no luck in efforts to obtain a dispensation on her behalf. At this point, Rose Kennedy seems to have assumed that Kick, in the absence of a dispensation, would back off from marrying Billy. But in the wake of the campaign, things were no longer so simple. When, presently, Kick visited Churchdale Hall for two days, she knew in advance that the Reverend Edward Keble Talbot, chaplain to the King, would be there to talk to her at the request of Billy's mother. The clergyman spoke of the Cavendish family's religious role, explaining why it would be impossible for Billy's son to be raised as a Roman Catholic, and reviewed the differences between the Anglican and Roman churches. Kick, in turn, said that it would be very hard to find a substitute for the faith in which she had been raised. The clergyman and the duchess responded that they did not wish for her to give up anything. They hoped only that she might discover an equivalent in Anglicanism. Kick felt that would be impossible.

Yet her letter to her parents afterward hinted that she might be ready to make an accommodation. She said she wanted to do what was right, but hoped she was not giving up the most important thing in her life. The duchess sympathized with Kick, alone in Britain without her mother and father as she faced an overwhelming decision. The duke, who continued to detest the idea of his son's marriage to a Roman Catholic, promised that, whatever Billy decided to do about Kick, he would never be cut off—not even, or so the duke seemed to imply, if he agreed to raise his own heir as a Roman Catholic. Billy did not want to put his father to that test. Kick wrote home that Billy was very sad. He saw that his duty must come first, and Kick suggested to her parents that such an attitude was what had made Britain great.

Not long after the visit to Churchdale Hall, Kick spent four days at Cliveden, where Nancy Astor strongly encouraged her to find a way to marry Billy. Kick, she advised, could only be happy in England. Kick later declared that these talks with "Aunt Nancy" had helped her to see her own mind. Lady Astor had promised Rose Kennedy to "watch over" her child as though she were her own, but in this matter she and Rose were working at cross purposes.

On April 4, 1944, Kick had just returned from Cliveden when Billy called to say he had little hope of leave to come to London. He could, however, manage to see her at Jean Lloyd's house, which was near to where he was stationed in Yorkshire. If he came for just the night, it would not count as leave. Two weeks later, Kick traveled north by train in expectation of meeting him the following evening. In 1938, at Cliveden, Jean had eased Kick's way into the group. At Cortachy Castle, she had given the romance with Billy an opportunity to flourish. Now, six years later, she would provide the setting in which Kick finally made her decision. The Lloyds still lacked a telephone, and Kick arrived at their modest house, three miles outside Scarborough, to find Jean's leg in plaster. Several days previously, when Billy came by unannounced as he often did, she had tripped on the way upstairs to make up a bed for him.

Kick spent the evening of April 20 with her hosts. The next morning at about seven, she was in the kitchen chatting with David Lloyd, as Jean prepared eggs and bacon, when the door opened. There stood a beaming Billy, carrying a sack of oranges—a rarity in wartime, as they had to be imported—which he tossed to Kick. Then, rubbing the palms of his hands together, he exclaimed, "We're off!" Jean, to whom her cousin had first communicated his anguish after the evacuation at Dunkirk, knew at once what he meant. The invasion of France was imminent. Billy had been haunted by images of his own escape in a commandeered car and by a desperate desire to go back. It was a huge relief to know that he would soon have his chance.

That evening, the couples feasted on lobsters and champagne, which Billy had managed to secure. When the Lloyds went up to bed, Kick and Billy, as in the past, talked till dawn, and did so again the following night. By the third morning, Kick, driven to make up her mind before Billy went off again to war, had agreed to marry on his terms. As they prepared to leave, Jean took a photograph of them on the day Billy finally had the two things he wanted most: Kick, and the chance to tend to unfinished business in France and Belgium. The photograph captured what was for him a moment of perfect happiness.

Back in London, Kick wrote to the Kennedys on April 24 that she had definitely made up her mind to marry. As there had been no dispensation, the Kennedys knew immediately what Kick's decision must mean. Rose launched a battle that would cause her daughter the most acute grief, though it did not change her mind. "Mrs. Kennedy telegraphed Kick begging her not to do it," remembered Jean Lloyd. "She was very worried that Kick would go to hell." "I don't think she felt damned," added Anne Tree, to whom Kick appeared perfectly at peace with her decision. On April 30, Billy wrote a long letter to Rose Kennedy in an effort to explain why, given his responsibilities, he could not be the one to compromise. In the absence of those responsibilities, he assured her, he would never have felt justified in asking Kick to agree that their children be brought up in the Church of England. He asked Mrs. Kennedy not to think too harshly of him for what he acknowledged must seem to her a tyrannical attitude. After his initial upset, Joe Kennedy finally chose to approve, but Rose continued to hold out.

On the eve of the wedding, Kick contacted her father to say she was convinced she had taken the right step. She asked him to beseech Rose not to worry. Nonetheless, on Kick's wedding day—May 6, 1944— Rose had Archbishop Francis Spellman ask the apostolic delegate in Britain to remind her that her mother was greatly distressed and urge her to put off the marriage. The marriage took place anyway, at the

Chelsea Register Office, as Kick had stipulated that she would not agree to an Anglican service.

The Duke and Duchess of Devonshire attended with Elizabeth and Anne. Billy's grandmothers were there, as was Nancy Astor, who had done much to make the day possible. Joe Junior, who had been flying anti-submarine patrols out of Britain since the previous September, was the sole Kennedy present. Young Joe had proven supportive through-out, and he wrote home enthusiastically of the couple's love for each other. Andrew, then fighting in Italy, missed his brother's wedding, as did Debo, who had recently given birth to a son—the future 12th Duke of Devonshire. Following a reception in Belgravia, the Marquess and Marchioness of Hartington had a week's honeymoon at Compton Place. Later, they moved to a small hotel, the Swan, near to where Billy was stationed, as he and his battalion prepared to leave. He expected to be part of the first wave of troops on D-Day, but to his immense frus-tration he was ordered to stay behind to command the reinforcements. Even as he rejoiced in having as much time as possible with his bride, he remained desperately eager to return to the fight. All told, he and Kick had only five weeks together before he finally went off to war on June 20. He left, a friend later remembered, "so utterly happy, so con-vinced that all that had happened to him was for the very best."

CHAPTER SEVEN

What about You?

J UST AS BILLY HARTINGTON'S WAR RESUMED, JACK'S WAS COMING
to an end. In June 1944, Jack had been awarded the Navy and Marine
Corps Medal for heroism in the PT 109 incident. "Unmindful of personal danger," the citation read, "Lieutenant Kennedy unhesitatingly
braved the difficulties and hazards of darkness to direct rescue operations, swimming many hours to secure aid and food after he had succeeded in getting his crew ashore. His outstanding courage, endurance
and leadership contributed to the saving of several lives and were in
keeping with the highest traditions of the United States Naval service."

Despite the damage to his health, Jack had returned to duty within
eight days, saying of those people who had given him up for dead that
they had "misjudged the durability of a Kennedy." For nearly four
months he continued to serve, apparently persuaded that in some way
his actions might yet avenge the men he had lost. During this time he
experienced severe abdominal pain and was diagnosed with a duodenal
ulcer and an irritable colon. The pain down his left leg was so intense
that he could barely carry out his duties and had to spend most of his
off-duty time resting. Finally, in December 1943, Jack was sent home.
He arrived in California on January 7, 1944, and stopped off in Los
Angeles to see Inga Arvad, with whom he had corresponded from the
South Pacific. She had not remarried, but in California she had become
involved with another man, and Jack failed to revive his affair with her.

Jack's next stop was Minnesota, where he met up with his father to confer with doctors at the Mayo Clinic. Then he went on to Palm Beach, where Rose Kennedy, though joyous at his return, worried about his physical and psychological condition. He was thin and drawn, as well as exceedingly nervous. Rose recorded in her diary that he would start outside to the patio and dart in and out several times, unable to settle down. A family friend compared him to a racehorse that had been highly geared and needed to be gradually unwound. Meanwhile, his back and abdominal pain persisted, and in February doctors at the Lahey Clinic diagnosed a herniated disc. Released to active duty in Miami, he put off the recommended operation until spring.

On June 23, 1944, three days after Billy left England for France, Jack underwent surgery at the Lahey Clinic at New England Baptist Hospital. The herniated disc was removed, and initially he seemed to do well, but once he was up and about "severe muscle spasms in the lower back" required "fairly large doses of narcotics in order to keep him comfortable." Dr. James Poppen noted that he had performed more than five hundred such procedures and that only nine other patients had had a similar outcome; in every case, their pain had subsided in a matter of days or weeks. "I am indeed sorry that this has had to happen with Lieutenant Kennedy," the surgeon commented, adding that it would be "at least six months before he can return to active duty." Severe abdominal pain and a bout of malaria further complicated Jack's situation.

Meanwhile, *The New Yorker* magazine published an article about PT 109, by John Hersey, that highlighted Jack's heroism. Between his bestselling book and his valor in the Pacific theater, Jack had stored up a great deal of capital for the future. Nonetheless, that future looked bleak as Jack left the hospital in worse condition than when he had checked in. Instead of providing relief, the operation seemed merely to have exacerbated his suffering. But Jack had to cope with more than physical pain as he sought to recover from his war experience.

He had returned from the Pacific a hero, yet the entire episode had had a terrible emptiness for him because he did not have the comfort of believing deeply in the cause for which he and his men had suffered and in some cases died. Shortly after his boat was rammed, he had written dryly to Inga that fighting on islands "belonging to . . . a British concern making soap" made it hard to see his efforts in terms of any larger cause. Echoing his father's cynicism about why governments send men off to die, Jack went on, "I suppose if we were stockholders we would perhaps be doing better, but to see that by dying at Munda you are helping to insure peace in our time takes a larger imagination than most men possess." Summing up his experiences, Jack wrote of the war, "This thing is so stupid, that while it has a sickening fascination for some of us, myself included, I want to leave it far behind me when I go." Jack had returned from combat having yet to discover anything like the beliefs Inga had encouraged him to seek. When on various occasions Jack protested at being called a hero ("None of that hero stuff about me"), his remarks came off as becoming modesty. But it was also the case that, based on his reading, Jack's idea of a hero was someone willing to sacrifice everything for his convictions. How, in his own terms, could Jack feel like a hero when he persisted in questioning what his sacrifices had been for?

Jack was an outpatient at the US Naval Hospital in Chelsea, Massachusetts, when Joe Junior wrote to him for the last time. Joe had completed his anti-submarine missions and was due to leave Britain shortly after Kick's wedding. Instead, he volunteered to stay on. Part of this was because, as he said, the end of the war seemed near and he wanted to be in Britain when it came. Part was because he wished to spend more time with a married woman named Pat Wilson (who had already been divorced once), with whom some people believed he was in love. And part was because, confronted with his brother's triumphs, he longed to have a few of his own. Nearly a year had passed since Joe Timilty had heard Joe Junior weep after a toast to Jack's heroism. To judge by Joe's letter of August 10, 1944, his brother's exploits in the South Pacific continued to irk him. Jack still grieved for the crewmen lost under his command and wondered whether there was anything he might have done to avert the incident, so Joe was pouring salt on an open wound when he wrote apropos the *New Yorker* article, "What I really want to know, is where the hell were you when the destroyer hove into sight, and exactly what were your moves, and where the hell was your radar." Hotheaded and cruel to the end, Joe had his eye not just on the magazine piece but also on the medal. His last words to Jack were to congratulate him on his award and to add pointedly, "It looks like I shall return home with the European campaign medal if I'm lucky. Your devoted brother Joe."

Two days later, Joe embarked on a highly dangerous volunteer mission for which he had trained in secret. Since June, Britain had endured a new sort of attack by strange, slow, noisy, low-flying pilotless planes, each carrying a ton of explosives. There were predictions that the robot planes would soon make substantial inroads on the nerves of people who had once seemed unshakable. Joe Junior's mission targeted what was thought to be a launch site, near Calais. He and a co-pilot were to fly a naval plane armed with a massive quantity of explosives to a set point and then parachute out, after having activated a remote-control mechanism to guide the aircraft to its destination. It was a magnificent feat of courage, but it did not go as planned. The plane exploded in midair before either man had a chance to escape.

On August 13, 1944, word reached Hyannis Port that young Joe had been killed. Kick was in London with the Duke and Duchess of Devonshire when she received the terrible news. At least, the duke would say, she had not been alone at the time and he wrote the Kennedys to say she had been splendid and very brave. She knew immediately that she must go home to her parents, for she understood the toll Joe's death would take on them. With Billy also in danger, fighting in France, there was some feeling that she ought not to leave Britain, but Kick was intent on returning to America. On August 16, she arrived at Logan Airport in Boston, where Jack was waiting for her. She had not seen Jack since before he left for the Solomon Islands in 1943, and though she had long been accustomed to the sight of him suffering with one illness or another, nothing could have prepared her for the ravaged figure that greeted her. He had failed to regain the weight lost in the South Pacific, and his skin had the sickly hue of malaria. In the aftermath of the operation, he had been treated with procaine injections, antispasmodic medication and other remedies, yet the pain persisted. Reporters looked on as Jack and Kick embraced, and she fell on his shoulder in a flood of tears.

Both parents had been devastated by Joe's death, but Joe Senior took it hardest. He had never believed that the war was worth fighting, and he did not change his mind now. At length, Joe was posthumously awarded the Navy Cross, the Navy's highest decoration. His citation read in part:

> Well knowing the extreme dangers involved and totally uncon-
> cerned for his own safety, Lieutenant Kennedy unhesitatingly vol-
> unteered to conduct an exceptionally hazardous and special
> operational mission. Intrepid and daring in his tactics and with
> unwavering confidence in the vital importance of his task, he will-
> ingly risked his life in the supreme measure of service and, by his
> great personal valor and fortitude in carrying out a perilous under-
> taking, sustained and enhanced the finest traditions of the United
> States Naval Service.

The ambassador appreciated the reports of Joe's bravery, but insisted he had no illusions that his son had died for a great cause. Ever the cynic, he dismissed such thinking as "hocus-pocus." He had argued with all his heart against this war. He had urged Britain and the United States to come to terms with Hitler. But his words and actions had gone unheeded, and young Joe, he believed, had died, like others, "as a result of the stupidity of our generation." When Jack and young Joe were boys, their father had often bitterly recalled the soldiers who had died "for nothing" in the Somme fighting of 1916. His firstborn's death had no more meaning than theirs. In his grief, he expressed a wish to be like Lord Halifax, who had reacted to the death of one son and the mutila-tion of another by continuing bravely and uncomplainingly and by working too hard for his mind to dwell on sorrow. Nonetheless, when Joe's final letter to his parents arrived, his father collapsed in despair.

At home, young Joe's death restored the family dynamics to what they had been before Jack began to surpass his brother. In their father's eyes, Joe once again became the best and most gifted of the boys. Once again he became the son with the brilliant political future, the one for whom greatness had been foreordained. Since the success of *Why England Slept*, reality had begun to impinge on the myth of Joe's superi-ority. His death expunged recent history. Never again would Joe Junior fall short of a father's dreams.

Kick's presence did her parents considerable good. It was not just that, as the last Kennedy to see Joe alive, she could speak of his final weeks. In

Jack's testimony, her "great happiness" in having finally married Billy "even shone through her sadness over Joe's death." That happiness might have been incongruous in an atmosphere of intense mourning, yet it had a healing effect. It "was so manifest and so infectious," Jack wrote, "that it did much to ease the grief of our mother and father."

Shortly before she returned to America, Kick had had a personal triumph, as well as an exhilarating preview of what life with Billy promised to be like after the war. The newlyweds had shared a dream of a political partnership, but neither had expected that, in the end, she would make her political debut alone. The new marchioness's first official public appearance occurred in Derbyshire on August 8. The setting was the Derby Red Cross and St. John Carnival at Bakewell market, where, six months previously, Billy had made his own rather inauspicious debut on a rostrum with his opponent Charles White. At the time of the by-election, Kick had been required mostly to stay in the shadows. There was no such constraint now that she was Lady Hartington. Dressed in a Red Cross uniform and accompanied by her husband's grandmother the dowager duchess, she toured various stalls, made purchases and climbed atop a platform to pose with a sheep that wore a cloth emblazoned with the Red Cross symbol. Kick delivered a spirited speech, and it was not lost on the duke's longtime political agent, who watched from the sidelines, that the crowd loved her.

Having once charmed the cousinhood, she proceeded to do the same with the constituency, whose votes Conservatives were eager to retrieve. Many of those in attendance at the carnival were the very electors who had wrested the traditional Cavendish seat in Parliament out of family hands, so their approval was significant. Her performance proved Billy to have been shrewd in his estimate of her potential. For six years he had sensed that Kick's personal magnetism and passion for politics could be tremendous assets in his own career. The political agent wrote to the duke, who, though still smarting from the by-election, finally perceived the possibilities. He sent word to Kick's father of his daughter's natural political skills, describing her impact on the crowd at Bakewell and predicting that if Billy could not win the seat back for himself, his marchioness would win it back for him.

In Hyannis Port, Kick proudly spoke to Jack about Billy's determination to return to battle. She managed to make Jack understand her and her young husband's great happiness, as well as the convictions that made Billy so eager, in spite of all that happiness, to go back to finish the fight he had been forced to abandon in 1940. Germany was on the verge of military defeat, but, as Kick knew, danger persisted. It was especially hard on the families of those who, like Joe, died in these months, to reflect that the lives had been lost so close to the end. Recent casualties had included an uncle of Billy's, as well as his cousins Charlie Lansdowne (one of the young men at Cortachy Castle in 1938) and Charlie's younger brother, Ned Fitzmaurice. Billy's own brother, Andrew, now a captain in the Coldstream Guards, had narrowly escaped death on the Italian front. Trapped by enemy forces on three sides and by flames on the fourth, his company endured massive shellfire and an absence of food and water for a day and a half. Andrew, by a combination of intrepidity, dash and good cheer, managed to keep up the troops' morale until they were relieved. He was later awarded a Military Cross for "personal gallantry" that had been "an inspiration to his men."

Billy was mindful that death might come at any time. He had written in July, before Kick left for the United States, "I have been spending a lovely hour on the ground and thinking in a nice vague sleepy way about you & what a lot I've got to look forward to if I come through this all right. I feel I may talk about it for the moment as I'm not in danger so I'll just say that if anything should happen to me I shall be wanting you to try to isolate our life together, to face its finish, and to start a new one as soon as you feel you can. I hope that you will marry again, quite soon—someone good & nice." By August Billy was fighting in Normandy, where his battalion sustained heavy casualties. Two commanding officers were wounded in the space of twelve hours, and Billy, as senior officer, led the battalion for three critical days. On the final day the battalion was counterattacked continuously from six in the morning until ten at night. Billy stayed cool throughout and held the position. Promoted to major, he pushed on through France and crossed the Somme.

He participated in the liberation of Belgium and, perched on a tank as it rolled into Brussels, nearly wept for joy. He wrote to Kick of the Belgians' intense gratitude to their liberators. Cheering crowds rushed toward the British tanks and threw their arms round Billy and other

Jack (second from left), age eight, with his older brother Joe Junior, and their sisters Rosemary, Kathleen and Eunice. COURTESY JOHN F. KENNEDY LIBRARY

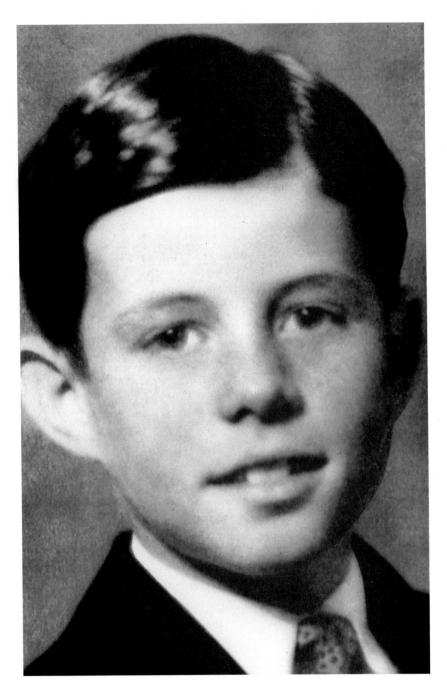

Jack, age ten, was an avid reader. His taste ran to the heroes of English
and Scottish history. He was drawn to tales of adventure and chivalry,
of the strong who protected the weak and of causes worth dying for.

Jack, age eighteen, on his first trip abroad in 1935. For the past three years he had been absorbed in the books and speeches of Winston Churchill. In London, he became fascinated by the 1935 general election, of which he would often speak a quarter century later when he ran for president.

COURTESY JOHN F. KENNEDY LIBRARY

In youth, Jack was often ill and confined to bed, and endured several life-threatening episodes.

COURTESY JOHN F. KENNEDY LIBRARY

Joe and Rose Kennedy in 1938, shortly after Joe took up
his post as US ambassador to the Court of St. James's.

Joe Junior, Ambassador Kennedy and Jack arriving in Britain on July 4, 1938. "He looked very much a boy," remembered one of the London debutantes Jack met that summer, "all long skinny arms and legs, but very, very attractive!" COURTESY JOHN F. KENNEDY LIBRARY

The Set

On his arrival during the last weeks of the 1938 London Season, Jack discovered that his sister Kick had become part of a group of young aristocrats.

TOP LEFT:
Andrew Cavendish.
MIDDLE ROW:
David Ormsby
Gore,
Debo Mitford.
BOTTOM ROW:
Jean Ogilvy,
Jakie Astor.

TOP ROW: Tony Loughborough, Sissie Lloyd Thomas.

MIDDLE ROW: Hugh Fraser, Fiona Gore.

BOTTOM ROW: Billy Hartington, Robert Cecil.

The Second Sons' Club

Jack Kennedy joined David Ormsby Gore and Andrew Cavendish in the second sons' club, comprised of those who had drawn "the short straw in life."

Jack Kennedy

COURTESY JOHN F. KENNEDY LIBRARY

ABOVE: Andrew Cavendish.

COURTESY JEAN LLOYD

LEFT: David Ormsby Gore.

COURTESY JEAN LLOYD

Kick Kennedy and Billy Hartington

Within the aristocratic cousinhood, it was soon "taken for granted" that the US ambassador's daughter and the 10th Duke of Devonshire's heir were falling in love.

BOTH PHOTOS COURTESY
JEAN LLOYD

In September 1938, Neville Chamberlain and Adolf Hitler met in Munich to decide Czechoslovakia's fate. Kick and her friends monitored the Czech crisis from Scotland. Pictured (left to right) are Debo Mitford; Jean Ogilvy; Kick Kennedy; Mabell, Dowager Countess of Airlie; Robert Cecil; Ivar Colquhoun; Billy Hartington; David Ormsby Gore.

In London during the crisis, Ambassador Kennedy was constantly in and out of 10 Downing Street. He sought to ensure that the prime minister adhered to the policy of appeasement.

Jack avidly followed the crisis from the United States, where he had returned to begin the fall term at Harvard. The Munich agreement was to become a critical point of reference in Jack's future reflections on international affairs.

In March 1939 Jack joined the Kennedys in Rome for the coronation of Pope Pius XII. While they were there, word came that German troops had seized the rest of Czechoslovakia in flagrant violation of the Munich agreement. COURTESY JOHN F. KENNEDY LIBRARY

On the eve of war, Jack was constantly on the move because, he wrote, "the only way you can really know what is going on is to go to all the countries."

Joe Junior, Kick and
Jack on their way to the
House of Commons on
September 3, 1939, the
day Britain declared
war on Germany.

Jack graduated from
Harvard in June 1940,
with a senior honors
thesis on the Munich
agreement.

Despite his long history of fragile health, in 1941 Jack passed a Navy physical and took up a post in naval intelligence in Washington, DC.

Jack and Kick in Palm Beach. They were so close that friends compared them to twins.

Kick married Billy Hartington in London on May 6, 1944. They had only five weeks together before he went off to war.

Debo Cavendish; Evelyn, Dowager Duchess of Devonshire; and Kick Hartington at Bakewell Market on August 8, 1944. A month later Billy Hartington was killed in action at the age of twenty-six.

The war hero. Jack's experiences in the South
Pacific left him in ravaged physical condition.

soldiers. He reported that having lived in "reasonable comfort and safety" while the Belgians had suffered under Hitler, he felt somehow unworthy of so much gratitude. Still, he had put the anguish of Dunkirk behind him at last, and, as a fellow soldier would later attest, Billy in the last days of his life seemed "perfectly at peace with himself." Further along the route, fighting resumed. In the thick of combat, according to an eyewitness, Billy seemed so calm it was as though he were in the garden at Compton Place rather than at war. Finally, on September 10, he was targeted by a German sniper, presumably on account of the pale corduroy trousers that identified him as an officer. In a letter published in *The Times* that would later seize Jack's imagination, Captain Charles Waterhouse wrote of Billy's final moments: "Leading the infantry forward, ahead of the tanks, completely calm and casual, carrying his cap and saying rather languidly, 'Come on, you fellows, buck up!' death came to him instantly."

Three days after Billy was killed in action, a telegram addressed to the marchioness reached the Devonshires. Moucher wrote to Kick: "All your life I shall love you—not only for yourself but that you gave such perfect happiness to my son whom I loved above anything in the world." Jack stayed up with Kick an entire night as she talked about Billy and why she had loved him so. Nothing Jack did or said seemed to lessen her pain, and he later told Betty Coxe that it had been the worst night of his life. A few weeks previously, Kick had demanded to return to America after her brother's death. Now all she wanted was to go back to Britain. As she would explain to her parents, when a brother dies a sister is very sad but does not have the "gnawing pain" associated with losing "a part of oneself" that the loss of her husband caused her to feel. On September 20, she was offered passage on an aircraft from Quebec carrying General Sir Alan Brooke, the chief of the British Imperial General Staff and Billy's commander at the time of the Dunkirk evacuation, who was on his way back from Churchill's meeting with Roosevelt to plan the war's final phase and address the question of their respective zones of occupation in postwar Germany. Contemplating her future as a widow as she waited for the aircraft to leave Quebec, Kick pictured herself living on in companionship with Jack. She wrote to Joe and Rose asking that they tell Jack not to get married for a long time. She promised to keep house for him.

Upon landing in Britain, Kick traveled to London on the general's special train. The duke waited for her at the station. He was said by his daughters never to have been the same after Billy's death, and in his wallet he had a picture he would carry with him for the rest of his life. It was Jean Lloyd's photograph of Kick and Billy on a spring morning in Yorkshire, after he had learned that the invasion of France was near and after she had consented to be his wife. The duke escorted the young widow to Compton Place, where she impressed Billy's mother by her lack of selfishness and the care she took "not to upset others." Still, as the duchess later told Jack, it broke her heart to observe his sister's "desolate face."

The day after Kick flew out of Quebec, Jack, at Hyannis Port, composed a letter to Moucher Devonshire. Jack and his sister's husband had had a history of arguing past one another. After hearing Kick talk at length about her husband, Jack finally understood the sense of honor and duty that had driven him. Two years after Billy had enquired whether he still thought the British decadent, Jack answered anew. To Billy, Jack had proclaimed that the likes of Raymond Asquith no longer existed in Britain. Now, calling the news of Billy's death "about the saddest I have ever had," he paid his brother-in-law the highest tribute by comparing him to the man Jack himself had taken for a model. He wrote: "When I read Captain Waterhouse's letter about the cool and gallant way Billy died, I couldn't help but think of what John Buchan had written about Raymond Asquith. 'Our roll of honor is long, but it holds no nobler figure. He will stand to those of us who are left as an incarnation of the spirit of the land he loved. . . . He loved his youth, and his youth has become eternal. Debonair and brilliant and brave, he is now part of that immortal England which knows not age or weariness or defeat.' I think that those words could be so well applied to Billy. I feel extremely proud that he was my sister's husband." Both Jack and Billy had been war heroes, and both had demonstrated enormous physical courage, but there was a crucial difference between them. Like Asquith, Billy had beliefs he was willing to die for. Ambivalent about the war and much else, Jack did not yet have such beliefs himself—though he longed to have them.

Jack's letter, particularly the reference to Asquith, deeply moved Moucher Devonshire. She and Jack had never met, but the letter impelled her to reach out to him and share her own sense of the son she had loved so intensely. She replied to Jack with a long, beautiful letter, which, after she had sent it off, she felt "rather embarrassed" at having written; but Kick assured her Jack would be pleased—and he was. Billy's mother wrote of his courage, but also of Jack's. "I do hope you are better yourself," she told him, "for you must have had a frightful time. Kick showed us the account of your awful experience. What a tremendous thing it was & how proud all your family must be of you. Everyone here was thrilled by the account. We should love to hear you talk of it. Kick tells us there is quite an outside chance you might come over here early next year. How lovely that would be. We do hope it may come off." Kick, too, was greatly moved by Jack's tribute. She reread *Pilgrim's Way* and discussed it with the Devonshires, who, she reported, had known most of the cast of characters in Buchan's memoir—"especially the people that were killed in the last war." The duchess, she said in an effort to persuade Jack to come over, was "keen as mustard" to have a visit from him.

It appeared he would soon be free. As early as October 3 the Naval Medical Board had declared Jack unfit for duty for an indefinite time. In November, he had been home for nearly eleven months when the board issued a diagnosis of chronic colitis and ruled him permanently unfit for service. "The background of his present physical status," it was noted in his naval record on October 25, "is an exhausting combat experience in the South Pacific. Recovery in his case is dependent on a long period of rest in a secluded outdoor environment." Another month passed before the Naval Retiring Board in Washington, DC, discharged him, his release to become final in March.

Staying in Arizona for his health, Jack worked on what was to become a privately printed book, *We Remember Joe*, along the lines of the memorial volumes produced by grieving families of the golden youth sacrificed in the First World War. Kick assembled her reminiscences and solicited tributes from some of those who had encountered Joe Junior in Britain. Jack composed an essay, which captured, among other traits, the ceaseless striving and straining from which the second son had long sought to differentiate himself. Jack wrote of young Joe, "Though at a glance Joe's record shows that he had great success, things did not come particularly easy for him. I think his accomplishments were due chiefly to the amazing intensity with which he applied himself to the job on hand. I do not think I can ever remember him sit back in a chair and relax." In that passage, Jack described the very opposite of the personal style he most admired, one of Raymond Asquith's distinguishing characteristics having been the ease with which he did everything. Jack had bested Joe repeatedly when he was alive, and for all his talk now of the "great accomplishments" which had lain in Joe's future, the second son's final triumph may have been to transform Joe's life into material for, in his own icy phrase, "the best writing I ever did."

Jack planned to go on to law school in the fall—Harvard, rather than Yale, now that Joe would not be in attendance. "And then if something good comes up while I am there I will run for it," he wrote to Lem Billings of his political ambitions. "I have my eye on something good now if it comes through." First, after a holiday in Los Angeles, Jack returned to the Mayo Clinic for another evaluation of his back. He was weighing a recommendation of further surgery when his father produced an enticing offer. The *Chicago Herald–American* invited the author of *Why England Slept* to cover, from a serviceman's perspective, one of the last great wartime conferences, the meeting to plan the founding of the United Nations.

Jack postponed the back operation and was in San Francisco the week of April 25 when delegates from fifty countries convened to discuss the international security organization that was supposed to be the bit of good to emerge from two world wars. Though billed as a peace conference, the proceedings were highly contentious from the outset. In a dispatch which his father arranged to have published in other Hearst papers as well, Jack compared them to "an international football game," with the Soviet representative "carrying the ball" while the Americans and the British "tried to tackle him all over the field." He was writing of events in 1945, but he might as well have meant international affairs in the next decades.

Already there were signs of the conflict that would fracture the post-war world. Indeed, it harked back to the European scene when Jack had first arrived in London with his father and brother. In 1938, there had been twin threats: Germany and the Soviet Union. The latter had struck many in Britain, including Ambassador Kennedy, as the more obnoxious, and the policy of appeasement had arisen in part from a belief that

Germany offered a defense against the spread of Communism. When, in spite of the non-aggression pact, Nazi Germany invaded the Soviet Union in June 1941, not a few observers considered that Hitler and Stalin ought to be permitted, even encouraged, to disembowel one another. Churchill, much as he loathed Communism, took a different view. He insisted it was Britain's duty to come to the aid of the Russians, as he preferred to call them in an effort to distinguish between the people and the ideology. Pragmatic considerations lay behind his wish to help. In embracing the Soviets as friends and allies, Churchill focused on the goal of victory over Hitler and put aside for the moment anything that might happen later. The Allied victory owed much to, in Churchill's words, "the mighty military achievements of the Russian people."

With the end of the war in Europe, the old tensions reemerged and the Soviet Union's demeanor toward the West altered. Suddenly, or so it struck Churchill, the entire relationship with the Russians was again "in flux," every question about the future unsettled. Churchill brooded about the potential for a Soviet-dominated continent and about a new global conflict—"another bloodbath"—if nothing was done to stop the Communist onslaught; American troops must not withdraw from the Soviet zone in Germany until there was a firm agreement as to the temporary nature of the Soviet occupation. He feared that much the Allies had fought for was already being "brushed aside," and that the world organization then in the process of formation in San Francisco threatened to become "an idle name." Without a trace of exaggeration, he declared that he looked on the future of Europe "with as much anxiety" as he had before the outbreak of war.

The issue of a settlement with the Soviet Union seemed to Churchill to dwarf all other matters. At the Yalta Conference in February, Roosevelt had stunned Churchill with the announcement that the United States would do what it could to preserve the peace, but not at the expense of maintaining a large military force in Europe. The American occupation would last no more than two years. Appalled by what he saw as America's lack of strategic thinking, Churchill later made the grim forecast that the sooner US troops went home, the sooner they would have to return.

On Jack Kennedy's first night in London in 1938, he had seen Anthony Eden warn of Fascist aggression; in 1945, it was the Communists that Eden, the lead British delegate in San Francisco, pointed to with alarm. Prior to the conference, Eden had gone so far as to propose that it be postponed altogether until the matter of Soviet efforts to establish a satellite government in Warsaw was settled. At Yalta, Churchill had pointed out that Britain had entered the war on account of German aggression in Poland, and that it regarded Polish independence in the postwar period as a matter of honor. Stalin in turn had declared that, as in the past thirty years the Germans had twice passed through Poland, the Soviet Union saw that country as a necessary bulwark to its own security. In his reports on the distrust of Moscow that permeated the proceedings in San Francisco, Jack drew on conversations with Eden and with other members of the British contingent, including Cranborne, Halifax and Kick's great friend Richard Wood. Jack wrote, "It is this distrust—which is becoming deeper—that is causing grave concern and considerable discouragement." To Jack's mind, hope was fast evaporating for "winning any lasting peace from this war." He even heard talk from British friends that a fight with the Soviets could be imminent.

The conference was in progress when VE Day, the day of victory in Europe for the Allies, was celebrated on May 8. Churchill's pleasure was alloyed by frustration at American reluctance to recast yesterday's co-belligerents as tomorrow's enemies. In early April he had told Roosevelt of his wish that the Allies "should join forces with the Russian armies as far to the east as possible, and, if circumstances allow, enter Berlin." In his final message before he died on April 12, Roosevelt, loath to jeopardize Soviet commitment to the Pacific war and to the conference in San Francisco that had been his brainchild, had urged Churchill "to minimize the general Soviet problem as much as possible, because these problems, in one form or another, seem to arise every day, and most of them straighten out." Harry Truman, Roosevelt's successor, rejected Churchill's request that US troops retain the territory gained in the fighting, which overlapped with the previously designated Soviet zone of occupation. When US and British forces withdrew to their allotted zones, Churchill declared it "a fateful milestone for mankind."

That Soviet power had thus been permitted to establish itself, as Churchill wrote, "in the heart of Europe" was not the only abrupt and monumental shift in the order of things now that Germany and Italy had lost the war. In one of his articles, Jack told of the upcoming election in Britain that threatened to remove Churchill from office at his triumphant moment. "The British Labour Party is out for blood," Jack informed American readers. "They are going all the way: Public ownership of the Bank of England, Government control of rents and prices, gradual Government ownership of mines, transportation, planned farming—the works. . . . While everyone knows Churchill's strengths, they are not sure that he can buck the recent strong surge to the left."

It had always been understood that victory in Europe would mean the end of the coalition government. Still, in the afterglow of VE Day, many observers round the world found it inconceivable that Britain could fail to return to power its wartime leader and national hero. The view within Britain was strikingly different, as Kick reported in a letter to Jack. On April 26, 1945, the Tories had experienced a smashing defeat in the Chelmsford by-election. Kick wrote to her brother, "All the Conservatives have been very shocked by the result of the by-election held at Chelmsford on Thursday. I am sending you some clippings on it from today's paper. It is of special interest to us as Billy was beaten by Common Wealth with a much smaller majority. With the war nearly at an end & doing so well this result was amazing."

Chelmsford, like West Derbyshire, spawned predictions that the British electorate would demand fresh leadership once Hitler had been beaten. In both by-elections, the determining factor had been not Churchill's conduct of the war but what the general populace thought postwar Britain ought to be like. Churchill had become prime minister as a consequence of the war. Had he saved Britain only to assure his own demise? Polling day, July 5, would be the ultimate test. Churchill, for his part, had wanted to postpone the election and carry on the coalition until after the Japanese had been dealt with, but the Labour Party resisted his appeals to be allowed to "finish the job." The UN conference had yet to conclude when Eden handed the reins to Lord Cranborne and went home early in anticipation of the contest over who would guide the nation into the postwar era.

Kick took a keen if bittersweet interest in the election, in which Billy's brother, Andrew, and friends such as Hugh Fraser, Robert Cecil, Michael Astor, Julian Amery and Tom Egerton came forward as candidates. Young men who had talked of politics all their lives were about to start their political careers together. Billy, naturally, would have been among them had he lived, and Kick would have had an opportunity to prove the duke correct about her ability to help win back the family seat. She wrote to Jack, "Nearly all the boys that you knew here have been adopted by various constituencies for the General Election. Of course they will stand as Conservatives. . . . What about you? What are your plans?" Before Jack went to the South Pacific, Kick had heard him speak of his presidential ambitions. As he faced his new life after the war, she sought to use the example of their British friends to spur him to launch a political career of his own.

When Jack completed his assignment to cover the founding of the UN, it was a natural next step to go on to report the British general election. Both were part of the same big story: the conformation of the postwar world. He had last visited London on the eve of war, and a very stimulating encounter it had been. He knew from Kick's letters that a major social change was in the air and he wanted to be there to see it.

CHAPTER EIGHT

By Watching England
We Will Have Much to Learn

AS JACK STRUGGLED TO FIND HIS WAY IN THE AFTERMATH of the war, he was supremely aware of the toll Billy's death had taken on Kick. He had urged their friends to write to her after she returned to Britain, and he had involved her in his own project of assembling a memorial book about young Joe. As they had once done when Kick was in Washington and Jack in Charleston, they again wrote back and forth about matters of style and substance. But while Kick often managed to sound like her old self, Jack knew that she was far from all right. In San Francisco, he had discussed her at length with Richard Wood, and part of his eagerness to get to London was to see for himself how she was. He wanted to talk to her about her plans for the future, as well as his own.

When Kick first returned to Britain after Billy was killed, Billy's sister Elizabeth had had to sleep on a mattress on the floor of the young widow's room at Compton Place. Kick, she remembered, "couldn't be left alone at night." Kick wrote home that the realization of Billy's death had come to her very strongly at Compton Place, and she wondered whether she might have spared herself a great deal of pain had she remained in America. Everything seemed to remind her of him. His black standard poodle, Lupin, left roughly cut "just the way Billy liked him," still darted about as though his master were about to come back.

As Kick went through Billy's possessions she picked out a photograph of him with Lupin as a present for Jean Lloyd. She found the diamond and sapphire cufflinks his father had given him for his twenty-first birthday and made a gift of them to Billy's young godson, Andrew Parker Bowles. She pored over the letters that fellow officers had written to the duchess about Billy's last days, and she declared, "I thank God every night I married him and I think it must have been God's way of making Billy's life, though short completely happy."

She was less sure of God's plan for her own life. "Before it had its purpose," Kick told her parents. "I knew what it would be. Now I feel like a small cork that is tossing around. I know that there are hundreds like me, and lots more unfortunate, but it doesn't heal the wound." Her relationship with Billy had been based on the shared dream of a useful life together. He had seen her as a partner both in his political career and—though he questioned whether he would ever really get to live at Chatsworth—in his aspiration to revive the ancestral home of the Devonshire dukes as a center of political and cultural power. She had shared his exhilaration during the West Derbyshire by-election and delighted in her own efficacy when, as the Marchioness of Hartington, she addressed the constituency at Bakewell market. She had looked forward to taking a benevolent interest in the lives of those who lived and worked on the duke's estates. Billy had been clear about what he was offering her, and she had found that level of certainty tremendously appealing. Now that he was gone Kick wondered how she would live, what she would do. A month and a half after Billy's death she wrote to Jack, "It just seems the pattern of life for me has been destroyed."

She told Jack that when she was with people she liked and knew well it would be all right for a while—"and then I just start thinking and it's no good. I'm much better down here just with the family and I can't face going out in London with a crowd which everyone thinks would cheer me up." Eventually she consented to move to London, where she shared a flat with Billy's aunt Anne Hunloke. In the beginning, she continued to find it difficult to go out in public, even to shop. "I don't like to go into shops," she told Jean Lloyd, who saw a good deal of her in this period, "because I feel people are looking at me, wondering how I'm taking it."

She braced herself to return to the Red Cross, and at the duchess's request she went to Derbyshire to speak to the Women's Institute about the American housewife in wartime. The mayor introduced Lady Hartington, and as at Bakewell she charmed the crowd. By the end of the session, audience members were shouting, "Give the English country housewife the recognition she deserves—more freedom for women!" (The mayor privately confessed afterward, "We have always considered our women chattels.") Amused by their response and by the thought of what her traditionally-minded husband's reaction would have been had he heard her urge the women on "to bigger and better things," Kick nearly managed to seem like her old self.

Still, her agitation persisted. Faced with the end of the war in Europe and the return of Andrew and the other boys, she asked Jack—the person to whom she remained closest—what she ought to do. Her status as an American made things more difficult. Should she—could she—remain in Britain? Would it be better for her, and for Billy's family, if she returned to the United States? "I write you every minute for advice but none seems to come through," Kick scrawled on April 1, 1945, to Jack. "The war, we think, has ended. Am pleased but rather agonized. Seeing Andrew and all the others come home." Seven years after Kick had first encountered Andrew on the staircase at Cliveden, she found the sight of the surviving Cavendish brother difficult to bear. "It nearly kills me to see him," she told her parents, "not that he is really at all like Billy but the whole idea of seeing Andy makes Billy's absence so much more noticeable."

Kick felt that, without Billy, she did not "fit into any design." Andrew, for his part, was immediately constrained by the inviolable pattern imposed by his brother's death. Training for the Coldstream Guards had come as a jolt to a young man who had never been a paragon of discipline, but in the end he had been transformed by the experience and even rather glad for it. On the Italian front he had emerged as a hero and a leader of men, and earned a Military Cross for gallantry in the field. He had prized the camaraderie and the opportunity to serve as an officer. To his dismay, in the aftermath of Billy's death Harold Macmillan had moved to shield the new heir to the Devonshire dukedom. In his capacity as Minister Resident at Allied headquarters, Macmillan had quietly arranged for his wife's nephew to be taken off the front lines lest Moucher Devonshire lose not one son but two. Macmillan was exceptionally close to Moucher, who had "held his hand" and done what she could to keep his marriage intact when his wife, the duke's sister Dorothy, took a lover. "I never forgave him," Andrew Devonshire would say many years afterward of Macmillan's intervention. Andrew, who had yet to learn the reason for his reassignment to a training camp in Naples, spent three "miserable" months feeling "bored and ashamed." When he rejoined his battalion shortly before it went home, he was so mortified that he felt unable to look his comrades in the eye.

On his return to Britain, Andrew was expected to take up his brother's identity when, by his accomplishments in the military, he had just begun to reformulate his own. In years past, "the boy who couldn't wait to grow up" had often seemed to claim for himself anything that was Billy's. He had striven to have the same friends, the same debs, the same party guests; whatever his brother had, Andrew had desired. Yet, in his efforts to keep up, Andrew had been able to go only so far. Jack, conceivably, might have displaced his elder brother had the latter survived, but no such possibility had been available to Andrew. The eldest son and heir might be a dunce, but as long as he lived there was no way a second son could usurp his position.

A German sniper's bullet had changed everything, and Andrew, presented with Billy's life, in the form of his title and inheritance, was by no means certain he wanted it. He appeared as conflicted about his future as Billy had been serene. Before the war, Andrew, considered by some of their friends "the more intellectually stimulating" of the duke's sons, had looked forward to a double career in publishing and politics like that of his uncle Harold Macmillan. With his talents and interests, Andrew had seemed ideally positioned to use and appreciate the liberty that was the consolation prize of the second son. Though it was common for second sons to resent their fate, it was also the case that they were free to become, as David Cecil most triumphantly had, the men they wished to be, while firstborn male children often became slaves to their inheritance.

Billy's life had ended, but so in a sense had Andrew's—at least, life as he had known and savored it to date. Suddenly his future was plotted in a way it never had been before; the free-spirited, irrepressible Andrew had to abandon all expectation of a private existence and be groomed for the life of a duke. Whatever his ambivalence, he and Debo were to replace Billy and Kick as the Marquess and Marchioness of Hartington. One day, Andrew would inherit everything that, to his mind, ought to have been Billy's—vast property, but also vast responsibilities. Both as heir and, later, as duke, Andrew, by his own account, would never permit himself to forget that he was acting "by proxy." Those two words circumscribed his fate. Yet on his homecoming that March there was still one thing Andrew could do, not "by proxy" and not as Marquess of Hartington, but as himself. In the general election, using the name Lord Andrew Cavendish for the last time, he stood as the Conservative candidate for Chesterfield.

Kick spent the evening of VE Day in the company of David and Sissie Ormsby Gore and Hugh Fraser. The questions of Hitler's reputed invincibility and Britain's will to fight another war, which had been debated in David and Hugh's nose-to-nose discussions at Cliveden in 1938 when Kick first met them, had finally and definitively been answered that afternoon. Churchill, cheered by all in the Commons "except the recently elected cad for Chelmsford," had announced the Nazis' surrender and proposed that "this House do now attend at the Church of St. Margaret's, Westminster, to give humble and reverend thanks to Almighty God for our deliverance from the threat of German domination."

That night, the weather was exceptionally warm and "thousands of searchlights swept the sky" as all of London seemed to pour out onto the streets. Kick, Hugh and the Ormsby Gores, part of an immense crowd in front of Buckingham Palace, cheered as the King and Queen appeared on a floodlit balcony. On their way to Piccadilly, they paused to watch a massive bonfire beneath the trees in Green Park. Celebrants fed the flames with barricades of wood and air-raid shelter doorways; the fire, as recorded by the diarist James Lees-Milne, was reflected "upon thousands of faces, packed on the pavement, squatting on the grass and cramming the windows of the Piccadilly houses." Piccadilly was "absolute bedlam," Kick reported in a letter to her family. There were fireworks and dancing in the streets, and people climbed lampposts to plant flags on top "amid tumultuous applause from bystanders."

In the midst of the festivities, Kick's isolation persisted. As she told Jack, only one other girl she knew well—Hugh Fraser's sister Veronica—had also been widowed in the war. Sissie, Debo, Jean and the rest of Kick's female friends all had their husbands still. Kick was glad for them, of course, but that did not make her feel any less alone. Of all the individuals Kick knew in London, Moucher Devonshire perhaps best understood what she still found it hard to accept. The night after the victory revels, Kick dined quietly with Moucher, whom she sometimes affectionately referred to as "the Dutch." Speaking of herself but also of Kick, whose anguish she shared, Moucher expressed the opinion that it was time to set-tle down to facing life without the best ones, who would never come back.

The general election campaign began in earnest before Jack arrived in London. For Churchill, the launch was a calamitous radio address on June 5. Accustomed in wartime to "wander on as long as he liked," Churchill was appalled when the BBC asked that he limit himself to twenty minutes. His physician, Lord Moran, perceived the request as "a sign of the times." From then on, Churchill would "be treated like other men" and was sure to be unhappy about it. Gesturing at the microphone as though he were speaking before a vast audience instead of in a small study at Chequers, the prime minister warned that socialism in Britain would inevitably lead to political repression and Gestapo-like tactics. This heavy pounding was unpopular. As Julian Amery observed, "the vio-lence of his invective . . . seemed out of tune with the country's mood." The public found it hard to understand how Churchill could "turn and rend" former colleagues in his own coalition government.

Neither distaste for the prime minister's rhetoric nor displeasure with his warnings about the Russian menace prevented enthusiastic crowds from coming out to see him on his thousand-mile electoral tour. "If ever there existed any doubt about the continuing popularity of the Prime Minister among all classes in the country it was com-pletely dissipated today," said *The Times*, ". . . his reception was so tumultuous and overwhelming that his programme was seriously delayed." Repeatedly throngs closed in on his open car and progress slowed to nearly a walking pace. Throughout the war, the British had been comforted and inspired by Churchill's radio broadcasts. Many who came out to greet him that spring of 1945 had, by Macmillan's reckoning, "hardly seen him in person since the beginning of the war." By their cheers and cries of "Good old Winnie!" they seemed "to wish to thank him for what he had done for them."

Churchill felt keenly the "incongruity" between "party excitement and clamor" and his preoccupation with the matters that must be settled at his upcoming encounter with Stalin, a task that had been made no easier by a lack of strategic thinking on the American side. By turns he confessed to anxiety "about this damned election" and took comfort that no one who had witnessed his reception "could have any doubt as to the result." Still, gratitude for Churchill's vision and leadership during the war years was one thing, and a desire that he remain in office another. The crowds, apparently, made a definitive distinction between Churchill the savior of his country and Churchill the politician. Even as they applauded the former, they were about to dismiss the latter.

Jack had previously suggested to his sister that Billy Hartington's Britain would not survive the war, and her recounting of Billy's election experiences had confirmed him in that belief. In mid-June, he crossed the Atlantic with the expectation of writing its requiem. Ambassador Kennedy had been wrong in his prediction that Britain would be licked by Germany, but his warnings about the postwar rise of socialism seemed about to come spectacularly true. Even before Jack surveyed the scene, he had heard from Kick that none of their friends who were to stand as Conservatives in the election "really expect to get in as a terrific swing to the Left is expected." The young men who were just starting their political careers represented an old order that was on its way out.

Jack's first dispatch, under the eye-opening headline, "Churchill May Lose Election," told American readers to prepare for the unthinkable.

> Britishers will go to the polls on July 5th in the first general election in almost ten years, and there is a definite possibility that Prime Minister Winston Churchill and his Conservative party may be defeated. This may come as a surprise to most Americans, who feel Churchill is as indomitable at the polls as he was in war. However, Churchill is fighting a tide that is surging through Europe, washing away monarchies and conservative governments everywhere, and that tide flows powerfully in England. England is moving toward some form of socialism—if not in this election then surely at the next.

In future dispatches, Jack laid out for Americans some of the reasons for the sea change. He highlighted the British public's dismay at social and economic conditions under Tory rule; sentiment that, Churchill notwithstanding, the Conservative Party bore responsibility for the failed policy of appeasement; and the popular appeal of the Labour Party's emphasis on class struggle.

> The Conservatives offer Churchill, their conduct during the war and the firm belief that Socialism cannot work in England. Whether this platform will suffice to carry the Conservatives through cannot be said at this time. But what one can be sure of is that England will carry through in the next few years some economic changes that many people in America and England feel cannot be made without an important limitation on democratic government. By watching England we will have much to learn.

It was no secret among Jack's friends in London that he was observing the electioneering with an eye to his own political future. Every afternoon at about five, young aristocrats Jack had known before the war turned up for drinks and political talk in a suite at the Grosvenor House hotel which he shared with Patrick Lannan, an American friend also on assignment to cover the election. David Ormsby Gore came; so did William Douglas Home and Hugh Fraser. All were fascinated by what had become of the younger Kennedy brother. In 1939, Jack had been far less formidable and promising than Joe. When he returned in 1945 at the age of twenty-eight, a celebrated war hero and successful author, he had utterly confounded expectations.

Even David Ormsby Gore, who with Tony Rosslyn was closest to Jack, had judged him—as he had judged himself—not very serious-minded. After reading *Why England Slept*, David had revised his opinion. Jack wore his accomplishments lightly and still joked and laughed at his own expense. Nonetheless, David perceived that in the 1930s Jack must have been thinking about certain issues more deeply than even David, despite their many conversations, had suspected at the time.

David and Jack seamlessly reverted to the familiar repartee. As the political terra firma shifted beneath their feet and monuments crumbled on all sides, the friends had much to talk about. If there existed an even greater degree of intimacy than before the war, it was on account of Kick. David and Sissie had embraced Billy's widow, and they did the same with

Jack. He had become "another cousin"—no small matter in the Ormsby Gores' aristocratic world. David and Jack had always delighted in one another's company and shared a good many interests, but a "family connection" deepened the bond and permitted it to evolve.

When Jack first met David in 1938, they were both exceptionally bright fellows who, each for reasons of his own, seemed to lack the focus and drive of a Hugh Fraser or Joe Kennedy Junior. Seven years later they differed in important respects. Jack had repeatedly outdistanced Joe Junior when the latter was alive, and appeared confidently and resolutely to have taken up the role of family "prime runner" now that Joe was gone, untroubled by any sense that he would be acting "by proxy." David, in contrast, continued to lack ambition. His older brother had been dead for a decade, but David still did not feel at ease with the expectation that he assume the political career that, by family tradition, ought to have been Gerard's. What exactly did David want to do now that the war in Europe was over? Despite an abiding interest in politics, for the moment his answer was no different from the one he gave in 1938: "I haven't got a clue." He knew what he thought on a good many issues, but he had yet to make up his mind about himself. David believed it his duty to learn to manage the family estates, and to that end he planned to spend time with his father, Lord Harlech, who had been in South Africa for much of the war as UK High Commissioner. Though Andrew Cavendish, Hugh Fraser, David's brother-in-law Maurice Macmillan (married to his sister Katharine), and other close friends had chosen to stand for Parliament, David was not among them.

Moucher Devonshire had longed to meet Jack Kennedy since his letter about Billy. She and Elizabeth had come in to London to dine with him soon after his arrival, but his visit to Compton Place on June 29 was his first encounter with the duke. It was also his first chance to observe his sister in her role as a member of Billy's family. By then, remembered Anne Tree, Kick had been "completely amalgamated into our family—it had become her family." The duchess, whom Jack described in his diary as "a woman of intense personal charm and complete selflessness," treated Kick as though she was her own daughter, and for all the trouble the duke had caused early on it was evident that he loved her as well. The Devonshires welcomed Jack as though he—like David, who joined them at Compton Place—was part of the family. So, from then on, he would be. The duchess had been greatly moved when Jack in his letter compared Billy to Raymond Asquith, and now the talk abounded with references to those who had perished in the First World War. By speaking of such figures it was as if they were speaking of Billy.

There was also much talk of the upcoming election, and if Jack required confirmation of his own view that the aristocrats' time was up, he had it from a most improbable source. Billy's father, alone among the Conservatives Jack interviewed, predicted "an overwhelming victory" for Labour. The duke had been saying as much in the family circle for some time. He persisted in the belief that aristocratic political leadership was best, but the West Derbyshire by-election had convinced him that that had come to an end. In his diary afterward, Jack characterized his host as "an eighteenth-century story book Duke in his beliefs—if not in his appearance." Pursuing a familiar theme, he called him "an anachronism with hardly the adaptability necessary to meet the changing tides of the present day." Jack had previously said more or less the same about Billy. When Jack later referred to the duke as "a statesman of mediocre ability but outstanding integrity," David—like Billy, never shy about defending the values of his class—countered that it was by their contribution of integrity that figures such as the duke earned their keep.

Kick joined Jack in observing the electioneering, but soon it became too painful to watch Billy's group launch their political careers and she accepted Richard Wood's offer of sanctuary at Garrowby. Jack, as in the past, feasted on Churchill's speeches. He also spent several days observing Hugh Fraser, the Conservative candidate for the Staffordshire and Stone constituency, whom Evelyn Waugh dubbed "the hope of the Catholics" in the general election. Before the war, it had been natural for the most ambitious and promising young man in the set to pair off with Joe Junior. In 1945 Hugh regarded Jack as a compeer, and Jack, in turn, hoped to pick up "a pointer or two" by watching Hugh in action. Jack bombarded him with questions about speech construction and delivery, and the former Oxford Union president agreed to come to London after the poll to make a recording so that Jack might study his oratorical technique when he returned to America.

Churchill struck a confident pose to the end. "I feel it in my bones that you are going to send me back to power with a great majority," he declared in an eve-of-the-poll address. "The eyes of the world will be on us tomorrow. If we go down, then all the ninepins of Europe will go down with us." The electorate went to the polls on July 5, a beautiful warm cloudless day. Afterward, policemen carted off boxes in which the votes remained sealed for three weeks while the service vote came in from around the world. Jack had insisted to Hugh Fraser that Labour would triumph, but when next he addressed American newspaper readers, on July 6, he forecast a close vote that "the Conservatives should win this time."

In the meantime, Churchill departed to face Stalin. On July 15 he arrived in Berlin, where the palace of the German Crown Prince in nearby Potsdam provided the setting for the last of the wartime summits. Joint sessions of the Big Three were scheduled for July 17–August 2, with a forty-eight-hour intermission when Churchill would return to England on July 25 for the results of the poll. He had been in Germany for two days when he learned that the United States had successfully developed an atomic bomb to be used on Japan should its government refuse to surrender. "Here then was a speedy end to the Second World War," Churchill wrote in his war memoir, "and perhaps to much else besides." He welcomed the news of the powerful weapon that, as he saw it then, would "bring peace to the world" and, by making it unnecessary to "quell the Japanese resistance man by man and conquer the country yard by yard," miraculously "save the lives alike of friend and foe."

In the atomic bomb, which only the United States then possessed, Churchill seems also to have sensed something more. He told Lord Camrose, proprietor and editor in chief of the *Daily Telegraph*, that the bomb would permit America to "dominate the world for the next five years." If the American government could be so convinced, Churchill planned to use that power "to restrain the Russians" and to pressure them "to behave responsibly and decently in Europe." Whether Churchill, had he continued in office, really would have bullied Stalin with the bomb one cannot know. He did later record that he had planned "to come to grips with the Soviet government" at the end of the Potsdam conference, to have a "show-down" with Stalin on the matter of Russian expansionism. "That," as Geoffrey Best has written, "was how he looked back on it after five years of the Cold War. Was he really so determined at the time? . . . The world . . . was never to know what he would actually have done and to what effect."

The election was a landslide for Labour. Of the young aristocrats in Kick's orbit, only Hugh Fraser and Michael Astor won their seats. Andrew Cavendish, Robert Cecil, Julian Amery and the rest had been caught up in the Conservative rout. Evelyn Waugh, in his diary, called the outcome "a prodigious surprise" and Harold Nicolson wrote, "Nobody foresaw this at all." It was not merely the fact of the wartime leader's defeat that was astonishing, but its magnitude. Churchill might have waited to take his dismissal from the House of Commons, a tactic that would have permitted him to return to Potsdam. Instead, in view of the overwhelming verdict, he asked for an audience with the King that evening. He tendered his resignation at seven, and half an hour later the King received the Labour Party leader, Clement Attlee, and invited him to form a government. Directly, a statement dictated by Churchill was broadcast on the radio: "Immense responsibilities abroad and at home fall upon the new Government, and we must all hope they will be successful in bearing them."

After the results were in, Jack tried to explain the Conservative debacle to US readers:

> Looking back over the campaign, I think the Socialist victory is due chiefly to two factors. First, the general feeling that after 10 years of Conservative government, it was "time for a change." . . . Second and most important is the fact that living conditions in England have always been difficult for the workingman. . . . The Socialists promised that "things will be better for the workingman" and to the Socialist Party, just everyone is a workingman. Churchill, on the other hand, took the same line in this campaign that had been so successful in 1940. He offered them nothing but "toil and sweat" and said the Conservative Party would make no glib promises it could not keep. Unfortunately for the Conservatives, the people of this island have been on a diet of toil and sweat for the past five years. The British people will take that diet in an emergency but they feel the emergency has passed.

Not long afterward, Jack recorded in his diary a striking image of the impermanence of power. As part of a group led by his father's friend US Navy Secretary James Forrestal, Jack landed in Berlin just after the prime minister's aircraft had touched down. Jack looked on as Clement Attlee reviewed the same honor guard Churchill had reviewed "only a few days before."

Jack went on to set down a disturbing omen of the postwar world. "We drove immediately to Potsdam through miles of Russian soldiers. They were stationed on both sides of the road at about 40 yard intervals—green-hatted and green epauleted—Stalin's personal and picked guard. They looked rugged and tough, unsmiling but with perfect discipline. As the cars drove by, they presented arms." He continued, "One opinion here is that the Russians are never going to pull out of their zone of occupation but plan to make their part of Germany a Soviet Socialist Republic." That eventuality was precisely what Churchill had hoped to avert had he returned to the summit.

Following a bout of illness in London, Jack flew home on August 6, the day the first atomic bomb fell on Hiroshima. Two days later, the Soviets declared war on Japan. After a second atomic bomb was dropped on Nagasaki, the Japanese surrendered unconditionally on August 14. Kick celebrated with Hugh Fraser, Evelyn Waugh and other friends. There was mass revelry in London, where the paper-littered streets resembled, in Chips Channon's description, "a Victorian paperweight." The bomb seemed to many, as it had to Churchill, "a miracle of deliverance," but it also provoked much somber reflection. "I think for any intelligent young man living through the period '38–'45," David Ormsby Gore would say years afterward, ". . . unless you were moronic on the subject of politics, inevitably your mind turned to thinking of what ought to be done about this world. . . . Clearly, our elders and betters had not made a great success of conducting the affairs of the world. You had a strong feeling that somehow, after 1945, an effort must be made to see that human affairs were conducted in a more responsible and sensible way than they had in the past and that you couldn't afford another world war with nuclear weapons around."

The old questions had been put to rest, and the young men began to argue about new matters. Though only two of the friends had joined the Conservative benches in the House of Commons, several careers had been launched. Jack, in his role as observer, had shared in the excitement. Subsequent claims (largely emanating from Jack) that when he returned to America in 1945 he entered politics reluctantly

must have come as a surprise to those who had seen him study the electioneering in Britain unabashedly with an eye to his own future. Jack
and his British friends were on parallel tracks, and a sense that he and
they were starting in politics at roughly the same time added to the fun.

On August 25, Hugh Fraser telegraphed Hyannis Port to announce
his maiden speech in the Commons and to wish Jack well in his own
impending efforts. That fall Jack was to speak before the Kiwanis Club
of Worcester, Massachusetts, the Erie Society of Boston, the Boston
Association of Geography Teachers, the Lions Club of Attleboro,
Massachusetts, and numerous other groups. Though it had yet to be
determined precisely which elective office he would seek, the schedule
of appearances aimed to put John F. Kennedy on the political map in
Massachusetts. Capitalizing on his recent trip, he planned to make his
debut with remarks on the defeat of Churchill and the Conservative
Party, as well as on the war's aftermath elsewhere in Europe.

Elizabeth Cavendish recalled that during the war she and many
other young people had lived essentially in the moment: "There was no
past, there was no future, there was nothing—you lived for now." Their
outlook changed abruptly once peace was declared: "It was as if a curtain came down. Suddenly there was a future again, and you started to
move forward." That, Billy's sister explained, is how his widow dealt
with all she had lost in the war. Rather than dwell on the fact that, after
the interminable wait to marry, she and Billy had had only five weeks
together, Kick simply "turned it off and moved on." To do otherwise,
thought Elizabeth, who had grown "very, very, very" close to her, would
have been unendurable.

Hugh Fraser's arrival in the House of Commons did much to help
Kick start over. She joined him there often during what Michael Astor
called "an enthralling moment in history" when curiosity abounded
about Labour's new position of power. There was nothing of romance
in Kick's friendship with Hugh; she reveled in his boisterous, always
stimulating conversation. His successful candidacy at a moment of
broad Conservative disappointment seemed to confirm his reputation
as the most promising young man in their set. Kick spent much time
with him and with Michael Astor, Christopher Hollis, the new
Conservative member for Devizes, Tony Rosslyn, who sat in the Lords,
and Evelyn Waugh, who after one "enjoyable and drunken evening at

the House of Commons" claimed that "the widow Hartington" was in love with him. Waugh was partly right. Kick had fallen in love—with the world of Westminster.

She began to perceive the outlines of how she would live, what she would do. "She longed to play an important part in this country, which she would have done, I am quite convinced, if Billy hadn't been killed," explained Richard Holderness. "It sounds as if Kick were terribly ambitious for herself. I don't think she was. I think she was ambitious to play a part as great ladies of the past have played a part." She was by this time a very different person from the high-spirited teenager who had captivated London before the war. She spoke and carried herself more authoritatively, was altogether more knowledgeable and had a broader outlook. She could no longer expect to preside over the salon she and Billy had hoped to establish at Chatsworth. But, she told Richard, she believed she might play a similar role, on a much smaller scale, as a Conservative hostess in London.

Kick bought a charming little house in Smith Square so that friends would be able to stop by on their way to and from Parliament, a few minutes' walk away. By the time she returned to America for a visit in November 1945, she had found a new design for her life. Her father thought she ought to come back for good and could not comprehend what attracted her to war-scarred Britain. But Kick had determined to make her home there and create a useful new life for herself based on the dreams of political efficacy that Billy had imparted to her.

Jack, too, began to see his own future more clearly that fall. As he continued to address various organizations on "the European situation," he strove to overcome significant physical and vocal disadvantages. Kennedy, as Lord Moran once said of Churchill, was not "designed by nature" for the part of an orator. His boyish features and scrawny frame led to comments that he looked like a child dressed up in his father's clothing. His tense, harsh, high-pitched voice sounded at times as though he were pressing a finger against one side of his nose. He had a brutal way of using words, as well as a tendency to stumble over them, as if ideas came more quickly than speech. But when that happened he would flash the high-voltage smile that became his trademark, and more often than not people were charmed. Audiences responded to the strength and style of Jack's personality, and that gave him time to evolve as a speaker.

When Kick sat down to Thanksgiving dinner with the rest of the family, Jack was weighing a run for Congress. A seat in the House of Representatives for the Eleventh District had become vacant that month when its occupant, James Michael Curley, was elected mayor of Boston. The district was staunchly Democratic, so the party candidate was almost certain to win the following November. At this point Jack needed only to decide whether to participate in a June primary. An alternative was to seek the lieutenant governorship of Massachusetts on a ticket with his father's friend Maurice Tobin when Tobin ran for reelection. Joe Kennedy initially favored the latter prospect, but old-time Boston political manager Joe Kane, Kennedy's cousin, persuaded him it would be the riskier of the two.

Meanwhile, at a moment when Kennedy's opinion that all Americans (not just Kick) should turn their sights back to America seemed to reflect that of a majority of citizens, Churchill descended on the United States to argue the opposite position. Some six months had passed since the British had toppled their wartime leader when, on January 31, 1946, Churchill had a chance meeting with Joe Kennedy at the Hialeah racetrack in Florida—their first encounter since the war. In the past, the two huge influences in Jack's life had differed sharply, and they did so again now. By Kennedy's account, Churchill said, "You had a terrible time during the war; your losses were very great. I felt so sad for you and hope you received my messages." He added, "The world seems to be in frightful condition."

Kennedy agreed. "Yes. After all, what did we accomplish by this war?"

"Well, at least we have our lives," Churchill answered.

"Not all of us," Kennedy shot back.

Churchill's comment on the "frightful condition" of the world anticipated his landmark speech on March 5 at Westminster College in Fulton, Missouri—the first installment of a major body of thought that would at length change the way Jack Kennedy and a good many others looked at the problems of the postwar world. In his familiar role as a teller of unpleasant but necessary truths, Churchill planned to address what he saw as a new international crisis, and urge the need for the United States, however war-weary, to shoulder the responsibility that went with being the most powerful nation in the world and again to involve itself in European affairs. Kennedy's bitter riposte to

Churchill, presumably a reference to the loss of Joe Junior, suggested the prevailing isolationism that would have to be overcome if America were to be persuaded to cease disarming and to accept the necessity of further sacrifice.

The Fulton speech, titled "The Sinews of Peace," was Churchill's clarion call to confront the threat of Soviet expansionism. The concerns he had previously communicated to Roosevelt, Truman and others he now shared with the public. "From Stettin in the Baltic to Trieste in the Adriatic," he announced, "an iron curtain has descended across the Continent. Behind that line lie all the capitals of the ancient states of Central and Eastern Europe. Warsaw, Berlin, Prague, Vienna, Budapest, Belgrade, Bucharest, and Sofia, all these famous cities and the populations around them lie in what I must call the Soviet sphere, and all are subject in one form or another, not only to Soviet influence but to a very high and, in many cases, increasing measure of control from Moscow." This, Churchill warned, was not the liberated Europe which the western democracies had fought to establish. Nor did the altered map of Europe contain the essentials of a permanent peace. He stated as his "over-all strategic concept" a wish to avert another war, reminding listeners that he had seen the last war coming and had cried out to his countrymen in vain. He suggested that had the British acted in time the world might have been spared the horrors Hitler had let loose upon humanity; "there never was a war in all history easier to prevent by timely action," he said, than the one that had just been waged against Hitler. "It could have been prevented in my belief without the firing of a single shot . . . but no one would listen and one by one we were all sucked into the awful whirlpool."

Churchill urged an audience that included Harry Truman, who had invited him to Fulton, not to make the same mistake. In an echo of "The Locust Years," he warned that events must not be permitted to drift along until it was too late. He rejoiced that the atomic bomb was, for now, solely in American hands and noted that that advantage gave the Western democracies "a breathing space to set our house in order" before the other side caught up. Another war would be "incomparably more rigorous than that from which we have just been released. The dark ages may return, the Stone Age may return on the gleaming wings of science, and what might now shower immeasurable material blessings on mankind, may even bring about its total destruction."

He rejected the notion that a new war was either imminent or inevitable. In his view the Soviets did not want war, "only the fruits of war and the indefinite expansion of their power and doctrines." There was nothing the men in Moscow respected so much as strength, and nothing for which they had less respect than weakness. The Western democracies might still control their own fortunes if only, instead of disarming, they confronted Moscow with overwhelming strength, and if only Britain and the United States united in a "special relationship" to contain and defuse the Soviet menace. "Our difficulties and dangers will not be removed by closing our eyes to them," he said, as he had in the 1930s. "They will not be removed by mere waiting to see what happens; nor will they be removed by a policy of appeasement. What is needed is a settlement, and the longer this is delayed, the more difficult it will be and the greater our dangers will become."

The speech was at first widely reviled in the United States. Stalin, like Hitler before him, accused Churchill of being a "warmonger"—a coincidence that seemed to amuse Churchill as much as American resistance to his ideas vexed him. As evidenced by its title, Churchill's speech was anything but a call for war. Even as he warned the free world to recognize the Soviet peril, Churchill had begun to sketch the outlines of a path to peace. If only the dangers of war and tyranny could be removed, he argued, science and cooperation would be able to bring to the world "an expansion of material well-being beyond anything that has yet occurred in human experience." Mankind, he suggested, had a choice. Fifteen years later, a young American president would make a strikingly similar point in his inaugural address.

Kick had returned to London by the time her brother announced his candidacy for a seat in Congress, but the public annoyance the announcement provoked would have been familiar to her. It was reminiscent of the hostility Billy Hartington, another rich man's son, had faced when he stood for Parliament. Jack was widely attacked for his family wealth, his age and inexperience, his failure ever to have held public office and his lack of knowledge on the issues vital to the district he hoped to represent. Critics accused the Kennedys of seeking to buy the election and of insulting voters by a shameless effort to put forth a ludicrously unqualified candidate. "Congress seat for sale," the *East Boston Leader* mocked. "No experience necessary. Applicant must live in New York or Florida. Only millionaires need apply." What, it was asked, had Jack Kennedy ever done to merit people's votes? How could a "poor little rich kid" who had never had a regular job understand the needs of average people? Were they to elect him simply because he bore the names "Fitzgerald" and "Kennedy"? With the exception of the carpetbagger accusation, comparable charges had been heard in West Derbyshire in 1944.

One crucial difference was that Billy Hartington—and the fellows Jack had seen defeated in the 1945 general election—had, though young, represented an old order. Jack, from the first, emphatically presented himself as the voice of the new. Rather than downplay his age and political inexperience, he strove to make virtues of them. The young hero had returned from battle to help guide America into the postwar world—a world, he emphasized in his first radio address as a candidate, "capable of destroying itself" with the atomic bomb. In a year when the veterans' vote promised to be an important factor, it was no accident that young veterans formed the public face of the Kennedy campaign. The highly effective campaign motto, "The New Generation Offers a Leader," laid stress on youth and a fresh outlook; the old hand Joe Kane had come up with the slogan, yet he believed they ought to go only so far with what it suggested. He repeatedly prodded Jack to wear a hat, on the argument that otherwise he looked too young. Jack persisted in going hatless.

Though Joe Kennedy is supposed to have remarked that for all the money he spent on the campaign he could as easily have elected his chauffeur, Jack worked hard to dispel any notion that a congressional seat was being purchased on his behalf. Every week he spent a full day in each of the district's communities—Cambridge, Charlestown, Somerville, Brighton, East Boston and the wards of downtown Boston. He pumped workers' hands at factory entrances and on docks. He knocked on doors, visited barbershops and bars, post offices and pool halls—anywhere he could meet and talk to people. He concentrated in his remarks not on the foreign-policy questions that had long absorbed him but on employment, housing and other issues that mattered to voters.

Jack's oft-repeated insistence that he sought office only because Joe Junior could not blunted perceptions of the fierce ambition that had driven him repeatedly to surpass his older brother. Deadpan humor deflected hostility to a tycoon's son from Harvard. On one occasion, he entered an auditorium where Cambridge favorite son Mike Neville, one of ten candidates for the nomination, had begun to speak. "Here comes the opposition," Neville sneered. "Maybe he's going to talk to you about money and how to manage a bank." Jack shot back, "I'm not going to talk about banking, Mike. I'm going to talk about you." The audience exploded in laughter and so, unavoidably, did Neville. Another time, a moderator, by way of disparaging comment on Jack, introduced all the speakers but the last as somebody who had come up "the hard way." Jack remarked to the audience, "I seem to be the only person here tonight who did not come up the hard way. I hope you will not hold it against me." In the end the candidate of the "New Generation" won the primary with a decisive 42 percent of the vote.

In 1944, Kick had reported every detail of the West Derbyshire by-election to her family in Hyannis Port; two years later, she kept abreast of the minutiae of Jack's campaign. She studied newspaper clippings sent to London at her request, and talked incessantly of the Boston Democratic primary as though it were a political event of worldwide significance. As she wrote to Jack in the course of a week-long stay at Garrowby with Richard Wood and his parents, "there's nothing they don't know about the Eleventh Congressional District."

When Jack won the party nomination, Kick, half in earnest and half in jest, sighed that London's *Daily Telegraph* had failed to take note. "Everyone says you were so good in the election," she wrote to her brother, "and the outcome must have been a source of great satisfaction. . . . The folks here think you are madly pro-British so don't start destroying that illusion until I get my house fixed. The painters might just not like your attitude!" Kick knew well that, notwithstanding his passion for British history, culture and politics, Jack agreed with their father's opinion that her "second home" was a land in decline.

For her, it was a place to build a future. The interior of the house she put together in the political heart of London made a strong visual statement of what she expected that future to be like. The tiny drawing room was crammed with armchairs—"and nothing else!" exclaimed Jean Lloyd, recalling her own initial surprise and delight at the décor. What other furniture was necessary given Kick's intention to establish a Conservative salon? She had fashioned a setting where, among other friends, Hugh Fraser and David Ormsby Gore could argue "nose to nose," as they used to at Lady Astor's before the war. When Eunice Kennedy visited that fall, she reported to her parents that Lady Hartington (a name Kick now shared with Debo) held "a salon every night from 6 to 8 here at home." That, the younger sister emphasized, was about the only time one could be certain to find Kick at Smith Square. She was constantly out and about. She haunted Parliament. She dined with friends. She had invitations to all the best parties in London.

In addition to Nancy Astor, who continued to advise her following Billy's death, two other formidable women had taken Kick under their wing. Kick had met Mabell Airlie, Jean Lloyd's grandmother, in Scotland in 1938. After the war, Lady Airlie, who had herself been widowed at a young age, took a keen interest in Kick's reemergence on the London scene. Lady Melbourne's biographer was someone with whom Kick could discuss the "great ladies of the past" who fascinated and inspired her. Another of Kick's mentors during this time was Ava Anderson, the wife of Sir John Anderson, Churchill's chancellor of the exchequer. Kick had first met her at Compton Place in 1943, and later gasped at the audacity of Lady Anderson's "great plans" for her. Lady Anderson encouraged her to see herself as someone in a position to "straighten out Anglo-American relations" in the postwar world.

The previous July, Billy had written to say that should anything happen to him in the war he wanted Kick to start a new life as soon as she felt she could, and to marry again—"someone good & nice." In early 1946, it seemed as if that person might be Richard Wood. By his own account, he had fallen in love with her. He had long been her close friend and adviser, and Kick, who had once described him to her parents as one of the best and most understanding friends she had in the world, had begun to see that he might become something more. She and Richard were of different faiths, but, though deeply religious, he had no objection to his children being raised as Roman Catholics. He was not Lord Halifax's heir, and the particular problems Billy had faced as heir to the Duke of Devonshire simply did not exist for him. Richard brilliantly transcended his war injuries and managed to drive, ride, swim and shoot. He wanted a life in politics and understood that that was what Kick wanted as well. He was a brave, kind, learned man, and

her best friends in London—people Richard had known all his life—
would have been pleased had she married him.

Jean Lloyd was at Smith Square one evening when the phone rang
in the middle of dinner. Kick slipped off for a bit, and when she came
back said that it had been Peter.

"Is that Peter Cazalet?" Jean asked.

"No," Kick replied. "Peter Fitzwilliam."

Not a word more was said, but it was Jean's first inkling of Kick's
romantic involvement with an older, married aristocrat, who moved in
"rather a more racy group" than that of the young people she had
known since 1938.

No one, Elizabeth Cavendish remembered, any longer lived at quite
the level of opulence the 8th Earl Fitzwilliam enjoyed. In an era when
most of his class had had to retrench, Peter Fitzwilliam kept several vast
estates staffed with a full complement of servants in the event he
decided to appear without notice, at any hour, with a large party of
guests. A war hero, racehorse owner and sportsman, he was also an
inveterate gambler, philanderer and heavy drinker, whose marital status
meant that his liaison with Kick, ten years his junior, must be conducted in shadow. Fitzwilliam, who was characterized by Evelyn
Waugh, who had first known him in the Commandos, as "a king dandy
and scum," was an entirely different sort of man from Billy Hartington.

It seemed to Richard Wood that Kick, when she spoke of him,
focused rather improbably on the similarities. Fitzwilliam, like Billy, was
heir to great rank and property—far greater than any Richard or most
other suitors could offer. Fitzwilliam's ancestors had played a venerable
role in Whig history, and Kick, an ardent admirer of Whiggery, seemed
to believe she could recapture with her new lover some of the dreams and
ideals she had shared with Billy. But Fitzwilliam was interested in pleasure, not politics, and whatever Kick insisted to her friends and, perhaps,
to herself, his forebears' principles concerned him not at all.

Certain of Kick's friends, such as Fiona Gore, guessed that her
attraction to Fitzwilliam was mainly sexual. At the same time, as Richard
Wood perceived, Kick clung to the belief that were Fitzwilliam, as he
promised, to make her his wife, his wealth and position would allow
her to take up the "important part" in Britain she would have played
had Billy survived. Jean Lloyd viewed that belief as wishful thinking.

Elizabeth Cavendish, who remained tremendously protective of her brother's widow, wondered whether a marriage to a man of Fitzwilliam's habits had any chance of lasting. Billy had regarded the position of a great territorial noble as an opportunity to be useful. By contrast, Fitzwilliam's life was one of self-indulgence, and David and Sissie Ormsby Gore urged Kick to consider that such an existence might not make her happy. Kick was adamant that she planned to go forward with Fitzwilliam, but Elizabeth Cavendish thought she seemed "terrified" of her parents' reaction. It had been bad enough that Billy was a Protestant. Fitzwilliam had a wife and daughter and would have to obtain a divorce.

Jack was the first Kennedy to whom Kick spoke of her attachment. In September 1947 she presided over a house party at Lismore Castle in Ireland, which the Duke of Devonshire's late brother had left to Andrew. Hugh Fraser and Tony Rosslyn were present; so was Anthony Eden, who, having sat next to Kick at a dinner party for the Duke and Duchess of Windsor, had joined her list of cavaliers. Jack had handily won his race the previous November to represent the Eleventh District in the House of Representatives; in Britain on a congressional fact-finding mission, he was able to join the party at Lismore.

Jack had troubles of his own at the time, though, as was his nature, he made little of them. Before he left the United States he had seen a doctor on account of an alarming ulceration on his left calf and a peculiar tint to his skin, and had promised to put himself in a physician's care as soon as he arrived in Ireland. Instead, foolishly perhaps, it was not until after Kick's house party, nearly a month later, that he finally sought medical help in London. One of Kick's guests, Pamela Churchill, the former wife of the ex-prime minister's son Randolph, had accompanied Jack there. She knew him to have been unwell at Lismore, and when his blood pressure plummeted she called her own doctor, Sir Daniel Davis, who put him in the London Clinic. Davis diagnosed Addison's disease, a disturbance of the suprarenal glands known to produce low blood pressure, extreme weakness and a brownish skin cast, and said to Pamela Churchill, "That American friend of yours, he hasn't got a year to live." The congressman's office issued a press release that attributed his hospitalization to a recurrence of malaria contracted during the war, and a Kennedy family nurse, sent over from Boston, took Jack home by ocean liner in October. When the ship reached America, Jack's condition was so grave that a priest gave him the last rites before he was carried ashore on a stretcher.

Jack began treatment for Addison's at the Lahey Clinic and was much absent from the House of Representatives. Meanwhile, he kept his promise to Kick not to tell their parents about Fitzwilliam. As she prepared to go to America to make her difficult announcement, she asked Elizabeth Cavendish to travel with her. From the moment they arrived in February 1948 for a two-month visit, Kick hesitated to mention her fiancé's name to her parents, let alone reveal her marriage plans. Despite the tension, Kick and Elizabeth had great fun on the trip. They visited the Kennedys in Palm Beach, then went to Washington to stay with Jack and Eunice in Georgetown. The atmosphere was so lighthearted that, many years later, it seemed impossible to Elizabeth that Kick could have had any inkling that a physician had given Jack a year to live. The sole but unrelenting pressure had been the necessity for Kick to speak about Fitzwilliam to her parents. She waited until shortly before she and Elizabeth sailed for Europe on April 22. Rose's reaction was to vow to disown Kick if she married a divorced man. Joe Kennedy's silence implied that he agreed with his wife.

But, as Rose would write to Nancy Astor less than two months later, Kick was her father's "favorite of all the children." She hoped she might yet bring him round. He was going to be in Paris, and Kick persuaded him to meet her fiancé there on May 15. On May 13, Fitzwilliam and Kick were on a chartered plane en route to Cannes, where they planned to spend two nights, when they landed at Le Bourget Field outside Paris to refuel. They went into town to dine with friends, and returned to reports of heavy rain. The pilot urged them to wait, but Fitzwilliam demanded they take off immediately. It was a reckless decision for which they paid with their lives. Buffeted by a thunderstorm, the small aircraft crashed into the side of a mountain.

The next morning, Joe Kennedy was given the news at his hotel in Paris. In Washington, Jack, Eunice and Pat gathered in Georgetown. The gramophone played ceaselessly and, remembered Dinah Brand, who came by after she had heard the news, the atmosphere was characterized by "a grim, tragic restlessness." The first reports stated only that Lady Hartington had been killed, and there was some confusion as to whether that meant Kick or Debo. As it happened, Andrew and Debo had been spending the night at David and Jean Lloyd's house in London when Tom Egerton called with the news. Andrew set off at once on a round of newspaper proprietors to ensure that no mention was made in print of Kick's affair with a married man. Thanks to his influence, it was written only that she and Fitzwilliam had been passengers on the same plane. Joe Kennedy, meanwhile, had gone to the crash site, and once a positive identification had been made he collapsed in despair.

Kick's body was transported to Paris. At first, her father seemed to expect Jack to arrange to have her buried in the United States. On May 15, the day Joe was to have met Kick and her fiancé, he telegraphed Jack in Hyannis Port, "Would like to hear burial plans." When days passed and Jack came forth with no plan, Moucher Devonshire stepped in. Kick had had only five weeks of marriage to Billy, but her connection to the Devonshires had lasted a decade. If the Kennedys would agree, they proposed to bury Kick with other Cavendishes in the Edensor churchyard. In a gesture that expressed the depth of their love, the Devonshires offered to arrange a Roman Catholic funeral, the duke's perfervid anti-Catholicism notwithstanding.

Joe Kennedy assented, and Jack sent word that he would come over for the service on Thursday, May 20. He arrived in New York on the Tuesday in anticipation of flying to London that night. Such was his state of distraction that at the last minute he had been unable to locate his passport. His Washington office set to work to obtain an emergency replacement, which an assistant promised to rush to New York. Suddenly, however, Jack turned back, as if he could not bear to attend the funeral. With Rose and her remaining children notably missing, Kick's father was the sole Kennedy present at a requiem Mass arranged by the Devonshires.

The friends, young and old, that Kick had made in Britain since 1938 filled the Farm Street church in Mayfair, London. The suitors, the mentors, the habitués of her salon in Smith Square—all came to say goodbye. She had enchanted London with what a tribute printed in *The Times* that morning called her "infectious gaiety." When Randolph Churchill asked one young woman why she had come to a funeral in a hat so flamboyant and gay, the woman replied, "Because I thought it's exactly what Kick would have wanted me to wear!" There were also moments of ineffable sadness at the church service, as when Sissie

Ormsby Gore, as she passed the coffin, dropped to her knees, laid her head sideways on the casket and began to wail.

Afterward, many people boarded a special train for those who wished to be present at the cemetery. The duke had refused to move back to Chatsworth after the war because he strongly associated the house with Billy. When he, his wife and children, and other mourners arrived following the Mass, estate employees lined the road to Kick's grave. A committee of Roman Catholic priests made certain that everything was done as Rose Kennedy—though she had declined to attend her daughter's funeral—might have wished. The duchess herself had selected the epitaph for the gravestone. A wreath sent by Winston Churchill was among those adorning the casket. Joe Kennedy, by all accounts, cut a lonely, pathetic figure at the graveside. "He wore a crumpled blue suit," Debo Devonshire remembered, "and he was crumpled just like the suit. I never saw anything like it."

Back in America, Jack thought constantly, often uncontrollably, of Kick. He confided to Lem Billings that he might be at a congressional hearing when suddenly he would find himself musing on all he and Kick had done together and all the friends they had shared. In the beginning, Kick had been the one Kennedy to idolize Jack rather than young Joe. She had perceived—and prized—who Jack really was. She had been the favorite sister to whom he could tell everything because, as he said, he always knew she loved him. Kick had laughed and schemed with him; she had critiqued his writing and corrected his spelling; she had been an enthusiastic supporter of his early dreams of the presidency, even with young Joe still alive; she had encouraged him to join "nearly all the boys that you knew" in Britain in launching a political career; she had cheered his congressional campaign from afar. Now, overwhelmed by memories of her, Jack found it difficult to fall asleep at night. He told Lem that as soon as he shut his eyes he would start to think about all the nights when he and Kick had stayed up talking. In the aftermath of his sister's death, Jack found it easier to rest with a young woman at his side. Imagining her to be a friend of Kick's, he would picture the three of them having breakfast together the next morning, and the fantasy would help him to sleep.

CHAPTER NINE

A Divided Nature

S IX WEEKS AFTER KICK'S FUNERAL, JACK TURNED UP IN LONDON. He went to the house in Smith Square, which remained much as it had been when Kick had left for Cannes with Fitzwilliam. A pair of Hungarian maids, who had yet to move out, recounted Lady Harting-ton's last days. A senior partner with the firm Messrs Currey & Co., which had looked after the financial affairs of Devonshire dukes for as long as anyone could remember, laboriously detailed the affairs of her estate. Moucher Devonshire, who had urged Kick to accept that they must both settle down to facing life without the best ones, who would never come back, strove to console Jack. His graceful letter comparing her son to Raymond Asquith had moved the duchess so, and now she did what she could to assuage his pain at the loss of someone whom she herself had come to regard as a daughter. David Ormsby Gore recog-nized that the display of emotion was anathema to Jack, but anguish at the loss of a sister he persisted in calling his best friend was visible nonetheless. When the time came to travel to the Edensor village churchyard to see her grave, Jack simply could not bring himself to go.

A decade had passed since that first night at Nancy Astor's dinner dance during the 1938 Season, when Kick brought Jack into the circle of the aristocratic cousinhood. For Jack, friendships, conversations and much else crucial to his formation remained inextricably bound up with her. All told, he had spent a relatively short time in Britain, but it had been one of supreme excitement and intensity. Prior to 1938 Jack had merely read about how wars begin. In London he observed the spectacle of the prelude to the Second World War, saw the debates, noted the momentum and the miscalculations. He was present at "the closing of an age" and moved among young people who knew that their families' traditional way of life might be at an end and that they themselves might soon die. London on the eve of war had served as Jack's campus; in 1939, though seemingly more under his father's influence than ever, he had returned to Harvard with a stock of knowledge and ideas that he would draw on significantly in his political career. His experience in Britain had enabled him to write the senior honors thesis that later became a bestselling book—a book which had dramatically altered his position at home. By the time of Kick's death, one might have thought London had given him all it could. But when he came back in June 1948, he solidified ties of friendship and family that would lead to the critical next phase of the education of the future president.

Officially, Jack was in London in his capacity as a US congressman. A similar junket the previous year had been canceled when Jack fell ill after his stay at Lismore. This summer he traveled on behalf of the US House of Representatives Committee on Education and Labor to collect information on the "labor situation" in Britain, France and Italy. His travel companion was his former Harvard roommate Torby Macdonald, who worked for the National Labor Relations Board. All that spring there had been escalating anxiety in Europe over Soviet intentions, as well as rampant talk of "the possibilities of war." In Czechoslovakia there had been a brutal Communist takeover in February, and in Germany the Soviets had repeatedly interfered with Allied access to West Berlin. Though the city was divided into Western and Communist sectors, it lay entirely within the Soviet zone of occupation, and the Russians had begun to insist on the right to board all incoming trains. On June 24, 1948, in response to an American and British decision to merge their occupation zones and to introduce a new currency that would render an independent West Germany economically viable, Stalin severed road and rail access to Berlin. The Berlin blockade, as it would come to be known, began the day Jack and Torby sailed for Britain.

General Lucius Clay, the commander of US forces in Germany,

warned Washington that the fall of West Berlin, coming hard on the Communist takeover in Czechoslovakia, would mean West Germany was next. American troops in Germany, depleted in spite of Churchill's warnings, could hardly match Stalin's seventeen Red Army divisions in the Soviet zone. Once West Germany was incorporated into the Soviet bloc, Stalin's forces would be in a position to continue through Europe as far as the English Channel. In short, Berlin emerged as the decisive point of resistance. The Soviets must not be appeased there, for, given their superior conventional forces, should they undertake further aggression the only way to stop them would be to use the bomb.

Two days after the blockade began, Jack was halfway across the Atlantic when Churchill, in an address to a Conservative Party gathering, compared the crisis in Berlin to the critical episode of Munich in 1938. He made it clear that, in the present instance, all would hinge on how firmly the West responded to Stalin's challenge. With reference to the campaign of harassment that had culminated in the blockade, Churchill spoke in support of the position taken by the Labour government's foreign secretary Ernest Bevin that the Western powers were in Berlin "as of right" and that they intended to remain there. The Communist leadership in Moscow, Churchill declared, had clearly decided to try to drive the Allies out of Berlin and to turn the Russian zone of Germany into a Soviet satellite. The Allies, he argued, ought to have learned by now that there could be no safety in yielding to dictators, whether Nazi or Communist. The only hope of peace was to be strong and to make it plain that the free nations would defend themselves against aggression. "I cannot guarantee that even a firm and resolute course will ward off the dangers which now threaten us," Churchill went on, "but I am sure that such a course is not merely the best but the only chance of preventing a third war in which the most fearful agencies of destruction yet known to man will be used to the fullest extent."

The day Churchill, in speaking of the blockade, cited the precedent of Munich, President Truman launched the Berlin airlift, whereby American and British fliers, by provisioning West Berlin, asserted the Western powers' right to be there. The airlift was the opposite of Chamberlain's actions in 1938 when he yielded to the dictator's threats, and for Jack there would be an enormous amount to contemplate during the year that followed as the fliers triumphantly sustained the West Berliners until Stalin, in May 1949, finally gave up. But at the time Jack arrived in London, on June 29, 1948, it was still too early to predict the outcome. People questioned whether a city of two and a half million people could be sustained by air. They wondered whether Stalin would dare shoot down an American or British plane and what Washington's response would be if he did. They asked if Soviet actions in Berlin might be the prelude to a new world war. Three years after Jack wrote Churchill's political obituary in the Hearst newspapers, the talk in certain circles was nearly as much about Churchill renascent as about the airlift.

Despite the opinion of some that the seventy-three-year-old Churchill was too old and sick to lead the country again, he was predicting that he would return to office the following year, or in 1950, with a three-figure majority. The serialization in the *Daily Telegraph* of *The Gathering Storm*, the first volume of Churchill's Second World War memoir—a book Jack would consult, as well as cite, during his presidency—sparked discussion among the young men who had argued about *Arms and the Covenant* a decade before. Churchill's literary treatment of the road to war stimulated much impassioned talk of Munich and the other signal events they had all lived through, and also of how the lessons of those events could be applied to relations with the Soviets and especially to the unfolding Berlin crisis. Jack, as he had on first arriving in London in the 1930s, plunged into these discussions with relish.

Though Jack's congressional assignment concerned labor matters in Britain, France and Italy, he was determined to see the tense situation in Berlin for himself. He had taken a similar course in the 1930s when, in keeping with the credo that "the only way you can really know what is going on is to go to all the countries," he had wandered about Europe on the eve of war and interviewed diplomats, government officials and other possessors of privileged information. After a week in London, Jack headed to Paris and the Hôtel Georges V, where his father had been in residence when he learned of Kick's death. Meanwhile, though he had no foreign-policy role and no official reason to visit Berlin, he arranged to add Germany to his itinerary. A decade before, Jack's status as Ambassador Kennedy's son had gained him entrée to the places where history was being made. In 1948, he used his credentials as a congressman to schedule briefings by General Lucius Clay and other military figures in Berlin. Jack had been to Berlin in 1939 before the war, and again in 1945 just as the war ended. Berlin would preoccupy him during his presidency, and he would look back on the blockade as the Soviets' most direct challenge to the West until their effort to put missiles in Cuba in 1962.

Jack's 1948 visit to Berlin highlighted his frustration as a congressman who, for all his eagerness to win in 1946, had been disappointed by the reality of his first term in office. He had been palpably bored in Congress, where he was relegated to domestic matters that in truth held little interest for him. Typically, that summer, he had been assigned to labor issues when it was foreign-policy questions that fired his imagination—specifically the Berlin crisis and what it augured for future relations with the Soviets. His restlessness and dissatisfaction persisted when, shortly after his return from Europe, he was elected to a second term. Still, if Jack was not yet in a position to make world history, the Berlin visit at least suggested that the title of congressman might permit him to reclaim the front-row seat he had used to great advantage in the 1930s. There would be other trips abroad when, during congressional recesses, he would store up information and perspective in preparation for the moment when he finally had an opportunity to move on.

On his return from Europe in 1948 Jack continued to follow the drama of Churchill's political rebirth. Like many Americans in those years, he had yet to grasp how Churchill's mind was working as, in a series of speeches, the wartime leader staked out a new policy to deal with the Soviet threat. On October 9, 1948, prior to Jack's election to a second term, Churchill, in an address to the annual Conservative Party conference, propounded two ideas that would at length have a decisive impact on the young American. With reference to Czechoslovakia and Berlin, as well as to the dispersal of US forces after the war which left Soviet forces in Europe exceeding "those of all the western countries put together," Churchill underscored the importance of the fact that to date America alone had the bomb. "I hope you will give full consideration to my words," he urged. "I have not always been wrong. Nothing stands between Europe today and complete subjugation to Communist tyranny but the atomic bomb in American possession." He went on to warn that if the Soviets had dared to act as fiercely as they had of late, matters would surely be far worse when they too possessed atomic weapons. In a line which Jack would cite as a presidential contender, Churchill made his point by dramatically echoing Luke 23: "If these things are done in the green wood, what will be done in the dry?" Churchill had always believed in the wisdom of negotiating from a position of strength, and he now argued the necessity of pursuing a settlement while the West retained its advantage. He had suggested as much in "The Sinews of Peace," his Fulton speech, but now he laid particular stress on the point. The Western powers, he maintained, would be far more likely to attain "a lasting settlement, without bloodshed," if they put forth their just demands before the Soviets had atomic capability. Belying his image as a warmonger, Churchill's interest in the avoidance of bloodshed recalled his stance at the time of the Rhineland episode, when he also had sought to thwart the enemy without any spillage of blood.

The second idea articulated in Churchill's address to the Conservative Party conference of which Kennedy would later make crucial use would be followed up in speeches in March 1949, at a dinner given by Henry Luce in Churchill's honor in New York, and in May 1949, at the time of the signing of the Atlantic Alliance and the creation of NATO. Expanding on his already famous metaphor of an Iron Curtain, Churchill suggested some ways to infiltrate the closed Communist society and in so doing to subvert and ultimately vanquish Soviet power. In the 1930s he had elucidated the danger that contact with democracies posed to dictatorships, and now he argued that Russia's leaders dreaded the friendship of the free world as much as they did its hostility. If the Iron Curtain were lifted and free intercourse, commercial and cultural, permitted between people on both sides, the power of the leaders in Moscow would soon be broken. Therefore, every instance of contact and intermingling with the West posed a threat to them. Talk of atomic bombs and the leverage provided was the natural attention-grabber, but this speech, along with others like it, signaled that Churchill had begun to think about ways to defeat the Soviets not by weaponry, but by the friendly intercourse and breaking down of barriers he believed a closed society could not withstand.

Though on inauguration day, 1961, Kennedy's Soviet strategy would owe much to that idea, he would by that time have come a long way from his congressional days. He started out in public life as a gar-den-variety "strong" anti-Communist, with none of the flexibility and sophistication he would demonstrate in later years. In this, the young congressman's politics reflected a particular time and place. Despite the Fulton speech's negative reception in the United States in 1946, the notion that yesterday's co-belligerent had become today's adversary and that America needed to rearm was soon generally accepted. Were he to deliver the identical speech again, Churchill said in 1947, Americans would receive his harsh portrait of the Soviets as "a stream of tepid plat-itudes." When Churchill spoke at Fulton, Truman had been quick to distance himself from his remarks. Still, the president's subsequent actions to quell Soviet expansionism had been highly pleasing to Churchill. The Truman Doctrine acknowledged the need to combat efforts to impose Soviet totalitarianism; in expounding it, as the histo-rian Martin Gilbert has pointed out, Truman took over "the role which Churchill had urged upon him a year earlier" at Fulton. The Berlin air-lift confirmed American readiness again to come to Europe's defense, and in October 1948 Churchill rejoiced that the United States was "rearming on a large scale." But that was only part of what Churchill had urged in "The Sinews of Peace," which would long be misinter-preted as solely a call to arms. Unlike his warnings about the Soviets, Churchill's call for negotiations and a peaceful settlement had made lit-tle impact in America. Once the nation had geared up to confront the threat of Communist domination, most Americans were in no mood to entertain the desirability of a settlement and contact. In London, anxi-ety about a revival of American isolationism was soon replaced by con-cern about the mounting anti-Communist fervor in the United States and about the possibility that a lack of flexibility in the American posi-tion might lead to a third world war.

Jack Kennedy, even as he continued to read and ponder, focused on one part of Churchill's argument in "The Sinews of Peace" to the exclu-sion of the other. He had learned well the lessons of the 1930s. He was supremely alert to the Soviet peril and a vocal proponent of rearma-ment; he supported the Truman Doctrine and the Marshall Plan. But at this point in his public life he remained among the many whom Churchill targeted in arguing that it was not the West that ought to feel threatened by the prospect of contact, but the Soviets.

Jack's presentation to an informal gathering of students and faculty at Harvard University on November 10, 1950, three days after his election to a third term in Congress, encapsulated his public posture at a time when much of America, far from viewing contact as a way to undermine Soviet power, had grown obsessed with the specter of Communist infiltration at high levels of the US government. That year Wisconsin senator Joseph McCarthy had claimed that Communists at the State Department directed US foreign policy. According to one person present, Jack suggested that he "rather respected McCarthy," that he believed he "knew Joe pretty well," and that McCarthy "may have something." At a moment when McCarthy was portraying Democrats, as a group, as soft on Communism, Jack maintained that "not enough" was being done about "Communists in government." Massachusetts Democrats, many of them Catholic, had a reputation for being more militantly anti-Communist than Republicans, and Jack pointed out that his views reflected those of his constituents, who wished to see "more done" about Communism.

In the aftermath of midterm elections characterized—notably in Richard Nixon's vicious campaign against Helen Gahagan Douglas in California—by a good deal of red-baiting, Jack assured listeners at his alma mater that he was "personally very happy" that Douglas had been defeated in her Senate campaign. Speaking of matters that ignited fierce passions on all sides, Jack employed the cool, detached style he had favored since his Harvard thesis. He created the impression that "his reasons for these views were not so much ideological as a matter of casual intuitive feeling." He professed to like McCarthy "on a personal basis" and stated that Helen Gahagan Douglas was "not the sort of person I like working with on committees."

The latter statement was significant: Jack left no doubt in his Harvard talk that he hoped to launch a Senate bid of his own in 1952. His ambition was no particular secret, as he had regularly devoted weekends to appearances before virtually any local group in Massachusetts that would have him. What most people did not know was the part health considerations played in driving him on to the Senate. Jack had known since 1947 that he had Addison's disease, though the nature of his illness had been kept secret lest it hobble him politically. While he had disproved the doctor's prediction to Pamela Churchill that he had less than a year to live, he remained at high risk of infection and deadly crises. Since the loss of Kick, following as it had on young Joe's demise, Jack had struck friends as being preoccupied with death, and was known to say in private conversation that he did not expect to live "more than ten years or so." Far from indulging in self-pity, however, he seemed, like Asquith and the other First World War heroes he revered, to make a point of smiling at fate. He spoke openly of his intention to take his pleasures in life while he could, but it was also the case that a time lock lent urgency to his determination to seek higher office.

Jack was intent that the upcoming term in Congress would be his last. In December 1950 he spotted an opportunity to attract national press attention and to bolster his credibility on foreign policy. Truman's plan to send additional US forces to Europe to serve in NATO under its newly appointed supreme commander, General Dwight D. Eisenhower, had provoked vehement protests from those who regarded it as folly to commit troops when Europe was officially at peace and the United States was fighting in Korea. Joe Kennedy, again draping himself in the isolationist banner, argued that the United States should pull out of Europe altogether and that if Europe went Communist as a consequence, so be it. America's "only real hope," the elder Kennedy maintained, was "to keep Russia, if she chooses to march, on the other side of the Atlantic." To deflect criticism by former president Herbert Hoover and Senator Robert Taft that the United States ought not accept the burden of the defense of Europe when the Europeans themselves were unwilling to bear their fair share, Eisenhower planned an eleven-capital tour in January 1951 to win assurances that Europe's leaders intended to do their part. A decade previously, Jack had made rearmament a signature issue with the publication of *Why England Slept,* and he now perceived in Eisenhower's trip a chance to propel himself into the national debate.

Though no one asked him to go, Jack announced plans of his own to visit Europe. According to one report, "Congressman Kennedy explained that any decision by Congress to send troops to Europe will depend in large measure on what effort Europe makes to rearm itself. And to discover just how far these various nations plan to go, Kennedy plans to have clear-cut personal observations which he will secure by

personal interviews with the heads of countries involved." Even before
he left home, Jack benefited immeasurably from attaching himself, if
only in the public mind, to Eisenhower's well-publicized tour. Through
radio interviews and cleverly orchestrated press releases describing his
encounters with European dignitaries, Jack claimed a prominent part
in the news coverage. Reports set Kennedy's remarks on the defense of
Europe alongside those of the NATO Supreme Commander. The effect
was to lend an aura of weight and significance to all that the young
Senate hopeful had to say.

On January 8, 1951, Jack arrived in London. He was soon comparing notes with British friends about the progress of their respective
careers in politics. Andrew, David and others from their group had
stood for Parliament in the 1950 general election, with varying results.
Churchill's hopes for a Conservative victory that would return him to
Number 10 had been disappointed, but, in contrast to 1945, the
Labour majority was a slender one.

Like Jack, Andrew felt the pressure of time in his political life.
Whereas Jack's horizons were limited by health concerns, Andrew's
were defined by the requirement that on his father's death he resign
from the Commons to take his seat in the House of Lords. Given that
in 1950 the duke was only fifty-five and apparently in robust health,
Andrew had seemed likely to have a good many years to pursue the
career on which, before Billy's death, he had trained his sights. He had
been defeated in 1945 in Chesterfield, where he and Debo had been
spat upon and otherwise harassed. Unable to get adopted for a safe
Tory seat, Andrew fought the battle anew in Chesterfield, this time as
the Marquess of Hartington (a courtesy title which did not give him a
seat in the Lords). The constituency's boundaries had been redrawn in
the interim, making it even more of a Labour stronghold. Although he
was defeated again in 1950, Andrew, intent on a political career, had
the consolation that, in view of Labour's narrow majority, there was
likely to be another election before long. Without a trace of the
ambivalence that had long characterized his cousin David Ormsby
Gore, Andrew was resolved that when the opportunity presented itself
he would try again.

Uncertain whether he was quite up to the political career that would
have come naturally to his older brother, David Ormsby Gore had cho-

sen to sit out the 1945 general election, preferring to return to school to study business and agriculture, and learn to oversee the family dairy farms in Shropshire. He knew that he would like to get into politics someday, but despite also being heir to a peerage, he altogether lacked Andrew's sense of urgency. While Andrew was nursing the constituency at Chesterfield in anticipation of the 1950 election, David merely put his name on the list of Conservative candidates, with no real intention of going to Parliament. He had it in mind to stand for a "fairly hopeless seat" and thereby to acquire seasoning in anticipation of trying again later. So he was disconcerted when his local Conservative Association asked if he would be their candidate for the borough of Oswestry in Shropshire, which traditionally voted Conservative. He allowed his name to go forward, though he "secretly rather hoped" that someone else would be selected so that he could revert to his original plan. Partly because of his status as the son of the preeminent local family and partly because of his deep familiarity with the agricultural matters of particular concern to the constituency, the committee picked him. He received the news with mingled emotions.

For all his initial uncertainty, David, at thirty-one, had found a niche in the Commons by the time Jack arrived in London in January 1951. Though he never warmed to the demands of public speaking, he loved to sit on the back benches and listen to the debates—particularly when Churchill was the speaker. It was less Churchill's maneuvers as party leader that fascinated David than his ideas about the problems of the postwar world. Still, though foreign policy had long been David's abiding interest, he started out in public life with a concentration on finance and the budget, and it was in this capacity that he came into the orbit of Selwyn Lloyd, the Opposition spokesman on finance. David had discovered a political mentor, and in ways no one could have imagined in 1951 the connection would be critically important to Jack as, through conversation and the exchange of ideas, his and David's careers intertwined. Much that David acquired by an association with Selwyn Lloyd would prove essential not only to his own political future, but to Jack's. As president, Jack would make it possible for David to bring certain of the things he cared about to fruition; it was also the case that, without David, Jack might never have emerged as the leader he finally became.

As for Andrew, by the time of Jack's 1951 visit, the 10th Duke of Devonshire's sudden death on November 26, 1950, had ruled out the possibility of another attempt at the House of Commons. Andrew was now the 11th Duke, with a seat in the House of Lords. David, Jack and the others were just starting their lives in politics when Andrew found his dreams of a political career suddenly at an end. Because of a change in the inheritance laws under Labour, the 10th Duke had made complicated legal arrangements whereby, so long as he lived until March 1951, his son could inherit without having to pay death duties. The duke's death fourteen weeks too early forced his heir to immerse himself in efforts to preserve as much as possible of the family estates and fortune. The top rate of death duties was 80 percent, and Andrew faced the need to raise millions of pounds. He might have sold off everything and lived comfortably free from debt, but he saw it as his duty to fulfill, however imperfectly, his father's "overwhelming ambition" to keep the estates and fortune intact.

Besides seeing old friends in London, Jack interviewed government officials about rearmament. He continued his research in France, Italy, West Germany, Yugoslavia and Spain. On his return to the United States his comments on national radio and in congressional testimony were consistently linked to Eisenhower's, whose spotlight, much to the latter's irritation, he managed to share. "These reports by General Eisenhower and Kennedy are regarded as of history-making importance and upon them may depend to a considerable extent, future courses in US action on the arming of Western Europe program," declared an announcer at the Mutual–Yankee Networks, on which both the older man and the younger were scheduled to speak during the first week of February. Jack emphasized that the Europeans must accept their fair share of the burden of defense efforts. "If Europe is to be saved," he said in the February 6 broadcast, "Europe must commence to make the sacrifices sufficient for that purpose and commensurate with the danger that threatens to engulf her peoples. The plain and brutal fact today is that Europe is not making these sacrifices."

He delivered a similar message before the Senate Foreign Relations Committee on February 22. While he was in favor of the dispatch of four American divisions, he believed that no further troops ought to be sent until the Europeans committed thirty-six divisions to Eisenhower's command. Acknowledging that the Truman administration opposed any such restrictions by Congress, Jack pointed out that, of all the Western European nations, only Great Britain had so far made an effort comparable to that of the United States. The rearmament of Europe, he warned, must not become "simply an American enterprise." Asked about his father's isolationism, Jack noted that to Ambassador Kennedy, as to a great many other Americans, the creation of a strong, unified European military force seemed a nearly hopeless enterprise. Nonetheless, Jack declared that after looking at the situation "as cold-bloodedly as I can," he was convinced the risk ought to be taken. "That is my position," Jack said crisply. "I think you should ask my father directly as to his position."

Pleased with the jolt of publicity provided by his European visit, Jack undertook another fact-finding tour later the same year, this time to the Far and Middle East. But in Okinawa, Japan, an Addisonian crisis landed him in a military hospital. His temperature spiked above 106 degrees, and doctors feared he might not survive. He recovered quickly, but the incident highlighted the danger of such episodes and served as a reminder, if any had been necessary, of how little time he might have to chase his political dreams. On his return to the United States in November 1951, though there was less public attention to be had without the tie-in to Eisenhower, Jack claimed the spotlight by speaking out on topics such as his opposition to US support of French colonial forces as they struggled against a nationalist uprising in Indochina. America, Kennedy argued, ought to take no part in France's "desperate effort . . . to hang on to the remnants of empire."

Jack was in the Far East when a new general election in Britain—the second in eighteen months—returned Churchill and the Conservative Party to power with a small majority. Before the poll, Churchill had enunciated the "double-barreled policy" he hoped to implement as postwar prime minister. In a radio address on October 8, he stressed that, although he was pleased by US-led rearmament efforts in conjunction with the Korean conflict, rearmament was "only half a policy." Were he to become prime minister again, he intended to execute the vital second part of his program for dealing with the Russians—the part America, caught up in the maelstrom of McCarthyism, had failed to grasp. Churchill explained that he had urged the West to make itself strong in order that it might be in a position to press for "a reasonable and lasting" settlement. In words that would undergird presidential policy in the Kennedy years, Churchill declared, "I do not hold that we should rearm in order to fight. I hold that we should rearm in order to parley."

No sooner had the electorate sent Churchill back to Number 10, on October 26, 1951, than he seized the opportunity to put theory into practice. The Polish ambassador had suggested that the Soviet Union might be amenable to informal settlement discussions, and the sixth annual UN General Assembly, held in Paris that November, emerged as Churchill's first chance as postwar prime minister to parley with the Communists. Anthony Eden, now again foreign secretary, was to head the British delegation, but responsibility for much of the day-to-day work went to Selwyn Lloyd, newly appointed minister of state in the Foreign Office. With the General Assembly looming, Lloyd needed to appoint a parliamentary private secretary immediately. He chose David Ormsby Gore. David underwent what amounted to a crash course in Churchill's Soviet policy, a fundamental tenet of which was that, rather than try to settle everything at once, both sides would do well to begin with limited areas of dispute where agreement seemed possible.

It soon became evident that the Soviets were far from interested in settlement talks, informal or otherwise. Nor did US Secretary of State Dean Acheson seem in any mood for conciliation. Early on, Acheson delivered an address whose "harshness," the *New York Times* reported, prompted expressions of regret from several Western European delegates. In turn, Stalin's foreign minister, Andrei Vishinsky, was mocking and confrontational. In a role that would often fall to the British, Eden endeavored to bring the temperature down.

At Selwyn Lloyd's side, David began to rack up experience that would later serve him—and Jack—well. He saw for himself the fierce resistance to negotiations, from both the Soviets and the Americans, that would have to be overcome in order to avert another world war. He became attuned to nuances of what Churchill perceived as the "dominating problem" of Germany. Disarmament was one of the main items on the agenda, the Soviets having acquired the bomb two years previously, and David plunged headlong into a complicated subject that would emerge as the focus of his political life. Eden delivered the opening remarks on disarmament, but Lloyd represented Britain at subsequent sessions where, in the Soviets' adamant refusal of demands for verification and inspections, David had a first glimpse of the Communist leaders' determination to keep their society closed.

David had launched his political career three years after Jack, but while the latter was still hoping to place himself in a position where he might concentrate on foreign policy, David, with minimal preparation, was already tackling issues that would come to dominate both men's careers. For David, postwar relations with the Soviets were no longer merely a theoretical matter. In Paris they became a reality grounded in experience. Due to his ongoing work with Selwyn Lloyd as well as to his personal association with Harold Macmillan, now minister of housing and local government, David continued to benefit from a close-up view of the evolution of Churchill's Soviet strategy. Macmillan regarded Churchill, in whose Cabinet he served, as "the great figure and the greatest inspiration of my life," and Michael Astor dubbed Macmillan Churchill's "intellectual heir." Macmillan was the father-in-law of David's sister Katharine, and at family gatherings he and David would move off to a corner of the room and spend the better part of the evening deep in conversations that proved central to the younger man's political education. By the time David returned to Paris with Selwyn Lloyd in January 1952 for further UN meetings and disarmament talks, he was on his way to becoming the man Macmillan, as prime minister, would appoint ambassador to Washington.

Jack, by contrast, was still far from the man who, within eight years, would be elected president. He had not yet begun to assemble the core policy or even certain of the fundamental beliefs with which he would run for the White House. That policy would owe much to Churchill, but on January 17, 1952, as he watched the prime minister address a joint session of Congress, Jack, persuaded though he long had been of the need to rearm, had yet to make the imaginative leap to the essential second part of Churchill's policy.

On his first US visit as postwar prime minister, Churchill evoked a changed world in which "former allies have becomes foes" and "former foes have become allies." He lauded the "vast process" of US rearmament as a deterrent to a third world war, and expressed hope that "a new mood" would soon reign behind the Iron Curtain and that the removal of the threat of war would permit "the great forward bound in progress and prosperity" for which mankind longed. Speaking of politics in Britain by way of an oblique comment on circumstances in the United States, Churchill addressed the need to separate, as far as possible, "what is done to make a party win" from "what is done to make the nation live and serve high causes." He was hinting at what he had stated explicitly on previous occasions: the need for a more flexible approach to the Soviets. Given the political climate in the United States, it was an approach likely to carry enormous risks to anyone in public life who embraced it. In 1952, Jack, who since boyhood had been tracking Churchill's speeches and writings, judged the seventy-seven-year-old Churchill's eloquence "undimmed." His deep engagement with Churchill's ideas about Soviet relations, however, was yet to come.

At the time, Jack was preparing to run against popular three-time Massachusetts senator Henry Cabot Lodge Jr. Joe Kennedy declared that when his son had beaten Lodge he would have beaten the best, so why try for anything less? It would be no greater challenge to be elected president, the elder Kennedy said, than to defeat Lodge. Jack, by his travels to every corner of the state, had spent the past few years building name recognition and good will. Now, Joe Kennedy pumped so much money into the campaign that, a wag remarked at the time, one could live the rest of one's life on his billboard budget alone. Bobby Kennedy built and oversaw a well-oiled statewide campaign machine. Other Kennedys knocked on doors, hosted parties and teas, gave speeches and made television appearances on the candidate's behalf. Lodge had the reputation of a moderate, and some commentators saw him as the Republican Party's best chance to "emerge from the depths of McCarthyist Neanderthalism." The Kennedy campaign perceived a significant political vulnerability in Lodge's lack of appeal to conservative Republicans, and actively chased the votes of those who, having backed Robert Taft for their party's presidential nomination, resented Lodge's vehement support for Eisenhower. A vocal Republicans-for-Kennedy movement arose in Massachusetts. The movement, composed in large part of disgruntled Taftians, seemed at times less pro-Kennedy than anti-Lodge, but it was founded on the belief that the Democrat was the stauncher anti-Communist.

Audiences warmed to Jack's attractive appearance, charming manner and flashes of humor. One published account on the eve of the election described him as "an Irishman of family—and breeding—rare in a state where almost all Democratic leaders are self-made, one-generation and often crude in manner and appearance." When the "first Irish Brahmin," as Kennedy was called, debated Lodge, the "Yankee blue blood," it was not the discussion of issues that seemed to absorb spectators so much as the fact that the challenger came off as sharper and more confident. The wisdom inside the Kennedy camp was that, in the words of aides Kenny O'Donnell and Dave Powers, "generally speaking the voters in that election were not interested in issues. Kennedy won on his personality." In the end, Eisenhower vanquished Democratic presidential candidate Adlai Stevenson, but despite the landslide the thirty-five-year-old Kennedy bested Lodge by more than seventy thousand votes.

Jack had served three terms in Congress during a time of intense hostility and perilous confrontation between East and West. These had been the years of the brutal Communist takeover in Czechoslovakia, of the Berlin blockade, and of the Korean War. In the Soviet Union, Stalin's rule continued, which meant that there had been little opportunity for any significant erosion of barriers. In the United States, the period had been one of harsh anti-Communist sentiment and feverish anxiety about domestic subversion. The national mood had been far from receptive to any suggestion of the desirability of negotiations with the Soviets. During most of Jack's time in the House, Churchill had been out of office; it was only when he again became prime minister, as Jack was planning his Senate campaign, that he finally had an opportunity to try to shift the Western agenda to the second part of his double-barreled policy. Jack, as it happened, came to the Senate at a time of enormous change in the postwar world. Two months after he was sworn in, Stalin died on March 5, 1953—an event, Churchill perceived, with vast implications for East–West relations and the transformation of Soviet society.

Not only was Stalin gone, but there was a new president in the White House. Churchill had enjoyed a warm personal relationship with Eisenhower during the war, and he hoped that would help him persuade Eisenhower to move swiftly and forcefully to take full advantage of the altered situation in Moscow. Stalin was replaced with a collective leadership comprising Chairman of the Council of Ministers Georgi Malenkov, First Secretary of the Communist Party Nikita Khrushchev, Foreign Minister Vyacheslav Molotov, Minister of Defense Marshal Nikolai Bulganin and Minister of State for Security Lavrenti Beria. Churchill had no illusion that the new group would bring down the Iron Curtain, but he did hope that in Stalin's absence Russia would allow itself to become a little less isolated and that there would be fresh opportunities for the infiltration he believed fatal to Communism. Six days after Stalin died, Churchill wrote to Eisenhower to suggest a joint approach to the new leadership. In a subsequent letter, he cited the maxim that the most dangerous moment for evil governments is when they begin to reform, and he argued that the present moment might prove such an occasion. On May 11, 1953, Churchill spoke in the Commons of his sense of a change of mood at the Kremlin. Urging that a conference of the leading powers be convened without delay, he argued that rather than concentrate on points of dispute, East and West ought to look for areas where they might actually agree. In words Kennedy would later take to heart, Churchill said, "It would I think be a mistake to assume that nothing can be settled with Soviet Russia until everything is settled. . . . Piecemeal solutions should not be disdained or improvidently put aside." The point was to look for areas of common interest and then to go on from there, one agreement at a time—but first they had to make a start.

Churchill's efforts to seize the moment were interrupted when he suffered a stroke the following month. He fought bravely and secretly to recover, telling his physician that he did not wish to be "kicked out" of office till he had had "a shot at settling this Russian business." Against considerable odds he was soon back on his feet, and in an address to the Commons on November 3, 1953, he cautioned that no one should think that an all-encompassing settlement with the Soviets was at hand. "Time will undoubtedly be needed—more time than some of us here are likely to see," he declared poignantly. He argued that the only sure guide to the actions of mighty governments was an estimate of what they would consider to be their own interests; it seemed likely that the present Soviet leadership sought internal prosperity, not another major war. He touched on a cherished theme when he spoke of the goals that, in the event of a settlement, both sides might wish to pursue: "There is no doubt that if the human race are to have their dearest wish and to be free from the dread of mass destruction, they could have, as an alternative, what many of them might prefer, namely, the swiftest expansion of material well-being that has ever been within their reach, or even within their dreams." In a sentiment Kennedy would echo on his inauguration day, Churchill posited that in a world transformed by the existence of all-annihilating weapons, humanity faced a choice. "We, and all nations, stand, at this hour in human history, before the portals of supreme catastrophe and of measureless reward."

To Churchill's exasperation, Eisenhower did not regard Stalin's demise or the advent of all-annihilating weapons as turning points. When the president and the prime minister conferred in Bermuda in December 1953, it became evident that Eisenhower saw the world as no different from what it had been previously. Face to face with the president, Churchill proposed that the West approach the new Soviet leaders with a show of military strength on the one hand and an offer of friendship on the other. He touted the desirability of contact and other forms of infiltration. Eisenhower responded with what John Colville, Churchill's private secretary, described in his diary as "a short, very violent statement, in the coarsest terms." The president expressed skepticism of Churchill's claim that the mood in Moscow had changed. Russia, Eisenhower insisted, "was a woman of the streets and whether her dress was new, or just the old one patched, it was certainly the same whore underneath." The United States intended "to drive her off her present 'beat' into the back streets." Adding to the alarm on the British side was Eisenhower's statement to Colville that whereas Churchill regarded atomic weapons as "something new and terrible," he viewed them as "just the latest improvement in military weapons." Eisenhower suggested that there was in fact "no distinction between 'conventional weapons' and atomic weapons" and that all weapons in due course became conventional.

Eisenhower disagreed with Churchill about the significance of Stalin's death and of the new weaponry, but the monumental changes wrought would be central to foreign policy during his successor's presidency. Churchill understood that the hydrogen bomb, first exploded by the United States in 1952, had transported mankind into dimensions previously confined to the realm of the imagination. It was no longer a question of entire cities being destroyed, but of all civilization. War was no longer an option for rational men. Churchill saw the extreme, militant form of anti-Communism that prevailed in the United States in the 1950s as an ironic reflection of the lamentable absence of strategic thinking that had minimized the Soviet threat at the close of the war. With a torrent of words written and spoken, he struggled in vain to convince Eisenhower that Communism should be outmaneuvered by contact rather than by confrontation.

Not unconnected to Churchill's thoughts about Stalin and the bomb was the tremendous hope invested in the coronation of Queen Elizabeth in June 1953, "at a time," the prime minister declared, "when a tormented mankind stands poised between world catastrophe and a golden age." Among the American journalists in London to cover the crowning of the young Queen was Jacqueline Bouvier. Jackie, as she was known, was on assignment for the *Washington Times–Herald*, the newspaper where Kick had worked during the war. Curiously, Joe Kennedy's friend Arthur Krock had recommended both Kick and Jackie for their positions at the paper; editor Frank Waldrop had hired both; and journalist John White had dated them both as well. Since the previous summer Jack Kennedy had been dating Jackie, who was twelve years his junior, and in January the newly elected senator had escorted her to Eisenhower's inaugural ball. In important ways, Jack and Jackie were kindred spirits. As children, both had found solace and sustenance in books, and both had subsequently invented themselves out of their reading. Both were preoccupied with history, he with that of Britain and she with France. Both had a special fascination with the eighteenth century, and both enjoyed memorizing the other's favorite poems. They gossiped and bantered, and he prized her sense of humor, which was by turns fey and corrosive.

When Jackie was a girl, her mother, Janet Bouvier, had warned that she had better hide her love of books and learning if she hoped to capture a husband. Janet had also drummed into Jackie, who had inherited her father's broad square face, wide-set eyes, and dark coloring, that she lacked physical allure. Jackie's parents had separated for the first time in 1936 when Jackie was seven, and they divorced three years later. From then on, Janet seemed to vent her rage on Jackie, who by her very appearance constantly brought her philandering, hard-drinking stock-broker father to mind. Jackie reveled in the attentions of handsome Jack Kennedy. At least in the beginning, his reputation as a ladies' man was an advantage in the eyes of his future wife, for it meant that her mother had been wrong about her unattractiveness.

Jack had turned thirty-six in May and, given his political aspira-tions, the time had clearly come for him to marry. Even so, his courtship of Jackie, if it could really be called that, remained to her frustration an intermittent one. By the spring of 1953 a marriage pro-posal had yet to materialize, and Jackie, who knew full well that Jack saw many other women, had reason to doubt that it ever would. That changed on her return from London with a suitcase stuffed full of books on British history and politics that he had asked her to find. Jack had called her there frequently, and, both on the telephone and in let-ters, she had regaled him with tales of the coronation celebration in which Andrew and Debo Devonshire and others he had first known in the 1930s took a prominent part. The extravagance of the festivities marked an end to the austerity and constraint of recent years in Britain and appeared, in John Colville's words, "to usher in a period of prosper-ity and relaxation." Jackie's witty, exuberant accounts of her adventures in London reminded Jack of Kick. To her surprise and delight, when her plane touched down in Boston Jack came on board and asked her to be his wife.

Jack's friends would remember being mystified by the lackluster physical appearance of his future bride, who was then far from the epit-ome of style she would later become. To Jewel Reed, who was married to a former Navy friend of Jack's, Jackie seemed "almost homely . . . an odd choice for him." Betty Spalding also responded with astonishment; Jack's taste in women usually ran to stunning beauties like the stat-uesque blonde Inga Arvad. But Betty, who (as Betty Coxe) had lived with Kick in Washington and observed her great intimacy with Jack, soon perceived that Jack was drawn to Jackie precisely because he asso-ciated her with the late sister he had called his best friend. Significantly, when Jack brought Jackie home to meet his father, Joe Kennedy also found in her, in Betty's words, "a substitute for Kick"—a bright, spir-ited girl he could laugh with and tease. As far as his father was concerned, Jack could hardly have selected a better wife. Three months after the proposal, at a ceremony at the Newport, Rhode Island, estate of Janet and her second husband, the investment banker Hugh D. Auchincloss, Jackie became Mrs. John F. Kennedy.

Having entered the Senate and taken a wife, Jack was putting the pieces in place to seek higher office. On April 6, 1954, he gave his first major Senate speech. Jack addressed the vexed question of US military intervention in Indochina. With France's long war in Indochina approaching a climax, the United States was considering military action and the Russians and Chinese were themselves threatening to come in. As he had done to great effect in *Why England Slept*, Jack bolstered his case with personal testimony. Basing his comments on what he had seen "firsthand" on his visit to the region three years previously, he argued against the commitment of US forces. Recalling his observation three years previously that the United States had done wrong to ally itself with a colonial regime that had no real support from the people, he argued that to send troops to the jungles of Indochina would be "dangerously futile and self-destructive."

That summer Jack published an essay, "Foreign Policy is the People's Business," which suggested that he was in the process of drastically revising his approach to the Communist menace. Addressing the myths and misconceptions that, in his view, clouded US policy, he trained his sights on those Americans who rejected diplomacy as a method of dealing with international disputes. In the utterly new circumstances of what he called "the hydrogen age," the decisions of leaders, he wrote, might affect "the very existence of mankind." The duty of a leader in a democratic society was, he stated, not to pander to people's false beliefs in an effort to win votes, but rather to take steps to educate and enlighten public opinion. He who in recent memory had expressed personal affection for Joseph McCarthy, who had favored the red-baiting Nixon over Helen Gahagan Douglas, and who had campaigned as the stauncher anti-Communist against Lodge, now expressed distaste for those who would "exploit public opinion for partisan purposes." Given the deep suspicion of the Soviets that prevailed in the United States, it was politically dangerous to argue, as Churchill did, that diplomatic solutions were preferable to confrontation. Nonetheless Kennedy's essay, which appeared in the *New York Times Magazine* on August 8,

1954, signaled his recognition of the need for a change in the way Americans looked at the postwar world.

That he remained at odds with himself, however, is suggested by what he did four days later. McCarthy had attacked Democrats for "twenty years of treason" and Herbert Hoover had blamed them for years of Communist advances; the Democrats' supposed softness on Communism was sure to be an issue in the next congressional elections. On August 12, Hubert Humphrey, joined by Democratic senator Kennedy of Massachusetts and Independent senator Wayne Morse of Oregon, moved to outdo Republicans on the issue of anti-Communism. Senate Republicans had proposed a bill that would deprive Communist-infiltrated labor unions of the right to collective bargaining; the trio introduced an amendment that would ban the Communist Party altogether. The political motivation behind the Humphrey–Kennedy–Morse amendment, as it was called, was openly discussed in the press at the time. Jack, with his high-profile involvement in the attempt to hijack the Republicans' bill, had engaged in precisely the sort of exploitation of public opinion for partisan purposes that he had criticized in print just days before. Rather than undertake to educate the public, he catered to what, by the evidence of his *Times* piece, he had come to regard as its myths and misconceptions. By this time, he understood that the problem was not a matter of softness toward the Communists, but of an ineffective Soviet policy. Like Stanley Baldwin, he seemed to know what was right yet, with an eye on the upcoming election, took a different course. The conflict between politician and statesman was to tug Kennedy in opposite directions for years to come.

By contrast, the other great question that absorbed Jack then had to be resolved immediately. His back condition had worsened markedly in recent years. Since his arrival in the Senate he had been unwell much of the time and often absent. At times, he found it difficult to walk even with crutches. By 1954 the pain had escalated to a degree at which, for all of his insistence on smiling at fate, he showed signs of having reached his limit. When the Senate went into summer recess, he and Jackie left for Hyannis Port, where he agonized over whether to have an operation. On the one hand his back problem threatened to become totally incapacitating, but on the other his

Addison's disease made surgery an extremely dangerous proposition. In itself, an operation could trigger a possibly fatal Addisonian crisis; furthermore, Addison's made patients highly susceptible to infection, which could also prove fatal. Physicians at the Lahey Clinic, where Jack had been treated for Addison's since 1947, ruled out what they regarded as elective surgery, and Joe Kennedy urged his son to accept their decision. But Jack could not. Informed that the chances he would survive an operation were about fifty-fifty, he pounded his crutches with his fist and declared that he would rather die than spend the rest of his life on them. Figuring that surgery would either kill him or cure him, Jack made up his mind to be operated on in New York during the second week of October 1954. Jackie, who had had little idea of the severity of Jack's health problems when they married, was shaken by his decision and by all that faced them.

On September 21, David Ormsby Gore arrived in New York with Selwyn Lloyd as part of the British delegation to the United Nations General Assembly. That weekend, he visited Jack in Hyannis Port. It proved a momentous occasion, as the setting for what David would call Jack's "twenty-five-year conversation" with British friends shifted to US soil. David had walked in at a time of crisis for Jack—and not just on account of the impending operation. David was aware of his friend's primitive anti-Communism of recent years and of how it harmonized with the political atmosphere in McCarthy-era America, but there was also evidence that Jack had begun to see the need for a suppler, more effective approach. David warmly encouraged this development. In their discussions through the years Jack had taken the view that a politician must look to his own interests, but David also perceived the huge appeal that a willingness to risk everything for ideals exerted upon him. David remained confident that he knew the kind of man Jack wanted to be, and he believed him capable of becoming that man. As David's daughter Jane would say many years afterward, he acknowledged Jack's faults, but viewed them as insignificant when weighed against his potential for good. David, recognizing a divided nature, never wavered in his faith that Jack had the "right instincts" and that they would win out in the end.

David arrived at Hyannis Port uniquely qualified to help Jack work out his doubts about committing himself to a sea change in US policy toward the Soviets. David had had the benefit of conversations—with Selwyn Lloyd, Macmillan, Eden and others—about Churchill's ideas on Russia and the postwar world, and he had been actively engaged in efforts to put those ideas into practice. Starting in Paris in 1951, and as recently as that summer of 1954 in London when he had assisted during the latest round of disarmament talks, he had had direct experience of negotiations with the Soviets. He could testify first-hand that since Stalin's death tensions had eased and Soviet attitudes shifted for the better. Having worked with Lloyd in the preparation of speeches elucidating the distinction between negotiations and appeasement, he was amply prepared to counter the accusations that a more sophisticated approach to Soviet relations would provoke in the United States. He could attest that Churchill's policy was no updated version of "living with the dictators," but rather a fully-fledged strategy to bring about the downfall of Soviet Communism.

Jack had already grappled with some of these issues on his own. David both clarified matters and suggested a new emphasis. Selwyn Lloyd had established himself as an expert on disarmament; work in that area had provisioned David with a great deal of information and insight. Jack had always had a knack for asking questions, and that weekend at Cape Cod Jackie took notes as, at her husband's prompting, David poured out the bounty of what he had learned during his service to the Churchill government. For the first time, David and Jack spoke of some of the great things the latter might accomplish in the next phase of his political career—if only he lived through the operation. Their discussions, situating disarmament in the context of a new approach to Soviet relations, planted a seed that would come to fruition during the Kennedy presidency. The friends continued to talk at the hospital in New York, where Jack's operation was repeatedly postponed while doctors assessed his condition. David had to return to London unexpectedly, after a Cabinet reshuffle resulted in Selwyn Lloyd being reassigned as minister of supply. Nonetheless, by the time Jack underwent surgery on October 21, he had, in the course of conversations with David, begun to move decisively toward assembling the policy and beliefs that would carry him to the White House and guide his actions as president.

After the operation, in which doctors attempted to stabilize the spine with a bone graft and a metal plate—a procedure known as a lumbar fusion—there was doubt whether Jack would survive. He developed an infection and, as he hovered near death, a priest again administered the last rites. Joe Kennedy, who had stood vigil at Jack's bedside during previous scrapes with death, wept at the seeming certainty that this time he would lose his son after all. But Jack did not die, and in December Jackie walked alongside and whispered words of encouragement as he was carried out of the hospital on a stretcher. They spent Christmas at the family home in Palm Beach, but the gaping wound in his back refused to heal. Jack drifted into a deep depression. Most uncharacteristically, he seemed to lose the will to live, and Joe Kennedy feared that even if his son survived his spirit might be crushed. In February 1955, Jack was flown north for a second operation, to remove the metal plate.

Back in Florida he began to recover, but it became apparent that while surgery had failed to kill, it had not cured either. Still, seven months after the first operation, Jack emerged from his ordeal a stronger and more determined man. The improvement was less physical than intellectual. Far from having wasted his hiatus from the Senate, he had used the time to begin to reinvent himself. He returned to the world with the manuscript of a book that documented where his thinking and reading had taken him—and where, if he could find it in himself to do so, he might go next.

CHAPTER TEN

To Find a Beginning

 JACK'S RETURN TO THE SENATE IN MAY 1955 WAS FOLLOWED BY
several trips to the hospital owing to complications. During the
recess, he planned to spend a week in Scandinavia with Torby
Macdonald, in anticipation of going on to meet Jackie at the Hôtel
du Cap in Cap d'Antibes. Before Jack sailed for Europe, he sent on to
his father the first and last chapters of the book he had been working
on—assisted by Jackie, his aide Theodore Sorensen and others—in
the months since the second operation. Rose Kennedy had already
hand-delivered the body of the manuscript to her husband when she
joined him in the south of France at the start of their summer holiday. In 1940, the delivery of a manuscript to Jack's father had marked
a watershed in its young author's life. Fifteen years later, *Profiles in
Courage* would prove to be another turning point in his career. The
manuscripts, though separated by more than a decade, were connected in other ways as well, for both addressed the question of the
responsibilities of leadership in a democratic society. In 1940, Jack
had sided with Baldwin on the necessity of doing whatever it takes to
get elected. In 1955, he lauded those men in American public life who
had found the courage to take an unpopular stand at whatever personal
and political cost to themselves.

Some fellow Democrats would read *Profiles in Courage* in terms of
Jack's silence the previous December when the Senate voted to con-

demn Joseph McCarthy, who remained popular in Massachusetts. On the grounds that to oppose McCarthy would be political suicide, Jack—who, though hospitalized, might have recorded his vote through an aide—had been the sole Democrat not to take a stand against the demagogue. Certain of Jack's detractors within the party would interpret his book as an "act of contrition" for the McCarthy affair. But, with its call for a new way of thinking about the Soviet threat and its acknowledgment of the likely political consequences, *Profiles in Courage* is also usefully read in terms of the pivotal talks Jack had with David Ormsby Gore before he underwent surgery.

During his convalescence Jack had read deeply in Edmund Burke, and he chose as an epigraph a passage from a 1783 speech in praise of Charles James Fox, who had risked power for an unpopular stand in the matter of the East India Bill.

> He well knows what snares are spread about his path, from personal animosity . . . and possibly from popular delusion. But he has put to hazard his ease, his security, his interest, his power, even his . . . popularity. . . . He is traduced and abused for his supposed motives. He will remember that obloquy is a necessary ingredient in the composition of all true glory: he will remember . . . that calumny and abuse are essential parts of triumph. . . . He may live long, he may do much. But here is the summit. He can never exceed what he does this day.

Jack wrote of US senators who had taken a principled stand and thereby defied the "angry power" of the voters on whom their political future depended. Their stories had taken place in the past, but Jack, writing in 1955, used them to make an important point about the present—and the future. In his Harvard thesis he had written of the susceptibility of elected leaders in 1930s' Britain to the pressure of popular opinion, and he had labored to justify Baldwin's failure to rearm. Fifteen years later, shifting his focus to America during the Cold War, Jack again perceived a disparity between what the leader ought to do on behalf of his country and what, in light of public opinion, he must do to win votes. In the introduction to *Profiles in Courage*, he came down on the side of those prepared to display "political courage" in seeking new and unorthodox ways to deal with the "powerful enemy" in Moscow. The man who three years previously had claimed simply to reflect the views of a constituency that wanted "more done" about Communism now paraphrased Burke in pointing out that senators came to Washington not as special pleaders for their state or section but as "members of the deliberative assembly of one nation with one interest."

Informing Jack's remarks was a sense that the rigidity and dogmatism that continued to dominate American opinion about the Soviets would no longer do. He suggested that only a fresh approach—one likely to be unpopular with the American public—would prove effective in defeating a "foreign ideology that fears free thought more than it fears hydrogen bombs." In that phrase he drew on Churchill's insight about the Soviet leaders' fear of words and ideas as a threat to their closed society. Lest anyone think that Jack intended his comments as a disparagement of popular rule, he alluded to a 1947 speech in which Churchill broached the matter of democracy's imperfection. Jack wrote, "The stories of men who accomplished good in the face of cruel calumnies from the public are not final proof that we should at all times ignore the feelings of voters on national issues. For, as Winston Churchill has said, 'Democracy is the worst form of government— except all those other forms that have been tried from time to time.'"

Interestingly, Jack's labors on *Profiles in Courage* had overlapped with Churchill's final months in office. In the words of Violet Bonham Carter, the prime minister had been "in great agony of mind" about when to relinquish power. To the exasperation of many, he had seemed to clutch at any excuse to remain "in harness" longer than he claimed to have wished or planned. On March 1, 1955, as the time for resignation approached, Churchill delivered an address that formed the final installment of his reflections on the postwar world. He spoke of a world in which both sides possessed the obliterating weapons of the nuclear age. There was no absolute defense against the hydrogen bomb, nor, he went on, was there any method in sight by which nations might be guaranteed against the devastation that it threatened to inflict on vast regions. At the same time, in both sides' ability to destroy the other he discerned a chance for peace, for who would be so foolish as to strike the first blow knowing that retaliation would be swift and overwhelming? A worldwide agreement on disarmament remained Churchill's goal, but in its absence he perceived only one rational policy, which he called defense through deterrents. Always a proponent of negotiating from a position of strength, he cautioned that for now the West must maintain a capacity for retaliation so enormous as to deter any Soviet plan to launch a surprise attack. The deterrent, he added ominously, did not cover the case of lunatics or dictators in the mood of Hitler in his bunker—hence the urgency of efforts to prevent nuclear weapons from falling into many hands. Churchill's speech on the deterrent was his swan song, his farewell to colleagues and to the electorate. He would address the Commons again, but this was his last great appearance. He resigned on April 5, 1955, and Anthony Eden became prime minister.

In the end, Churchill had failed to launch the new era in East–West relations which he saw as leading to the peaceful defeat of Soviet Communism, but *Profiles in Courage* quietly suggested that in his absence from public life that dream might be taken up by others. Jack's call for the United States to adopt a new Soviet strategy was a statement of belief, as well as an acknowledgment of the courage required by anyone in public life who chose to fight for such a fundamental shift in American foreign policy. Whether Jack himself had yet fully made up his mind to become that figure was another matter. His book made no promises. But Jack's argument worried his father nonetheless. In 1940, when Joe Kennedy read the manuscript that would become Jack's first book, he had stumbled over the passages about Stanley Baldwin. In *Profiles in Courage*, he read with alarm Jack's call for a new way of thinking about the Communist peril. Joe studied the worrisome passages three times, and professed to be confused. He had found his way to the core of his son's meditation on the theme of political courage, but this time the sentiments that caused him distress would remain intact.

Jack was thirty-eight when he returned to the Senate that fall. Illness had kept him from public life for the better part of a year. He had had two major operations, against the advice of doctors. He had had another brush with death. More than ever, the young politician who had privately declared that he did not expect to live past the age of forty-five perceived the pressure of time if he was to achieve the goal, stated to his wife, of claiming his "place in history." Certainly, the world had changed lately in ways that suggested it might be possible to sell a fresh Soviet strategy to the American electorate. Censured by the US Senate, McCarthy had fallen; and in July 1955 the new Soviet leadership of Bulganin, the nominal head of the government, and Khrushchev, the party chief with whom the real power lay, had emerged from behind the Iron Curtain for the first time to meet at Geneva with their American, British and French counterparts in the high-level talks for which Churchill had long hoped. If ever there was a possibility for the friendly intercourse by which Churchill had proposed to defeat the Communists, it was now.

Jack, meanwhile, was "very intrigued" by rumors that he was under consideration as a possible vice presidential candidate on a ticket with Adlai Stevenson in 1956. On the face of it, his barely-launched Senate career hardly seemed capable of supporting a claim to higher office. Still, his defeat of Lodge in 1952 had riveted his party's attention. More recently he had benefited from a good deal of positive publicity about his hospitalization. The fact that press accounts of Jack's tribulations came so soon after the photographs of his society wedding made his personal struggle more poignant. Pictures of Jack on crutches entering the hospital, while Jackie, at his side, did her best to smile bravely, generated national interest in the story of the first-term senator who refused to succumb to physical defeat. The publication in January 1956 of *Profiles in Courage*, which went on to win the Pulitzer Prize, set off a new burst of publicity that reinforced Jack's image as one of the Democrats' young stars. He was portrayed by turns as an intellectual, a fearless war hero and a courageous fighter against his own physical limitations.

As the possibility strengthened that Jack might be chosen as a vice presidential candidate, both he and his father began to have reservations. Joe Kennedy doubted that Stevenson had a chance against Eisenhower, and feared that Democrats would blame the loss on Jack's Catholicism. That would doom Jack's aspirations to be his party's presidential candidate someday, for the verdict would be that a Catholic was unelectable. Though Jack acknowledged the power of his father's argument, he did finally decide to seek the number two spot on the ticket. At the Democratic convention in August, formidable opposition emerged from those who refused to forgive his failure to take a stand in the McCarthy affair, and Senator Estes Kefauver of Tennessee was chosen instead. Jack conceded gracefully, and, having already excited the delegates with his narration of a film on the history of the party, he nominated Stevenson with a speech that made a vivid impression, particularly on television viewers. Following a holiday in the south of France, Jack built up further credit within his party by vigorously campaigning nationwide for Stevenson. As Joe Kennedy had predicted, Eisenhower and his vice president Richard Nixon triumphed in November, and Jack rejoiced that he had avoided a spot on a losing ticket. Instead, he had gained both national attention and a reputation for party loyalty that promised to serve him well next time. The popular Eisenhower would not be able to run again, and, as Jack saw it, Stevenson's second loss provided fodder for the argument that a Kennedy candidacy would give the Democrats a better chance in 1960.

A presidential bid would be out of the question unless Jack settled a private matter that threatened to derail him politically. A crisis had erupted in his marriage that nearly caused Jackie to leave him. Jack, apparently expecting to live as his father had, had been unfaithful from the first. For all their rapport, Jackie had never been his physical type, and during their honeymoon in Mexico he had been so restless that he proposed she go back to Washington on her own while he enjoyed a few days in California. A perplexed Jackie had resisted that suggestion, but hardly had they returned to Washington together when the womanizing that would blight their marriage began. Time and again, Jackie found herself abandoned at parties while her husband disappeared with other women. Jackie had entered the marriage, said Jack's friend Jane Suydam, with eyes "filled with dreams," and the reality of life with a philandering husband left her reeling. Remembering her mother's cruel judgment that no man would find her attractive, Jackie blamed herself for her husband's infidelity. She chopped off her mop of naturally curly hair in favor of an Audrey Hepburn–style pixie cut and outfitted herself with an elegant wardrobe from Paris, but nothing seemed to work. The problem naturally subsided when Jack lay ill in the aftermath of two operations. Jackie read to him and entertained him with gossip and caustic observations, and, in the absence of other women, husband and wife seemed wonderfully at peace. To Jackie's dismay, that changed as soon as Jack was able to get about again. The couple's problems came to a head after the Democratic convention, when Jack went off to the south of France despite the fact that Jackie was seven months' pregnant and, having already suffered one miscarriage, forbidden by her doctor to travel abroad. In Cap d'Antibes Jack had a friend arrange dates with bikini-clad women on his behalf. On August 23, 1956, he had gone off sailing with one of these women, along with a group of friends, when Jackie gave birth by cesarean section to a stillborn girl. Three days passed before Jack could be reached, and Bobby Kennedy stepped in to comfort Jackie and arrange to bury his brother's daughter. Joe Kennedy finally managed to find Jack and let him know what had happened— and Jack saw no reason to come home. Only when Joe angrily pointed out the danger to his political career if he failed to return at once did Jack reluctantly consent. He arrived to discover Jackie ready to seek a divorce, but at length he persuaded her to give their marriage another chance. Three weeks after Eisenhower's reelection, Jackie was at her husband's side when, at the Kennedy Thanksgiving dinner at Hyannis Port, he told the family that he had made up his mind to seek his party's presidential nomination in 1960.

Even as Jack had been conferring with his father over his decision, in Britain events had begun to take shape that would influence the policies with which he would lay claim to the White House. David Ormsby Gore, who had left the Foreign Office but remained in Parliament after Selwyn Lloyd's recall from the UN in 1954, was on the rise again. Lloyd now served as foreign secretary, and when one of Eden's ministers resigned as a consequence of the Suez crisis David's mentor recommended him as joint parliamentary under-secretary of state for foreign affairs. Only a short time after David joined the government, he happened to be shooting at Sandringham, the Queen's country estate in Norfolk, when Eden, done in by Suez, turned up to submit his resignation. Harold Macmillan kissed hands as prime minister; and on forming a government he named to junior posts some of the young men whom Jack had first known in London before the war: Julian Amery, Hugh Fraser, Richard Wood, and David Ormsby Gore. At exactly the moment when Jack began his efforts to win the premier spot on the Democratic ticket, David, as minister of state for foreign affairs, prepared again to take up an issue—disarmament—which would prove decisive to his friend's campaign and, later, to the Kennedy presidency.

Jack calculated that if he was to have any chance for the nomination in 1960, he had better start his campaign immediately. As a congress-man intent on a move to the Senate he had worked hard to make him-self known outside his district, and that tactic had served him brilliantly in 1952. Four years later he decided to do the same, though on a much larger scale, and began to travel relentlessly throughout the United States. Nearly every weekend when the Senate was in session Jack was off to deliver speeches, appear on local television and radio, and build alliances with local political figures. His goal was to visit every state and talk to Democrats in all walks of life. The strain of so much travel on his health was immense. Not only did he have to cope with back and stomach pain, throat and urinary tract infections and bouts of spiking fever, but he had to appear consistently youthful, vig-orous and charming in public if his efforts were to pay off. In September 1957, an abscess on his back sent him to New York Hospital for three weeks. Eventually the abscess was drained in a surgical proce-dure, and Jack resumed the travels and speaking engagements that had become the focus of his existence.

Jack's schedule severely tested a marriage that had already nearly failed. At the outset Jackie was able to travel with him some of the time, but by the spring of 1957 she was pregnant again and her medical his-tory forced her to withdraw from the campaign duties she disliked any-way. Husband and wife were apart most weekends, and when they were together there was the pressure of illness and anxiety on both sides. It was hardly a prescription to repair a fragile marriage. Yet the arrange-ment did have one curious advantage. Though Jack did not become a faithful husband, he tended to confine his womanizing to those periods when he was away from home. Jackie found a way to retain her dignity as long as she was not confronted directly with his infidelities.

Finally, exactly one year after Jack had made up his mind to chase the presidential nomination, Jackie gave birth to a healthy girl at Lying-In Hospital in New York on November 27, 1957. For Jack, who since boyhood had trained himself to keep his feelings in check, the arrival of baby Caroline was a hugely emotional event. Having learned early on to shield himself against a sense that his parents did not value him as he might have wished, Jack seemed to realize that with little Caroline no such defenses were necessary. He was unreserved in his love, deter-mined, he said, to be physically affectionate as his own mother had never been. His child would experience no sad longing for the embraces that, in Jack's memory, Rose had failed to provide. Jackie, for her part, proved more physically reserved than Jack, but she quickly found her own ways of making certain that the baby knew how much she was adored. The parents' shared passion for Caroline—and later for John Junior, born in 1960—created a powerful bond that would do much to hold the marriage together in the difficult times to come.

Now that Jackie was a mother, she was even less anxious to spend weekends on the road. A pattern established itself whereby, more often than not, Jack traveled on his own while Jackie remained behind with Caroline in the brick house in Georgetown that he had purchased as a gift to his wife after she gave birth. In those days, Jackie would complain, she and her husband rarely spent two consecutive days together. Jack did not, however, lack for female companionship. If he was unable to pick up someone at a campaign rally, there always seemed to be a local politician or businessman eager to ingratiate himself by providing a pretty girl for the evening. If all else failed, there was usually an available girl or two among the campaign workers. He was known to call female staff members at the end of the day, and if a young woman turned him down Jack, never one to sacrifice his good humor at such moments, would simply make another call. Jackie had no illusions about his activities with other women, but she taught herself to focus on the good times, when he was at home with his young family, and to do her best to seem oblivious to the rest. With some of Jack's male friends she affected the pose that though she knew about his philandering she just did not care.

For all the relentless travel, Jack had yet to make a compelling case for why people ought to vote for him. His full campaign strategy began to emerge in the summer of 1958, when, about to run for a second Senate term, he attacked the Eisenhower administration for allowing America to become perilously weak in the face of Soviet might. Jack's speech in the Senate on August 14, 1958, was part of a move by a number of prominent Democrats to depict themselves as fiercer anti-Communists than those who had long derided their party as soft. The Soviets' 1957 launch of the Sputnik satellite, followed by a US government paper, the Gaither Report, which suggested that America was about to become second to Russia in nuclear strength, provided the openings Democrats sought. Senators J. William Fulbright of Arkansas, Stewart Symington of Missouri and Lyndon Johnson of Texas criticized the administration's defense policy, but it was Kennedy who most sharply articulated the charges in a speech that prompted a tumultuous response from Republicans rattled by the spectacle of a Democrat capable of recasting himself and his party as the true hardliners.

Kennedy prophesied an imminent "missile gap," when the United States would cede nuclear superiority to the Soviets. To date, he observed, the United States had possessed a capacity for retaliation so great as to deter a potential aggressor from launching a direct attack. But in "the years of the gap," America's threat of massive retaliation would lose most of its force and the nation would no longer be safe. He argued that even as the Eisenhower administration had been concentrating on economic strength, the United States had been steadily losing its chance to maintain a lead against Russia in missile capacity. Appropriating Churchill's rhetoric of the 1930s, Kennedy declared, "These were the vital years, the years the locusts have eaten, and it is quite obvious we obtained economic security at the expense of military security, and that this policy will bring us into great danger within the next few years." He insisted that to sound the alarm was neither to panic nor to provide encouragement to the enemy. It was instead to warn Americans that time was running out and that the facts, however disturbing, must be faced. Kennedy went on, "In the words of Sir Winston Churchill in a dark time of England's history: 'Come then— let us to the task, to the battle and the toil—each to our part, each to our station. . . . Let us go forward together in all parts of the [land]. There is not a week, nor a day, nor an hour to be lost.'"

Senator Homer Capehart of Indiana was so distressed by Kennedy's remarks that he talked of clearing the galleries of spectators. He insisted that Kennedy, by his speech, had provided comfort to the Russians and thereby weakened the United States. Senator Leverett Saltonstall of Massachusetts mounted a robust defense of Eisenhower's record on missile development, and the president himself soon weighed in with assurances that Defense Department programs were perfectly adequate and that there could be no missile gap. Eisenhower knew, but could not say, that secret U-2 reconnaissance photographs showed that claims of a missile gap were baseless.

Jack had begun to discover a voice as a presidential candidate. Other Democrats might be equally critical of the White House, but extensive knowledge of Churchill's speeches helped Kennedy to fashion a sharper critique. It was not merely a question of quotation, though here and in later campaign speeches he did cite Churchill to splendid effect. Kennedy's assault on Eisenhower-era policies echoed Churchill's indictment of the Baldwin and Chamberlain governments' failure to rearm and of their willingness to squander Britain's advantage over Germany after the First World War. The candidate would refine and develop this approach over time, but already in the missile gap speech Jack emphatically cast himself in the mold of the 1930s' Churchill, campaigning as a strong leader who would tell the people the truth about the world situation and demand the sacrifices necessary to restore his country's supremacy. His warnings about a missile gap attracted a great deal of publicity and helped bring about a massive victory in the November 1958 Senate race. He had said in advance that he needed a big win in Massachusetts in order to prove to his party that he could be a formidable vote-getter. He won by a record-setting 874,608 votes, a margin of victory that instantly bestowed credibility on his presidential aspirations.

From then on, Jack ran for president, as Harold Macmillan later said, "on the Churchill ticket." He examined the current scene through the lens of Britain in the interwar years. He noted that in 1939, when Churchill cautioned the British people that they could not escape their dangers by recoiling from them, he seemed to have inherited the fate of Cassandra, whose prophecies, though accurate, were not believed. Churchill had been much derided "for his warnings of danger and his calls for sacrifice at a time when the hopes for relaxation were high." In America in 1959, the hopes for relaxation were similarly high. Jack warned his audiences that Americans, like the British twenty years previously, would be unable to escape their own dangers by recoiling or by allowing themselves to be lulled to sleep.

This line of argument attained its fullest expression on November 13, 1959, when Jack made his keynote address to the annual convention of the Democratic Party of Wisconsin, in Milwaukee. The speech was cast as an extended reference to "The Locust Years," one of Churchill's speeches, then lately printed in *Arms and the Covenant*, much argued over by Billy Hartington, Andrew Cavendish, David

Ormsby Gore and the other young men in their set when Jack first arrived in London in 1938. Jack called his own remarks "The Years the Locusts Have Eaten" and deployed the metaphors of sleep and drift to accuse the Republican administration in Washington of having allowed the United States to plummet from superiority to second best. This time it was not Germany but the Soviet Union that had seized the advantage. And this time, ironically, it was the wartime hero Eisenhower who—like Baldwin, the target of Churchill's original speech—had permitted his nation to slumber while the enemy methodically gained strength.

"Twenty-three years ago," Jack began, "in a bitter debate in the House of Commons, Winston Churchill charged the British Government with acute blindness to the menace of Nazi Germany, with gross negligence in the maintenance of the island's defenses, and with indifferent, indecisive leadership of British foreign policy and British public opinion. The preceding years of drift and impotence, he said, were 'the years the locusts have eaten.'" Since January 1953, Jack went on, the United States had passed through a similar period, when it drifted and "sought the easy way" while, on the other side of the globe, another mighty power had been working steadily to surpass America. When Khrushchev, who had replaced Bulganin as prime minister in 1958, vowed to "bury" the United States, it was not so much by war that he intended to do so, Jack contended, as "by possessing the most powerful military establishments, by boasting the most impressive scientific achievements, by dominating the most markets and trade routes, by influencing the most needy or neutral nations through aid and trade and diplomatic penetration." Like Churchill, Jack conjured up a vision of preeminence inexcusably squandered. He insisted that the American people had yet to be made aware of the seven-year record of Soviet gains and US gaps, and that as a consequence they had grown dangerously complacent and easy-going. He promised that, if only America would heed his call, it was not too late to make up for the years the locusts had eaten, to close the gaps and pull ahead.

It was one thing to attack Eisenhower's failed policies, quite another to suggest how a Kennedy administration would deal differently with the Soviets. In the fall of 1959, further conversations with David Ormsby Gore, then the head of the British delegation to the United

Nations General Assembly in New York, enabled Kennedy to fill out the picture. David's experience during the past year as chief British delegate to the Three-Power Conference on the Discontinuance of Nuclear Tests, held at Geneva, had led him to conclude that an agreement with the Soviets on a nuclear test ban was suddenly a very real possibility. Building on Churchill's ideas about defeating the Communists by contact and agreements, David seized on the nuclear test ban treaty as the place where a first agreement might be possible—a breakthrough important not only in itself, but even more so in terms of the many agreements to follow. For all the ambivalence with which he had embarked on a political career, David became in this period deeply, emotionally committed to the notion of the test ban treaty as quite possibly the beginning of the end of Soviet Communism. Upon Macmillan's triumph in the October 1959 general election, David drafted a letter about his own immediate future to the prime minister. Aware that Macmillan might intend to promote him, David asked to be allowed to stay on at Geneva, a post he held in addition to his responsibilities at the UN in New York. He gave as his reason his strong sense that a shift in the Soviet position might soon result in major progress toward a test ban. He did not wish to go off to work in some other area until a treaty was in place.

With Jack in and out of New York that fall as he continued to travel and speak, the friends had their first chance to discuss things since David had gone to Geneva the previous year. In the course of these discussions, David communicated his great hopes for the test ban as a first step toward the peaceful defeat of Soviet Communism. And at length, Jack's program for dealing with the Soviets—what he would call his "strategy of peace"—finally crystallized. At the time of *Profiles in Courage*, Jack had recognized the desirability of a new beginning in East–West relations but had not yet been prepared to declare himself the man to fight for it. Now he was ready, though by David's assessment, his commitment was as yet strictly rational and intellectual; the emotional commitment was still to come. Nonetheless, by December 11, 1959, when Jack delivered a major speech on disarmament, the man who would be president had emerged in full. Jack finally had in hand the Churchillian double-barreled policy with which he would lay claim to the White House. He had spoken of the nuclear test ban treaty on previous occasions, but here he encouraged voters to see it as something much larger than an end in itself. Emphasizing that in the meantime the United States must be sure to remain strong, Jack argued for a dramatic intervention to break the vicious cycle of the Cold War. "The problem is to find a beginning," he asserted. ". . . It may be that an agreement on the control and limitation of nuclear tests will be the beginning." Three weeks before Jack officially declared himself a candidate for supreme office, his remarks on the test ban treaty as a possible new beginning went to the very heart of what he hoped to accomplish as president.

CHAPTER ELEVEN

On the Churchill Ticket

O N JANUARY 2, 1960, JACK KENNEDY FORMALLY ANNOUNCED
to reporters who crowded into the Senate Caucus Room that he hoped
to become the next president of the United States. Cheered on by some
three hundred supporters who gave the news conference the buoyant
air of a campaign rally, Jack spoke of the tasks ahead. Calling the presidency the most powerful office in the free world, he cited some of the
crucial decisions that would face a new American leader during the
next four years. Much of what Jack had to say reflected his campaign
theme of lost supremacy. He spoke of the need to end or alter the arms
race, where Soviet gains had begun to pose a threat to America's existence; the diminished stature of American science and education; setbacks in the farm economy and the decay of American cities; and the
need to achieve, without further inflation or unemployment, economic
growth that benefited everyone. Above all, he highlighted the necessity
of awakening Americans to the dangers and opportunities that confronted them. Having spent the past forty months touring every state
in the Union and meeting Democrats in every walk of life, Jack was
confident that he could win both his party's nomination and the
national election.

Privately, however, Jack acknowledged that America might be in no
mood to listen to, let alone believe, his warnings of national decline. As
1960 opened, the country's mood was "comfortable and complacent,"

in the words of Britain's ambassador in Washington, Sir Harold Caccia, a shrewd observer of the American scene. "In the first part of the year," Caccia noted in his annual report to London, "Americans felt that under President Eisenhower's personal diplomacy their country was successfully exercising world leadership." Eisenhower, beloved by the people and almost certain to have been reelected had he not been prohibited from running for a third term, "appeared to be firmly at the head of the leadership of the Western world. . . . His evident determination to make his record in the last year of his presidency seemed to assure a strong hand on the tiller."

For the moment, voters also had reason to be pleased with the economy. Caccia noted that despite 5 percent unemployment and other indicators of a gradual downward trend, many Americans "enjoyed record prosperity." So, too, Eisenhower's "insistence upon sound finance and an orthodox budget was reassuring." In such an atmosphere, Kennedy's cries of alarm and his call to sacrifice might well prove unpopular with "a public used to being told in fatherly tones that all was well." At the same time, Caccia observed that in the course of history America had "alternated between periods of revolutionary change and consolidation, and the periods of consolidation have seldom lasted long." Kennedy's historical sense, the British ambassador theorized, had "told him the time was ripe for another swing of the pendulum." Thus his decision to seize on campaign themes that, to some eyes, might have seemed likely in an environment of contentment to do more harm that good. The politician was betting that he had history on his side.

In his newspaper reportage on the 1945 general election in Britain, Jack had attempted to explain Churchill's defeat by pointing out that whereas the electorate had accepted a diet of toil and sweat in times of emergency, by the end of the war they believed the emergency had passed. Fifteen years later it fell to the presidential candidate to persuade American voters that a new emergency was at hand. "This administration may go out of office on a crest of 'peace' popularity," Jack remarked at the time, "but it will leave on the next administration's doorstep the most critical problems we have ever faced. . . . This administration has not faced up to these . . . problems squarely—nor have they been willing to tell the American people the truth about them—if they themselves know the truth—what they mean in terms of real danger and what it will take to ease those dangers."

Jack Kennedy clearly ran a risk by speaking of unpleasant matters—and he made the willingness to risk his own standing an issue of the campaign. He portrayed it as a characteristic of leadership. In an address to the California Democratic Clubs Convention in Fresno, he said, "In 1960 we must elect a President who will lead the people—who will risk, if he must, his popularity for his responsibility." In his Harvard thesis, Jack had written sympathetically of Baldwin's response to Churchill's "Locust Years" speech. Twenty years later he argued on the side of Churchill, the teller of harsh but necessary truths. He said that the president must strive to "educate" the people, to be their "guide" and to "lead the way."

Jack criticized Eisenhower's failure to say the harsh things and take the harsh steps that, however necessary, threatened to be unpopular or inconvenient. He spoke approvingly of Thomas Jefferson's decision to purchase the Louisiana Territory despite complaints from the "budget-cutters" of his day, and of George Washington's commitment to the Jay Treaty despite being abused, as he wrote, "in such exaggerated and indecent terms as could scarcely be applied to Nero, to a notorious defaulter or even to a common pickpocket." Jack contrasted these presidents with Madison, McKinley, Harding and Coolidge, who, by his analysis, had "yielded to public pressure instead of educating it."

Jack Kennedy's insistence that America needed a "strong" president was an indictment of Eisenhower's preference for—in Macmillan's words—"the devolution of authority wherever possible." Eisenhower had organized his administration "on military lines and with an essentially military staff structure." As in wartime, Eisenhower relied on others to "sift and sort" problems and, more often than not, to submit "a final solution" for his approval. For better or worse, Eisenhower had established his style of leadership long before he ran for president. So, to a degree, had Kennedy. Confronted with a problem, Kennedy tended to ask questions, listen to clashing opinions, examine great numbers of documents and then reach his own conclusions. He made it clear that he intended to do the same in the White House. "The President's responsibility cannot be delegated," he argued. "For he is the one focal point of responsibility. . . . He does not have to wait for unanimous agreement below, summed up in one-page memoranda that stifle dissent. He does not have to wait for crises to spur decisions that are long overdue. He must look ahead—and sometimes act alone."

David Ormsby Gore, in a visit to Washington in early 1960, experienced first-hand some of the very limitations of the Eisenhower presidency that Jack targeted. In addition to his duties as lead negotiator at the test ban talks, he had been assigned to head the British delegation to the ten-power talks on disarmament set to begin in March, also in Geneva. Prior to the talks, which had been convened in the wake of a disarmament proposal put forth by Khrushchev at the UN the year before, David came to Washington in order to devise a unified Western disarmament position. From the outset he was troubled by problems on the American side. He reported to London:

> The meetings of the Heads of Delegations to prepare the Western position for Geneva were a frustrating experience. . . . The embarrassing situation in which the Americans found themselves during the discussion seems to be symptomatic of the present state of affairs in the Administration. There appears to be no one driving the machine. . . . This results in there being little agreement upon policy even within a Department, let alone between different Departments and Agencies. . . . It seems to take months to arrive at any decision, and when it has taken shape the attempt to satisfy so many warring factions often results in its containing an inner contradiction. The implications of all this for the disarmament negotiations and for the Summit are not encouraging.

Ormsby Gore noted that at the time of Khrushchev's US visit in 1959, Eisenhower had put his name to a communiqué that called general disarmament the most important question facing the world today. The United States had also signed on to a similar statement in the form of a UN resolution. Yet the committee that was to have prepared a report for the present meeting had taken a stand "against any comprehensive plan of disarmament." In light of that contradiction, the report, which was never actually seen by the British, had been withheld.

Meanwhile, it struck Ormsby Gore that certain of the Americans had begun "to try to pretend that the objective of general disarmament was a

Soviet idea put forward for propaganda reasons"—and that therefore the Western powers ought to oppose it. "Again and again," he wrote, "I had to say that this was not our view, and that in any case this line did not square with the Camp David communiqué which the President himself had signed; nor with the United Nations resolution for which we had all voted." At length the Americans did manage to produce a document cleared, they emphasized, by both the Secretary of State and the Department of Defense. Ormsby Gore lamented that, "in addition to being quite worthless," the paper on "ultimate goals" was "written in English so deplorable as to make it almost incomprehensible."

Though he made no mention of it in his report to the Foreign Office, David had a chance to vent his frustration in a long talk with Jack at home in Georgetown. Jack planned to leave late that night for Wisconsin in order to be at the factory gates at five-thirty the next morning to campaign in the Democratic primary. David spoke at length of "the situation" in Washington, and Jack made it his cause to ensure that there would be "well prepared" US positions in Geneva, rather than the disgraceful lack of positive proposals David described. David reviewed the British position on disarmament, and thereafter Jack, according to Robert Kennedy, "stuck very closely to the line" of that conversation.

David Ormsby Gore was in Geneva when Jack Kennedy, in a speech at the University of Wisconsin in Madison on March 26, drew on their private discussion of the previous month to lambast the administration's inept preparations for the ten-power disarmament talks. "Last week," he began,

> ten nations began negotiations on the most important and com-
> plex problem facing the world today—the problem of disarma-
> ment. But despite the fact that these critical negotiations have
> already begun—despite our nation's basic desire to channel the
> immense sums now being spent on arms into peaceful activity—
> despite the absolute necessity of ending today's disastrous arms
> race if we are to reduce world tensions and move toward a lasting
> peace—despite these things, the US has put forward a hurriedly
> prepared disarmament plan—compounded of old proposals and a
> lack of new, creative thinking.

Jack noted that there had been presidential speeches, presidential advisers and presidential commissions on disarmament—but no policy. The United States had participated in previous conferences on disarmament and nuclear testing, but its conferees in every instance had been poorly prepared and inadequately instructed. The Eisenhower administration had played host to the Western allies in January in order to complete joint preparations for the Geneva Conference, but had put forth no positive proposals of its own.

Moscow, meanwhile, had unexpectedly signaled a new willingness to allow in Western inspection teams whenever an earth tremor provoked questions as to whether the cause was natural or artificial. It was a huge step for a closed society that had tended to view Western demands for an inspection mechanism as a pretext for espionage. Further, the Soviets came forward with a new proposal for a ban on all nuclear explosions above a certain magnitude and a moratorium on small tests while scientists worked to discover how these too might be made subject to detection. Jack, emphasizing that much remained to be explored and negotiated, and that the new Soviet proposal might well prove deceptive, urged Washington at least to consider it seriously.

Kennedy did not wish to give the impression of minimizing the Soviet threat. The Russians, he noted, still hoped to bury the United States "economically, politically, culturally and in every other sphere of interest." Nor, Jack stressed, did he harbor any illusion that a disarmament agreement would be possible in the absence of a rigorous inspection system. Nonetheless, he did believe that under what seemed to be the "more fluid and rational atmosphere" in Moscow since Stalin's death, the Soviet leaders would perceive comprehensive arms control to be in their own self-interest. In this he reflected Churchill's emphasis on the use of Russian self-interest as a guideline in negotiations.

Importantly, Jack again made it clear that he did not see the goal of a nuclear test ban treaty as an end in itself. Such an agreement would be "only a limited step forward." It would constitute neither true arms control nor an end to the arms race. "But," he continued, "we will have begun the first great experiment in international cooperation—the first real system of international inspection and control—and perhaps we will have begun the first halting moves toward an end to weapons and the dawn of a new era of world peace."

Macmillan saw the Soviet offer as "a conspicuous advance," and two days after Kennedy's speech he went to Washington at Eisenhower's invitation. Eisenhower, he knew from Caccia, was under terrific pressure from within his own camp to regard the offer as "an inevitable trap." Macmillan and Eisenhower had been great friends since the war, when they served together during the North African campaign, and at length, despite strong opposition from the Pentagon and other elements in Washington, the prime minister prevailed. On March 28, 1960, he and Eisenhower released the Camp David communiqué widely viewed as "an acceptance of the Russians' proposals."

A number of points remained, but Macmillan returned to London with a sense that "all the omens were good" for Geneva, as well as for the upcoming summit in Paris. Macmillan had striven to bring about the four-power conference, after a clash with Khrushchev in Moscow in 1959 led him to conclude that only a summit would make it possible to avoid a new and potentially cataclysmic confrontation over Western access to Berlin. The bad news for Jack Kennedy was that within days of his big speech on disarmament, the Camp David communiqué appeared to render a fair amount of his criticism in Wisconsin irrelevant. The administration's approach might not be so inept after all. Eisenhower seemed, in Caccia's estimate, "both firm and flexible." Progress in Geneva would bode well for the summit, to begin on May 16, where, it was hoped, a final agreement on a test ban might be reached. After Paris, Eisenhower was set to go on to the Soviet Union as Khrushchev's guest.

In conversation with Caccia, Richard Nixon predicted that his own party would benefit politically from a positive outcome in Paris. He also calculated that any public perception that the administration had "muffed it at the summit" would give the Democrats an edge. In mid-April, when the vice president made those remarks, the former possibility seemed the more likely, despite an ominous note struck by Khrushchev's vow to go forward with a peace treaty with East Germany in the event the Paris talks failed. The mood in Geneva, according to the Soviet delegate Semyon Tsarapkin, was "favorable," and Eisenhower was poised to leave office with his image as an effective world leader triumphantly intact.

Two weeks after Nixon's talk with the British ambassador, the

Soviets shot down a U-2 reconnaissance plane over Russia. The flight, requested by Allen Dulles and Richard Bissell at the CIA to monitor missile development, had originally been scheduled to take place before April 25. Eisenhower wanted no chance of an incident that might jeopardize the summit, but in the end weather conditions had led him to consent reluctantly to the mission going ahead on May 1. The misstep, in its way, was a perfect example of the leadership style Kennedy had criticized. Rather than listening to Dulles and Bissell, the president would have been wiser to follow the dictates of his own judgment. Washington responded to news of the downed plane with what Robert Menzies, the Australian prime minister, despairingly called a "curious set of conflicting statements" that made short work of the administration's credibility and left a good many top-level figures in Washington "ashamed of the ineptitude of their own Administration."

First, the National Aeronautics and Space Administration claimed the purpose of the flight had been to explore meteorological conditions at high altitudes. Then the State Department claimed that the U-2, though equipped for intelligence aims, had lacked presidential authorization to fly over Soviet territory. James Reston speculated in the *New York Times*, "If this particular flight of the U-2 was not authorized here, it could only be assumed that someone in the chain of the command in the Middle East or Europe had given the order." The very suggestion provided ammunition to those like Jack Kennedy who complained that Eisenhower exerted too little personal control. For a time the State Department suggested that Eisenhower had known nothing about the flight, but at length there came an admission that he had been responsible after all. "This was a sad and perplexed capital tonight, caught in a swirl of charges of clumsy administration, bad judgment and bad faith," Reston reported. "It was depressed and humiliated by the United States having been caught spying over the Soviet Union and trying to cover up its activities in a series of misleading official announcements." In effect the administration had been forced to confess it had lied, and in private Eisenhower went so far as to speak of a wish to resign.

Initially, Khrushchev had preferred not to believe that his counterpart was responsible for the spy plane. Convinced that on his visit to America he and Eisenhower had established a true bond of friendship and that the president was a man of peace, he looked to Allen Dulles and others in the CIA and the military as the likely culprits. He publicly suggested that the episode might have been the doing of "Pentagon militarists" who acted "without the President's knowledge." When Eisenhower unapologetically confessed involvement, Khrushchev felt betrayed. He did not refuse to come to Paris, as Macmillan feared. Instead, he used the summit as a podium from which to express his outrage.

Macmillan, in his diary, described the scene at the clamorous first session at the Elysée Palace in Paris, when Khrushchev rose to address his American, French and British counterparts. "With a gesture reminiscent of Mr. Micawber . . . [he] pulled a large wad of folio typewritten papers out of his pocket and began to speak. . . . Khrushchev tried to pulverize Ike (as Micawber did Heep) by a mixture of abuse, vitriolic and offensive, and legal argument." Khrushchev insisted the summit be postponed for six to eight months—that is, until after Eisenhower left office. The invitation to Eisenhower to visit the Soviet Union was withdrawn.

Khrushchev's harangue made Eisenhower turn crimson, but he waited until afterward in private with Macmillan to denounce him as "a real S.O.B." He refused to give in to Khrushchev's demand for an apology for the U-2 incident. Back in the States, Kennedy was insistent that words must not be confused with strength and maintained that the president should have expressed regret if that would have saved the summit; Nixon held that any sort of apology would have been appeasement. Kennedy, while being careful not to oppose espionage per se, did publicly question the wisdom of a U-2 flight so soon before the summit. Meanwhile, at a press conference in Paris, Khrushchev threatened, ranted and cursed in a performance, said Macmillan, "reminiscent of Hitler at his worst." The long-hoped-for summit "broke up in a disorderly and discreditable way." In a related development, the Soviets torpedoed the ten-power Geneva talks on disarmament soon afterward. Macmillan traced the reversal in the Soviet attitude towards détente to Khrushchev's feeling of betrayal. Of all that had been lost, Macmillan wrote in his diary, "For me, it is perhaps the work of two or three years. For Eisenhower, it means an ignominious end to his Presidency. For Khrushchev, a set-back to his more conciliatory and sensible ideas. For the world, a step nearer ultimate disaster."

Caccia also perceived an effect on the US presidential campaign. He regarded the U-2 incident and the collapse of the summit as the first two of five "hammer strokes" that shattered the comfortable and complacent mood of the American electorate. During the early part of 1960 there appeared to be wide confidence in Eisenhower. But, Caccia noted, "from the U2 incident onwards this was manifestly no longer true and Americans felt puzzled and angry." Eisenhower returned from Paris with his prestige badly tarnished, and from then on, said the British ambassador, "it could no longer be pretended that America was successfully leading the Western world."

That made a tremendous difference to the Kennedy campaign. Suddenly, for Jack Kennedy, it was not only a question of having history on his side, but fortune as well. "Fortune," wrote Caccia, "since international events outside his control conspired to give point to his criticism."

Jack wasted no time in seizing the advantage. When he addressed the Senate on June 14, he used recent events to substantiate his theme of national decline. The cancellation of the summit, in exposing the very problems he had sought to bring to the attention of voters, made him much less likely to suffer the fate of Cassandra. Jack argued that May 17, 1960, the day the summit collapsed, "marked the end of an era—an era of illusion." The fiasco in Paris had been inevitable because the president had allowed the United States to sleep while the Soviet Union grew in strength. The summit had been doomed from the start, because the United States had failed for the past eight years to develop the position of strength vital to effective negotiation, and because the American contingent had arrived in Paris unprepared with new ideas for the settlement of outstanding substantive issues. In his Harvard thesis, Jack had pointed to Munich as the event that had shocked Britain into action; here he expressed the hope that the failed summit might have a similar impact on America.

Notably, Kennedy ended with a jibe not at Eisenhower but at Nixon. He took the likely Republican presidential candidate to task for his recent claim that America was the world's "strongest country" militarily, economically and otherwise. Jack reiterated that his own warnings stood "in sharp contrast with the rosy assurances of the Administration." He strove to make the election a referendum on the Eisenhower years and to distinguish himself from those who wished only to maintain the status quo. He put Nixon on the defensive for Eisenhower's record and chipped away at the perception, privately expressed even by Nixon himself, that in a Kennedy–Nixon contest there would be no significant differences on foreign-policy questions.

Two days after Kennedy spoke on America's diminished position in the world, Eisenhower suffered yet another international embarrassment. Prior to Khrushchev's announcement that Eisenhower would no longer be welcome in the Soviet Union, the president had planned to go on from there to Japan. When the trip to Moscow fell through, Eisenhower decided on a two-week goodwill tour of the Philippines, Korea and Formosa. He began his trip on June 12 and was in Manila when Nobusuke Kishi, the Japanese prime minister, suggested it would be better if he did not come. Riots in protest at Eisenhower's arrival and at the use of bases on Japanese soil for the launch of future U-2 flights made it necessary to "postpone" the visit as officials could not guarantee the president's safety. The announcement that Eisenhower had been asked not to come to Japan served as further confirmation, if any were necessary, of the dismal picture painted by Kennedy in his Senate address and other speeches. Kennedy used the episode to illustrate further the loss of American power and prestige. Before two weeks had passed there was more calamitous news for the administration. On July 1, the Soviets shot down an RB-47 reconnaissance aircraft and recovered two pilots. Moscow claimed the plane had been targeted over Soviet territorial waters; Washington firmly, and this time univocally, denied it.

The cancellation of Eisenhower's trip to Japan and the downing of yet another plane were the third and fourth hammer strokes that, by Caccia's analysis, shattered the complacent mood of American voters as the presidential election drew near. The fifth was the drastic deterioration of US relations with Cuba, which led to Fidel Castro's seizure of oil refineries, sugar mills, utility companies and other US holdings on the island in the summer of 1960. Irked by Havana's romance with Moscow, Eisenhower had in March secretly approved a CIA plan to eliminate Castro that included preparations for an invasion by Cuban exiles. He also slashed the Cuban sugar quota. Meanwhile, Caccia reported to London, "The spectacle of the heavy-weight champion of the world being pushed around in his own backyard by such a fly-weight as Cuba was trying to American tempers and may be a portent of things to come." In this context, Kennedy's Churchillian message could scarcely have been timelier.

Jack Kennedy gained the presidential nomination on July 13, 1960, on the first ballot at the Democratic National Convention in Los Angeles. He had won all seven primaries he entered (New Hampshire, Wisconsin, Indiana, Nebraska, West Virginia, Maryland and Oregon) as well as in the three (Illinois, Massachusetts and Pennsylvania) where he had been a write-in candidate. He had not done as well as he had hoped against Hubert Humphrey in the Wisconsin race on April 5; that Kennedy had brought out the Roman Catholic vote in Wisconsin there could be no doubt, but there was anxiety that the achievement could boomerang by causing Protestants of both parties to join against him. His big victory on May 10 in West Virginia—a "Protestant state" where a Kennedy win, Richard Nixon had predicted in April, would assure his nomination—suggested that fears of a Protestant reaction to his candidacy were baseless.

In Los Angeles, Kennedy needed 761 votes to win the nomination, but garnered a total of 806 to Johnson's 409, Symington's 86 and Stevenson's 79^1/$_2$. The next day, Kennedy provided what some observers saw as the convention's "only real surprise" when he selected Johnson as his running mate rather than Symington, Senator Jackson of Washington or Governor Freeman of Minnesota.

In his acceptance speech, Kennedy alluded to Churchill's 1940 address, "Their Finest Hour," in which the new prime minister, speaking after the Battle of France, rejected the notion of an inquest in the House of Commons on the conduct of past governments. Kennedy took a similar approach to the mistakes of the Eisenhower years. He told the convention:

> I think the American people expect more from us than cries of
> indignation and attack. The times are too grave, the challenge too
> urgent, and the stakes too high to permit the customary passions
> of political debate. We are not here to curse the darkness, but to
> light the candle that can guide us through that darkness to a safe
> and sane future. As Winston Churchill said on taking office some
> twenty years ago: If we open a quarrel between the present and the
> past, we shall be in danger of losing the future.

Like Churchill at the close of that speech, Kennedy concluded that in events soon to come, his country must not fail. "All mankind waits upon our decision," the nominee declared. "A whole world looks to see what we will do. We cannot fail their trust, we cannot fail to try."

The Kennedy of the acceptance speech had something else in common with the Churchill of 1940. When Kennedy became the Democratic nominee, he made it clear that his campaign would be based not on what he intended to do for people, but on what he intended to ask of them. Pointedly, he held out the promise "of more sacrifice instead of more security."

Prior to the Democratic convention, Nixon had remarked to Selwyn Lloyd that of all likely candidates Kennedy would make the most formidable opponent. In the afterglow of Los Angeles, Kennedy and his running mate did seem impressive when they arrived in Washington in August for a rump session of Congress. But efforts to showcase the forty-three-year-old nominee's leadership ended in fiasco when a coalition of Republicans and Southern Democrats blocked legislation on medical aid to the aged, a comprehensive minimum hourly wage bill, and federal aid to education that Kennedy had intended to push through as part of his program to make America second to none. That he had failed, even with Johnson's adroit assistance, called his efficacy into question—a huge embarrassment to a candidate who had vowed to be a strong leader. Nixon pounced on Kennedy's inability to get the bills passed because they had been "too extreme" and because "the people" opposed them.

To make matters worse, rumors abounded that not all Democrats would necessarily be behind Kennedy in November. His nomination had displeased certain party members from the south, and the choice of Johnson had had a similar effect on liberals. By contrast, the Republicans, including conservatives led by Senator Barry Goldwater of Arizona and moderates led by Governor Nelson Rockefeller of New York, had united solidly behind Nixon after he was nominated in Chicago. Suspicions about Kennedy's youth and inexperience dogged his candidacy, while polls showed that voters regarded Nixon as the more seasoned. Nixon certainly was the better known, despite Kennedy's relentless campaigning. Early polls gave the vice president a healthy lead, 50 percent to 44, with 6 percent undecided. When Jack sought to debate Nixon on television, Eisenhower argued that Nixon ought not to permit Kennedy to share his spotlight. But Nixon, vain of his skills as a debater, agreed.

International affairs had significantly affected the presidential contest in recent weeks, and that continued to be the case in the fall when events at the United Nations provided a backdrop for the Kennedy–Nixon debates. On September 16, Khrushchev came to New York to attend the fifteenth session of the UN General Assembly, where seventeen new members—sixteen from Africa—were to be admitted. Khrushchev's theatrics, in the words of Britain's ambassador to the UN, Patrick Dean, attracted "continuous front page treatment, which relegated the presidential elections in the US to the inside columns." From the outset, Khrushchev found the perfect acting partner in Fidel Castro, who had also come to stir things up at the General Assembly. There was speculation at the time that the main purpose of Khrushchev's trip might be to embarrass Eisenhower in the election season. If Khrushchev sought to tweak the president on his home ground he could not have chosen a better helper than Castro, who had recently done a considerable amount of tweaking of his own when he nationalized many millions of dollars of US property in Cuba. In an effort to display solidarity with Cuba as well as with revolutionary forces across Latin America, Khrushchev went to Harlem's Theresa Hotel, where, with much fanfare, Castro had moved after an argument with the management of a midtown hotel and bitter threats to camp out in Central Park. Though the Soviet Union was the colossus, Khrushchev made the symbolic gesture of calling on Castro.

Cameras clicked as the Russian and the Cuban, who had never met before, embraced. Then they headed upstairs for a chat through interpreters. "You can imagine the uproar this episode caused in the American press and elsewhere as well," Khrushchev exulted in his memoirs. That uproar, it seems, had been precisely the point. Later, at the UN, in a marvelous bit of choreography Khrushchev strode from his seat to the front row where he again embraced Castro. This very public courtship left no doubt of Soviet intentions to intervene in all parts of the globe—even on America's very doorstep.

In addition to his main speech in the general debate, Khrushchev, in the course of twenty-five days, made four big speeches to the Assembly.

He often intervened on points of order or to claim his right of reply. He held forth on disarmament, imperialism, Chinese representation and Soviet claims of US aggression. He insisted that colonialism in all its forms was evil and ought to be abolished at once, and advertised the Soviet Union as the natural ally of exploited peoples. He sought the support of the uncommitted countries and boasted of Moscow's premier role in world affairs.

UN Secretary-General Dag Hammarskjold was denounced as a representative of the colonialist powers, and Khrushchev by turns urged Hammarskjold to quit and vowed that Russia would itself pull out of the UN. He assailed the structure of the UN, proposed to replace the secretary-general with a troika representing "the Western military bloc, the socialist states and the neutralist states," and demanded the world body move from New York. He ran the gamut of emotions, alternating between obnoxious threats and denunciations and seemingly heartfelt expressions of concern for the fate of mankind. His fury was laced with proverbs and homespun humor presumably designed to project the image of "a benign and basically 'simpatico' figure with whom business could be done." When Khrushchev was not actually speaking, he made his presence felt by leading energetic applause or by banging the desk in front of him with his fist or his shoe. Over in the British delegation, David Ormsby Gore, still a jazz aficionado, would lightly drum his own desk in mock reply.

Tension over the Russian's undignified behavior came to a head on the day Macmillan spoke. During Macmillan's address, Khrushchev banged the table with displeasure. Macmillan, also a consummate showman, paused to ask in a calculatedly calm voice, "Mr. President, perhaps we could have a translation. I could not quite follow." The auditorium dissolved in laughter at Khrushchev's expense, and the presiding assembly president pounded his gavel at the unruly Soviet leader. The press made much of the incident, and many were the contrasts between "British phlegm" and "Russian excitability."

Macmillan wrote in his diary that most participants, himself included, had "secretly enjoyed" Khrushchev's histrionics. Khrushchev made the entire city his stage, as when he appeared on a balcony at the Soviet Mission and sang a chorus of the workers' and Communists' anthem "The Internationale" to reporters below. In Macmillan's view, only Castro's retreat to Harlem and his four-and-a-quarter-hour anti-US diatribe had managed to snatch the limelight away from Khrushchev. By contrast, Eisenhower had delivered a lackluster address. "The President made a good enough speech," Macmillan wrote in his diary, "but it had no fire in it nor was it especially adroit. . . . The most powerful country in the world has, at the moment, weak leadership."

Macmillan, rather to his own surprise, much admired Jack Kennedy in the first of four nationally televised debates. It aired from Chicago while the rancorous UN session was still in progress. Macmillan watched it with David Ormsby Gore in his suite at the Waldorf–Astoria. The previous month at Bolton Abbey, the Devonshires' Yorkshire estate, Macmillan had confided to his nephew Andrew Devonshire that if Nixon became president he would send a professional diplomat to Washington, but that if Kennedy won he would send Ormsby Gore. At that point, Macmillan had been rooting for Nixon as the natural successor to his great friend Eisenhower. Eisenhower had told Macmillan that he knew what many people said against Nixon, but insisted he had "come on a lot" as vice president and it would be a "tragedy" if he were defeated. Most importantly, from Macmillan's perspective, Eisenhower had promised that in a Nixon presidency everything would be as the last administration had left it. Eisenhower would "certainly" continue to exert influence; he would make speeches and otherwise remain visible. Nixon would be "grateful" because he would know that Eisenhower had "made him." As to the Democratic candidate, Eisenhower at the time said he thought the opposition would be wise to choose a "respectable" man, such as Lyndon Johnson.

Since that conversation, Macmillan had heard from Robert Menzies, the Australian prime minister, that "old Joe Kennedy" had already poured "literally millions of dollars" into his son's campaign. Menzies quoted the sardonic comment of one prominent Democrat apropos the Catholic issue, "I am not afraid of the Pope. I am afraid of Papa!" Macmillan was a strong believer in Churchill's dictum that Britain and the United States must stand together in a special relationship against the menace of Soviet territorial ambitions, and had vivid memories of Joe Kennedy's anti-British stance in the 1930s. The news that old Joe had invested heavily in the presidential campaign led the prime minister to worry about Jack. "He wondered," observed Lord Stockton,

Macmillan's grandson, "whether this man was going to be his own master or whether Joe would be pulling the strings." That, added to concerns about how he would get on with a president so young and inexperienced, left the prime minister "apprehensive" about the Democratic candidate—even after the first debate.

The encounter had been billed as a discussion of domestic affairs, but Kennedy, who as his campaign had made clear viewed such matters in terms of America's vanished supremacy, was quick to invoke his overarching international theme. He also tied his remarks to Khrushchev's performance at the UN. "We discuss tonight domestic issues," Kennedy said in the first opening statement, "but I would not want that to be any implication that this does not involve directly our struggle with Mr. Khrushchev for survival. Mr. Khrushchev is in New York, and he maintains the Communist offensive throughout the world because of the productive power of the Soviet Union itself. . . . The kind of country we have here, the kind of society we have, the kind of strength we build in the US will be the defense of freedom. If we do well here, if we meet our obligations, if we're moving ahead, then I think freedom will be secure around the world. If we fail, then freedom fails. Therefore, I think the question before the American people is: Are we doing as much as we can do? Are we as strong as we should be? Are we as strong as we must be if we're going to maintain our independence, and if we're going to maintain and hold out the hand of friendship to those who look to us for assistance, to those who look to us for survival? I should make it very clear that I do not think we're doing enough, that I am not satisfied as an American with the progress that we're making."

As in "The Years the Locusts Have Eaten," Kennedy cited areas—economic growth, the production of scientists and engineers, power output, and so forth—in which, by his estimate, the United States had lost ground against the Soviets. He showed how that had diminished America's stature around the world, saying:

> I don't believe in big government, but I believe in effective governmental action. And I think that's the only way that the US is going to maintain its freedom. It's the only way that we're going to move ahead. I think we can do a better job. I think we're going to

have to do a better job if we are going to meet our responsibilities, which time and events have placed on us. We cannot turn the job over to anyone else. If the US fails, then the whole cause of freedom fails. And I think it depends in great measure on what we do here in this country. The reason Franklin Roosevelt was a good neighbor in Latin America was because he was a good neighbor in the US Because they felt that the American society was moving again. I want us to recapture that image. I want people in Latin America and Africa and Asia to start to look to America; to see how we're doing things; to wonder what the President of the US is doing; and not to look at Khrushchev, or look at the Chinese Communists. This is the obligation upon our generation. . . . I think it's time America started moving again.

Nixon went into the debates with a lead over Kennedy. Yet as soon as the debate began, his opponent put him on the defensive. Kennedy repeated his assertion that America had declined in the Eisenhower years, and the vice president was forced to insist that it had not. Rather than making a positive statement, Nixon cast his opening remarks in the form of a reply to Kennedy.

The things that Senator Kennedy has said many of us can agree with. There is no question but that we cannot discuss our internal affairs in the US without recognizing that they have a tremendous bearing on our international position. There is no question but that this nation cannot stand still, because we are in a deadly competition, a competition not only with the men in the Kremlin, but the men in Peking. . . . I subscribe completely to the spirit that Senator Kennedy has expressed tonight, the spirit that the US should move ahead. Where, then, do we disagree? I think we disagree on the implication of his remarks tonight and on the statements that he has made on many occasions during his campaign to the effect that the US has been standing still. . . . Let's look at the record. Is the US standing still? Is it true that the Administration, as Senator Kennedy has charged, has been an Administration of retreat, of defeat, of stagnation?

Nixon devoted the rest of his opening statement to an effort to disprove Kennedy's claims. In effect, Kennedy had set the agenda for this and future debates. Nixon was further handicapped by a wish to counter his image as "a man with an instinct for the jugular." His efforts to seem moderate and responsible compelled him, according to Caccia, "to avoid the sort of all-out attack which might have rallied the faithful." Then there was the matter of the vice president's physical appearance. Macmillan, on the basis of the first debate, jested that Nixon, with his dark, furtive face, looked like "a convicted criminal" while Kennedy resembled "a rather engaging undergraduate."

The prime minister, never one to emphasize the medium at the expense of the message, had also quickly spotted that Jack Kennedy had brains. That, according to his grandson, intrigued Macmillan. Kennedy later admitted that, aware of a family connection through Kick, he had been observing the prime minister for some time, but September 26 was Macmillan's first sustained look at the younger man. Whatever his anxieties, there could be no denying that he liked what he saw and heard.

"Your chap's beat," Macmillan needled Eisenhower over breakfast the next morning at the Waldorf-Astoria. Eisenhower claimed he had not watched the debate and lamented Nixon's decision to face Kennedy. "In his heart," Macmillan wrote at the time, "it seemed as if President Eisenhower thought that Mr. Nixon might lose." Since March, when he and Macmillan had last talked about the election, Eisenhower's enthusiasm for a Nixon presidency appeared to have diminished. On September 27, he told the prime minister that whoever won, "the position over defense matters and with the allies would be much more difficult" because neither candidate knew "anything about war." He proposed that he and Macmillan ought to talk after the election to decide "how best to handle the future."

In the aftermath of the first debate, Jack Kennedy was widely perceived to be fighting the vice president "on equal terms." In the next three encounters, on October 7, 13, and 21, Nixon struggled to regain ground. Khrushchev was still in the United States at the time of the second debate, and in light of the drama—some might say farce—at the UN, Nixon sought to prove himself the better equipped to deal with the Russian. He knew Khrushchev, after all, and had confronted him aggressively in the past. He insisted that with Khrushchev in the country, Kennedy ought to refrain from claims that American prestige was at an all-time low. He scolded the senator for "running down America" and argued that Kennedy, by spotlighting areas where the United States had slipped to second place, had himself diminished America's image abroad. He maintained that, contrary to anything Kennedy might say, Soviet prestige was at an all-time low and American prestige at a high.

From his opening statement in the first debate Nixon had been on the defensive, and there, despite his best efforts, he tended to remain. By contrast, Kennedy managed by turns to criticize the administration and to suggest what he would do to restore supremacy. He talked fluently of the economy, of civil rights and of the space program in terms of how improvements in those areas would bolster US prestige. Western interests in Berlin would be protected, and US military might augmented in anticipation of an imminent crisis there. He quoted Churchill on the policy of arming to parley, and promised to go back to the table in Geneva immediately for "one last effort to secure an agreement on the cessation of nuclear tests."

Nixon did himself no favors with his performance in the debates. Arguably he scored one body blow, though the damage would not be fully evident till after Kennedy became president. The islands of Quemoy and Matsu near the Chinese mainland had figured prominently in the Churchill–Eisenhower correspondence, and they also played an important role in the Kennedy–Nixon debates. Kennedy, in essence, took the Churchill view that while the United States ought certainly to defend Formosa against the Chinese Communists, it should take no steps to protect Quemoy and Matsu on behalf of Chiang Kai-shek. Nixon echoed Eisenhower's argument that to give in on the offshore islands would only encourage further Communist belligerency. Eisenhower had urged Churchill to consider that to capitulate on Quemoy and Matsu would be even "worse than a Munich," as Hitler at least had pledged "to cease expansion and to keep the peace" while the Chinese Communists had promised nothing. The specter of appeasement reappeared in the presidential debates when Nixon, attacking Kennedy on the subject, seemed by his choice of words to remind voters that his opponent was the son of a man who had urged America to learn to live with the dictators. "This is the history of dealing with dictators," said Nixon. "This is something that Mr. Kennedy and all Americans must know. We tried this with Hitler. It didn't work. He wanted first Austria, and then he went on to the Sudetenland and then Danzig, and each time it was thought this is all that he wanted." Nixon repeated the charges later in the debates. Kennedy, in turn, mocked Nixon's determination to defend "islands five miles off the coast of the Republic of China when he's never really protested the Communists seizing Cuba, ninety miles off the coast of the US." He suggested that the administration had been soft on Cuba, and Nixon, though aware of the secret invasion plans, was in no position to reveal them. The "appeaser" label was one that Kennedy would have to deal with as president, but in the campaign it proved less damaging than Nixon must have hoped.

Jack Kennedy later said that without the debates he would never have won the election. Exposure on national television blunted the charge that Kennedy was immature. Caccia reported back to London that viewers had seen Kennedy "answering questions at least as aggressively, maturely and responsibly as Mr. Nixon and with an even greater wealth of information and statistics at his command." That Kennedy's looks and manner better suited him for television there could be no doubt, but Caccia believed that the more important sources of his triumph lay in the force of his message and the breadth of his knowledge. In a similar vein, Walter Lippmann wrote in the *New York Herald Tribune*, "It has been truly impressive to see the precision of Mr. Kennedy's mind, his immense command of the facts, his instinct for the crucial point, his singular lack of demagoguery and sloganeering, his intense concern and interest in the subject itself, the stability and steadfastness of his nerves and his coolness and his courage. And through it all have transpired the recognizable marks of the man who, besides being highly trained, is a natural leader, organizer and ruler of men." Nixon was later said to have blamed his loss of the election on biased newspaper coverage, but as the British ambassador pointed out, the televised debates had given voters an opportunity to see and judge for themselves.

Meanwhile, Kennedy methodically hammered away with references to Churchill and Britain in the 1930s. He told voters in Grand Rapids, Michigan, that the best way to understand the present was "to study the history of the thirties." "I know what happens to a nation that sleeps too long," he declared at the New York Coliseum. "I saw the British deceive themselves before World War II, as Winston Churchill tried in vain to awaken them and while England slept, Hitler rearmed; and if we sleep too long in the sixties, Mr. Khrushchev will 'bury' us yet."

Again and again he returned to a favorite theme—the 1935 general election, whose dramatic prelude Jack had witnessed in his youth. He told a crowd in Philadelphia, Pennsylvania, "I spent some time in England before World War II and I recall very clearly the election of 1935, when Winston Churchill was warning of the danger of a rearmed Germany. Stanley Baldwin, the head of the Conservative Party of England at that time, chose to go to the people in that election telling them that all was well, that their future was peaceful, and, as a result, the British lost two years which could have been devoted to preparing for action." Before Kennedy had the nomination he had compared Eisenhower to Baldwin. Now it was Nixon he compared to the candidate who had failed to tell the public the truth. Kennedy attacked Nixon for telling voters that US prestige in the world had never been higher. "I recall in 1935," Jack said at a rally in the Bronx, New York, "when Winston Churchill was warning of the dangers of the Nazi rise, Stanley Baldwin, the leader of the Conservative Party, told the people of England that everything was being done in its own good time. He won that election and England almost lost the war." In New Haven, Connecticut, Jack remarked of Nixon, "I do not recall any candidate for office whose speeches have shown less reaction to the actual facts since Stanley Baldwin."

Jack Kennedy made the question of whether Nixon actually believed the United States was still ahead of Russia a campaign theme. "If he really believes these things he says, in my opinion he disqualifies himself," Kennedy told an audience in Kansas City. "If he does not believe them, and runs on that program, he makes the same mistake that Stanley Baldwin made in England in 1935, which almost destroyed Great Britain, by misleading the people of England. . . . By not telling them the truth, he prevented them from arming at a time when it might have been possible to prevent the disaster of Munich."

Repeatedly Jack Kennedy identified himself with the man who had warned Britain about Hitler. At a campaign stop in St. Louis, Missouri, he spoke of the Churchill who had urged Americans to wake up to the Soviet threat. He reminded voters of Churchill's speech in nearby Fulton and of his assertion that there was nothing the Soviets admired so much as strength and nothing for which they had less respect than weakness. He argued that Churchill's "prophetic" words of 1946—"We cannot afford, if we can help it, to work on narrow margins offering temptations to a trial of strength"—had even greater significance in 1960. Jack went on, "If we are to protect our heritage of freedom—if we are to maintain it around the world—we must be strong—militarily, economically, educationally and morally strong. And that is why I am dedicating this campaign to the goal of a stronger America—to the proposition that this Nation is strong but can and must be stronger."

In the end the voters chose Kennedy by a slim margin. He won the popular vote by a mere 118,574, though the electoral college vote was 303–219 in his favor. The numbers suggested that Kennedy would have to be careful of his credit with Congress and with voters. At the same time, Eisenhower's announcement within a week of the election that confidence in the dollar was threatened—a crisis long in the making—seemed vividly to confirm the national decline Kennedy had vowed to reverse. In private, Eisenhower used "barrack-room language" about the man who had become his successor by portraying his two terms in Washington as the years the locusts had eaten.

Jack Kennedy's decision to run "on the Churchill ticket" had served him brilliantly. And on November 11, 1960, the giant whose words Jack had been poring over since boyhood addressed a telegram to the president-elect: "On the occasion of your election to your great Office I salute you. The thoughts of the Free World will be with you in the challenging tasks that lie ahead. May I add my own warm good wishes. Winston S. Churchill."

CHAPTER TWELVE

What the Man Would Like to Be

O N JANUARY 20, 1961, WASHINGTON WAS BURIED BENEATH nearly eight inches of snow when Jack Kennedy took the oath of office as America's thirty-fifth president. A cluster of Kennedys sat on the platform just behind him, and none seemed prouder than his father. Sporting a top hat, Joseph P. Kennedy looked rather as he had when he served as Ambassador to the Court of St. James's. To those who knew him well, it seemed as if the old man had never been happier than on the day Jack became president. Yet, given Joe's history, there was something decidedly ironic in his son having campaigned "on the Churchill ticket," and even more so in the fact that Jack came to office with a set of goals drawn from Churchill's ideas about the postwar world.

Twenty-three years after Joe Kennedy, when he became ambassador in London, positioned himself as the adversary of Winston Churchill, Jack Kennedy took up Churchill's mantle. Though he did not mention Churchill by name, in the inaugural address he laid out a Soviet strategy based on postwar speeches from "The Sinews of Peace" on. Like Churchill, President Kennedy took as a starting point the manner in which the existence of all-annihilating weapons had transformed the world. Eisenhower, who at Bermuda in 1953 had exasperated Churchill by his refusal to acknowledge the monumental changes that the new weapons had wrought, looked on as his successor declared, "The world is very different now. For man holds in his mortal hands the power to abolish all forms of human poverty and all forms of human life." Churchill had, on various occasions, laid out precisely that choice. Like Churchill, Kennedy called on both sides in the Cold War to "begin anew the quest for peace, before the dark powers of destruction unleashed by science engulf all humanity in planned or accidental self-destruction." Echoing the Churchillian dictum about arming not for war but for peace, Kennedy insisted that the United States must avoid tempting the other side with weakness. "For only when our arms are sufficient beyond doubt," he said, "can we be certain beyond doubt that they will never be employed." And he repeated Churchill's call for negotiations based on limited areas of common interest where both sides might agree, no matter how far apart otherwise. "Let us never negotiate out of fear, but let us never fear to negotiate," Kennedy proposed. "Let both sides explore what problems unite us, instead of belaboring those problems which divide us."

As to where it might be possible to find a confluence of interest Kennedy, having often discussed that question with David Ormsby Gore, continued, "Let both sides, for the first time, formulate serious and precise proposals for the inspection and control of arms—and bring the absolute power to destroy other nations under the absolute control of all nations." The aged, ailing Churchill, in speaking of the goal of a settlement with the Soviets, had poignantly declared in 1953, "Time will undoubtedly be needed—more time than some of us here are likely to see." So, too, Kennedy, though only forty-three, said of the program outlined in his inaugural address, "All this will not be finished in the first one hundred days, nor in the life of this administration, nor even perhaps in our lifetime on this planet. But let us begin." Churchill had been gratified when the West rearmed after the war, but by the time he left office in 1955 he had failed to realize the second part of his double-barreled policy. A first agreement with Moscow—the start of the process of infiltration whereby so long as war could be avoided the closed Soviet society would at length be defeated without bloodshed— had eluded him. That breakthrough agreement was the "beginning" to which Kennedy had referred during the campaign ("The problem is to find a beginning") and to which he repeatedly came back in his inaugural address ("begin anew the quest for peace," "So let us begin anew," "But let us begin"). With those words he enunciated a central theme of his presidency. As he saw it, the effort to secure a new beginning in East–West relations had nothing to do with appeasement. In 1938, Jack Kennedy had written to his father in praise of the ambassador's position on Munich and the need to learn to live with the dictators; in 1961, far from proposing to live with the dictators in Moscow, he followed Churchill in viewing contact and agreements as part of a fully-fledged battle plan to bring about the downfall of Soviet Communism in an age when war was no longer an option for rational men. Various hands—writers and advice-givers—contributed to the final version of the address, which had many strands and sources. But at the heart of the address were Churchill's ideas for how to beat the Russians peacefully.

Years of reading and discussion had led Jack Kennedy to embrace those ideas, though he had started out in political life with a very different approach. Still, there is a difference between speaking of great ideas and actually striving to put them into practice, and Harold Caccia found himself wondering whether Kennedy was prepared to do the latter given an electorate that, for all the rapturous applause on inauguration day, had a history of favoring a confrontational stance toward the Soviets and disdaining those on their own side who seemed soft. There could be no doubt that the young, vigorous, charismatic new leader had scored an oratorical triumph and persuaded many people that he was the man to reverse the humiliations of Eisenhower's last months in office. Still, the British ambassador said privately of the speech, "It is what the man would like to be." Whether Kennedy had it in him to become that president remained to be seen. In his political career to date he had been largely untested, having done remarkably little besides run for office. "Time alone," Caccia decreed after the inauguration, "will show whether Mr. Kennedy will live up to the high purpose which he has enunciated."

In the heady early weeks of the presidency, there were indications that he might soon live up to it. Kennedy had called for a shift in relations with the Soviets, and Moscow from the first appeared eager to cooperate. On a number of occasions since the election, Mikhail Menshikov, the Soviet ambassador in Washington, had conveyed Khrushchev's optimism about a new administration. Menshikov had asked Robert Kennedy and others with access to the president-elect to tell him of Khrushchev's desire for better relations, as well as his confidence that in private conversation he and the new American leader would be able to reach agreement on the key issues of disarmament and Berlin. The day after the inauguration, Khrushchev, having ordered Kennedy's speech published in the Soviet press, publicly signaled his response to the president's proposals. In a sign of Moscow's wish to start afresh, Khrushchev announced the release of the two American pilots captured the previous July after their RB-47 reconnaissance aircraft was shot down over what Moscow had insisted were Russian territorial waters. The downing of the plane had been one of several episodes, starting with the U-2 incident, that had undermined voter confidence in the Republican administration and made it easier to argue for the necessity of new leadership. To Kennedy, the prisoners' release, coming as it did so soon after he had publicly and emphatically situated détente at the center of his presidential aspirations, was the happiest possible way to start in office.

Under other circumstances Kennedy might have been more skeptical and cautious, but in the atmosphere of euphoria that followed the inauguration he was tempted by Khrushchev's suggestion of an early informal encounter. The US ambassador in Moscow, Llewellyn Thompson, liked the idea and advised that such a meeting, before the new president could be expected to have formulated fixed positions, might have the advantage of allowing him to persuade his counterpart of his sincere desire for negotiations, as well as establishing which issue he and Khrushchev would "tackle first, which I assume would be atomic testing." At this point, Thompson suggested, no substantive discussions would occur, only an effort to set the agenda to Kennedy's liking. At the very least, an early meeting would offer an opportunity for the leaders to take one another's measure. During the campaign, Kennedy had had much to say about the foolishness of going to the Paris summit without adequate preparation, yet there was also an element in him drawn to Churchill's notion of summitry not so much as negotiations but as frank conversation between equals. Kennedy, made overconfident perhaps by the cheers of the crowd, failed to consider that Churchill's faith in what might be accomplished at a top-level meeting had been based on decades of personal experience of a kind that the new president entirely lacked.

It seemed to Jack Kennedy at the outset of his presidency that, in the short term, he and Khrushchev wanted the same thing. The long term, he recognized, was another matter: While the American leader hoped peacefully to outmaneuver the Communists, the Russian believed that Communism, given a chance to thrive, would inevitably prevail. At a meeting with Soviet analysts including Thompson, Averell Harriman, Charles Bohlen and George Kennan, Kennedy heard the experts agree that Khrushchev's "deepest desire" was to avoid a military conflict and thereby "gain time" for his side to make the economic advances by which he fully expected to defeat the West. The experts confirmed that at that moment East and West seemed to have "one common enemy"—war. They concurred that Khrushchev was hungry for a disarmament agreement and other diplomatic successes in 1961. Buoyed by everything he had seen and heard thus far, and after poring over the record of Khrushchev's 1959 talks with Eisenhower, Kennedy wrote to the Russian leader on February 22 to express the hope for an "early informal exchange of views."

Every element appeared to be on track to accomplish Jack Kennedy's overriding goal of a first major postwar agreement with the Soviets in the form of a nuclear test ban treaty. He had come to view the test ban as important not only in itself, but as the start of a process of trust that might lead over time to the opening up of the closed Communist society and the undoing of Soviet power. He had campaigned hard for his strategy of peace, a fundamental component of which was the test ban as a possible new beginning. In the inaugural address he had powerfully evoked the theme of beginnings, and two weeks later he had sent word to the Russians, via Secretary of State Dean Rusk, that "priority attention" would be given to the push for an agreement on nuclear testing. Ormsby Gore had conveyed the need for the British and American teams to arrive in Geneva with a meticulously prepared joint negotiating position; as president-elect, Kennedy had arranged to shift the talks' start date from February to March 21 to give their side time to do its homework. When he and Ormsby Gore had conferred in New York in December, he had asked David, in his capacity as head of the British delegation at Geneva, to come to Washington following the inauguration to help the American negotiators formulate the fresh proposals expected of a new administration. The signals from Moscow in recent weeks seemed amply to confirm Ormsby Gore's optimism. As the

Geneva talks drew near, Kennedy exulted in the likelihood of a swift breakthrough.

On the evening of February 28, 1961, Kennedy, in the Oval Office, also found reason to rejoice in a newly released Gallup poll. In November he had been disappointed by his slender margin of victory and the tenuous mandate it afforded, so a 72 percent approval rating after a month in office was most welcome. Particularly pleased that his numbers were even better than Eisenhower's at the end of his first month, he took the elevator upstairs to the family quarters shortly after eight. But his delight was not unalloyed. He knew what he wanted to accomplish in office and he acknowledged, as he had not at the time of his Harvard thesis, that it was a leader's duty to act regardless of the political risks. He had reflected in *Profiles in Courage* on the "political courage" required of anyone in American public life who pursued new and unorthodox ways of dealing with the enemy in Moscow. Though he had once adamantly defended Stanley Baldwin, he had since come out firmly against that prime minister's willingness to jeopardize the national well-being for his own political self-interest. During the campaign he had criticized Eisenhower and Nixon for what he saw as an abdication of duty comparable to Baldwin's. But when he made that criticism he had been speaking theoretically, as one not yet confronted with the reality of leadership—and with the temptation, which anyone might feel, to do what it takes to hold on to power and to rationalize the reasons for doing so. Now that Kennedy was "playing the part" himself, as Macmillan liked to say, the superb approval ratings suggested all that he had to lose. As would become clear that night, his feelings about Baldwin remained divided. He might now think that Baldwin had been wrong when, operating as a politician rather than a statesman, he succumbed to the pressure of public opinion and took the politically safe course of failing to ensure that Britain rearmed adequately. Yet, in spite of himself, part of him remained attracted to Baldwin's argument that he had had no choice but to act as he had lest he fail to win reelection and see a man with a less positive agenda take his place.

Jack Kennedy had first debated the role and responsibilities of a leader in a democratic society in 1938, when the inclusion in *Arms and the Covenant* of the Churchill–Baldwin exchange on the 1935 election, along with Randolph Churchill's prefatory remarks about the difference between the politician and the statesman, ignited ardent discussion among Jack's young British friends. They argued about how much attention a leader ought to pay to public opinion; and they argued about whether, in cases where there was a disparity between a leader's views and the public's, he ought to wait for the people to catch up, as Baldwin claimed to have done, or strive à la Churchill to educate an electorate that might well punish him at the polls for his efforts. More than two decades later, the debate continued at the White House when on the night of February 28 David Ormsby Gore joined Jack in the book-filled West Sitting Room in the family quarters. Now the discussion was no longer academic. The Jack Kennedy who persisted in wrestling with the meaning of leadership was himself now the leader of the most powerful nation in the world. Ormsby Gore, having done much since 1954 to convert his old friend to some of the very ideas that threatened to be politically problematic when Jack tried to realize them, was eager to keep him on course.

In contrast to Kennedy, who loved the spotlight, Ormsby Gore was self-effacing by nature. His sole concern was that the issues he cared about were effectively advanced. It has been said that the role of the aristocrats in Macmillan's government was largely decorative and marginal, but Ormsby Gore's quiet, persistent, behind-the-scenes work during the next three years would be nothing of the sort. Without question, times had changed and his class had lost much of its power, yet he was determined, as Captain Charles Waterhouse wrote in 1944 of Billy Hartington, "to play his part in directing the current and not merely to be swept away by it." Ormsby Gore later recalled that from the outset of his career in government his ambition had been to move events "in certain directions which I believed in." "And if that is your motive," he reflected, "you want to get some kind of hand on the levers of power. . . . One hoped for the day one might be given the opportunity." Jack Kennedy's election offered precisely such an opportunity, and Ormsby Gore had wasted no time positioning himself to make good use of it. He had already had a huge influence in helping Jack to devise a more flexible and intelligent approach to Soviet relations in the nuclear age, and now he aspired to do more.

At the time of the election David had been posted to the UN in New York. After Jack's victory he had written to Alec Home (formerly

Lord Dunglass), the foreign secretary, for approval to approach the president-elect both as a friend and as a representative of the British government. After all, Jack was no longer just David's intimate since 1938 when, both overshadowed by older brothers, they had seemed the least ambitious and least promising fellows in their London set. He was the US president-elect and David a member of the Macmillan government, and there must be no mixed signals from the British end. Jack would be aware that David, in his official capacity, was likely to report the content of their talks back to London. Yet their long intimacy and shared frame of reference promised to make those talks especially productive.

Ormsby Gore's message, though welcome at the Foreign Office, was met with a dash of nervousness. Could he really, as he claimed, engineer an invitation to see the president-elect "at almost any time"? Could he really just invite himself to stay with Kennedy's brother in order to have an opportunity to meet with the president-elect "on a wholly informal basis"? Was he really in a position to assume that he would be asked to stay with the Kennedys in Florida? Though his friendship with the Kennedy family was no secret, and though Macmillan himself had already spoken to Andrew Devonshire of sending David to Washington as Britain's ambassador, his superiors found it hard to grasp that a minister of state in the Foreign Office could enjoy quite the entrée, let alone the influence implied. There was concern on the British side that there be no perception that they were somehow "running after" America's new leader. Caccia, on the phone from Washington, pointed out that there was likely to be a large number of supplicants, both domestic and foreign, and that Ormsby Gore must avoid making it seem as if the British wished "to join or crash the queue."

Presently, to the amazement of just about everyone on the British side except David, and before any kind of overture was made, he heard suddenly from Jack. The president-elect intended to be in New York in December to interview candidates for high-level appointments, and he asked to see David then. In short, there had been no need to request a meeting, let alone finagle one. The two men had been talking on and off since the eve of the Second World War, and Kennedy, who had profited immensely from those talks, did not intend for them to cease.

Besides, as Robert Kennedy would later say, David was "part of the family." Kick and Billy's determination to be together in spite of formidable obstacles, as well as her decision to remain in London as a widow, had given Jack's friendship with David a chance to ripen. By the time of Kick's death in 1948 they were not merely friends with a great fund of shared interests and pleasures, but family.

Over lunch at the Carlyle Hotel in New York on December 7, 1960, David, for the first time but not the last, walked a delicate line between his roles as close personal friend and the representative of a foreign government. He had been under orders—though none would have been necessary—to make it clear that both Home and Macmillan knew and warmly approved of the encounter. Home had suggested a number of topics on which the Foreign Office hoped to learn the president-elect's views, but by and large David was free to proceed as he thought best. Though the session had its official moments, for the most part the friends bantered, sparred and debated as always. The fact that they had conferred regularly during the campaign and that David had done much to help assemble vital policy facilitated the brisk pace both had long favored. Anxious by his own account not to create an impression that he was "just pumping" Jack, David frequently digressed from international affairs. Yet, as his reports to the Foreign Office demonstrate, the repartee established two decades previously allowed the men to cover an enormous amount of serious ground in an hour and a half. No less important than their shared past were the goals they had in common—goals that might never have been articulated had it not been for David's decade's worth of experience in Soviet affairs, and that might never be realized were it not for Jack's position of power.

By the time David came to the White House in February for their first meeting since the inauguration, any traces of awkwardness that had arisen from the monumental shift in Jack's status had vanished. Jack, by his own account surrounded by a good many people he barely knew—both new appointees and holdovers from the prior administration—and as yet uncertain about whose judgment to trust, welcomed the chance for a long, frank talk. He did of course have his brother Robert, whom he had appointed attorney general. But Bobby, the president's "most loyal supporter and admirer," besides being young and inexperienced in the foreign-policy issues that urgently confronted the new leader was, by Harold Caccia's assessment at any rate, "not an 'ideas man.'" As his own comments then and later left no doubt, Bobby, who in emulation of his brother had cultivated a close friendship of his own with Ormsby Gore in London after the war, prized the latter's influence on Jack.

From "Appeasement at Munich," through *Profiles in Courage*, through his public statements during the presidential campaign, the Baldwin question had been a preoccupation of Jack's. That it would emerge as a motif of his presidency suggested itself when Jack, having boasted to David that his approval ratings were 4 percent higher than Eisenhower's after his first month in office, went on to speak repeatedly of areas where, if he acted on his convictions, those ratings might quickly plummet. He had worked for years to become president, and to his electoral triumph was added the sort of personal acclaim it would be hard for anyone to put at risk. For a new leader hoping to take bold measures that were a departure from anything the electorate had accepted in the past, the soaring approval ratings in their way made the task ahead more difficult.

Tonight was not the first time David had confronted the possibility that Jack's enduring ambivalence about the Baldwin question—his undeniable attraction to what Churchill in "The Violation of the Rhineland" had called "the easy applause of public opinion"—might stand in the way of his actually doing some of the things he believed right for the country. The previous December in New York, Jack had told David of a tense meeting with Eisenhower the day before, when the president and president-elect had discussed the question of whether Communist China should be admitted to the UN. Kennedy had maintained that it would be foolish to exclude China. Eisenhower had strongly disagreed, and though he professed to recognize that former presidents should not speak out on foreign policy, he vowed to comment publicly in the event of any move to admit or recognize the Chinese. When he recounted the incident to David, Jack had seemed "shaken" by Eisenhower's attitude and by the potential for public embarrassment to himself. During the campaign Jack had attacked Eisenhower for a lack of willingness to make unpopular decisions, but hardly was the election over when Jack began to speak privately of waiting six or nine months to see where his prestige stood in the United

States before deciding whether to take such risks himself. He told David that if his prestige was high he might be able to take decisive action on China, but that if he were "in low water" it would be better not to risk denunciation by "a figure as respected as Eisenhower" as well as by other political adversaries. The day before Jack took office, Eisenhower had again warned him about the vehemence of his own opinion on China. Now that he was president, Jack appeared more worried than ever about a political attack from his predecessor should he follow his convictions.

China was not the only area where he worried about jeopardizing his political standing. He returned to the identical theme when, with regard to an even more pressing matter, he went on to speak of the tough decisions that faced him in Laos, and here again he seemed tempted to protect himself politically by backing off from the policy he thought best. During the Eisenhower years, the United States had supported the right-wing military regime of Phoumi Nosavan against the Communist Pathet Lao because the former had declared itself pro-American. Kennedy came to office determined to alter the Eisenhower policy. In the belief that efforts to prop up a corrupt and unpopular regime were foolhardy and that the United States could not hope to succeed militarily in Laos, he had concluded that the best hope for Laos would be a neutral government to serve as a buffer between Vietnam and Thailand. Though Eisenhower had warned the president-elect that Laos was the key to Southeast Asia and that the United States must be prepared to intervene unilaterally to prevent that country from falling to the Communists, and though people at the Pentagon and the State Department, as well as some on the ground in Southeast Asia, had since urged him to reaffirm US support for Phoumi, Kennedy persisted in his belief in the desirability of a neutral Laos. On the evening of the 28th, he confided his anxieties to Ormsby Gore, who, by the testimony of Bobby Kennedy, had been "instrumental" in persuading Jack of the need for a change in US policy there. Again, at the close of his first month in office the thing that worried Jack most was the potential for political damage to himself. He worried that after an agreement to establish a neutral Laos had been reached at the conference table, or perhaps even before, the country might indeed go Communist and that he would look soft for having accepted a Communist takeover without a fight. Seeing that political considerations were causing Jack to waver, David joined him in methodically reviewing the lengthy reasoning process that had led him to commit to the idea of a neutral government in the first place. The discussion helped him to stay the course.

Jack needed such a conversation with someone he could trust for, by his own account, he had found that the early weeks of a new presidency could be a perilous period for the nation. Whereas in Britain a new prime minister would have previously worked with every member of his Cabinet, as the new president, Jack found it difficult to evaluate the recommendations of team members he as yet barely knew. That, at any rate, had been his experience on being advised repeatedly that it would be best to continue US support for Phoumi. In the matter of Laos, he had at least had the benefit of input from David, but when it came to the other "mess"—as Jack called it—that Eisenhower had left behind for him to "clean up," he would of necessity be on his own in weighing the advice he had been given. A plan to eliminate Castro, authorized by Eisenhower the previous March, would soon lead to a debacle which, the president later judged, might have been avoided had he not had to take a decision before he was familiar with the particular men urging him to go forward. The plan's authors and chief boosters, Allen Dulles and Richard Bissell at the CIA, were the same experts who had urged on the U-2 spy mission that wrecked the Paris summit, drastically diminished voter confidence in Eisenhower, and gave Kennedy a crucial opportunity to attack the administration's incompetence. Now that Kennedy was president, they lavished advice on him. Within six to eight weeks of Kennedy's first day in office, the CIA intended to put a strike force of more than seven hundred Cuban exiles on a beachhead in Cuba. In preparation, three US Special Forces teams were overseeing a secret training program in Guatemala. Dulles and Bissell insisted that the attack on Cuba would trigger widespread uprisings and a civil war. At worst, should the uprisings fail to materialize, the brigade would disperse to the mountains, where they would transform themselves into a guerrilla force such as Castro himself had once led. In any case, in the absence of overt US military support, no one need ever know of Washington's involvement in the attack.

Dulles and Bissell were pressing for a quick decision, as they argued the attack had to take place no later than early April. The reasons were manifold: Guatemala was unwilling to permit the exile force to be housed there beyond that date; the exiles themselves, after months of training in spartan facilities, threatened to grow restive; the onset of the rainy season in Guatemala would sap the forces' morale and make their landing in Cuba more difficult; the Castro regime was steadily consolidating its control; Havana was reportedly about to take delivery of a shipment of Soviet jets and a contingent of Cuban pilots was soon to return from training in Czechoslovakia. Without an immediate go-ahead, the opportunity to be rid of Castro would be lost and, when word of his decision inevitably leaked out, Kennedy would be perceived as soft, or so the CIA assured him. At a moment when Jack believed himself to be on the verge of an agreement in Geneva, an invasion would of course be blatantly antithetical to everything he hoped to accomplish, but despite a gut dislike for the inherited plan he continued to weigh the CIA's arguments. The plan's clandestine nature made it impossible to spell out his quandary to David Ormsby Gore on the evening of February 28. Jack did, however, speak of it generally and rather ruefully as one of the left-behind messes that, if he failed to make the right decision, threatened him politically.

For all his anxiety, Jack remained focused on everything that had gone spectacularly right in his first month as president—culminating in that night's poll numbers. As the friends dined together and Jackie flitted in and out of an adjoining bedroom to model for her husband's appraisal the latest additions to her wardrobe, Jack spoke of the possibility of an early informal meeting with Khrushchev. Told that Kennedy had already written to suggest such an encounter, David was dismayed. He doubted Thompson's certainty that there would be no question of getting down to serious talks at this stage. David thought it unwise, as he put it, "to hang out an invitation sign with no real intention of talking substance on any single issue." Having long studied Khrushchev, he expressed doubt that the Russian leader would be satisfied with anything so benign as the get-acquainted meeting Jack anticipated. Calling a top-level encounter "premature," he urged his friend not to proceed. But though Thompson had yet to deliver the president's letter to Khrushchev, Kennedy was not prepared to reconsider. While on the one hand he seemed to perceive political danger everywhere, on the other, his spirits were so high that he appeared to believe nothing could really go wrong.

Indeed, the overall tone of the friends' discussion, which stretched past midnight, was ebullient and festive on both sides. As far as Jack was concerned, the best was yet to come. Most of the evening was devoted to going over the details of the upcoming resumption of the Geneva test ban talks. For Jack, as for David, nothing could be more important than what happened in Geneva. All of their conversations since the eve of Jack's life-threatening back surgery in 1954 had been leading to the moment when Moscow signed on to a first major post-war agreement. Whatever the signs that night that, in certain areas, President Kennedy might be prepared à la Baldwin to subordinate his convictions to political self-interest, he showed no such inclination here. He had assembled a first-rate US delegation headed by Arthur Dean, and David had been working with his American counterparts to make all the changes in the Western position which he believed were necessary for a deal. In addition to the favorable signs from Moscow on the general prospects for détente, American and British scientists had returned from a conference in the Soviet Union in December with high hopes that the Russians were indeed ready to come to terms on a test ban treaty. Moscow's acceptance of the US–British proposals, which seemed likely to occur as early as Jack's second month in office, would be a first significant step in launching his strategy of peace—a brilliant start to his presidency.

Ormsby Gore went to Geneva with an enormous sense of anticipation, but two days before the test ban talks reopened there were distressing signs. In a conversation with Llewellyn Thompson on March 19, Soviet First Deputy Foreign Minister Vasili Kuznetsov, citing the military budget increases announced in Kennedy's State of the Union address in January, expressed suspicion that by talking disarmament the Americans, like the Germans after the First World War, were merely stalling in order to give themselves time to rearm. Things only got worse on the first day in Geneva, when it became clear that the Soviet position had hardened substantially during the recess. Since the two sides had last met, the Soviet negotiators had changed their minds in vital areas. Ormsby Gore's optimism dissolved as he listened to a demand for a troika or three-man council—with one representative each for the Soviet Union, the Western powers, and the uncommitted countries—to replace the single impartial administrator previously agreed upon. Echoing as it did Khrushchev's demand of a troika to oversee the UN, the surprise proposal led to concern on the Western side that acceptance of it might lay the foundations for a serious attack on the UN. To Ormsby Gore's further dismay, Moscow also reversed itself on the matter of an independent inspection system. The Soviets went back to demanding to police themselves, and that was unacceptable. The talks dragged on, but it had become evident that if a treaty were to be had at all there would be much difficulty along the way. For Kennedy, the disappointment was more than just the inability to secure the test ban. Two months into his presidency, he had lost, at least for the moment, the beginning he had spoken of so movingly during the campaign and in his inaugural address.

By the last week in March, the signs from Moscow were dramatically different from most since the election. The change—which observers in London and Washington attributed by turns to internal pressure on Khrushchev's leadership and to a desire on his part to bolster his nation's position with respect to China—did not manifest itself only at the test ban talks. In what seemed from Kennedy's perspective a related development, five or six battalions of the Communist Pathet Lao, with Soviet arms and equipment, were forcing the demoralized Laotian government forces to retreat. In the best of circumstances, Kennedy had been nervous about the political consequences to himself of his decision to depart from Eisenhower's Laos policy, and now, in view of the darkening picture there, he was under even greater pressure from the Pentagon to abandon his commitment to a neutral government and order immediate military intervention. But Kennedy persisted in his preference for a diplomatic settlement. The day after the test ban talks opened so disappointingly, Kennedy sent word to the British that intervention in Laos might soon be necessary to save at least some of the country. At the same time he encouraged the British, in their capacity as co-chairs of the international commission responsible for the Indochina peace settlement, to persuade Moscow to agree to a ceasefire in anticipation of a conference, attended by all sides, to establish an authentically neutral and independent Laos. He hoped the Soviets would assent to a ceasefire; the trouble, as he saw it, was what would happen if they declined. In a televised news conference on March 23, Kennedy told the American people of his support for efforts to establish Laos as a neutral nation, but he added pointedly that that might change if there were no halt to the ongoing attack by externally supported Communists. The next day, troubled by an ambiguous telegram from Macmillan that seemed to indicate that even if the Russians proved uncooperative Britain might withhold support for military intervention and leave the United States to go in alone, Kennedy proposed an impromptu meeting with the British leader. Viewing Laos and Southeast Asia as part of the general Soviet problem, he wanted to be certain that the United States and the United Kingdom were in accord before he received the Soviet foreign minister, Andrei Gromyko, in Washington on March 27. As Macmillan was to be in Trinidad at the start of a tour of the West Indies and was not scheduled to come to Washington until April 5, Kennedy telegraphed to ask him to fly to the military base in Key West, Florida, on Sunday, March 26, to review the options in Laos.

It was 4 a.m. on Saturday morning in Trinidad when the sixty-seven-year-old Macmillan, exhausted after a long flight, was awakened to read Kennedy's emergency telegram. The summons to Key West disconcerted him not only because of the hour, but also because traveling "1800 miles to luncheon," as he would say, was not the sort of thing he usually did. For a meeting such as this, a first session with his most important ally, a man with whom it was crucial he get on well, the prime minister expected to have the opportunity to strategize and prepare laboriously. The previous November, faced with the need to compose a congratulatory message to the victor in the presidential election, he had agonized over the precise wording of his letter and consulted with David Ormsby Gore and others about whether it would be presumptuous to include a reference to Billy Hartington having been his nephew. (Macmillan had eventually decided against the reference and had been fascinated to learn that when Kennedy was handed the message by the British consul general in Boston he spoke "at some length of his family connection with the Prime Minister through his sister" and went on to explain that "this, as well as politics, had always given him a special interest in the Prime Minister.") Given Macmillan's customary caution and attention to detail, the idea of rescheduling on a few hours' notice was unsettling, to say the least. On reflection, it also struck him as deeply exciting. That mixture of nervousness and excitement would be the keynote of his relationship with, and at length great affection for, President Kennedy. As Andrew Devonshire would say with amusement years afterward, there was a part of his uncle Harold that would have given almost anything to be the sort of man, like Jack Kennedy, to whom the idea of going "1800 miles to luncheon" seemed perfectly natural. In the end, it was the gravity of the crisis and the knowledge, based on Ormsby Gore's report of his February 28 conversation at the White House, that Kennedy might prove susceptible to domestic political considerations in deciding what to do in Laos that compelled him to go.

At the airfield in Key West, Kennedy met Macmillan—to the latter's surprise and delight—with a large guard of honor and a nineteen-gun salute. A Navy and Marine band played the British national anthem. As he stood beside Kennedy at the welcoming ceremony, the prime minister could hardly have seemed more unlike his youthful counterpart. Even as a comparatively young man, Macmillan had appeared old. In 1961 he had crinkly, drooping eyes and a bristly mustache, and was sluggish of movement and stilted in manner. His walk was a slow, stiff shuffle. But when, shortly after noon, Kennedy and Macmillan began to discuss the events in Laos, in the presence of US military officers on the one side and Harold Caccia on the other, it instantly became apparent that, for all their differences, the president and the prime minister had a tremendous amount in common. Not least, because Britain had been critical to the American's intellectual formation, they shared a frame of reference. For both leaders, the Rhineland episode, the Munich agreement and other British errors in dealing with Hitler in the 1930s provided a lens through which to view their present relations with the Soviets. They also shared a preference for the style of conversation Jack had first encountered in London and at country-house weekends before the war, when he had talked politics with young men who were themselves now part of the Macmillan government. That Kennedy and Macmillan clicked should not have been entirely surprising to either, for though they had never met previously, each had heard about the other from David Ormsby Gore, Andrew Devonshire, Moucher Devonshire and others with great personal affection for both men. Kennedy had been tracking Macmillan's career for years and knew of his close association with Churchill, notably in the postwar era when Churchill worked out his ideas about how to deal with the Soviets based on the mistakes of the 1930s. Macmillan, for his part, had pored over the text of Kennedy's inaugural address, as well as—on Ormsby Gore's recommendation—a book-length collection of his major speeches, *The Strategy of Peace*, published at the time of the campaign. If others had failed to perceive the Churchillian underpinnings of Kennedy's strategy of peace—indeed, to grasp why it was a strategy at all—Macmillan certainly had not. When, early in their talk, Kennedy declared that if the Russians thought the Americans would refrain from military action in Laos, "there would be no negotiations—or such negotiations as there were would fail," the allusion to Munich was not lost on Macmillan. In return, Kennedy was a receptive listener when Macmillan addressed the question of whether it was worth the effort to save Laos by declaring, "The occupation of the Rhineland was not by itself perhaps an important step but if action had been taken to stop it, subsequent history would have been entirely different." Kennedy and Macmillan shared the understanding that, as analyzed by Churchill, the lesson of the Rhineland episode was not so much that it had been the moment to fight Hitler, but that it had been the moment when a show of force might have persuaded the Führer that the British would fight. Conceivably, had a small action been taken when the opportunity presented itself, the Second World War might have been prevented. At Key West, Kennedy and Macmillan agreed that that lesson might be well applied to the Laotian crisis. As it turned out, they were not far apart on the matter of how to proceed in Laos. Macmillan believed that if the Soviets refused to back a ceasefire they would be testing the new American leader, and that a show of military force would be required to prove—as the British had failed to do at the time of the Rhineland episode—that the United States was prepared to fight.

Following an elaborate presentation by the Pentagon of a plan to secure Laos, Macmillan lunched privately with Kennedy and expressed dismay at the large-scale operations proposed. The president agreed that, if the need for military action presented itself, a much smaller operation would be preferable—a show of strength designed both to communicate that the United States was serious and to get the Soviets to the conference table. The first objective was to secure Soviet acceptance of a ceasefire; if intervention was required its goal must not be military victory, as the military men expected, but a negotiated settlement.

Where the president and the prime minister differed was on the request for an immediate commitment of British troops in the event of a negative response from Moscow. Macmillan worried that Kennedy's military advisers sought, with their ornate plans, to build momentum toward full-scale intervention before Moscow had had a chance to respond to the ceasefire proposal. In an effort to slow that momentum, Macmillan said that he could not commit any troops until he had conferred with his Cabinet. In short, even as he privately reassured the president that the United States would not be alone in the event of a problem with the Soviets, he strove to cool him down in advance of the following day's encounter with Gromyko.

Kennedy had used the back-and-forth with Macmillan to run through his thinking on Laos—why a ceasefire and an international conference were necessary, and what, based on the lessons of the 1930s, the United States must do if the Soviets refused—before he discussed the Laotian crisis with the Soviet foreign minister. But he also seemed to be shoring up his position against those on his own side who wanted him to revert to the Eisenhower policy, which rejected the idea of a neutral Laos on the principle that military might was the only way to stop the Communists in the area. It was the sort of conversation Kennedy had often found invaluable with Ormsby Gore, and an important outcome of the meeting in Key West, apart from the dealings on Laos, was Kennedy's discovery that Macmillan, because of all they so improbably shared, was someone he could talk to in this manner. At Key West, the prime minister joined Kennedy's "twenty-five-year conversation" with British friends. The closest of those friends had been Ormsby Gore, and at lunch Macmillan had broached the idea of sending him to Washington as ambassador. The president naturally was "emphatic" in his enthusiasm. Macmillan came away from their meeting with a sense of Jack Kennedy as "a curious mixture of qualities—courteous, quiet, quick, decisive—and tough." At the session with the military officers, Kennedy had shown that he was "in control of the Pentagon, not the other way around." Despite the pressure to alter his views, and despite his own abiding concern at the risk to his popularity, he had stuck to his convictions and clearly meant to push for a diplomatic settlement and neutrality in Laos. After the meeting, the White House issued a joint communiqué to the effect that Kennedy and

Macmillan, having agreed that the situation in Laos could not be permitted to deteriorate, strongly hoped that Moscow would reply positively and constructively to the British proposals to end the fighting and pave the way for the creation of a truly neutral state. Kennedy flew back to Washington to await the next day's session with Gromyko, where he hoped to receive a sign of whether the Russians would assent to a ceasefire.

The portents seemed good when Gromyko—whom a young Jack Kennedy had first met as a reporter for the Hearst papers at the San Francisco Conference in 1945—came to the White House on Monday, March 27. Gromyko noted that while his government had yet to complete its study of the British proposals for an international conference to lead to the establishment of a neutral Laos, it believed they might form the basis for a settlement. Kennedy, pleased, underscored the importance of a ceasefire. In its absence, he noted, the flow of Soviet and US supplies would continue and that would only inflame matters. Kennedy asked that Moscow reply formally to the British overture as soon as possible. Everything must be done, he asserted, to prevent an escalation of the Laotian crisis.

Having been frustrated by the derailment of his plan to use the test ban talks to start anew with Moscow, Kennedy seized on the opportunity provided by this face-to-face encounter with a major Soviet official to get the process back on track. For Kennedy the point was to avoid a war and to defeat the Soviets peacefully. At Key West, the Rhineland episode and Munich had provided the historical backdrop for the discussion; now it was the First World War and Churchill's perceptions in *The World Crisis* that the momentum toward a war neither side really wanted could take on a life of its own, and that discussion was more difficult when both parties teetered on the edge of the precipice where a war could easily be set off by accident. Kennedy stressed the need in the present East–West conflict to establish an environment where problems might be addressed "without approaching the brink of a military situation." Clearly he was thinking of the lead-up to the First World War when, after formal talks in the presence of their respective teams, he conferred privately in the Rose Garden with Gromyko. Specifically recalling "the 1914 situation," Kennedy expressed the hope that Washington and Moscow would do what they could to avoid a development "where both sides would be moving in" toward a collision and suddenly find they were unable to stop. After getting an encouraging response from Gromyko on Laos, he alluded to the other "mess" Eisenhower had left behind by making an oblique reference to "the belligerent attitude of the Cuban government." By complaining about Havana's belligerence, it was as if, even as he preached the need for both sides to steer clear of the edge of the precipice, he was reaching in advance for a justification of what he might be about to undertake in Cuba.

Kennedy, whose main goal as president was to shift the dynamics of East–West relations, would certainly not have put the idea of an invasion of Cuba into play. But the plan existed, and Kennedy, burdened with this unwanted legacy, had to decide on it urgently. In the days that followed his talk with Gromyko, there were indications that Kennedy might reject the CIA plan. He was aware that as he juggled decisions on Laos, Cuba and other areas where American and Soviet interests conflicted, the strategy of peace on which he had staked his presidency hung in the balance. The much-anticipated Geneva test ban talks had been cause for huge disappointment, but both sides were after all still at the negotiating table, which meant that hope had not been extinguished. Gromyko had just suggested that the Laotian crisis might end in a negotiated settlement if, as seemed likely, Moscow accepted the British proposals. Though the CIA and Joint Chiefs of Staff advised Kennedy to proceed with the Cuban invasion, from the first there had been a number of strong voices within the administration opposing the plan. Under-Secretary of State Chester Bowles had argued that a US-supported attack would violate treaty obligations that ought to be binding in law and conscience, and would also deprive America of its moral edge by blurring the differences that distinguished it from the Soviet Union. Special Assistant Arthur Schlesinger Jr. had warned that the assault on Cuba would dissipate the good will that had arisen toward the United States since Kennedy's inauguration and "fix a malevolent image of the new Administration in the minds of millions." By March 30, when Kennedy left to spend Easter with his family in Florida, it struck Schlesinger, who had attended a meeting on Cuba with Kennedy the previous day, that in view of the president's growing skepticism the tide had turned against the invasion plan.

In the course of the six days Kennedy spent at Palm Beach with Jackie and the children, a number of critically important events took place. On Saturday, April 1, the Soviets officially accepted the British proposals on Laos, and that same day Khrushchev notified Llewellyn Thompson that he agreed to an early informal meeting with Kennedy. On April 3, dates were set for the president to visit Paris to meet the French president, General Charles de Gaulle; that day, Kennedy also sent word to Moscow suggesting that he and Khrushchev meet on June 3 and 4. As he prepared to return to Washington, Kennedy faced the likelihood that his politically risky decision to seek a neutral government in Laos was about to be put to the test. His intention to meet the Soviet leader would also have to be announced, at some later date, and he worried about how to present it "to American public opinion in such a way as to be acceptable." Kennedy knew that, for all his soaring poll numbers, his message of a fresh approach to Soviet relations remained largely unassimilated by the electorate. He was hugely popular, to be sure; and his thrilling call to service and sacrifice, like Churchill's similar appeal on taking office as wartime prime minister, had inspired many Americans. Still, he recognized that his views on how best to deal with the Communist menace were out of harmony with the large segment of the public that continued to favor the militant style of anti-Communism he himself had once embraced, and he was concerned that they would perceive his willingness to sit down with Khrushchev as a sign that he was weak and an appeaser. Eisenhower, in meeting Khrushchev, had run no such risk, for, as Khrushchev himself would later point out, Eisenhower's record of leadership during the war insulated him; in contrast to his young successor, he had had the authority to take whatever stance he wished toward the Soviets, and, in Khrushchev's words, "no one would dare accuse him of being afraid." Kennedy did face the possibility, even the likelihood, of such accusations. At the family home in Palm Beach he had, in the presence of his father, a vivid reminder of the crushing effect that charges of appeasement could have on a public career.

On April 4, Kennedy flew back to Washington. It was late afternoon by the time his helicopter touched down on the White House lawn and he went directly to the Oval Office. To the President's Special Assistant for National Security Affairs McGeorge Bundy, it was immediately apparent that Kennedy's position on the Cuban invasion had altered. Suddenly, it seemed, the president "really wanted to do this." Others soon noticed the same thing, and some attributed the change, at least in part, to his father's influence. Kennedy's conversations with Macmillan, who arrived for several days of meetings beginning on April 5, provide a fascinating window on the president's thinking about Laos and Cuba—and the considerations driving his actions in both. In Kennedy's mind, Eisenhower's two "messes" were inextricably connected. In the end, concern about the political consequences of his decisions on one influenced his course of action in the other.

In the matter of Laos, Kennedy had resolved to act without regard for political considerations, but that did not mean he had mastered his anxiety about the price he might have to pay for the decision to seek a diplomatic rather than a military solution. Having voiced concern to Ormsby Gore that his Laos policy would make him look soft, he now talked to Macmillan of his fear of being charged with appeasement. He who had relentlessly pummeled Eisenhower during the campaign had come to dread the political damage should his predecessor openly question his judgment in office. Kennedy asked Macmillan to urge Eisenhower to remain silent. He wanted Macmillan to assure his old friend that the current administration had no intention of permitting Laos to fall to the Communists and that the president believed diplomatic efforts would prove successful in averting a Communist takeover. Above all, Kennedy hoped Macmillan could persuade Eisenhower not to charge him with appeasement.

Concern about that charge shadowed Kennedy's thinking at precisely the moment he had to decide about the Cuban invasion. He had stuck to his convictions on Laos—could he really afford to do the same in the matter of Cuba? Could he twice reject military action and the advice of the generals that intervention was best? Could he twice provoke accusations of softness and appeasement from Eisenhower? As Ormsby Gore would later report, when he learned the details from Kennedy himself, the president had been "anxious not to appear less active against Communism than the previous Administration." Ironically, Moscow's acceptance of the British proposals on Laos did much to influence Kennedy to go "tough" on Cuba. Looking back on the whole episode, Ormsby Gore concluded that because Kennedy had already overruled the military on Laos, he was inclined to take their advice in Cuba lest another refusal so early in the administration "might make him look as though he was a weak president." Ormsby Gore later reported that the president believed that his own campaign statements had "virtually committed" him to proceed with the invasion. In the presidential debates, Kennedy, stung by charges that his position on Quemoy and Matsu made him an appeaser, had mocked Nixon for seeking to guarantee those islands off the coast of China when he had "never really protested the Communists seizing Cuba, ninety miles off the coast of the United States." The Kennedy campaign, apparently without the candidate's knowledge but decidedly in keeping with the impression given in the debate, had put out a statement: "We must attempt to strengthen the non-Batista democratic anti-Castro forces in exile, and in Cuba itself, who offer eventually hope of overthrowing Castro. Thus far these fighters for freedom have had virtually no support from our Government." They had, of course, but Nixon had not been at liberty to reveal that information in his defense. In conversation with Macmillan, though he did not spell out the details of the invasion plan, Kennedy expressed anxiety about what the Cuban exiles might do in the event he refused to support them. Were the CIA to bring the exiles back to the United States after months of training, Kennedy had been reminded, they would almost certainly speak out in public against a president who had pledged support during the campaign but had flinched when the time came to act.

Still torn between Baldwin and Churchill, he tried to be both. On the test ban negotiations and Laos he had acted as a statesman, doing what he thought best for the country however unpopular his course of action might prove in a national climate that preferred confrontation with the Soviets to contact. On Cuba he acted as a politician; in light of Laos and his statements during the campaign, he judged it to be in his own political self-interest to approve the invasion despite his instinctive dislike of the plan. This assessment of his actions is neither harsh nor unreasonable, for it is the standard he himself had applied during the campaign to Eisenhower and Nixon.

The deadline for the "go" order for air strikes designed to obliterate Castro's air force in anticipation of the landing on the beachhead by the Cuban Expeditionary Force, was Friday, April 14—less than a week after Macmillan sent off a letter asking Eisenhower to refrain from accusations of appeasement with regard to administration policy in Laos. Until the last minute, it was evident that Kennedy was uneasy. Though he was usually decisive, he hesitated at this step, as he did at each point of decision to follow. Again and again, he sought to make certain that the exiles understood that whatever happened there would be no support from the US military. Finally, at noon on April 14, Kennedy, after a walk on the South Lawn with his wife, picked up the phone in the Oval Office and, tapping his ornately carved oak desk for luck, ordered an air assault at dawn the next day.

The first reports seemed positive. Saturday's dawn air strikes appeared to have destroyed the better part of Castro's air force, and the cover story invented by the CIA to suggest that the dictator's own people were responsible was holding. A bullet-scarred B-26 had touched down in Miami and its pilot, a CIA man impersonating a defector from the Cuban Air Force, claimed to have participated in the air strikes and to have made off afterward with the aircraft. Thus far, no one had questioned his account. Complications arose when Castro called for an emergency UN session to charge Washington with aggression, and Moscow's ambassador to the UN warned that Cuba's friends would not hesitate to participate in the island's defense. Jackie and the children had already left for Glen Ora, the family's weekend home in the Virginia hunt country, and despite the trouble at the UN the president went off to join them for lunch, in keeping with the cover story which provided for his absence from the White House when the landing of the troops started. He had until Sunday at noon to approve the next phase of the assault—or call off the whole thing.

On Sunday morning, the phones at Glen Ora rang constantly, and virtually all the news was bad. The press had unmasked the impostor who had landed at Miami International Airport the previous day, and intelligence reports that the Cuban Air Force had been annihilated proved false. Instead of the devastation previously claimed, only five Cuban aircraft had been destroyed. Kennedy, unready to give the final go-ahead, went off to Mass with Jackie shortly before twelve. Still unprepared to commit when they came back at 12:30, he lunched with his wife, his sister Jean and her husband Stephen Smith. After the meal, Jack picked up a golf club and headed outside to a pasture where he hit balls for nearly half an hour. It was a quarter to two when he suddenly dropped his club and, followed by Jackie, marched back into the house. An hour and forty-five minutes after he had silently allowed the deadline to pass, he called Bissell and directed that the landing of the troops should proceed.

That evening at nine, Jack and Jackie had already gone to bed when Dean Rusk, who had previously opined that the invasion could not succeed, urged the president to call off the next round of air strikes, which were to resume at dawn. The specifics of the attack had been altered numerous times, and—this being a covert operation—no one had ever written down a full account of what was to take place. Rusk pointed out that further air attacks from Nicaragua were obviously to precede the landing by sea, and that it would instantly be apparent that the assault could not have come from within Cuba. "I'm not signed on to this!" Kennedy shouted into the phone, realizing that he had only a hazy idea of the operation. Like Rusk, Kennedy had been allowed to assume that on the day of the invasion the air strikes would be launched not from another country but from the beachhead at the Bay of Pigs. At the secretary of state's behest, Kennedy canceled the next round of air strikes. He and Rusk agreed that no strikes would take place until such time as they could conceivably be launched from the beachhead. Following the conversation, Kennedy nervously paced the bedroom, appalled that he had lost control. At 4:30 a.m., Rusk called back to report that the deputy director of the CIA, General Charles Cabell, had come to his apartment to ask that US jets provide air cover for the exile forces, which had already begun to land. Kennedy, who would gradually conclude that the CIA had promised the exiles US backup in spite of everything he had said, declined the general's request. After he hung up, he was too agitated to go back to sleep, and Jackie sat up with him until daybreak.

That day, the Kennedys flew back in a helicopter to a White House pervaded by a sense of futility. Castro's air force had proven vastly more formidable than expected. Two of the exile brigade's ships had been struck, including, importantly, a freighter carrying communications paraphernalia and more than a week's stock of ammunition. By mid-morning, word reached the Oval Office that both vessels had been lost, and that in the absence of air support the four ships that remained must move out to sea in flight from Castro's planes. Jack and Jackie went through the motions of presiding over a luncheon in the State Dining Room in honor of Prime Minister and Mrs. Karamanlis of Greece, who had arrived that afternoon for a three-day visit. When, after three, Kennedy finally managed to detach himself from Karamanlis, he learned that Cuban government tanks had begun to appear on the beachhead. The president had been awake since half past four that morning; still, having approved a brigade air strike on Cuba's main air base to take place at dawn the following day, he wandered out the Northwest Gate with the First Lady after ten in the evening. Trailed by Secret Service agents, the couple took a walk in the city streets just beyond the White House grounds. During his first months in office Kennedy had often been known to walk at night, alone or in the company of male friends. Tonight, confronted with a debacle brought on by his own bad judgment, he preferred to be with his wife.

Jack Kennedy had come to office calling on both sides in the Cold War to "begin anew the quest for peace" before all-annihilating weapons engulfed mankind "in planned or accidental self-destruction." The great plans outlined in the inaugural address had represented "what the man would like to be." Now, in an effort to protect himself politically, he had jeopardized everything he believed in and had hoped to accomplish. The full measure of what he had just done presented itself unavoidably on Tuesday morning when he received a scathing letter from Khrushchev. Given the upper hand by Kennedy's own actions, Khrushchev lamented all that the new young president had so quickly squandered. He sneered at claims that the United States had had nothing to do with the attack on Cuba, which the whole world knew to be false. He recalled how "only recently" both Moscow and Washington had expressed their mutual desire to improve relations and eliminate the dangers of war. He warned Kennedy—who, as Khrushchev well knew, had spoken along similar lines to Gromyko when they talked in March—that a small war could "touch off a chain reaction in all parts of the globe" and thereby "lead the world to military catastrophe." By citing the hopes and beliefs with which Kennedy had begun in office and by showing how his actions in the interim had contradicted those beliefs, Khrushchev confronted him with the fact that he had just betrayed his own strategy of peace. Soon the letter reached a wider audience, when a Soviet representative read the text aloud at the UN. Suddenly Khrushchev was the leader who was publicly calling for peace and warning of the need to avoid the uncontrollable momentum toward war.

On inauguration day, Jack Kennedy had persuaded many Americans that he was the man to reverse the humiliations of Eisenhower's final months in office. As it turned out, those humiliations had been nothing compared to the fiasco at the Bay of Pigs. As the second day of the invasion unfolded, Kennedy learned that low thick cloud and a soupy mist had ruined the morning's air attack on Castro's principal airfield and that the brigade, trapped on the beaches, was about to be surrounded by Cuban forces. At length, a US Navy reconnaissance mission, attempting to assess the situation at one of two landing sites, discovered only charred Cuban Expeditionary Force trucks and tanks and no sign of the exiles. They were presumed to have been "wiped out" and the survivors to have fled to another beach. Throughout the day, on the grounds that he had told the press that he would not involve US forces in the operation, Kennedy resisted CIA pressure to authorize the use of Navy jets on a US aircraft carrier then positioned just beyond Cuba's territorial waters. But late that night, a desperate message from the brigade commander on the beachhead—"Do you people realize how desperate this situation is? Do you back us up or quit? All we want is low jet cover and jet close support . . . I will not be evacuated. Will fight to the end if we have to"—prompted the president to direct six unmarked US jet aircraft to provide cover for a B-26 attack from Nicaragua designed to hit Cuban tanks. It was after 3 a.m. when he reluctantly gave the order. Afterward, Kenny O'Donnell and press secretary Pierre Salinger observed from the Oval Office as Kennedy, jacketless, head bent and hands stuffed into his pockets, wandered alone in the Rose Garden for almost an hour.

After a few hours' sleep in the family quarters, Kennedy awakened to news of further ineptitude. The military planners had failed to take into consideration the one-hour time difference between Nicaragua and Cuba, so that when the B-26s arrived, the promised air cover failed to materialize and Castro's forces handily picked off two of the aircraft. At a meeting with the Greek prime minister that morning Kennedy railed against Eisenhower, who had passed on to him the scheme to overthrow Castro. In response to Karamanlis's expression of surprise at "the unpreparedness of the landing," Kennedy alternated between reiterating that it had not been his fault and promising to take personal responsibility for the fiasco. Later, in the family quarters, Kennedy plunged into a mood such as Jackie had not witnessed since his deep depression following the back surgery in 1954. Long experience of life-threatening illness had taught him to greet the most appalling events with detachment and good humor, as his hero Raymond Asquith had done. But at the time of his back operation and now again in the aftermath of the Bay of Pigs, Jack fell into an uncharacteristic despair. Jackie listened as he complained bitterly of all those he held responsible for his present troubles—Eisenhower for having bequeathed the plan to him and the CIA and Joint Chiefs of Staff for having counseled him to go forward. Jack was so distraught that his father, who had conferred with him and with Bobby throughout the crisis, moaned to Rose that he felt as if he himself might die.

Four days after the first air strike, Castro, who had taken nearly two thousand prisoners, crowed that the invaders had been vanquished. In advance of the operation the president had been assured that, at worst, the brigade would disperse to the mountains, but it turned out that that had never been a possibility. The mountains lay on the other side of an impassable swamp, and the exiles—in the event they had to withdraw—had had instructions to move toward the sea and wait to be picked up. Clearly Kennedy had been lied to repeatedly by some of his own people, and, as he had told David Ormsby Gore prior to the fiasco, he had not yet known whose judgment to trust. When he appeared at a Cabinet meeting on April 20, the day of Castro's announcement, he struck Chester Bowles as a "shattered" man, like someone who had just endured "an acute shock." Never before had he failed like this. The invasion had damaged not the Castro regime but Kennedy's own presidency. Kennedy, usually terse, rambled on for twenty-five minutes, but it seemed to Fred Dutton, assistant secretary of state for congressional affairs, that "he was really talking more to himself than anyone else." In the end, whatever the ferocity of his private resentments, the president chose, at least in public, to take full blame for the debacle. At a news conference the following day he told a reporter who had been fishing for a story about divisions within the administration, "There is an old saying that victory has a hundred fathers and defeat is an orphan. I am the responsible officer of this government."

At an explosive meeting with Eisenhower at Camp David on April 22, their first since Kennedy's inauguration, Kennedy reverted to the picture of himself as having merely approved a plan recommended by both the CIA and the Joint Chiefs of Staff. Of the blame, which in conversation with Jackie, Karamanlis and others he had bitterly heaped on his predecessor, he made no mention. Four days previously, Eisenhower had replied to Macmillan's appeal on the new young leader's behalf. Scornful of efforts to secure a neutral Laos, he had reminded the prime minister that the Communists' word was worthless and that a neutrality agreement threatened merely to "serve as a cloak" for those who hoped to communize the area. As to whether he would cry appeasement, Eisenhower pointedly made no promises. So, when he faced his successor in the aftermath of the fiasco in Cuba, he was well aware that Kennedy feared what he might say in public. Eisenhower, for his part, had been enraged by Kennedy's campaign accusations of lassitude and complacency. Kennedy the candidate had targeted the inept preparations for the Geneva disarmament talks and the Paris summit, had questioned the poor timing of the U-2 flight and Eisenhower's clumsy handling of the incident, and had insisted that fiasco in Paris had been inevitable because the president, by his refusal to say the harsh things and take the harsh steps that, however necessary for the country, promised to be unpopular or inconvenient, had allowed the United States to fall into second place. At Camp David, Eisenhower made full use of the opportunity to humiliate Kennedy by enumerating the errors, both of preparation and execution, that had led to defeat in Cuba. Eisenhower insisted that, by refusing to provide backup for the expedition force, Kennedy had communicated to Khrushchev that he was weak. Afterward the former and current presidents met with reporters, and Eisenhower, though he had excoriated Kennedy in private, offered a strained, perfunctory show of support.

Visibly "devastated" by the violence of Eisenhower's scolding, Kennedy joined Jackie and the children at Glen Ora, where he had asked Chuck and Betty Spalding to spend the weekend. A quarter of an hour after he arrived, he headed outdoors to practice his golf swing with Betty. But as Jack mechanically chipped balls back and forth, it became evident that his mind was elsewhere. Whatever the mistakes of others—Eisenhower, the CIA or the Joint Chiefs of Staff—he believed that by his decision to go forward he had brought the disaster on himself and shattered the confidence and sense of purpose that had marked his early weeks in office.

"How can I have been so stupid?" Jack groaned repeatedly. "How could I have made that mistake?"

CHAPTER THIRTEEN

The Meaning of "Miscalculation"

E VEN BEFORE THE CUBAN AFFAIR, JACK KENNEDY HAD BEEN
worried about how the American public would receive the news that he
intended to meet Khrushchev. Part of his rationale for the Cuban
adventure had been to secure political capital before the meeting was
announced. Of course, the botched invasion would be no bulwark
against charges of softness and appeasement; far from having made
Kennedy look tough, it had, as Eisenhower had angrily pointed out,
created an impression of weakness. Instead of making it easier to
announce a meeting with Khrushchev, the Cuban attack, by the president's estimate, had actually made it much more difficult.

On the day of his scolding by Eisenhower at Camp David, Kennedy
sent word to Macmillan, via Caccia, seeking advice about the political
difficulties that faced him over the planned meeting with Khrushchev.
As a consequence of the debacle, an announcement at any time "in the
immediate future" would make it seem as if Kennedy was "going to
lead from a position of weakness" following a defeat at the hands of
Castro. To make matters worse, Khrushchev seemed determined to cast
the encounter as "an American initiative"; though early on he had sent
numerous verbal messages via Menshikov to propose a meeting,
Kennedy had been the first to suggest it in writing. No matter what the
original sequence of events, the American public would therefore perceive its president as having reached out to Khrushchev, and that could

add significantly to the damage. Kennedy wanted to know whether Macmillan thought the meeting with Khrushchev would be "a serious mistake at this time," and indicated that he would give "great weight" to the prime minister's advice. He had yet to have final word from Khrushchev as to the dates and location for the talks, and he could still quietly back out. Thus far there had been "no vestige of rumor or leak" about the proposed meeting. Kennedy asked Macmillan to keep the information "within the narrowest possible circle."

The meeting, as Macmillan was quick to reply, was not so secret as the president believed. Walter Lippmann, who had recently passed through London on his way home from Moscow, had told Macmillan of Khrushchev's pleasure at Kennedy's suggestion of a meeting in either Stockholm or Vienna, and that Khrushchev had expressed a preference for the latter. All of this, Macmillan well understood, further complicated Kennedy's predicament, for the information that the president had initiated the session and that Khrushchev had been receptive was now in a journalist's hands. Should Kennedy decide against the meeting, it was still likely to become public knowledge that one had been planned, that Kennedy had been the driving force behind it, and, perhaps worst of all, that he had withdrawn on account of Cuba. Whether or not Kennedy went through with the meeting, he would be the target of criticism from those who opposed any talk with the Soviets.

As far as Macmillan could see, Kennedy was boxed in. Should Khrushchev decide to go forward with an early meeting, the president would be wisest to proceed. Macmillan did not presume to advise on how the American public might react to the announcement, but he did note, for whatever it was worth, that in Britain public opinion would regard it "as a courageous initiative by the President in circumstances which, because of Cuba, are not particularly easy for him." Macmillan did, however, issue a word of warning. In his message, the president had again insisted that he would be meeting Khrushchev at this early date not to enter into negotiations but to take the measure of the man and to allow Khrushchev to take his measure. Macmillan, like Ormsby Gore, thought such an assumption naive, and he cautioned that the leaders would after all "have to talk about something." Based on long experience of Khrushchev, Macmillan predicted that the Russian was bound to raise Berlin, disarmament and other topics, which Kennedy, like it or not, would have little choice but to address. In short, Kennedy had better be prepared for the reality he faced rather than the situation he hoped for.

In the days that followed, Kennedy waited for Khrushchev's move. When no word came, he began to hope that Khrushchev had abandoned the idea for the moment. The Cuban fiasco had created a contentious atmosphere which was the very opposite of what Kennedy had proposed on inauguration day, but at least, in the absence of a message from Khrushchev, he would be spared the need to face his Soviet counterpart from a position of extreme weakness. A delay would give him time to recover and to think through how to get the strategy of peace back on track. Meanwhile, as May began and the first Gallup poll numbers since Cuba were reported, the president was darkly amused to learn that his approval rating, far from having sunk, had soared. In domestic terms, anyway, it seemed as if the decision not to cancel the invasion had been the right one after all. Directly, his hopes that the summit meeting might be off were dashed, when on May 4 Llewellyn Thompson reported from Moscow that Gromyko had called to read him a carefully crafted statement to the effect that Khrushchev did indeed wish to meet Kennedy. Sounding rather as Kennedy himself had upon taking office, Khrushchev cited the need for both sides to live together and settle their differences peacefully. If in the aftermath of Cuba, Kennedy's offer to meet remained valid, Khrushchev was eager to go forward. In fact, the Soviets believed that recent events made it even more urgent that contact be undertaken at the highest level. The statement was so worded that if the meeting was to be canceled, it was Kennedy who would have to do it and thereby abandon the very principles he had enunciated in his inaugural address.

Anticipating the president's anxieties, Thompson acknowledged that at this point the meeting with Khrushchev would present "domestic political problems." He suggested that those difficulties might be assuaged were the president to make it clear that his original proposal had predated the attack on Cuba. In other words, it would be best to communicate to the American people that Kennedy's February 22, 1961, letter to Khrushchev, written as it had been before the debacle, had not been a vanquished leader's plea to talk. Before two days had passed, the White House tentatively confirmed to Thompson Kennedy's intention to meet Khrushchev at Vienna, but, in a sign of the president's abiding preoccupation, Rusk's message stressed that "for domestic political reasons" Kennedy would want to be able to announce specific subjects, such as the nuclear test ban, which he planned to take up with Khrushchev—topics, notably, where there would be "some prospect of progress." Kennedy, who had previously insisted that no negotiations would occur, now hoped for tangible evidence of progress in East–West relations to bring back to the American people. After the colossal ineptitude of the Cuban invasion, such progress would reassert his effectiveness. Admittedly based on political considerations, this new determination not to return from Vienna empty-handed marked a significant shift in Kennedy's thinking, and under the circumstances it would lead to trouble. One of Kennedy's favorite lines in Burke was, "The concessions of the weak are the concessions of fear." That idea underpinned the particularly splendid moment in the inaugural address when he declared, "Let us never negotiate out of fear, but let us never fear to negotiate." A student of Burke and Churchill, Kennedy well knew the perils of negotiating from weakness, but, enfeebled by Cuba, that was precisely what he set out to do in advance of his encounter with Khrushchev.

Bobby Kennedy, at his brother's direction, tried to establish an unofficial line of communication with Khrushchev via Georgi Bolshakov, a known Soviet intelligence agent stationed in Washington as an employee of the news agency TASS. On May 9, 1961, three days after the telegram tentatively confirming the president's request for a meeting, Bobby took a walk with Bolshakov in the streets of Washington. His goal was to make a deal in advance of the Vienna session, in order to ensure that President Kennedy would emerge from the talks with a concrete success in the form of a nuclear test ban treaty. Bobby conveyed to Bolshakov his brother's offer of a compromise designed to produce an agreement at Geneva, so that the American and Soviet leaders could sign the treaty when they met. A major point of disagreement had been the number of inspections on each side. Though the United States had been insisting on twenty inspections annually, Bobby informed Bolshakov that in the interest of a deal the president would accept half that number. But, he added, domestic political constraints dictated that President Kennedy could only assent to ten inspections per year "if this were in response to a Soviet proposal." Let the Soviet delegation at the ongoing talks in Geneva come forward with the number ten and, Bobby assured Bolshakov, the United States would agree. Bobby insisted that his brother was not interested in a meeting "where leaders just exchange views"; he sought "agreements on major issues" at Vienna.

Certainly it would be a triumph to secure a first major postwar agreement with the Soviets and thereby return to the hopeful path outlined on inauguration day. But by sending the attorney general to make a back-channel offer, Kennedy inadvertently conveyed to Khrushchev a number of important things about himself: that in the aftermath of Cuba he was nervous that Vienna be perceived as a success; that in order to come home with a deal he was willing to make deep compromises; that he perceived himself to lack popular support on vital issues and was ready to complain to the Russians—his enemies after all—of the disparity between his views and those of a large segment of the electorate; that, rather than acting decisively according to his convictions, he preferred to seek political cover; and that he was willing to deceive the American people, who, at his instigation, were to be told that the offer of ten inspections had come from the Soviet negotiators rather than from him. In sum, he bared his vulnerabilities to an opponent well able to take advantage of them.

The president went off to Palm Beach on May 11, still awaiting a response from Bolshakov. He planned to rest and play golf in anticipation of a state visit to Canada the following week, and of the longer and far more demanding journey to Paris, Vienna and London two weeks after that. Jack also had a private reason for the holiday in Florida, where he hoped something might be done to relieve Jackie of the bouts of depression that had plagued her on and off since the start of the presidency. She had taken up her role as First Lady only two months after the birth of John Junior. The pregnancy had been difficult, the baby premature. Young John's underdeveloped lungs had been a source of immense worry to a mother who had previously suffered a miscarriage and a stillbirth. Adding to Jackie's strain had been the fact that she had had to recover in the crowded and chaotic setting of her father-in-law's house in Palm Beach, where, in the weeks prior to the inauguration, she had enjoyed little peace or privacy. At a moment when she should have been recuperating, she had had to make countless decisions about the family's move to the White House.

Those decisions had been especially complicated in Jackie's case, for the Kennedys' new life in Washington promised entirely to undo the tacit arrangement that had previously allowed her to live with at least some degree of dignity with a perpetually unfaithful husband. So long as Jack had confined his philandering to those times when he and Jackie were apart, she had been able to sustain the pretense of obliviousness to his many other women. Not everyone had been prepared to look with such a forgiving eye on the candidate's extramarital affairs. The journalist and family friend Arthur Krock had cautioned Joe Kennedy that Jack's frequent visits to the New York nightclub El Morocco with various young women threatened to provoke an exposé that could prove devastating to his presidential hopes. (Joe, despite great affection for Jackie, approved of Jack's exploits and responded to Krock's friendly warning by insisting that American voters cared not at all "how many times he gets laid.") A woman named Florence Kater, who as the landlady of one of Jack's girlfriends had grown annoyed by the married politician's late-night visits to her building, mounted a vigorous campaign to expose him. Mrs. Kater wrote letters to newspapers and to dignitaries such as Eleanor Roosevelt, and when she confronted the candidate at a political event Jackie was hard pressed to ignore the woman who had been so publicly indignant on her behalf. Jackie was not so naive as to think that Jack would suddenly evolve into a model husband now that he was president. In a curious way it fell to her to devise a new arrangement that would permit her to retain a morsel of dignity, while Jack, as he would have in any circumstances, continued to cheat.

As soon as Glen Ora was ready, the new First Lady had begun to spend a great deal of time there. Kennedy's Secret Service agents noticed that no sooner had she and the children left for the country than her husband, as if on cue, would head to the White House swimming pool or the family quarters with one or more female companions—either White House employees (whom some co-workers called "bimbos" on account of their willingness to have sex with the boss) or women brought in by procurers such as Kennedy's long-time aide Dave Powers. Jackie's absences shielded her from things she preferred not to see or know about. But when she returned to the White House, she had to face a great many people who knew what her husband had been up to while she was gone, including some of the very women who regularly dallied with him in the family quarters that the fiercely private Jackie had conceived of as her sanctum sanctorum. In her bedroom at the White House, Jackie had positioned one of Jack's special cattle-hair mattresses beside her own to accommodate his bad back. In her absence, the president often used her bed, which as a result was more spacious than the one in his own room, for three-way sex. She found it increasingly painful to be in Washington, and she was often depressed. That she questioned whether she had it in her to go on in this appalling new life is not difficult to understand.

Jackie had been marvelously supportive during the Cuban crisis when Jack, miserable at what he had brought on himself, repeatedly sought comfort from his wife. On the day of his dressing-down by Eisenhower, it had been evident to Betty Spalding, visiting at Glen Ora, that Jackie had been desperately concerned about Jack, and he about the impact of the ordeal on her. Yet only days later, as soon as Jackie's limousine left the White House en route to Glen Ora, a government car was sent to pick up a woman with whom Jack had begun an affair during the presidential campaign, the month Jackie became pregnant with John Junior. Judith Campbell, who also had a relationship with the gangster Sam Giancana, was staying at the Mayflower Hotel in a room reserved by Kennedy's secretary. Nothing had changed, and, as the time approached when it would be her duty to accompany her husband to Canada and then Europe for crucial encounters with de Gaulle, Khrushchev and Macmillan, Jackie seemed to reach an emotional nadir. Doubt arose as to whether she would be in any mental or physical condition to participate in the state visits.

Finally, on May 12, Kennedy invited Max Jacobson, a New York physician known to his elite clientele as Dr. Feel Good, to visit the Charles Wrightsman estate in Palm Beach where he and the First Lady, along with their guests the Spaldings, were staying in the owner's absence. Chuck Spalding, a devotee of Jacobson's mood-lifting methamphetamine injections, had introduced Jack to the doctor during the campaign. The candidate, complaining of weakness and fatigue, had been about to debate Richard Nixon for the first time, and Jacobson had administered an injection of what some patients referred to as his "joy juice." He had a special blend for every need, and though he refused to disclose the ingredients they usually included methamphetamines, steroids, calcium, monkey placenta and procaine. Patients reported a sudden blast of energy, racing thoughts, a boundless sense of elation and even a feeling of being lit up from within. Jack had very much liked the effects of the shot, except for the fact that it had also made him feel "out of control," and for that reason he did not intend to have another. He did, however, arrange for Jacobson and his wife to attend the inauguration, and in early May Dr. Janet Travell, Kennedy's personal physician, had conducted a telephone interview with Jacobson about his techniques for the treatment of stress. When the White House asked Jacobson to fly to Palm Beach, he assumed he was being hired to treat the president. But when Kennedy greeted Jacobson at the Wrightsman estate, he asked him to see the First Lady.

Jackie was not exactly welcoming when Jacobson, hulking and unkempt with black-stained fingernails, was shown into the bedroom where she lay in seclusion with the lights out and curtains drawn. She complained vaguely of a headache and the doctor, who had a sonorous voice and a heavy accent that one patient said made him sound like a caricature of Freud, told her he might be able to help. When he injected Jackie, the throbbing in her head instantly vanished and she appeared to relax. Since arriving in Palm Beach she had spent most of the time apart from her husband and the Spaldings, but soon Jacobson led a radiant Jackie out to the pool to see the others and report how much better she felt. At the time, the only noticeable drawback, as far as Jackie could tell, was a dry mouth, which at intervals drove her to lick her lips. Miraculously, not only was her headache gone but her depression seemed to have abated as well. To Jack's relief, it appeared as if she might be able to accompany him abroad after all.

Scarcely had Jack addressed the problem of his wife's depression when an enormous new problem emerged, with significant implications for the impending talks with Khrushchev. On May 14, racial violence erupted in the South. Two weeks before the president was scheduled to go to Vienna and argue the virtues of US-style democracy over Soviet Communism, the violence threatened substantially to undermine his argument. Ten days previously, on May 3, unbeknownst to the president or the attorney general, a group of thirteen "Freedom Riders" had set out in two buses from Washington. Their plan had been to ride through the South in order to test a December 1960 Supreme Court ruling that restaurants in interstate bus stations must serve black patrons. When, on May 14, one of the buses rolled into Anniston, Alabama, a crowd of whites torched the vehicle and seriously beat the travelers. That same day, the second bus arrived in Birmingham, Alabama, where local authorities were rumored to have assured the Ku Klux Klan that it would have fifteen minutes to do as it wished before the police intervened. In response to those rumors, a large press contingent had descended on Birmingham and was there to witness as, for fifteen minutes, Klansmen attacked the Freedom Riders. By the time the police arrived, the Klansmen had withdrawn and the bus station was filled with beaten, bloodied people, including some journalists. The police chief later claimed that his men had been off duty in recognition of Mother's Day. After a magazine writer called the Justice Department to express concern that the Freedom Riders could not safely escape Birmingham, Bobby Kennedy finally learned what was happening.

In Palm Beach, the president awakened on the morning of May 15 to front-page pictures of the burning bus in Alabama. To make matters worse, news of the violence had made front pages around the world—a disastrous blow to Kennedy's efforts, central to his strategy of peace, to convince emerging African nations to draw closer to Washington rather than to Moscow. At this point, America's civil rights problems were of concern to the president principally as they related to a foreign policy that aimed to defeat the Soviets by the slow, peaceful process of infiltration. Kennedy had argued during the campaign that while that process was given a chance to play itself out, the West must also move to win the minds and souls of emerging nations in Africa and elsewhere, thereby slowing the spread of Communism. The racial difficulties in the United States, as Kennedy perceived them, presented an obstacle to efforts to make America seem attractive to the Africans and thereby undermined the larger goal of beating the Communists peacefully. To be sure, Kennedy did not condone racial injustice, but at that point he believed that the process of change must be a gradual one and he concerned himself with episodes such as the attacks on the Freedom Riders strictly in so far as they imperiled his international agenda. On the afternoon of May 15, by the time the Kennedys and the Spaldings had returned to Washington, Bobby seemed to have found a way to prevent further violence and spare the president additional embarrassment abroad. He had arranged to have the badly battered Freedom Riders flown to New Orleans, their original destination. It was hardly a perfect solution, but it did pull the story off the front pages, thereby allowing the possibility that it might be forgotten by the time of the summit meeting in Vienna.

Two days later, Jack and Jackie undertook the state visit to Canada that had been arranged as a kind of practice run before Paris, Vienna and London. Prime Minister John Diefenbaker, upon greeting the Kennedys at Government House in Ottawa, invited the president outside to plant a tree in honor of the occasion. As Kennedy lifted a bit of earth with a silver shovel he felt a sudden stabbing sensation in his back. He said nothing and managed to complete the ceremony, but he suspected that he had gravely injured himself. Through the years Jack had rarely been free of back pain, but, on a regimen of Novocain shots from Dr. Travell, he had actually been in remarkably good shape since inauguration day. He had played golf whenever he could, which his friends knew was a sign that his back was not giving him too much trouble.

That evening, after the tree-planting ceremony, it was all the president could do to get through a state dinner for one hundred people and the reception afterward for another four hundred guests. Long accustomed to masking physical pain, he hid his suffering from the Canadians. Jackie was a good deal less successful in concealing her moodiness. The First Lady's abrupt cancellation of a widely advertised interview, which she was to have undertaken in French, suggested to her husband that, in the absence of Max Jacobson's elixir, she might not be up to the formidable demands that faced her in Europe. Kennedy returned to Washington on May 18 determined that the public must not learn about his debilitating pain. Khrushchev had written officially to accept a meeting in Vienna and the announcement over which Kennedy had long agonized was due to be made on May 19. In the meantime, at a moment when he knew his position had been badly weakened by Cuba, he wanted there to be no photographs of him hobbling about on crutches. He spent as much time as possible in bed being treated with hot packs and Novocain, but nothing seemed to assuage the intensity of the pain.

On the morning of May 19, Jack was still in his pajamas, about to start breakfast, when Bobby arrived in the family quarters with two Justice Department aides. The attorney general informed his brother that the problem of the Freedom Riders had not been solved after all. A new contingent of Freedom Riders had arrived in Alabama. At present they were at the bus terminal in Birmingham, determined to test the law even at the risk of being beaten like their predecessors. The president, unable to see why the Freedom Riders had to choose this particular moment to assert their rights, wondered whether something might yet be done to restrain them from creating a problem on the eve of the Vienna summit. Advised that this would be impossible, he had the first inkling that his hope for a gradual approach to eradicating racial injustice in America was not going to be realized. As Kennedy prepared to face Khrushchev he might find it inconvenient to deal with civil rights, and he might believe that the Freedom Riders ought to understand that the United States could ill afford the international headlines their actions in Alabama promised to provoke, but, as Martin Luther King Jr. said, "I am not my father. I can't wait to be free." Many black Americans were tired of waiting for freedom, and Kennedy's strategic priorities were not theirs.

Bobby had already tried and failed to get the governor of Alabama to agree to protect the Freedom Riders; he told Jack that, like it or not, the federal government might soon have to send in troops. The governor viewed the Freedom Riders as rabble-rousers who had come to Alabama to make trouble and violate local laws, and as such they were in no position to complain when state authorities failed to shield them from the consequences of their actions. Bobby took the position that should the state authorities prove unwilling to preserve order, it was the federal government's clear duty to step in. In view of the president's desire to avoid press photographs of US soldiers acting against American citizens, the brothers came up with the idea of using US marshals, civilians without guns or uniforms. A further advantage of marshals was that, unlike soldiers who would have to be ordered in by the president himself, they could be authorized by the attorney general once the president had instructed him to take all necessary measures. Still, Jack was eager to avoid bringing in federal forces of any kind, particularly on the day of the announcement of his talks with Khrushchev. Governor John Patterson of Alabama had been the first Southern governor to endorse Kennedy for president, so Jack was confident he would succeed where his brother had failed. But when the president telephoned, an operator at the State House said that the governor could not be reached as he was off on a fishing trip. Jack, Bobby and the others present knew that the governor had simply ducked the call—a massive insult. Patterson also refused subsequent calls from the White House, but he did at length agree to meet with Justice Department special assistant John Siegenthaler, who wrested a promise from him to protect the Freedom Riders. In any event, the damage to Kennedy's prestige had been done. He had long worried about how the announcement that he planned to meet Khrushchev would play with the American people. He had worried about it before the Cuban invasion, and afterward even more when he calculated that the fiasco had exacerbated the problem to the point where it might have become "almost unmanageable." Never had he imagined that on the day most Americans first learned of the intended meeting, there would also be front-page stories informing the world that Kennedy had been unable to get Alabama's governor to take his call. To the president's horror, news coverage on May 20 made him seem astonishingly ineffectual.

Bobby, in the meantime, had finally heard from Bolshakov, who reported that Moscow had no interest in Kennedy's secret offer of a compromise to break the deadlock at the nuclear test ban talks. The president swiftly instructed Bobby, already scrambling to manage events in Alabama, to set up another meeting with the Soviet intelligence agent. On Sunday, May 21, at a third encounter with Bolshakov, Bobby conveyed the president's latest back-channel offer. Back in March, on the first day of the reconvened Geneva test ban talks, the Soviet delegation had surprised Ormsby Gore and others on the Western side by insisting on a troika rather than the single impartial administrator previously agreed upon. In the American delegation it had been thought that acceptance of a troika would lay the foundation for a serious attack on the UN, and the demand had ended hopes for a quick agreement. Now, two months later, Bobby signaled his brother's change of heart; the president was prepared to agree to a troika, though without the veto power for each member previously specified by Moscow. Jack was trying to protect himself politically by having a deal in place before he went to Vienna, but as it turned out the only result of his efforts was that the Soviets saw him sweat.

At 1 p.m. that afternoon the president boarded a helicopter for the short trip to Glen Ora, where he was to spend the remainder of the weekend. Jack began his flight in the belief that as the Freedom Riders had left Birmingham under the governor's protection, matters there were under control. By the time he touched down in Virginia, however, trouble had already erupted. The escorts provided by the governor had accompanied the bus only as far as the Montgomery city limits. When the bus pulled into the terminal, a waiting mob closed in and, in the absence of police who took ten minutes to arrive, beat everyone in sight. The victims included John Siegenthaler, who, in his capacity as the president's personal representative to Governor Patterson, had been there to observe. As the victims were carried off to the hospital, Bobby called Glen Ora, whereupon the president, though still wary of sending in troops, instructed him to take all appropriate and necessary action. Violence persisted the following day, when a mob of three thousand whites, hurling bricks, rocks and Molotov cocktails, stormed a church where Martin Luther King, Jr. was speaking to fifteen hundred people who had gathered in support of the Freedom Riders. US marshals fired tear gas on the attackers, but were unable to protect the people inside the church. Bobby, unwilling to preside over a repetition of the Cuban debacle when the failure to provide military backup had led to defeat and disgrace, concluded that his brother's only choice was to send in troops. The order had yet to be given, however, when Patterson declared martial law and dispatched the National Guard. President Kennedy had been spared the need to send in the military—but not the photographs and articles about racial violence in the American South that filled the international press for days.

It had been a ghastly weekend for the president: extensive news coverage of the Freedom Riders; the public humiliation of Governor Patterson's refusal to take his calls; the Soviets' rejection of efforts to negotiate a secret deal; and, on top of it all, unrelenting back pain combined with Dr. Travell's suggestion that it might be best to use crutches when he and the First Lady left presently for Europe. On his return to the White House on Monday, May 22, Jack Kennedy was at breaking point. The combination of acute stress and physical pain seems to have driven him to take what he himself well understood were desperate measures. With Jackie due to come in from the country the following day, he had a call placed to Max Jacobson in New York. The doctor whose treatments Jack had decided not to repeat because he believed that, whatever their positive effects, they also deprived him of control, was asked to come to the White House in the morning, with the stipulation that he carry an attaché case in lieu of his customary black leather physician's bag. Jacobson naturally thought that he was being summoned to provide a second methamphetamine treatment to Mrs. Kennedy. Indeed, shortly after her helicopter landed on the South Grounds at ten, he did give Jackie an injection. When he was done, the president's valet informed him that Kennedy wanted to see him as well. Kennedy, who had been waiting in his own bedroom, described what had happened in Ottawa. After Jacobson gave him a shot—Kennedy's first use of methamphetamine as president—the patient stood up and walked about the room, and declared that he felt "very much better." Not only did the injection relieve the physical pain that threatened his effectiveness with Khrushchev at Vienna, it helped with stress as well. Kennedy asked Jacobson to accompany him and the First Lady to Europe.

That same day, Khrushchev also undertook preparations for Vienna. Kennedy had tried in his back-channel offers to set the agenda for the Vienna talks, but by his eagerness to negotiate from a position of weakness he had merely suggested his own desperation. Now, in a stern, even threatening message sent via Llewellyn Thompson, Khrushchev signaled that it would be he who dictated the subject matter at Vienna. When Khrushchev spoke to Thompson at an American ice revue in Moscow on May 23, he emphasized his determination to settle the Berlin problem at once. He warned that, in the absence of a settlement, he would sign a separate treaty with the East Germans that would terminate Western access to Berlin. In a phrase that by its very ambiguity deeply troubled Kennedy when he read Thompson's telegram the next day, Khrushchev declared that while Western troops in Berlin would not be touched, "they might have to tighten their

THE MEANING OF "MISCALCULATION" | 303

belts." Kennedy sent Bobby to ask Bolshakov the meaning of Khrushchev's threat, but, like the Alabama governor who had refused the president's calls, Moscow deigned to respond neither to this question nor to Kennedy's second offer on the test ban.

To date, Kennedy had been worried primarily about the domestic political repercussions of his meeting with Khrushchev; he had focused on efforts to minimize the damage to himself by trying to be certain he had some tangible prize to bring home from Vienna. Thompson's telegram of the 24th abruptly shifted the president's attention to what he suddenly saw as the very real threat of war and the need to make it clear, lest Khrushchev miscalculate, that the United States would indeed defend its interests in Berlin. Kennedy had previously theorized that Khrushchev had refrained from moving on Berlin because the threat of Western response had acted as a "deterrent." Now, Kennedy had to face the possibility that his failure in Cuba had altered Khrushchev's perception of US resolve—or worse, efficacy. It was not that Kennedy had given the go-ahead for the invasion that seemed to have struck Khrushchev; it was that, when the attack faltered, he had declined to send in US forces. Word reached the White House via the Polish ambassador that Khrushchev saw this as a failure to finish the job and considered the president "a soft, not very decisive young man." In an effort to portray himself as strong Kennedy delivered a tough speech to a joint session of Congress on May 25. He sought two billion dollars to defend freedom around the world, and by his talk of strengthening the army's conventional forces he signaled his determination to fight in Berlin, where the Soviets' conventional forces were superior.

Following a Democratic Party dinner on Saturday, May 27, the president spent his last weekend prior to the European trip at Hyannis Port with the father to whom he had long been accustomed to turn in times of crisis. At this point in his life he looked to old Joe less for actual advice, though the ambassador never hesitated to make recommendations, than for reassurance and encouragement—and the love that more than any other had sustained him since boyhood. On May 29, the day before he was due to join Jackie in New York for the flight to Paris, Jack celebrated his forty-fourth birthday in the family house at Cape Cod. A week and a half previously, he had had a long private letter from David Ormsby Gore, expressing sympathy for all he knew his friend to be suffering in the wake of Cuba and saying that he did indeed plan to come to Washington in October as Britain's ambassador. At a time when much seemed to have gone calamitously wrong with the new administration, David's letter served as an eloquent reminder of his and Jack's shared hopes and as a statement of his unwavering belief that a Kennedy presidency offered the best possible chance to realize them.

Recalling their dinner in late February, when Jack had spoken of the "horrible messes" his predecessor had left to be cleaned up, David observed, "I do not think it is possible to win a hand when someone else has made the most monumental mess of playing the first ten cards and then passes the hand on to you to play the last three. This could be used to describe Cuba and Laos." He meant to encourage Jack to get beyond them and regain focus. At once David turned to the big themes, in particular the need to begin the lengthy process of defeating Communism peacefully, through contact rather than combat, that had formed the substance of many of the friends' conversations since 1954. "In many respects," David wrote, "our need is to gain time to regroup our forces, reorganize our free-world institutions and rethink our strategy and tactics before we can hope to turn the tide of history in our favor. I am buoyed up by the fact that I am convinced we can turn it in our favor and that Communism can be maneuvered into a fatal decline. I am further convinced that our best hope of beginning the process is during your presidency." The day before he left for Europe, Jack sent word to Macmillan that he would appreciate it if David could come in before the end of their private talk in London on June 5, after the encounter with Khrushchev. Jack sensed that whatever might happen in Vienna, he would very much want to confer with David afterward.

Also on May 29, Jack had his brother contact Bolshakov yet again, this time to see if Khrushchev might be amenable to meeting privately in Vienna, with only their interpreters present; in the absence of the leaders' respective teams, perhaps conversation would flow more freely. Bobby stressed the president's need to have an answer before he flew to Paris the following day, but by the time the Kennedys boarded *Air Force One* there had again been no reply. At the last minute, Kennedy decided that before they took off he wanted an injection from

Jacobson. In the interest of keeping it out of the press that Kennedy had joined Dr. Feel Good's roster of rich and powerful patients, it had been arranged for Jacobson to fly separately on Air France and to come to the president discreetly prior to his first set of talks with de Gaulle. Now, aides dashed to locate the doctor at a nearby hotel so he could give shots to both Kennedys before they left.

By the following morning, when the president's plane touched down at Orly Airport, Jacobson's cocktail of drugs had worn off and Kennedy's back pain had again become excruciating. But he was careful to let his French hosts see as little as possible of his acute physical discomfort. The imposing figure of the seventy-year-old General de Gaulle, dressed in a double-breasted gray suit, waited to greet the President and First Lady on a red carpet at the foot of the stairs leading from the aircraft. Kennedy gingerly descended the steps in front of his wife, and, after the leaders reviewed a military display, they were driven off together in an open limousine. An escort of fifty motorcycles led the way, while Jackie and the mousy, retiring Madame de Gaulle followed in a bubbletop Citroën. The general had proclaimed a national holiday, and as many as a million people lined the roads into Paris. Despite his physical condition, Kennedy repeatedly stood up to wave to the cheering, applauding, singing, flag-waving spectators. De Gaulle, whose motto was "There can be no authority without prestige, nor prestige unless one keeps one's distance," pointedly remained seated. In the course of the ten-mile motorcade, persistent cries of "Vive Jacqueline!" reflected a vast amount of public interest in Jackie, the result of a taped interview which had run on French television prior to the Kennedys' arrival. In impeccable French, Jackie had spoken charmingly and evocatively of her Gallic background and love of French culture. The broadcast had created a sensation, and de Gaulle attributed the surprising magnitude of the turnout to fascination with Mrs. Kennedy.

An hour remained before Jack's first meeting with de Gaulle when the motorcade reached the Quai d'Orsay, where the visitors were to be housed. Before he faced the general whom some called America's prickliest ally, Jack bathed in a steaming, gold-plated tub and had a revivifying shot from Dr. Jacobson. During the Kennedys' visit to Paris, Jacobson charged them up in advance of their official duties and soothed them in order that they might sleep comfortably at night. He made it possible for Jackie enthusiastically to undertake public appearances she almost certainly would otherwise have recoiled from, and he helped the president to function in spite of his back injury. But, then and later, the doctor's own erratic behavior suggested that there might be serious disadvantages to his treatments. In the first of such episodes, while tending to the First Lady in her bedroom at the Quai d'Orsay he refused to speak because he believed there was a microphone in the ceiling. Later, at the White House, he would complain to Secret Service agents that certain paintings were "bugged," that he was constantly observed through "eyes in the portraits" and that men "in the wall" listened to his every word. Jacobson's bouts of paranoia were probably caused and certainly exacerbated by his own prodigious intake of amphetamines. These were the same drugs that he had begun to pump into the Kennedys—just as the president was preparing to face Khrushchev.

Kennedy and de Gaulle took their places in facing armchairs in the French president's second-floor office at the Elysée Palace, and the talk turned on how to persuade Khrushchev of the United States's determination to stand firm on Berlin. There had been a time when Kennedy thought it would be relatively simple to put East–West relations on a new footing with a quick first agreement in Geneva. There had been a time, indeed only a few days before, when he hoped that a test ban treaty might yet be signed at Vienna. But Khrushchev's thunderclap, transmitted via Llewellyn Thompson on May 23, had made it clear that Berlin, rather than the nuclear test ban, would be the crucial topic when the leaders finally met. De Gaulle urged Kennedy not to overreact, maintaining that had Khrushchev really wished to go to war over Berlin he would already have done so. Khrushchev had made similar threats in the past, and would no doubt do so again. De Gaulle suggested that it would be best to leave no doubt that if Khrushchev wanted a war he would have it, but he reiterated that that did not appear to be the Russian's desire.

To date, Kennedy too had been operating on the premise that Khrushchev did not want war—an essential factor if the American leader was to succeed in executing the strategy of peace central to what he hoped to accomplish in office. Nonetheless, he believed that Khrushchev, however desirous to avoid war, might yet miscalculate.

Kennedy worried that in the mistaken belief that the United States had lost the will to fight Khrushchev might move to cut off access to Berlin—and thereby trigger a war neither side wanted. In 1939, a young Jack Kennedy had worried that the Germans, "counting on another Munich," would miscalculate in the matter of Danzig. But in those days, he had been merely an observer of world events. In 1961, it was Kennedy who by his own actions (or lack of them) in Cuba seemed to have caused Khrushchev to believe that should the Soviets move in Berlin the United States would remain passive; and it was Kennedy to whom, by his own reckoning, it now fell to prove otherwise at Vienna.

Jacobson's absence during the flight from New York had meant that at Orly Kennedy had had to face de Gaulle without the benefit of a shot. Nothing of the sort would do in Vienna, where on the day of his arrival Kennedy would be on an absurdly tight schedule. On Saturday morning, June 3, following three days of talks and ceremonies in Paris, he was due to fly in to Schwechat Airport, attend a welcoming ceremony, participate in a forty-five-minute motorcade and stop off to pay a courtesy call to the Austrian president—all before arriving at the American ambassador's residence minutes before Khrushchev was expected. To preclude the possibility that he might begin talks before Jacobson had had a chance to inject him, Kennedy, who had previously taken care to conceal Dr. Feel Good's presence, asked him to fly on *Air Force One*.

It was raining in Vienna on the morning of June 3 when the motorcade from the airport split in two, Jack's part headed to the Austrian president's residence, Jackie's directly to the American ambassador's. Jacobson traveled with the latter party and was waiting when, twenty minutes before Khrushchev was due to arrive, Kennedy hurried in. The president said that his talks with the Russian leader were likely to last a long time and directed Jacobson to see to it that his back gave him no trouble and that he would be able to get up and move about freely. After he had had a shot, he instructed Jacobson to remain in an anteroom so that he might be summoned if an additional treatment were needed in the course of the meeting. An aide brought a plate of ham sandwiches to occupy the doctor while he perched on a windowsill for the duration. Meanwhile, Kennedy himself, so energetic that press reports commented on it afterward, bounded out the front door of the gray stucco embassy residence and down some steps to greet Khrushchev, whose black limousine, with fluttering hammer-and-sickle flags, pulled up the gravel drive at a quarter to one.

Kenny O'Donnell, who through the years had accompanied Jack Kennedy on many campaign outings, watched the president put out his hand to Khrushchev and utter the phrase he had used with countless voters, "How are you? I'm glad to meet you." Then O'Donnell saw Kennedy step back and, thrusting his hands into the pockets of his gray suit jacket, stare at the sixty-seven-year-old Russian leader as though sizing up his adversary. Khrushchev, short, plump and bald with a bull neck, bright darting eyes and three prominent wens on his face, wore a bulky gray suit with a pair of star-shaped medals above the left pocket. When the leaders went indoors en route to the music room where they were to conduct their first session, it seemed to the president's secretary, Evelyn Lincoln, that Khrushchev's heavy footsteps caused the rafters to shake.

Over the course of two days of talks, Khrushchev's pounding style of argument would have a similar impact on Kennedy. At the opening session, Khrushchev was quick to claim the future for himself and to relegate the younger man, the self-styled representative of a new generation, to a dying past. He identified his own nation with progress and inevitability, and Kennedy's with a desire to preserve the status quo. He wondered aloud whether the United States wished to build a dam to halt human development and philosophized that it would not be possible. Adroitly he turned Kennedy's own words against him, making him sound like an opponent of the very change he had campaigned to bring about. He maneuvered Kennedy into a debate on Marxist theory, an area in which the president proved no match for the experienced Bolshevik agitator. He flashed displeasure when Kennedy, expressing the hope that the struggle between their two countries would remain one of ideas rather than arms, cited the dangers of miscalculation. Khrushchev complained of the vagueness of the term and professed uncertainty as to its meaning. Kennedy's attempts at clarification drove Khrushchev to explode, "Miscalculation! Miscalculation! Miscalculation! . . . You ought to take that word and bury it in cold storage and never use it again! I'm sick of it!" Kennedy, persuaded that no topic could be more important than the need to avoid an accidental war, doggedly returned to it after lunch. Long possessed of the ability to charm others by mocking himself, he offered as an example of a great power's miscalculation his own recent blunder in Cuba. He spoke almost as he had as a Canterbury boy when he conceded that he had been laughable on the football team. Through the years, most people had found Jack Kennedy's ability to laugh at himself irresistible—but not Khrushchev. To Kennedy's immense frustration, Khrushchev, "completely impervious" to his charm, perceived any confession of one's own mistakes as evidence of weakness. Accordingly, Kennedy had merely confirmed the image of himself he had hoped to alter. Upstairs afterward, Kennedy, pale and worn out, seemed "fidgety" to his secretary. He indicated that he wished to rest, but proved unable to. While Jackie had her hair set and a maid prepared her silvery-pink sheath evening dress in anticipation of that evening's state dinner at the former summer residence of the Hapsburg emperors, the president sent aides scrambling to locate a cigar. Later, Jack was pacing his room when Mrs. Lincoln finally asked how his day had gone. "Not too well," he replied.

On Sunday morning, June 4, the Kennedys attended Mass at St. Stephan's Cathedral. The president left the church at ten and, accompanied by Secretary of State Dean Rusk, proceeded to the Soviet embassy, where talks were scheduled to resume at a quarter past. Khrushchev had warned in advance that he meant to speak of Berlin, and today, as the leaders conferred on a small red damask sofa in the second-floor conference room, the conversation turned to the problem that had been festering since Churchill had failed to persuade Truman to delay the withdrawal of American troops from the Soviet occupation zone until after a settlement with Stalin at Potsdam. Khrushchev, observing that sixteen years had elapsed since the war, gave voice to the old argument that the Soviets' greater suffering in the war justified a policy of expansionism in the postwar world. What the West interpreted as aggression they, in the light of history, perceived as a reasonable quest for security. Recalling the vast devastation wrought upon the Soviet Union, Khrushchev noted that Germany, the nation that had "unleashed" the Second World War, had again acquired military power. Moscow, determined never again to face a unified Germany and certainly not a unified anti-Communist Germany, planned by the end of the year to sign a treaty with East Germany, with the result that Western rights of access to Berlin would devolve to the East Germans with whom in future the United States would have to negotiate.

Kennedy also harked back to the Second World War, but with a different emphasis. "We are in Berlin not because of someone's sufferance," he declared. "We fought our way there, although our casualties may have been not as high as the USSR's. We are in Berlin not by agreement of the East Germans but by contractual rights." He went on to emphasize, as Churchill had in 1939 with regard to Danzig, that the United States regarded Berlin as more than just a city. He argued that should the United States accept the loss of access rights, all future confidence in American pledges and commitments would be lost. To abandon West Berlin, Kennedy maintained, would be tantamount to abandoning Europe. "So when we are talking about Berlin," the president went on, "we are talking about West Europe." Under the assumption that Khrushchev too wished to avoid a nuclear war, Kennedy endeavored to spell out the American position on Berlin and thereby to avoid mistakes that had led to war in the past. Lest Khrushchev underestimate American resolve and thereby set off a war neither side wanted, Kennedy emphasized that the United States would not assent to any effort by East Germany to prevent the exercise of rights "won by war." And, most certainly, the United States would not accept an ultimatum. Khrushchev, unflinching, countered that should the Americans go to war there was nothing he could do. He reminded Kennedy that it would be the United States that had started the war and the Soviets who would be perceived as the defenders of peace. "History," Khrushchev warned, "will be the judge."

At lunch, Khrushchev struck a positive note when, with reference to the moratorium on nuclear tests that had lasted for three years while the Geneva talks proceeded, he voluntarily pledged that the Soviets would not be the first to resume testing. Noting that he understood Kennedy was under pressure to resume nuclear weapons tests and that he was under similar pressure himself, he declared that only if the Americans began to test would Moscow follow suit. Despite that promise, Kennedy grew troubled by a sense that Khrushchev in person seemed weirdly unconcerned by the threat of nuclear war. Kennedy's entire program for dealing with the Soviets was predicated on the assumption that in an age of all-annihilating weapons the other side, as rational men, did not want war and would act accordingly. Hopeful that the peaceful defeat of Soviet Communism was possible so long as war could be avoided, he had come to Vienna determined to persuade Khrushchev not to trigger an accidental war on the mistaken belief that the United States had lost the will to fight. But there had been nothing in this morning's session to make Kennedy think that Khrushchev had taken his point. Worse, Khrushchev had seemed blithely to accept the possibility that their differences over Berlin could lead to nuclear war. Now, at the end of the meal, the Russian seemed merrily to taunt his counterpart with a champagne toast that highlighted his own determination to defend Soviet interests no matter what.

When Khrushchev was done, Kennedy stood up to offer some remarks of his own. A model of the USS *Constitution*, which Kennedy had presented to Khrushchev as a gift, had provided a centerpiece at lunch. Declaring that he had traveled to Vienna in hopes of preventing a war that threatened to obliterate both his country and Khrushchev's, Kennedy pointed to the model ship. He noted that in their day Old Ironsides' cannons had carried no further than half a mile and had been capable of killing but a small number of people. By contrast, in an era of nuclear weapons seventy million deaths could result from a first exchange alone. Kennedy insisted that he and Khrushchev together must not permit such a thing to occur. The president, when he said that, looked hard at Khrushchev, and was appalled at what he took to be his response. At least to Kennedy's eyes, Khrushchev seemed to react blankly, indeed, almost to shrug as if the appeal to sanity had made no impact whatever. The impression of Khrushchev Kennedy formed at Vienna was critical, for it would be the reference point against which all later decisions would be taken—but could Kennedy, fueled by amphetamines that deprived him of his customary coolness and control, trust his own perception?

After lunch the meetings officially concluded. Frantic at Khrushchev's apparent lack of concern about the consequences of a nuclear showdown, Kennedy asked to see him again with only translators present. The deterrent, as Churchill had been careful to point out, did not cover the case of lunatics undaunted by the prospect of Armageddon. An additional meeting would be an opportunity to gauge whether Khrushchev was as heedless as he seemed.

Kennedy and Khrushchev faced each other one last time at the Soviet embassy at a quarter past three. In the course of a tense fifteen-minute conversation, Kennedy reiterated his wish that relations between the United States and the USSR would develop in a way that would avoid direct confrontation between them. At the same time, he strove to make "very plain" his position that the United States would not tolerate any interference with its access rights to Berlin. Khrushchev, unwavering in his determination by the end of the year to sign a treaty with the East Germans that would end those rights, shot back that force would be met by force and that if there was to be war, "then let it come now." "Then there will be war, Mr. Chairman," Kennedy warned, adding that it promised to be "a very cold winter."

If he hoped by such words to persuade Khrushchev of his firmness, his performance had no such effect. Khrushchev had already smelled Kennedy's desperation in advance of the meetings, and left Vienna convinced, in the words of the Soviet diplomat Arkady Shevchenko, that America's new young leader "would accept almost anything to avoid nuclear war." In spite of Kennedy's efforts, Vienna promised to be his Munich—the encounter that led the enemy to conclude that he did not have it in him to fight. Following his private talk with Khrushchev, Kennedy returned to the American embassy. The president tended to dislike and distrust emotion, yet he was unrestrainedly emotional when, in a dark room with the blinds shut, he spoke to James Reston of his ordeal. He talked of having been "savaged" by Khrushchev and called Vienna the "worst thing" in his life. Khrushchev, the president admitted from the sofa where he had collapsed, had "beat hell" out of him.

That night, in a scene reminiscent of Chamberlain's exultant return to London after the encounter with Hitler at Munich, cheering crowds lined the route from London Airport as Kennedy and Macmillan were driven in an open car, their wives following in a closed vehicle, to the home of Mrs. Kennedy's sister, Lee Radziwill, in Buckingham Place. The rapturous public reception was sharply at odds with Kennedy's private knowledge of how he had fared with Khrushchev. The masses of people who had come out to hail Kennedy acted as if he had triumphed in Vienna, when in his heart he knew it had been a rout. In 1941, Lord Halifax, then Britain's ambassador in Washington, had told a young Jack Kennedy about Chamberlain's grave political error on returning from Munich. When Chamberlain, ignoring the advice of his parliamentary private secretary, Lord Dunglass, not to exaggerate his accomplishments, faced the crowd from the first-floor window at Number 10 and claimed to have saved the world from war he had destroyed himself politically, for it had been inevitable that the truth would soon make itself known. In advance of Vienna, Kennedy had agonized about how the American people would respond to an announcement that he planned to meet with Khrushchev; in London, he wrestled with the problem of what he would say to them when he went home. Kennedy was determined not to make the same mistake as Chamberlain, who had pretended that Munich was a victory. Early in his administration, the president had allowed himself to be lulled by the cheers of the crowd; he was intent, after Vienna, that he would not let it happen to him again.

Kennedy's talks with Macmillan would have to wait until morning. The president did, however, hint at what was to come when he told Macmillan that the past few days had made him realize that the problems of the world were far more difficult than he had imagined before it fell to him as president to cope with them. As Kennedy had just discovered at Vienna, it was one thing to imagine from an observer's perspective how one would handle a summit meeting and quite another actually to have to face the enemy. Clearly he had been humbled by the experience. The next morning when Kennedy came to Admiralty House, where the prime minister was in residence while 10 Downing Street underwent renovations, it seemed to Macmillan that Khrushchev had "completely overwhelmed" Kennedy. Kennedy came from Vienna a beaten man, and Macmillan, perceiving the extremity of his upset, promptly took him upstairs where, apart from their advisers, the leaders remained closeted for two and a half hours, fortified by sandwiches and whisky.

After Kennedy recounted his ordeal, Macmillan, who over time had developed a certain fond appreciation for Khrushchev's theatrics, suggested that his brutality at Vienna might have been an act designed to unnerve the young president and test his character. He said that Khrushchev might, as threatened, sign a treaty with East Germany and announce that all rights reverted to the East Germans—yet, when the time came, do nothing to block Western access. But, Macmillan cautioned, the threats at Vienna might also be real. He and Kennedy agreed that in the event West Berlin became "a Danzig," as they referred to it in their shorthand, they would be left with little choice but to go to war. With Macmillan, Kennedy found himself in a unique situation, for, as the prime minister would later explain to Jackie, they along with Khrushchev were the only world leaders who lived with the knowledge that they might at any time be called on to launch a nuclear attack. Kennedy had emerged from Vienna with a first overwhelming sense of the reality of such a decision and of the appalling possibility that he might soon be pressed to make it. Vienna had shaken Kennedy's core assumption that the Soviets grasped the consequences of a nuclear confrontation. It was a great comfort to be able to talk to a fellow leader who shared his burdens and understood the magnitude of what Kennedy called his "loneliness" as president. Ormsby Gore, who, at the president's prior request joined them afterward, saw the private talk as "the beginning of a much closer understanding" between the two men, and Macmillan himself wrote to Jackie after her husband's death, "I shall never forget our talk alone (in London) when he was back from the first (and bad) visit to meet Khrushchev. He seemed to trust me—and as you know—for those of us who have had to play the so-called game of politics—national and international—this is something very rare but very precious."

Kennedy seemed much better after the private talk, and when he came downstairs for a luncheon attended by Andrew Devonshire, now under-secretary of state for Commonwealth relations, Debo Devonshire, Moucher Devonshire, the Ormsby Gores and others, there was no sign of the drained, devastated man Macmillan had seen that morning. During the course of the meal, which was very much a family celebration of "their" president's first visit to London since taking office, Jack appeared to relax and enjoy himself immensely, as he always did in that company. To look at him, no one would have thought anything was wrong. But no sooner had the luncheon ended than he again turned to the problem of how on his return to the United States he would portray his encounter with Khrushchev. Earlier he had asked David Ormsby Gore and Lord Home to help his aides prepare a draft of what he would say. Both men, for whom the experience of Munich had been formative, were in a position to understand his particular concerns about the speech—especially Home, who, as Lord Dunglass, had warned Chamberlain to be modest in his claims of what had been attained at the meeting with Hitler. Kennedy was determined that in future no one would say that in his own address after Vienna he had claimed too much or minimized the dangers. In view of Kennedy's optimism at the start of his presidency about the prospects for détente, there was a suggestion from the American side that he ought to offer a "crumb of comfort" by way of mentioning that he and Khrushchev had concurred on the desirability of a neutral Laos. In truth, there had been no substantive progress on the Laos question at Vienna; the Soviets, meanwhile, had been doing little to make the ceasefire hold and, more and more, it seemed likely that the country would indeed fall to Communism. In the interest of protecting himself politically, Kennedy was concerned not to suggest that there had been agreement of any sort in Vienna. Above all, he was concerned to avoid Chamberlain's politically suicidal error of suggesting that war had been averted. Were there to be a crisis presently, he did not want it to come as a total surprise. Following the christening of his and Jackie's niece and a reception afterward at the Radziwill home, Kennedy attended Queen Elizabeth's dinner in his honor. The setting, Buckingham Palace, had in her father's day been one of Chamberlain's triumphant stops on his return from Munich. Kennedy, preoccupied with the televised address he was to deliver the next night, June 6, from the Oval Office, spent much of the evening huddled with David Ormsby Gore, discussing what he would tell the American people about Vienna.

CHAPTER FOURTEEN

The Edge of the Precipice

J ACK KENNEDY LEFT BUCKINGHAM PALACE AT A QUARTER TO
eleven, en route to the airport. Jackie remained behind in London with
her sister and brother-in-law in anticipation of a private holiday. When
they had visited Washington during the time of the Cuban invasion,
Prime Minister and Mrs. Karamanlis, perceiving Jackie's exhaustion
and distress, had invited her to come to Greece in June as their guest. It
had seemed at the time that Jackie would welcome a chance to rest far
from the official demands that vexed her. But in the intervening eight
weeks, matters had developed very differently from what anyone might
have expected. Far from fatigued after the trip to Paris, Vienna and
London, Jackie was exhilarated. She had dazzled France, where, following a reception in the Hall of Mirrors at the Palace of Versailles, newspapers proclaimed, "Versailles Has a Queen." Having enchanted de
Gaulle, Jackie had charmed Khrushchev as well. "First Lady Wins
Khrushchev Too," reported the *New York Times* after their high-spirited
encounter at the state dinner, and "Smitten Khrushchev is Jackie's
Happy Escort," announced the *New York Herald Tribune*. Only three
weeks had passed since the president had brought in Max Jacobson;
methamphetamine shots seemed to have made all the difference. With
the exception of suggestions in the Viennese press, which had greatly
annoyed her husband, that Jackie had been drunk at the state dinner,
her press coverage had been brilliant. Therein, curiously, lay a problem

for the president as he headed back to the United States tended by Jacobson on *Air Force One*. After so much emphasis on the glitter and glamor of the Kennedys' visit to Europe, Jack had somehow to dampen the impression of the trip as a success.

The president returned to the White House in horrible physical condition. For three weeks he had managed to conceal his back injury, but the combination of pain and stress had left him greatly in need of rest. Kennedy arranged that, after hosting a luncheon for President Youlou of the Congo on June 8, he would fly to Palm Beach, where the Wrightsman estate had again been made available. Meanwhile, he limited his use of crutches to those times when he was out of public view. Since boyhood, on account of his own ill health and a favored older brother's robustness, he had been sensitive to any depiction of himself as physically weak. Now, when much depended on his ability to persuade Khrushchev of US resolve, it was even more important to him not to project any hint of weakness.

At a meeting with the congressional leadership the following day, June 6, Kennedy spoke of Khrushchev's toughness at Vienna and of his own sense that the Russian had met with him "to know whether we would fight." He repeated Khrushchev's chilling declaration that if there were to be a war, "then let it come now," and he commented on the contents of an aide-memoire Khrushchev had handed him which specified a December deadline for the signing of a treaty with the East Germans. Kennedy said that in his televised address that evening he would indicate that the situation was serious, but, in the interest of not alarming the people, avoid pressing it home too sharply. His private remarks to the legislators were disturbing, to say the least, and Senate Majority Leader Mike Mansfield came away from the presentation with a sense that Kennedy, "shaken" by his talks with Khrushchev, seemed to believe there was a strong chance that the conflict over Berlin would lead to war.

That night at seven, Kennedy, speaking from the Oval Office, told the American people that it was his obligation to report to them "candidly and publicly" on Vienna. Calling the meetings "a very sober two days," he stressed that no spectacular progress had been "either achieved or pretended." Asserting his original view of the encounter as not a summit meeting "where negotiations are attempted and new

agreements sought" but rather an "informal exchange" aimed at allowing the leaders to gain "insight and understanding of each other's policies," he avoided any mention of his own efforts to secure a deal to be
signed by both men at Vienna. Decidedly underplaying his impression—
privately conveyed to Macmillan and to the congressional leadership
—of Khrushchev as brutal and threatening, he assured the American
people that "there had been no discourtesy, no loss of temper, no
threats or ultimatums on either side." At the same time he noted that
his and Khrushchev's "most somber talks" had concerned Germany and
Berlin. Reiterating the United States's determination to retain uninter-
rupted access to Berlin, Kennedy omitted—as he had told the congressional leaders he would—any reference to Khrushchev's end-of-the-year
deadline.

As would become clear from Kennedy's private conversations in
Florida, that deadline loomed in his thoughts. Meanwhile, by the
morning of Thursday, June 8, his back pain had become so severe that
he doubted he would be able to ascend the steps to *Air Force One* without assistance. To date he had managed to conceal his injury, but he
sensed he could do it no more. It galled him to have to instruct Pierre
Salinger to notify the press that when he left for Florida that afternoon,
he would be on crutches. Tactically, the point of the announcement was
to make it clear that the present difficulty, the result of a specific injury,
was unrelated to Kennedy's previous grave back problems. Salinger
explained what had happened at the tree-planting ceremony in Ottawa,
spoke of Dr. Travell's Novocain and hot pack treatments (though not
Dr. Jacobson's methamphetamine shots), and cited Travell's assurances
that Kennedy's condition posed "no serious concern" and that he would
recover quickly. So the press had been informed, but even then Jack
simply could not bear to be seen on crutches. He called Salinger during
the press briefing to say that he planned not to use them after all.
Presently, when at Andrews Air Force Base he walked to his jet, he did
it without assistance. No more than a slight limp and awkwardness in
his manner of carrying himself was detectable.

Kennedy and Chuck Spalding were accompanied on the three-day
holiday in Florida not only by the president's doctor and chef but also
by two White House secretaries, who, when Jackie was away, routinely
made themselves sexually available to Kennedy. On this and similar

occasions, the president, for all his concern about his public image, seemed oddly oblivious to the potential for scandal should word get out about his other women.

In addition to relaxing in the Wrightsmans' heated pool, Jack spent much of the long weekend discussing Vienna and Khrushchev with Spalding. Had he read Khrushchev correctly? Why had he not been able to get through to him? Was Khrushchev really prepared to provoke a confrontation and set off a nuclear war? That the answer to the last question might be yes seemed to suggest itself when the news reached him in Florida that Khrushchev had released to the public the aide-memoire, which included the December deadline the president had hoped to keep from the American people. By Monday morning, as the flight back to Washington drew near, Kennedy's back pain had worsened. He was forced to accept that there was no chance he would be able to repeat the act of will he had managed on Thursday, when he climbed the airplane steps without assistance.

Four months previously, when Kennedy spoke in his inaugural address of the torch having passed to a new generation of Americans, he had seemed the epitome of youth and vigor. On June 12, not only was he photographed on crutches for the first time, but he was also shown being loaded onto *Air Force One* by a crane and taken off by a forklift. The images set off a flurry of rumors about a reprise of the back problems that, in the mid-1950s, had kept him out of the Senate for nearly a year. Even worse was the news that, in Geneva that day, the Soviets had effectively sabotaged the test ban talks by echoing Khrushchev's insistence at Vienna that they be folded into the more general talks on disarmament, a vaster and necessarily more complicated issue. At the same time, the Soviet delegate Semyon Tsarapkin angrily accused the Western negotiators of seeking a way to break off the talks and throw the blame on Moscow. Within days, US intelligence would judge that the test ban talks were essentially dead.

There was no time to mourn the talks on which Kennedy had pinned his hopes for a swift first agreement with the Soviets. Khrushchev's year-end deadline required Kennedy to plunge immediately into the search for a way to avert a crisis over Berlin. It was not the signing of a treaty per se that Kennedy saw as a threat but an effort to sever Western access, for the latter, as he had striven to make clear at Vienna, must

lead to war. To help him decide what to do, Kennedy had asked Dean
Acheson to examine the Berlin crisis. Truman's secretary of state, before
submitting a written report, offered some preliminary views at a session
of the Interdepartmental Coordinating Group on Berlin Contingency
Planning on June 16. Brilliant and imperious, Acheson, who affected a
British style of dress and personal manner, made no secret of his scorn
for all who differed with his opinions. In the present instance, he called
for emphatic military measures, to include the resumption of nuclear
tests, the swift buildup of nuclear and conventional forces and the declaration of a national emergency, all designed to impress Khrushchev
with US seriousness about Berlin. He stressed that the president, having embarked on such a program, must be ready "to go all the way"—
that is, to launch a nuclear attack if necessary. In the end, either the
Soviets would finally be persuaded of American resolve, or the United
States would be at war.

Key to Acheson's recommendations was the belief that negotiations
must wait until after a US-precipitated test of will and that attempts to
negotiate prior to such a demonstration would be interpreted in
Moscow as a sign of weakness. Obviously Acheson's suggestions were
antithetical to the strategy of peace Kennedy had enunciated during the
campaign and on inauguration day. He was urging the president to
propel both countries to the edge of the precipice and thereby repeat
certain of the factors—which Kennedy had been studying since boyhood—that had set off the First World War. By his insistence that the
test of will precede negotiations, he was suggesting something very different from the combination of strength and negotiations that characterized Churchill's double-barreled policy. At the same time, Acheson
spoke directly and forcefully to Kennedy's sense that the essential problem was to convince Khrushchev that, if pressed in Berlin, he would
indeed use nuclear weapons. In light of the deadline and, particularly,
of Kennedy's appalled impression at Vienna that Khrushchev might not
himself be averse to starting a war, the president was prepared to consider that it might be necessary to rethink substantially his approach to
Soviet relations.

It did not help that, even as Kennedy strove to make up his mind,
his health deteriorated sharply. Unable to do without crutches, he
avoided more press photographs of his debility by remaining in the car

rather than getting out to welcome the First Lady when she landed at
Andrews Air Force Base following her Greek holiday. On the evening of
June 16 the Kennedys left to spend the weekend at Glen Ora, but the
president was not well enough to accompany Jackie to a party at the
nearby estate of Paul Mellon, to which much of fashionable Washington
had been invited. He was back at the White House at the start of the
week in time for a state visit by Prime Minister and Mrs. Ikada of Japan,
but on Wednesday, June 21, following a two-hour Potomac cruise with
the Japanese leader, the president fell ill. What began as a sore throat
escalated to a 101-degree fever, and by the time Dr. Travell arrived after
Jackie had summoned her at midnight, the fever had risen to 103.
Extreme stress of any sort poses a grave danger to a sufferer of Addison's
disease, and it seemed as if the acute pain of recent weeks, coupled with
tension over Berlin, where a misstep could set off a nuclear war, might
have triggered an Addisonian crisis. In the course of the night Kennedy's
fever rose to 105, while Travell took blood cultures and started the president on large doses of penicillin for what seemed to be a recurrence of
infection at the site of the 1954–5 back surgery. Travell administered an
intravenous infusion and alcohol sponge baths, and by daybreak
Kennedy's temperature had returned to 101. Coming as it did so soon
after press pictures of Kennedy's return trip from Florida, the present
episode threatened further to undermine public confidence in him.
Accordingly, the White House tried to minimize the incident. Travell's
press release omitted the fact that Kennedy's temperature had spiked at
105, saying only that it had been 101 both when she was summoned to
his bedside and the next morning. Of course there was no mention of
its having been an Addisonian crisis, as Kennedy through the years had
persistently denied that he had Addison's disease. But there could be no
concealing that, though the crisis was over, the president remained so
unwell that he had to cancel all of his Thursday appointments. He
remained in bed, where Dr. Preston A. Wade, summoned from New
York, determined that, despite Dr. Travell's fears, there was no infection
in his back after all. By evening Kennedy's temperature was normal and
he insisted on getting up to greet visitors, despite Travell's admonitions,
though he was not well enough to go to a dinner at the Japanese
embassy, which Jackie attended with Vice President and Mrs. Johnson.
On Friday Kennedy held some meetings upstairs, but still lacked the

strength to come down to the Oval Office. Jackie and Lem Billings took him to Glen Ora for the weekend. On Sunday, June 25, when the Kennedys attended Mass in Middleburg, Virginia, Lem, who was not Catholic, went along in case his friend required physical support. In truth the president was not yet up to such an outing, but he believed it necessary to provide some press pictures that signaled recovery. In the days that followed, as he struggled with critical decisions about the direction of his presidency, he would remain seriously unwell.

Was Khrushchev referring to the ailing president when, in a speech on June 25, he spoke sardonically of the United States as a "worn-out runner"? Kennedy, particularly sensitive to such a characterization, brought up Khrushchev's metaphor when he met the following day with the Soviet leader's son-in-law Aleksei Adzhubei, the editor of the Russian newspaper *Izvestia*. This was one meeting that Kennedy would not hear of canceling, for to do so would seem like an admission of weakness. Georgi Bolshakov, the Soviet intelligence agent who had passed on Kennedy's back-channel messages in advance of Vienna, translated for Adzhubei as the president declared that he could not understand why Khrushchev wanted to force the United States out of Berlin. Kennedy noted that Americans regarded West Berlin as a symbol and that if he abandoned US rights in Berlin he would be "impeached by the American people." He did himself no favors by the latter remark, which Khrushchev, in an address to Warsaw Pact leaders on August 4, would cite with scorn. Coming on top of Kennedy's previous statements, transmitted via Bolshakov, about his domestic political problems, as well as his own comments at Vienna about the constraints on his ability to act, the reference to impeachment added to the picture that had begun to form in Moscow of a leader preoccupied with his own political vulnerability.

In other quarters, Kennedy's failure to produce a timely response to the Khrushchev aide-memoire was beginning to raise doubts about his leadership. Walter Lippmann, who had given him high marks at the time of the debates with Nixon, wrote that the president seemed unsure of himself. In a similar vein, Macmillan worried that his initial assessment of Kennedy's abilities might have been wrong. "I feel 'in my bones' that President K. is going to fail to produce any real leadership," the prime minister wrote in his diary on June 25. Macmillan feared that in the absence of decisive action, "we may drift to disaster over Berlin—a terrible diplomatic defeat or (out of sheer incompetence) a nuclear war." Alarmingly, Lord Home, recently back from Washington where Kennedy had invited him to confer on Berlin, was of the opinion that in the end the president might prove too weak to withstand Acheson's insistence that negotiations be put off till after a potentially cataclysmic test of will with the Soviets.

Acheson submitted his report on June 28, and the president had it in his battered black alligator briefcase when he left for Hyannis Port to spend the Fourth of July holiday at the family compound. On the surface, at least, it was a perfect Cape Cod weekend, replete with lobsters and fish chowder; bare feet, sailboats and sun; children running through the hedges; and nighttime film screenings in the basement of his father's house. Joe Kennedy took particular pleasure in the large number of neighbors and tourists who crowded in as close as possible to the property in order to catch a glimpse of the president—his son. Each day Jack went out with his father on the water, where he always seemed happiest and most at ease, and he participated fully in the holiday festivities. Still, he had taken the problem of Berlin along with him in the form of Acheson's report, and as the traditional fireworks celebrating American independence streaked the summer night sky, the president found himself facing a moment of decision. However comforting the mood of family celebration, there could be no escape from the grim reality of what was being demanded of him. In the interest of establishing US firmness, Acheson advised the president to take extreme military measures which, the report freely admitted, might provoke a nuclear exchange. It was everything Kennedy on coming to office had hoped to avoid. At the same time, the president unequivocally agreed that the deterrent which had previously kept Khrushchev from moving on Berlin must somehow be restored, and Acheson was nothing if not lucid about what needed to be done to that end. When he returned to the White House on July 5, Kennedy questioned National Security Adviser McGeorge Bundy about how in the short term they might improve Americans' chances of survival in the event of a nuclear war. What action did Bundy think they ought to ask citizens to take at present, and what should be required of them in case of an attack? Kennedy directed his civil defense experts to come up with an emergency program by the following week.

In this atmosphere of tense uncertainty, the Kennedys hosted a state dinner in honor of President Mohammed Ayub Khan of Pakistan that, to the president's pride and delight, Jackie had conceived as a riposte to Khrushchev's charges at Vienna that the United States stood against progress and change. The accusations had stung her husband, who, as part of his strategy of peace, was eager to win over emerging nations. The First Lady seized on the home of George Washington as the ideal setting for a spectacle aimed at reminding the world that the United States had itself been born in revolution. As Jackie saw it, there was a second part to the message sent out on the evening of July 11, when a fleet of yachts carried partygoers down the Potomac to Mount Vernon, which was illuminated—à la Versailles—with spotlights. In addition to the soldiers in red coats and powdered wigs who seemed to have stepped out of Washington's era, the trappings of present-day wealth and power suggested that if only the emerging nations followed America's revolutionary path, rather than Russia's, they too could hope someday to have all this. On the occasion of the Mount Vernon dinner, Jackie, attired in a white organza lace evening dress with a green silk sash round her waist, long white gloves and diamonds glittering in her hair, took up her role as chief image-maker, the individual responsible more than anyone else for creating the aura of style and sophistication that people would associate with the Kennedy presidency. She fashioned settings and events that projected a new and fresh idea of America, one more vibrant and alluring than that of the Eisenhower years. And lest the glamor and high style alienate some voters, they would be perfectly balanced, at Jack's instigation, by plenty of warm, reassuring pictures of the Kennedys and their children as a loving family.

Dean Acheson privately lamented what he saw as an excess of concern with "image" at the Kennedy White House and "a weakness of decision at the top." The day after Jackie's immensely successful party at Mount Vernon, Acheson, at a session of the Interdepartmental Coordinating Group on Germany and Berlin, complained that Kennedy needed to make up his mind "at the earliest possible moment" about the suggestions in his report. More than a month had passed since Khrushchev presented Kennedy with the aide-memoire on Berlin. Warning that there would be a revolt in Congress if the president failed to provide strong leadership on the Berlin question, Acheson argued that basic decisions must be taken soon. He returned the next day to put his demands directly to Kennedy at a meeting of the National Security Council, but the session concluded without any firm word one way or another from the president. Acheson was irritated, but it was one thing to advise the president to prepare to launch a nuclear war, and quite another to be the one who must carry out such a plan with the vast loss of life it entailed. More generally, the long delay reflected that Kennedy was also weighing whether to shift the overall direction of his presidency from the course he had so emphatically set on inauguration day. It was a huge decision, and Kennedy, unwilling to be rushed—certainly not after his rash actions in Cuba—deliberated for another six days. Acheson, meanwhile, carped that when Kennedy made foreign-policy decisions he seemed overly inclined to weigh the effects on his own personal fortunes and on those of his party. Ironically, while in certain instances to date, notably the Cuban invasion, Kennedy had indeed made politically-driven decisions, this was simply not the case with regard to Berlin and the Acheson Report. In the present instance, seeing as he did both sides of the argument—the reasons for departing from the strategy of peace and those for adhering to it—the president really was struggling to make the decision that would be best for the country. Indeed, at a moment when *Time* magazine was reporting that most Americans preferred to risk war over Berlin rather than appear to give in to Khrushchev, the line of action Kennedy finally decided upon was anything but tailored to benefit him politically.

In the end Kennedy decided to seek not a military but a diplomatic solution in Berlin. Having flirted with Acheson's hard-line approach, he returned to the double-barreled policy, combining strength and negotiation, on which he had campaigned. On July 19, though he accepted some of Acheson's proposals for beefing up US military might, he made it clear that he did not want matters to become "so dominated by the military aspects that fruitful negotiations might become impossible." He refused to declare a national emergency, and most importantly he declined to put off negotiations until after a military test of will. Far from ruling out talks at this stage, he intended vigorously to seek negotiations before Khrushchev signed the treaty with East Germany. To that end, he called for immediate discussions with the French and the Germans to devise a joint Western negotiating position. Kennedy seemed relieved not just to have taken a decision at long last, but also to have left behind the turbulent emotions that had characterized his reaction to Khrushchev at Vienna. Coolness and reason were again guiding his decisions, and he appeared much happier that way. Even his back seemed suddenly much improved. That weekend at Cape Cod he swam and sailed with Jackie and otherwise enjoyed himself. His sister Eunice reported to their mother that he was "feeling the best he has felt in six months" and was "in fantastically good humor."

After the disappointment of the test ban talks, fiasco in Cuba, and shock at Vienna, Jack Kennedy had retrieved both his balance and his sense of where he wanted to take the country. He went on national television on July 25 to explain his decisions. During the campaign, he had echoed Churchill's call to strengthen conventional forces lest the West be required "to unleash a full-scale nuclear war" in response to every Soviet provocation. Now he enumerated plans for a buildup of conventional forces that would give the United States "a wider choice than humiliation or all-out nuclear action." Kennedy spoke of larger defense appropriations; a doubling and even trebling of the draft; increases in Army, Navy and Air Force manpower; and additions to the stock of non-nuclear weapons, ammunition and equipment. After he had spelled out his intention to arm, he went on to proclaim a wish to parley. America's peacetime posture was traditionally defensive, Kennedy argued, but its diplomatic posture need not be. "Our response to the Berlin crisis will not be merely military or negative," he declared. "It will be more than merely standing firm." While the United States was prepared to defend its interests, it was also ready to seek peace in talks. As Churchill had in speeches both before and after the Second World War, the president emphasized that the preparations called for, and stipulations made, aimed not to start a war, but to prevent one. "The steps I have indicated tonight are aimed at avoiding . . . war. To sum it all up: we seek peace—but we shall not surrender. That is the central meaning of this crisis, and the meaning of your government's policy."

The day after the speech, Kennedy emphasized his determination to move swiftly on negotiations. He opened a session on Berlin attended by

Acheson, Rusk, Bundy and others by asking about "progress on our negotiating position." Even as Kennedy moved to execute the policy of
strength and negotiations he had announced the previous evening,
Khrushchev was exploding with rage at a text of the president's speech.
Like the many Americans who, at the time of "The Sinews of Peace"
speech, had focused on Churchill's call for strength but ignored his
equally important appeal for negotiations, Khrushchev concentrated on
Kennedy's tough talk to the exclusion of the rest. Khrushchev told White
House disarmament chief John McCloy, who would be sure to report his
comments back to Kennedy, that as far as he was concerned the president
had declared preliminary war. Despite protests from McCloy that
Kennedy in fact desired negotiations, Khrushchev insisted that the speech
had been an ultimatum "tantamount to war" and vowed that he too
would undertake drastic military measures. Professing regret that Kennedy
had chosen this course, he said he accepted the challenge and vowed not
to be deterred from a treaty with East Germany. By way of derisive comment on Kennedy's plan to build up conventional forces in hopes of averting a nuclear exchange, Khrushchev promised that the next war would be
nuclear, its outcome "decided not by infantry but by rockets and nuclear
bombs." He boasted that he had enough bombs already, and predicted
that while the United States and the USSR might survive, all of Europe
would undoubtedly be destroyed. He conceded that Kennedy seemed a
"reasonable young man full of energy," but grimly prophesied that in the
event of war he would be "the last president."

McCloy was struck by Khrushchev's "strong emotional tone" and
"rough war-like language." Over dinner with McCloy, Sir Frank
Roberts, Britain's ambassador in Moscow, suggested that the fit of temper had been merely an act, since Khrushchev's rage had not been
reflected in the comments of Gromyko and other senior Soviet officials
with whom the ambassador had discussed Kennedy's speech. Where
Khrushchev had claimed to interpret the speech as an ultimatum, the
other Russians had "clearly noted" the call for negotiations and a diplomatic rather than a military solution. Khrushchev, it would turn out,
was well aware of Kennedy's desire for talks, but the president's endless
complaints about political problems at home had led Khrushchev to
conclude that Kennedy, however much he wanted détente, would

finally be too fearful of the political consequences to act on his beliefs. At a secret meeting of Soviet scientists in July, as well as at a gathering of Warsaw Pact leaders in early August, Khrushchev ridiculed the president's susceptibility to domestic political considerations and mocked his appeals that Moscow sympathize with his desire to stay in office. On the assumption that Kennedy's dread of nuclear war would outweigh the fear of political damage to himself, Khrushchev set out to scare him into making a settlement that would give the Soviets time to complete the economic advances needed to beat capitalism. By the decision to go tough, Khrushchev was also covering himself politically with hardliners at home and with the Chinese Communists, who considered him soft for espousing a policy of peaceful coexistence.

For the moment, at any rate, Kennedy did not falter in the face of Khrushchev's threats. Having resisted Acheson's efforts to raise the emotional temperature, the president seemed serenely determined to press ahead with plans to seek negotiations on Berlin. And, having reaffirmed the beliefs with which he came to office, he looked anew at the test ban talks, which by most estimates had degenerated to the level of "farce." Khrushchev, in speaking to McCloy, had reiterated the point made at Vienna that, though he was under pressure to resume nuclear weapons tests, he would not be the first to do so. Kennedy took encouragement from this and, three days after announcing his Berlin policy, decided to send Arthur Dean back to Geneva later in the month to make one last concentrated effort to secure a breakthrough first agreement.

The president's eagerness at least to have opened negotiations on Berlin before Khrushchev signed a treaty with the East Germans was based on his sense that it would be more dangerous to negotiate at the edge of the precipice, where, Churchill wrote, one could so easily lose one's balance: "A touch, a gust of wind, a momentary dizziness, and all is precipitated into the abyss." Long fascinated by the causes of the First World War, Kennedy sought to keep clear of the accidents and mishaps that might suddenly, irreversibly set off a war. It was fitting that Dean Rusk began meetings with the French, British and Germans on August 4, 1961, the forty-seventh anniversary of the outbreak of the First World War, in order to work out a joint Western negotiating position in anticipation of beginning talks with the Soviets in October—two months before the threatened treaty would make everything much more difficult. The president also believed it essential that there be no sign of disunity on the Western side, which Khrushchev would of course take as weakness.

When Rusk began to speak of Kennedy's wish for negotiations, it soon became apparent that Maurice Couve de Murville and Heinrich von Brentano, the French and German foreign ministers respectively, were taken aback. This time, in contrast to Khrushchev's performance with McCloy, the distress was undoubtedly real. Kennedy's July 25 speech had been widely received in France and Germany as a welcome call to arms. The president's desire for negotiations had genuinely gone unnoticed, and Couve, for his part, seemed sincerely appalled to hear Rusk suggest that there might be talks at this point. Certainly the French wanted no part in preparing a joint negotiating position. Couve declared, "If the present situation is a trial of strength, it is essential to show no weakness." He pointed to Khrushchev's belief that the West would not fight to protect its position in Berlin and insisted that Kennedy's military measures had made an impression on the Russian leader that would be undone by an offer to negotiate. In an allusion to Munich and the policy of appeasement, Couve suggested that a deal with Moscow might make it possible to avoid a nuclear war in 1961, but that such action would merely lead to such a war in 1962 or 1963. "This is not a policy," Couve went on. "We have learned that in the past and must evaluate the present situation in this light." Only Britain's representative, Lord Home, was supportive when Rusk laid out Kennedy's plan. "We are arming," Rusk explained, "but part of our purpose for this is to support us in negotiation." Kennedy was a great believer in Burke's idea that so long as one maintained superior power it was possible to offer peace with honor and safety, and that such an offer would be attributed not to weakness but to magnanimity. Accordingly, the secretary of state pointed out Kennedy's conviction that so long as their side remained strong, a Western initiative on negotiations need not detract from its position of strength; instead it was "an essential part thereof." Rusk, for all his efforts, was unable to sell the Kennedy position to Couve or Brentano, and he fared no better at a separate session with de Gaulle. Kennedy, de Gaulle suggested, was free to do as he wished, but France would not assent to negotiations simply because Khrushchev had "whistled" at Vienna.

Four days after the Paris discussions ended with precisely the show of disunity Kennedy had hoped to avoid, Khrushchev took an action that by any measure went considerably beyond whistling. On August 13, the president was at Hyannis Port preparing to sail with Jackie to their friends Paul and Bunny Mellon's for lunch when word arrived that East German troops and police had sealed the border between East and West Berlin and begun to erect the barrier of barbed wire and rubble that became the Berlin Wall. Kennedy's first reaction was shock, for under the circumstances any move on Berlin threatened to spark off a nuclear war. But he soon grasped that, far from being an effort to deny Western access, which would have necessitated a US military response, the sealing of the border was in fact an attempt to prevent East German citizens from escaping to the West. After Vienna, the belief had been widespread in East Germany that an impasse between the Soviets and the Americans had been reached, and that war was imminent. So many refugees had fled to what they hoped would be safety in the West that the exodus imperiled the economy and stability of East Germany. Kennedy's July 25 speech had heightened fears on the Communist side, and finally the East German government had moved forcibly to keep people in. The border closing was not a show of power but, in Kennedy's estimate, a tacit admission of failure and desperation.

On the calculation that this was not the crisis moment, Kennedy was careful to keep his initial public response low-key. He issued a statement that the action violated the four-power status of Berlin and that a strong protest would follow. Washington's early restraint provoked anguish in West Germany, where there had long been fears that the Americans and British might prove all too ready to abandon their German allies in an effort to make a deal with the Soviet Union. Coming at precisely the moment when Kennedy was attempting to drag the very reluctant Germans into negotiations, the White House's muted response to the border closing spurred rumors throughout Germany that the United States planned gradually to withdraw from West Berlin. The US mission in Berlin sent word to Washington that the president's July 25 speech had been widely read as "a promise of firmness" and that "a crisis of confidence" would ensue in the absence of a more emphatic response. Kennedy, eager on the one hand to avoid unnecessarily triggering a war and on the other to persuade the

Germans to agree to the concept of negotiations on Berlin, began to see that he must make a gesture to show that the United States did not intend to abandon them. A request from Willy Brandt, mayor of West Berlin, that the United States fortify its garrison there as a display of commitment prompted Kennedy to send a symbolic force of fifteen hundred troops up the Autobahn to West Berlin on Saturday, August 19. Kennedy also dispatched Vice President Johnson and General Lucius Clay, the hero of the Berlin airlift, to hand-deliver to Brandt a message of support for the German people.

As the sealing of the border targeted East German refugees rather than Western access, Kennedy saw little real chance that the convoy would be stopped. Nonetheless, sensitive to the fact that a tiny incident could easily spiral out of control, he tensely monitored the convoy until it was through. When he was certain there had been no incident, he went up to Cape Cod for the rest of the weekend, but the tension had served as a reminder of just how explosive the Berlin situation was. On his return to the White House on Monday, August 21, Kennedy fired off a memo to Rusk to say that he wanted to "take a stronger lead on Berlin negotiations." Curiously, where the sealing of the border had reaffirmed Kennedy's conviction that talks must be entered into at once, they also confirmed de Gaulle in the belief that at this stage negotiations with the Soviets were out of the question. On August 26 he warned Kennedy that a willingness to negotiate in the present environment would be read in Moscow as "a notice of our surrender."

On the evening of Tuesday, August 29, Jack Kennedy and Senator George Smathers, accompanied by two young women, cruised the Potomac on the presidential yacht the *Honey Fitz*. Jackie was at the Cape, and Jack was due to join her there for the Labor Day weekend. Smathers, an old friend from congressional days, was often present when the presidential schedule provided for an evening with girls. Even as Kennedy was out relaxing on one of the last nights of summer, Khrushchev, in keeping with his plan to frighten the president into agreeing to a settlement advantageous to the Soviets, was preparing another surprise. On August 30, with Arthur Dean and David Ormsby Gore having gone to Geneva to try one last time for a test ban agreement, Moscow announced the resumption of nuclear testing. The president, in the Oval Office with Bobby, cursed and shouted on learning

the news. It was not the fact of the tests themselves that plunged
Kennedy into a fit of agitation; after all, on the previous day he had
himself approved a future announcement of "contingent preparations"
should he later decide to resume US nuclear testing. It was that at
Vienna Khrushchev had pledged that he would not be the first to test.
Significantly, Khrushchev had made the promise not to a former president or to one of Kennedy's representatives, but to Kennedy himself,
leader to leader, at a meeting which was supposed to have allowed both
men to take the first steps toward trust and clarity.

At a moment when Kennedy was struggling to convince the French
and the Germans to agree to Berlin negotiations, and when he faced
charges of appeasement within his own country for so much as considering a deal, he found it deeply troubling that Khrushchev would have
lied so brazenly. How was Kennedy to sell anyone on Berlin talks, when
the leader with whom he proposed to make a deal could not be trusted?
And more generally, how viable was a Soviet strategy based on contact
and agreements, when those agreements might soon prove worthless?
After Khrushchev's brutality in Vienna, Kennedy had had to call into
question all of his assumptions about the best way to deal with and
defeat the Soviets. He had seriously considered Acheson's hard-line proposals, which would have had him shift entirely his approach to Soviet
relations. In the end, his decision—based not on politics but on what
he sincerely believed best for the country—to revert to the double-
barreled policy of strength coupled with negotiations had permitted
him to remain serene in the face of Khrushchev's new threats and had
bolstered his resolve to push for Berlin talks despite determined opposition from US allies. Having gone through that process of reflection and
having taken a decision that reaffirmed his faith in the strategy of peace,
Kennedy was profoundly shaken by the news from Moscow. At best,
Khrushchev's lie would make it vastly more difficult to sell the concept
of negotiations to recalcitrant allies and to an electorate already distrust-
ful of the Russians. At worst, it left Kennedy's strategy of peace in tatters,
for how in the absence of trust would negotiations be possible?

After Vienna, Kennedy had been careful not to repeat Chamberlain's
error of pretending to have won a lasting peace at Munich. Three months
later, on the day the Soviets announced that they would resume nuclear
testing, Kennedy was left to ponder whether he had repeated Chamber-

lain's far more devastating mistake—the error that had led to war—of believing his opponent's lies. Hitler, stalling until he found it convenient to fight, had lied to Chamberlain, and the prime minister had foolishly trusted him. That Khrushchev had also lied to Kennedy seemed to confirm the president's worst fears at Vienna that the Russian leader was gearing up for battle and that efforts to talk were useless. As he prepared to join Jackie and the children at Cape Cod, Kennedy had to consider again whether it might be time to abandon the push for negotiations and to ready the nation for war.

CHAPTER FIFTEEN

The Go-Between

SHORTLY AFTER 6 P.M. ON SEPTEMBER 1, 1961, A LARGE DARK helicopter with a painted white top, followed by a chase helicopter, approached the Kennedy family compound in Hyannis Port. A Friday evening ritual had established itself in the Cape Cod village that had come to be known as America's "summer political capital." Jackie, on learning from a Secret Service agent that *Air Force One* had touched down at Otis Air Force Base, would take Caroline, and sometimes John Junior in his carriage, to the main house. Other young Kennedy cousins would gather near the landing pad that had been constructed on the lawn, and a crowd of neighbors and camera-wielding vacationers would collect on the other side of the tall green privacy hedges. As the helicopter prepared to land after a ten-minute flight, the president's father, who liked nothing better than to be there to offer an affectionate welcome, would come out onto the lawn. Tonight, as always, Jack Kennedy smiled and waved to the crowd. Unlike Jackie, who loathed being stared at and complained that at the Cape she felt as if she were living in a fishbowl with strangers peering in at her with enormous menacing eyes, Jack loved the attention. He tended to relax noticeably as soon as he arrived, and it seemed no different tonight, three hours after he had learned that the Soviets had, that very morning, exploded a nuclear bomb near the Mongolian border in Soviet Central Asia. Long-range American detecting devices estimated the blast to have been more powerful and destructive than that in Hiroshima in 1945.

The news was the culmination of two days of high tension. Kennedy had responded to the announcement on August 30 that the Soviets planned to resume nuclear testing with a scathing public denunciation of the decision and the recall of Arthur Dean from the Geneva test ban talks. The British government also recalled David Ormsby Gore. Saturday morning's explosion proved that the decision to test must have been made some time previously; otherwise, this first known test by one of the trio of nuclear powers to have agreed in 1958 to a moratorium could not have been accomplished so quickly. Khrushchev, meanwhile, had been heard to boast that he planned to test a 100-megaton bomb—a device whose destructive capacity, equivalent to that of 100,000,000 tons of TNT, made it virtually useless as a military weapon, as it would be impossible to direct with any degree of precision. The Central Asian blast had possessed nowhere near that force. Kennedy, in conference with Arthur Dean and John McCloy shortly before he left for the Labor Day weekend, struggled to comprehend an enemy who would talk gleefully of a nuclear device so large that it could only be employed, in Dean's chilling words, as "a weapon of mass terror." The president grew preoccupied with the enigma of Khrushchev the man. What, he would ask, were Khrushchev's real intentions? Had Khrushchev actually lied at Vienna when he pledged not to be the first to resume testing, or had he, in the interim, merely given in to the pressure of which he had spoken? Did he not want negotiations, but rather a test of strength? Kennedy repeatedly came back to these and related questions, on which some of his most important decisions must turn. Should it be the case that Khrushchev was a megalomaniac like Hitler, attempts to negotiate would be pointless. Clearly, when the time came to act, Kennedy would have little choice but to make a guess about his enemy's character and his plans.

At the Kennedy compound, the crowd that had gathered at the periphery of the property lingered after the president went indoors, it being part of the Friday night ritual that he would soon reemerge with three-year-old Caroline for their weekly excursion to stock up on sweets. The spectators were not disappointed. The president, casually dressed, came out at five past seven and, along with his blonde, sun-tanned daughter and some of the other youngsters, rode the golf cart Joe Kennedy had provided that year to ease his son's back troubles. En route to the News Stand, Jack exchanged pleasantries with his mainly Republican neighbors. Within hours, he would have to decide how to respond to that morning's explosion and to Khrushchev's promise of more and bigger blasts. Even before the Soviet announcement on August 30, prominent scientific, military and congressional figures had urged Kennedy to resume nuclear tests; the political pressure was certain to intensify in view of the Soviet provocation. The president told the Spaldings that he did not doubt that a vast segment of the American electorate would expect their government to reply to Khrushchev's nuclear blast with one of its own.

By Saturday morning he had decided not to bow to public pressure. Usually at his best when utterly cool and rational, Kennedy was determined to preserve his equanimity in a volatile situation. For the moment, he planned to continue to seek negotiations despite Khrushchev's posturing. Before the president went out sailing at 1 p.m., he phoned Rusk to convey his instructions. Rather than participate in the momentum toward war, Kennedy indicated that he wanted, along with the British should they prove amenable, to suggest to Khrushchev that the three powers join in an agreement to ban any further atmospheric tests that would produce radioactive fallout. No inspection mechanism would be required, for while underground tests might go undetected in the absence of the sort of controls the Soviets continued adamantly to refuse, atmospheric explosions could be monitored with existing equipment. Moscow would have six days to reply to Kennedy's proposal that both sides in effect agree to a partial test ban; as the president saw it, whatever Khrushchev's response, the offer would almost certainly benefit the United States. If, as Kennedy thought probable, Khrushchev declined, his rejection would have immense worldwide propaganda value for the American side. If, on the other hand, Khrushchev agreed, Washington would keep the advantage it already held in nuclear capacity. Mindful that the clock was ticking on Khrushchev's vow to make a treaty with East Germany, Kennedy also decided to use the crisis precipitated by the Soviet nuclear explosion as a spur for talks on Berlin. He directed Rusk to instruct Llewellyn Thompson in Moscow to broach with Foreign Minister Gromyko the possibility of exploratory discussions in New York later in the month to coincide with the UN General Assembly.

On Sunday, while the Kennedys sailed to Egg Island, a joint US–British proposal for a partial test ban was sent to Khrushchev. Kennedy knew there would be intense pressure, not just in the United States but abroad, to take a harder line. De Gaulle sent word via the US ambassador in Paris that Friday's nuclear blast had confirmed him in the belief that there was no room for talks with the Soviets in the present, increasingly hostile climate. At half past seven on Sunday evening, Jack walked over to his father's house for dinner and lingered until eleven. After the election, Joe Kennedy had agreed to steer clear of the White House lest it be rumored that the president was serving as his puppet. Still, while Jack now depended on his father less for specific ideas and advice, he continued to turn to him for the comfort and support the elder Kennedy had always provided in abundance. As he had been in youth, Jack was buoyed up by his father's optimism. The next day, when the Kennedys sailed to Oyster Harbor, Khrushchev replied to the proposal to ban atmospheric tests by detonating a second nuclear device in Central Asia. Again, American monitoring equipment detected the blast, which, like its predecessor, had a force greater than that at Hiroshima.

In the context of the Labor Day explosion, some acrid remarks by Tsarapkin in Geneva were interpreted as a strong sign that Khrushchev planned formally to reject the Kennedy–Macmillan overture. When Kennedy reached the White House on September 5, he conferred with Defense Secretary Robert McNamara and Atomic Energy Commission Chairman Glenn Seaborg, and indicated that he wanted to resume underground nuclear testing on September 15, on the assumption that Khrushchev would not agree to a ban on atmospheric tests. It would be fundamentally a theatrical gesture, for at that point there was little of military or scientific value to be gained from underground tests. On the matter of whether to test in the atmosphere, where significant information could be acquired, Kennedy reserved judgment. He thought it best to wait until after Khrushchev had responded formally to his and Macmillan's proposal before making any public announcement of his decision. In the course of the weekend, voices from around the world had been heard in denunciation of the Soviet tests, and for the moment the president preferred to keep the focus of international attention squarely on Khrushchev.

Kennedy had managed thus far to act shrewdly and objectively. He had chosen not to respond to the Soviet blasts tit for tat, as many of his critics would have had him do, and he had been careful to exploit the nuclear tests in Central Asia, as well as Khrushchev's vows soon to test a super-bomb, for maximum propaganda value. But when, shortly after the meeting with McNamara and Seaborg, Kennedy learned that Russia had set off a third explosion, he lost his composure and with it the ability to master his political fears. In a fury, he concluded that he must answer Khrushchev with an immediate show of US strength if he were not to come under devastating political criticism for what many would decry as a failure of nerve. Forgetting his own prior assessment that it would be wisest to wait until Khrushchev formally declined to join in a ban, Kennedy hurriedly ordered Salinger to make an immediate announcement of the resumption of US underground tests. Bundy was stunned by how quickly the process had been set in motion, the president having called his press secretary before anyone might have had a chance to stop him. The British were notified by telegram, but there was no consultation despite the fact that Macmillan had collaborated on that weekend's overture. At 5 p.m., Salinger announced the resumption of nuclear weapons tests "in the laboratory and underground, with no fallout." In view of continued testing by the Soviet government, he noted, the president had had "no other choice."

In Congress, cheers and applause from Democrats and Republicans alike greeted the statement by Representative Chet Holifield, Democratic chairman of the Joint Atomic Energy Commission, that Kennedy had ordered new nuclear tests. By contrast, there was no ovation in London, where Macmillan judged that the timing of the announcement effectively canceled much of the propaganda value of their initially calm, measured response. By not waiting for Khrushchev's formal response Kennedy had, in Macmillan's view, "relieved the Russians of some part of their presentational difficulties." Kennedy seemed to have taken the volley of nuclear explosions personally, and while Macmillan agreed that Khrushchev had been taunting the president, he lamented in his diary that Kennedy had responded "like a bull being teased by the darts of the picadors." For all of his carefully cultivated sangfroid, Kennedy had allowed his temper to get the better of him. On the morning of September 5, Jackie and the children had remained at the Cape when the president returned for what had proven to be a miserable day in Washington. Two and a half hours after the world learned that the United States planned to resume underground nuclear tests, Kennedy went sailing on the *Honey Fitz* with Senator Smathers, their friend Bill Thompson who, like Dave Powers, often served as the president's procurer, and two young women.

Khrushchev, as expected, soon publicly rejected the proposal for a partial ban, which, in related comments, Tsarapkin in Geneva denounced as a fraud. The United States requested a recess of the test ban talks, which had continued despite the recall of Dean and Ormsby Gore; notably, for the first time since the talks began in 1958, no date was set for their resumption. Jack Kennedy later called the talks' collapse the worst disappointment of his first year as president. On September 15 the first new US nuclear test, in the sands of Nevada, testified to the failure of the dream with which Kennedy had come to office. Kennedy, it seemed to Macmillan, had yet to recover from his encounter with Khrushchev at Vienna, where, as the prime minister wrote to Queen Elizabeth on September 15, he had been "completely overwhelmed by the ruthlessness and barbarity of the Russian Premier. It reminded me in a way of Lord Halifax or Mr. Neville Chamberlain trying to hold a conversation with Herr Hitler." On the day the United States resumed testing, Macmillan, in the same letter to the Queen, wrote of Kennedy, "He thinks all the time about politics."

Kennedy had hoped by the resumption of tests to mitigate some of the domestic political criticism of his leadership, but the drumbeat of his adversaries in the United States only intensified in the weeks that followed. When Eisenhower, on September 16, assailed the "indecision and uncertainty" currently prevailing at the White House, Kennedy did his best to laugh it off by remarking that his predecessor was becoming more interested in politics now than he had ever been as president. McNamara and Robert Kennedy riposted on the president's behalf when, on September 21, another Republican, Senator Margaret Chase Smith, caused a national sensation by charging in the Senate that Kennedy's response to the Berlin crisis, which stressed the buildup of conventional forces, had sent a message to Khrushchev that America lacked "the will to use the one power with which we can stop him"— nuclear weapons. Privately, the president took the view, expressed to Harold Caccia who had come in for a visit before he returned finally to London, that the American people, including certain of his political adversaries, had yet to comprehend fully what a nuclear exchange would mean. Unlike the previous administration, which to Churchill's exasperation had argued for the use of small nuclear weapons as conventional weapons, Kennedy—as he had made explicit during the presidential campaign—preferred to concentrate on conventional forces because the use of nuclear armaments, no matter how limited, threatened to tempt the enemy to raise the ante to all-out nuclear warfare. The leader who, under pressure, had himself acted rashly on September 5 could see how the enemy in Moscow might do the same.

More than ever, with Khrushchev's deadline fast approaching, Kennedy agonized about the potential for nuclear war. In conversation with the Indonesian president Sukarno, Kennedy suggested that in the absence of negotiations there might well be "war before Christmas." Talks in themselves, he stressed, would not be sufficient—they had to bear fruit. With Rusk set to begin exploratory talks with Gromyko in New York on September 19 to see if formal negotiations might be possible, Kennedy had scant encouragement when he sat down with Couve, Brentano and Home at the White House in an effort to fashion a joint negotiating position. When the French and German foreign ministers reiterated their opposition to talks at this stage, Kennedy voiced concern that Khrushchev would interpret the West's failure to speak with one voice as a sign of weakness. Couve and Brentano remained adamant. Kennedy could scarcely conceal his displeasure, nor did he seem to try.

Khrushchev blew hot and cold, alternating between public threats designed to scare the president and secret assurances, at times almost avuncular in tone, that he not only understood Kennedy's domestic political pressures but would help overcome them. He ranted in a *New York Times* interview about his intention to equip Soviet forces with "several" 100-megaton bombs, and privately conveyed a message via the *Times*'s C. L. Sulzberger that he was ready to do what he could to help minimize the political damage a Berlin deal might pose to Kennedy. In short, he was playing to Kennedy's political fears, which

Kennedy himself had shown him in his back-channel messages via Bolshakov and his remarks in Vienna. The Rusk–Gromyko talks were under way when Gromyko's press spokesman, Mikhail Kharlamov, conveyed a comparable message to Pierre Salinger, then in New York with the president who was set to address the UN General Assembly. Bolshakov again translated as Kharlamov delivered assurances that Khrushchev was prepared to listen to the president's suggestions for rapprochement on Berlin, but intended to leave the timing of a summit to Kennedy because of the latter's "obvious political difficulties." Khrushchev, the emissary declared, would give Kennedy time to prepare the American people for the compromises necessary to a settlement—but "not too much time."

Kennedy had gone out to the theater, after which he planned to have a late supper with friends, and it was 1 a.m. when Salinger found him in his suite at the Carlyle Hotel. Kennedy chewed on an unlit cigar as he sat up in bed with a book. He asked Salinger to repeat the key points of Khrushchev's message a number of times. Then he rose from his bed and stood by the window for a long while, gazing in silence at the New York skyline. Finally, he said that there was only one way to interpret Khrushchev's message. As he saw it, Khrushchev's readiness to listen to US views on the Berlin crisis meant that he was not going to sign the treaty with East Germany this year after all. On September 25, after Max Jacobson injected him in the larynx because he had been having trouble with his voice, Kennedy delivered a thirty-eight-minute speech at the UN, in which he pledged both to stand firm in Berlin and to be ready to negotiate. Kennedy reported that even as he spoke the possibilities for negotiation were being explored, but that it was too early to speculate on what the prospects might be.

In his diary the next day, Macmillan praised Kennedy's address as "simple and noble," but he went on to observe that the president was in "great political difficulty, which the Republicans, led—I am sorry to think—by Eisenhower, are trying to exploit. Kennedy got elected by attacking Eisenhower as 'weak' and on his slogan 'Wake up America!' So, elected on the Churchill ticket, he will now be accused of following a Chamberlain policy." So it happened, when the president's critics specifically compared his eagerness for a negotiated settlement of the Berlin crisis to Chamberlain's capitulation to Hitler at Munich.

While he waited to learn the outcome of the Rusk–Gromyko talks, Jack, Jackie and the children vacationed at her stepfather's estate in Newport, Rhode Island. The third and final meeting was scheduled to take place at Rusk's apartment at the Waldorf Towers on the morning of September 30. It was to be a long session, extending through lunch. Kennedy spent the morning in a neighbor's heated pool to ease the pain in his back, while Jackie played five holes of golf with a friend, the artist William Walton. Afterward, in balmy weather, the Kennedys went out sailing together on the *Honey Fitz*, and Jackie water-skied on Narragansett Bay. Fifteen minutes after Gromyko left Rusk's apartment at three, the *Honey Fitz* docked and Kennedy hurried indoors to confer by telephone with the secretary of state. In Rusk's judgment, the exploratory talks had succeeded and formal negotiations to end the Berlin crisis would now be possible. The good news was compounded when that same day Bolshakov delivered to Salinger a twenty-six-page secret letter from Khrushchev to Kennedy expressing the hope that the Rusk–Gromyko talks might lead to further discussion of the German question, and proposing that he and Kennedy open a confidential correspondence where they might exchange views without fear of their remarks turning up in the press and, by implication, harming Kennedy politically. Salinger called the letter "the most hopeful overture from Khrushchev" since the dramatic release of the American pilots the day after the inauguration had seemed to ratify Kennedy's decision to publicly place détente at the center of his presidential aims. Kennedy was now filled with high hopes that a diplomatic solution to the Berlin crisis might be in the offing.

In a further gesture, Khrushchev, in an address to the Twentieth Party Congress in Moscow on October 17, lifted the December deadline for a treaty with East Germany. Heretofore, Kennedy had been intent that there be negotiations before a treaty was signed, lest talks at the edge of the precipice multiply the chances for accidental war. With the removal of the deadline, he rejoiced that he had been given a "breathing space" to secure a deal on Berlin and thereby to solve one of the big problems that remained after the Second World War. Rusk's September 30 assessment of his talks with Gromyko, the first of the secret "pen pal" letters and the lifting of the deadline—all were highly positive indications. In the belief that an agreement was really possible,

Kennedy began to make plans to get the American people, and his French and German allies, ready for full negotiations.

On October 24, the newly knighted Sir David Ormsby Gore arrived in Washington to take up his post as ambassador. In the aftermath of the Rusk–Gromyko talks, the president was intensely focused on Berlin and full of optimism about the chances for a settlement even though he was under blistering political attack, not least the recent harangue by Eisenhower whose public opposition, David knew well, the president had long been keen to avert. Two decades after David, Jack, Billy Hartington and others in their group first contemplated the lessons of Munich, Munich was again much in the air. To Kennedy's delight, C. L. Sulzberger, in a piece titled "Berlin in the Light of Munich" that ran in the *New York Times* on the anniversary of the Munich agreement, had recently debunked the comparison by arguing that there appeared to be sufficient leeway in Khrushchev's position to make possible a negotiated settlement "without any Munich connotations."

The Ormsby Gores, along with three of their five children, had traveled by ship, and the youngsters had been up since four in the morning in anticipation of docking in New York at 6 a.m. Later in the day, as soon as they entered Washington's largest embassy, a cavernous building on Massachusetts Avenue of vast, high-ceilinged rooms with dark mirrors, glittering antique chandeliers and floors of black and white checkerboard tile, the phone rang with warm greetings from Jack Kennedy in Newport. At nearly the same moment, an aide rushed in with a stack of frantic messages from Macmillan. The Soviets, since resuming tests on September 1, had set off some three dozen nuclear blasts of escalating explosive force. On the previous day, Khrushchev had exploded a 30-megaton bomb, reports of which had flung Macmillan into a fit of rage. Tests on such a massive scale, Macmillan was convinced, were principally for psychological, not military, purposes. Insistent that an end be put to such folly before East and West obliterated each other, Macmillan wanted Kennedy to join Britain in a six-month voluntary moratorium on all atmospheric tests. Macmillan further wanted him to agree to pledge that in future all US and British tests would take place underground except for those few clearly proven and agreed by them to be militarily necessary. Aware that Kennedy was under acute political pressure in his own country to sanction atmospheric tests in addition to the underground explosions already under way, Macmillan left it to Ormsby Gore to persuade his old friend to flout American public opinion and go with the British plan.

It was a tall order, and David set to work, oblivious to the chaos of unopened suitcases and packing crates. Concentrating singlemindedly on the stack of papers in his red dispatch box, he scrawled notes and made plans for the urgent conversations that would ensue when he presented his credentials to the president on October 26. Prior to accepting the ambassadorship, David had worried that he would not by nature be suited for the post should he and Sissie be required to devote too much of their time in Washington to strictly social activities. He had told Macmillan point-blank that they could not be expected to attend "the cutting of every ribbon." For all his trepidation, within minutes of arrival at the embassy he had plunged deeply into the work he loved—a splendid start to "the most inspiring and pleasurable" years of his life when he served as Macmillan's "go-between" with Jack Kennedy.

Two days later, when the president returned from Newport, Ormsby Gore went to the White House to present his credentials. Ormsby Gore had not seen Kennedy since June, when the president had been on his way back to the States after the Vienna summit. Having heard rumors in London of his friend's gravely diminished health, Ormsby Gore was relieved to find him "extremely vigorous" and moving about "without any sign of discomfort." At the presentation ceremony, Ormsby Gore said that in light of the new challenge to the great principles their two countries held in common, and in view of the jeopardy in which the whole world and the civilization of centuries had been placed, it was essential that the United States and Britain work together in the closest harmony. He voiced confidence that their partnership would "flourish and prosper so long, in the words of Sir Winston Churchill, as we have 'faith in each other's purpose, hope in each other's future and charity towards each other's shortcomings.'" Kennedy, in turn, expressed pleasure at the Queen's decision (as it nominally was) "to appoint you, an old friend, as her representative in Washington." After the formalities, Jack and David, as they had long been known to do, peeled off together for a private talk. With many people the president tended to be more of a listener and a questioner than a talker, but in this first important conversation of Ormsby Gore's ambassadorship he "talked the whole time at a great rate." That was how it had always been between the friends, and it would be no different now. Kennedy spoke frankly of his exasperation with the French and the Germans and of his determination to get Adenauer to Washington as soon as possible to sell him on the idea of a Berlin settlement.

From the outset, the president's relationship with Britain's new ambassador was highly unusual. "He was almost a part of the government," recalled Bobby Kennedy of Ormsby Gore. The president, in Bobby's opinion, "would rather have his judgment than that of almost anybody else. . . . He'd rather have . . . his ideas, his suggestions and recommendations than even anybody in our own government." Speechwriter and special counsel Theodore Sorensen remembered that the president consulted with and confided in Ormsby Gore "as he would a member of his own staff." Kennedy told Sorensen, "I trust David as I would my own Cabinet." And Arthur Schlesinger Jr. wrote of the president's association with Ormsby Gore, "Their long, relaxed, confidential talks together, whether at Hyannis Port or Palm Beach or on quiet evenings in the White House, gave Kennedy probably his best opportunity to clarify his own purposes in world affairs."

Kennedy was quick to reject Macmillan's proposal, as conveyed by the new ambassador, of a voluntary six-month moratorium on atmospheric nuclear tests. In the current political climate, it was just not something he was prepared to do. Still, David knew his man: he knew his friend's ambivalence about the Baldwin question; he knew Jack's susceptibility to strictly political considerations; he also knew where his sympathies lay in the whole debate on nuclear testing. At length he managed to persuade him of the wisdom of pledging that the United States would undertake atmospheric tests only were there a clear military justification—not for show or for purely psychological effect. Kennedy, for his part, nursed the hope that the Soviet scientists were not learning much from the present set of explosions, and that when his own experts concluded as much he would have the political ammunition to decline to approve US atmospheric tests. On the phone to Macmillan the following day Kennedy suggested that in due course they both make public statements to the effect that they would test in the atmosphere only were it essential for military reasons.

Khrushchev's explosion of a 50-megaton bomb shortly thereafter prompted cries for an immediate tough response, but Kennedy still refused to approve the atmospheric blasts a good many influential voices were calling for. Instead he strove to placate the opposition by announcing preparations for such tests—with the proviso that the United States would not, as the Soviets had, resume atmospheric tests for merely psychological or political reasons. Kennedy vowed that only if it were "necessary to maintain our responsibilities for Free World security" would he set off explosions in the atmosphere. In the meantime, he declared that the United States had no need to explode 50-megaton bombs to prove that it had many times more nuclear power than any other country. In terms of total military strength the United States, Kennedy promised, was the strongest nation on earth. "We have taken major steps in the past year to maintain our lead—and we do not propose to lose it."

Ormsby Gore recognized this announcement as a stopgap to deflect political criticism while Kennedy tended to what he saw as the more urgent business of reaching a deal on Berlin. On the day Kennedy phoned Macmillan, a tense confrontation in Berlin, which had Soviet and American tanks facing one another head-on at the border, had threatened to escalate into an accidental war. The president had dissipated the crisis by sending a back-channel message via Bolshakov asking Khrushchev to pull back his tanks, and promising to do the same immediately thereafter. On this occasion the unofficial communication worked, but the episode had powerfully confirmed Kennedy in the belief that his priority must be to make full use of the breathing space provided by Khrushchev's lifting of the year-end deadline. The president wanted to settle the Berlin problem before both sides again began moving toward the edge of the precipice. As he told David, by contrast everything else felt like a distraction.

Yet he could not simply will away other problems, and no sooner had he settled the question of how to respond for now to Soviet atmospheric tests than another urgent matter pressed itself on his attention. The day after Kennedy made his announcement on nuclear testing, General Maxwell Taylor, just back from South Vietnam where the president had directed him to look into the Communist insurgency, presented his report.

In 1954, following the withdrawal of the French from Indochina,

Vietnam had been divided into the Communist North under the leadership of Ho Chi Minh and the anti-Communist South under Ngo Dinh Diem. Eisenhower had supported the Diem regime from its inception. Since that time, the situation had deteriorated as guerrilla attacks supported by the Communist regime in Hanoi pounded the South. Diem, under siege, sought increased assistance from Washington, and the purpose of the Taylor mission had been to assess the situation and report back to the president. On November 3, Taylor presented a report that urged Kennedy to send combat troops to South Vietnam and insisted a war there would be winnable. The passionate views expressed at a White House dinner party on November 8 attended by Ormsby Gore, Bundy, Schlesinger and US ambassador to India John Kenneth Galbraith suggest the pressure from both sides within the administration. For Ormsby Gore, this first opportunity "to have a ringside view of the President's technique" with some of his advisers was a mesmerizing experience. The discussion ran on for an hour and a quarter, the debate was "fast and furious," and "it was quite difficult to get a word in unless one shouted rather loud." (Shouting, fortunately, was something David did well.) Each of the guests had his own emphatic view of what to do about Vietnam. Galbraith opposed US military intervention and regarded Diem as "a broken reed." Schlesinger sided with Galbraith. Bundy strongly disagreed. The president affected a mask of inscrutability. In private with David he tended to express his views candidly and forthrightly, but he was very different in the advisers' company. "Although he constantly intervened in the debate with many pointed questions," Ormsby Gore wrote of the evening, "he never gave anything like a complete summary of his views on any of the points under discussion and no matter how hard he was pressed the decision he was finally likely to take remained wrapped in mystery."

It was no secret that Kennedy "instinctively" opposed the introduction of US forces into Vietnam and that he preferred the sort of diplomatic solution widely feared and distrusted by the South Vietnamese, who had little reason to believe that a negotiated settlement would have any effect on guerrilla activity. The Taylor Report was not the first occasion on which the president had been urged by members of his own government to seek a military victory in Vietnam. In the wake of the

Bay of Pigs fiasco, Deputy Special Assistant to the President for National Security Affairs Walt Rostow, who later accompanied General Taylor on his fact-finding trip, had urged Kennedy to turn his attention to Vietnam, where a clear-cut military victory against the Communists would provide an antidote to the Cuban debacle. More recently, on July 20, the day after Kennedy, having long struggled with Acheson's recommendations, signaled his preference for a diplomatic solution in Berlin, Robert Komer of the National Security Council staff had made an appeal of his own for US military intervention in Vietnam. Such advice demonstrated the philosophical chasm between the president, whose double-barreled policy combined "a readiness to look for peaceful solutions through negotiation" with "the maintenance of the necessary military strength," and those in the administration who leapt at military solutions to tensions with the Communists.

Further complicating the president's response to calls for military action in Vietnam was his abiding sense that, like Laos, Vietnam was not a vital interest of the United States. Kennedy's position reflected that of Churchill seven years previously, when, on being asked to join the United States in military intervention in Indochina, he had warned of "the danger of war at the fringes" and suggested that the West would do better to focus on "conversations at the center." In November 1961, the conversation at the center was decidedly that to do with Berlin. Kennedy did not want to be sucked into a prolonged commitment in Vietnam. Still, for both strategic and political reasons he worried about South Vietnam going Communist, along with Laos and the rest of Southeast Asia. He was acutely mindful of the fact that were South Vietnam to fall to the Communists during his watch, the loss would not play well with American voters already inclined to suspect him of softness. In the absence of other solutions the president had at least to consider proposals for military measures, though he did from the first balk at suggestions that the United States make "a Berlin-type commitment" to South Vietnam.

Kennedy subscribed to the tenet stated by Churchill as a guideline for the action of nations that a government ought to keep its word and act in accordance with treaty obligations to allies—exactly what Chamberlain had failed to do at Munich. On that basis Kennedy, however much he wished for a diplomatic settlement on Berlin, was ready to fight, even to use nuclear weapons, in the event that Western access was blocked. He was not prepared to make such a commitment in Vietnam. With McNamara, Deputy Secretary of Defence Roswell Gilpatric and the Joint Chiefs of Staff, among others, urging that the United States "commit to the clear objective of preventing the fall of South Vietnam to Communism and that we support this commitment by the necessary military actions," a decision had to be taken. He put it off as long as he could, but at a meeting on November 11, attended by Taylor, Rostow, Rusk, McNamara, Bundy, Robert Kennedy and others, the president refused to send combat troops or to make the Berlin-type commitment called for. Nonetheless, the session ended with considerable confusion as to what measures he would be willing to accept. There was a sense that nothing really had been settled, and the discussion of General Taylor's recommendations was set to continue at a National Security Council meeting on November 15, the day before Kennedy left for a tour of the western states "to explain to the American people once again the Administration's approach to world problems" and—more narrowly—to sell them on the prospect of negotiations with the Soviets over Berlin.

On the night of the 11th, the Kennedys hosted a lavish dinner dance in the Blue Room in honor of Jackie's sister. The fall season at the White House had been a triumph for Jackie, who had presided over a string of highly successful official events for distinguished guests from Peru, Sudan, Finland and India; the following week she was set to give the last state dinner of the season, a musical evening centered on a concert by the cellist Pablo Casals to welcome the governor of Puerto Rico to Washington. The party, by contrast, was a private occasion attended by eighty-nine friends and acquaintances of the Kennedys, who flew in from New York and Palm Beach. There was a great deal of drinking, the festivities did not break up until 4 a.m., and it was nearly daybreak when Jack and Jackie and a select group of guests who had been invited to accompany them the following day to Camp David, in Maryland's Catoctin Mountains, finally went to bed.

A helicopter had been ordered for half past eight, but when the time came to depart the group, badly hung over, was far from ready. The president summoned Max Jacobson, by this time a regular visitor at the White House. As the Kennedys and their guests sat talking in a bedroom, the doctor, whose rumpled trousers and jacket bulged with drug paraphernalia, passed among them methodically injecting them with methamphetamines. Nobody pretended that Dr. Feel Good had been called in to treat the president's bad back or other health problems. As Betty Spalding, one of the guests, remembered, it was strictly a matter of "cranking everybody up after an enormous night." "It was the damnedest performance I ever saw," she recalled. "I thought, 'These people are crazy to be doing this!'" Yet, for all of her horror, everyone else present, including her own husband, seemed to regard the sight of a group of people—the President and First Lady included—shooting up at the White House as perfectly natural. Jack, though he took other physicians' medications that threatened to mix disastrously with Jacobson's, casually had a shot in full view of the others. So did Jackie, despite the fact that Betty would have expected the First Lady, with her tightly controlled personality, to be the last person to become involved with addictive drugs.

When he left shortly before noon, Kennedy took with him a copy of the Taylor Report, Vietnam position papers by various administration members, and a new proposal by Averell Harriman, in which America's man at the ongoing Laos negotiations outlined a diplomatic solution to the Vietnamese problem that seemed closest to Kennedy's own thinking. The president studied the documents at intervals in the course of his brief stay at Camp David, where he had last been on the occasion of his scolding by Eisenhower. The following morning, as the Kennedys and their friends waited to return to Washington, Betty Spalding sat with him, surrounded by luggage, as he scrutinized General Taylor's fifty-five-page report one more time. Jack had spoken to her of his upset in the aftermath of Cuba, and now again he expressed frustration at the strong sentiment within his administration that he ought to intervene militarily despite his own instincts. Suddenly Jack broke off reading and hurled the Taylor Report in Betty's direction, exclaiming that he had no idea "what the hell" he planned to do about Vietnam.

That perplexity was reflected in his mixed actions upon his return to the White House. He steadfastly persisted in his refusal to commit US troops and spoke, at the National Security Council meeting on November 15, of his fear "of becoming involved simultaneously on two fronts on opposite sides of the world." He questioned "the wisdom of involvement" in Vietnam and highlighted the contrast between "the obscurity of the issues" there and "the clarity of the positions" in Berlin. In keeping with his own preference that the Vietnamese conflict be settled at the conference table rather than on the battlefield, he moved to appoint Harriman, who as Bundy and others recognized saw things much as the president did, assistant secretary for Far Eastern affairs. Having signaled Harriman to try to use the Laos talks to broach the possibility of a settlement on Vietnam, he wrote directly to Khrushchev to suggest a deal. Kennedy's letter of November 16 proposed that if Hanoi would withdraw guerrillas from the South, the United States would not have to consider, as it must at present, how best to back the South Vietnamese government in its struggle for independence and national integrity. He urged Khrushchev to ensure that those closely associated with him leave South Vietnam alone. In exchange, he offered to guarantee that North Vietnam would not be the object of direct or indirect aggression. But even as he did all that, in a gesture to his critics Kennedy approved a significant increase in the number of US military advisers in South Vietnam and modified their rules of engagement. In spite of himself, by that action he prepared the way for a greater US military role in Vietnam.

The morning after the NSC meeting, Kennedy, relieved again to have his eye "on the ball"—the urgent business of getting a Berlin deal in place—flew to Seattle, where he was to give the first of a series of speeches designed to narrow the disparity between his view of world problems and that of the American people. Kennedy remained personally popular overall, but in recent days an ugly incident had highlighted the intense hostility in certain quarters. At a White House luncheon hosted by the president, *Dallas Morning News* publisher Edward M. Dealey had claimed to speak for "many people in Texas and the Southwest" when he assailed Kennedy and his administration as "weak sisters." Calling for "a man on horseback to lead this nation" and to leave no doubt that "we can annihilate Russia," Dealey mocked Kennedy for "riding Caroline's tricycle" instead. Kennedy fired back that "the difference between you and me is that I was elected president of this country and you were not; and I have the responsibility for the lives of 180 million Americans, which you have not." The exchange had received a good deal of play in the press.

Perceiving a "resurgence of right-wing opinion" that might diminish his flexibility in the negotiations ahead, Kennedy viewed the western tour as a chance to launch a "counter-attack." He wanted to get away from Washington and, as in the long years of the campaign, talk to the people directly. He had laid out his Soviet strategy in the inaugural address, but since that time his speeches had mainly been to announce actions. That afternoon, dressed in a flowing red academic gown before a large audience at the University of Washington, the president had a broader purpose—to make good on his campaign promise to "educate" the people, to be their "guide" and "to lead the way." Determined to persuade the American people of the desirability of Berlin talks "at a time when a single clash could escalate overnight into a holocaust of mushroom clouds," he restated his policy of strength combined with negotiations and elaborated on his belief that the United States had nothing to fear from negotiations and nothing to gain by a refusal to take part in them. Expecting that he would again be disparaged as an appeaser, the president cited Britain's most famous opponent of the policy of appeasement by quoting from *The Gathering Storm*: "'How many wars,' Winston Churchill has written, 'have been averted by patience and by persisting good will! . . . How many wars have been precipitated by firebrands!'" Rather than bend to public opinion, Kennedy in the November 16 address sought to change it, acting as the kind of leader he had pledged—and wanted—to be.

That night, after he had appeared at a testimonial dinner for Senator Warren Magnuson in the grand ballroom of the Olympic Hotel in Seattle, Kennedy went up to the second floor, which had been wholly given over to the presidential party. The floor had been sealed, the president presumably having gone to bed, when a prominent local Democrat arrived with two call girls. Denied access by Secret Service agents Larry Newman and Roy Kellerman, the visitor, who seemed tipsy, indignantly insisted that he meant to deliver the women to President Kennedy. Finally, Dave Powers materialized and ushered the women, though not the local politico, into the president's suite. As Powers shut the door in the man's face, the latter shouted a warning to the girls that if they told anyone about this evening they would find themselves in the state mental hospital. Jack Kennedy had spent the afternoon striving to impart his ideas and ideals to the American people; a study in contrasts, he ended the day with a pair of prostitutes.

Twenty-nine-year-old Jack stands between his parents in June 1946 at a victory celebration after the Democratic congressional primary, his first political race. Five months later he was elected to the US Congress.

Kick was killed in a plane crash in May 1948. Her parents used this photograph on the Roman Catholic mass card they sent to her friends. COURTESY JEAN LLOYD

On September 12, 1953, Kennedy, now a US senator, married
Jacqueline Bouvier, age twenty-four, at her stepfather's home in
Newport, Rhode Island. COURTESY JOHN F. KENNEDY LIBRARY

Kennedy signing copies of his book *Profiles in Courage* in 1956.
By this time, he had begun to evolve the strategy on which he would
run for the US presidency. COURTESY JOHN F. KENNEDY LIBRARY

Kennedy campaigning for president in 1960. Borrowing crucial rhetoric and ideas from Winston Churchill, he ran "on the Churchill ticket." COURTESY JOHN F. KENNEDY LIBRARY

Jack Kennedy was sworn in as the thirty-fifth US president
on January 20, 1961. COURTESY JOHN F. KENNEDY LIBRARY

On April 22, 1961, Kennedy met with his predecessor, following the debacle at the Bay of Pigs. Eisenhower humiliated him by enumerating the errors that had led to defeat in Cuba.

Kennedy went to Vienna in June 1961 hoping to persuade Nikita
Khrushchev of his firmness on Berlin, but Khrushchev emerged from
the talks convinced that the president did not have it in him to fight.

In the aftermath of Vienna, Prime Minister Harold Macmillan and his wife, Lady Dorothy, welcomed Kennedy to London. For Kennedy, it was a great comfort to be able to talk to a fellow leader who shared his burdens and understood the magnitude of what Kennedy called his "loneliness" as president.

At Buckingham Palace, the Kennedys attended a dinner in their honor given by Queen Elizabeth and Prince Philip. Kennedy spent much of the evening huddled with David Ormsby Gore, discussing how best to avoid repeating Chamberlain's politically fatal errors after Munich.

Kennedy had to sell his Berlin policy to French and German allies who accused him of appeasement. Pictured here at a September 15, 1961, White House luncheon for Western foreign ministers (left to right): Heinrich von Brentano, President Kennedy, Maurice Couve de Murville, Vice President Lyndon Johnson, Lord Home, Dean Rusk. COURTESY JOHN F. KENNEDY LIBRARY

On October 26, 1961, David Ormsby Gore presented his credentials as Britain's new ambassador to Washington. "He was almost a part of the government," remembered Bobby Kennedy. The president "would rather have his judgment than that of almost anybody else. . . . He'd rather have . . . his ideas, his suggestions and recommendations than even anybody in our own government." David, said Bobby Kennedy, was "part of the family."

COURTESY JOHN F. KENNEDY LIBRARY

At Bermuda in December 1961, Harold Macmillan offered a dramatic lesson in the duty of a leader. COURTESY JOHN F. KENNEDY LIBRARY

At an April 29, 1962, White House luncheon, attended by the Kennedys, Harold Macmillan, and David and Sissie Ormsby Gore, the president and his guests discussed those moments in history when one must put everything at risk in order to change the course of events.

Kennedy on October 22, 1963, moments before he informed the
American people of the presence of Soviet offensive missiles in Cuba.

(Left to right: Kennedy, Macmillan, Ormsby Gore.) Since the eve of World War II, Kennedy and Ormsby Gore had been arguing about great things, and it was no different now. In the aftermath of the missile crisis, they would begin the final stage of their twenty-five-year conversation.

Winston Churchill was made an honorary US citizen on April 9, 1963. As Churchill was too frail to attend, his son Randolph came in his place. The ceremony meant a great deal to Kennedy, who had been shaped by Churchill's books.

Kennedy (with Caroline on his lap) and Ormsby Gore aboard the
Honey Fitz off Hyannis Port on July 28, 1963, where they were celebrating
the news that a nuclear test ban treaty—long the centerpiece of Kennedy's
Soviet strategy—had been agreed upon in Moscow a few days previously.

Kennedy signed the instrument of ratification of the nuclear test ban treaty on October 7, 1963. For Kennedy the test ban had never been an end in itself, but rather a first step toward further contact and agreements with Moscow and the peaceful defeat of Soviet Communism. "Today we have a beginning," Kennedy declared. One month later, he was assassinated in Dallas, Texas, at the age of forty-six. COURTESY JOHN F. KENNEDY LIBRARY

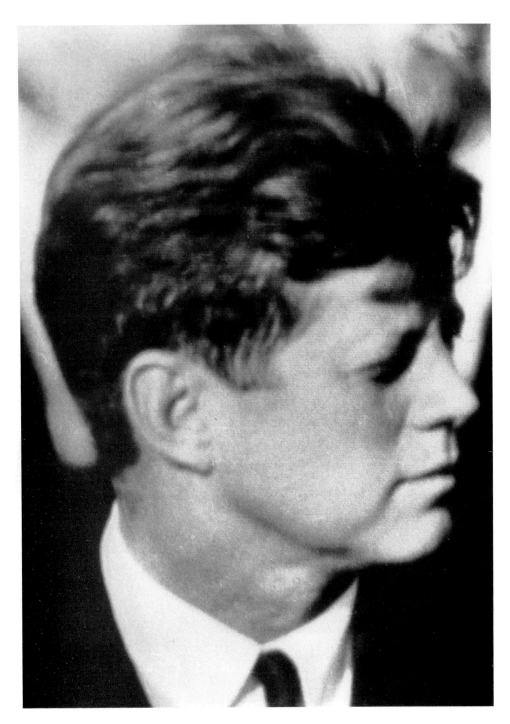

Picket signs proclaiming "Disarmament is National Suicide" and "Let's Get Out of the UN" greeted Kennedy when he spoke in Phoenix, Arizona, home state of the ultra-conservative senator Barry Goldwater, a contender to be the Republican presidential candidate in 1964. Following the president's speech, Goldwater called a press conference to denounce the "radicals in the White House" and to dub Kennedy the "wagon master" who was "riding on the left wheel all the time." Kennedy went on to California where, in Los Angeles he criticized those who called for "a man on horseback" to lead the nation against the Soviets at a time when negotiations, backed by strength, were the more rational course. Having completed the first part of his plan to get American voters, and his French and German allies, ready for Berlin talks, Kennedy returned to Washington on November 20 in anticipation of making his case to Adenauer, who would visit the White House the following day.

On the morning of November 21 Kennedy did not seem especially hopeful as he breakfasted with the British economist Barbara Ward, whom he had first met in 1945 when Kick had drafted her to drive him about to observe the general election campaign with an eye to his own political future. Instead of discussing African problems, as the schedule called for, he poured out his frustration at his inability to get the support of Adenauer and de Gaulle for negotiations on Berlin. Ward sensed that Kennedy's short temper was due to fatigue in the aftermath of the western tour, but she also noted that she had never previously seen him betray such hopelessness. As it happened, in the course of three days of discussions, Adenauer not only seemed to accept Kennedy's argument that they must talk to the Russians, but promised to write to de Gaulle immediately to declare his change of heart. As Kennedy saw it, it was essential to have the Germans on board, for any Berlin deal concluded in their absence could lead to the sort of grievances that in the aftermath of the First World War had led to the rise of Nazism. Even if France continued to balk at negotiations, a tripartite agreement such as he now appeared to have with Macmillan and Adenauer would make it possible for talks to proceed. Macmillan was set to see de Gaulle on November 24, and Adenauer's promise to try to enlist the French leader prior to that date meant that the Allies might soon have the joint negotiating position needed, by Kennedy's estimate, to negotiate with Khrushchev from a position of maximum strength. Macmillan, delighted by the news, which promised to make his own upcoming encounter with de Gaulle much simpler, telegraphed congratulations: "You seem to have collected a homer."

Directly, the president went off to celebrate Thanksgiving in Hyannis Port, where Joe Kennedy, his children and grandchildren traditionally spent the holiday together before he and Rose went off for the winter season in Palm Beach. The Adenauer visit had put Jack in an ebullient mood, and he decided to organize a celebration very much to his own liking by asking David and Sissie Ormsby Gore and Andrew and Debo Devonshire to join the presidential party the following weekend at the annual Army–Navy football game. Hardly had the invitations been issued when the president, on his return to Washington, learned that Adenauer had not kept his promise to intervene with de Gaulle. Worse, de Gaulle had reiterated his disdain for the idea of negotiations when he met Macmillan at Birch Grove, the prime minister's country house. He insisted that he had no intention of "doing a Munich" on Berlin, clearly implying that that was precisely what he thought Macmillan and Kennedy were about to do.

On December 2, Kennedy, joined by the Ormsby Gores and by Debo Devonshire, who was staying with them at the British embassy, attended the Army–Navy game at Municipal Stadium in Philadelphia. As more than 100,000 spectators cheered and applauded, the president shook both team captains' hands and flipped a coin by way of determining which side would kick off. In an effort to show no favoritism despite his status as a Navy man, Kennedy, mauling a fat cigar and pointedly doing without a topcoat until plunging temperatures forced him to give in, observed the first half from a box on the Army side and the second from the Navy's. In the end, he seemed unable to suppress his delight when Navy won 13–7. After the game, the party, which included three of the president's sisters and their husbands, headed to the Pennsylvania Railroad's Thirtieth Street Station, where a thirteen-car train waited to take them back to Washington. The presidential special departed shortly after four, and, as Sissie Ormsby Gore had known them to do regularly through the years, Jack and David peeled off from the group to have a long talk.

It became clear to David that Jack had returned from the western tour greatly frustrated by the gap that, for all of his efforts, remained between his own views on Soviet relations and those of many Americans. He had done his best to spell out his thinking on the wisdom of negotiations, but, as he explained to David, an attitude of complete distrust of the Soviets had been so effectively established by the American press that if he told people simply that it would be pointless to negotiate they would probably have agreed. David said he found it inconceivable that a democratic nation would be prepared to go to the brink of nuclear war without there having been any effort to talk to the enemy. Jack suggested that therein lay an important difference in the political climates of the United States and Britain. Personally he agreed with David; his problem was that many in the United States did not. In 1938 Jack and David had sparred about what Baldwin ought to have done confronted with a pacifist electorate; in 1961 Jack faced the opposite problem. Still, he appeared determined to do what he thought best, the mood of the electorate notwithstanding.

When the conversation turned to the question of nuclear tests, the old ambivalence began to show itself. Jack hardly had to tell David, who had spent three years attempting to negotiate a test ban treaty, that the last thing he wanted was to order atmospheric tests. When he and David had talked at the Carlyle in New York after the election, they had shared the fervent hope that they would soon have a first major agreement with the Soviets in the form of that treaty. Twelve months later, Jack had already ordered a round of underground tests and seemed ready to cater to public opinion in following them with atmospheric tests. David recognized that something more than just political pressure was influencing Jack to overrule his gut reluctance to atmospheric testing. Jack had been hoping that when US scientists analyzed the recent series of Soviet explosions, it would become evident that little significant knowledge had been gained. Such a finding would have offered the political cover he needed were he to rule against new tests. Instead, to his dismay, the experts had determined precisely the opposite. Russia's tests did appear to have been productive, and there was concern on the American side that if Moscow, building on the knowledge gained, planned a further round of tests in a year or two, the United States might suddenly find itself substantially behind. During the presidential campaign, Jack had accused Eisenhower of an abdication of duty comparable to Baldwin's when the latter allowed Hitler to seize the advantage, and he was extremely wary of presiding over locust years of his own. However much he loathed the idea of atmospheric tests, he had to consider that were he to decide against them he might permit the Soviets to gain nuclear superiority. That concern inevitably turned political, as he calculated that were the United States to sacrifice supremacy on his watch it would be nearly impossible to explain the years of inactivity to the American people. He told David that in light of public opinion he thought it quite likely that he would soon feel bound to authorize some aboveground tests.

In the December 2 conversation, as in others to come, though David saw that Jack was torn between politics and principle, and though he hoped that in the end his friend would resist the temptation to take the politically safe course, he strove not to be judgmental. He never let himself forget that were things to go disastrously wrong—as in the case of the United States losing nuclear superiority—history would blame not Macmillan or his go-between, but the American president. David was fond of citing his great-grandfather, the prime minister Lord Salisbury, who once compared conducting foreign policy in a democracy to playing a hand at bridge with various people standing behind your chair advising out loud which card you should play. In the present instance, while David was careful to refrain from telling Jack which card to play, he did emphatically remind him that he had pledged, along with Macmillan, to undertake atmospheric tests only in the event of clear military necessity. Jack replied that the trouble in all this was that people were likely to differ about the criteria for such a judgment. Of course there was truth in what he said.

By raising the issue, David had kept the question of testing open for Macmillan to take it up when the leaders met presently in Bermuda. Macmillan had been eager for a meeting since Kennedy, on what the prime minister saw as purely political grounds, had refused his October proposal for a six-month moratorium on atmospheric nuclear tests. On the train from Philadelphia, David began to firm up the dates, December 21 and 22. Kennedy looked forward to an opportunity to confer with Macmillan about how to handle de Gaulle and Adenauer on Berlin, among other matters. Macmillan had decidedly different ideas about what he and Kennedy needed urgently to discuss.

Kennedy, meanwhile, had been planning a trip to Latin America in conjunction with efforts to convince developing nations around the world of Washington's commitment to democratic revolution. To that end he had selected two countries, Venezuela and Colombia, whose leaders had prominently associated themselves with the ideal of progressive reform. At the White House there was much trepidation about the prospect of a visit to Venezuela, where, during the Eisenhower years, Nixon had encountered a stone-throwing mob. Shortly before President and Mrs. Kennedy were due to depart, Bobby Kennedy received word from the CIA of plans for an assassination attempt by Cuban agents, who were reported to be en route to Caracas. To Joe Kennedy's great alarm, his son and daughter-in-law went ahead with the trip. The old man had endured the deaths of the two people he had loved the most, Joe Junior and Kick, and the idea of anything happening to Jack and Jackie was almost too much to bear. He monitored their progress closely, and three days later, the trip having been completed without incident, Joe waited on the tarmac at the airport in Palm Beach when *Air Force One* landed at half past seven on the morning of December 18.

All three Kennedys went on to the borrowed house just down the beach from the family residence where Jackie was to remain with the children until after the Christmas holidays. Jack, recovering from a cold, planned to spend the day there in anticipation of heading back to Washington to prepare for the Bermuda Conference, after which he would return to Palm Beach. Early the next morning, Joe arrived at his son's house to see him off. The patriarch suggested that for the first time young John be taken along to participate in the leavetaking ceremony both men had grown to cherish, and shortly after 9 a.m. three generations of Kennedys drove off together. At Palm Beach International, Jack's seventy-three-year-old father—noticeably flush of face—and one-year-old son stood in the bright sunlight smiling and waving as *Air Force One* took off.

Jack Kennedy had not been long at the White House when he heard from Bobby that their father had suffered a massive stroke. He had been taken to St. Mary's Hospital in Palm Beach, where doctors did not expect him to survive. Jack flew back to Florida, and that evening he was at St. Mary's, where his father had already been given the last rites of the Catholic Church. In 1920, Joe's intensely emotional response to Jack's nearly fatal bout of scarlet fever had bonded the boy to his father. Now it was Jack's turn to perch at Joe's bedside as the old man hovered near death. In the morning, when Jack and Jackie returned to St. Mary's, it remained uncertain whether Joe would survive. After spending forty-five minutes with his father, who slept throughout, Jack and Jackie drove to St. Edward's Church, where they lit candles and, kneeling side by side, prayed that Joe would live. All that Jack could think about, Jackie would later remember, was that Joe must not die. Twice more that day they returned to the hospital, but it was only on the third visit that Jack believed his father actually recognized him. By nightfall Joe's condition seemed to have improved slightly, but doctors broke the news that even if he did live he almost certainly would never again be the man he had been. The stroke had frozen Joe's right arm, leg and face, and robbed him of the capacity to speak. At best, this once powerful and dynamic figure would be trapped in a body that did not work. At the age of two Jack had learned to look to his father for the tenderness and affection he craved. Now he was devastated.

CHAPTER SIXTEEN

A Lesson in Duty

WHEN JACK KENNEDY ARRIVED AT ST. MARY'S ON THURSDAY morning, four days before Christmas, he found his father's condition unchanged. Joe remained semi-comatose, unable to speak or eat, and was paralyzed on the right side. The Bermuda Conference was set to begin that day, and there had been a good deal of back-and-forth between the president's staff and Macmillan's, the prime minister having learned of the elder Kennedy's stroke only when he arrived in Bermuda that morning. Macmillan sent a message of sympathy and offered to fly to Palm Beach or, if the president preferred, to put off the meeting altogether and come to Washington after Christmas. The Kennedys' friend Charles Wrightsman had offered his estate for the prime minister's use should the conference be moved to Palm Beach. In the end, Jack accepted the doctors' verdict that his father's semi-comatose state might persist for weeks and there was really nothing he could do at the hospital, and decided to go to Bermuda as planned. For half an hour Jack sat at his father's bedside, then left for West Palm Beach Airport, where Joe and young John had so joyously seen him off earlier in the week.

As *Air Force One* touched down in Bermuda two hours later, Harold Macmillan waited on the tarmac in the tropical sunshine to greet the president. Despite his aged appearance and manner, the prime minister retained the ramrod posture of the Grenadier Guardsman he had once been. He clasped Kennedy's hand, leaning in closely to ask about Joe and offer words of comfort. After a brief welcoming ceremony, which ended with a public statement of Britain's sympathy for the president and his family, the leaders were driven to Government House, where they were both to stay. The vast, Italianate official residence of Major General Sir Julian Gascoigne, the governor-general, was set on a ridge on the north shore of the island overlooking the capital city of Hamilton. It would not ordinarily have been the setting for an event such as the Bermuda Conference, the Mid-Ocean Club being the more obvious choice, but Macmillan had seized on it for a reason. He wanted the talks to take place in "country-house conditions," with the leaders living under the same roof and taking meals together. Preferring not to array Kennedy and himself, and their respective teams, opposite each other at a conference table in a large, coldly impersonal room, Macmillan had commandeered an intimate drawing room where the conversation might flow freely as it had at Cliveden and the other great houses frequented by the Kennedys before the war. At Key West, nearly a year before, Macmillan had entered Jack Kennedy's "twenty-five-year conversation" with British friends. At Bermuda he hoped to replicate the atmosphere associated with the aristocratic cousinhood to which he and the president had come to belong by virtue, in his own case, of marriage to the 9th Duke of Devonshire's daughter, and in Jack's, of his sister's marriage to the 10th Duke's son. Macmillan had arrived in Bermuda bearing a gift that highlighted the Kennedy–Devonshire connection. Before he left London, Debo Devonshire had dropped by Admiralty House to deliver a set of silver buttons with the ducal coronet and crest. The buttons had once adorned the buff and blue livery of a footman at Chatsworth. A previous Duchess of Devonshire, Georgiana, had chosen the colors in homage to those worn by George Washington's soldiers—an emblem of her Foxite allegiance to the American rebels. The elegant gift sent by the current duchess recalled the Devonshires' support for the American Revolution in the eighteenth century and betokened their present fondness for their American "cousin" President Kennedy.

Macmillan came to Bermuda with great purposes that would require him to engage the president in the most personal fashion. When Kennedy rejected his proposal, in the wake of the Soviets' explosion of a 30-megaton bomb, that Washington and London declare a moratorium on aboveground tests and appeal to Khrushchev to halt atmospheric testing, the prime minister had concluded that he urgently needed to have another face-to-face talk with the president. Like Khrushchev, Macmillan had come to understand the preoccupation with political self-interest and the susceptibility to political pressure that were Kennedy's great weaknesses as a leader; Ormsby Gore's reports from Washington had detailed the president's feelings of being out of harmony with the views of many Americans and his worries about protecting himself from political damage. Macmillan recognized that the president was determined to move forward with talks to settle the Berlin problem and that he had tried during his western tour to explain his policy of negotiation to the American people. At the same time, Macmillan also perceived that a combination of extreme political pressure to resume nuclear testing in response to Soviet resumption, and Kennedy's own genuine confusion when confronted with Khrushchev's lies, had led him to waver on the whole test ban issue. Macmillan was convinced that a Berlin settlement, however desirable, would be far more difficult to achieve than an agreement on nuclear testing, for it was in the latter that the interests of East and West most nearly coincided. Accordingly, he had set himself the task of finding a way to address the conflict between Kennedy's political fears and Macmillan's own fervent belief that it was their responsibility as leaders to risk everything to secure a first agreement between East and West. At a moment when Kennedy had grown pessimistic about the possibility of securing a test ban treaty, Macmillan had come to Bermuda to persuade him that he must try once more. He believed that Kennedy had trusted him at their meeting after Vienna, and now he planned to put that trust to the test by speaking to Kennedy in ways in which, Ormsby Gore said, no one had ever quite spoken to him before. He had come to provide Kennedy with a lesson in duty.

For all of Macmillan's great plans, initially it was Kennedy who set the tone of the Bermuda sessions. He had come with an agenda of his own and he moved at once to pursue it. First there was a brief discussion of problems in the Congo, and it was Kennedy who quickly came up with a statement on which both sides could agree. Twenty minutes later, when the talks shifted to Berlin, Kennedy again took the lead. He explained that he had directed the US ambassador in Moscow, Llewellyn Thompson, to approach Soviet Foreign Minister Gromyko to arrange to pick up the exploratory talks that had been left off in September. Kennedy spoke of the specifics of the instructions he would give Thompson in advance of those talks. Following Kennedy's lead, soon everyone in the room—with the conspicuous exception of Macmillan—became absorbed in the discussion of such short-term matters as what Thompson would say and when, what the French were likely to do, and what the Germans would be told. Macmillan remained absolutely silent. While the others talked on, he appeared to brood. Finally, as Ormsby Gore was in the middle of making a remark about the Germans, Macmillan cut him off. In an instant, Macmillan shifted the direction of the talk from a consideration of next steps and practical details to the question of Kennedy's ultimate intentions in dealing with the Soviets. Again and again, Macmillan pushed the president to address the deeper, underlying issues, and repeatedly Kennedy tried to shift back to more immediate matters. Before long it became clear that, though there were other people present in the room, it was Kennedy alone whom Macmillan had come to address. By the time the first Berlin discussion ended, however, Macmillan seemed to have made little progress. The president appeared determined to avoid probing questions that raised issues with which he was uncomfortable and on which he clearly did not wish to commit himself. But when the sessions resumed in the morning, it became evident that Macmillan's steady probing had made an impression. This time, Kennedy seemed less resistant. Macmillan persisted in asking hard questions about his ultimate aims, and the president began to give answers.

When the discussion shifted to nuclear testing, it again became evident that Kennedy had arrived in Bermuda with a decidedly limited agenda. He was here to secure British agreement to the use of Christmas Island, a British territory in the Central Pacific, for the atmospheric tests he expected to order soon. Kennedy knew that to win such an agreement, in keeping with the criteria Ormsby Gore had convinced him to accept that fall, he would have to make a persuasive case that such tests were militarily necessary, that they were not being ordered merely for political reasons. To that end, the nuclear discussions opened with presentations by scientific experts evaluating the significance of the recent Soviet tests. At first it seemed, as it had the day before, that Kennedy was in control of the talks' direction. Macmillan went so far as to lead off, asking his own expert, Sir William Penney, to speak on technical matters. But when the president interrupted to ask Penney about the feasibility of a missile defense system, Macmillan pounced. It was not such matters he had come to discuss with Kennedy, but rather "the terrifying prospects of an indefinitely conducted and enormously expensive arms race." Berlin, Macmillan declared, was "very small beer compared to the destruction of mankind." Kennedy might think they had convened to consider the US request to use Christmas Island for nuclear testing, but Macmillan soon made it clear that he had much larger questions in mind. Macmillan insisted that they could not "sit in an ordinary little room three days before Christmas and talk about these terrible things without doing anything." Proceeding on the Churchillian assumption that a first agreement, however limited, would lead to others, Macmillan continued to maintain that, for all the many problems dividing East and West, that breakthrough was most likely to come in the form of a test ban treaty. Speaking with great passion, he made the case that, previous failures notwithstanding, they must try again to break the deadlock.

Macmillan undertook to show Kennedy his duty as president by forcing him to face the stark reality of the world situation in the postwar era. He wanted to make Kennedy understand that the dangers were now so great that they trumped any consideration of his own political self-interest that might prevent him from taking prompt action. Macmillan reminded the president that history found itself at a moment of supreme peril. East and West faced one another with nuclear weapons, and if history proceeded on its present course of confrontation, a crisis was inevitable. If the adversaries set off their bombs, mankind would be destroyed. As Macmillan painted the picture, it was that simple—and that terrible. This was the situation Macmillan insisted he and Kennedy could not passively accept. In Bermuda, Macmillan as yet offered no specifics as to what he was asking the president to do. For now his goal was simply to make the president recognize that, under the circumstances, it was his duty to do something.

Through the years Kennedy had gone back and forth as to where he stood on the responsibilities of a leader in a democratic society, wavering between Baldwin and Churchill. In Bermuda, Macmillan began the process of guiding him to act as a statesman. Macmillan, himself a tough, shrewd politician, possessed of no small dose of personal ambition and fondness for power, could well comprehend the demons driving the younger man. Still, he argued that Kennedy must be prepared to risk everything—even his own power—in an effort to get history off its present collision course and avert a nuclear holocaust. Macmillan's argument that action was urgently required of them if the great disaster was to be averted appealed to Kennedy, who had long been fascinated by those "moments in history when individual people had to take a very difficult judgment." It also helped that part of him had long instinctively been drawn to the concept of duty Macmillan expounded upon. That was the part of Jack Kennedy that idolized Raymond Asquith and the other heroes of the Somme. Not insignificantly, Macmillan was himself one of those heroes, having been gravely injured in the Somme fighting on the very day in 1916 that Asquith, his fellow Grenadier Guardsman, fell in battle. (In later years, the prime minister's shuffling walk testified to that injury.) Macmillan gave voice to the values of Kennedy's early reading—values sharply at odds with those of a father who had taught him to put self-interest first. At a time when it was inevitable that Joe Kennedy as a force would recede from his son's life, Macmillan stepped in to provide instruction which the father, for all his merits, had not had it in him to offer.

Some of Kennedy's advisers considered Macmillan hysterical, but the president did not agree. He was "very impressed" by the prime minister's arguments. In light of the limited agenda with which Kennedy had arrived in Bermuda, it was a measure of Macmillan's success that the leaders ended the talks by issuing a joint communiqué that included the statement, "The President and the Prime Minister . . . continue to believe that no task is more urgent than the search for paths toward effective disarmament, and they pledge themselves to intensive and continued efforts in this direction. Serious progress toward disarmament is the only way of breaking out of the dangerous contest so sharply renewed by the Soviet Union." Macmillan came away with the agreement that somehow—they did not know exactly by what means, and it was as yet far from clear just how much the president was prepared to do—they would try again to change the course of history from confrontation to détente.

Jackie was at the West Palm Beach airport when Jack flew in on the evening of Friday, December 22, physically and emotionally drained after Bermuda. Husband and wife drove directly to St. Mary's, where Joe Kennedy lay amid a tangle of medical equipment. The following day, the news that Joe had contracted pneumonia and was again near death sent Jack and Jackie to church again to pray for his life. By Christmas Eve, doctors had to cut into Joe's trachea and insert a tube by which he could take oxygen. Jack and Jackie, after spending much of the day at the hospital, went home briefly to hang stockings loaded with gifts for Caroline and young John before returning to St. Mary's where they remained till after midnight. For two days more, as the old man wavered between life and death, Jack sat vigil at his beside. Many times through the decades Joe had wept for a son on the brink of death, and now Jack did the same for him. By the 27th the crisis had passed, yet the sight of his drooling, helpless father, full of rage at the indignity of his condition, led Jack to wonder aloud to Jackie whether it might have been a mistake to pray for his life.

Throughout this wrenching personal crisis, the business of the presidency necessarily went on. From Palm Beach, the president monitored with intense interest the exploratory talks on Berlin, which, in the persons of Thompson and Gromyko, resumed on Moscow on January 2, 1962. He made another appeal to the French, this time in the form of a letter to de Gaulle, not to obstruct efforts to seek a negotiated settlement during the breathing space provided by the removal of the year-end deadline. Khrushchev, Kennedy maintained, "must sign the treaty [with East Germany] sooner or later; he is too far in to turn back now." In a letter to Lem Billings in 1939, a young Jack Kennedy had said much the same about Hitler with regard to Danzig. Twenty-three years later, he worried that another dictator's prideful unwillingness to pull back after having so publicly staked his claims might lead to war. On January 3, Kennedy met with McNamara, Gilpatric, Vice President Johnson and the Joint Chiefs of Staff to finalize the appointment of General Paul Harkins to the position of senior US commander in Vietnam. In the course of the discussion, the president stressed yet again "the importance of the United States not becoming further involved in the area." At the meeting he specified that, as he saw it, the US military role in South Vietnam was "for advice, training and support of the Vietnamese Armed Forces and not combat."

Macmillan had been pondering deeply the dangers he believed imminent if he and Kennedy did not act at once to break the deadlock between East and West. He had secured the president's agreement to do something to avert the coming catastrophe, and he spent the holidays considering how best to follow up on what had been begun at Bermuda. Part of this involved outlining a specific initiative, and part was a continuation of the campaign to persuade Kennedy to choose at last to be a statesman rather than a politician. Interestingly, as Macmillan labored over the Christmas holidays on a long letter asking that in spite of the political risks Kennedy join with him in a new initiative, he re-read Churchill's *Marlborough*. On the eve of the Second World War, Macmillan had been reminded of that work's powerful portrait of the 1st Duke of Marlborough when Churchill persisted in warning of the Nazi peril though the message was far from what most of his countrymen wished to hear. Macmillan's choice of reading matter while composing the letter was significant; a leader willing, like Churchill, to risk personal and party fortunes for the good of the nation was precisely what he was urging Kennedy to be. The Macmillan letter had a recent historical precedent: Churchill in 1953 had similarly appealed to President Eisenhower to join him in a détente initiative. The big difference in 1962 was that Kennedy had already embraced Churchill's Soviet strategy, which he believed to be in his country's best interests. But, as Ormsby Gore understood, that embrace had been intellectual rather than emotional, and the problem at this stage of the presidency was to convince him, despite Khrushchev's undeniable bad faith and despite the opposition of many voters, to take the risks necessary to give the strategy a chance to work. Based on conversations with John Wheeler-Bennett, who in the 1930s had provided a counterpoise to Joe Kennedy's influence, and with Ormsby Gore, who had done much to convert Jack to some of the very ideas that were now proving so politically troublesome, Macmillan sensed that, far from going against the grain, he was really only encouraging the president to become the man he wanted to be.

Macmillan wrote draft after draft until he was satisfied that his letter to Kennedy was exactly as he wished it to be, and on January 5 he finally finished. After reiterating his basic arguments in Bermuda about it being their duty as leaders to risk all in an effort to avert a nuclear holocaust, he asked the president to join him now in "a supreme effort . . . to unlock the present log-jam." As to the specific course of action he thought they ought to take, he proposed that he and Kennedy appeal to Khrushchev for a fresh initiative to get a test ban treaty. Eighteen nations were set to begin disarmament talks in Geneva in March, and Macmillan suggested that he and Kennedy propose to Khrushchev that within the framework of those talks the three nuclear powers ought to take it as their personal responsibility to actively seek a test ban treaty as a first step toward détente.

In his letter, Macmillan reminded the president that twice before there had been attempts to achieve détente, which had nearly suc-ceeded—at the time of the test ban treaty talks, and in 1960 at the time of the summit. As he had at Bermuda, he argued that it was their duty to try again, for if they did not, one of the many problems—all related to the confrontational relationship between East and West—was sure eventually to erupt into a crisis. Most importantly Macmillan argued that they could not sit by and watch passively as disaster unfolded. Nor could they afford to take minor actions. He saw this as a moment of maximum danger; the destruction of mankind was at stake if they failed to act, and as such it was their duty to make a supreme effort. When he wrote of those "moments in history when it is better to take a bolder choice and put a larger stake upon a more ambitious throw," it was clear that this was what he was appealing to Kennedy to do now. Macmillan's letter concluded with a reminder to the president: "It is, of course, easy to do nothing or to do nothing in particular. But, on the whole, it is not the things one did in one's life that one regrets but rather the opportunities missed."

Jack Kennedy, having left his wife in Florida to watch over Joe and take him home when he was ready to be discharged, had been back in Washington for three days when Macmillan's letter reached the Oval Office on January 8. The president barely had time to absorb the nine closely reasoned pages when he had to head upstairs to the family quar-ters where lunch guests were expected. The Ormsby Gores were coming along with their houseguests at the embassy, Secretary of State for Air Julian Amery and his wife, Macmillan's daughter Catherine. The letter was not the sort of document one could digest at a glance, and Jack told David that he would require a day or two to think it through. When Ormsby Gore returned on January 10 for a detailed discussion of Macmillan's letter, it was evident that while Macmillan's stark reminder at Bermuda of all that was at stake had made an impression on Kennedy, confronted with a request that he take specific actions the president was not about to move in an instant to disregard the political risks and act on the basis of duty.

As Ormsby Gore and Kennedy talked that winter morning in the White House, the former perceived at once that, though Macmillan's comments both spoken and written seemed to have brought home to Kennedy the urgent need to seek détente with the Soviets, the president continued to be haunted by the possibility of further lies from Khrushchev and the potential for political damage to himself. While skeptical of claims that the recent round of tests had given the Soviets a clear breakthrough, Kennedy worried about permitting Khrushchev to gain the military advantage, perhaps even to develop an anti-missile missile which would render the deterrent ineffective. In Bermuda, Macmillan had argued that while there was certainly a chance Khrushchev might again prove guilty of trickery, given all that was at stake it was a risk the United States and Britain would just have to take. Nonetheless, Kennedy worried how it would look to the American people if he allowed Khrushchev to fool him again.

Responding to the president's hesitation and knowing him as he did, David moved to supplement Macmillan's reflections on duty with a pitch designed to appeal to Jack's self-interest. He pointed out that there were also political risks if, by failing to act first, Jack permitted the Soviets to come forth with an initiative of their own at Geneva for no other reason than to show the world that they took disarmament more seriously than the United States did. He predicted that Khrushchev might propose to open discussions at Foreign Ministers or even Heads of Government level. Jack took David's point; he did not want to allow the Soviets to seize the advantage in the battle for world opinion. But while he was willing to consider sending Rusk to meet with other Foreign Ministers at Geneva, he made it clear that he was "allergic" to the idea of facing Khrushchev himself. Macmillan had urged that they must try again despite the risk of failure, but Kennedy remained preoccupied with the political cost of such a failure. As he talked to David that winter morning it was obvious that he did not have high hopes for what could be accomplished at Geneva, and he calculated that if he went so far as to appear there himself a failure to come home with solid results could be politically devastating. Mindful of the political damage to Eisenhower done by the Paris summit, Jack simply was not willing to risk another calamitous encounter with Khrushchev.

Still, for all of his political hesitations, Macmillan's portrayal of the dangers of the situation had had an impact on Kennedy. While he was not willing to risk a summit meeting, he was eager to find a way to participate in a joint initiative with the British if a satisfactory formula could be found. Afterward, in his 1962 State of the Union address, he echoed Macmillan's letter when he declared, "This nation has the will and the faith to make a supreme effort to break the log jam on disarmament and nuclear tests." In fact, Kennedy had intended to go even further, using the speech to make another offer to the Soviets of an atmospheric test ban, but strong behind-the-scenes opposition from the State and Defense departments caused him to change his mind.

Finally, it was agreed that Kennedy and Macmillan would appeal for a new initiative in a joint letter to Khrushchev. The task of formulating the letter itself was delegated to Dean Rusk and David Ormsby Gore. After much back and forth between Rusk and Ormsby Gore, a letter began to take shape in which Kennedy and Macmillan, on the argument that if nothing were done at once to make a start toward controlling the arms race, events might soon take their own course and lead to disaster, invited Khrushchev to join them in a "supreme effort" to assure progress at the disarmament talks to begin in March. As Kennedy continued privately to insist that under no circumstances would he himself face Khrushchev in Geneva, the document finally agreed upon asked only that the leaders accept "personal responsibility for directing the part to be played by our personal representatives in the forthcoming talks." Just what that personal responsibility might consist of remained unspecified.

The missive was sent off to Moscow on February 7, and two days later Kennedy seemed to have a sign that Khrushchev might be in the mood to react favorably. Lately, impasse at the Thompson–Gromyko talks in Moscow, coupled with harassment in the Berlin air corridors, had seemed to indicate otherwise. But on the evening of February 9 the hint that Khrushchev might be ready to release the U-2 pilot Francis Gary Powers, whose capture in 1960 had led Khrushchev to scuttle the Paris summit, suggested that this might have been the perfect moment to approach the Russians with a new initiative.

That night, as it happened, the Kennedys were to host a private dinner dance at the White House for more than one hundred guests. An invitation to the event had emerged as a highly coveted possession in Washington society, and finally Jackie had decided to give dinner to seventy-five of their closest friends, such as Lem Billings, the Spaldings and the Ormsby Gores, and to bring in a second wave of guests at 10 p.m. for the dancing. As last-minute preparations were being made for the party, Jack Kennedy believed the festivities might coincide with a dramatic swap of prisoners at Glienicker Bridge, which linked East and West Berlin, whereby Powers would be exchanged for Colonel Rudolf Abel, an East German spy held by the United States. The whole U-2 episode had a great deal of personal resonance for Kennedy, for in 1960 the presidential candidate had been quick to use it to substantiate his theme of national decline. The present deal, which had been long in the works, seemed a fulfillment of his pledge to reverse the humiliations of the Eisenhower presidency. He had not been alone in interpreting Khrushchev's release of two captured American pilots on the day after his inauguration as a sign of the Soviet leader's desire to start afresh with a new administration. The present gesture, if and when it took place, seemed similarly loaded with significance.

As soon as Lester Lanin's New York society orchestra began to play, the president, who was as protective of David and Sissie's daughter Jane as he had once been of his sisters, asked the shy eighteen-year-old for the first dance. Afterward, to the puzzlement and fascination of his guests, he spent much of the evening darting in and out of the crowded, candlelit ground-floor state rooms as he sought updates on the progress of the top-secret spy exchange. However, not every one of Kennedy's mysterious disappearances in the course of the evening had to do with the U-2 pilot. Among the guests to arrive at 10 p.m. was Mary Meyer, an artist with whom Jack had begun an affair two weeks previously while Jackie and the children were at Glen Ora. Betty Spalding, who was recovering from a skiing injury, had left the party to rest on the third floor, which housed various guest rooms and Caroline Kennedy's schoolroom. The only person on the floor at the time, Spalding was on her way back down to the party when she was surprised to see Jack and Mary Meyer arrive upstairs. Unfazed that they had been spotted, the couple headed into Caroline's schoolroom for a quick sexual encounter.

It was after 2 a.m. when Jack finally received the official confirmation from Berlin that he had been waiting for all night. He had already quietly given the spy swap story to Ben Bradlee of *Newsweek*, Mary Meyer's brother-in-law; now he authorized Salinger to announce the news at a 3 a.m. press briefing. Delighted at the prospect of splendid press coverage, Jack enjoyed several celebratory glasses of champagne and, seemingly "a bit high," talked and laughed with friends until half past four.

His elation was short-lived. The following day, he was at Glen Ora when Khrushchev's reply to the Kennedy–Macmillan letter came in. The problem, at least as Kennedy saw it, was not that Khrushchev was unfavorable to the proposal that the three leaders take personal responsibility to reverse the arms race. On the contrary, the Russian seemed to burst with enthusiasm. In line with Ormsby Gore's prediction, Khrushchev said he had been at work on a similar proposal of his own in conjunction with the Eighteen-Power Conference. But whereas Kennedy and Macmillan had suggested a meeting of foreign ministers, Khrushchev had a better idea. "Who," Khrushchev asked rhetorically, "can most quickly step over the routine conceptions and disagreements which, like a snowball, accumulate on disarmament negotiations as soon as these have begun? I should think that this must first of all lie on the shoulders of those who are invested with the greatest trust of all the peoples and who have the full breadth of authority." In short, Khrushchev was proposing exactly what the president had been anxious to avoid: a heads of government meeting at Geneva attended by himself, Kennedy and Macmillan. Apparently, by releasing the U-2 pilot at that particular moment he had been signaling his desire for another top-level conference.

Kennedy remained adamant that he would not be forced into a direct encounter with Khrushchev. After a flurry of telephone conversations with Macmillan, he replied to Moscow rejecting a top-level meeting and suggesting that they revert to the notion of sending their respective foreign ministers instead. Though Ormsby Gore understood his friend's reluctance to face Khrushchev again without a guarantee of a firm deal to bring back to the American people, he pointed out during a private visit to Glen Ora that, even were there to be no concrete results, a meeting could have significant benefits nonetheless. David reminded Jack that though the 1955 summit had produced no tangible results it had created "an atmosphere of détente," which had been "quickly followed by the rise to power of Gomulka in Poland and an anti-Communist revolution in Hungary." In line with Churchill's theory of infiltration, David argued that the Soviets had far more to fear from such encounters than the West. But Jack, for the moment decidedly less interested in the benefits for Eastern Europe than in the political impact on himself, was not biting.

In these weeks, as Macmillan and Ormsby Gore pressed Kennedy to make a new initiative on détente via a test ban treaty, the pressure on the president to resume atmospheric tests continued to mount. As it mounted, the conflict between Macmillan's calls of duty and responsibility and Kennedy's instincts for political self-preservation intensified. In the aftermath of the first Soviet explosion back in September, many Americans had been eager for the United States to respond with aboveground blasts of its own. Six months later, Kennedy's critics voiced astonishment that he would be willing to provide the enemy with—in the words of a hostile questioner at a presidential news conference—"a gift of that length of time." Nor was the chorus of those who urged the need to test so as not to lose vital ground to Khrushchev limited to the president's political enemies. There was strong sentiment within the administration to test aboveground, and on February 20 Dean Rusk handed the president a memo expressing his own support for resumption. It seemed to Glenn Seaborg that by the end of 1961 Kennedy himself had all but made the decision to resume tests. "Yet two months more were to elapse before the decision was announced," the Atomic Energy Commission chairman recalled. "During this period the president repeatedly sought reassurance, in meeting after meeting, that it was the right thing to do, that there was no alternative. . . . What Kennedy seemed to hope for was some eleventh-hour agreement with the Russians that would make testing unnecessary." On more than one occasion he expressed the wish to Ormsby Gore that progress at Geneva would enable him not to go forward with atmospheric testing. But after his secretary of state came down in favor of tests, Kennedy phoned Ormsby Gore to say that he would make up his mind once and for all following a National Security Council meeting on February 23, when senior advisers were due to offer their views on nuclear testing. He planned to announce his decision in a speech on March 1, with an eye toward starting tests on April 1.

David understood that this was not the moment to argue the other side. What he did say, however, was that it would be unwise to make the announcement a full two weeks before the 18-Power Conference. Such a statement by the president before the talks had even started would greatly diminish the chances for success. Whatever Jack might decide after the NSC meeting—and it seemed obvious what that decision would be—he urged him at least to withhold any announcement. Jack, torn between a desire on the one hand to cover himself politically and on the other to give the Geneva sessions a chance to succeed, at last agreed. It was a substantial concession, for the longer the president put off a public announcement of the resumption of testing the more he would be criticized for weakness and indecision. Kennedy followed up by letting Bundy know that instead of making a straightforward public statement after the NSC meeting, as previously planned, he would announce only that preparations for aboveground tests were nearing completion.

That week, as Jack Kennedy was being widely criticized—as once he had criticized Eisenhower—for allowing his country to fall behind the Russians, he rejoiced along with other Americans when the United States finally matched the Soviet ability, which had been triumphantly demonstrated ten months before, to put a man into orbit around the earth. On February 20, John Glenn circled the earth three times. Kennedy was so delighted that he made plans to go to Florida to congratulate Glenn personally at Cape Canaveral. The NSC meeting to hear what his advisers had to say about atmospheric testing was delayed four days, to February 27. Publicly the Florida trip was a jubilant occasion, but the receipt of a jeering letter from Khrushchev before he flew down on the afternoon of February 22 privately and profoundly altered his mood. Khrushchev pointed to the contradiction between Kennedy's insistence that the three leaders take personal responsibility for progress at the Eighteen-Power Conference and his resistance to the proposal that they meet there themselves. He accused him, for all his noble words, of not really believing that success was possible in Geneva: it was that very lack of conviction that impelled Kennedy to demand that the foreign ministers, rather than heads of government, bear the brunt of the talks' failure. The clear implication was that Kennedy saw the initiative as no more than a device to soften his image at a moment when he was about to resume atmospheric tests. What made Khrushchev's long letter so insidious was that it was so accurate. Kennedy really did not want to attend another meeting with Khrushchev, where he might be perceived to fail. In large part he really had decided to participate in the initiative not because he believed the Geneva talks could succeed, but on Ormsby Gore's argument that it would be in his interest to make an overture before Khrushchev made one to him.

Without giving himself time to cool down, Kennedy, robbed of even the pretense of detachment, responded emotionally to Khrushchev's taunts. Less than forty-eight hours after Khrushchev's letter arrived at the State Department, a letter containing Kennedy's own accusations was on its way to Moscow. There was much truth in what Kennedy said as well. He pointed to contradictions in Khrushchev's arguments, noting the absurdity of calling the resumption of above-ground tests by the United States aggression when it was the Soviets who had violated the moratorium in the first place. When Macmillan learned of the president's February 24 letter, he was furious that Kennedy had chosen to trade barbs with Khrushchev without so much as alerting the British, even though Britain had been a full partner in both the initiative and the letter rejecting Khrushchev's proposal of a top-level meeting. To the prime minister's mind, such a dangerous moment in human history was hardly the time to indulge oneself by losing one's temper and acting impetuously, yet that was precisely what the president had done.

Kennedy returned from Florida on February 26 in time to attend the rescheduled National Security Council meeting the following morning. Bundy still assumed that the president meant to keep to his decision to make no firm announcement one way or another afterward. But Kennedy's anger over Khrushchev's letter had changed his mind. In the course of the meeting, Rusk reiterated his position that in view of Soviet progress in recent months, "common prudence" required the United States to test, adding that they must not allow a time to come when the United States was, or was thought to be, behind the Russians in nuclear strength. McNamara concurred that the United States "must neither fall behind nor appear to fall behind." General Lemnitzer, speaking for the Joint Chiefs of Staff, expressed concern that the Soviets might have made "a major breakthrough" in their recent round of tests. The Chiefs, Lemnitzer reported, strongly favored the resumption of tests. So the discussion went; the judgment of the president's senior advisers was unanimous in favor of testing. As soon as the meeting concluded, Kennedy phoned the British embassy to ask Ormsby Gore to come to the family quarters later in the day.

When Ormsby Gore arrived in the West Sitting Room shortly after four that afternoon, Jack informed him that he had had a change of heart since their conversation the previous week. He had made a firm decision to resume atmospheric tests on April 15, and he planned to announce it in a televised speech to the nation on Thursday evening, March 1. Stunned, Ormsby Gore was not sure he understood correctly. Had they not agreed that it would be best to give the disarmament conference a chance to succeed before any decision was taken? Jack confirmed that that had been his position, but, he went on, only an agreement on a test ban or, alternatively, on the Berlin question would have permitted him to put off testing. Test ban talks, Jack pointed out, had been going on for three years, and the current discussions in Moscow showed no sign of any softening of the Soviet position on Berlin. Now that the National Security Council had unanimously urged him to resume aboveground tests, he thought he had better announce his decision before the senior advisers' views began to leak out, with all the political damage that would entail. The Soviets would have a chance to sign a test ban treaty in Geneva before April 15, and if they did there would be no need for the tests to begin. By this point, however, Jack believed such an agreement unlikely.

Hearing this was a terrible experience for David. Their discussions through the years had bristled, as young men's conversations will, with the promise of all the great things they and their generation hoped to accomplish. From the time of their talks on the eve of Jack's 1954 back surgery, as well as the conversations in New York in 1959 when he was running for president, the friends had come to share an approach founded on the strategy laid out by Churchill in postwar speeches from "The Sinews of Peace" on. The central goals presented in Jack's inaugural address were based on ideas worked out through the years in discussion with David. Exactly one year before, on February 28, 1961, when David visited Washington for the first time since inauguration day, he and Jack had sat together in this very room excitedly discussing the new president's plans to implement his strategy of peace. The mood was drastically different this day, as Jack outlined a plan of action that threatened to take the arms race to a new level, perhaps to destroy all he himself had hoped to accomplish as president, perhaps even to lead to the nuclear confrontation Macmillan had warned of at Bermuda if bold measures were not immediately taken. For David personally, it was the demise of all he had been working for, from the time of his apprenticeship under Selwyn Lloyd through recent days, when he had been lobbying to be certain that the proposal presented at Geneva on March 14 would be fresh and strong enough to have a chance to succeed rather than being a mere exercise in public relations. Hesitantly, as though he knew the answer already and could not bear to hear it, David inquired whether the test ban treaty Jack planned to ask the Soviets to sign this time round was the same document tabled by the United States and Britain the previous April. Should the proposal be unchanged from the one already rejected by the Soviets, the Geneva talks were certain to fail. Jack confirmed that he intended to put forth the identical proposal. There being nothing more David could think of to say, he suggested that Macmillan would surely want to discuss all of this with the president immediately. Jack, who had already handed him a letter to Macmillan explaining his decision, said he would welcome a chance to talk by phone. It was nearly five o'clock when David returned sadly to the embassy where, for more than four hours, he labored over his report to the prime minister.

On February 28, Macmillan awakened to David's message. Aghast at Kennedy's change of heart, he made two quick calculations. First, he decided that, although he had much to say to the president, he must not attempt to do it by phone. Macmillan was as uncomfortable on the phone as Kennedy was famously at ease. He had been effective with Kennedy in Bermuda, but hours before the president's televised address to the American people there was no time to arrange another face-to-face encounter. So his immediate reply to Kennedy's letter was to notify him of his intention to respond in writing. Lest Kennedy be tempted to call first, Macmillan emphasized that he would not be available. Directly, he plunged into work on a letter that he hoped might have as much of an impact as the one of January 5, though this time there would be no opportunity to produce draft after draft. Within less than twenty-four hours Kennedy must have his reply.

Macmillan's second calculation was that in view of the pressure under which Kennedy had been operating, it would be pointless to try to change his mind about either the tests themselves or the announcement. Enraged though he was by the president's decision, Macmillan saw that his best chance to influence events would be calmly to try to persuade Kennedy of two things. Based on all that Ormsby Gore had said in the past, it was likely that Kennedy, having made his decision reluctantly, would welcome an excuse to put off the tests so long as it did not damage him politically. Macmillan asked the president to push the date of the first test from April 15 to May 3 so as to give the Geneva talks a chance to produce results. And, reminding Kennedy of their publicly-stated joint commitment to make a supreme effort to break the deadlock on nuclear disarmament, he asked him to reconsider his plan to put forth a proposal the Soviets had already rejected and were certain to reject again. Macmillan recognized the impossibility of pinning Kennedy down to specifics so soon before his televised speech, but he took pains to prevent him from saying anything on the air that closed off the possibility of a fresh proposal. Appealing to Kennedy's preoccupation with image, Macmillan made the case that it would be best to show the world that the United States sincerely wanted a deal at Geneva. Finally, though he had previously acquiesced to Kennedy's insistence that it not be the leaders themselves who met at Geneva, Macmillan asked him to remain open to the possibility that Khrushchev might really want to meet "for some constructive purpose."

No sooner had the letter gone off than Macmillan began to doubt that Kennedy would respond favorably. In the absence of any positive action by the president, Macmillan was intent on making profitable use of the six weeks that would remain between the televised announcement of the resumption of tests and the first explosion in the series. While he planned publicly to support Kennedy's decision as right "in the circumstances of today," he would try to alter those circumstances, it being "the duty of a statesman not just to follow events, but to seek also to lead." In his view, the coming collision he had warned of at Bermuda made it far too dangerous not to act. Though it would hardly be as good as acting in concert with the United States—by far the greater power—Macmillan planned in the aftermath of Kennedy's broadcast to contact Khrushchev on his own. He would suggest that the two of them meet, whether in Geneva, Moscow or London, to see if together they might work out a treaty to end nuclear tests.

Macmillan abandoned the idea of a solo approach to Khrushchev after Kennedy's reply on March 1 seemed to offer a glimmer of hope. This was a terribly complicated moment for Kennedy, who was intellectually convinced of the need to make a breakthrough with the Soviets yet hamstrung by his own political fears and by his dread of again allowing Khrushchev to trick him. Reminded that he had publicly committed himself to a supreme effort at Geneva, Kennedy agreed not to send the same proposal the Soviets had already turned down. He reported that he had assigned his experts "to work at full steam" with Macmillan's to come up with a new offer that had a chance of acceptance. While he rejected Macmillan's suggestion of a May 3 test date, he did agree to say that he would not test until the latter part of April; he assured the prime minister that no tests would go off until after April 22, which would give the Soviets "a considerable space of time" in which to make up their minds on the test ban. As to Macmillan's comment on Khrushchev's possible motive for seeking a top-level meeting, Kennedy, still stewing over Khrushchev's taunts, declared, "It may be that Khrushchev really wants to talk with us, but I must say I think his last letter is a strange way of showing it."

When Kennedy appeared on television on the evening of Friday, March 2, his address reflected the discord within him. On the one hand, he was responding to the mood of the electorate, as well as shielding himself against further charges of weakness and indecision, when he announced the resumption of atmospheric testing. (Senator Everett Dirksen of Illinois, the Republican floor leader, commented that Kennedy was to be "applauded" for a measure the Republican leadership had been demanding for months.) On the other hand, his genuine desire to achieve a breakthrough with the Soviets was suggested by his pledge to send to Geneva a fresh offer for a test ban, and to cancel the tests in the event a treaty were signed. Still, his remarks did not quite represent the supreme effort to try to change the direction of history, at whatever cost to his own popularity and power, that Macmillan urged on him. Jack Kennedy was not yet ready to make such an effort—at least not in public. But a sense of disappointment with his own decision to order atmospheric testing galvanized him to find some way to postpone it, and on the very day of his broadcast speech he made a secret overture to Khrushchev bolder than anything hinted at on the air. Bobby Kennedy sent another back-channel message via the Soviet intelligence agent Bolshakov, conveying the president's offer of an atmospheric test ban treaty. Had the president made the offer publicly, he would have faced severe criticism from the American people whether or not it was accepted. By making it in secret, he ensured that he would only have to tell the public in the event of a favorable response from Moscow. He would be subjected to attack in any case, but at least with a deal in place he could limit the political damage by arguing that a first major step had been taken toward détente.

Khrushchev turned down the back channel offer, and Kennedy, under pressure from within his administration, did not fulfill his pledge to improve on the previous year's draft treaty. The disarmament conference stumbled along, but there was no agreement on a test ban. In view of the stalemate at the Thompson–Gromyko talks in Moscow, Kennedy directed Rusk to approach Gromyko in Geneva about what Churchill had called a modus vivendi on Berlin, in effect an agreement to disagree which, in the absence of a more lasting settlement, would at least prevent both sides from flying to arms. Kennedy judged that Khrushchev would soon revert to his plan to sign a treaty with the East Germans, with all the consequences that might entail. At Bermuda, the president had vowed not to go to war without one final attempt to negotiate, but, as he told Ormsby Gore, it would be almost impossible to negotiate effectively at the precipice, for the American people would regard as appeasement any substantial concessions made in an atmosphere of crisis. He hoped to get a deal, however temporary and imperfect, on the principle articulated in *The World Crisis* that "a war postponed may be a war averted. Circumstances change, combinations change, new groupings arise, old interests are superseded by new." On the afternoon of March 22, Rusk handed Gromyko a written proposal for the modus vivendi. While the president waited for Moscow's response he traveled to California for the weekend, where, at the Bing Crosby estate in Palm Desert, he spent a night with the actress Marilyn Monroe.

On his return to Washington Monday morning, Kennedy had a message from Rusk registering the absolute failure of the Geneva talks. At Bermuda, Macmillan had warned that if bold measures were not taken immediately, mankind might soon destroy itself. Now he asked Kennedy to join him in a final urgent appeal to Khrushchev for a test ban treaty, before the United States set off its first atmospheric nuclear test. Kennedy refused on the explanation that "opinion in this country would not hold that a further appeal from me to Khrushchev was appropriate or constructive." Though he agreed that an additional Western appeal might be helpful, and though he encouraged Macmillan to contact Khrushchev on his own, Kennedy was unwilling to take such a political risk. Macmillan, offering one last lesson in duty, replied that he himself did not worry much about public opinion. "In my experience," he wrote, "[public opinion] always stabilizes itself in the long run behind what is right and sensible." As chance would have it, the day after he received this letter Kennedy had a visit at the White House from Moucher Devonshire, with whose elder son he had jousted in the 1930s about the competing claims of duty and self-interest. In the end Billy Hartington had risked everything for ideals—precisely what Macmillan, Billy's uncle, maintained a leader must be ready to do, and what he was asking Jack Kennedy to do now.

On April 25, 1962, three days after Easter, the United States conducted its first aboveground nuclear test since 1958 near Christmas Island. Before the round was completed, there would be a total of thirty-six explosions. The arms race, which Jack Kennedy had sincerely hoped to avert, had resumed in earnest, the assumption in Washington being that the Soviet Union would react with a new series of blasts. When the first American test was fired, the president was in Palm Beach, where he had spent Easter with his wife and children and invalid father, who remained paralyzed and unable to speak. He was not due back in Washington until two days later, when Macmillan was to arrive for three days of talks. Indeed, one of the reasons to set off the first device on the 25th had been Kennedy's determination to start the series before the prime minister's visit. Aware of his own susceptibility to Macmillan's eloquence, particularly when they were in a room together, he did not care to risk a last-minute attempt to enlist him in another move to put off testing. Much as Kennedy did not want the tests to go forward, he was determined to proceed.

The day after the first explosion, Macmillan delivered an address to the American Newspaper Publishers Association convention at the Waldorf–Astoria in New York. The previous December, on the train after the Army–Navy game, Jack had complained to David Ormsby Gore of the complete distrust of the Soviets that the press had instilled in many Americans. In anticipation of Macmillan's trip to the United States, Ormsby Gore, noting that many Americans had not even glimpsed an alternative to a policy of confrontation, proposed that the prime minister talk up a very different Soviet strategy to those who by their control of the press played a decisive role in shaping public opinion. In his remarks to the newspaper publishers, Macmillan argued that in spite of the failure at Geneva, the United States and Britain must not abandon efforts to find areas where agreement might be possible with the Soviets. Noting that many people continued to believe in the inevitability of a "final conflict" between Communism and the free world, he suggested that "apocalyptic dogma" was ill suited to the nuclear age. By enumerating the positive changes in the Soviet Union since Stalin's death, he offered evidence that Churchill's plan gradually and peacefully to lift the Iron Curtain had begun to work. Macmillan believed that the more the Russian people saw of the West, the more they would want Western things—and that could only work to the detriment of the closed Soviet society. One day after the nuclear blast at Christmas Island attested to diplomatic failure, he urged the newspaper publishers to consider that the struggle against Communism promised to be a long one and victory likely if their side managed to avoid a war. Typically, Macmillan cast his argument in terms of duty. "Our duty is surely simple—to be firm but patient; never to yield and never to give ground, but never to take provocative action ourselves; and to wait maybe one, maybe two generations, maybe more, until in God's good time the ordinary peoples of that vast area, encouraged by higher standards of material life, begin to look again for that spiritual food, without which man has never lived for prolonged periods since he came into the world." In short, he was making a case for the peaceful defeat of Communism by contact and agreements.

On April 29, at the close of official meetings between the two leaders at the White House, Jackie Kennedy presided over an informal Sunday lunch in the family quarters for just Jack and herself, Macmillan, and the Ormsby Gores. The lunch marked a new stage in Kennedy's relationship with Macmillan. In undertaking to show Kennedy his duty as a leader, Macmillan had emerged as a mentor, even a substitute father, to the younger man. In the months after Bermuda, Kennedy, in attempting to act on the basis of what was right rather than what was politically safe, had moved forward one step then back another, as Macmillan described the process to Wheeler-Bennett. Yet during that time their personal bond had grown stronger; and at the lunch it seemed to Jackie that she had never seen her husband "so relaxed outside his own family circle." Jack and his guests discussed "everything in the world," and afterward both the president and the prime minister reported to David a sense that the lunch represented the "complete family atmosphere" that had developed between them since Bermuda. Inevitably, given the participants' literary cast of mind, the conversation turned to books, and Jack spoke enthusiastically of Barbara Tuchman's newly published *The Guns of August*. Tuchman's study of the first month of the First World War took its epigraph, "The terrible ifs accumulate," from *The World Crisis*, and reprised a number of Churchill's central themes, such as accidental war and the momentum toward war. Macmillan had yet to read the book, but Ormsby Gore argued that Tuchman had been unfair in her treatment of the decision by Sir John French, commander of the British Expeditionary Force, to order his troops to retreat. David compared the general's decision to that of Churchill and Gort at the time of Dunkirk, and the comparison launched a discussion of those moments in history when one must put everything at risk in order to change the course of events. In Bermuda and afterward, Macmillan had urged Jack Kennedy to see the current crisis as such a moment. In the wake of the failure at Geneva, as the trio talked about European and American history they were speaking obliquely of the difficult choices facing the president if together they were to prevent East and West from mutual destruction.

CHAPTER SEVENTEEN

In Reading the History of Past Wars and How They Began

T HE INITIATIVE HAD FAILED; EAST AND WEST REMAINED ON A collision course. The arms race was on again, and Soviet rejection of Kennedy's proposal for an agreement to disagree over Berlin meant that the breathing space provided by Khrushchev the previous October would almost certainly soon come to an end. At Geneva, Gromyko had suggested that Rusk might want to continue talking about Berlin to Soviet ambassador Anatoly Dobrynin in Washington. Kennedy thought it important for those discussions to be under way before the first US aboveground test, and by the time Macmillan came to Washington Rusk had already conferred with Dobrynin on three occasions. Even after Adenauer protested, the sessions with Dobrynin went on. Kennedy was intent that both sides keep talking in an effort to prevent them from reaching the edge of the precipice. Macmillan agreed that the modus vivendi now seemed their best hope for avoiding imminent confrontation. With further talks with Dobrynin set for May, Kennedy sent Rusk to Europe to talk to US allies and, especially, to do what he could to assuage Adenauer's fears by arguing that greater trouble loomed were Khrushchev to sign the long-threatened treaty with East Germany. But no sooner had Rusk conferred with the Germans than Adenauer denounced Kennedy to the American journalist Daniel Shorr. Privately Kennedy was livid and he would later send off an angry message to

Adenauer, but at a press conference on May 9 he managed to suppress his rage when asked about the German chancellor's objections to US efforts to get a deal on Berlin. "As Winston Churchill said, 'It is better to jaw-jaw than to war-war,' and we shall continue to jaw-jaw, and see if we can produce a useful result," Kennedy responded. "We may fail, but in my opinion the effort is worth it when we're dealing with such dangerous matters."

He was also determined to jaw-jaw over Laos, where an unexpected crisis had erupted that week. At the time of Macmillan's visit, Kennedy had taken solace for the disarmament conference's failure in the fact that the agreement to establish a neutral Laos seemed about to materialize. On May 6, the ceasefire suddenly collapsed and Phoumi's forces, under attack by the Communist Pathet Lao, fled Nam Tha in the northern part of the country. From one day to the next, the situation in Laos had gone from "encouraging" to "ugly and dangerous." On May 10, US ambassador Winthrop Brown sent word that the Soviet refusal thus far to do anything suggested that Moscow's desire for a peaceful settlement had "to say the least, substantially diminished." Kennedy again found himself called on to send in US troops, and he again feared that if he resisted being dragged into a war he believed could not be won Eisenhower would speak out against him. He sent an urgent message via Dobrynin to Khrushchev, asking his help in getting both sides back on the path of negotiations. Kennedy had yet to have a response from Khrushchev when the next day he sent CIA director John McCone and National Security Council staff member James Forrestal to brief Eisenhower on Laos and to attempt to discern what his public position would be. Eisenhower indicated that he leaned toward intervention, and that in the event US troops were sent over he favored doing whatever it took to win, including the use of tactical nuclear weapons.

Kennedy now sensed that his efforts to avoid a war were being generally undermined—by Adenauer and de Gaulle, who opposed his efforts with Khrushchev; by Khrushchev, who did not get back to him immediately on Laos; and by Eisenhower, who was making noises about nuclear weapons. He was, therefore, in an irascible mood when he received the French Minister of State for Cultural Affairs, André Malraux, in the Cabinet Room on the afternoon of May 11. Jackie had invited Malraux to Washington as an expression of gratitude for his personal kindness to her during the Kennedys' visit to Paris. That evening she was to preside over a grand dinner in his honor, attended by some of America's most celebrated artists, writers, performers and other cultural figures. It was well known at the White House that of all the social events staged by the First Lady, this was the one in which she seemed to have the greatest personal stake. Malraux had come to the White House as the Kennedys' personal guest, so when he went in to say hello to the president at half past four he was totally unprepared for the tirade that greeted him. Kennedy had managed to remain calm at the press conference at the beginning of the week, but in private he permitted himself to let fly. He accused the French and Germans of "a latent, almost female hostility" toward the United States, and declared that if they did not appreciate his efforts to seek peace in Europe he would be happy to get out. He said he felt like a man carrying a 200-pound sack of potatoes, while everyone else just stands around criticizing his performance; he was tired of such treatment and would put up with it no more.

In an early phone call to David Ormsby Gore the following morning, Kennedy complained bitterly about the French, the Germans and especially Khrushchev. Three days after he had sent a message asking for cooperation in Laos, Khrushchev had not even bothered to respond. Kennedy interpreted his silence as a gesture of contempt. He told Ormsby Gore he could not believe he was being treated so, and he indignantly raised the possibility of notifying Moscow that he intended to cut off the Berlin talks. But, as Ormsby Gore perceived, such threats were simply a way of blowing off steam. In the days that followed, the president, relieved to learn that Eisenhower did not after all intend to speak out on behalf of immediate intervention in Laos, strove to get both sides back to the conference table. He approved a plan to move some four thousand US troops to Thailand, specifying privately that his aim was not to intervene militarily but to scare the Laotians to start talking again. Indeed, the day after the troop deployment was announced, the Pathet Lao agreed to resume negotiations—a good sign. "The great danger is of a shooting war in Asia—in the jungles of Asia," Kennedy said at a press conference on May 18, "and it is our object to bring about a diplomatic solution which will make the chances of such a war far less likely." There was as yet no Laotian settlement, but at least the adversaries were talking rather than fighting, and there was reason to hope that the development augured well generally for Kennedy's plan to keep away from the edge of the precipice.

The president's spirits were noticeably improved when, that same day, he went to New York to attend a political fundraiser in the form of a gala celebration of his forty-fifth birthday, attended by some fifteen thousand Democrats. On the evening of Saturday, May 19, Jack Kennedy, puffing on a cigar and enjoying himself hugely, sat with his feet up on the railing of the presidential box at a red-white-and-blue-festooned Madison Square Garden, as Marilyn Monroe, in a gauzy, skin-tight, flesh-toned gown encrusted with rhinestones, serenaded him from the stage. As soon as Marilyn began to sing in her signature breathy voice, it became apparent that she was high. Eyes closed, she licked her lips and ran her hands up her thighs and over her stomach. The Broadway columnist Dorothy Kilgallen, writing of the telecast, described Marilyn's performance as "making love to the President in direct view of forty million Americans," and Kennedy when he came on stage afterward jested that he could now "retire from politics after having had 'Happy Birthday' sung to me in such a sweet, wholesome way." Later that night he went on to a private celebration at the Upper East Side townhouse of United Artists chairman Arthur Krim.

As Kennedy frolicked with Marilyn into the early hours of Sunday, May 20, Khrushchev was launching a plan to force the confrontation at the edge of the precipice the president had been striving to avoid. On May 20, Khrushchev spoke to Gromyko and others of his idea of placing Soviet missiles in Cuba. For many months Khrushchev had been telling Kennedy, both privately and publicly, that he considered the German problem the most important unresolved issue between East and West, the area of dispute that must be settled at once. Khrushchev had staked his personal prestige on securing a German settlement, and in some quarters it was said that he had begun to look foolish for having threatened so long to bring matters to a head without actually having done so. As Kennedy understood, Khrushchev's desire to get a German settlement was far more than a matter of prestige; he was fueled by the very real fear of a reunified Germany with all that that might mean for Russia, which had suffered so greatly at German hands in two world wars. Now, with Kennedy hoping that a modus vivendi on Berlin would make it possible to avoid a crisis, Khrushchev quietly and systematically moved to create a crisis that would force the president to accept the Soviets' terms: the abandonment of any idea of German reunification, diplomatic recognition of East Germany, and the withdrawal of Western troops from Berlin. Once Khrushchev had his missiles in Cuba, he intended to appear in New York in the latter part of November and demand that Kennedy agree to the Berlin settlement Moscow proposed. Kennedy's behavior in Vienna had persuaded Khrushchev that America's young leader would accept almost anything if it meant avoiding a nuclear war. Eleven months later, Khrushchev calculated that with missiles so close to the United States, Kennedy's fear of a nuclear confrontation would outweigh his dread of being labeled an appeaser. Khrushchev was confident that he had come to know his enemy; if Kennedy were forced to decide between war and a settlement on Soviet terms, he would choose the latter. Certainly, from Khrushchev's point of view, there were other benefits to putting the missiles in Cuba, where they would guard against another invasion and equalize the balance of power between Moscow and Washington, the United States already having missiles of its own close to Russia in Turkey. But at the heart of what would come to be known as the Cuban missile crisis was Khrushchev's determination to force Kennedy to make major concessions over Berlin.

On May 21, Khrushchev presented the missile plan to his Defense Council, and three days later the Presidium of the Central Committee of the Communist Party of the Soviet Union conferred tentative approval in anticipation of a delegation being sent to Castro. On May 27, while Kennedy enjoyed a quiet weekend with Jackie and the children at Glen Ora, Khrushchev met with the delegation before it left for Cuba. Khrushchev explained to the delegates that once the missiles were in place he did not actually intend to use them. Their purpose was strictly to "scare" and "restrain" the Americans. Khrushchev did not intend to go to war, only to bend Kennedy to his will.

Khrushchev, playing what Kennedy would later call his "double game," both professed concern about progress at the Rusk–Dobrynin talks on Berlin, which resumed in Washington on May 30, and persisted in his plan to put missiles in Cuba and precipitate a crisis. Shortly after word arrived on June 11 that at long last a diplomatic settlement in Laos was near, Khrushchev warmly expressed the hope to Kennedy that progress in resolving the Laotian problem might presage agreements in other areas of dispute between East and West. Kennedy had reason to take this as a positive sign on Berlin, and wasted no time agreeing. Unbeknownst to Kennedy, two days before Khrushchev's optimistic letter of June 12 the Presidium had confirmed its approval of the Cuban missile plan, to which Castro had agreed. Khrushchev's suggestion of the possibility of a thaw in East–West relations even as he undertook preparations to move men and matériel to Cuba was exactly the sort of trickery Kennedy had been so worried about since Moscow's announcement of the resumption of nuclear tests.

Khrushchev followed up with a message relayed via Bolshakov to Bobby Kennedy asking the president to withdraw US troops from Thailand now that matters in Laos had been settled. Bobby, after conferring with his brother, responded that the United States would begin to pull out within ten days. Contrary to the hopes expressed by both leaders—sincerely in Kennedy's case, insincerely in Khrushchev's—there was no comparable agreement at the Berlin talks in Washington. On the day Bolshakov approached Bobby about the troops in Thailand, Rusk and Dobrynin seemed to have reached an impasse, the latter again insisting that Western troops must leave Berlin and the former that the US presence there was not negotiable. Directly, Khrushchev contacted Kennedy to say that, given the standstill, he hoped to "speed up" matters by offering a Berlin proposal of his own, but the White House quickly saw that the supposedly new offer was nothing more than a repackaging of previous Soviet demands for the withdrawal of Western troops from Berlin. Still, Khrushchev made it seem as if he really wished to keep talking. He did, in truth, but only to stall while he sent ships to Cuba. Far from aiming to expedite the present talks, he was marking time in anticipation of talks of a very different sort, when he and Kennedy would themselves meet again and settle the Berlin question on Khrushchev's terms.

As the time approached for the foreign ministers to meet in Geneva to sign an accord on Laos, Kennedy took personal action to see if the occasion might not also serve to forestall the impending crisis in Berlin. Assessing correctly that Khrushchev still did not think he would fight to protect the US position in Berlin, Kennedy asked to see Dobrynin alone at the White House on July 17 to underscore that defeat over Berlin was something he could never contemplate. On other matters, he suggested, he might be prepared "to press the Germans quite hard," but on the question of the presence of Allied troops he would not be moved. That day Kennedy also sent off a letter to Khrushchev in which, taking a page from Macmillan's argument at Bermuda, he maintained that as leaders in the nuclear age he and Khrushchev could not afford to be passive. The president made the case that at a time when mankind's very existence was threatened by the prospect of nuclear war, it was their joint duty to try to alter the course of history, and strive to resolve differences "rather than move step-by-step towards a major confrontation." Noting that when Rusk and Gromyko were in Geneva the following week for the signing of the Laos agreement they would undoubtedly have a chance to speak of Berlin, Kennedy urged Khrushchev to consider anew the US proposal of a modus vivendi, which though it did not purport to settle matters to either side's satisfaction would at least ease tensions. On arriving in the Oval Office that morning, Kennedy had had news of a plane-buzzing episode in the Berlin corridor. It was precisely the sort of small incident capable of flaring up into something major that the president was speaking of when he warned again of the peril of accidental war: "In reading the history of past wars and how they began, we cannot help but be impressed how frequently the failure of communication, misunderstanding and mutual irritation have played an important role in the events leading up to fateful decisions for war."

Kennedy would have to wait until Rusk saw Gromyko the following week before learning if his personal intervention had had any effect. In the meantime, the president invited Ormsby Gore to Hyannis Port for their last long talks before David returned to Britain for a vacation. Lem Billings would also be in residence with Jack and Jackie, and the astronaut John Glenn and his family would be Bobby's houseguests. Jack and David flew up together on Friday, July 20, the same day Rusk left for Geneva. Protesting that she did not wish to spend another summer in the fishbowl of the Kennedy compound, Jackie had persuaded Jack to accept the singer Morton Downey's offer of the use of a secluded property on nearby Squaw Island. She planned to pass July there, and then spend much of August with her sister in the Italian resort of Ravello.

On his arrival, Jack's first stop was to visit his father. No longer the energetic, provocative figure David had first known in the 1930s, the old man was a spectral presence, confined to a wheelchair and unable to speak. On at least one occasion in the course of the weekend he sat grimly to one side, perhaps listening, perhaps not, as Jack and David talked. In the days that followed, both indoors and on various family boats, Jack spoke to David of his need to turn his attentions to domestic politics as the mid-term congressional elections loomed in November. Eager to have a Congress more sympathetic to his policies, he planned to campaign vigorously for Democratic candidates and to launch a series of televised "fireside chats," inspired by Roosevelt's on the radio, to convey his ideas directly to voters. On Berlin and on nuclear testing, he wanted to do something "big," but congressional opposition limited his options. Macmillan had warned of an inevitable crisis if action were not taken to shift onto a path to détente, and Jack hoped by his personal appeal to Khrushchev to get at least a temporary agreement on Berlin good for two or three years. What neither he nor David knew that weekend as they awaited Khrushchev's response was that the *Maria Ulyanova*, named for Lenin's sister, the first of eighty-five ships carrying men and matériel, was headed for Cuba.

When Kennedy returned to Washington, he had disappointing news from Geneva. Despite his personal intervention the previous week, Rusk had made no headway with Gromyko on Berlin. Meanwhile, Khrushchev needed time and secrecy. On July 25, one day before the first vessel was due to reach Cuba, Khrushchev, drawing on his understanding of Kennedy's political susceptibilities, moved to trick the president into helping to further his plan. Conveying his message orally via Llewellyn Thompson in Moscow, and specifying that he wished it to be transmitted not to the State Department but directly to the president himself, Khrushchev asked whether it would be better for Kennedy for the Berlin question to be "brought to a head" before or after the congressional elections. Khrushchev indicated that he did not want to make things more difficult for the president; in fact, he would like to be of help. In the same conversation Khrushchev also spoke to Thompson of another pressing concern, his distress at the harassment of Soviet ships by American aircraft attempting to photograph their cargoes. Though he did not say so, Khrushchev was aware, on the basis of the May 9, 1961, back-channel message in advance of Vienna, that Kennedy was not above a secret deal with the enemy if it would cover him politically. That, in effect, was what he was proposing here. If Kennedy would stop buzzing his ships, Khrushchev would put off the Berlin crisis until after the congressional elections. Neither a permanent settlement nor the modus vivendi proposed by Kennedy in the interest of averting an imminent war, the arrangement would merely allow the president to face the midterm elections without fear of an international crisis during the campaign and without the need to make concessions that would leave him open to politically devastating charges of appeasement. Khrushchev's goal, of course, was to prevent US planes from photographing the ships en route to Cuba. Lest Kennedy fail to grasp what Khrushchev was asking of him, Bolshakov delivered a message protesting the harassment of Soviet vessels by American aircraft. As Khrushchev had reckoned, Kennedy proved eager to make a deal. He instructed his brother to bring Bolshakov to the Oval Office for an off-the-record meeting at the close of the working day on July 31. When Bobby produced the Soviet intelligence agent at a quarter to seven that evening, the president, who considered what he had to say so important that he insisted on communicating it himself, sent word to Khrushchev that he would indeed terminate the buzzing of Soviet ships—and that he would prefer the German problem to be put "on ice" till after the elections.

In the belief that he had a deal with Moscow, Kennedy assumed he could safely turn his attention to domestic politics. Hardly had he done so when there began to appear in the press mentions of a mysterious stream of ships heading for Cuba. On August 7, in a report cited in the next day's *New York Times*, a Spanish-language radio broadcast from Miami, basing its claims on information provided by travelers from Cuba, announced that more than four thousand Soviet troops had landed in July. Before long, rumors began to fly. While US officials expressed skepticism of claims of massive troop landings, Cuban exile leaders insisted that the ships were indeed delivering Soviet-bloc soldiers as part of a scheme to master South America, and that the United States ought to move at once "against the Communist invaders." By

August 20, Washington was willing to confirm the arrival of fifteen Russian vessels the previous month, but continued to scoff at reports of troop movements. Administration analysts suggested instead that the ships were carrying equipment and technical personnel to render agricultural, industrial and military assistance.

Kennedy had so far managed to stay out of the news coverage, but two days later a reporter at the president's press conference elicited a first comment. Asked whether he had any information about Soviet bloc troops or new supplies having landed in Cuba recently, Kennedy replied, "Yes, new supplies definitely, in large quantities. Troops? We do not have information, but an increased number of technicians." As to what it all meant, Kennedy would say only that he was examining the situation. An hour and a half later, McCone briefed the president on what was known about the Soviet shipments, and in essence the CIA chief knew little more than an ordinary citizen might have learned from the press. McCone reported that a large number of ships carrying men and matériel had come in to Cuba. Many of the ships had been unloaded in the dark of night in areas cleared of all Cubans. There had been numerous large cases, possibly containing missile parts or the fuselages of fighter planes. But nothing was certain, there having been no fresh reconnaissance information since August 5 due to poor weather conditions. They would have to wait for new U-2 flights in order to get a better idea of what was going on.

By the next day, Kennedy had a basic plan of action in place. On August 23, at his first big meeting with Rusk, McNamara, Bundy, McCone and other advisers about a possible new crisis over Cuba, the president, applying the lessons of the first volume of *The World Crisis*, outlined the steps he might have to take. First, on the model of Lloyd George, who during the Agadir crisis of 1911 prevented a catastrophe by issuing a firm, clear statement to the Germans of British intent, Kennedy asked that a draft statement be prepared to make it clear to Khrushchev that he would not tolerate offensive missiles in Cuba. In the event that the enemy did not really want war, such a statement, as Churchill had suggested, promised to avoid dangerous miscalculation. If the other side did seek war, however, Churchill believed that conflict might yet be averted by negotiations. Accordingly, the second step was to prepare a negotiating position, and on that principle the president asked to have a report on the possibility of offering to remove US missiles stationed in Turkey. Finally, according to Churchill, a leader must plan for war in the event negotiations fail, and to that end Kennedy directed the Joint Chiefs of Staff to draw up the appropriate military reports.

Meanwhile, until weather conditions improved, Kennedy could only speculate as to what he was actually dealing with in Cuba. While he waited, both for the U-2 flights and for the various papers he had demanded, his Republican adversaries seemed to have struck political gold. Leaping with glee on the president's remarks of August 22, Senator Homer Capehart, an old nemesis of Kennedy's, maintained that, contrary to the president's claim, the majority of the Russians shipped to Cuba in recent weeks were indeed combat troops and would soon be followed by more. In 1958, when Jack Kennedy, finding his voice as a presidential candidate, accused Eisenhower of ceding nuclear superiority, it had been Capehart who had argued that Kennedy, in saying so, had weakened the United States and provided comfort to the Russians. At the time, Senate Republicans had been aghast at the spectacle of a Democrat effectively casting himself as the authentic hardliner. Four years later, Capehart's insistence that Kennedy knew about the Soviet military buildup in Cuba and had prevaricated in his press conference had the tang of sweet revenge. Once Kennedy had excoriated a Republican administration for misleading voters and failing to act; now Capehart accused Kennedy of minimizing Soviet activity in Cuba. He called for an immediate US invasion of Cuba to halt the flow of Soviet troops and equipment.

The day Capehart's remarks appeared in newspapers Kennedy held another press conference. Asked about the charge that the Soviets were sending troops to Cuba, not technicians as he had stated the previous week, Kennedy fired back, "We've no evidence of troops." Confronted with the Indiana Republican's call for an invasion, Kennedy pointed to the potential impact on the Berlin situation and insisted that a strike on Cuba would be "a mistake." With no further knowledge of what Khrushchev was up to than he had had the week before, the best Kennedy could say on August 29 was that he was "continuing to watch" Cuba "with the closest attention" and would be "glad to announce any new information if it should come, immediately." It seemed there would soon be crucial new information. That day, the weather cleared and the first U-2 reconnaissance missions since August 5 flew over Cuba.

Two days later, on August 31, Kennedy was preparing to leave for Newport to spend the Labor Day weekend with Jackie and the children when he received the results. Exactly a year previously, on the eve of Labor Day weekend, he had been aghast to learn that Khrushchev intended to resume nuclear testing. This year the news was worse: Khrushchev was building missile sites in Cuba. Intelligence photography showed the construction of at least eight surface-to-air missile sites, which looked as if they might be operational in a week or two. In contrast to surface-to-surface missile sites, these were defensive rather than offensive in nature—but they were missile sites nonetheless. Kennedy instructed the CIA to put the information "back in the box and nail it tight." He did not want word to get out until he had had time to reflect, though he accepted that it was only a matter of time before the Republicans learned about the missile sites. On his departure he took with him the various papers and reports he had called for on August 23.

It was nearly seven in the evening when *Air Force One* touched down at Quonset Point Naval Air Station in Rhode Island. There the president was reunited with Jackie and Caroline, who had just completed a three-week holiday in Italy. Half an hour later, a helicopter transported the trio to Hammersmith Farm, where in his mother's absence young John had been cared for by his maternal grandmother and a nanny. In the days that followed, Jack Kennedy and his family swam at Bailey's Beach, cruised on the *Honey Fitz* and partook of other pleasures. He and his daughter took a side trip to Hyannis Port to visit Joe Kennedy, who waited on the porch in a wheelchair for their arrival. Outwardly it was a long holiday weekend like any other. But from first to last, the day loomed when Kennedy would have to respond to the discovery of the missile sites.

In part, Kennedy's deliberations focused on the enemy in Moscow, in part on his political adversaries in the United States. The missiles detected thus far were of the defensive type useful to the Communists solely to prevent the invasion Castro had been insisting was imminent. In the wake of the Bay of Pigs debacle Kennedy had authorized operations to provoke a revolution from within Cuba itself, but contrary to claims by the Cuban government no invasion by US forces was currently in the works. At a moment when Kennedy had been hoping for a period of calm to concentrate on efforts to avert a nuclear confrontation over Berlin, a US attack on Cuba would have been the last sort of thing to appeal to him. The defensive missiles—if indeed that was all that was there—were not in themselves a threat to the United States. Therefore, the problem for Kennedy was mainly political. As Bundy pointed out in one of the many reports the president scrutinized that weekend, any missile deployment whatever would strengthen critics of the administration's "softness" on Cuba. Such criticism could be mitigated by words and deeds, Bundy argued, but it could not be prevented altogether so long as the missiles remained.

Kennedy saw a further difficulty. Though the Republicans possessed no hard evidence, such as the president already had in hand, they strongly suspected Khrushchev of building missile bases. That weekend, Senator Kenneth Keating of New York, attacking the White House's "do-nothing" attitude toward Soviet activity in Cuba, demanded an inter-American mission to search for missile bases. Senator Capehart had previously accused the president of misleading the American people about Cuba. The fact that Kennedy had not known about the missile bases at the time of his press conferences would seem irrelevant when, inevitably, their presence was revealed and Republican claims vindicated. Eager to minimize the damage, Kennedy decided to put out the news before Republicans could beat him to it. As he said at a White House meeting on Tuesday, September 4, "We can't permit somebody to break this story before we do." During the presidential campaign Kennedy had compared himself to the man who warned Britain about Hitler; now he did not wish to appear the sort of leader content to tell people all was well while Republicans, Churchill-like, pointed to the dangers that must be faced. Kennedy released a public statement announcing the discovery within the past four days of evidence that the Soviets had provided the Cuban government with anti-aircraft defense missiles. At the same time, he pointed out that there were no indications that the Cubans had "significant offensive capability." "Were it to be otherwise," he added pointedly, "the gravest issues would arise." He pledged that the United States would employ "whatever means may be necessary" to prevent aggression issuing from Cuba. That last was a warning to Khrushchev not to miscalculate in Cuba, not to proceed on the assumption that the United States would back off from a fight.

By way of response, Dobrynin told Bobby Kennedy and Theodore Sorensen, in separate meetings, that the missiles in Cuba were strictly defensive. On September 6, Khrushchev himself sent an identical message to the president via US Secretary of the Interior Stewart Udall, who was then on a visit to the Soviet Union. But those assurances were made in private. On September 11, the Soviet news agency TASS made the declaration public. For a time, CIA analysts suspected that a surface-to-surface missile site might be under construction after all, but two days after the TASS statement further photographic analysis determined that, in line with Soviet claims, the missile site did appear to be exclusively defensive. Moscow's assurances, coupled with the most recent CIA analysis as well as the absence, noted by Kennedy's Soviet specialists, of any historical precedent for the Soviets placing missiles outside their own territory, led the president to conclude that in all probability the missile sites were indeed for defense only. At a press conference on September 13, Kennedy, mindful that Republicans had decided to make the military buildup in Cuba a major issue in the midterm elections, took pains to diminish the frenzy. At a time when Republicans were sounding alarms about Cuba, Kennedy, in the belief that his remarks were consistent with the facts, emphatically downplayed the danger. "I will repeat the conclusion that I reported last week: that these new shipments do not constitute a serious threat to any other part of this hemisphere." Taking aim at his political critics, he declared, "Rash talk is cheap, particularly on the part of those who do not have the responsibility." Yet even as he undertook to calm the nerves of the American people, Kennedy reiterated his warning of September 4, stressing that if the Soviet buildup should pose a threat to the United States he would take all necessary steps to safeguard the nation's security.

The president, accompanied by David and Sissie Ormsby Gore, left for Newport the following day believing he had done what he could to resolve the Cuban situation, at least for the time being. Contrary to claims that day by Barry Goldwater that Kennedy had "virtually promised" the Communists not to take action to remove the Soviet military threat in Cuba, the president had in fact issued firm, clear warnings that were Cuba to become an offensive military base for the Soviet Union Khrushchev could expect him to take strong action. Plainly differentiating between defensive and offensive military capacity, Kennedy had drawn what seemed to him a clear line in the sand, and as of September 14, he really did not expect that there would be a major East–West confrontation over Cuba anytime soon.

He did, however, privately fear that the crisis Macmillan had warned of at Bermuda was indeed imminent over Berlin. That weekend he discussed his fears with Ormsby Gore. In June, Khrushchev had sent word via Llewellyn Thompson seemingly offering to defer the Berlin question until after the November elections. Since that time, Khrushchev's rhetoric about Berlin had hardened. Along with his claims of having placed only defensive weaponry in Cuba, Stewart Udall had reported Khrushchev's promise to create a situation that would force Kennedy to come to terms on Berlin under threat of a war which Khrushchev was convinced he did not have the stomach to fight. Kennedy worried desperately that a Soviet effort to block Western access or even to seize West Berlin would almost certainly occur soon after the midterm elections—and that the confrontation thereby provoked might lead to nuclear war.

When Kennedy arrived with the Ormsby Gores, Newport was crowded with visitors gathered for the opening of the America's Cup international yacht races the next day. On Friday evening, Jack and Jackie, with their houseguests David and Sissie, attended a dinner party for three hundred hosted by Australian ambassador Sir Howard Beale in the vast marble and gilt dining room of the rococo mansion known as The Breakers. On Saturday morning, the *Honey Fitz* collected the two couples, along with Jackie's mother and stepfather, at the dock at Hammersmith Farm and transported them to the base where the destroyer USS *Joseph P. Kennedy Jr.* waited. The Kennedy party transferred to the destroyer and, as military planes flew overhead, the ship named for the young Kennedy killed in the Second World War traveled fourteen miles to the site of the first race.

To watch Jack Kennedy, smiling and ebullient, attired in gray flannels and blue yachting blazer, the polished metal of his coat buttons gleaming in the sunlight, one would hardly have guessed he was a man contemplating the possibility of another world war. Then and at other times that

weekend he appeared utterly devoted to the pleasures of the moment—
the races, the glamorous parties in great houses, the laughter and lighthearted conversation with friends. But there were also times when Jack
broke away to talk in private with David, and then his smile would fade
and his mood turn somber. He spoke of Khrushchev's intention to come
to New York in November after the elections to announce his terms for
settling the German question, and he noted that lately the Soviet leader
had boasted to several Western visitors that he could do whatever he liked
in Berlin without fear of a fight. He showed David a report received that
very day in which Khrushchev, in a last interview with the departing
German ambassador Hans Kroll, confidently proclaimed that the
Western allies would never go to war over Berlin, insisting that he knew
all about the NATO contingency plans for countermeasures and that
they did not worry him in the least. Jack called Khrushchev's complacency "dangerous" and "disturbing." He knew he had to find some way
to impress on Khrushchev the certainty that, if provoked in Berlin, the
United States would fight. Still, he had yet to decide quite "how to play
the hand" when the crisis came, as he felt certain it would. That was
something he would continue to ponder in the days that followed.
Meanwhile, both men savored the festive atmosphere that weekend
much as they had the last London Season before the war, the difference
being that they alone among the revelers in Newport shared an acute
sense of the possibility that this world of wealth, power and privilege
might soon vanish in the devastation to come.

Back in Washington, on September 28, a letter arrived from Khrushchev that seemed to confirm the president's fears of a November crisis. Explicitly echoing Kennedy's back-channel message, Khrushchev
promised to put the German problem "on ice" until after the midterm
congressional elections. "After the elections," Khrushchev continued,
"apparently in the second half of November, it would be necessary in
our opinion to continue the dialogue. Of great importance for finding
the ways to solve both this problem and other pressing international
problems are personal contacts of statesmen on the highest level." The
day after receiving the letter, Kennedy, in an effort to probe the enigma
of Khrushchev's actions, conferred with the Soviet specialists Llewellyn
Thompson—who had been brought back to Washington to serve as a
general adviser to the president on Soviet affairs, under the title

Ambassador at Large—and Charles Bohlen. What, Kennedy wanted to know, could Khrushchev's motive be for repeatedly announcing that the Americans would not fight? Why was Khrushchev pressing so hard in Cuba? Did Khrushchev not understand that the Cuban situation would make it politically more difficult for Kennedy to deal on Berlin? Khrushchev's letter focused Kennedy on puzzling out a connection between Cuba and Berlin. By Sunday, September 30, when he met over lunch at the White House with Ormsby Gore, Home, Rusk and US ambassador to Britain David Bruce, Kennedy thought he finally knew why Khrushchev, contrary to his claims, was deliberately causing trouble before the election. It seemed to Kennedy that Khrushchev had predicted the massive pressure now being brought to bear on the administration to intervene in Cuba, and that the outcry by Republicans had been part of his calculations. At Sunday lunch, Kennedy voiced suspicion that Khrushchev was trying to goad him to invade Cuba, thus giving the Soviets a pretext to seize West Berlin.

The lunch took place against the backdrop of a violent civil rights crisis, where federal troops were required to make it possible for James Meredith, a black veteran of nine years in the Air Force, to register at the University of Mississippi. Kennedy's meeting with Home, who was in the United States for the opening of the UN General Assembly, had originally been scheduled to take place at Hammersmith Farm, but in light of the unfolding crisis in Mississippi, in which two people would be killed and many wounded, the president had decided to return to the White House. There he spoke to Home and the others of Khrushchev's plan to come to New York after the elections, and he suggested that he might refuse to meet with him. Rusk and Home in turn proposed that there might be some advantage to asking for another deputy foreign ministers' meeting, which would offer Khrushchev a new excuse to put off signing a treaty with the East Germans. Kennedy dismissed the idea. Pointing out that the military balance was more favorable to the West at present than it was likely to be in the future, Kennedy suggested that it might actually "be better to allow a confrontation to develop over Berlin now rather than later." Two days previously at the UN, Home had tried to impress on Gromyko that unless the Berlin problem was handled "with extreme caution" it might lead to war and that the Russians must not miscalculate about the West's willingness to fight. Having done what he could to caution and restrain Khrushchev, Home was disturbed to hear Kennedy so rashly express the opinion that it might be best for their side to have an immediate confrontation. But as Ormsby Gore, who knew him better, understood, Kennedy was still deciding "how to play the hand." Nothing had been settled in his mind, and his remarks at lunch were merely by way of considering all the possibilities.

As the elections drew near, Kennedy planned to spend weekends campaigning for Democratic candidates. McCone was insisting that, contrary to what others in the administration might think, the Soviets were indeed preparing or already installing offensive missiles in Cuba, and he requested further U-2 flights over a part of the island last photographed in August. Kennedy was wary. The previous month Moscow had protested when a U-2 flight strayed into Soviet territory, and Kennedy had apologized to Khrushchev, precisely as he had urged Eisenhower to do during the Paris summit. The United States had discontinued such flights over Soviet territory after the 1960 incident, which had drastically diminished voter confidence in Eisenhower and provided an invaluable opening to the Kennedy campaign. On the eve of the 1962 midterm elections, Kennedy feared that a U-2 episode over Cuba could do to him what the earlier incident had done to his predecessor. Nonetheless, on October 9, prodded by McCone, Kennedy reluctantly agreed to further reconnaissance. The next day, McCone showed the president intelligence photographs of crates en route to Cuba likely to contain medium-range bombers. Kennedy asked that the images be withheld until after the election, claiming that were his political adversaries to obtain them, his independence of action would be limited. When McCone said the pictures could no longer be restricted as they had already been released to the intelligence community and were set for publication in the CIA Bulletin later in the week, Kennedy, to the CIA chief's chagrin, asked that any additional information of the sort be suppressed. In the meantime, due to the weather, the flight approved on the 9th did not take place until Sunday, October 14.

On the morning of October 16, the president, in dressing gown and pajamas, lay in bed propped up against pillows as he brooded about press accounts of disparaging comments by Eisenhower. The former president had compared Kennedy's foreign-policy record unfavorably to that of his own administration, during which no "threatening foreign bases" had been established. Kennedy had spent the past two weekends campaigning and was due to go out again in three days' time; he was about to sound off on Eisenhower when Bundy announced that the United States had obtained hard photographic evidence that the Soviets had offensive missiles in Cuba. "He can't do that to me!" Kennedy exclaimed, the focus of his anger abruptly shifting to Khrushchev. He had assured the American people that the shipments to Cuba did not pose a serious threat, and he saw at once the potential impact on his own political fortunes and on those of his adversaries. That morning, he ruefully told Kenny O'Donnell that the reelection of Capehart in Indiana was assured and that Keating would probably be the next president.

Kennedy was furious that Khrushchev had lied again. The offensive missiles in Cuba were, in his view, the most direct challenge by the Soviets since Stalin launched the Berlin blockade in 1948. When the initial shock wore off, the fact remained that Kennedy had been fully anticipating a crisis, though he had expected it to come after the elections and in Berlin, not Cuba. At length, the president, adjusting his sense of the link between Berlin and Cuba, saw that Khrushchev had expected to complete the shipments by the time he arrived in New York in the second half of November, when he planned to confront Kennedy with the missiles' existence ninety miles from US shores and use them to demand major concessions over Berlin. Meanwhile, the Americans' discovery had drastically upset Khrushchev's timetable, though for the moment only Kennedy knew it. That, he perceived, was a distinct advantage. Also in Kennedy's favor were the many hours he had devoted to deciding on an appropriate response should Khrushchev finally move to cut off Western access or seize West Berlin outright. Kennedy, who tended to be at his best when coolly detached and at his worst when excitable and impetuous, benefited greatly from having already blown off a good deal of steam in expectation of a November crisis. In that sense, Khrushchev, with his threats and taunts, had done him a favor. Still, no amount of preparation, psychological or otherwise, could diminish Kennedy's horror that the crisis was actually upon him, the moment Macmillan had pleaded with such feeling that they must risk everything, even their own power, to avoid.

Like Khrushchev when he launched his plan to force a confrontation at the edge of the precipice, now it was Kennedy who needed time and secrecy. Whatever he might decide in the next few days, he aimed both to preserve the element of surprise to the Soviets and to avoid domestic political pressure on himself at a moment when Republicans were calling Cuba a "symbol of the tragic irresolution of the Administration" and insisting that their candidates would "offer the alternative of a resolute foreign policy." It would be nearly a week before the existence of the missiles became public knowledge, during which time Kennedy held intense secret meetings with the Executive Committee of the National Security Council (Ex Comm) devoted to the missile crisis. He talked face to face with Gromyko, who continued to lie brazenly. And he maintained a busy campaign schedule of travel and speaking engagements, lest suspicion arise that something was wrong.

On Saturday, October 20, the president was in Chicago when he received word from Bobby Kennedy that his advisers were ready to present their positions as to whether to launch an air strike to take out the missiles or settle for the milder remedy of a blockade to prevent additional men and matériel from coming in. Cutting short his trip on the pretext that he had developed a cold, Jack called Jackie at Glen Ora to ask that she and the children go to the White House immediately. He wanted them nearby when he made the "terrible" choices that faced him. On his return, Kennedy decided on a blockade. He would address the nation on Monday to explain what the Soviets had been up to in Cuba and to announce his response. In the meantime US forces would gather in the course of a week in case it became necessary to invade. On Sunday morning, the president called to ask Ormsby Gore to "come unseen" to the White House shortly before lunch. He was in a meeting in the Yellow Oval Room when his friend arrived, and it was half past twelve before he was ready for him.

When David entered and closed the door, they had a long talk utterly unlike any in their association to date. This was without question the most difficult moment of Jack's life. One wrong move and he could set off a nuclear exchange that might end in annihilation for all. Not surprisingly he sought, as in the past, to review his reasoning process with David. First, he explained that David would be the first person outside the US government to be informed of what was happening. Reconnaissance flights over Cuba had shown that the Soviets were putting in two types of offensive missiles, one with a range of 2,000 miles, the other of 1,500. In addition to between thirty and forty missiles already on the island, more were en route. Jack said he had to assume the missiles would be equipped with nuclear warheads. He did not yet know whether the warheads had arrived, but he could say with certainty that underground storage facilities had been constructed. In his clear public statement on September 13, he had declared that if Cuba became an offensive military base of significant capacity for the Soviets the United States would have to take steps to protect its own security and that of its allies. His straightforward differentiation between defensive and offensive capacity had constituted an unambiguous warning of where he intended to draw the line, and, he continued, in light of the reconnaissance photographs, he would now have to act.

He told David that he and his advisers saw two alternatives. On Monday morning, the United States could launch an all-out air strike on the missile sites. This, he had been informed by his generals, would eliminate at least half the Cuban missile potential, but it would also kill many Russians and Cubans and leave open the possibility of a return strike on the United States with the missiles that remained. The air strike would be followed by a blockade of Cuba to keep additional men and matériel out. The second alternative was simply to impose a blockade without an air strike first. Though this would mean leaving Cuba's present offensive capacity to be dealt with later, it would display US determination not to permit the military buildup to continue. After laying out the options, Jack, without disclosing the decision he had already taken, asked which of them David thought best.

David saw serious drawbacks to an air strike. He argued that very few people outside the United States would regard the Cuban government's provocation as grave enough to merit an attack, and that such an action would damage the United States politically around the world. David also worried that an air strike on Cuba might embolden the Soviets to move against Berlin. Therefore, of the two alternatives put to him he would favor the second, though even a blockade, he warned, might spur the Soviets to act in Berlin. Jack confirmed that he too favored a blockade, and admitted a grudging admiration for the Soviets' strategy. If he reacted violently to their challenge in Cuba, he would be giving Khrushchev a pretext to seize West Berlin; if he did nothing, he would communicate to the Latin Americans and other US allies a lack of will to resist the encroachments of Communism.

Jack made it clear that he hoped the crisis would be resolved "through negotiations and discussions" to get the missiles out. He said that he was considering trading US missiles in Turkey for the removal of Soviet missiles in Cuba; though he was uncertain he would be able to do so politically, he saw no military reasons not to make the offer. In the meantime, while there had been some thought of attempting to open talks at once, Jack had concluded that a blockade would permit him to establish a position of strength from which to negotiate. When those negotiations took place, he explained, he expected them to reach well beyond the current crisis, to include—in addition to Cuba—Berlin, foreign bases, disarmament and other matters of East–West dispute. Confronted with offensive missiles in Cuba and with the possibility of something going disastrously wrong when he moved to get them out, Jack reflected that the existence of nuclear weapons made "a secure and rational world" impossible. Speaking with a frankness that deeply unsettled David, Jack said they had somehow to find a means of getting rid of all such weapons. David knew that the display of emotion was anathema to his friend; he perceived in these remarks the germ of a new emotional commitment to ideas that Jack had long accepted intellectually.

The discussion lasted about an hour, after which David had lunch in the family quarters with Jack and Jackie and promised to return that evening with Sissie. It would be the last night before Jack addressed the American people, and he used the occasion of dinner with the Ormsby Gores—just the four of them—to run through his reasoning yet again. There was no telling how Khrushchev would react to the news that the secret had been discovered before he had completed his shipments to Cuba, and the idea haunted Jack that the Soviet leader would respond with an assault on the United States. Jack confessed to David that he did not, could not know whether his choice of a blockade was the right one. Perhaps he should have approved an air strike; perhaps he should do nothing at all. For now, he lived with an excruciating sense of uncertainty.

The next day, before he went on the air at 7 p.m., Kennedy endured a tense session with the congressional leadership. He had previously assured them that the Soviet shipments posed no serious threat, and now his plan for a blockade struck some legislators, Democrats prominent among them, as too weak a response. In light of new warnings from Moscow that if the United States tried to stop their ships it would mean war, Kennedy told the congressional leaders that the United States might find itself at war within twenty-four hours. If, as feared, the Russians moved to "grab" Berlin, the present intention was "to fire our nuclear weapons at them."

Speaking to the American people from his desk in the Oval Office, Kennedy detailed the discovery of the offensive missile sites in Cuba and catalogued Soviet lies, from the public statement on September 11 to Gromyko's assurances the previous Thursday that the armaments shipped to Cuba were solely for defense. At the heart of Kennedy's speech, once again, was his use of Britain's mistakes with Hitler in the 1930s as a guideline for present action. "The 1930s taught us a clear lesson. Aggressive conduct, if allowed to grow unchecked and unchallenged, ultimately leads to war." He announced his plan to block the further shipment of weapons to Cuba. All vessels would be halted and, if found to carry offensive military equipment, they would be turned back. Kennedy stressed that he would view any nuclear missile launched from Cuba against any nation in the western hemisphere as a Soviet assault on the United States, necessitating a full retaliatory response upon the Soviet Union. He called for the prompt dismantling and withdrawal of all offensive weapons in Cuba under the supervision of UN observers, and he vowed to act should the Soviets move against West Berlin or other US allies around the world.

The danger that Macmillan had warned of at Bermuda almost a year earlier had come to pass: East and West were face to face with their nuclear bombs, and mankind was at risk of being destroyed. It was thus hardly surprising that Kennedy would regularly phone the prime minister throughout the crisis to talk through the situation and seek his advice. Immediately following his broadcast that night, Kennedy made a call to Macmillan, whom he had informed of his intentions by secure Teletype the previous day. In this first talk, Kennedy explained his purpose in moving to stop Khrushchev before he had all the missiles in place in time to "squeeze" the American government on Berlin in November. He said that were he to allow the military buildup to continue, the Russians would soon double the number of missiles they were able to bring to bear upon the United States. Worse, those missiles, coming as they would from the south, had the capacity to overcome the inadequate warning systems the United States currently had in place, and Kennedy worried that that would permit Moscow "to face us with such a dangerous situation over Berlin that we would have to quit." He therefore felt compelled to act at once, though he stressed that his actions would be tempered by awareness that anything he did might set off a nuclear war—thus the decision to go with a blockade rather than an air strike. Macmillan, assuming a role first consciously played at Bermuda, offered the words of comfort the president in his lonely solitude seemed to crave, and which Joe Kennedy was no longer in a position to provide. But no kindness could unburden the president of his sense that the actions he had just taken might have catastrophic consequences should Khrushchev, who at Vienna had struck him as weirdly unconcerned about the threat of nuclear war, respond irrationally.

"I think it was very significant that we were here this morning," Dean Rusk remarked at an Ex-Comm meeting the following day, Tuesday, October 23. "We've passed the one contingency: an immediate, sudden, irrational strike." Though Khrushchev, who had also had a letter from the president warning him not to miscalculate, now knew that his lies had been uncovered, the blockade itself would not go into effect until Wednesday. "So," said Kennedy, "I think we're going to have all our troubles tomorrow morning." In the meantime, the president, who, along with Jackie and the children and various essential members of government had access to an underground shelter in a Virginia mountain, asked what could be done to protect the many Americans within reach of the Soviet missiles already in Cuba. Especially in the event that US forces went on to invade Cuba, Kennedy worried desperately about the Russians firing off even one missile against the United States. Assistant Secretary of Defense for Civil Defense Steuart Pittman informed the president that 92 million people in fifty-eight cities would be affected. Desperate to find some way to protect the people, Kennedy asked if the government might evacuate them to rural areas prior to launching an invasion. Pittman replied that evacuation might make sense if the authorities could be certain the Soviet response would not be nuclear. People would find little or no protection from nuclear fallout in the country and

would be better off in the city. At this point, substantial measures to prepare the population for an attack ran the risk of creating mass panic. The
president had to face the chilling fact that, in McCone's words, "not very
much could or would be done" for the Americans within range of the
missiles. For all the nation's vast power, there was little Kennedy could do
to guard 92 million people against a course of events he himself had set in
motion by intervening to halt the Soviet military buildup in Cuba.

Presently he left the Cabinet Room en route to the Oval Office,
where he was to be photographed as he signed the formal quarantine
proclamation. The responsibility for all those lives weighed heavily on
him, and afterward, alone with his brother, he struggled to reassure
himself that he had had no choice but to act as he had. "How does it
look?" Bobby asked. "Ah, looks like hell—looks real mean, doesn't it?"
Jack replied. "But, on the other hand, there is no other choice. If they
get this mean on this one, it's just a question of where they go about it
next. No choice. I don't think there was a choice." This was the lesson
of the 1930s evoked in the president's speech the night before. A young
Jack Kennedy had himself witnessed the refusal to stop Hitler that,
inevitably, had led to war.

At half past seven he went up to the family quarters, where he and
the First Lady were to preside over a dinner arranged some time previously. There he found some of the very people he had known on the
eve of the Second World War, when Hitler's bombs were about to rain
on London and when Baldwin's warning that the bomber would
"always get through" was on many minds. Jack himself had invited the
Ormsby Gores, the Devonshires and Jakie Astor and his wife before he
had any inkling of the particular crisis that was now upon him. He
had first known them all as young people wildly in love with life even
as they acknowledged that a dictator's bombs and bullets might soon
snatch their lives away. In those days, he and David had seemed the
least promising young men in their group; and it was not lost on Jakie
Astor that those same two fellows went off together after dinner to
strategize in advance of the imminent confrontation—the first
attempt to halt a Soviet ship—which they all feared might be the prelude to nuclear holocaust.

As they talked on, Jack agreed to David's proposal that the line of
interception be moved closer to Cuba in order to delay the confronta-

tion and give Khrushchev the maximum time to consider. As would become clear when Bobby joined them at a quarter past ten, David was also concerned that nothing be done to encourage their adversary to underestimate US resolve. At the president's direction, Bobby had been to see Dobrynin in the hope that he might start the process of a negotiated settlement. David understood why Jack had sent Bobby to the Soviet ambassador, and he worried that Jack, whom he knew to be passionately concerned about the many lives in his hands and whose own adored children were asleep just down the hall, might be too eager for any deal that would avert a war. In the aftermath of the Bay of Pigs debacle, the president, by indicating a willingness to make deep concessions in order to secure an agreement at Vienna, had committed the fatal error of allowing Khrushchev to see him sweat. David, like Jack a student of Munich, reminded him that any attempt at negotiation that left Khrushchev with the impression that he was prepared to make unilateral concessions would be "disastrous."

The quarantine was set to go into effect at 10 a.m. on Wednesday, October 24, and no one knew quite how the Soviets would react when US forces intercepted and boarded their ships. The moment of confrontation seemed to draw near as two vessels, menacingly accompanied by submarines, approached the quarantine zone. Then, suddenly, McCone burst in to an Ex-Comm meeting with the news that the ships had either stopped or reversed direction. No one as yet knew what it meant, but Rusk whispered to Bundy that he believed the Soviets had just blinked. As the day wore on, however, it seemed that Khrushchev had not in fact retreated from a faceoff; rather, he had merely turned back ships carrying missiles and military equipment that he did not wish to fall into enemy hands. Khrushchev fired off a letter to accuse the United States of "pushing mankind toward the abyss of a world-missile nuclear war" and to vow that he would order the captains of Soviet vessels bound for Cuba not to heed the instructions of American naval forces blockading the island. In short, he was directing his ships to run the blockade.

Under-Secretary of State George Ball told Kennedy that Khrushchev left them no choice but to put the matter to the test when a Soviet tanker reached the quarantine zone in the morning. "There is not much time," the president said, his anguish visible. ". . . The time is so short." The man who in 1939 had told Lem Billings that the Germans had gone so far with their Danzig propaganda that it was "hard to see them backing down" now searched for a way to permit Khrushchev to back down without sacrificing his dignity before the world. In the belief that nothing he said at this point would influence Khrushchev, Kennedy hit on the idea of asking UN Secretary-General U Thant to intervene in such a way as to give the Soviets "enough of an out to stop their shipments without looking like they completely crawled down." Thant, awakened in the night, agreed to convey to the Soviets that if they would consent to halt their shipments for the time being, the United States wanted to talk. "Otherwise," Kennedy said sadly at the close of a late-night phone conversation with Ball, "we just have to go with this thing."

On Thursday morning the United States intercepted a Soviet oil tanker, the *Bucharest*, bound for Cuba, but it was allowed to proceed in the interest of doing nothing to impede U Thant's efforts. As Kennedy told Macmillan when they spoke on the phone, he did not want to sink a Soviet vessel at a time when Thant had just made a diplomatic appeal to Moscow. Still, Khrushchev's ships kept coming, and "sooner or later," Kennedy said, "probably by tomorrow evening, we'll have to accost one of these and board it." On Friday morning, the USS *Joseph P. Kennedy Jr.* and a second destroyer stopped a Lebanese freighter under Soviet charter, the *Marucla*. The ship's Greek crew offered no resistance, and the first instance of boarding and inspecting a vessel was peacefully accomplished. Later that morning Khrushchev sent word that, in accordance with the Secretary General's appeal, he had ordered the masters of Soviet ships headed to Cuba but not yet within reach of the Americans' "piratical activities" to remain outside the interception area. That was splendid news, but as Kennedy saw he would need a clear agreement by the Soviets and Cubans to allow UN verification of a halt to work on the missile sites while talks progressed. Verification had long been a sticking point with Moscow, but the president could not afford to allow Khrushchev to fool him again by using the interlude to finish erecting missile sites in Cuba.

These and related considerations were still in play when, on Friday evening, word arrived that appeared to change everything. Khrushchev offered to remove his missiles from Cuba if the United States would pledge not to invade and to restrain others—presumably Cuban refugees—from doing so. In the absence of any threat to Cuba,

Khrushchev declared, the armaments would not be necessary. The previous evening Kennedy had been at pains to permit Khrushchev to withdraw without undue loss of face. Khrushchev accomplished that very nicely for himself in his letter of October 26; rather than admit that the military buildup had anything to do with Berlin, he made it seem as if his sole concern had been to defend Cuba against the threat of a US attack. Kennedy took the letter as a hopeful sign that Khrushchev had begun to back away from the edge of the precipice to which he had endeavored to drag both powers.

The following morning, Khrushchev publicly released a second letter offering to remove the missiles if Kennedy, in addition to pledging not to invade Cuba, also withdrew US missiles from Turkey. Khrushchev's decision to alter his terms provoked consternation at the White House and caused Defense Secretary Robert McNamara to question whether it was possible to negotiate with the man at all. "How," he asked, "can we negotiate with somebody who changes his deal before we even get a chance to reply, and announces publicly his deal before we receive it?" Kennedy for his part remained remarkably unruffled by Khrushchev's behavior. Half an hour after the White House learned of the second letter, David Ormsby Gore, who had been summoned to the Oval Office along with Andrew and Debo Devonshire, arrived to find the president "completely relaxed." Andrew, recently promoted to minister of state, was struck by the fact that Jack showed no sign of the tension that surrounded him at this moment of supreme crisis.

His air of serenity was a good indication, and as the day progressed it became evident that he knew exactly what he wanted and was determined to achieve it. He had previously told David that he hoped to get the missiles out through negotiations, and events on Saturday, October 27, strongly confirmed him in that objective. That day there occurred two incidents of the sort he feared could lead to accidental war. The first involved a U-2 straying into Soviet air space near the Chukotka peninsula. In the second incident, a U-2 was shot down over Cuba and its pilot killed. With the Joint Chiefs calling for an invasion and with US forces now in place in the southeastern United States in readiness for an attack, the president knew he had better get a deal before the momentum toward war raced out of control.

Unlike those of his advisers who disdained the idea of sacrificing the

Turkish missiles, he had first considered a swap on August 23, but he had worried that it might prove politically impossible. Judging that to be the case, Kennedy concluded that he could not publicly agree to the proposal in Khrushchev's second letter. From a military point of view, submarine-based Polaris missiles in the Mediterranean rendered the the Jupiter missiles in Turkey superfluous; still, in an atmosphere of crisis, to give in on the Jupiter missiles, however unnecessary to US or for that matter Turkish security, might play to American voters as a Munich-like betrayal of an ally. Kennedy's tactic was simply to pretend that Khrushchev's second letter—the one with the demand about the Jupiter missiles—did not exist. The president's own letter of October 27, in which he accepted Khrushchev's earlier offer to remove the missiles in exchange for a promise not to invade, became in effect the public face of the settlement of the Cuban missile crisis. Privately, he assigned his brother to convey to Dobrynin what could not be put in writing lest it provoke catcalls of appeasement.

Bobby Kennedy saw the Soviet ambassador that evening at the Justice Department. Speaking with the authority conferred by the massive buildup of US troops now ready to invade, the attorney general argued that time was running out and that the two sides in the conflict had better not lose their chance to avert a nuclear war in which millions of Russians and Americans would die. He warned that because of the downed U-2 plane, the president was under intense pressure to give orders to respond with fire if fired upon, which might provoke a "chain reaction" that could be very hard to stop. The White House would have to make "certain decisions" within the next twelve or possibly twenty-four hours—hence the urgency that the Soviets agree to dismantle the missile bases and remove all offensive weapons from Cuba in exchange for a pledge not to permit an invasion from US soil.

"What about Turkey?" Dobrynin interjected.

Once again, as he had on May 9, 1961, Bobby Kennedy carried out his brother's instructions and proposed a deal that would allow the president to do in secret what he feared to do in public. As before, the clandestine nature of the offer afforded Kennedy the political cover to make concessions he judged many voters would find intolerable. Bobby said that while the president could neither agree openly to a swap nor declare his intentions in writing, he was prepared to remove the Jupiter missiles in four or five months' time. The attorney general insisted that his remarks on the elimination of the missiles in Turkey were "extremely confidential" and that there must be no expectation that the president would ever comment publicly. If the Soviets spoke of the arrangement to others, President Kennedy would simply deny that it had ever happened and the deal would be off. Shortly thereafter, Khrushchev announced plans to withdraw the missiles in exchange for a pledge not to invade Cuba.

Kennedy, having mounted a blockade and gathered US forces in the event it were necessary to attack, had negotiated from a position of strength, precisely as he had long said a leader should. But because the trading that ended the standoff was done in secret, the public had the impression that something entirely different had occurred. The version of events put out to the world was the reverse of the truth. To all appearances, Kennedy, by standing his ground and declining to concede any point, had forced the removal of the missiles. In fact, the president had ended the crisis by negotiation, but in the interest of protecting himself politically he let people think he had won by a refusal to negotiate. Though Kennedy's political adversaries questioned whether Khrushchev would be true to his word, and though the president, having been lied to in the past, had reason to wonder himself, there was public rejoicing at the triumphant resolution of the crisis. Kennedy's handling of the stand-off, assessed Ormsby Gore of that part of the story which people saw at the time, "caught the mood of the public and the Russian back-down confirmed the average man's view that toughness rather than talk is the proper way for America to do business with Russia."

How often had the president been derided as soft; how often had he been tagged an appeaser. On the eve of the midterm congressional elections, Kennedy, to borrow a phrase from his Harvard thesis, had managed brilliantly to recast himself in "the form most pleasing to his audience." As he was soon to discover, the transformation, though useful in the short term, would come at great cost.

CHAPTER EIGHTEEN

Before It Is Too Late

J ACK KENNEDY HAD FACED THE ULTIMATE CONFRONTATION Macmillan had warned of at Bermuda. He had felt the full weight of his own personal responsibility for many millions of lives. He had learned what it was like to feel that time was running out before the clash that set off a nuclear war. In the past he had spoken eloquently of how all-annihilating weapons had made the world a different place and of how humanity must be prevented from destroying itself, but during the Cuban missile crisis he had had a direct and overwhelming emotional experience of matters he had previously grasped solely in intellectual terms. The president had gone to bed each night of the crisis a few feet from where his son and daughter slept, and he had come to see the world's first nuclear confrontation "in terms of children, his children and everybody else's children," Ormsby Gore would recall. "And that's where his passion came in, that's when his emotion came in."

The terrifying thirteen days in October lent a new sense of urgency to the strategy of peace. But the ordeal also made it considerably harder to sell the American people on the wisdom of efforts to improve relations with the Soviet Union. Moscow's lies, enumerated by Kennedy himself in his October 22 speech, confirmed the widely-held belief that the Soviets could not be trusted. And the misconception, strongly encouraged by Kennedy, that he had triumphed by standing tough and refusing to negotiate did much to bolster many Americans' preference for a policy of confrontation and to confuse people about the vital distinction between negotiation and appeasement. The White House went so far as to put out a story that the president had avoided another Munich by his refusal to consider trading missiles in Turkey for those in Cuba. Kennedy emerged from the crisis more popular than ever, admired not because he had proceeded in accordance with the beliefs with which he had come to office—notably the double-barreled policy of strength coupled with negotiation—but because he seemed by an act of nerve to have forced Khrushchev to back down. The president knew that in fact he had ended the faceoff by negotiation, and he knew that there had been no trace of appeasement in his decision to sacrifice the Turkish missiles; he also knew that as the midterm elections loomed and as he himself prepared to gear up for the 1964 presidential campaign, the public's good opinion was a precious asset. Indeed, when voters went to the polls on November 6, 1962, the results were better than any incumbent administration had enjoyed since 1934. Understandably, Kennedy was eager not to lose that popularity before he ran for reelection.

Further complicating Kennedy's actions in the wake of the missile crisis was the fact that though he had come to believe more than ever that East and West must find a way to détente, he was also troubled more than ever by doubts as to whether it was possible to make effective agreements with the Soviets. Khrushchev had lied at Vienna about nuclear tests, and he had lied again about the missiles in Cuba. Kennedy, who had complained privately in the past of the complete distrust of the Soviets inculcated in the people by the American press, came out of the missile crisis with new questions of his own about Khrushchev's trustworthiness. He told Adenauer that as a consequence of Khrushchev's lies he had "no confidence" in him and that rather than take the initiative on Berlin he thought it best at this point to wait for the Soviets to act. Perhaps, the president speculated, Khrushchev might become even "more unreasonable" as a consequence of his present difficulties, or perhaps he might be prompted to seek some kind of a settlement. Kennedy felt as though he were "acting blind" with Khrushchev. Deeply unsettled by his own and his advisers' inability to read the Soviets and anticipate their actions, he planned to stand back and let his adversary make the first move, whatever it might be. In the meantime, he insisted that nothing else could be considered until Cuba was settled and he concentrated on making sure that Khrushchev withdrew the weapons and that the removal was properly verified. Even after his announcement on November 20 lifting the quarantine, as the Soviets appeared to have fulfilled their promise to remove the missiles and dismantle the missile sites, Kennedy proved reluctant to take the initiative in other areas of East–West dispute.

That reluctance was a source of frustration to David Ormsby Gore. Euphoric at the resolution of the Cuban affair, he argued that this was precisely the right moment to seek out contact with the Soviets and to try to make progress on other issues. He maintained that there was a better chance of getting East and West to come to terms while the experience of being on the verge of nuclear war was still fresh in everyone's memory. He also saw a distinct advantage in talking to Khrushchev at a time when the Russian leader was vulnerable, having just lost the card he had expected to play when he appeared in New York after the elections. David saw that Jack was now personally and emotionally invested in the need to move from confrontation to détente, but he also saw the extent to which the political climate in the United States had shifted as a consequence of the missile crisis, and he recognized that Jack had again begun to waver about how best to deal with Moscow. Macmillan and Kennedy were set to meet again in Nassau on December 19–20, and David viewed the encounter as an opportunity to shore up the president's commitment to the Churchillian strategy for the peaceful defeat of Soviet Communism. Macmillan, congratulating Kennedy on the removal of the missiles, declared the hope that he and the president might discuss "the long-term implications of all this" when they conferred in December. He was insistent that their side must not lose the initiative gained over Cuba.

The missile crisis had been everything Macmillan had predicted would happen eventually unless they found some way to get a genuine détente with the Soviets. For thirteen terrible days, East and West had faced one another with their nuclear missiles, and the fate of mankind had hung in the balance. This time mankind had escaped, but the confrontation had materialized exactly as Macmillan had said it would, and there was no way to know if the world would be so lucky again. To Macmillan, the need to change the course of history seemed more urgent than ever.

Before the Nassau sessions began, however, a crisis in British–American relations abruptly and drastically shifted the focus of the talks. While Kennedy had been absorbed in the aftermath of Cuba, the US government had moved to discontinue production of the Skybolt missile, on which Britain's independent nuclear deterrent was based. As a result of a series of misunderstandings and miscommunications, Britain suddenly found itself faced not just with the loss of a weapon but—far more importantly—of its right to a place at the table when some of the most urgent matters of the day were discussed. Churchill had believed that only with an independent nuclear deterrent, however small and symbolic, would Britain wield significant influence in the postwar world. On that principle, Macmillan had secured an agreement with Eisenhower on Skybolt. In Macmillan's view, to deprive Britain of Skybolt, as the US government now proposed to do, would be to deprive it of its voice in international affairs. He found that intolerable. Putting aside all thought of the major strategic review he had initially contemplated, Macmillan went to the Bahamas determined to do all he could to sustain Britain's role and beneficent influence in the postwar world. He arrived knowing from Ormsby Gore that Kennedy had not sought to provoke the present crisis; he had simply failed to comprehend the dimensions of the problem posed to Britain by the cancellation of Skybolt, and he believed himself morally obliged to find a satisfactory alternative. Ormsby Gore accompanied Kennedy on *Air Force One*, and by the time three days of talks concluded the president had agreed to provide Macmillan with a credible substitute for Skybolt in the form of Polaris nuclear missiles.

The agreement came just in time, for the Nassau talks were still in progress when a surprise message from Khrushchev arrived. For the first time since 1960, Khrushchev appeared ready to agree to a nuclear test ban treaty that provided for verification and inspection within the borders of the Soviet Union. He had repeatedly denounced the concept of verification as a pretext for espionage, so the present offer was a breakthrough. Kennedy, Macmillan and Ormsby Gore were jubilant. Khrushchev had not only made the first move, as Kennedy had believed he must; he had also made a substantial concession to Western demands. His willingness to allow inspectors to verify that the Soviets were living up to the terms of a treaty did much to address concerns that, having lied in the past, he would lie again. From the time of their 1959 conversations in New York, when Ormsby Gore had convinced Kennedy that a ban on nuclear testing was the place to get a critical first agreement with the Russians, the goal of a test ban treaty had been central to Kennedy's strategy of peace. It was especially gratifying now that the president might be able to follow up his triumph over Cuba with a test ban, which was important not just as an end in itself but even more so in terms of the many agreements to follow—the start of a long process of infiltration whereby the closed Soviet society could be defeated without bloodshed. Within weeks of confrontation on the brink of the nuclear abyss, it seemed as if East and West might finally be about to make real progress toward détente.

The Nassau talks ended in a mood of celebration, and Jack went on to Palm Beach with David to spend the holiday with their families and, naturally, to discuss Khrushchev's letter of December 19. Jack and David both assumed that Khrushchev had put forth his offer of two to three yearly on-site inspections on Soviet territory by way of opening a fully-fledged negotiation. Three days after Christmas, the Ormsby Gores were still the Kennedys' houseguests when the president wrote to welcome Khrushchev's proposal and to suggest that, though the precise numbers offered were far from acceptable, both sides meet either in New York or Geneva to work out a deal. Khrushchev agreed to have his representatives meet the Americans in New York. Macmillan had no objection to the bilateral nature of the talks, but Ormsby Gore did worry about the political climate in the United States. He feared that, despite the president's enthusiasm, the American contingent might be more concerned with what Congress would accept than with actually getting a treaty. On the argument that in the absence of British influence the Americans might flinch at making a deal, Ormsby Gore proposed that London needed to send a representative of its own. The day before the talks opened in New York on January 14, 1963, Macmillan wrote Kennedy to suggest that Ormsby Gore himself be permitted to join in. The president was quick to say yes, but the Soviets did not agree until the end of the first week, and David finally entered the discussions when they transferred to Washington on January 22. That day, Kennedy signalled his determination to make the talks a success by directing the Atomic Energy Commission—over the objections of its chairman, Glenn Seaborg—to postpone the scheduled underground tests for two to three weeks while American, British and Soviet negotiators met.

As soon as the president issued those instructions, Ormsby Gore's anxieties about the American political climate were abundantly realized. To Republican chagrin, Kennedy had emerged from his faceoff with Khrushchev with the image of a Cold Warrior par excellence. Now, Republicans were quick to seize on the opening provided by the test ban talks in New York and Washington to suggest that the hero of the missile crisis might prove himself an appeaser yet. On January 24, Congressman Craig Hosmer of California, a ranking member of the Joint Congressional Committee on Atomic Energy, made a speech in the House of Representatives expressing concern that the United States might accept the numbers proposed in Khrushchev's December 19 letter. When on January 26 Kennedy publicly announced the postponement of underground tests in Nevada, Hosmer responded by charging that the president was so anxious to get a test ban agreement that the United States now risked "losing its nuclear shirt." But it was another politician's comments that most forcefully suggested that Republicans intended to make the test ban treaty a major issue in the 1964 presidential campaign. On January 29, Governor Nelson Rockefeller of New York, a moderate widely seen as a potential Republican challenger to Kennedy, and by Kennedy's own private admission the candidate he most feared running against, attacked the postponement of tests in Nevada. Rockefeller accused the president of a readiness to make concessions that threatened to jeopardize the future security of the United States and of the entire free world.

The Republican onslaught would have been trouble enough had the test ban talks fulfilled Kennedy's great hopes. To his perplexity, the Soviets seemed unwilling to budge from Khrushchev's original offer of two to three inspections. Repeatedly the Western negotiators made it clear that they could improve their offer if only the Soviets would improve their own, but those efforts were in vain. What neither Kennedy nor Ormsby Gore knew at that point was that Khrushchev was equally surprised and disappointed by the inability to secure a deal. The source of the problem was a misunderstanding on the Soviet side about the number of inspections acceptable to the United States. As the missile crisis drew to a close, Khrushchev had tried to save face by claiming that he had protected Cuba from an invasion by US forces. Thereafter, in line with his new image as a man of peace, he had moved to become the world leader responsible for initiating progress toward a test ban treaty, an accomplishment that promised to earn credit with the neutral nations. In the apparently sincere belief that the previous October Arthur Dean had said that Soviet acceptance of two to four yearly inspections would be enough to get an agreement—a statement Dean later denied having made—Khrushchev had gone to his Council of Ministers for authorization to make an offer of three. Asked by the council whether that number would be sufficient, Khrushchev had guaranteed that it would be. Hence his mounting rage when American and British negotiators insisted they needed a higher number. The outcome of the missile crisis had been humiliation enough; Khrushchev did not care to be humiliated anew by the test ban talks. To make matters worse, he was convinced that inspections were no more than a political requirement to enable Kennedy to get a treaty ratified in the Senate. Now that Khrushchev had made such a major concession and, as far as he could see, given Kennedy the required political cover, he was bewildered when a deal failed to materialize. Finally, on January 31 in New York, the Soviets announced that they were ending the present set of talks and that the test ban negotiations would continue within the context of the eighteen-nation disarmament talks due to resume in Geneva on February 12.

For Kennedy and Ormsby Gore, it was a great disappointment. David, who would not himself go on to Geneva, saw a glimmer of hope in the fact that at least both sides were still talking. Jack, for his part, remained keen to get a deal at a moment when, for all the difficulty thus far, Khrushchev's acceptance of the concept of verification and inspections made a treaty seem achingly within reach. But the Republican attacks, especially Rockefeller's, had unsettled the president, and on the day the New York talks dissolved Kennedy responded to the criticism by ordering the resumption of underground testing in Nevada. His detractors did not let up, and on February 1 the *New York Times* ran a story spelling out the Republicans' intention to launch an unprecedented "concerted attack" on the very idea of a test ban. The newly formed House Republican Committee on Nuclear Testing, under Hosmer's chairmanship, released a warning by the nuclear physicist Dr. Edward Teller that a test ban treaty would involve "Munich-type concessions" by the United States that would endanger American security and "help the Soviet Union in its plan to conquer the world." Prominent Democrats, including Senators Henry Jackson, Stuart Symington, and Thomas J. Dodd, were soon themselves publicly expressing dismay at what Dodd called Kennedy's willingness to make "many grave concessions" to the Soviets in the test ban talks. The whole issue of the nuclear test ban treaty was becoming political poison for Kennedy at a time when he had had reason to hope that public perception of his handling of the missile crisis would help reelect him by a wide margin.

After the Geneva talks also ended in deadlock—the Soviets still frozen at an offer of three inspections and the United States and Britain at seven—Kennedy flew down to Palm Beach with Ormsby Gore on February 21 for a long weekend. Two months had passed since the friends had come here in a mood of exhilaration, fresh from Nassau and Khrushchev's surprise offer of on-site inspections. In December they had believed that a first agreement and all it represented might finally be at hand. Now, as February drew to a close, both men conceded that success had again eluded them, though they were not sure why. In Geneva the Soviets seemed suddenly to have lost interest in a test ban, and David wondered aloud whether that apparent change of heart was genuine or a tactic to wrest further concessions. As if to explain why he must now abandon the goal that had absorbed them both for so long, Jack spoke of his own limited ability to maneuver politically and of his belief that a test ban treaty, even if they had managed to get one, was unlikely to win Senate ratification at a time when Democrats and Republicans alike had begun to militate against it. He made it clear that though he was willing to take some risks with the Senate, he was not prepared to set himself up for almost certain defeat. David, for his part, acknowledged that the political environment after the missile crisis, coupled with the Soviets' exasperating refusal to give an inch on the numbers, made it impossible for the president to do much more. In short, they appeared to have failed again—and meanwhile East and West remained on a collision course.

Macmillan, who learned all this from Ormsby Gore, found the complete deadlock in Geneva most depressing. But, on reflection, he disagreed that there really was nothing more to be done. His conscience told him otherwise. He saw Khrushchev's acceptance of the concept of verification and inspections as a tremendous turning point, a moment of opportunity that might not come again. The missile crisis had amply confirmed him in the belief that they could not continue to live with such danger without doing everything in their power to lessen the chance of war. He therefore began work on a long letter to urge Kennedy that it was their duty as leaders to keep trying. Macmillan was aware that his renewed pleas might be most unwelcome in Washington and that he might be thought annoying and even alarmist. But in the 1930s Churchill had cared not at all what people thought of him when he persisted in warning about the dangers of Nazi Germany, and in the postwar years he had taken a similar attitude when he steadfastly warned of the need for détente with the Soviets, though Eisenhower and even some members of Churchill's own government expressed annoyance at his repeated pleas. So too, Macmillan believed that the stakes were simply too high to care what anyone thought of him. Like Churchill, Macmillan kept trying because he saw it as his duty to do so.

Macmillan felt he must get to the president immediately, before the United States became so consumed by the 1964 election that any action on Kennedy's part really would be impossible. Before he addressed him directly, however, he believed he must first enlist his ambassador's support. Ormsby Gore had lately bristled at a suggestion from the British delegation in Geneva that it might be useful for Britain to make an independent effort to break the deadlock. Stating vehemently that Jack Kennedy had again and again demonstrated his keen desire for an agreement, David warned against any British intervention that might aggravate the president's problems with Congress. In light of this, Macmillan wrote to David to say that he did not think they could be content to leave things as they were. Though he recognized Kennedy's difficulties with Congress, he believed political considerations must be put aside in favor of the more important question of avoiding a new world war. He was writing to David for advice on how best to approach Kennedy about all of this, but also for his go-ahead to approach him at all.

The prime minister was not optimistic that his ambassador would approve of another appeal to Kennedy, so he was surprised and delighted when David wrote back enthusiastically. The timing of

Macmillan's approach, David cautioned, was anything but auspicious. The president seemed "despondent" about the prospects for progress with the Soviets, and though he believed as firmly as ever in the importance of a test ban treaty he was "genuinely fearful" that an agreement would not win Senate approval. David proposed that he and the prime minister "might need a little time to work on him and he in turn on Congress and other doubters here."

The effort was on. With Ormsby Gore's blessing, Macmillan resumed the process, launched in Bermuda, of instructing Kennedy in matters of duty. On March 16, 1963, he wrote to make the case that the urgent need to change the course of history overrode any strictly political reasons to do nothing. Ormsby Gore had informed Macmillan of the practical concerns that prevented Kennedy from going forward, and the prime minister addressed those concerns head-on. Though aware of Kennedy's readiness at times to subordinate principle to politics, Macmillan spoke to him as if he were already the man he wanted to be; he expressed confidence that the president would choose to do the right thing. "Of course," Macmillan acknowledged, "there are very strong arguments for doing nothing. Strong logical arguments, strong political arguments. But this is not the spirit in which you, who carry the largest responsibility, before God and man, have faced your duty, nor that in which I have tried to do the same." Five months after the world's first confrontation of nuclear powers, Macmillan once again portrayed the test ban as "the most important step" they could take as leaders "towards unraveling this frightful tangle of fear and suspicion in East/West relations." A year earlier, Kennedy had been much moved by Macmillan's passionate depiction of the dangerous realities of the postwar situation. In this letter, Macmillan again spoke of what he saw as their duty to try to alter that situation.

Duty and responsibility were Macmillan's prevailing theme, and near the end of his deeply moving thirteen-page appeal to the president he hit a wistfully Churchillian note in referring to his own mortality and his sense of responsibility to finish the work while time remained. "I am so sorry to inflict so long a letter on you," Macmillan wrote to the younger man, "but I feel this very deep personal obligation upon me and it is one which in some form or another, I must discharge, before it is too late."

Ormsby Gore met with Kennedy at the White House on March 21 to discuss Macmillan's letter. In important ways, the friends' encounter on this occasion was the most dramatic of their "twenty-five-year conversation." After much argument through the years, the moment when Kennedy would have to choose between Churchill and Baldwin was finally at hand. Macmillan's renewed plea to try to change the course of history came at what both he and Ormsby Gore understood to be the last possible moment to get Kennedy to act before the launch of his reelection campaign. In their view, it would be perhaps three years before they would again have any hope of spurring him to action, and there was no telling what might happen in the interim. Hovering over the conversation of March 21 was a sense that, for the time being at least, Kennedy was confronting his last chance to decide to act as a statesman. In the past he may have had the luxury of vacillating, but not this time. It was a particularly tense encounter for Ormsby Gore. His and Macmillan's efforts to influence the president would either pay off now or they would have failed. Everything depended on Kennedy's reaction to Macmillan's letter. The experience of the missile crisis had had an enormous impact on the president, who finally felt, rather than simply accepted intellectually, that one could not proceed rationally in an environment of confrontation with both sides armed with nuclear weapons. But even as he agreed fully with Macmillan that they must find some way to change the situation, it was by no means certain that Kennedy would be able to bring himself to act, given the enormous political risks. Ormsby Gore went into the conversation with no clear idea of what his friend would do, and as it turned out Kennedy was not sure himself.

At first, the signs were encouraging. Jack began by saying that while he needed more time to consider Macmillan's letter, he was in complete sympathy with the prime minister's general approach and remained anxious to do all he could to secure a test ban treaty. Nonetheless, almost as soon as the two friends began to talk about the letter, Kennedy's political fears began to surface in response to one of Macmillan's proposals. After much thought about what had gone wrong after the high promise of the latest talks, Ormsby Gore had concluded that the deadlock at Geneva must have been due to a genuine misunderstanding on Khrushchev's part, and Macmillan had suggested as much to Kennedy in his letter. Knowing that Vienna had left Kennedy highly resistant to the idea of another meeting with Khrushchev, Macmillan was convinced nonetheless that at this point the only way to get a test ban agreement was for the Heads of Government—Kennedy, Khrushchev and Macmillan himself—to sit down together and work it out. Now, based on an idea of Ormsby Gore's designed to allay the president's fears, Macmillan had suggested that instead of going to see Khrushchev himself, Kennedy might prefer to send a special emissary on his behalf.

After the president had talked for a bit, David, as he had told Macmillan he would, proceeded to go over some of the prime minister's main points, notably the need to make direct contact with Khrushchev, perhaps in the form of a special emissary. Again, Kennedy's initial reaction was promising. Jack displayed enthusiasm for the idea and noted that if he did send someone it would almost certainly be Averell Harriman. He was quick to add that the emissary would have to travel with a "cover story." Though he fully accepted the usefulness, even the necessity, of direct contact with Khrushchev, he said it would not do for it to be publicly stated that he had sent someone to Moscow to talk about a nuclear test ban. In an instant, Jack had laid bare his fears. Not only was he loath to risk another catastrophic personal encounter with Khrushchev; at a time when Republicans were moving to make the test ban a major campaign issue, he would not even go so far as openly to send a representative to discuss it.

David, aware of the magnitude of Jack's political fears but also of the instincts driving him to do what was right, moved to counter those fears. With exquisite tact, rather than tell Jack what he ought to do he began to speak of how Macmillan saw his own duty as a world leader. The prime minister, David said, was convinced he must try to do something to break the deadlock, not simply because he had made a public commitment to the test ban, but for much more personal reasons. Macmillan, he explained, believed that men of power had "a duty to try and change the course of history and guide it in a direction which would be of benefit to our peoples." Jack replied that he too would like to change the course of history, then instantly launched into a discussion of all the reasons not to try. Though prepared to wage a major campaign with Congress, he could not ignore the "political pitfalls" that might cause him to lose the 1964 election. He did not want to secure a treaty only to fail to win ratification. He worried too that in the event he did manage to drive a treaty through the Senate, were the Chinese Communists to explode an atomic weapon six months later it would almost certainly finish him politically.

Then, having spoken of his fears, Jack went on to justify basing his actions on them rather than on his responsibilities as a leader. After many years of going back and forth with Jack on the Churchill-Baldwin debate, David was in a unique position to hear the echoes in the president's words when he warned that were Nelson Rockefeller to defeat him in 1964 nuclear testing would go on indefinitely, as this was the course Rockefeller favored. His comment recalled the argument put forth by Stanley Baldwin to defend his failure to rearm lest he be defeated in 1935 by the Socialists, whose policies would have left the country far worse than under Baldwin's watch. Jack had recycled Baldwin's self-justifying argument in his Harvard thesis, and now again he used it on his own behalf, substituting Rockefeller for the Socialists. Jack, who had criticized Nixon for acting like Baldwin in the 1935 general election, was now himself imitating Baldwin. Like Baldwin, he suggested that it was not personal ambition that impelled him to subordinate his convictions to the need to be reelected, but a sincere concern for the good of the country. Macmillan had written as if he assumed Jack Kennedy was not the sort of leader to refuse to act for fear of damaging himself politically. Jack's preliminary remarks to David suggested that though part of him wanted to do what was right, the other part remained unwilling to risk any action that might hurt his chances in 1964. The conversation ended with David having no better idea of what Jack was about to do than when they began. One thing, however, was clear. In the coming days, circumstances were going to require the president to make up his mind not just about the test ban, but about whether he would be a politician or a statesman.

While the president had been divided in his reaction to Macmillan's letter, the State Department was emphatically opposed. Hardly had the letter been delivered to the White House when the State Department's leading Soviet expert began to exert intense pressure to reject Macmillan's appeal. Llewellyn Thompson insisted to the president that it was the wrong moment for another approach to Moscow. In the Soviet specialist's judgment, the situation had changed drastically since the beginning of the year, and Khrushchev now seemed too preoccupied with internal problems and with his differences with the Chinese Communists to take an interest in agreements with the West. There were also indications that Khrushchev was trying to decide whether to persist with the policy of peaceful coexistence or whether to shift to a more confrontational posture. Were he involved in a process of self-examination, it seemed unlikely that he would want to discuss a nuclear test ban treaty with Kennedy and Macmillan or their emissaries. Of course, no one knew for certain what was really happening at the Kremlin, but Thompson could say unequivocally that Macmillan's timing was simply wrong. These arguments provided justification for Kennedy's impulse to leave matters where they were. Why risk so much politically when the effort to break the deadlock was doomed anyway?

For a week after his receipt of the prime minister's letter and his talk with Ormsby Gore, the president—with Thompson's objections on his desk—pondered the situation but made no further response. Finally, on March 28, a letter drafted at the State Department went out over Kennedy's signature to inform Macmillan that Khrushchev probably had "too many problems on his hands right now" to give serious consideration to the test ban. Kennedy proposed that perhaps he and Macmillan ought to consider sending a joint letter to Khrushchev to see what the prospects were for progress in the immediate future, and he enclosed a draft also prepared by the State Department. Ormsby Gore found the package immensely disappointing. In all the speculation about what Khrushchev might or might not be up to, he detected at once the hand of Thompson and the other "Kremlin demonologists." He complained to Macmillan that the president's letter had the effect of surrendering the initiative to the Soviets at a time when it was essential to take positive action and not simply permit events to drift. And he saw the draft letter to Khrushchev as ludicrously self-defeating in the way it attempted to spar with Khrushchev and force him to make concessions in advance.

For all of David's annoyance, he had predicted from the first that Jack would be wary of a further approach to Khrushchev and that it might be necessary to work on him over time. So he was quick to urge Macmillan "to return to the charge with the President and get the argument back on the higher plane which was typified by your own letter." Jack may have said no initially, but based on years of intimacy David, like Jackie, knew that Jack's ambitions extended beyond the mere possession of power. David remained confident about the powerful appeal arguments such as Macmillan's about duty and history exerted on him, and he remained steadfast in the hope they would win out in the end. David also thought he and Macmillan might cast a new initiative in such a way as to make it appeal to the president on a practical basis. He knew that in the months since the missile crisis Jack had expressed frustration with how wrong the Soviet experts had proven in their judgments and forecasts, and with his own predicament of having had to operate "blind" with Khrushchev. David advised Macmillan to suggest that rather than speculate about Khrushchev's intentions just now, the best way to find out what he might be prepared to do was to send a personal emissary to ask him directly in a serious way. He urged Macmillan to present Kennedy with a joint letter to Khrushchev that, in contrast to the jargon-laced State Department draft, seemed "worthy of the occasion." Macmillan argued that, rather than debating with Khrushchev in a manner certain to irritate him, they should propose simply and sincerely that he join them in an effort to break the impasse. The battle lines were drawn.

On the one side Kennedy's political instincts told him not to act: there was sentiment within the administration that it was the wrong time to move with Khrushchev, as well as outright opposition to the test ban; and opinion in both Congress and the electorate was hugely discouraging. On the other side were the call of duty and his desire to take up Churchill's mantle and move for the critical first agreement with the Soviets that had eluded Churchill himself. Kennedy was torn between two kinds of ambition: the desire to hold on to power and the desire, spoken of to his wife, to do great things and claim his place in history.

Ormsby Gore followed up on Macmillan's appeal by noting that even if it were true that Khrushchev and the other party leaders were of two minds as to future Soviet policy, that made it all the more important to let them know that progress toward peaceful coexistence was by no means closed. He argued that, contrary to the recommendations of the State Department, the West should not "sit supine" while an internal discussion developed at the Kremlin. He insisted that a Western initiative could well influence the outcome of that crucial debate and that this could be their last chance to get to Khrushchev before a shift in Soviet policy made détente unlikely.

While these discussions raged on, preparations were under way for a White House ceremony to mark the signing of a proclamation making Winston Churchill an honorary US citizen. Churchill had turned down an offer of honorary citizenship in 1958, but when Congress made a second offer he decided he must accept. He was now too frail to attend the ceremony, and his son Randolph, who had been Kick's friend after the war, was set to come in his place. The day had special meaning for the president, who, Jackie later said, regarded it as a gift to the man whose books had shaped him. Arrangements were made to broadcast the ceremony in the Rose Garden on national television in the United States, as well as in Britain via satellite. When April 9 came, it rained in Washington and Jack worried that the afternoon would turn out a disaster. After a morning of meetings he had a swim, then lunch and a rest upstairs where his invalid father, en route to Florida, was to spend the night. At a quarter to two, Jack and Jackie went down to the Oval Office where a small group waited. There was Randolph Churchill, whose preface to *Arms and the Covenant* had spelled out for Jack the difference between the politician and the statesman. There was Randolph's great friend Kay Halle, the woman who had entered a Boston hospital room in 1932 to find young Jack Kennedy absorbed in *The World Crisis*, which had exposed the fifteen-year-old to values sharply at odds with those of his father. And there was David Ormsby Gore, who in recent days had been working to persuade the president, in effect, to act in line with those values and to put duty before self-interest, as Kennedy himself had said during the campaign a leader must do.

As the others looked on, the president signed the proclamation declaring Churchill an honorary citizen. At 3 p.m. the French doors swung open and the group went outside, where the sun had come out and a larger gathering had assembled. Members of the Cabinet and Congress, senior members of the administration, members of the British Embassy staff, diplomatic representatives of the Commonwealth, and personal friends and former colleagues of Churchill were present. Kennedy was first to speak, and Jackie, aware of how anxious her husband was that all go well, found she could hardly listen. Randolph Churchill spoke next. He read his father's message, a meditation on the special relationship between Kennedy's nation and his own. Winston Churchill reflected on Britain's great partnership with the United States in past wars, and, at a moment when some people seemed inclined to count the British out, he pointedly remarked on the need for his country to continue to play a decisive role in the post-war world: "Let no man underrate our energies, our potentialities and our abiding power for good." Those remarks were especially fitting, as Britain had done so much through the years to contribute to the intellectual formation of America's thirty-fifth president, and as, even now, Macmillan and Ormsby Gore were mounting a passionate campaign to influence him anew.

Following the ceremony, the president invited guests to the East Room for champagne. He was about to head back to the Oval Office when Ormsby Gore asked whether he had yet replied to Macmillan's second letter. Kennedy said he had not, but it soon became apparent that the day had galvanized him, reminding him of what he had come to the White House to achieve—and clarifying what he must do now. If he was to take up Churchill's mantle and try for a first agreement, he was going to have to act regardless of the possible political cost to himself.

Finally, Kennedy accepted Macmillan's proposal that together they attempt to make direct personal contact with Khrushchev. He had chosen to act as Churchill, not Baldwin, as a statesman rather than a politician, taking the stand he believed in at whatever cost to himself and his political fortunes. On April 11, he called Macmillan to say he had decided to participate in a new initiative. He agreed basically to go with Macmillan's draft letter to Khrushchev, with the notable exception that he still did not wish to raise the possibility of a summit meeting. Macmillan, delighted by how far the president had come, was careful not to press. A personal emissary would be fine, and he would be pleased if it were Harriman.

That afternoon, the president headed for Florida for a long holiday weekend. The previous Easter had been overshadowed by his decision to resume atmospheric tests and by the knowledge that he had acted to re-ignite the arms race with all of the danger of a devastating war it had been his great wish to avert. In 1962, Kennedy had not yet been prepared to take the risks Macmillan had urged upon him; this year—after the experience of the missile crisis and after another sustained campaign by Macmillan and Ormsby Gore—he was ready. The day after Easter, a letter from Kennedy and Macmillan proposing to send personal emissaries went off to Moscow, where the American and British ambassadors were to present it to Khrushchev. That Kennedy was very much on his own with this at the White House became clear at a meeting of senior advisers on the day of his return, April 17. General Taylor, speaking for the Joint Chiefs, expressed opposition to a test ban treaty. Rusk seemed to feel it was unobtainable and he was at best lukewarm. McCone, though he voiced no opinion on this occasion, had previously made his opposition clear to the president. McNamara believed a treaty to be in the nation's interest, but he pointed nonetheless to mounting congressional resistance. When word arrived from the new US ambassador to Moscow, Foy Kohler, on April 24 that Khrushchev's initial reaction on being handed the letter had been "almost entirely negative," Llewellyn Thompson leapt on the news as confirmation that this was simply the wrong time for an overture.

On May 8, Khrushchev fired off an angry letter to Kennedy, which depicted his previous offer of three inspections as a gesture to the president's political situation. He insisted that he had made the concession not because he agreed that inspections were necessary but because Kennedy had repeatedly insisted that without a minimum number he would never get a treaty through the Senate. Khrushchev grudgingly agreed to receive the emissaries, but predicted that the talks would amount to nothing more than further "haggling over inspections, but at a higher level."

The letter came as a massive disappointment to Kennedy. Despite Khrushchev's willingness to see the emissaries, it was impossible to overlook the letter's relentlessly negative, even sarcastic tone. The president's mood was apparent at a press conference that same day. Asked about the prospects for a test ban, he replied, "I am not hopeful at all. . . . We thought maybe we were moving toward it in December, now we seem to be moving away from it. If we don't get it now, I would think generally perhaps the genie is out of the bottle and we will not get him back in again." Macmillan worried that Kennedy would interpret the letter as an absolute rejection and that he would be inclined to make a hasty reply that might again bring matters to an abrupt halt. Indeed, the president, deprived of hope, began again to waver about whether to proceed with Khrushchev at all. The possibility presented itself that those who had warned against the initiative had been right and that it might be best to pull back now before it became another failed attempt that could damage him in 1964.

As Kennedy considered how best to respond to Khrushchev, both Macmillan and Ormsby Gore urged him to do nothing just yet. Macmillan pointed out that at least Khrushchev had agreed to talk to the emissaries, and he argued that even if the effort came to naught it would be wrong to stop before they had gone some way further to explore the possibilities. Ormsby Gore, who had been summoned to London to strategize with the prime minister about how best to deal with both Kennedy and Khrushchev, wrested an agreement from Jack at least to make no reply to Khrushchev until his return. On the argument that new nuclear tests would send all the wrong signals while an initiative was under way, David also persuaded him to postpone a test scheduled for the end of the month. Aware that Jack was again at a point of decision and that the impulse to give in to political considerations was very strong, David hit on a way to remind him of the man he wanted to be. Raymond Asquith's sister, Churchill's great friend Violet Bonham Carter, happened to be in Washington just then, and David sent a note to Jack to say he was sure the president would enjoy meeting her.

On May 14, 1963, Violet Bonham Carter visited Jack Kennedy at the White House. She sat on a sofa, he in a rocking chair beside her. Though he knew in advance, he politely asked what relation she was to Raymond Asquith, then went on to say that he had read about him in Churchill's *Great Contemporaries* and John Buchan's *Pilgrim's Way*. To Bonham Carter's astonishment, he recited from memory Churchill's lines about her brother: "The War which found the measure of so many never got to the bottom of him, and when the Grenadiers strode into the crash and thunder of the Somme, he went to his fate, cool, poised, resolute, matter-of-fact, debonair." She was enchanted. She did not know, as Ormsby Gore did, quite what her brother had meant to Jack. In 1944, when Jack compared Billy Hartington to Asquith, it had been because of both men's willingness to risk everything for ideals—and that, as David well understood, was the sort of man Jack wanted to be. He had never lacked physical courage; but "political courage," a very different article, would be required if he were to put his own reelection at risk for the sake of what he sincerely believed was the nation's best interest. Jack asked his visitor about Churchill in the 1930s, when he had struggled to impart a message the people were in no mood to hear. Bonham Carter said he had been "despised and rejected of men."

"Did he make no impression?" Kennedy asked.

"None," she replied. "The country wanted poppy and mandragora. The governments gave it. Awakening came with the fulfillment of the doom he prophesied."

As promised, Kennedy made no reply to Khrushchev while Ormsby Gore was in London. Soon the prime minister wrote to say that after much thought and discussion, he had concluded that although Khrushchev's letter was not very helpful on substance, he and Kennedy ought to take up his acceptance of their proposal to send emissaries to Moscow. Macmillan enclosed a draft letter to Khrushchev for the president's consideration. In the meantime, the White House had worked up a draft of its own which seemed likely to doom the initiative. When Ormsby Gore returned, Kennedy told him that he had directed his people to work from Macmillan's draft and to make "as few changes as possible."

Having decided to go forward in spite of formidable opposition, Kennedy stated at a press conference on May 22 that he intended to "push very hard" for a test ban. He seemed a changed man from the one who had insisted on March 21 that were he to send an emissary to Khrushchev he would have to travel with a cover story. After two months of introspection and debate, including many private talks with Ormsby Gore, Kennedy had not only chosen to commit to the initiative; he had decided to do so openly. During the last presidential campaign he had said, "In 1960 we must elect a President who will lead the people—who will risk, if he must, his popularity for his responsibility." He had expressed the view that it is for a leader to try to educate public opinion rather than simply yield to it.

Such leadership was precisely what Kennedy undertook to provide when, on June 10, he delivered an address at American University in Washington, DC, in which he urged Americans to reexamine their attitude toward the Soviet Union. Asking them to rethink in rational rather than emotional terms how best to deal with the Soviets in the nuclear age, Kennedy rejected "a strategy of annihilation" in favor of "a strategy of peace." After the Cuban missile crisis, a call for contact and agreements with the Soviets was unlikely to appeal to many voters, but Kennedy had decided to speak his mind and try to re-educate the public though it made him "despised and rejected of men." As Churchill had in "The Sinews of Peace," from which key elements of the American University address were drawn, Kennedy argued that mankind must assume responsibility for its own future and that another world war was not inevitable. He made the case for a treaty to outlaw nuclear tests, and he went on to announce that Khrushchev, Macmillan and he had now agreed that high-level discussions would shortly begin in Moscow. In spite of previous criticism from Rockefeller and others of his willingness to put off nuclear testing in advance of negotiations, Kennedy, to make clear his good faith in the present talks, pledged that the United States would conduct no nuclear tests in the atmosphere so long as other states refrained from doing so.

The test ban had never been an end in itself for Kennedy, and its significance extended well beyond arms control. Once there was a first major postwar agreement, the point was to move directly to others. Hoping that the next might be a settlement of the Berlin question, Kennedy traveled to Germany at the end of the month to make a series of speeches—including a speech in Berlin which became known as the "I am a Berliner" speech—whose aggressive posture toward the Soviets contrasted markedly with his "peace speech," as the American University address came to be known. Among those to voice perplexity was Khrushchev, who commented that in the president's German speeches it was "as though he were quite a different person" from the Kennedy of the peace speech. But there was no contradiction as far as Kennedy was concerned. If, in the aftermath of a test ban treaty, he was going to make any headway on Berlin, he believed he needed to gain German trust and allay the widespread fears of betrayal that had arisen in the wake of the 1961 talks. Kennedy privately expressed satisfaction that as a result of his visit the Germans—both the people and their government—had grown less anxious about US intentions, and that could only prove helpful to new negotiations to get a German settlement.

From Germany, Kennedy flew on to Ireland, where he suddenly decided to make an unscheduled visit to Kick's grave at Chatsworth. In 1948, her death had left him bereft and alone. But as recent events had just made clear, she had also left him with a legacy that had proven invaluable in his struggle to become the man he wanted to be. Not only had she managed before her death to make her brother understand the role of duty and belief in Billy Hartington's life, but she had bequeathed him a familial connection to David Ormsby Gore, who having assumed a brotherly role in her life after Billy died went on to do the same with Jack. Now, after the tumultuous conversations of that climactic spring of 1963, as David fought with all that was in him to help the president make the most difficult decisions of his life, Jack was finally able to bring himself to visit Kick's last resting place. After his visit to Chatsworth, Kennedy went on to Birch Grove, where he and Macmillan conferred about the test ban negotiations to begin in Moscow on July 15 and all that might flow from them. It struck Macmillan that the president had undergone a palpable transformation. Though obviously in great pain on account of his back, Kennedy projected "a greater degree of authority" than previously. At long last he was "clearly willing to risk a great deal to achieve what he thought was right." To Macmillan's fond eye, he seemed much the better for it.

Back in America on the eve of the Moscow meetings, Kennedy spent the weekend of July 12–14 in Hyannis Port with Ormsby Gore, whose 1954 talks with him there, about disarmament in the context of a new approach to Soviet relations, were about to come to fruition. Once again, Jackie, now heavily pregnant with the couple's second son, took notes as Jack and David talked. Two days previously, at his final meeting with Harriman before the envoy's departure, the president had made it clear that he was sending him to Moscow to do considerably more than negotiate a test ban treaty. He instructed Harriman also to lay the groundwork for future agreements on Berlin and other outstanding problems with the Soviets. The president knew that Harriman and Macmillan's emissary, Lord Hailsham—who as Quintin Hogg had participated in the prewar King and Country debate at the Oxford Union that had enthralled a young Jack Kennedy—faced difficult negotiations with Khrushchev; nonetheless, he was extremely hopeful. That weekend, as his back was much improved, he and David played a good deal of golf. After one final game on Sunday evening, they returned to Washington in the morning to monitor the Moscow talks set to open that day.

At the first meeting, Harriman handed Khrushchev a letter from Kennedy saying that, though he continued to hope for a comprehensive test ban treaty and regretted the misunderstanding over inspection numbers, in the interest of getting an agreement a ban on atmospheric testing only—which would require no inspections—would do. The talks went on for ten days, and after a last-minute hitch that Macmillan feared might ruin their chances after all, a deal was in place. On July 25, 1963, Kennedy, with Ormsby Gore at his side, told Macmillan on the phone that at that very moment in Moscow a treaty was being initialed. The prime minister wept at the news. Later he sent a message of gratitude to the president: "I found myself unable to express my real feelings on the telephone tonight. My task here has been relatively easy but I do understand the high degree of courage and faith which you have shown." Kennedy understood all too clearly the role that Macmillan had actually played with his relentless determination to ensure that the president moved to pursue the strategy of peace, and he wanted to thank him. With the treaty at last initialed, Kennedy wrote to Macmillan, "What no one can doubt is the importance in all of this of your own persistent pursuit of a solution. You have never given up for a minute, and more than once your initiative is what had got things started again. I want you to know that this indispensable contribution is well understood and highly valued." Both men grasped that this was no simple arms agreement, but rather the first expression of trust between the Soviets and the West since the end of the war. By opening the way to further contact and agreements, it was also, they hoped, the beginning of the end of the closed Soviet society.

Kennedy announced the treaty to the American people in a televised address on the evening of Friday, July 26. After the speech, he and Ormsby Gore left for Hyannis Port to celebrate—and to chart their next moves. That Sunday, the friends had gone off for a swim when Bobby Kennedy joined them on the beach. As the trio stood together in the water, Bobby suggested that Jack's next step might be to go to the Soviet Union. David chimed in that he had long been of the opinion that had Eisenhower gone to Russia as planned before the U-2 debacle, and had the Russian people been able to see for themselves that an American leader lacked "horns and a tail," subsequent East–West relations would have been very different. A visit by Kennedy in the wake of the test ban treaty, David theorized, would do much to break down the barriers and ease the way to further agreements. It was precisely such friendly intercourse that, Churchill had taught, the closed Communist society ultimately could not withstand. Despite the others' excitement, Jack was noncommittal about such a trip. But over dinner at the White House in November, he suddenly reminded David of their conversation and said he had made up his mind to go to Russia, probably after the election.

For now, the next steps were the official signing of the treaty and then the ratification process in the Senate. Kennedy sent Dean Rusk to Moscow both to participate in the ceremony and to follow up on Harriman's efforts to move on to other areas of agreement. Rusk signed the treaty on August 5, and Kennedy was avidly monitoring the progress of the talks that followed when his attention was wrenched away from public affairs by an urgent call from Cape Cod on the 7th. Jackie had gone into labor prematurely and was being rushed to the hospital at Otis Air Force Base. The baby's chances, the president learned, were fifty-fifty. As soon as a plane could be prepared, Kennedy was en route to Otis. By the time he appeared at the hospital, Jackie had already given birth. The tiny baby boy weighed only four pounds, ten and a half ounces and suffered from hyaline membrane disease, the lung ailment that had afflicted young John. While Jackie slept, Jack mobilized the best possible medical care and arranged to transfer the child, baptized Patrick, to Children's Hospital in Boston. When his wife awakened, he told her the baby needed further treatment, but he offered no hint of the gravity of his condition. Aware that this might be Jackie's only chance to see and hold their second son, Jack wheeled Patrick's incubator into her room and placed the infant in his mother's arms. When the child was transported to Boston by ambulance, the president followed.

The next day Patrick's condition deteriorated, and in hopes of keeping his lungs open doctors decided to bring in a pressure chamber used in open-heart surgery. After conferring with physicians for two hours, the president was taken to the Ritz–Carlton Hotel to rest, but he found that he could not stay away from his son. Hardly had he arrived at the hotel when he turned round and headed back to the hospital. For an hour he stood alone next to the fragile figure and watched helplessly as he struggled to breathe, much as his own father had often hovered at his bedside when Jack himself lay near death. Refusing to leave the hospital again, he finally lay down in a nearby room, only to be called at 2 a.m. and told that Patrick had taken a bad turn. For the next two hours, Jack sat beside Patrick and held his tiny fingers. He was still touching them when the child died shortly after four. Informed that he was gone, Jack said in a soft voice, "He put up quite a fight." Presently, Jack went to his room and asked to be left alone for a bit. When the door closed, aide Dave Powers could hear his sobs in the hall. Later that morning the president returned to Otis, and when he entered Jackie's room he fell to his knees beside her bed and cried convulsively. Then he flew to Hyannis Port to explain to Caroline and young John that the brother they had excitedly awaited would not be coming home after all.

Finally Jack went to his father's house. Joe Kennedy could no longer soothe him with the words he once would have used. Nonetheless, the president, in his grief, sought out the physical presence of the man who had so often comforted and consoled him. Joe Kennedy may not have had it in him to teach his son certain important lessons, which it had been left to others to impart, but he had given Jack the gift of unreserved love. When the news about Patrick reached Harold Macmillan, who lately had become a kind of second father to Jack, he was in Norway; Jackie would later say that his letter of condolence seemed to bind her husband to the prime minister even more closely than before. When the letter arrived, Jack read it aloud to Jackie. Macmillan wrote, "The burdens of public affairs are more or less tolerable, because they are in a sense impersonal. But private grief is poignant and cruel."

While the president was preoccupied with his dying son, the test ban treaty went to the Senate on August 8. In view of the climate of opinion since the Cuban affair, Kennedy hoped for an emphatic vote of support, and worried that the coalition of Republicans and Southern Democrats that had embarrassed him during the rump session of Congress in 1960 would deny him even the two-thirds necessary for ratification. He also worried that the Republicans, having seized on the test ban as an issue for the 1964 presidential campaign, would enlist Eisenhower to speak against ratification. At the White House's request, Macmillan again wrote to intervene with his old friend. The Senate

Committee on Foreign Relations began hearings on August 12, and such were the fireworks that Anatoly Dobrynin remarked to Kennedy that the proceedings sounded more like "a step toward war than toward peace." Nonetheless, the committee issued a positive report, and after two weeks of debate the Senate gave its consent to ratification of the partial test ban on September 24. The vote of eighty to nineteen gave Kennedy fourteen votes beyond the two-thirds majority he needed—a solid endorsement.

At the outset of his presidency, Jack Kennedy had hoped that his first few months in office would coincide with the start of a new era in East–West relations, and all that that might bring. When, on inauguration day, Kennedy expressed the wish for a new beginning, Harold Caccia observed that time alone would show whether the president could "live up to the high purpose" he set forth. It took nearly three years to secure the first major postwar agreement with the Soviets, and in an effort to change the course of history Kennedy had had to overcome great obstacles, both externally and within himself. When he finally signed the instruments of ratification, on October 7, 1963, in the Treaty Room at the White House, appropriately he returned to the theme of beginnings.

"For the first time we have been able to reach an agreement which can limit the dangers of the age," he said. ". . . Today we have a beginning."

Jack Kennedy had set precisely that new beginning as the central strategic goal of his presidency, and now he had achieved it. In partnership with Macmillan, he had secured the precious first agreement with the Soviets that Churchill had dreamed of, but had been unable to attain as postwar prime minister. For Kennedy, the test ban treaty was also a beginning in strictly personal terms: By the time of his death he had yet to make the total commitment to act in spite of the political risks that had characterized Churchill's career. He had, however, taken a first important step toward becoming the statesman he longed to be, the sort of hero, first admired in his boyhood books, who sets principle before self-interest. Whether Kennedy would have continued along that path had he lived is impossible to know, but he had begun.

One month later, Jack Kennedy was assassinated in Dallas, Texas, at the age of forty-six.

Epilogue

EIGHTEEN MONTHS AFTER THE ASSASSINATION, THE UNLIKELY story that began in prewar London and culminated in the signing of the first major postwar agreement with the Soviets had drawn to a close. Not only was the president gone, but the other key players had retreated from history's stage as well. On a glorious spring day, the survivors gathered together for a final act of memory and homage, to honor Jack Kennedy and in a sense to mark the end of the history they had shared.

At Runnymede on May 14, 1965, the sun loomed hot and brilliant over green meadows washed with the yellow of buttercups and dandelions. By 3 p.m. a crowd of perhaps 5,000 people had already assembled. Many had made impromptu hats out of folded newspapers to shield against the intense glare. Invited dignitaries took their places in a special enclosure, and some of the afternoon's speakers began to collect on a raised blue-and-gold platform. Soft white fluff from the poplar trees filled the air, and the effect, one observer noted, was "almost like snow in May."

That afternoon, Queen Elizabeth was to dedicate Great Britain's memorial to the American leader who had had such a powerful bond with Britain and its history. In the meadow overlooking the island in the River Thames where in 1215 King John had met with his rebellious barons to sign Magna Carta, the foundation of constitutional government, the Queen was to give in perpetuity to the American people three acres of this sacred ground in memory of President Kennedy. Shortly after three, the Queen emerged from the woods with a small party, including the president's widow, his seven-year-old daughter and four-year-old son, his two surviving brothers, two of his sisters—and David Ormsby Gore, who had become Lord Harlech on the recent death of his father.

Two months previously, David had resigned his post as ambassador in Washington. Broken-hearted after the assassination, he had wanted nothing more than to leave the United States immediately, but he felt it was his duty to stay on in an effort to ensure that the things for which he and Jack had worked together might continue. Shy and modest in the extreme, he had been the perfect partner for Kennedy, who had loved the spotlight as much as David preferred to work in the background. Poised for two and a half years between two ferociously ambitious figures—Kennedy and Macmillan—the self-effacing Ormsby Gore had been pivotal in making that triangular relationship work to such great effect. Now, all that was past. As Ormsby Gore himself had written to Macmillan shortly after Jack's death, "The sun has gone down and Washington seems desolate and dull in comparison with the still so recent past. . . . I myself know that my two years as your go-between will probably have been the most inspiring and pleasurable of my life."

In the end, as he tried to adjust to life with a new American president, David had felt that what he missed most were the "conversations." Years later, he would explain that when Lyndon Johnson summoned him to the White House, "it wasn't like the old days when we had a proper exchange of views. He expressed views that he wanted me to report to London. We didn't really get into a debate about the issues, which obviously I had done with President Kennedy." A Cecil bred to love good talk, David had treasured his "twenty-five-year conversation" with Jack Kennedy; though he was much too modest to say so, he must have known what it had meant to Jack as well. Having played his great role in history—largely off-stage, in keeping with his nature—David was now ready to withdraw. Though he would remain quietly active in British public life for another two decades, henceforth he would operate on a considerably smaller scale. In 1985, at the age of sixty-six, David, like his beloved Sissie before him, would die in an automobile crash.

Waiting on the speaker's platform as David escorted the Queen to her seat was the prime minister he had served so faithfully and so well. The seventy-one-year-old Harold Macmillan, recovered from the ill health that had precipitated his resignation just after the test ban treaty went into effect, was the first speaker. His words expressed the shock, anger and disbelief of the much older man who had spoken to Jack

Kennedy of his fear that he might not live to see their work completed. Now, he was mourning the loss of the young American leader who had come to seem almost like a son to him. As Macmillan began to speak of "that grim day nearly two years ago when we heard the news," a look of sharp pain crossed the face of the president's widow, seated just behind him. Jacqueline Kennedy had made an exception in agreeing to appear at this public tribute to her husband, for as she struggled to recover from the assassination, she had consciously tried to put Jack out of her mind for the sake of their children. As she later privately told Macmillan, she had found listening to his speech the hardest part of the day. For both of them, as she well understood, the emotions stirred up by Jack's death were still extremely raw.

If Macmillan's anguish was apparent in his speech, the Queen's personal warmth and affection for the slain president imbued her presentation. She began, "This soil is now bequeathed in perpetuity to the American people in memory of John F. Kennedy, whom in death my people still mourn and whom in life, they loved and admired." The Queen herself had first met Jack Kennedy when she was a little girl, and after Billy Hartington's death she had visited Compton Place and seen for herself Kick's gallant determination to find some way to go on alone. In the hot afternoon sun at Runnymede, the Queen spoke fondly of Kick and of the fact that she was buried in an English churchyard.

As it happened, the previous afternoon had been the seventeenth anniversary of Kick's death. Her two surviving brothers and two of her sisters had made the pilgrimage to Chatsworth, where Andrew Devonshire had taken them to the churchyard as two years previously he had taken Jack. Like David, Andrew had remained in government when Macmillan's foreign secretary, Alec Douglas-Home, succeeded him as prime minister. But by the time of Runnymede, Andrew's years of active political life were behind him. Although he remained deeply concerned with politics, what he would later refer to as the happiest years of his life had ended with the Conservative defeat in 1964.

Missing from the ceremony that May was the Englishman who, by his writings and example, had played the most important role of all in the life of the American president. Only four months before, the Queen had presided over the state funeral of Winston Churchill. Churchill's son Randolph did come to Runnymede, where he spoke to

Jacqueline Kennedy of his intention to have a complete set of first editions of his father's works beautifully bound in memory of her husband. A few months later, a painted tin trunk filled with the books arrived at the Kennedy apartment in New York—a gift for young John. "Maybe," Jackie wrote of the gift, "Randolph will be the one to draw John to the books that shaped John's father."

Jackie had come to Runnymede with the intention of making a brief speech, to conclude with John Buchan's lines on Raymond Asquith that Jack had once applied to Billy Hartington. In the event, she found that she was just too emotional to speak. After the ceremony she released a statement to express gratitude to the British people and to offer a last word on their country's influence on President Kennedy. "Your literature and the lives of your great men shaped him, as did no other part of his education. In a sense, he returns today to the tradition from which he sprang."

Acknowledgments

M Y FIRST DEBT OF GRATITUDE IS TO THE PEOPLE WHO, by sharing their memories and perceptions, did so much to help me tell the story of Britain's influence on President John F. Kennedy. I could never have completed this book without the generosity of the Duke and Duchess of Devonshire, Lady Lloyd, Lady Anne Tree, Lady Elizabeth Cavendish and Lord Holderness. Lord Stockton spoke to me about his grandfather Harold Macmillan, and Jane Rainey and Victoria Lloyd discussed their father, David Ormsby Gore. Many, many thanks to all.

I also want to acknowledge the kind help of Lady Arran, Brigadier Andrew Parker Bowles, Betty Spalding, Larry Newman, Susan Newman, Lady Kennard, Lord Rosslyn, Helen Marchant, Michael Cockerell, and Brian Porter.

Special thanks to Helen Langley and the staff at the Bodleian Library, Oxford University; Richard Groocock and other staff members at the Public Record Office in London; Sharon Kelly, Megan Desnoyers, June Payne, and Maura Porter at the John F. Kennedy Library; Michael Bott at the University of Reading Library; Ann Marie Gleason at the Franklin Delano Roosevelt Library; Tessa Sterling at the Cabinet Office Historical Section; Sue Donnelly at the London School of Economics; Kate Dubose at the Massachusetts Historical Society; Godfrey Waller and other staff members at Cambridge University Library; Jackie Tarrant-Barton at Eton College; Mark Dionne at the University of Rhode Island; Bryan Dyson at the University of Hull; and the librarians at Sterling Library and the Beinecke Rare Book and Manuscript Library, Yale University. I am also grateful to Lord Harlech for allowing me access to an interview with his father on deposit at the London School of Economics.

Ion Trewin, editor-in-chief at Weidenfeld & Nicolson in London, was the first person to whom I spoke of this book when it was little more than a half-formed idea. The book would never have become a reality without his astute advice and encouragement. We have now done four books together, and with each new project I realize how fortunate I am to have him as my editor. As all of his authors know, he is an oasis of calm and wisdom. I have benefited immensely from his guidance. Starling Lawrence, editor-in-chief at W. W. Norton in New York, was immediately enthusiastic about the project. I am grateful for his many helpful comments and suggestions, and for making it possible to do a book that has been a great adventure for me. Allegra Huston, formerly editorial director at Weidenfeld, has worked with me on six books. She is a gifted editor with a remarkable sense of narrative. Always determined to make a book the best it can be, she is unfailingly generous in finding ways to make that possible. I also wish to express gratitude to Juliet Ewers at Orion in London for all of her help on this and past projects. Thanks as well to Anna Herve at Weidenfeld and Morgen Van Vorst at Norton.

Also to my agents, Lois Wallace in New York and Bill Hamilton in London, my thanks for all of their wonderful support.

Thank you as well to Kelly Horgan for her many kindnesses during the writing of this book.

I must also acknowledge Rafael Guevara, both for his patience and for his acute sense of drama.

Finally, I wish to thank my husband, David. He carried endless boxes of photocopies from Kew to Eaton Place, spent countless hours discussing Churchill, the Whigs, and every aspect of Jack Kennedy's life, and made the last four years of work on this book possible in ways too numerous to mention. He has always been incredibly generous with his ideas—but never more so than on this book. It would not exist without him.

Source Notes

ABBREVIATIONS

JFK   John Fitzgerald Kennedy
PRO   Public Record Office, London
FRUS   *Foreign Relations of the United States, 1961–1963*, vols. 1–16
(Washington, DC: United States Government Printing Office, 1996)
PPP   *Public Papers of the Presidents, John F. Kennedy 1961–1963*
(Washington, DC: United States Government Printing Office, 1964)
BLO   Bodleian Library, Oxford
JFKL   John F. Kennedy Library, Boston, Massachusetts
FDRL   Franklin D. Roosevelt Library, Hyde Park, New York
LBJL   Lyndon B. Johnson Library, Austin, Texas
MHS   Massachusetts Historical Society, Boston, Massachusetts
UR   University of Reading

CHAPTER ONE: THE TWENTY-FIVE-YEAR CONVERSATION

p. 9:   visit to Chatsworth: Andrew Devonshire, author interview; Deborah Devonshire, author interview; Philip de Zulueta to J.O. Wright, June 28, 1963, FO 371/173293, PRO; Confidential Timetable, FO 371/173293, PRO; Deborah Devonshire's scrapbook.

p. 11:   "twenty-five-year conversation": Jane Rainey, author interview.

p. 12:   Background on marriage of Joe and Rose Kennedy: Rose Fitzgerald Kennedy, *Times to Remember* (New York: Bantam Books, 1975); Amanda Smith, ed., *Hostage to Fortune: The Letters of Joseph P. Kennedy* (New York: Viking, 2001); Doris Kearns Goodwin, *The Kennedys and the Fitzgeralds* (New York: Simon & Schuster, 1987); Peter Collier and David Horowitz, *The Kennedys* (New York: Summit Books, 1984); Richard J. Whalen, *The Founding Father: The Story of Joseph P. Kennedy* (New York: New American Library, 1964); Betty Spalding, author interview.

p. 13: at odds with friends: Whalen, *The Founding Father*; Rose Kennedy quoted in Goodwin, *The Fitzgeralds and the Kennedys*.

p. 13: "just long enough": Rose Kennedy, *Times to Remember*.

p. 13: as he remembered years afterward: Betty Spalding, author interview.

p. 13: the entries in her diary: Rose Kennedy, *Times to Remember*.

p. 14: could not remember a hug: Deborah Devonshire, author interview.

p. 15: Joe later confessed: Joseph P. Kennedy to Dr. Place, July 2, 1920, in Smith, ed., *Hostage to Fortune*.

p. 15: "Gee, you're a": Rose Kennedy, *Times to Remember*.

p. 16: Jack's poor health: Rose Kennedy, child health record, 1928, JFKL.

p. 17: the ability to laugh at himself: Andrew Devonshire, author interview.

p. 18: "favorite of all": Rose Kennedy to Nancy Astor, June 14, 1948, UR.

p. 18: "heresy": Kick Kennedy quoted in Betty Spalding, author interview.

p. 18: "I always knew": JFK quoted in Betty Spalding, author interview.

p. 19: "When Joe came": JFK to Joseph P. Kennedy, December 29, 1929, JFKL.

p. 20: "5 lb. heavier": JFK to Rose Kennedy, n.d., JFKL.

p. 20: "My nose my leg": JFK to Rose Kennedy, n.d., JFKL.

p. 20: "I am made": JFK to Rose Kennedy, n.d., JFKL.

p. 20: "We are reading": JFK to Joseph P. Kennedy, n.d., JFKL.

p. 21: "one of the": Mrs. George St. John to Rose Kennedy, October 7, 1931, JFKL.

p. 21: "the boy that": quoted in "John F. Kennedy: Fiftieth Reunion of 1000 Days at School," MHS.

p. 21: "inability to concentrate": quoted in "John F. Kennedy: Fiftieth Reunion of 1000 Days at School," MHS.

p. 21: Jack reading *The World Crisis*: Kay Halle, interview, JFKL.

p. 22: "for nothing": Kick Kennedy quoted in Jean Lloyd, author interview.

p. 22: "delusion": Kick Kennedy quoted in Jean Lloyd, author interview.

p. 23: "so surrounded by": Kay Halle, interview, JFKL.

p. 23: "problem child": Joseph P. Kennedy to George St. John, September 1, 1943, MHS.

p. 23: "every single day": Ralph Horton, interview, JFKL.

p. 23: "I'll read it": JFK quoted in Ralph Horton, interview, JFKL.

p. 24: "the opening gun": JFK, "Appeasement at Munich," JFKL.

p. 24: "deeply and profoundly": JFK, "Appeasement at Munich," JFKL.

p. 24: "within the first": Stanley Baldwin, speech, November 10, 1932.

p. 24: "no power on": Baldwin, speech, November 10, 1932.

p. 24: "The bomber will": Baldwin, speech, November 10, 1932.

p. 24: "the return of": Winston Churchill, speech, November 23, 1932.

p. 24: "they principally and": Baldwin, speech, November 10, 1932.

p. 25: "the curl of": Churchill, speech, February 17, 1932.

p. 25: "decadent": Kick Kennedy to JFK, February 13, 1942, JFKL.

p. 25: "every single thing": Kay Halle, interview, JFKL.

p. 26: confesses to Lem: Lem Billings quoted in Goodwin, *The Fitzgeralds and the Kennedys*.

p. 26: "I feel very": Joseph P. Kennedy to George St. John, September 25, 1933, JFKL.

p. 27: "I can't tell": Joseph P. Kennedy to George St. John, November 21, 1933, JFKL.

p. 28: "about five": Joseph P. Kennedy to Joseph Kennedy Jr., May 4, 1934, JFKL.

p. 29: "the dirtiest-minded": JFK to Lem Billings, June 30, 1934, JFKL.

p. 29: "I had": JFK to Lem Billings, June 19, 1934, JFKL.

p. 29: "The nurses are": JFK to Lem Billings, June 30, 1934, JFKL.

p. 30: "I wanted power": Joseph P. Kennedy quoted in Ralph Martin, *A Hero for Our Time* (New York: Fawcett, 1983).

p. 30: "practically ignored": Ralph Horton, interview, JFKL.

p. 30: "rather curtly": Ralph Horton, interview, JFKL.

p. 31: "go to great": Ralph Horton, interview, JFKL.

p. 31: "corrupting the morals": Ralph Horton, interview, JFKL.

p. 31: "the worst kind": Ralph Horton, interview, JFKL.

p. 31: "highly irate": Ralph Horton, interview, JFKL.

p. 31: reportedly on the basis of the King and Country resolution: Winston Churchill, *The Gathering Storm* (Boston: Houghton Mifflin Co., 1985).

p. 31: "Am definitely coming": JFK to Lem Billings, October 9, 1935, JFKL.

p. 33: "My blood count": JFK to Lem Billings, January 18, 1936, JFKL.

p. 34: "but a step": Churchill, speech, March 26, 1936.

p. 34: "the beginning of": Joseph P. Kennedy to Delmar Leighton, August 28, 1936, JFKL.

p. 35: he loved her too much: Betty Spalding, author interview.

p. 36: with the flu: naval records, JFKL.

p. 36: "a program of": Churchill, speech, March 14, 1938.

p. 37: "firmly of the": Anne Tree, author interview.

p. 38: Pilgrims' Club speech: *New York Times*, March 19, 1938.

p. 38: "the most isolationist": quoted in Thomas Jones, *A Diary with Letters, 1931–1950* (London: Oxford University Press, 1954).

p. 38: background on Joe Kennedy's political views: correspondence of Joseph P. Kennedy, FDRL.

CHAPTER TWO: THE ARISTOCRATIC COUSINHOOD

p. 40: Kennedy and Eden at the Dorchester: *Daily Telegraph*, London, July 5, 1938; *The Times*, London, July 5, 1938; John Harvey, ed., *The Diplomatic Diaries of Oliver Harvey 1937–1940* (London: Collins, 1970).

p. 41: Rose Kennedy's dinner and Lady Astor's dance: Jean Lloyd, author interview; Jean Ogilvy diary.

p. 42: "He looked very": Jean Lloyd, author interview.

p. 42: "the ugliest voice": Veronica Maclean, *Past Forgetting* (London: Review, 2002).

p. 42: "one might meet": Harold Macmillan, *Winds of Change* (New York: Harper & Row, 1966).

p. 42: "tight little circle": Jean Lloyd, author interview.

p. 43: "She had a": Jean Lloyd, author interview.

p. 43: "was just a": Anne Tree, author interview.

p. 43: "a very narrow": Fiona Arran, author interview.

p. 43: "rather difficult": Kick Kennedy to Nancy Astor, November 28, 1938, UR.

p. 43: loneliness: Kick Kennedy to Nancy Astor, April 19, 1938, UR.

p. 44: her first country-house weekend: Cliveden visitors' book, UR; Jean Ogilvy diary; Andrew Devonshire, author interview; Jean Lloyd, author interview.

p. 44: "the best thing": Kick Kennedy to Nancy Astor, November 28, 1938, UR.

p. 44: "rather lost": Jean Lloyd, author interview.

p. 45: formation of the group of young people: Jean Lloyd's scrapbooks; Jean Lloyd, author interview.

p. 45: "It was her": Andrew Devonshire, author interview.

p. 46: "He didn't like": Jean Lloyd, author interview.

p. 46: "one too many": Jean Lloyd, author interview.

p. 46: "little face": Jean Lloyd, author interview.

p. 47: "talked all the": Macmillan, *Winds of Change*.

p. 47: "expected to be": David Cecil, *The Cecils of Hatfield House* (Boston: Houghton Mifflin Co., 1973).

p. 47: "with all the": Cecil, *The Cecils of Hatfield House*.

p. 47: "David, I have": quoted by Anne Tree, author interview.

p. 47: "as a brother": Andrew Devonshire, author interview.

p. 48: arrival of Hugh Fraser: Cliveden visitors' book, UR.

p. 48: "Hugh and David": Jean Lloyd, author interview.

p. 49: "just about everything": Jean Lloyd, author interview.

p. 49: "at every party": Jean Lloyd, author interview.

p. 50: "the Big One": Fiona Arran, author interview.

p. 50: Joe's temper flared: Jean Lloyd, author interview.

p. 50: visit to Eton: Richard Holderness, author interview.

p. 51: background on JFK's friendship with David Ormsby Gore: Jane Rainey, author interview; Victoria Lloyd, author interview; Jean Lloyd, author interview; Andrew Devonshire, author interview; Richard Holderness, author interview.

p. 51: "the short straw": Andrew Devonshire, author interview.

p. 51: "pushed to the fore": Victoria Lloyd, author interview.

p. 51: "prime runner": Victoria Lloyd, author interview.

p. 51: "anything more ghastly": Jane Rainey, author interview.

p. 52: lacked the ruthlessness: Richard Holderness, author interview.

p. 53: "repartee": Jane Rainey, author interview.

p. 54: imbued with the spirit: Macmillan, *Winds of Change*.

p. 54: "spoke as": Macmillan, *Winds of Change*.

p. 54: "the luxury of": Randolph Churchill, preface to Winston Churchill, *Arms and the Covenant* (London: Harrap, 1938).

p. 55: read and debated *Arms and the Covenant*: Andrew Devonshire, author interview.

p. 57: "The War which": Winston Churchill, *Great Contemporaries* (London: Thornton Butterworth Ltd., 1937).

p. 57: decadence conversation: Jean Lloyd, author interview.

p. 57: based his assessment on the King and Country resolution: Andrew Devonshire, author interview.

p. 57: Background on Billy Hartington: Andrew Devonshire, author interview; Deborah Devonshire, author interview; Anne Tree, author interview; Elizabeth Cavendish, author interview; Jean Lloyd, author interview.

p. 58: playfully refer back to it: Kick Kennedy to JFK, February 13, 1942, JFKL.

p. 59: lunches and teas in London: Jean Ogilvy diary; Jean Lloyd, author interview.

p. 59: "fancied her": Andrew Devonshire, author interview.

p. 59: "Conversation took precedence": Julian Fane, *Best Friends* (London: Trafalgar House, 1991).

p. 59: "loved conversation": Anne Tree, author interview.

p. 60: "passionate love of politics": Anne Tree, author interview.

p. 60: "taken for granted": Jean Lloyd, author interview.

p. 60: "almost go mad": Rose Kennedy's diary quoted in Rose Kennedy, *Times to Remember*.

p. 60: planned to start Harvard Law School: *New York Times*, September 28, 1938.

p. 61: "disquieting signs": Churchill, speech, August 27, 1938.

p. 62: "which could be": Joseph P. Kennedy draft speech, FDRL.

CHAPTER THREE: SUNSET GLOW BEFORE THE STORM

p. 63: returns to United States and heads for Hyannis Port: JFK to Lem Billings, October 4, 1938, JFKL.

p. 64: telephoned Roosevelt: Harvey, ed., *The Diplomatic Diaries of Oliver Harvey*.

p. 64: "to clear Hitler's mind": Harvey, ed., *The Diplomatic Diaries of Oliver Harvey*.

p. 64: "in rotten shape": JFK to Lem Billings, October 4, 1938, JFKL.

p. 64: came back a different man: Torbert Macdonald, interview, JFKL.

p. 65: got up, dressed and ate by their radios: Jones, *A Diary with Letters*.

p. 65: The First Lord of the Admiralty countered: Duff Cooper, *Old Men Forget* (London: Century Publishing, 1986).

p. 65: Joe Kennedy summons Lindbergh: Charles Lindbergh, *The Wartime Journals* (New York: Harcourt Brace Jovanovich, 1970); Anne Morrow Lindbergh, *The Flower and the Nettle: Diaries and Letters of Anne Morrow Lindbergh, 1936–1939* (New York: Harcourt Brace Jovanovich, 1976); Jones, *A Diary with Letters*; Joseph P. Kennedy files, FDRL.

p. 67: followed "the crisis" at Cortachy Castle: Jean Lloyd, author interview.

p. 67: Cortachy house party: Jean Lloyd's scrapbook.

p. 67: "All you can hear": Kick Kennedy to Lem Billings, September 23, 1938, JFKL.

p. 67: a sense of foreboding: Jean Lloyd, author interview.

p. 67: Billy never in love before: Anne Tree, author interview.

p. 68: "Black Wednesday dawned": John Wheeler-Bennett, *Munich: Prologue to Tragedy*, (London: Macmillan, 1948).

p. 68: "Said I should": Rose Kennedy, *Times to Remember*.

p. 68: Kick at Perth: Jean Lloyd, author interview; Rose Kennedy, *Times to Remember*.

p. 68: "entitled": Andrew Devonshire, author interview.

p. 69: "silent and seated": Macmillan, *Winds of Change*.

p. 69: "I find an": Nigel Nicolson, ed., *Harold Nicolson Diaries and Letters 1930–39* (New York: Atheneum, 1966).

p. 69: "nothing else but": Jean Lloyd, author interview.

p. 69: "had inflicted": John Wheeler-Bennett, *Munich*.

p. 69: "the Man of": Robert Rhodes James, ed., *Chips: The Diaries of Sir Henry Channon* (London: Phoenix, 1996).

p. 70: "It was not": Cooper, *Old Men Forget*.

p. 70: "a most ordinary": Joe Kennedy diary, October 3, 1938, in Smith, ed., *Hostage to Fortune*.

p. 71: Macmillan and Taylor on Cooper's speech: Cooper, *Old Men Forget*.

p. 72: "The Navy Day": JFK to Joseph P. Kennedy, November 1, 1938, JFKL.

p. 72: Wheeler-Bennett meets JFK: John Wheeler-Bennett, *Special Relationships* (London: Macmillan, 1975).

p. 74: "tutor": Macmillan to JFK, May 19, 1963, JFKL.

p. 75: did not leave him feeling sick: JFK to Lem Billings, n.d., JFKL.

p. 75: aftermath of Munich: Andrew Devonshire, author interview.

p. 76: Billy's study of Talleyrand: Anne Tree, author interview.

p. 76: "quite important" . . . "a great deal of time": JFK to Lem Billings, n.d., JFKL.

p. 77: "not bearing fruit": Edward Devonshire quoted in Robert Shepherd, *A Class Divided* (London: Macmillan, 1988).

p. 77: united by its sense of shame: Andrew Devonshire, author interview.

p. 77: "the safety catch": Andrew Devonshire, author interview.

p. 78: "Everyone thinks war": JFK to Lem Billings, March 23, 1939, JFKL.

p. 78: "During the crisis": *New York Times*, February 17, 1939.

p. 78: "Well, I'm on": Joseph Kennedy Jr. to Joseph P. Kennedy, February 10, 1939, JFKL.

p. 78: guests at Cliveden: Cliveden visitors' book, UR.

p. 79: "international publicity": Joseph P. Kennedy to Paul Murphy, April 18, 1939, JFKL.

p. 79: a series on Communism: Joseph P. Kennedy to Paul Murphy, April 18, 1939, JFKL.

p. 79: a piece by Joe on Spain: Joseph P. Kennedy to Geoffrey Dawson, May 1, 1939, JFKL.

p. 79: "access to a": Torbert Macdonald, interview, JFKL.

p. 80: "Just listened to Hitler's": JFK to Lem Billings, April 28, 1939, JFKL.

p. 80: "gravitas": Hugh Fraser, interview, JFKL.

p. 80: a book-length collection: Joseph P. Kennedy to John B. Kennedy, May 12, 1939, in Smith, ed., *Hostage to Fortune*.

p. 81: "like Jack in a wig": Jakie Astor quoted by Deborah Devonshire, author interview.

p. 81: Jack visits Danzig: JFK to Lem Billings, n.d., JFKL.

p. 81: "The Poles are": JFK to Lem Billings, n.d., JFKL.

p. 81: Hugh Fraser and Julian Amery at the Oxford Union: Julian Amery, *Approach March* (London: Hutchinson, 1973); David Walter, *The Oxford Union: Playground of Power*, (London: Macdonald & Co, 1984); Edward Heath, *The Course of My Life: My Autobiography* (London: Hodder & Stoughton, 1998).

p. 82: Kennedy–Churchill encounter: Nicolson, ed., *Harold Nicolson Diaries and Letters*.

p. 83: film screening: Fiona Arran, author interview; Jean Lloyd, author interview.

p. 84: Billy's undergraduate thesis: Andrew Devonshire, author interview.

p. 84: "often talked to her": Richard Holderness, author interview.

p. 84: "the role he": Richard Holderness, author interview.

p. 84: passion for politics: Anne Tree, author interview.

p. 85: "ideal partner": Richard Holderness, author interview.

p. 85: lent a certain energy: Jean Lloyd, author interview.

p. 85: "grow up more": Jean Lloyd, author interview.

p. 86: "My father had": Anne Tree, author interview.

p. 86: "felt that he": Anne Tree, author interview.

p. 87: "These Catholic girls": Lord Richard Cavendish quoted by Jean Lloyd, author interview.

p. 87: RossKennedy: Tony Rosslyn to JFK, November 18, 1940, JFKL.

p. 87: Tony's admiration for Ambassador Kennedy: Tony Rosslyn to JFK, December 4, 1940, JFKL.

p. 88: "sunset glow before": Rhodes James, ed., *Chips*.

p. 88: "never again open": Rhodes James, ed., *Chips*.

p. 88: "by a sense of": Amery, *Approach March*.

p. 88: "Jack was very": Elizabeth Leveson-Gower quoted in Angela Lambert, *1939: The Last Season of Peace* (London: Weidenfeld & Nicolson, 1989).

p. 88: Tony's trousers: Tony Rosslyn to JFK, December 18, 1940, JFKL.

p. 88: Bleinheim ball: JFK to Lem Billings, July 17, 1939, JFKL.

p. 88: Chips Channon's luncheon: Rhodes James, ed., *Chips*.

p. 89: "Never had a": JFK to Lem Billings, July 17, 1939, JFKL.

p. 89: that thrilled David: David Ormsby Gore, interview, JFKL.

p. 89: "hard to see": JFK to Lem Billings, August 20, 1939, JFKL.

p. 89: "England seems firm": JFK to Lem Billings, August 20, 1939, JFKL.

p. 89: Billy's coming-of-age celebration: Jean Lloyd, author interview; Jean Lloyd's scrapbooks.

p. 90: "The atmosphere had": Andrew Devonshire, *Accidents of Fortune* (Norwich: Michael Russell, 2004).

p. 91: undermine Churchill in Roosevelt's eyes: Joseph P. Kennedy to Franklin D. Roosevelt, November 3, 1939, FDRL.

p. 92: "Yesterday my son": Joseph P. Kennedy to Cordell Hull, September 8, 1939, FDRL.

p. 93: her real life and real friends: Jean Lloyd, author interview.

p. 93: "distraught": Jean Lloyd, author interview.

p. 93: farewell dinner: minute book, September, 1939, FO 371/2287, PRO; Jean Lloyd, author interview.

p. 94: "Only fear, violent fear": JFK, "Appeasement at Munich," JFKL.

CHAPTER FOUR: THE FORM MOST PLEASING TO HIS AUDIENCE

p. 95: status as a "seer": JFK to Joseph P. Kennedy, n.d., JFKL.

p. 95: "savior": Joseph P. Kennedy to Franklin D. Roosevelt, September 11, 1939, FDRL.

p. 95: "The people of": Cordell Hull to Joseph P. Kennedy, September 11, 1939, FDRL.

p. 96: "Peace in Our Time": *Harvard Crimson*, October 9, 1939.

p. 97: "Everyone here is": JFK to Joseph P. Kennedy, n.d., JFKL.

p. 97: "might lead to": JFK to Joseph P. Kennedy, n.d., JFKL.

p. 97: "like a beautiful": Kick Kennedy to Joseph P. Kennedy, September 18, 1939, in Smith, ed., *Hostage to Fortune*.

p. 98: "not to his": Rhodes James, ed., *Chips*.

p. 98:   "Someday—somehow": Kick Kennedy to Rose Kennedy, July 6, 1944, JFKL.

p. 98:   "They bemoaned": Nancy Astor to Kick Kennedy, n.d., UR.

p. 98:   "The Government had not": Nicolson, ed., *Harold Nicolson Diaries and Letters*.

p. 99:   "I trust that": Rhodes James, ed., *Chips*.

p. 99:   "defeatist attitude": secret memo to Lord Lothian, October 3, 1939, FO 371/ 22827, PRO.

p. 99:   Foreign Office monitored Kennedy in US: FO 371/2287, PRO.

p. 100: "The vast majority": Harold Nicolson, "People and Things," *The Spectator*, March 8, 1940.

p. 100: Nancy Astor's candy: Jean Lloyd, author interview.

p. 100: "an open forum": Macmillan, *Winds of Change*.

p. 100: eager to see America come in: Nancy Astor to Kick Kennedy, December 13, 1940, UR.

p. 100: "scandalous": Nancy Astor to Joseph Kennedy Jr., February 2, 1940, UR.

p. 100: to change her friend's mind: Nancy Astor to Kick Kennedy, December 13, 1940, UR.

p. 101: "They have friends": Joseph P. Kennedy to Rose Kennedy, March 14, 1940, JFKL.

p. 101: "a cloud of": JFK, "Appeasement at Munich," JFKL.

p. 101: "a 'realist' policy": JFK, "Appeasement at Munich," JFKL.

p. 102: "Most of the": JFK, "Appeasement at Munich," JFKL.

p. 102: "A politician will": JFK, "Appeasement at Munich," JFKL.

p. 102: "on the pan for": JFK, "Appeasement at Munich," JFKL.

p. 102: "To blame one": JFK, "Appeasement at Munich," JFKL.

p. 103: "The nation was": JFK, "Appeasement at Munich," JFKL.

p. 104: "seemed to represent": quoted in Hank Searls, *The Lost Prince: Young Joe, the Forgotten Kennedy* (Cleveland: World Publishing, 1969).

p. 104: "disastrously true": Cooper, *Old Men Forget*.

p. 105: "The basis of": Joseph P. Kennedy to JFK, May 20, 1940, JFKL.

p. 106: "failure to awaken": John F. Kennedy, *Why England Slept* (New York: Funk, 1961).

p. 106: "He admits he": JFK, *Why England Slept*.

p. 106: "The moral": William Douglas Home to JFK, July 24, 1945, JFKL.

p. 106: "the only man": JFK, *Why England Slept*.

p. 106: "With this new": JFK, *Why England Slept*.

p. 107: "failure to bring": JFK, *Why England Slept*.

p. 107: "We must always": JFK, *Why England Slept*.

p. 107: Begged for news of Billy: Kick Kennedy to Joseph P. Kennedy, May 21, 1940, JFKL.

p. 108: "But what was": Winston Churchill, *Their Finest Hour* (Boston: Houghton Mifflin Co., 1985).

p. 108: Billy left behind in Flanders: Nancy Astor to Philip Lothian, June 10, 1940, UR.

p. 108: nobody knew where he was: Nancy Astor to Philip Lothian, June 16, 1940, UR.

p. 109: Billy appears at Jean's door: Jean Ogilvy diary.

p. 109: Scene in mews cottage: Jean Lloyd, author interview.

p. 109: "Of this I": Churchill, speech, June 18, 1940.

p. 110: ghosted the manuscript: Wheeler-Bennett, *Special Relationships*.

p. 110: Joe went to California: Joseph Kennedy Jr. to Nancy Astor, August 23, 1940, UR.

p. 111: "Health is OK": JFK to Joseph P. Kennedy, n.d., JFKL.

p. 111: "I couldn't be": Joseph P. Kennedy to JFK, September 10, 1940, JFKL.

p. 111: "quiet defiance": Wheeler-Bennett, *Special Relationships*.

p. 111: wished Hitler could see the British response: Nancy Astor to Bob Brand, March 31, 1941, UR.

p. 112: "thoroughly frightened," "lost his nerve" and "gone to pieces": FO 371/24251, PRO.

p. 112: "the most frightened": Douglas Fairbanks Jr. to Roosevelt, November 19, 1940, FDRL.

p. 112: "Rarely as a": Joseph P. Kennedy to Roosevelt, August 27, 1940, FDRL.

p. 112: "The United States": Lord Halifax to Lord Lothian, October 10, 1940, FO 371/24251, PRO.

p. 112: "an indictment of": Halifax to Lothian, October 10, 1940, FO 371/24251, PRO.

p. 112: "of considerable importance": Halifax to Lothian, October 10, 1940, FO 371/24251, PRO.

p. 112: did not want him to come home: Rose Kennedy to Joseph P. Kennedy, October 7, 1940, JFKL.

p. 113: cablegram demanding permission to leave: Arthur Krock, *Memoirs* (New York: Funk & Wagnalls, 1968).

p. 113: telephoned Welles: Krock, *Memoirs*.

p. 113: "interests in Wall Street": Memorandum on the Retirement of Mr. Joseph Kennedy from the Embassy of the United States in London, FO 371/24251, PRO.

p. 113: "decided to go along": Memorandum on the Retirement of Mr. Joseph Kennedy from the Embassy of the United States in London, FO 371/24251, PRO.

p. 113: effective radio address: Joseph P. Kennedy speech, October 29, 1940, JFKL.

p. 114: "Proud to have": JFK to Joseph P. Kennedy, October 30, 1940, JFKL.

p. 115: "They will never": JFK to Lem Billings, November 14, 1940, JFKL.

p. 115: "I think in": Joseph Kennedy Jr. to Joseph P. Kennedy, November 2, 1940, JFKL.

p. 116: "the man who": *New York Tribune*, November 12, 1940.

p. 116: controversial remarks in Boston: FO 371/24251, PRO.

p. 117: "A year ago": *New York Tribune*, November 12, 1940.

p. 117: Los Angeles luncheon and aftermath: E. A. Cleugh to Richard Ford, November 22, 1940, FO 371/2451, PRO; Fairbanks to Roosevelt, November 19, 1940, FDRL.

p. 118: confessed to William Randolph Hearst: Joseph P. Kennedy to William Randolph Hearst, November 26, 1940, JFKL.

p. 118: "My plan": *New York Times*, December 2, 1940.

p. 119: "rough outline" to help "clear the record": JFK to Joseph P. Kennedy, December 6, 1940, JFKL.

p. 121: "usual childhood illnesses": naval records, JFKL.

CHAPTER FIVE: BILLY HARTINGTON WANTS TO KNOW

p. 122: JFK's arrival in Washington: Betty Spalding, author interview.

p. 122: Inga's memories: Inga Arvad, "1941–1942," MHS.

p. 123: Billy had decided to marry: Kick Kennedy to Joseph P. Kennedy, October 20, 1941, JFKL.

p. 123: A letter arrived from Billy: Kick Kennedy to Joseph P. Kennedy, n.d., JFKL.

p. 123: "nearly going mad": Kick Kennedy to Joseph P. Kennedy, October 20, 1941, JFKL.

p. 124: "Jack's Future": Betty Spalding, author interview.

p. 124: "die-hard position on the war": JFK, notes on dinner at Mrs. Patterson's, JFKL.

p. 124: "fluid" and "flexible": JFK, notes on dinner at Mrs. Patterson's, JFKL.

p. 124: "the effort necessary": JFK, notes on dinner at Mrs. Patterson's, JFKL.

p. 124: John White also saw them that way: Goodwin, *The Fitzgeralds and the Kennedys*.

p. 125: "wonderful talker": Betty Spalding, author interview.

p. 125: "a boy with a future": Inga Arvad, Washington *Times–Herald*, November 27, 1941.

p. 125: Inga as espionage suspect: memorandum for the attorney general, Re: Mrs. Paul Fejos, nee Inga Arvad, Espionage, Internal Security, January 21, 1942, FBI; memorandum for the director, Re: Mrs. Paul Fejos nee Inga Arvad, December 12, 1941, FBI; Betty Spalding, author interview.

p. 126: "They certainly transfer": Kick Kennedy to Rose Kennedy, January 20, 1942, JFKL.

p. 126: a jubilant message: Nancy Astor to Kick Kennedy, December 24, 1941, UR.

p. 126: "My mother was": Anne Tree, author interview.

p. 126: Georgiana's letters: Anne Tree, author interview.

p. 126: "I long to": Kick Kennedy to Nancy Astor, n.d., UR.

p. 126: Kick's attempts to return to England: Betty Spalding, author interview.

p. 126: "countless dukes": Lem Billings to JFK, n.d., JFKL.

p. 126: Kick would sit cross-legged: Betty Spalding, author interview.

p. 127: "Billy Hartington wants": Kick Kennedy to JFK, February 13, 1942, JFKL.

p. 127: "In 1915": quoted in Nicolson, ed., *Harold Nicolson Diaries and Letters*.

p. 128: spoke of Churchill's speech: report, Re: Mrs. Paul Fejos, with aliases, Espionage, – G, February 23, 1942, FBI.

p. 128: "After reading the": JFK to Kick Kennedy, March 10, 1942, JFKL.

p. 130: "the drippings from": Kick Kennedy to JFK, February 13, 1942, JFKL.

p. 130: "average reader": Kick Kennedy to JFK, n.d., JFKL.

p. 130: a play she had not seen: Kick Kennedy to JFK, February 13, 1942, JFKL.

p. 130: sent it first to Kick: Kick Kennedy to JFK, n.d., JFKL.

p. 131: Clare Boothe Luce declared: Inga Arvad to JFK, February 23, 1942, JFKL.

p. 131: "If you can": Inga Arvad to JFK, February 23, 1942, JFKL.

p. 131: "Our roll of": John Buchan, *Pilgrim's Way* (Cambridge: Riverside Press, 1940).

p. 132: sought to model himself on Asquith: Betty Spalding, author interview.

p. 132: "He looks like": telephone transcript, July 24, 1942, FBI.

p. 133: "The requirements are": JFK to Lem Billings, n.d., JFKL.

p. 133: Kick joins Red Cross: Betty Spalding, author interview.

p. 134: Kick's friendship with Richard Wood: Richard Holderness, author interview.

p. 134: "immensely taken": Richard Holderness, author interview.

p. 135: "In regard to": JFK to Lem Billings, May 6, 1943, JFKL.

p. 136: "When she came back": Anne Tree, author interview.

p. 136: "second home": Kick Kennedy to JFK, July 29, 1943, JFKL.

p. 136: "Billy is just": Kick Kennedy to JFK, July 29, 1943, JFKL.

p. 137: with a sleeping bag: Fiona Arran, author interview.

p. 137: "more like a bed": Fiona Arran, author interview.

p. 137: "liked to sit": Jean Lloyd, author interview.

CHAPTER SIX: STRAW IN THE WIND

p. 138: rugged conditions: JFK, round-robin letter, n.d., JFKL.

p. 138: "All in all": JFK, round-robin letter, n.d., JFKL.

p. 139: "O.K.": JFK, round-robin letter, August 13, 1943, JFKL.

p. 139: physical condition after the rescue: naval records, JFKL.

p. 140: Joe's anguish showed itself: Joe Timilty, interview, JFKL.

p. 140: "very, very upset": Jean Lloyd, author interview.

p. 140: "He's got a": Billy Hartington quoted by Jean Lloyd, author interview.

p. 141: "he adored her": Anne Tree, author interview.

p. 141: Billy's proposal: Jean Lloyd, author interview.

p. 141: Kick began to develop breadth: Elizabeth Cavendish, author interview.

p. 142: background on by-election: Andrew Devonshire, author interview; Deborah Devonshire, author interview.

p. 142: "walkover": Harold Macmillan, *War Diaries* (London: Macmillan, 1984).

p. 143: "wearing rather thin": Macmillan, *War Diaries*.

p. 143: "It was a mistake": Andrew Devonshire, author interview.

p. 143: "in the fight": Deborah Devonshire's scrapbook.

p. 143: "hated soldiering": Moucher Devonshire to JFK, October 18, 1944, JFKL.

p. 143: he had awaited the day: Jean Lloyd, author interview.

p. 143: visit to Richard Wood: Richard Holderness, author interview.

p. 145: "political manners": Deborah Devonshire's scrapbook.

p. 145: "absolutely bound": Deborah Devonshire's scrapbook.

p. 145: "This must mean": Deborah Devonshire's scrapbook.

p. 146: "bobby dazzler": Deborah Devonshire's scrapbook.

p. 146: "It was too": Deborah Devonshire's scrapbook.

p. 147: "'propaganda' and untrue": Nicolson, ed., *Harold Nicolson Diaries and Letters*.

p. 147: "in mute comment": Deborah Devonshire's scrapbook.

p. 147: "My brother is": Billy Hartington quoted in Deborah Devonshire's scrapbook.

p. 147: Churchill's letter: quoted in John Pearson, *The Serpent and the Stag* (New York: Holt, Rinehart, 1984).

p. 148: "straw in the wind": Deborah Devonshire, author interview.

p. 148: "all day to": Moucher Devonshire to JFK, October 19, 1944, JFKL.

p. 149: "It has been": Billy Hartington quoted in Deborah Devonshire's scrapbook.

p. 149: "I don't know what the people want": Edward Devonshire quoted in Kick Kennedy, round-robin letter, February 22, 1944, JFKL.

p. 149: "caused a pall": John Colville, *The Fringes of Power* (London: Hodder & Stoughton, 1985).

p. 149: "disastrous": Rhodes James, ed., *Chips*.

p. 149: "ignominious": Rhodes James, ed., *Chips*.

p. 149: "proof that Britain": Sir Richard Acland quoted in Deborah Devonshire's scrapbook.

p. 150: "Duchesses' kisses": Duchess of Westminster quoted in Rhodes James, ed., *Chips*.

p. 150: "no less determined": Captain Charles Waterhouse quoted in Deborah Devonshire's scrapbook.

p. 150: "That's really the": Kick Kennedy, round-robin letter, February 22, 1944, JFKL.

p. 150: Kick's visit to Churchdale Hall: Kick Kennedy, round-robin letter, March 22, 1944, in Smith, ed., *Hostage to Fortune*.

p. 151: helped her to see her own mind: Kick Kennedy to Nancy Astor, n.d., UR.

p. 151: "watch over": Nancy Astor to Rose Kennedy, August 18, 1943, JFKL.

p. 151: visit to the Lloyds: Jean Lloyd, author interview.

p. 151: "We're off!": Billy Hartington quoted in Jean Lloyd, author interview.

p. 152: made up her mind to marry: Kick Kennedy, round-robin letter, April 24, 1944, in Smith, ed., *Hostage to Fortune*.

p. 152: "Mrs. Kennedy telegraphed": Jean Lloyd, author interview.

p. 152: "I don't think": Anne Tree, author interview.

p. 152: a long letter to Rose Kennedy: Billy Hartington to Rose Kennedy, April 30, 1944, in Smith, ed., *Hostage to Fortune*.

p. 153: part of the first wave of troops: Deborah Devonshire's scrapbook.

p. 153: "so utterly happy": Deborah Devonshire's scrapbook.

CHAPTER SEVEN: WHAT ABOUT YOU?

p. 154: "misjudged the durability": JFK, round-robin letter, n.d., JFKL.

p. 154: JFK's physical condition: naval records, JFKL.

p. 155: Rose recorded in her diary: diary entry, 1944, in Smith, ed., *Hostage to Fortune*.

p. 155: "I am indeed sorry": Dr. James Poppen to Captain Frederic Conklin, August 1, 1944, in JFK's naval records, JFKL.

p. 156: "belonging to a": JFK to Inga Arvad, September 26, 1943, quoted in Nigel Hamilton, *JFK: Reckless Youth* (New York: Random House, 1992).

p. 156: "What I really": Joseph Kennedy Jr. to JFK, August 10, 1944, JFKL.

p. 158: "hocus-pocus": Joseph P. Kennedy to Arthur Houghton, May 26, 1945, JFKL.

p. 158: expressed the wish to be like Lord Halifax: Rose Kennedy, "Joe Jr.'s Death," in Smith, ed., *Hostage to Fortune*.

p. 159: "great happiness": JFK to Moucher Devonshire, September 21, 1944, Chatsworth.

p. 159: Derby Red Cross and St. John Carnival: Deborah Devonshire's scrapbook.

p. 159: proudly spoke to Jack: Betty Spalding, author interview.

p. 160: Andrew in Italy: Deborah Devonshire's scrapbook.

p. 160: "I have been": quoted in Goodwin, *The Fitzgeralds and the Kennedys*.

p. 160: Billy in France and Belgium: Deborah Devonshire's scrapbook.

p. 161: "perfectly at peace": Deborah Devonshire's scrapbook.

p. 161: "All your life": Moucher Devonshire to Kick Kennedy, September 13, 1944, in Smith, ed., *Hostage to Fortune*.

p. 161: stayed up with Kick: Betty Spalding, author interview.

p. 161: "gnawing pain": Kick Kennedy to Rose and Joseph P. Kennedy, September 20, 1944, JFKL.

p. 161: offered passage: Field Marshal Lord Alan Brooke, *War Diaries* (London: Weidenfeld & Nicolson, 2001).

p. 162: Duke carries photo: Jean Lloyd, author interview.

p. 162: "not to upset others": Moucher Devonshire to Jack Kennedy, October 18, 1944, JFKL.

p. 162: "about the saddest": JFK to Moucher Devonshire, September 21, 1944, Chatsworth.

p. 163: "rather embarrassed": Kick Kennedy to JFK, n.d., JFKL.

p. 163: "I do hope": Moucher Devonshire to JFK, October 18, 1944, JFKL.

p. 163: "especially the people": Kick Kennedy to JFK, n.d., JFKL.

p. 163: "keen as mustard": Kick Kennedy to JFK, December 7, 1944, JFKL.

p. 163: declared Jack unfit: Rulings of Naval Medical Board and Naval Retiring Board, naval records, JFKL.

p. 163: "The background of": naval records, JFKL.

p. 163: composition of book: JFK's files on *As We Remember Joe*, JFKL.

p. 163: "Though at a": *As We Remember Joe*, privately printed, JFKL.

p. 164: "the best writing": JFK to Lem Billings, February 20, 1945, JFKL.

p. 164: "And then if": JFK to Lem Billings, February 20, 1945, JFKL.

p. 164: JFK in San Francisco: Richard Holderness, author interview; Charles Spalding, interview, JFKL; Betty Spalding, author interview; John F. Kennedy, *Prelude to Leadership: The Postwar Diary of John F. Kennedy* (Washington DC: Regnery,1995).

p. 164: "an international football": JFK, *Chicago Herald–American*, May 2, 1945.

p. 165: "in flux": Winston Churchill, *Triumph and Tragedy* (Boston: Houghton Mifflin Co., 1985).

p. 165: "another bloodbath": Churchill quoted in Martin Gilbert, *Never Despair* (Boston: Houghton Mifflin Co., 1988).

p. 166: "It is this": JFK, *Chicago Herald–American*, May 18, 1945.

p. 167: "All the Conservatives": Kick Kennedy to JFK, n.d., JFKL.

p. 167: a keen if bittersweet interest: Richard Holderness, author interview.

p. 168: "Nearly all the": Kick Kennedy to JFK, February 27, 1945, JFKL.

p. 168: wanted to be there to see it: Richard Holderness, author interview.

CHAPTER EIGHT: BY WATCHING ENGLAND WE WILL HAVE MUCH TO LEARN

p. 169: discussed her at length with Richard Wood: Richard Holderness, author interview.

p. 169: "couldn't be left alone": Elizabeth Cavendish, author interview.

p. 169: "just the way": Anne Tree, author interview.

p. 170: gift to Billy's godson: Andrew Parker Bowles, author interview.

p. 170: "It just seems": Kick Kennedy to JFK, October 31, 1944, JFKL.

p. 170: "I don't like": Kick Kennedy quoted by Jean Lloyd, author interview.

p. 171: "I write you": Kick Kennedy to JFK, April 1, 1945, JFKL.

p. 172: "I never forgave": Andrew Devonshire, author interview.

p. 172: training camp in Naples: Devonshire, *Accidents of Fortune*; Macmillan, *War Diaries*.

p. 172: as conflicted as Billy had been serene: Jean Lloyd, author interview.

p. 172: "the more intellectually stimulating": Richard Holderness, author interview.

p. 173: "by proxy": Andrew Devonshire, author interview.

p. 173: "except the recently": Rhodes James, ed., *Chips*.

p. 173: "this House do now attend": quoted in Nicolson, ed., *Harold Nicolson Diaries and Letters*.

p. 173: "thousands of searchlights": James Lees-Milne, *Prophesying Peace* (London: Faber & Faber, 1977).

p. 173: "absolute bedlam": Kick Kennedy, round-robin letter, May 12, 1945, JFKL.

p. 173: Only one other girl: Kick Kennedy to JFK, April 1, 1945, JFKL.

p. 174: "wander on as": Lord Moran, *Churchill* (Boston: Houghton Mifflin Co., 1966).

p. 174: "be treated like": Moran, *Churchill*.

p. 174: gesturing at the microphone: Colville, *The Fringes of Power*.

p. 174: "the violence of": Amery, *Approach March*.

p. 174: "If there ever": *The Times*, London, June 26, 1945.

p. 175: "about this damned": Moran, *Churchill*.

p. 175: "really expect to": Kick Kennedy to JFK, n.d., JFKL.

p. 175: "Britishers will go": JFK, *New York Journal–American*, June 24, 1945.

p. 176: with an eye to his own political future: Richard Holderness, author interview.

p. 176: thinking about certain issues more deeply: David Ormsby Gore, interview, JFKL.

p. 177: "another cousin": Alexander Stockton, author interview.

p. 177: Ormsby Gore after the war: Jane Rainey, author interview; Victoria Lloyd, author interview.

p. 177: "I haven't got": Victoria Lloyd, author interview.

p. 177: "completely amalgamated into": Anne Tree, author interview.

p. 177: "a woman of": JFK, *Prelude to Leadership*.

p. 177: as though she were her own daughter: Anne Tree, author interview.

p. 178: "an overwhelming victory": JFK, *Prelude to Leadership*.

p. 178: saying as much in the family circle: Anne Tree, author interview.

p. 178: "a statesman of": JFK, *Prelude to Leadership*.

p. 178: too painful for her to watch: Richard Holderness, author interview.

p. 178: JFK observes election: Barbara Ward, interview, JFKL; William Douglas Home to JFK, July 1945, JFKL; George Bilainkin, *Second Diary of a Diplomatic Correspondent* (London: Sampson Low, Marston & Co., 1946); JFK, *Prelude to Leadership.*

p. 178: JFK studies Hugh Fraser: Bilainkin, *Second Diary of a Diplomatic Correspondent*; Hugh Fraser, interview, JFKL; Hugh Fraser campaign materials, JFKL; William Douglas Home to JFK, July 1945, JFKL; Veronica Maclean to JFK, August, 1945, JFKL.

p. 178: "a pointer or two": Maclean, *Past Forgetting.*

p. 178: "I feel it": Churchill quoted in Bilainkin, *Second Diary of a Diplomatic Correspondent.*

p. 179: "Here then was": Churchill, *Triumph and Tragedy.*

p. 179: "to restrain the Russians": quoted in Gilbert, *Never Despair.*

p. 179: "That was how": Geoffrey Best, *Churchill: A Study in Greatness*, (London: Hambledon & London, 2001).

p. 180: "Nobody foresaw this": Nicolson, ed., *Harold Nicolson Diaries and Letters.*

p. 181: "only a few": JFK, *Prelude to Leadership.*

p. 181: "We drove immediately": JFK, *Prelude to Leadership.*

p. 181: JFK ill in London: naval records, JFKL.

p. 181: "a Victorian paperweight": Rhodes James, ed., *Chips.*

p. 181: "I think for": David Ormsby Gore, interview, JFKL.

p. 182: Hugh Fraser telegraphed Hyannis Port: Hugh Fraser to JFK, August 25, 1945, JFKL.

p. 182: "There was no": Elizabeth Cavendish, author interview.

p. 182: "It was as": Elizabeth Cavendish, author interview.

p. 182: "turned it off": Elizabeth Cavendish, author interview.

p. 182: "very, very, very": Elizabeth Cavendish, author interview.

p. 182: "an enthralling moment": Michael Astor, *Tribal Feeling* (London: John Murray, 1963).

p. 182: "enjoyable and drunken": Michael Davie, ed., *The Diaries of Evelyn Waugh* (London: Phoenix, 1995).

p. 183: in love with Waugh: Evelyn Waugh to Laura Waugh, August 29, 1945, in Mark Amory, ed., *The Letters of Evelyn Waugh* (New York: Penguin, 1980).

p. 183: "She longed to": Richard Holderness, author interview.

p. 183: a very different person: Elizabeth Cavendish, author interview.

p. 183: as a Conservative hostess in London: Richard Holderness, author interview.

p. 183: "the European situation": Joseph P. Kennedy to Cissy Patterson, November 26, 1945, JFKL.

p. 183: "designed by nature": Moran, *Churchill.*

p. 184: "You had a": Joseph P. Kennedy, memorandum of conversation with Churchill, JFKL.

p. 185: "From Stettin in": Churchill, speech, March 5, 1946.

p. 186: "warmonger": Joseph Stalin quoted in Gilbert, *Never Despair*.

p. 186: "Congress seat for sale": *East Boston Leader*, n.d., JFKL.

p. 188: "Here comes the": Mike Neville quoted in Kenneth P. O'Donnell and David F. Powers, *Johnny, We Hardly Knew Ye*, (Boston: Little, Brown & Co., 1970).

p. 188: sent to London at her request: Lady Hartington's secretary to JFK, May 27, 1946, JFKL.

p. 188: "There's nothing they": Kick Kennedy to JFK, July 13, 1946, JFKL.

p. 188: "Everyone says you": Kick Kennedy to JFK, January 13, 1946, JFKL.

p. 188: "and nothing else!": Jean Lloyd, author interview.

p. 189: "a salon every": Eunice Kennedy to Rose and Joseph P. Kennedy, October 1, 1946, JFKL.

p. 189: friendship with Mabell Airlie: Jean Lloyd, author interview.

p. 189: "great ladies of": Richard Holderness, author interview.

p. 189: "straighten out Anglo-American": Kick Kennedy to Rose and Joseph P. Kennedy, March 10, 1945, JFKL.

p. 189: had fallen in love with her: Richard Holderness, author interview.

p. 190: "Is that Peter": Jean Lloyd, author interview.

p. 190: background on Peter Fitzwilliam: Elizabeth Cavendish, author interview; Richard Holderness, author interview; Fiona Arran, author interview.

p. 190: quite the level of opulence: Elizabeth Cavendish, author interview.

p. 190: "a king dandy": Evelyn Waugh to Laura Waugh, November 1940, in Amory, ed., *The Letters of Evelyn Waugh*.

p. 190: focused rather improbably on the similarities: Richard Holderness, author interview.

p. 190: attraction mainly sexual: Fiona Arran, author interview.

p. 190: Kick clung to the belief: Richard Holderness, author interview.

p. 190: wishful thinking: Jean Lloyd, author interview.

p. 191: marriage to a man of Fitzwilliam's habits: Elizabeth Cavendish, author interview.

p. 191: "terrified": Elizabeth Cavendish, author interview.

p. 191: "That American friend": Sir Daniel Davis quoted in Joan and Clay Blair, *The Search for JFK*, (New York: Putnam, 1974).

p. 192: Kick's trip to America: Elizabeth Cavendish, author interview.

p. 192: "favorite of all": Rose Kennedy to Nancy Astor, June 14, 1948, UR.

p. 192: "a grim, tragic": Dinah Brand, interview, JFKL.

p. 193: Andrew set off at once: Jean Lloyd, author interview.

p. 193: "Would like to": Joseph P. Kennedy to JFK, May 15, 1948, JFKL.

p. 193: lost passport: Richmond to Shipley, May 18, 1948, JFKL; T. J. Reardon to Mrs. Shipley, May 18, 1948, JFKL.

p. 193: "infectious gaiety": *The Times*, London, May 20, 1948.

p. 193: When Randolph Churchill asked: Jean Lloyd, author interview.

p. 193: Sissie . . . began to wail: Jean Lloyd, author interview.

p. 194: "He wore a": Deborah Devonshire, author interview.

p. 194: picture the three of them: Lem Billings quoted in Goodwin, *The Fitzgeralds and the Kennedys*.

CHAPTER NINE: A DIVIDED NATURE

p. 196: "labor situation": Fred A. Hartley Jr. to JFK, June 8, 1948, JFKL.

p. 196: "the possibilities of war": Mark Pottle, ed., *Daring to Hope: The Diaries and Letters of Violet Bonham Carter, 1946–1969* (London: Weidenfeld & Nicolson, 2000).

p. 197: compared the crisis in Berlin to the critical episode in Munich: Churchill, speech, June 26, 1948.

p. 198: with a three-figure majority: Rhodes James, ed., *Chips*.

p. 199: briefings by General Clay: JFK to General Lucius Clay, August 13, 1948, JFKL.

p. 199: "I hope you will": Churchill, speech, October 9, 1948.

p. 201: "the role which": Gilbert, *Never Despair*.

p. 202: "rather respected McCarthy": John P. Mallan, "Massachusetts: Liberal and Corrupt," *New Republic*, October 13, 1952.

p. 203: preoccupied with death: Betty Spalding, author interview.

p. 203: "more than ten": Joseph Alsop, interview, JFKL.

p. 203: "Congressman Kennedy explained": Mutual–Yankee Networks transcript, JFKL.

p. 204: Andrew's political activities: Devonshire, *Accidents of Fortune*; Andrew Devonshire, author interview.

p. 204: Ormsby Gore's political activities: David Ormsby Gore, interview, London School of Economics.

p. 205: "fairly hopeless seat": David Ormsby Gore, interview, London School of Economics.

p. 205: the orbit of Selwyn Lloyd: David Ormsby Gore, interview, London School of Economics.

p. 206: "overwhelming ambition": Devonshire, *Accidents of Fortune*.

p. 206: "These reports by": Mutual–Yankee Networks transcript, JFKL.

p. 206: "If Europe is": Mutual–Yankee Networks transcript, JFKL.

p. 207: "simply an American": transcript of JFK's Senate testimony, February 22, 1951, JFKL.

p. 207: "only half a policy": Churchill, speech, October 8, 1951.

p. 208: "harshness": *New York Times*, November 9, 1951.

p. 208: Eden endeavored to bring the temperature down: *New York Times*, November 13, 1961.

p. 209: "the great figure": Harold Macmillan, *The Past Masters: Politics and Politicians 1906–1939*, (New York: Harper & Row, 1975).

p. 209: "intellectual heir": Astor, *Tribal Feeling*.

p. 209: move off to a corner: Jane Rainey, author interview.

p. 210: "what is done": Churchill, speech, January 17, 1952.

p. 210: "undimmed": JFK, Annual Message to the Congress on the State of the Union, January 30, 1961, PPP.

p. 210: "emerge from the depths": Mallan, "Massachusetts: Liberal and Corrupt."

p. 211: "generally speaking the": O'Donnell and Powers, *Johnny, We Hardly Knew Ye*.

p. 212: when they begin to reform: Winston Churchill to Dwight Eisenhower, April 11, 1953, in Peter G. Boyle, ed., *The Churchill–Eisenhower Correspondence* (Chapel Hill: University of North Carolina Press, 1990).

p. 212: a change of mood at the Kremlin: Churchill, speech, May 11, 1953.

p. 212: "kicked out": Moran, *Churchill*.

p. 212: "Time will undoubtedly": Churchill, speech, November 3, 1953.

p. 213: "a short, very": Colville, *The Fringes of Power*.

p. 213: "was a woman": Colville, *The Fringes of Power*.

p. 215: "to usher in": Colville, *The Fringes of Power*.

p. 215: "almost homely": Jewel Reed, author interview.

p. 215: responded with astonishment: Betty Spalding, author interview.

p. 215: "a substitute for Kick": Betty Spalding, author interview.

p. 216: "dangerously futile": JFK, speech, April 6, 1954, JFKL.

p. 216: "the hydrogen age": John F. Kennedy, "Foreign Policy is the People's Business," *New York Times Magazine*, August 8, 1954.

p. 216: "exploit public opinion": JFK, "Foreign Policy is the People's Business."

p. 217: amendment to ban the Communist Party: *New York Times*, August 13, 1954.

p. 218: pounded his crutches with his fist: O'Donnell and Powers, *Johnny, We Hardly Knew Ye*.

p. 218: Ormsby Gore in New York: David Ormsby Gore, interview, London School of Economics.

p. 218: visited Jack in Hyannis Port: David Ormsby Gore, interview, JFKL; Ormsby Gore quoted in Martin, *A Hero for Our Time*.

p. 219: Jackie took notes: David Ormsby Gore quoted in Martin, *A Hero for Our Time*.

p. 219: but viewed them as insignificant: Jane Rainey, author interview.

p. 220: drifted into a deep depression: Betty Spalding, author interview.

CHAPTER TEN: TO FIND A BEGINNING

p. 221: sends first and last chapters to father: JFK to Joseph P. Kennedy, n.d., JFKL.

p. 222: "act of contrition": O'Donnell and Powers, *Johnny, We Hardly Knew Ye.*

p. 222: "angry power": John F. Kennedy, *Profiles in Courage* (New York: Harper & Brothers, 1956).

p. 222: "political courage": JFK, *Profiles in Courage.*

p. 223: "in great agony of mind": Violet Bonham Carter quoted in Gilbert, *Never Despair.*

p. 224: defense through deterrents: Churchill, speech, March 1, 1955.

p. 224: swan song: Moran, *Churchill.*

p. 224: studied the worrisome passages three times: Joseph P. Kennedy to Theodore Sorensen, August 15, 1955, in Smith, ed. *Hostage to Fortune.*

p. 224: "place in history": Jacqueline Kennedy to Macmillan, January 31, 1964, BLO.

p. 224: "very intrigued": Joseph P. Kennedy to Edward Kennedy, September 3, 1955, JFKL.

p. 226: proposed she go back to Washington: Jewel Reed, author interview.

p. 226: "eyes filled with dreams": Jane Suydam, author interview.

p. 226: seemed wonderfully at peace: Betty Spalding, author interview.

p. 227: Only when Joe angrily pointed out: Betty Spalding, author interview.

p. 228: a hugely emotional event: Betty Spalding, author interview.

p. 228: to be physically affectionate: Deborah Devonshire, author interview.

p. 229: rarely spent two consecutive days together: Jacqueline Kennedy, interview, LBJL.

p. 230: "missile gap": JFK, speech, August 14, 1958, JFKL.

p. 231: "on the Churchill ticket": Macmillan diary, BLO.

p. 231: "for his warnings": JFK, speech, October 1, 1959, JFKL.

p. 232: "Twenty-three years": JFK, speech, November 13, 1959, JFKL.

p. 233: major progress toward a test ban: Ormsby Gore to Macmillan, October 9, 1959, Macmillan papers, BLO.

p. 233: JFK and Ormsby Gore discuss the test ban in New York in 1959: Ormsby Gore, interview, JFKL.

p. 233: the emotional commitment was still to come: Ormsby Gore quoted in Martin, *A Hero for Our Time.*

p. 233: Ormsby Gore's influence in making the test ban a major area of interest in the campaign: Edwin O. Guthman and Jeffrey Shulman, *Robert Kennedy, in His Own Words: The Unpublished Recollections of the Kennedy Years* (New York: Bantam Books, 1988); Ormsby Gore to Alec Home, November 14, 1960, FO 371/152108, PRO; Ormsby Gore, interview, JFKL.

p. 234: "The problem is": JFK, speech, December 11, 1959, JFKL.

CHAPTER ELEVEN: ON THE CHURCHILL TICKET

p. 235: "comfortable and complacent": Sir Harold Caccia, annual review for 1960, January 1, 1961, Foreign Office, PRO.

p. 236: "alternated between periods": Caccia, "The Presidential Election 1960," January 11, 1961, Foreign Office, PRO.

p. 236: "This administration may": JFK, discussion with John Fischer, December 9, 1959 in Allan Nevins, ed., *The Strategy of Peace* (New York: Popular Library, 1961).

p. 237: "In 1960 we must": JFK, speech, February 12, 1960, JFKL.

p. 237: "the devolution of": Harold Macmillan, *Pointing the Way* (Harper & Row, New York, 1972).

p. 237: "on military lines": Caccia, "The Handover to the New Administration," November 27, 1960, Foreign Office, PRO.

p. 237: "a final solution": Caccia, "The Handover to the New Administration," November 27, 1960, Foreign Office, PRO.

p. 237: "The President's responsibility": JFK, speech, February 12, 1960, JFKL.

p. 238: Ormsby Gore's visit to Washington: Ormsby Gore, interview, JFKL; Ormsby Gore to Foreign Office, February 24, 1960, FO 371/149394, PRO.

p. 238: "The meetings of": Ormsby Gore, "Views on Disarmament and Nuclear Tests formed on his visit to Washington," February 24, 1960, FO 371/149394, PRO.

p. 239: "Again and again": Ormsby Gore, "Views on Disarmament and Nuclear Tests formed on his visit to Washington," February 24, 1960, FO 371/149394, PRO.

p. 239: at home in Georgetown: Ormsby Gore, interview, JFKL.

p. 239: "stuck very closely to the line": Robert Kennedy quoted in Ormsby Gore to Home, December 6, 1960, FO 371/ 152108, PRO.

p. 239: "Last week, ten": JFK, speech, March 26, 1960, JFKL.

p. 241: "an acceptance of": Macmillan, *Pointing the Way*.

p. 241: "both firm and": Caccia, annual review for 1960, January 1, 1961, Foreign Office, PRO.

p. 241: "muffed it at": Caccia to Selwyn Lloyd, April 15, 1960, Foreign Office, PRO.

p. 241: "favorable": Semyon Tsarapkin quoted in Glenn Seaborg, *Kennedy, Khrushchev, and the Test Ban* (Berkeley: University of California Press, 1981).

p. 242: "curious set of": Sir Robert Menzies to Macmillan, June 28, 1960, PREM 11/3170, PRO.

p. 242: "If this particular": *New York Times*, May 8, 1960.

p. 242: "This was a": *New York Times*, May 9, 1960.

p. 243: "Pentagon militarists": Khrushchev quoted in William Taubman, *Khrushchev: The Man and His Era* (New York: W. W. Norton & Company, 2003).

p. 243: "With a gesture": Macmillan, *Pointing the Way*.

p. 244: "hammer strokes": Caccia, annual review for 1960, January 1, 1961, Foreign Office, PRO.

p. 244: "point to his criticism": Caccia, "The Presidential Election 1960," January 11, 1961, Foreign Office, PRO.

p. 244: "marked the end": JFK, speech, June 14, 1960, JFKL.

p. 245: "The spectacle of": Caccia, annual review for 1960, January 1, 1961, Foreign Office, PRO.

p. 246: Nixon had predicted in April: Selwyn Lloyd, record of conversation with the vice president of the US, April 13, 1960, Foreign Office, PRO.

p. 246: "I think the": JFK, speech, July 15, 1960, JFKL.

p. 247: the most formidable opponent: Selwyn Lloyd, record of conversation with the vice president of the United States, April 13, 1960, Foreign Office, PRO.

p. 248: to share his spotlight: record of parts of a conversation between the prime minister and President Eisenhower, September 27, 1960, PREM 11/3609, PRO.

p. 248: Khrushchev at the UN in 1960: FO 371/153638, PRO; Home to Macmillan, September 24, 1960, PREM 11/3780, PRO.

p. 248: "continuous front page": Patrick Dean to Home, November 12, 1960, FO 371/153638, PRO.

p. 248: "You can imagine": Nikita Khrushchev, *Khrushchev Remembers* (Boston: Little, Brown & Co., 1990).

p. 249: "a benign and": Patrick Dean to Home, November 12, 1960, FO 371/153638, PRO.

p. 249: lightly drum his own desk: Jane Rainey, author interview.

p. 249: Macmillan's UN speech: Home to Macmillan, September 24, 1960, PREM 11/3780, PRO.

p. 250: "The President made": Macmillan, *Pointing the Way*.

p. 250: much admired Jack Kennedy: Alexander Stockton, author interview.

p. 250: confided to his nephew: Devonshire, *Accidents of Fortune*.

p. 250: "come on a lot": note by the prime minister, March 28, 1960, PREM 11/3609, PRO.

p. 250: Menzies on Joe Kennedy: Menzies to Macmillan, June 28, 1960, PREM 11/3170, PRO.

p. 250: "He wondered": Alexander Stockton, author interview.

p. 251: "apprehensive": Alexander Stockton, author interview.

p. 253: "a man with": Caccia, "The Presidential Election 1960," January 11, 1961, Foreign Office, PRO.

p. 253: "a convicted criminal": quoted in Alistair Horne, *Macmillan*, vol. 2 (New York: Viking, 1989).

p. 253: intrigued Macmillan: Alexander Stockton, author interview.

p. 253: "Your chap's beat": quoted in Horne, *Macmillan*.

p. 253: "In his heart": record of conversation between the prime minister and President Eisenhower, September 27, 1960, PREM 11/3609, PRO.

p. 254: Churchill on Quemoy and Matsu: Boyle, ed., *The Churchill–Eisenhower Correspondence*.

p. 255: "answering questions": Caccia, "The Presidential Election 1960," January 11, 1961, Foreign Office, PRO.

p. 255: "to study the": JFK, speech, October 14, 1960, JFKL.

p. 256: "I know what": JFK, speech, November 5, 1960, JFKL.

p. 256: "I spent some": JFK, speech, October 31, 1960, JFKL.

p. 256: "I recall in": JFK, speech, November 5, 1960, JFKL.

p. 256: "I do not": JFK, speech, November 6, 1960, JFKL.

p. 256: "If he really": JFK, speech, October 22, 1960, JFKL.

p. 257: Churchill's "prophetic" words: JFK, speech, October 2, 1960, JFKL.

p. 257: "barrack-room language": Caccia to Foreign Office, November 26, 1960, Foreign Office, PRO.

CHAPTER TWELVE: WHAT THE MAN WOULD LIKE TO BE

p. 258: Joe Kennedy's mood: Betty Spalding, author interview.

p. 258: "on the Churchill ticket": Macmillan diary, BLO.

p. 258: inaugural address: January 20, 1961, PPP.

p. 260: "it is what . . . enunciated": Caccia to Macmillan, January 21, 1961, PREM 11/3609, PRO; Caccia to Home, January 25, 1961, FO 371/156437, PRO.

p. 260: Menshikov approaches: David K. E. Bruce diary, January 5, 1961, FRUS 5.

p. 261: release of RB-47 pilots: Llewellyn Thompson to Dept of State, January 21, 1961, FRUS 5; Thompson to Dept of State, January 21, 1961, FRUS 5.

p. 261: Thompson advises meeting: Thompson to Dept of State, January 28, 1961, FRUS 5.

p. 262: meeting with Soviet analysts: notes on discussion, February 11, 1961, FRUS 5.

p. 262: "early informal exchange of views": JFK to Khrushchev, February 22, 1961, FRUS 6.

p. 262: "priority attention": memo of conversation, February 3, 1961, Dean Rusk and Mikhail Menshikov, FRUS 5.

p. 262: shift the talks' start date: memo of conversation, February 3, 1961, Menshikov and Rusk, FRUS 5.

p. 262: asked David to come to Washington: Ormsby Gore to Home, December 9, 1960, FO 371/152108, PRO.

p. 263: Gallup poll: Ormsby Gore to Macmillan, March 1, 1961, PREM 11/3326, PRO.

p. 263: JFK–Ormsby Gore meeting of February 28, 1961: Ormsby Gore to Macmillan, March 1, 1961, PREM 11/3326, PRO; Ormsby Gore to JFK, May 18, 1961, JFKL; Ormsby Gore interview, JFKL.

p. 264: "to play his part": Deborah Devonshire's scrapbook.

p. 264: "in certain directions I believed in": Ormsby Gore interview, London School of Economics.

p. 265: approval to approach: Ormsby Gore to Home, November 14, 1960, FO 371/152108, PRO.

p. 265: met with a dash of nervousness: Home to Ormsby Gore, November 17, 1960, FO 371/152108, PRO.

p. 265: had already spoken to Andrew Devonshire: Devonshire, *Accidents of Fortune*.

p. 265: "to join or crash": Caccia to Home, November 21, 1960, FO 371/152108, PRO.

p. 265: asked to see David then: Ormsby Gore to Home, November 29, 1960, FO 371/152108, PRO.

p. 265: "part of the family": Guthman and Shulman, eds., *Robert Kennedy, in His Own Words*.

p. 265: lunch at the Carlyle Hotel: Ormsby Gore to Home, December 7, 1960, FO 37/152108, PRO; Ormsby Gore to Home, December 9, 1960, FO 371/152108, PRO.

p. 267: "not an 'ideas man'": Caccia to Foreign Office, December 16, 1960, Foreign Office, PRO.

p. 267: waiting six or nine months on China: Ormsby Gore, December 7, 1960, FO 371/152108, PRO.

p. 268: "instrumental": Guthman and Shulman, eds., *Robert Kennedy, in His Own Words*.

p. 268: change of Laos policy: Caccia to Foreign Office, July 14, 1961, FO 371/156349, PRO.

p. 269: CIA's Cuba plan: Colonel Jack Hawkins to J. D. Esterline, January 4, 1961, FRUS 10; CIA, "Evaluation of Possible Courses of Action in Cuba," January 16, 1961, FRUS 10; C. Tracy Barnes to J. D. Esterline, January 18, 1961, FRUS 10; "Meeting on Cuba," memo, January 22, 1961, FRUS 10; "Conclusions of Dean Rusk's Meeting on Cuba," January 22, 1961, FRUS 10; General Andrew Goodpaster, memo of conference of President Kennedy and Joint Chiefs of Staff, January 25, 1961, FRUS 10; Richard Bissell, "Concept of the Operation," January 26, 1961, FRUS 10; General L. L. Lemnitzer to Robert McNamara, January 27, 1961, FRUS 10; "Memorandum of Discussion of Cuba," January 28, 1961, FRUS 10; JFK to Rusk, January 31, 1961, FRUS 10; McGeorge Bundy to JFK, "Memorandum of February 8, 1961, Meeting with President Kennedy," February 8, 1961, FRUS 10; Bundy to JFK, February 18, 1961, FRUS 10; National Security action memoranda, March 11, 1961, FRUS 10; Arthur Schlesinger Jr. to JFK, March 15, 1961, FRUS 10; Bundy to JFK, March 15, 1961, FRUS 10; General David Gray, notes on meeting of March 15, 1961, FRUS 10; Gray, notes on meeting of March 16, 1961, FRUS 10; Gray, notes on meeting of March 29, 1961, FRUS 10; Gray, notes on meeting of April 6, 1961, FRUS 10; Gray, notes on meeting of April 11, 1961, FRUS 10; Gray, notes on meeting of April 12, 1961, FRUS 10; CIA, "Cuban Operation," April 12, 1961, FRUS 10; Bundy to Rusk, April 13, 1961, FRUS 10.

Background on invasion: Peter Wyden, *Bay of Pigs: The Untold Story* (New York: Simon & Schuster, 1979); Peter Kornbluh, ed., *Bay of Pigs Declassified: The Secret CIA Report on the Invasion of Cuba* (New York: New Press, 1998); Richard Bissell, *Confessions of a Cold Warrior* (New Haven: Yale University Press, 1996); Chester Bowles, *Promises to Keep* (New York: Harper & Row, 1971); Richard Goodwin, *Remembering America* (Boston: Little, Brown & Co., 1988); Arthur Schlesinger Jr., *A Thousand Days* (Boston: Houghton Mifflin Co., 1965); Michael Beschloss, *The Crisis Years: Kennedy and Khrushchev 1960–1963* (New York: HarperCollins, 1991).

p. 271: Thompson conversation with Kuznetsov: Thompson to Dept of State, March 20, 1961, FRUS 5.

p. 271: turnaround at Geneva talks: FRUS 7; Ormsby Gore, interview, JFKL.

p. 272: Laos situation at time of Key West meeting: C.C. (61) 16th conclusions, March 23, 1961, CAB 128/35, PRO; C.C.17 (61), PRO; Macmillan to JFK, March 24, 1961, PREM 11/4052, PRO. C.C.18 (61), PRO; Bowles to Rusk, March 24, 1961, JFKL; Charles Bohlen to Bowles, March 25, 1961, JFKL; "Laos and U.S.–U.S.S.R. Relations," memorandum of conversation between JFK, Andrei Gromyko, et al., March 27, 1961, JFKL; Thompson to Rusk, April 1, 1961, JFKL; L. D. Battle to Ralph Dungan, April 4, 1961, JFKL; Macmillan to JFK, April 28, 1961, JFKL; JFK to Macmillan, April 29, 1961, JFKL; Charles Bohlen, interview, JFKL.

p. 272: March 23, 1961 press conference: PPP.

p. 273: March 26, 1961 Key West meeting: record of discussion held at the United States Naval Base, Key West, Florida, March 26, 1961, PREM

11/3313, PRO; memos of conversations, March 26, 1961, Key West, Florida, JFKL; Macmillan to the Queen, March 27, 1961, PREM 11/3280, PRO; Ormsby Gore interview, JFKL; Ormsby Gore interview, London School of Economics; Macmillan diary, BLO; Macmillan, *Pointing the Way*; Caccia to Tim Bligh, April 17, 1961, PREM 11/3617, PRO; Minister of Defence to Macmillan, March 30, 1961, PREM 11/3280, PRO; Macmillan to Minister of Defence, March 30, 1961, PREM 11/3280, PRO; Home, "Laos and the Americans," notes, March 30, 1961, PREM 11/3280, PRO; Macmillan to Home, April 1, 1961, PREM 11/328, PRO; Macmillan to Jacqueline Kennedy, February 18, 1964, BLO; JFK and Macmillan, joint communiqué, March 26, 1961, JFKL; Prime Minister's Diaries, March 24–26, 1961, BLO; Hervé Alphand, interview, JFKL; Charles Bohlen, interview, JFKL; Bowles to Rusk, March 24, 1961, JFKL; Bohlen to Bowles, March 25, 1961, JFKL; Macmillan to JFK, March 26, 1961, JFKL; Caccia to JFK, March 27, 1961, JFKL; Bundy to JFK, April 4, 1961, JFKL.

p. 276: to Washington as ambassador: Ormsby Gore interview, London School of Economics; Macmillan diary, BLO; Macmillan, *Pointing the Way*; Jane Rainey, author interview; Victoria Lloyd, author interview.

p. 277: Gromyko–JFK meeting of March 27, 1961: FRUS 5.

p. 278: an encouraging response from Gromyko: Macmillan to the Queen, April 5, 1961, PREM 11/3281, PRO; note, p. 122, FRUS 5; C.C. 20 (61), PRO.

p. 278: had to decide on it urgently: Bowles to Rusk, March 31, 1961, JFKL; Schlesinger to JFK, February 11, 1961, JFKL.

p. 279: accepted the British proposals on Laos: Sir Frank Roberts to Foreign Office, April 1, 1961, PREM 11/3281, PRO.

p. 279: JFK sets dates for meeting with Khrushchev: Rusk to Thompson, April 5, 1961, FRUS 5.

p. 280: "really wanted to do this": Beschloss, *The Crisis Years*.

p. 280: JFK–Macmillan April 1961 talks: "The Prime Minister's Objectives in Washington," February 24, 1961, PREM 11/3326, PRO; memos of conversations, April 1961 talks, JFKL; Macmillan, *Pointing the Way*; British notes on Washington talks, April 1961, PREM 11/3326, PRO.

p. 280: JFK's concern about Eisenhower and Laos: JFK, notes on meeting with Eisenhower, January 19, 1961, JFKL; McNamara to JFK, January 24, 1961, JFKL; Clark Clifford to JFK, January 24, 1961, JFKL.

p. 280: urge Eisenhower to remain silent: Macmillan to Eisenhower, April 9, 1961, JFKL; Caccia to JFK, April 9, 1961, JFKL; Zulueta to Samuel, April 26, 1961, PREM 11/3602, PRO; Macmillan to Eisenhower, April 9, PREM 11/3602, PRO; Eisenhower to Macmillan, April 18, 1961, PREM 11/3602, PRO; C.C. 20 (61), PRO; Home to Menzies, April 12,

1961, PREM 11/3281, PRO; Home to Menzies, April 13, 1961, PREM11/3281, PRO.

p. 280: "anxious not to appear": Ormsby Gore to Home, January 2, 1962, FO 371/162586, PRO.

p. 281: "might make him look": Ormsby Gore interview, JFKL.

p. 281: "virtually committed": Ormsby Gore to Home, January 2, 1962, FO 371/162586, PRO.

p. 281: JFK and Macmillan talk about Cuba plans: "Note by the Prime Minister re April 6, 1961 private meeting with JFK at WH," PREM 11/3311, PRO.

p. 282: Cuban invasion: FRUS 10.

p. 283: Dean Rusk's call: Admiral Arleigh Burke, notes of conversation with JFK, May 16, 1961, JFKL.

p. 283: "I'm not signed on": Schlesinger, *A Thousand Days*.

p. 283: Rusk called at 4:30 a.m.: General C. P. Cabell to General Maxwell D. Taylor, May 9, 1961, JFKL.

p. 283: too agitated to go back to sleep: Schlesinger, *A Thousand Days*.

p. 284: Karamanlis luncheon: White House file, luncheon, April 17, 1961, JFKL.

p. 284: Khrushchev's letter: Khrushchev to JFK, April 18, 1961, FRUS 6.

p. 285: six unmarked jets: Joint Chiefs of Staff to Admiral Robert Dennison, April 19, 1961, JFKL.

p. 285: railed against Eisenhower: Constantine Karamanlis interview, JFKL.

p. 286: plunged into a mood: Rose Kennedy, *Times to Remember*.

p. 286: Joe Kennedy feels he might die: Rose Kennedy, *Times to Remember*.

p. 286: Castro crows: Wymberley Coerr to Rusk, April 10, 1961, JFKL.

p. 286: "shattered": Bowles, notes on Cuban crisis, April 20, 1960, JFKL.

p. 287: "There is an old saying": JFK press conference, April 21, 1961, PPP.

p. 287: Eisenhower had replied to Macmillan: Eisenhower to Macmillan, April 18, 1961, PREM 11/3602, PRO.

p. 287: JFK–Eisenhower meeting: Richard Reeves, *President Kennedy* (New York: Simon & Schuster, 1994).

p. 287: JFK at Glen Ora: Charles Spalding interview, JFKL; Betty Spalding, author interview.

p. 288: "How can I": Betty Spalding, author interview.

CHAPTER THIRTEEN: THE MEANING OF "MISCALCULATION"

p. 289: seeking advice: Caccia to Macmillan, April 21, 1961, PREM 11/3316, PRO.

p. 290: not so secret: Macmillan to Caccia, April 24, 1961, PREM 11/3316, PRO.

p. 290: "as a courageous initiative": Macmillan to Caccia, April 24, 1961, PREM 11/3316, PRO.

p. 290: "have to talk about something": Macmillan to Caccia, April 24, 1961, PREM 11/3316, PRO.

p. 291: Gromyko had called: Thompson to Dept of State, May 4, 1961, FRUS 5.

p. 291: "domestic political problems": Thompson to Dept of State, May 4, 1961, FRUS 5.

p. 292: "The concessions of the weak": Edmund Burke, "Mr. Burke's Speech on Moving His Resolutions for Conciliation with the Colonies," in David Bromwich, ed., *On Empire, Liberty, and Reform: Speeches and Letters of Edmund Burke* (New Haven: Yale University Press, 2000).

p. 292: Bobby Kennedy meets Bolshakov: Aleksandr Fursenko and Timothy Naftali, *"One Hell of a Gamble": Khrushchev, Castro, and Kennedy* (New York: W. W. Norton & Company, 1997).

p. 293: Palm Beach trip: Betty Spalding, author interview.

p. 294: Krock's warning: Arthur Krock interview, MHS.

p. 294: Kater campaign: Florence Kater to Eleanor Roosevelt, April 30, 1959, and June 18, 1960, FDRL.

p. 295: Judith Campbell: "Alleged Assassination Plots Involving Foreign Leaders, An Interim Report of the Select Committee to Study Governmental Operations with Respect to Intelligence Activities, United States Senate," (Washington: United States Government Printing Office, 1975); Judith Campbell Exner, *My Story* (New York: Grove Press, 1977); Courtney Evans to Alan Belmont, "Subject: Judith E. Campbell, Associate of Hoodlums, Criminal Intelligence Matter," March 20, 1962, FBI.

p. 295: Spalding introduces Jacobson: Betty Spalding, author interview.

p. 296: Kennedy and Jacobson: Max Jacobson, unpublished memoir, MHS.

p. 296: Jacobson visit to Palm Beach: Jacobson, unpublished memoir, MHS; Betty Spalding, author interview.

p. 296: background on Max Jacobson: Patrick O'Neal, author interview.

p. 296: licking her lips: Betty Spalding, author interview.

p. 297: Freedom Riders: Caccia report, May 24, 1961, FO 371/156507, PRO; Burke Marshall interview, JFKL; Taylor Branch, *Parting the Waters: America in the King Years 1954–63* (New York: Simon & Schuster, 1988).

p. 297: Freedom Riders: Burke Marshall, interview, JFKL; John Siegenthaler, interview, JFKL; Branch, *Parting the Waters*.

p. 300: Bobby Kennedy hears from Bolshakov: Fursenko and Naftali, *"One Hell of a Gamble."*

p. 301: deprived him of control: Betty Spalding, author interview.

p. 301: Jacobson's first White House visit: Jacobson, unpublished memoir, MHS.

p. 302: Khrushchev at ice revue: Thompson to State Dept, May 24, 1961, FRUS 14.

p. 303: JFK sends Bobby Kennedy to Bolshakov: Fursenko and Naftali, *"One Hell of a Gamble."*

p. 303: "a soft, not very decisive": Bowles interview, JFKL.

p. 303: Letter from Ormsby Gore: Ormsby Gore to JFK, May 18, 1961, JFKL.

p. 304: JFK requests Ormsby Gore's presence: John Wyndham to Macmillan, May 29, 1961, PREM 11/3328, PRO; Norman Brook to Macmillan, May 29, 1961, PREM 11/3328, PRO.

p. 304: JFK has Bobby Kennedy contact Bolshakov: Fursenko and Naftali, *"One Hell of a Gamble."*

p. 305: Jacobson and France: Jacobson, unpublished memoir, MHS.

p. 305: French trip: memoranda of conversations, JFK–Charles de Gaulle, May 31–June 2, 1961, JFKL; talking points reviewing conversations between President Kennedy and President de Gaulle, May 31–June 2, 1961, JFKL; Macmillan to JFK, April 28, 1961, PREM 11/3328, PRO; JFK to Macmillan, May 8, 1961, PREM 11/3328, PRO; Sir P. Dixon to Foreign Office, June 1, 1961, FO 371/160444, PRO; JFK to de Gaulle, February 2, 1961, JFKL; JFK to de Gaulle, February 23, 1961, JFKL; Walter Stoessel Jr. to Ralph Dungan, February 27, 1961, JFKL; Bundy to JFK, April 5, 1961, JFKL; Bundy, memorandum of conversation with Caccia, May 12, 1962, JFKL; JFK to Macmillan, May 22, 1961, JFKL; Macmillan to JFK, May 25, 1961, JFKL; "Talking Points for President," May 27, 1961, JFKL; JFK to Bundy, May 29, 1961, JFKL; Bundy to JFK, May 30, 1961, JFKL; Martin (Geneva) to JFK, May 31, 1961, JFKL; confidential background paper, President's visit to de Gaulle, May 31–June 2, 1961, "De Gaulle's Personality, Motivations and Essential Philosophy," JFKL; Ambassador Gavin to Bowles, May 31, 1961, JFKL; Hervé Alphand, interview, JFKL; Charles Bohlen, interview, JFKL; Angier Biddle Duke, interview, JFKL; Letitia Baldrige, interview, JFKL; daily programs and scenarios, JFKL; security schedules, JFKL; Hervé Alphand, *L'étonnement d'être, Journal 1939–1973* (Paris: Fayard, 1977); Charles de Gaulle, *Memoirs of Hope: Renewal and Endeavor* (New York: Simon & Schuster, 1971). .

p. 306: "eyes in the portraits": Larry Newman, author interview.

p. 306: de Gaulle to JFK on Berlin: memo of conversations, May 31, 1961, FRUS 14.

p. 307: Vienna visit: program and scenario for Vienna Visit, JFKL; Caccia to Bundy, April 24, 1961, JFKL; Macmillan to JFK, April 27, 1961, JFKL; Thompson to Rusk, May 6, 1961, JFKL; Khrushchev to JFK, May 16, 1961, JFKL; Dept of State scope paper, "President's Meeting with Khrushchev," May 23, 1961, JFKL; Dept of State, "Talking Points for President's Meeting with Khrushchev," May 23, 1961, JFKL; Adlai Stevenson to JFK, May 24, 1961, JFKL; Thompson to Rusk, May 24,

1961, JFKL; Dept of State Background Paper, "Soviet Aims and Expectations President's Meeting with Khrushchev," May 25, 1961, JFKL; Thompson to Rusk, May 25, 1961, JFKL; Allan Lightner to Rusk, May 25, 1961, JFKL; Mansfield to JFK, May 26, 1961, JFKL; Thompson to Rusk, May 27, 1961, JFKL; memorandum for the President, June 2, 1961, JFKL; special background paper, "Line of Approach to Khrushchev," June 1, 1961, JFKL; biographic briefing book, President Kennedy's Meeting with Khrushchev, Vienna, JFKL; George Kennan to Rusk, June 2, 1961, JFKL; Foy Kohler, interview, JFKL; Charles Bohlen, interview, JFKL; Peter Lisagor, interview, JFKL; Paul Nitze, *From Hiroshima to Glasnost* (New York: Grove Weidenfeld, 1989); Charles Bohlen, *Witness to History* (New York: W. W. Norton & Company, 1973); Dean Rusk, *As I Saw It* (New York: W. W. Norton & Company, 1990).

p. 308: "How are you?": O'Donnell and Powers, *Johnny, We Hardly Knew Ye.*

p. 308: Vienna talks: memo of conversations, JFK–Khrushchev, June 4–5, 1961, JFKL; "Talking Points Reviewing Conversations between President Kennedy and Chairman Khrushchev," June 3–4, 1961, JFKL; Rusk, summary of talks, June 4, 1961, JFKL; Rusk, summary of talks, June 5, 1961, JFKL; memorandum of conversation with the President and the congressional leadership, June 6, 1961, JFKL; meeting of the Policy Planning Council, June 7, 1961, JFKL; Dept of State report to all diplomatic and consular posts, June 8, 1961, JFKL; Dept of State, "Talking Points Reviewing Conversations Between President Kennedy and Chairman Khrushchev," June 12, 1961, JFKL; Charles Bohlen, interview, JFKL.

p. 309: "Not too well": Evelyn Lincoln, *My Twelve Years with John F. Kennedy* (New York: David McKay Co., 1965).

p. 312: "savaged": Reston quoted in Reeves, *President Kennedy.*

p. 312: London visit: trip schedule, JFKL; Caccia to Bundy, April 19, 1961, JFKL; Macmillan diary, BLO; Horne, *Macmillan*, vol. 2; Macmillan, *Pointing the Way*; Prime Minister's Diaries, April 4–5, 1961, BLO; Caccia to Bundy, April 11, 1961, JFKL; Bundy to Caccia, April 14, 1961, JFKL; Caccia to Bundy, April 15, 1961, JFKL; Caccia to Bundy, April 19, 1961, JFKL; Bundy to Caccia, April 21, 1961, JFKL; Caccia to Bundy, April 24, 1961, JFKL; Caccia to Bundy, May 19, 1961, JFKL; Bundy to Caccia, May 20, 1961, JFKL; Caccia to Bundy, May 22, 1961, JFKL; JFK to Macmillan, May 22, 1961, JFKL; JFK and Macmillan, joint communiqué, June 5, 1961, JFKL; Bundy to Lucius Battle, June 8, 1961, JFKL; Bundy to JFK, June 9, 1961, JFKL; British program and scenario for visit of President Kennedy, June 4–5, 1961, JFKL; Bundy to Rusk, n.d., JFKL; Dinah Bridge (Dinah Brand), interview, JFKL; Joseph Alsop, interview, JFKL; William Douglas Home, interview, JFKL; David Ormsby Gore, interview, JFKL.

p. 312: JFK–Halifax talk: JFK, notes on talk with Lord Halifax, January 23, 1942, JFKL.

p. 313: JFK–Macmillan talks at Admiralty House: Macmillan, *Pointing the Way*; Macmillan to Jacqueline Kennedy, February 18, 1964, BLO; memorandum of conversation, JFK and Macmillan, April 6, 1961, JFKL; Macmillan diary, BLO; Sir David Eccles to Macmillan, June 8, 1961, PREM 11/3328, PRO; Macmillan to Sir Milton Margai, June 19, 1961, PREM 11/3328, PRO; C.C. 30 (61), PRO; Ormsby Gore interview, JFKL; JFK to congressional leaders, June 6, 1961, FRUS 5; JFK to Macmillan, July 20, 1961, JFKL; JFK to Macmillan, June 10, 1961, PREM 11/3328, PRO; record of conversation, JFK–Macmillan, June 5, 1961, FRUS 14.

p. 314: "loneliness": Horne, *Macmillan*, vol. 2.

p. 314: Admiralty House lunch: Andrew Devonshire, author interview; Deborah Devonshire, author interview; Macmillan diary, BLO; Macmillan, *Pointing the Way*.

p. 314: help drafting speech: Bundy to Rusk, June 5, 1961, JFKL.

p. 315: Queen's dinner: Ormsby Gore interview, JFKL; Macmillan diary, BLO.

CHAPTER FOURTEEN: THE EDGE OF THE PRECIPICE

p. 317: loan of Wrightsman estate: Charles Wrightsman to JFK, June 9, 1961, JFKL.

p. 317: meeting with congressional leadership: June 6, 1961, FRUS 5.

p. 318: "no discourtesy": radio and television report to the American people on returning from Europe, June 6, 1961, PPP.

p. 318: Palm Beach trip: trip file, 1961 Palm Beach, McHugh papers, JFKL.

p. 318: JFK's entourage: *Air Force One* passenger lists: flight Andrews Air Force Base, Maryland, to West Palm Beach, Florida, June 8, 1961, flight West Palm Beach, Florida, to Andrews Air Force Base, Maryland, June 12, 1961, both JFKL; Charles Spalding, interview, JFKL.

p. 319: JFK talks about Khrushchev to Spalding: Charles Spalding interview, JFKL.

p. 319: sabotage of test ban talks: Current Intelligence Weekly Review, June 15, 1961, FRUS 5.

p. 319: test ban talks dead: Current Intelligence Weekly Review, June 15, 1961, FRUS 5; Macmillan diary, BLO.

p. 320: "to go all the way": Interdepartmental Coordinating Group on Berlin contingency planning meeting, June 16, 1961, FRUS 14.

p. 320: Acheson's position: Interdepartmental Coordinating Group on Berlin contingency planning meeting, June 16, 1961, FRUS 14; memo of conversation, June 14, 1961, FRUS 14.

p. 320: JFK's health: Janet Travell, interview, JFKL; Hugh Sidey, *John F. Kennedy, President* (New York: Atheneum, 1964).

p. 322: JFK's meeting with Adzhubei: memo of conversation, June 26, 1961, FRUS 5.

p. 322: unsure of himself: Walter Lippmann quoted in Reeves, *President Kennedy*.

p. 322: "I feel 'in my bones'": Macmillan diary, BLO.

p. 323: Acheson report: Dean Acheson, June 28, 1961, FRUS 14.

p. 323: JFK questions Bundy: JFK to Bundy, July 5, 1961, JFKL.

p. 324: Ayub Khan visit: program and scenario for state visit of Ayub Khan, July 11–18, 1961, JFKL; National Intelligence Estimate Prospects for Pakistan, July 5, 1961, JFKL; briefing papers for visit of Ayub Khan, JFKL; Dept of State, biography of Ayub Khan, July 6, 1961, JFKL; memorandum of conversation, JFK–Ayub, July 11, 1961, JFKL; Richard Goodkin to Evelyn Lincoln, July 11, 1961, JFKL; Elizabeth Carpenter, interview, LBJL; Angier Biddle Duke, interview, JFKL.

p. 324: "a weakness of decision": Acheson to Harry S. Truman, July 14, 1961, in David S. McLellan and David C. Acheson, eds., *Among Friends: Personal Letters of Dean Acheson* (New York: Dodd, Mead & Co., 1980).

p. 325: July 13, 1961 NSC meeting: National Security Council memo of discussion, July 13, 1961, FRUS 14.

p. 325: JFK's decisions: minutes of the National Security Council meeting, July 19, 1961, FRUS 14; National Security action memorandum No. 62, July 24, 1961, FRUS 14; JFK to Macmillan, July 20, 1961, JFKL.

p. 326: "feeling the best": Rose Kennedy, *Times to Remember*.

p. 326: JFK's television speech: July 25, 1961, PPP.

p. 327: "progress on our negotiating": minutes of meeting, July 26, 1961, FRUS 14.

p. 327: Khrushchev's talk with McCloy: Thompson to Dept of State, July 28, 1961, FRUS 14; McCloy to Rusk, July 29, 1961, FRUS 14.

p. 328: Khrushchev ridicules JFK: speech of August 4, 1961, quoted in Taubman, *Khrushchev*.

p. 328: Khrushchev assures McCloy he will not test: Thompson to Dept of State, July 28, 1961, FRUS 7.

p. 328: JFK makes new test ban try: memo by Bundy, July 28, 1961, FRUS 7.

p. 328: Rusk meets with Allies re Berlin: memorandum of conversations, ministerial consultations on Berlin, Paris, August 4–9, 1961, FRUS 14; Macmillan diary, BLO; Home to Cabinet, September 1, 1961, C.C. (61) 132, PRO.

p. 330: Berlin Wall: note, p. 325, FRUS 14; Bundy to JFK, August 14, 1961, FRUS 14; JFK to Rusk, August 14, 1961, FRUS 14; minutes, Berlin

Steering Group, August 15, 1961, FRUS 14; Special National Intelligence Estimate, August 24, 1961, FRUS 5; JFK to Rusk, August 21, 1961, FRUS 14; minutes, Berlin Steering Group, August 15, 1961, and August 17, 1961, JFKL; JFK to Willy Brandt, August 18, 1961, JFKL; Joseph Alsop, interview, JFKL; Foy Kohler, interview, JFKL.

p. 330: "a crisis of confidence": Lightner to Dept of State, August 16, 1961, FRUS 14.

p. 331: Willy Brandt request: Brandt to JFK, August 16, 1961, FRUS 14.

p. 331: JFK's response: minutes, Berlin Steering Group, August 17, 1961, FRUS 14.

p. 331: "to take a stronger lead": JFK to Rusk, August 21, 1961, FRUS 14.

p. 331: "a notice of our surrender": de Gaulle to JFK, August 26, 1961, note, p. 280, FRUS 5.

p. 331: Moscow announces test resumption: TASS announcement, August 30, 1961, FRUS 7; statement, August 30, 1961, PPP.

p. 332: "contingent preparations": memo by Bundy, August 29, 1961, FRUS 7.

CHAPTER FIFTEEN: THE GO-BETWEEN

p. 334: Jackie loathed being stared at . . . Jack loved the attention: Betty Spalding, author interview; Ormsby Gore, interview, JFKL.

p. 336: JFK instructions to Rusk on testing: note, p. 158–9, FRUS 7.

p. 337: US–British test ban proposal sent: note, p. 160, FRUS 7; joint statement, September 3, 1961, PPP; Macmillan to JFK, September 5, 1961, PREM 11/4052, PRO.

p. 337: JFK's instructions to Rusk on Berlin talks: Rusk to Thompson, September 3, 1961, FRUS 14.

p. 337: de Gaulle reaction: Gavin to Dept of State, September 2, 1961, FRUS 13.

p. 338: JFK wants to resume underground testing: Seaborg journal, quoted p. 161, FRUS 7; National Security action memorandum No. 87, September 5, 1961, FRUS 7.

p. 338: JFK's precipitous action: Bundy to Rusk, September 5, 1961, FRUS 7; JFK to Macmillan, September 5, 1961, JFKL; JFK, statement, September 5, 1961, PPP.

p. 338: "relieved the Russians": Macmillan, *Pointing the Way*.

p. 338: "like a bull": Macmillan, *Pointing the Way*.

p. 339: "completely overwhelmed": Macmillan to the Queen, September 15, 1961, in Macmillan, *At the End of the Day*.

p. 339: Kennedy had hoped: record of phone call, JFK to Macmillan, September 14, 1961, PRO; Macmillan diary, BLO.

p. 339: "indecision and uncertainty": Eisenhower speech, September 16, 1961, quoted in *New York Times*, September 17, 1961.

p. 339: JFK tries to laugh off Eisenhower's remark: Caccia to Sir F.H. Millar, September 21, 1961, Foreign Office, PRO.

p. 339: Senator Margaret Chase Smith speech: Caccia to Foreign Office, September 25, 1961, Foreign Office, PRO.

p. 340: JFK's talk with Caccia: Caccia to Sir F.H. Millar, September 21, 1961, Foreign Office, PRO.

p. 340: "war before Christmas": memo of conversation, JFK and Sukarno, September 12, 1961, FRUS 5.

p. 340: JFK talks with foreign ministers: memo of conversation, September 15, 1961, FRUS 14.

p. 340: Khrushchev to Sulzberger: C. L. Sulzberger, *The Last of the Giants* (New York: The Macmillan Company, 1970); *New York Times*, September 8, 1961.

p. 341: Khrushchev's message to Salinger: Pierre Salinger, *With Kennedy* (New York: Doubleday, 1966).

p. 341: Jacobson injection: Jacobson unpublished memoir, MHS.

p. 341: JFK's UN speech: September 25, 1961, PPP.

p. 341: "simple and noble": Macmillan diary, BLO.

p. 342: Rusk's assessment of talks: David K. E. Bruce diary, October 2, 1961, FRUS 14; Bundy to JFK, October 2, 1961, FRUS 14.

p. 342: Khrushchev's private letter to JFK: Khrushchev to JFK, September 29, 1961, FRUS 6.

p. 343: Ormsby Gore's arrival: Ormsby Gore to Home, November 4, 1961, PREM 11/4166, PRO.

p. 343: Macmillan proposes six-month moratorium: Rusk to US Embassy in UK, October 27, 1961, FRUS 7; Macmillan, *Pointing the Way*.

p. 344: David had worried: Ormsby Gore to JFK, May 18, 1961, JFKL; Jane Rainey, author interview; Victoria Lloyd, author interview; Jean Lloyd, author interview.

p. 344: "the most inspiring": Ormsby Gore to Macmillan, February 1, 1964, Macmillan papers, BLO.

p. 344: "extremely vigorous": Ormsby Gore to Home, November 4, 1961, PREM 11/4166, PRO.

p. 344: credentials ceremony: transcript of October 26, 1961 speeches by JFK and Ormsby Gore, FO 371/156510, PRO.

p. 345: "talked the whole time": Ormsby Gore to Home, November 4, 1961, PREM 11/4166, PRO.

p. 345: "He was almost a part": quoted in Guthman and Shulman, eds., *Robert Kennedy, in His Own Words*.

p. 345: "as he would a member": Theodore C. Sorensen, *Kennedy* (New York: Bantam Books, 1966).

p. 345: "Their long, relaxed": Schlesinger, *A Thousand Days*.

p. 345: Kennedy rejects Macmillan proposal: Rusk to US Embassy in UK, October 27, 1961, FRUS 7; Macmillan diary, BLO; Macmillan to JFK, November 3, 1961, FRUS 7.

p. 345: JFK refuses to approve atmospheric tests: memo for the record, November 2, 1961, FRUS 7.

p. 346: "necessary to maintain our": November 2, 1961 JFK statement, quoted in Ormsby Gore to FO No. 2931, PREM 11/3246, PRO; Ormsby Gore to Home, November 4, 1961, PREM 11/4166, PRO.

p. 346: a back-channel message: Fursenko and Naftali, *"One Hell of a Gamble."*

p. 346: felt like a distraction: Ormsby Gore to Home, December 15, 1961, PREM 11/4166, PRO.

p. 346: Taylor report: Taylor Report, November 3, 1961, FRUS 1; notes, November 6, 1961, FRUS 1.

p. 347: November 8 dinner party: Ormsby Gore to Home, November 13, 1961, PREM 11/4166, PRO.

p. 347: "instinctively" opposed: memo for the record, November 6, 1961, FRUS 1.

p. 348: Rostow had urged: Walt Rostow to McNamara, April 24, 1961, FRUS 10.

p. 348: Komer's appeal: Robert W. Komer to Rostow, July 20, 1961, FRUS 1.

p. 348: "a Berlin-type commitment": Under-Secretary Johnson to Rusk, November 5, 1961, FRUS 1.

p. 349: "commit to the clear objective": McNamara to JFK, November 8, 1961, FRUS 1.

p. 349: November 11 meeting on Vietnam: "Notes of a Meeting, The White House," November 11, 1961, FRUS 1.

p. 349: ends with confusion: memo of telephone conversation, Rusk to Taylor, November 13, 1961, FRUS 1.

p. 349: "to explain to the American people": Ormsby Gore to Foreign Office, November 22, 1961, Foreign Office, PRO.

p. 350: Jacobson injects group: Betty Spalding, author interview.

p. 350: new Harriman proposal: draft memo, Harriman to JFK, November 11, 1961, FRUS 1.

p. 350: "what the hell": Betty Spalding, author interview.

p. 350: "of becoming involved simultaneously": notes on NSC meeting, November 15, 1961, FRUS 1.

p. 351: letter to Khrushchev: JFK to Khrushchev, November 16, 1961, FRUS 6.

p. 351: goal of western speeches: Ormsby Gore to Foreign Office, November 22, 1961, PRO.

p. 352: launch a "counter-attack": Ormsby Gore to Foreign Office, November 22, 1961, PRO.

p. 352: Seattle speech: November 16, 1961, PPP.

p. 352: girls at hotel: Larry Newman, author interview.

p. 353: meeting with Barbara Ward: Barbara Ward interview, JFKL.

p. 353: JFK talks with Adenauer: memo of conversation, November 22, 1961, FRUS 14; JFK to Macmillan, November 22, 1961, FRUS 14; Macmillan, *Pointing the Way*; Macmillan diary, BLO.

p. 354: "You seem to have": Macmillan to JFK, November 23, 1961, PREM 11/4052, PRO.

p. 354: JFK organizes celebration: Macmillan to Wyndham, November 27, 1961, Macmillan papers, BLO.

p. 354: de Gaulle meeting with Macmillan: Macmillan, *Pointing the Way*; Macmillan diary, BLO.

p. 354: Army–Navy Game: Deborah Devonshire, author interview; Ormsby Gore to Home, December 4, 1961, PREM 11/4166, PRO.

p. 356: citing his great-grandfather: Ormsby Gore to JFK, May 18, 1961, JFKL.

p. 356: try to keep question of testing open: Ormsby Gore to Macmillan, November 15, 1961, PREM 11/3246, PRO.

p. 356: JFK plans for Bermuda talks: Suggested US agenda for talks, December 1961, JFKL.

p. 356: Macmillan plans for talks: Macmillan diary, BLO; Macmillan, *Pointing the Way*.

p. 357: alarm over Latin American trip: Richard Helms to Robert Kennedy, December 13, 1961, JFKL.

CHAPTER SIXTEEN: A LESSON IN DUTY

p. 359: Macmillan sent word: Macmillan to JFK, December 20, 1961, JFKL; Zulueta to Bundy, December 20, 1961, JFKL.

p. 360: "country-house conditions": Ormsby Gore, interview, JFKL.

p. 360: Debo Devonshire's gift: Macmillan diary, BLO.

p. 361: prime minister had concluded: Macmillan diary, BLO; Macmillan, *At the End of the Day*.

p. 361: believed Kennedy had trusted him: Macmillan to Jacqueline Kennedy, February 18, 1964, BLO.

p. 361: no one had ever quite spoken: Ormsby Gore interview, JFKL.

p. 361: Bermuda talks: notes of conversations, Bermuda, December 1961, FRUS 14; British Bermuda meeting records, PREM 11/3782, PRO; Ormsby Gore interview, JFKL; Macmillan, *At the End of the Day*; Macmillan diary, BLO; Dept of State, objectives paper, December 16, 1961, JFKL; "The Prime Minister's Visit to Bermuda 20–23rd December 1961," FO 371/166967, PRO; Macmillan to JFK, December 22, 1961, JFKL; Macmillan memo to Cabinet re Christmas Island, January 1, 1962, PRO.

p. 364: "moments in history": Ormsby Gore interview, JFKL.

p. 365: "must sign the treaty": JFK to de Gaulle, January 1, 1962, FRUS 14.

p. 365: "the importance of the United States": notes on meeting in Palm Beach, Florida, January 3, 1962 meeting, FRUS 2.

p. 366: Macmillan works on letter: Macmillan to Home, December 29, 1961, PREM 11/3246, PRO.

p. 366: reread *Marlborough*: Macmillan diary, BLO.

p. 366: Macmillan's letter: Macmillan to JFK, January 5, 1962, PREM 11/4052, PRO.

p. 367: January 8 lunch: Ormsby Gore to Macmillan, January 8, 1962, FO 371/163113, PRO.

p. 368: meeting with Ormsby Gore: Ormsby Gore to Macmillan, January 10, 1962, FO 371/163113, PRO.

p. 369: State of the Union message: January 11, 1962, PPP.

p. 369: had intended to go even further: Schlesinger, *A Thousand Days*.

p. 369: agree to joint letter: Ormsby Gore to Macmillan, January 17, 1962, FO 371/163113, PRO.

p. 369: Rusk and Ormsby Gore formulate letter: JFK to Macmillan, January 13, 1962, FRUS 7; Ormsby Gore to Macmillan, January 13, 1962, FO 371/163113, PRO; Ormsby Gore to Macmillan, January 19, 1962, FO 371/163113, PRO; Fisher to Rusk, January 31, 1962, FRUS 7; Macmillan to JFK, January 16, 1962, PREM 11/4052, PRO.

p. 369: "personal responsibility": JFK and Macmillan to Khrushchev, February 7, 1962, FRUS 7.

p. 369: dinner dance: White House file, dinner dance, February 9, 1962; Benjamin Bradlee, *Conversations with Kennedy* (New York: W. W. Norton & Company, 1975); William Tyler to Rusk, January 2, 1962, JFKL; Jane Rainey, author interview; Betty Spalding, author interview.

p. 371: "Who can most quickly step": Khrushchev to JFK and Macmillan, February 10, 1962, FRUS 6.

p. 371: JFK's reply: JFK to Khrushchev, February 14, 1962, FRUS 6.

p. 372: "a gift of that length": press conference, January 17, 1962, PPP.

p. 372: Rusk recommends: Rusk to JFK, n.d., c. February 20, 1962, FRUS 7.

p. 372: "Yet two months": Seaborg, *Kennedy, Khrushchev, and the Test Ban*.

p. 373: February 20 phone call to Ormsby Gore: Ormsby Gore to Home, February 21, 1962, FO 371/163115, PRO; Macmillan to JFK, February 23, 1962, PREM 11/4052, PRO.

p. 373: jeering letter: Khrushchev to JFK, February 21, 1962, FRUS 6.

p. 374: JFK's response: JFK to Khrushchev, February 24, 1962, FRUS 6.

p. 374: Bundy still assumed: memo for the record, February 26, 1962, FRUS 7.

p. 374: February 27 NSC meeting: memo of NSC meeting, February 27, 1962, FRUS 7.

p. 375: February 27 meeting with Ormsby Gore: Ormsby Gore to Foreign Office, February 27, 1962, FO 371/163115, PRO.

p. 376: letter to Macmillan: JFK to Macmillan, February 27, 1962, FRUS 7.

p. 376: not attempt to do it by phone: Foreign Office to Ormsby Gore, Feburary 28, 1962, FO 371/163115, PRO.

p. 376: Macmillan uncomfortable on phone: Ormsby Gore interview, JFKL.

p. 377: Macmillan's reply: Macmillan to JFK, February 28, 1962, PREM 11/4052, PRO.

p. 378: Macmillan plan to contact Khrushchev: PM's Personal Minute Serial No. M63/62 to Foreign Secretary, re nuclear tests, March 1, 1962, Macmillan papers, BLO.

p. 378: JFK's reply: JFK to Macmillan, March 1, 1962, FO 371/163115, PRO.

p. 378: Macmillan's reaction: Macmillan to Ormsby Gore, March 1, 1962, FO 371/163115, PRO; Macmillan to Ormsby Gore, March 1, 1962, FO 371/163115, PRO.

p. 378: television speech: March 2, 1962, PPP.

p. 379: JFK sends Bobby Kennedy to Bolshakov: Fursenko and Naftali, *"One Hell of a Gamble."*

p. 379: Khrushchev rejects offer: Khrushchev to JFK, March 10, 1962, FRUS 15.

p. 379: JFK did not improve draft treaty: delegation to Dept of State, March 12, 1962, FRUS 7.

p. 379: JFK directed Rusk re modus vivendi: JFK to Rusk, March 11, 1962, FRUS 15; JFK to Macmillan, March 10, 1962, PREM 11/3805, PRO.

p. 380: Rusk reports absolute failure: Rusk to JFK, March 26, 1962, FRUS 15.

p. 380: "opinion in this country": JFK to Macmillan, April 3, 1962, FRUS 7.

p. 380: "In my experience": Macmillan to JFK, April 5, 1962, PREM 11/4052, PRO.

p. 381: Ormsby Gore suggests Macmillan talk: Ormsby Gore to Home, April 16, 1962, PREM 11/4052, PRO.

p. 381: Macmillan speech: Macmillan April 26, 1962 speech to American Newspaper Publishers Association Convention, New York, PREM 11/4052, PRO.

p. 382: April 29 lunch: Ormsby Gore interview, JFKL.

p. 382: Tuchman book: Barbara W. Tuchman, *The Guns of August* (New York: Ballantine Books, 1994).

CHAPTER SEVENTEEN: IN READING THE HISTORY OF PAST WARS AND HOW THEY BEGAN

p. 383: Gromyko suggests talks: Rusk to Dept of State, March 26, 1962, FRUS 15.

p. 383: talks before tests start: Bundy to Rusk, April 7, 1962, FRUS 15.

p. 383: Adenauer protests talks: Adenauer to JFK, April 14, 1962, FRUS 15.

p. 383: JFK was intent: summary of discussion, April 28, 1962, FRUS 15.

p. 383: angry message: Dept of State to Embassy in Germany, May 12, 1962, FRUS 15.

p. 384: May 9 press conference: May 9, 1962, PPP.

p. 384: "encouraging": Winthrop Brown to Dept of State, May 10, 1962, FRUS 5.

p. 384: Eisenhower on Laos: David E. Kaiser, *American Tragedy: Kennedy, Johnson, and the Origins of the Vietnam War* (Cambridge: Harvard University Press, 2000).

p. 384: meeting with Malraux: memo of meeting, May 11, 1962, FRUS 13; Gavin to Rusk, May 28, 1962, FRUS 13.

p. 385: phone call to Ormsby Gore: Ormsby Gore to Foreign Office, May 12, 1962, FO 371/162587, PRO.

p. 385: sends troops to Laos: Ormsby Gore, annual review for 1962, January 1, 1963, FO 371/168405, PRO.

p. 385: "The great danger": JFK, press conference, May 18, 1962, PPP.

p. 386: Khrushchev spoke to Gromyko: Fursenko and Naftali, *"One Hell of a Gamble"*; Taubman, *Khrushchev.*

p. 387: May 21 meeting: Fursenko and Naftali, *"One Hell of a Gamble"*; Taubman, *Khrushchev.*

p. 387: "scare": Fursenko and Naftali, *"One Hell of a Gamble"*; Taubman, *Khrushchev.*

p. 387: "double game": transcript of phone conversation, JFK and Macmillan, October 22, 1962, PREM 11/3689, PRO.

p. 388: Khrushchev warmly expressed: Khrushchev to JFK, June 12, 1962, FRUS 6.

p. 388: JFK wasted no time: JFK to Khrushchev, June 12, 1962, FRUS 6.

p. 388: reached an impasse: Rusk to Dept of State, June 20, 1962, FRUS 13.

p. 388: "speed up": Khrushchev to JFK, n.d., FRUS 15.

p. 388: White House quickly saw: Bohlen to Rusk, July 6, 1962, FRUS 15.

p. 389: JFK meets Dobrynin: memo of conversation, Kennedy and Dobrynin, July 17, 1962, FRUS 15; record of conversation: Rusk, Home, Kohler, Schuckburgh, July 21, 1962, PREM 11/3806, PRO; record of conversation, Home and Rusk, July 21, 1962, PREM 11/3806, PRO.

p. 389: letter to Khrushchev: JFK to Khrushchev, July 17, 1962, FRUS 6.

p. 389: "In reading the history": JFK to Khrushchev, July 17, 1962, FRUS 6.

p. 389: talks with Ormsby Gore at Hyannis Port: Ormsby Gore to Home, July 24, 1962, PREM 11/4166, PRO; Macmillan diary, BLO.

p. 390: "brought to a head": Thompson to Rusk, July 25, 1962, FRUS 15.

p. 390: "on ice": Fursenko and Naftali, *"One Hell of a Gamble."*

p. 392: Cuban missile crisis meetings: In addition to documents cited below, my accounts of the meetings and quotations from participants during the Cuban crisis between August 1962 and November 1962 are based on the taped transcripts printed in *The Presidential Recordings, John F. Kennedy: The Great Crises*, vol. 1, Timothy Naftali, ed., vol. 2, Timothy Naftali and Philip Zelikow, eds., and vol. 3, Philip Zelikow and Ernest May, eds. (New York: W. W. Norton & Company, 2001), plus the accounts by notetakers present at the meetings contained in the documents in FRUS 10 and 11.

p. 392: "Yes, new supplies": press conference, August 22, 1962, PPP.

p. 392: McCone briefs JFK: JFK and McCone, August 22, 1962, *The Presidential Recordings*, vol. 1.

p. 392: JFK at August 23 meeting: FRUS 10.

p. 393: Capehart attack: *New York Times*, August 29, 1962.

p. 393: "We've no evidence": press conference, August 29, 1962, PPP.

p. 394: August 29 flight: Ray Cline to Marshall Carter, September 3, 1962, FRUS 10.

p. 394: "back in the box": note, p. 968, FRUS 10.

p. 395: Bundy report: Bundy to JFK, August 31, 1962, FRUS 10.

p. 395: "do-nothing" attitude: *New York Times*, September 3, 1962.

p. 395: September 4 statement: Statement by President John F. Kennedy on Cuba, September 4, 1962, JFKL.

p. 396: TASS statement: TASS statement, September 11, 1962, JFKL.

p. 396: CIA analysts suspected: Current Intelligence memorandum, September 13, 1962, FRUS 10.

p. 396: "I will repeat": press conference, September 13, 1962, PPP.

p. 396: "virtually promised": *New York Times*, September 15, 1962.

p. 397: JFK's private fears: Ormsby Gore to Home, September 19, 1962, PREM 11/4166, PRO; Ormsby Gore to Foreign Office, September 14, 1962, FO 371/162581, PRO.

p. 397: Khrushchev to Udall: memo of conversation, Udall and Khrushchev, September 6, 1962, FRUS 15.

p. 397: talks with Ormsby Gore in Newport: Ormsby Gore to Home, September 19, 1962, PREM 11/4166, PRO.

p. 398: "After the elections, apparently": Khrushchev to JFK, September 28, 1962, FRUS 6.

p. 398: JFK confers with Thompson and Bohlen: meeting on the Soviet Union, September 29, 1962, *The Presidential Recordings*, vol. 2.

p. 399: JFK lunch with Ormsby Gore, Home et al.: Home to Macmillan, October 1, 1962, FO 371/166970, PRO; Home to Macmillan, October 2, 1962, PREM 11/3806, PRO; record of conversation, Home and Gromyko, September 28, 1962, Prem 11/3806, PRO; Macmillan to Kennedy, October 5, 1962, FO 371/166970, PRO.

p. 399: civil rights crisis: meetings on the crisis at the University of Mississippi, September 29–October 1, 1962, *The Presidential Recordings*, vol. 2.

p. 400: McCone prodding: *The Presidential Recordings*, vol. 2; FRUS 11.

p. 400: that images be withheld: memo by McCone of meeting with President, October 11, 1962, FRUS 11.

p. 401: "He can't do that": Kai Bird, *The Color of Truth: McGeorge Bundy and William Bundy* (New York: Simon & Schuster, 1998).

p. 402: "a symbol of the tragic irresolution": Ormsby Gore to Foreign Office, October 20, 1962, PREM 11/3689, PRO.

p. 402: JFK summons Jacqueline Kennedy and children: Ormsby Gore, interview, JFKL.

p. 402: JFK's conversation with Ormsby Gore on Sunday: Ormsby Gore to Prime Minister, October 22, 1962, PREM 11/3689, PRO; Ormsby Gore to Macmillan, October 23, 1962, PREM 11/3689, PRO; Ormsby Gore to Macmillan, October 21, 1962, PREM 11/3689, PRO; Ormsby Gore interview, JFKL.

p. 405: "to fire our nuclear": JFK meeting with congressional leadership, 5:30–6:30 p.m., October 22, 1962, *The Presidential Recordings*, vol. 3.

p. 405: JFK speech: October 22, 1962, PPP.

p. 405: phone call to Macmillan: transcript of phone call, JFK to Macmillan, October 22, 1962, PREM 11/3689, PRO; Macmillan to Hugh Gaitskell, October 23, 1962, PREM 11/3689, PRO.

p. 406: October 23 talk with Ormsby Gore after dinner: Ormsby Gore to Macmillan, October 24, 1962, PREM 11/3690, PRO; Ormsby Gore interview, JFKL.

p. 408: Bobby Kennedy's talk with Dobrynin: Fursenko and Naftali, *"One Hell of a Gamble."*

p. 408: "pushing mankind toward the abyss": Khrushchev to JFK, October 24, 1962, FRUS 6.

p. 409: JFK calls with George Ball: transcripts of calls, JFK and Ball, October 24, 1962, FRUS 11.

p. 409: JFK tells Macmillan on phone: transcript of phone call, JFK and Macmillan, October 25, 1962, PREM 11/3690, PRO.

p. 409: need for verification: Ormsby Gore to Home, October 26, 1962, PREM 11/3690, PRO.

p. 409: Khrushchev's letter: Khrushchev to JFK, October 26, 1962, FRUS 6.

p. 410: Khrushchev's second letter: *The Presidential Recordings*, vol. 3.

p. 410: JFK summons Ormsby Gore and the Devonshires: Andrew Devonshire, author interview; Devonshire, *Accidents of Fortune*.

p. 410: JFK previously told Ormsby Gore: Ormsby Gore to Macmillan, October 23, 1962, PREM 11/3689, PRO.

p. 411: secret resolution to crisis: *The Presidential Recordings*, vol. 3; FRUS 11; Robert Kennedy, memo of Dobrynin talk, *The Presidential Recordings*, vol. 3; Dobrynin to USSR Foreign Ministry, October 27, 1962, in Fursenko and Naftali, *"One Hell of a Gamble."*

p. 412: "caught the mood of the public": Ormsby Gore, annual review for 1962, January 1, 1963, FO 371/168405, PRO.

CHAPTER EIGHTEEN: BEFORE IT IS TOO LATE

p. 413: "in terms of children": Ormsby Gore quoted in Martin, *A Hero for Our Times.*

p. 414: "no confidence": memo of conversation, JFK and Adenauer, November 14, 1962, FRUS 15.

p. 415: announces lifting of quarantine: press conference, November 20, 1962, PPP.

p. 415: Ormsby Gore's frustration in missile crisis aftermath: Ormsby Gore to Home, October 30, 1962, PREM 11/3806, PRO; Ormsby Gore to Home, November 10, 1962, FO 371/166970, PRO; Ormsby Gore to Home, December 8, 1962, FO 371/166971, PRO.

p. 415: "the long-term implications": Macmillan to JFK, November 22, 1962, PREM 11/4052, PRO.

p. 416: focus of talks shifts: Zulueta to Ormsby Gore, December 11, 1962, PREM 11/4229, PRO; "Talking Points for President Kennedy," PREM 11/4229, PRO; Ormsby Gore to Home, December 8, 1962, FO 371/166971, PRO; Ormsby Gore interview, JFKL.

p. 416: Nassau talks: British record of December 1962 meetings, FO 371/173292, PRO; memos of conversations, December 19–20, 1962, FRUS 13; Macmillan diary, BLO; CAB 128/37, meeting January 3, 1963, PRO; Ormsby Gore to Macmillan, December 28, 1962, PREM 11/4229, PRO.

p. 416: surprise message from Khrushchev: Khrushchev to JFK, December 19, 1962, FRUS 6.

p. 416: were jubilant: Ormsby Gore interview, JFKL; Ormsby Gore report at Chequers, May 18, 1963, record of meeting, FO 371/173293, PRO.

p. 417: JFK wrote to welcome: JFK to Khrushchev, December 28, 1962, FRUS 6.

p. 417: Macmillan had no objection: Macmillan to JFK, January 5, 1963, FRUS 7.

p. 417: Ormsby Gore proposed: Ormsby Gore to Home, January 9, 1963, PREM 11/4554, PRO.

p. 417: Macmillan wrote to suggest: Macmillan to JFK, January 13, 1963, PREM 11/4593, PRO.

p. 417: president was quick: JFK to Macmillan, January 13, 1963, FRUS 7.

p. 418: JFK postpones tests: Seaborg, *Kennedy, Khrushchev, and the Test Ban*; note, p. 636, FRUS 7.

p. 418: "losing its nuclear shirt": *New York Times*, January 28, 1963.

p. 418: Rockefeller accused: *New York Times*, January 30, 1963.

p. 419: Khrushchev had gone to his Council: quoted in Seaborg, *Kennedy, Khrushchev, and the Test Ban*.

p. 419: Soviets end New York talks: note, p. 634, FRUS 7.

p. 419: Ormsby Gore saw a glimmer of hope: Ormsby Gore to Foreign Office, February 1, 1963, FO 371/171216, PRO.

p. 419: ordering the resumption of underground testing: Seaborg, *Kennedy, Khrushchev, and the Test Ban*; Ormsby Gore to Home, February 1, 1963, FO 371/171216, PRO.

p. 420: Palm Beach weekend: Ormsby Gore to Home, February 26, 1963, FO 371/171231, PRO.

p. 421: Macmillan decides to take action: Macmillan to Home, March 4, 1963, Macmillan papers, BLO; Macmillan diary, BLO; Macmillan to JFK, March 8, 1963, PREM 11/4593, PRO.

p. 421: before the US became so consumed: Macmillan to Ormsby Gore, March 27, 1963, FO 371/171219, PRO.

p. 421: Ormsby Gore had lately bristled: Ormsby Gore to Foreign Office, February 15, 1963, FO 371/171235, PRO; Sir P. Mason to Foreign Office, February 19, 1963, FO 371/171235, PRO; Home to Ormsby Gore, February 27, 1963, FO 371/171235; Washington Embassy to Foreign Office, February 27, 1963, FO 371/171235, PRO.

p. 421: Macmillan did not think they could be content: Macmillan to Ormsby Gore, March 12, 1963, FO 371/171235, PRO.

p. 421: Ormsby Gore wrote back enthusiastically: Ormsby Gore to Macmillan, March 14, 1963, FO 371/171235, PRO.

p. 422: March 16 letter: Macmillan to JFK, March 16, 1963, JFKL.

p. 422: JFK and Ormsby Gore March 21 meeting: Ormsby Gore to Macmillan, March 21, 1963, FO 371/171219, PRO.

p. 425: Thompson's opposition: Thompson to Rusk, March 21, 1963, FRUS 7; note, p. 656, FRUS 7; Ormsby Gore to Foreign Office, March 27, 1963, PREM 11/4262, PRO.

p. 426: "too many problems": JFK to Macmillan, March 28, 1963, FO 371/171216, PRO.

p. 426: Ormsby Gore's response: Ormsby Gore to Macmillan, March 28, 1963, FO 371/171216, PRO; Ormsby Gore to Macmillan, April 1, 1963, PRO.

p. 427: JFK's ambitions extended: Ormsby Gore interview, JFKL; Macmillan diary, BLO; Jacqueline Kennedy to Macmillan, January 31, 1964, BLO.

p. 427: "worthy of the occasion": Ormsby Gore to Macmillan, March 28, 1963, FO 371/171216, PRO.

p. 427: JFK's desire to do great things: Jacqueline Kennedy to Macmillan,

January 31, 1964, BLO; Ormsby Gore interview, JFKL; Macmillan diary, BLO.

p. 428: "sit supine": Ormsby Gore to Macmillan, April 8, 1963, FO 371/171235, PRO.

p. 428: citizenship ceremony: Jacqueline Kennedy quoted in Kay Halle, *The Grand Original: Portraits of Randolph Churchill by his Friends* (Boston: Houghton Mifflin Co., 1971); "Honorary American Citizenship for Sir Winston Churchill: Details of the ceremony," January 25, 1963, February 18, 1963, February 20, 1963, February 25, 1963, February 28, 1963, March 21, 1963, April 3, 1963, April 9, 1963, FO 371/168490, PRO.

p. 429: phone call to Macmillan: Ormsby Gore to Macmillan, April 11, 1963, FO 371/171216, PRO; Macmillan to Ormsby Gore, April 12, 1963, FO 371/171216, PRO.

p. 429: letter from Kennedy and Macmillan to Khrushchev: JFK to Khrushchev, April 15, 1963, FRUS 6; Macmillan to JFK, April 15, 1963, FO 371/171216, PRO; Macmillan to Ormsby Gore, April 15, 1963, FO 371/171216, PRO.

p. 430: April 17 meeting of senior advisers: John McCone, memo for the record, meeting of April 17, 1963, FRUS 7.

p. 430: "almost entirely negative": Kohler to State Dept, April 24, 1963, FRUS 7.

p. 430: Thompson leapt on the news: Thompson to Rusk, April 24, 1963, FRUS 7.

p. 430: Khrushchev's letter: Khrushchev to JFK, May 8, 1963, FRUS 6.

p. 430: "I am not hopeful": press conference, May 8, 1963, PPP.

p. 431: Macmillan worried: Macmillan diary, BLO.

p. 431: Macmillan pointed out: Macmillan to JFK, May 9, 1963, PREM 11/4593, PRO.

p. 431: Ormsby Gore's assessment: Ormsby Gore report at Chequers, May 18, 1963, record of meeting, FO 371/173293, PRO.

p. 431: Ormsby Gore sent a note: Ormsby Gore to JFK, May 1963, JFKL.

p. 431: Violet Bonham Carter's visit: Pottle, ed., *Daring to Hope*.

p. 432: prime minister wrote: Macmillan to JFK, May 20, 1963, PREM 11/4593, PRO.

p. 432: "as few changes as possible": Ormsby Gore to Macmillan, May 22, 1963, FO 371/173293, PRO; Macmillan to Ormsby Gore, May 20, 1963, PREM 11/4593, PRO.

p. 432: "push very hard": press conference, May 22, 1963, PPP.

p. 432: American University speech: June 10, 1963, PPP.

p. 433: "as though he were quite a different": Khrushchev to Macmillan, aide-memoire, July 11, 1963, PREM 11/4491, PRO.

p. 433: privately expressed satisfaction: JFK and Harriman meeting of July 10, 1963, FRUS 7.

p. 434: visit to Chatsworth: Deborah Devonshire, author interview; Andrew Devonshire, author interview; Zulueta to J. O. Wright, June 28, 1963, FO 371/173293, PRO; confidential timetable, FO 371/173293, PRO; Deborah Devonshire's scrapbook.

p. 434: talks at Birch Grove: memos of conversations, June 29–30, 1963, FRUS 7; Macmillan to the Queen, July 5, 1963, PREM 11/4586, PRO; "Visit to the United Kingdom by the President and Secretary of State of the United States, Jun 27–30, 1963," PREM 11/4586, PRO; Macmillan diary, BLO.

p. 434: "a greater degree of authority": memorandum by the prime minister, July 1, 1963, PREM 11/4586, PRO.

p. 434: Ormsby Gore to Hyannis Port: Ormsby Gore interview, JFKL.

p. 434: final meeting with Harriman: "Instructions for Honorable W. Averell Harriman," July 10, 1963, FRUS 7; memo for the record, July 10, 1963, FRUS 7.

p. 435: Harriman handed Khrushchev a letter: JFK to Khrushchev, in July 12, 1963 letter to Harriman, FRUS 7.

p. 435: Macmillan feared: Macmillan diary, BLO; Macmillan, *At the End of the Day*.

p. 435: "I found myself unable": Macmillan to JFK, July 25, 1963, PREM 11/4593, PRO.

p. 435: "What no one can doubt": JFK to Macmillan, July 26, 1963, Macmillan papers, BLO.

p. 436: "horns and a tail": Ormsby Gore interview, JFKL.

p. 436: JFK sent Rusk to follow up: JFK meeting with Rusk, August 2, 1963, FRUS 5.

p. 436: birth and death of Patrick: Mary Barelli Gallagher, *My Life with Jacqueline Kennedy* (New York: David McKay Co., 1969); Janet Auchincloss, interview, JFKL; Richard Cardinal Cushing, interview, JFKL; Janet Travell, interview, JFKL; Roy Heffernan, interview, JFKL; David Ormsby Gore, interview, JFKL; Francis Morrissey, interview, JFKL; Maud Shaw, interview, JFKL; Betty Spalding, author interview; Larry Newman, author interview.

p. 437: fell to his knees: as described by Jacqueline Kennedy, Betty Spalding, author interview.

p. 437: "The burdens of public affairs": Macmillan to JFK, August 14, 1963, JFKL.

p. 438: "a step toward war": memo of conversation, Dobrynin and Kennedy, August 26, 1963, FRUS 5.

p. 438: "For the first time we have": speech, October 7, 1963, PPP.

EPILOGUE

p. 439: Runnymede: Secret Service memorandum, Hanly to Chief, "Subject: Security Survey Report for Trip of Mrs. Kennedy and children to London," June 2, 1965, LBJL; Jacqueline Kennedy to Lyndon Johnson, March 28, 1965, LBJL; *The Times*, London, May 15, 1965; *Daily Telegraph*, London, May 15, 1965; *Guardian*, Manchester, May 15, 1965; *New York Times*, May 15, 1965; *Washington Post*, May 14, 1965, May 15, 1965; *Boston Globe*, May 13, 1965, May 14, 1965, May 15, 1965.

p. 440: "The sun has gone down": Ormsby Gore to Macmillan, February 1, 1964, Macmillan papers, BLO.

p. 440: "it wasn't like the old days": Ormsby Gore, interview, London School of Economics.

p. 441: consciously tried: Jacqueline Kennedy to Macmillan, May 17, 1965, BLO.

p. 441: she had found listening: Jacqueline Kennedy to Macmillan, May 17, 1965, BLO.

p. 441: happiest years of his life: Andrew Devonshire, author interview.

p. 442: "Maybe Randolph will be the one": quoted in Halle, *The Grand Original*.

p. 442: "Your literature": statement issued by the United States Embassy, London, May 14, 1965, quoted in *Daily Telegraph*, London, May 15, 1965.

Index